Microwave Cookbook
The Complete Guide

by Pat Jester

Microwave Cookbook
The Complete Guide

Contents

Publishers: Bill and Helen Fisher; Executive Editor: Rick Bailey
Editorial Director: Veronica Durie; Art Director: Don Burton

Research Assistants: Karla Tillotson, Carol Miller, Diann Peyton
Food Stylists: Mable Hoffman, Pat Jester, Karla Tillotson, Carol Miller, Diann Peyton
Photography: Bob Hawks; George de Gennaro Studios

Published by HPBooks, P.O. Box 5367, Tucson, AZ 85703   602/888-2150
ISBN 0-89586-169-0
Library of Congress Catalog Card No. 82-80143
©1982 Fisher Publishing, Inc. Printed in U.S.A.

Pat Jester

Pat Jester, author of *Easy Suppers* and *Brunch Cookery*, is one of the leading experts on microwave cooking in the United States. She has worked with a major microwave manufacturer on five of its cookbooks and many use-and-care guides and booklets on microwave cooking accessories. A former food editor with Better Homes and Gardens, Pat now heads her own company, Creative Foods Ltd., in West Des Moines, Iowa. She has her own test kitchen where she does recipe testing and development for all her projects. Pat is a member of the International Microwave Power Institute.

How to Use this Book

You are the owner of the most informative and comprehensive microwave cookbook available. Each of the more than 700 recipes has been test-kitchen approved. You'll be proud to serve the delicious results to your family and friends. Over 490 color photographs show many interesting microwave techniques, menu suggestions and garnishing ideas. You never dreamed that your microwave could do so much!

You'll notice colorful, tabbed chapter-divider cards at the back of your book. Insert them at the beginning of chapters, using the page numbers on the divider cards as a guide for placement. These tabbed cards will allow you to find chapters easily and quickly.

SELECT-A-SIZE™ RECIPES

The unique recipe format of this book saves you time and money by eliminating costly leftovers. Here's how to use the exclusive *Select-A-Size™* recipes:

- Decide how many servings you need to make. The first line of the recipe gives the number of servings or yield. Select the column that fits the number of people you plan to serve.

- Gather the amount of ingredients listed in the column under the number of servings you are making.

- Get out the baking dish specified for the number of servings you selected. Microwave timings vary with the size of baking dish used. Be sure to use a dish similar to the size called for in the recipe.

- Use the microwave cooking power levels and timings called for under the number of servings you are making.

- The recipe method below the columns applies to any number of servings. Directions are written clearly and simply. Many recipes are illustrated with step-by-step photographs so you can see exactly how food should look each step of the way.

BONUS FEATURES

In addition to the Select-A-Size™ recipes, your book has these exciting features:

- **Tips:** In every chapter you'll find cooking tips to give you the "why" of recipe instructions. These tips also pass along information gained during extensive recipe development in the test kitchens.

- **Reheating Tips:** Wherever possible, we've included directions on how to chill and reheat portions. You'll find this extremely helpful when cooking for one, or when faced with feeding a hungry teenager between meals. In fact, this may become your favorite feature of the book!

- **Microwave Cautions:** Not every food cooks best in a microwave. This book indicates which recipes are best cooked conventionally and what cooking techniques to avoid using with your microwave. Look for *Microwave Cautions* throughout the book and follow their good advice.

- **Adapting Recipes:** Sometimes, all you want to know is how to cook Aunt Minnie's chicken recipe in your microwave. Now you can learn to do that, too! Look for the many tips throughout this book for adapting conventional recipes to your microwave.

Note: Select-A-Size™ is a trademark of HPBooks.

Getting to Know Your Microwave Oven

Getting To Know Your Microwave Oven

This comprehensive guide will help you enjoy the full potential of the most revolutionary addition to today's kitchen—the microwave. Revised standard recipes and delicious new ones, demonstrate the time-saving versatility of this exciting appliance.

In-depth information and over 450 full-color how-to photographs will enable you to make the microwave work for you as never before. Recipes include complete instructions for different size servings based on the package sizes available in the grocery store. Brand new defrosting techniques have been developed especially for this book. You will find many useful tips for adapting your favorite recipes so they can be cooked in the microwave.

This incredible appliance is geared to your busy lifestyle. Get to know it with the help of this book.

Q. What are the main advantages of cooking with a microwave?

A. Compared with conventional cooking, the greatest advantage is fast cooking time for all but a few items. This in turn saves energy and reduces the heat output into your kitchen—a tremendous plus during the summer. The fast cooking encourages maximum retention of vitamins and flavor in vegetables and other foods.

Q. Can you stir or check food in the microwave while the oven is operating?

A. The microwave power will automatically shut off when you open the oven door. Check on the food, close the oven door and then restart the microwave. Or, if the food is done, turn the timer to OFF.

Q. Can you change power levels while the microwave is operating?

A. You certainly can. If food is boiling too hard, for example, change the power to a lower level to cook more slowly. It's similar to using a burner on top of the range.

Q. What are microwave *hot spots*?

A. Most microwaves have one area that has a concentration of microwaves and consequently cooks food more quickly. This explains why it is necessary to stir and rearrange foods or turn dishes during cooking. This action rotates the food through the hot spot and contributes to even cooking. Some rearranging is also recommended for ovens with the carousel or rotating feature.

Q. How do you know where the hot spot is in a particular microwave?

A. Watch which area of food in a large casserole starts to bubble first or which area of cheese on top of a casserole melts first. This is a good indication of where the hot spot is.

Q. Why does the amount of food affect the microwave cooking time?

A. Unlike conventional cooking, six baked potatoes will not cook in the same length of time in the microwave as two potatoes. Foods have to absorb microwave energy in order to cook. More food absorbing microwave energy means less microwave energy is available for each item. The same is true for the contents of a casserole. The amount in a large casserole takes longer to heat than the amount in a small casserole. For this reason, the recipes in this book give cooking times for different size portions of the same recipe.

6 Shown on the divider: Grilled T-Bone Steak and Baked Onions with Herb Butter

Q. What other factors affect microwave cooking times?

A. The starting temperature of food affects the cooking time. Frozen peas, for example, take longer to cook than canned peas that start at room temperature. The shape of food also affects microwave cooking times. Microwave ovens cook food from the outside toward the inside. Therefore, thin foods cook faster than thick foods. The center of a dish heats more slowly than the edges. Select foods that are uniform in size and shape for more even microwave cooking. The composition of foods also affects the microwave cooking time. Foods high in fat and sugar cook faster in the microwave.

Q. Which utensils can be used in the microwave?

A. Refer to your manufacturer's use-and-care guide. Generally, ovenproof glass, ceramic and pottery dishes, including clay pots, with no metallic trim or parts, glass-ceramic, oven cooking bags and frozen-food pouches can all be used for microwave cooking. Paper should be used only for short cooking times. Plastics vary widely—check the plastic cookware package description to find plastic utensils recommended for microwave cooking. Some will melt or distort, especially if used with foods high in fat or sugar content. Baskets and wooden boards without any metal parts can be used in the microwave for brief reheating of foods such as rolls. Many specially designed microwave utensils are available. They include browning skillets, plastic or ceramic meat-roasting racks, fluted tube dishes, muffin dishes and ring molds.

Q. Which utensils cannot be used in the microwave?

A. Metal in any form should not be used unless the manufacturer of your oven states otherwise. This includes metal twist ties and dishes with decorative metal trim. There are two reasons for this. The most important is that it may cause *arcing* which looks and sounds like lightning or sparks inside the oven. The other reason for not using metal is that it reflects microwaves away from itself rather than allowing them to pass through the material and cause the food to become hot. This shielding effect of metal can be used to advantage when cooking large items such as roast meat or poultry. During the longer cooking time required for these items, some areas tend to cook faster than others. To prevent overbrowning, these areas can be shielded with small pieces of foil held in place with wooden picks. Never allow the foil to touch the oven walls.

Q. How do you know if a dish is safe to use in a microwave?

A. Place 1 cup of cool water in the microwave beside the dish you are testing. Microwave at full power (HIGH) for 1 minute. If the dish is warm, it is absorbing microwave energy and should not be used in the microwave.

Q. Is it true that food cooked in the microwave comes out looking pale?

A. Baked goods and meats that are cooked in a very short time do not have the browned appearance we are used to. If you feel that this is a disadvantage, here are some ways to overcome it. You will find many recipes in this book for glazes and basting sauces to make the appearance of poultry and meat chops more attractive. The browning skillet called for in some recipes is particularly recommended for cooking steak. You can also use one of the color-enhancing products now on the market. Frosting or a number of toppings using ingredients such as brown sugar, spices and nuts can be added to baked goods to increase their eye-appeal.

Microwave Techniques & Tips

Deep casseroles and baking dishes—Both utensils hold 2 quarts. The soup is in a deep 2-quart casserole, the chicken in a 12" x 7" baking dish. Be sure to use a deep casserole when it is called for in a recipe.

Browning skillets—A special substance on the outside bottom of these skillets causes this area to become extremely hot. Food placed in the preheated skillet is seared and browns attractively. Shown here are a 10-inch square microwave browning skillet and a round, 6-1/2-inch microwave browning skillet.

Pie plates—Both pie plates are marked as 10-inch plates but one holds 7 cups and the other holds 4-1/2 cups! Measure the volume of pie plates with water so you know how much food they will hold.

Ring molds—The spaghetti is in a microwave ring mold made of ovenproof glass. Plastic and ceramic rings are also available. To make your own ring mold, place a custard cup in the center of a pie plate.

Shielding—Use small pieces of foil secured with wooden picks to cover areas that are overbrowning. This is important for whole poultry and roasts. Also shield areas that are becoming warm during defrosting.

Cover—Use a casserole lid unless the recipe states to cover in some other manner. If your casserole does not have a lid, cover it with vented plastic wrap.

Cover with paper towel—Use white paper towels to cover foods that might spatter and require only a loose cover. Dye from colored paper towels may transfer to foods if the towels become moist.

Cover with waxed paper—Use waxed paper for a loose-fitting cover that allows steam to escape. Corn on the cob and artichokes can be wrapped in waxed paper for cooking.

Microwave Techniques & Tips

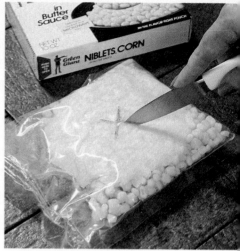

Cover with vented plastic wrap—This is the method to use when you are using a dish without a lid. There are two ways to vent plastic wrap: Either fold back a corner as on the squash rings or cut a few small slits with a knife. The vent is necessary to prevent a build-up of steam. Use good-quality plastic wrap.

Cut a small slit in pouch—The red "X" marks 1-inch slit that should be cut with a knife to ver frozen pouches of vegetables, fruits or entree: To serve, finish cutting the "X" from corner t corner.

Stir—Always stir the outside edges toward the center and the center toward the outside edge. The outside edges will cook first. Stirring moves the uncooked center portion to the outside edge, thus promoting more even cooking.

Rearrange—Move items from the center to th outside edge, and items at the edge to th center. Do this once or several times durin cooking, depending on the recipe. This is use for large items that can't be stirred to promot more even cooking.

Arrange thickest portion toward outside—The outside edges cook more quickly. Placing drumsticks with the meaty portion toward the edge of the dish will promote more even cooking.

Pierce or prick—Foods with membranes or tight skins such as egg yolks, oysters, chicken livers, baked potatoes and whole acorn squash are pierced with a large fork or wooden pick to prevent them from exploding during cooking.

Give dish a half turn—Look at the tomato in the bottom skillet. When the skillet is given a half turn in the microwave, the tomato will be in the same position as the tomato in the top skillet.

Give dish a quarter turn—Look at the green pear above. If the dish is given a quarter turn in the microwave, the pear in the bottom dish will be in the same position as the pear in the top dish.

Microwave Power Settings

Q. How can I work out the wattage of my microwave oven?

A. There are many ways to measure the power output or so-called wattage of micro
wave ovens. The most accepted way has been a matter of controversy for some time
Depending on the test used, the same microwave oven will give different wattage re
sults. Here is a simple test you can do yourself. It is the same one used to determine th
power levels for testing the recipes in this book.

Fill a 4-cup glass measuring cup with 1 liter (34 ounces) of cool water. Record the tem
perature of the water. Place the water in the center of your microwave. Microwave a
full power (HIGH) for exactly 2 minutes. Immediately stir the water with the ther
mometer and record the temperature again. Subtract the starting temperature of th
water from the heated temperature of the water. If you are using the Fahrenheit scale
multiply the answer by 19.5. If you are using the Celsius scale, multiply the answer b
35. This figure is the approximate power output or wattage for your microwave operat
ing at full power (HIGH).

Q. How else can I find out the wattage of my microwave oven?

A. Some manufacturers are including this information in the use-and-care literature
that comes with the microwave. You can call or write the consumer service departmen
of the manufacturer. Another possibility is to contact the dealer who sold you the oven
It is still a good idea to test your own unit because they vary in wattage even when the
come from the same manufacturer and are the same model. There is also the possibilit
that the manufacturer could have used a different test to determine wattage and migh
have a different result.

Q. Does anything affect the wattage of the microwave oven?

A. The wattage will be affected by the power load in your community at differen
times of the day and year. In addition, no other appliance should be plugged into the
same circuit as your microwave. This could drastically affect the wattage when both
appliances are operating at the same time.

Q. How can you figure out the wattage at different settings?

A. Refer to the chart below. The variable-power settings are expressed as a percentage
of full power (HIGH). To find the wattage of a variable-power level, multiply the
HIGH wattage by the percent of HIGH power for that particular power level. If your
microwave is operating at 647 watts at HIGH power, it will operate at 30% of this power
or 194 watts when the variable-power control is set at MEDIUM LOW or 3.

POWER LEVEL SETTINGS

Word Designation	Numerical Designation	Power Output at Setting	Percentage of HIGH Setting
HIGH	10	650 watts	100%
MEDIUM HIGH	7	455 watts	70%
MEDIUM	5	325 watts	50%
MEDIUM LOW	3	195 watts	30%
LOW	1	65 watts	10%

Appetizers & Beverages

Lengthy cooking time is eliminated with the microwave. Keep a few basic ingredients on hand and you will be able to serve speedy snacks when friends drop in.

Q. What are the advantages of cooking appetizers and beverages in the microwave?

A. Many appetizers, such as cocktail meatballs and stuffed vegetables, are precooked but require reheating before serving. The microwave does this quickly and efficiently. Individual servings of beverages can be heated or reheated in mugs using the microwave.

Q. Which appetizers and beverages do not cook satisfactorily in the microwave?

A. It is extremely dangerous to attempt any kind of deep-frying in the microwave. This means that deep-fried appetizers, such as egg rolls, cannot be cooked in the microwave. Breaded snacks and puff-pastry appetizers will not cook well. Drinks with a high proportion of eggs, such as eggnog, can only be warmed or they will curdle.

Q. How are appetizers and beverages cooked in the microwave?

A. Dips with cream-cheese bases are heated at 70% (MEDIUM HIGH) until they begin to get warm. Cracker toppers with cream-cheese or mayonnaise bases are warmed at 30% (MEDIUM LOW). Cocktail meatballs and franks heat quickly at full power (HIGH), as do sandwiches, stuffed mushrooms and stuffed artichokes. Stuffed oysters heat more gently at 50% (MEDIUM). It's easy to toast nuts, seeds and coconut in small batches at full power (HIGH). Snack mixes in large volume toast slowly at 30% (MEDIUM LOW). Most beverages are heated quickly at full power (HIGH). Some are brought to boiling at full power (HIGH) and then simmered at 30% (MEDIUM LOW) to develop flavors.

Q. How do you know when appetizers and beverages are done?

A. Drinks and soups without eggs are heated to 170F (75C). Be sure to stir drinks and soups to distribute the heat before deciding they are ready to serve. Dips with a cream-cheese base should be just warm; they may curdle if they become hot. Sandwiches should also be heated until just warm or the bread will be tough and dry.

Q. How do you convert favorite beverage recipes to the microwave?

A. Use instructions for boiling water, heating milk and reheating refrigerated drinks or room-temperature coffee as guidelines for drink timings. Most drinks without eggs can be easily adapted if you compare them to a similar recipe in the chapter.

Q. Are any special utensils needed for preparing appetizers and beverages in the microwave?

A. A large heatproof pitcher, 1- and 2-quart glass measuring cups and heatproof mugs are all useful for microwaving and serving hot drinks and soups. You can use trays made of wood or straw and straw baskets for warming food in the microwave. None of the utensils should have any metal parts.

Shown on the divider: Clockwise starting from the top left: Tomato Tang; Dilly Ham Dip; Curried Chicken Snack Sandwiches; Bacon-Olive Cracker Melts; Rumaki.

How to Defrost Juice Concentrates

Place the unopened can of frozen juice concentrate briefly under hot water to loosen. Empty the frozen block of concentrate into a glass measuring cup or heatproof pitcher.

Microwave the concentrate until nearly thawed, breaking up several times with a fork. To use as a beverage, stir in some crushed ice for part of the water listed on the can.

Defrosting Juice Concentrates

YIELD	2 cups	1-1/2 cups	3/4 cup
INGREDIENTS frozen juice concentrate	1 (16-oz.) can	1 (12-oz.) can	1 (6-oz.) can
GLASS MEASURING CUP	2-qt.	2-qt.	1-qt.
TIME AT HIGH	3 to 4 minutes	2 to 3 minutes	1 to 1-1/2 minutes

Place unopened juice can under hot running water to loosen frozen concentrate. Empty frozen concentrate into a glass measuring cup, see size in chart above. Microwave at full power (HIGH) for time in chart above or until almost thawed, stirring and breaking up two or three times. Use as a concentrate in recipes or add cold water and ice cubes and use as a beverage.

Defrosting Frozen Dip

Remove frozen avocado dip from 6-ounce carton and place in a 2-cup bowl. Microwave at 30% (MEDIUM LOW) 4 to 4-1/2 minutes or until thawed, breaking up dip as soon as possible and stirring twice. Let stand 2 minutes.

Hot Chocolate

SERVINGS	6 to 8		
INGREDIENTS			
sweetened condensed milk	1 (14-oz.) can		
semisweet chocolate pieces	1 (6-oz.) pkg.		
milk	6 cups		
ground cinnamon	1/4 teaspoon		
ground cloves	1/8 teaspoon		
large marshmallows	6 to 8		
BAKING DISH	deep 3-qt. casserole		
MUGS	6 to 8		
TIME AT HIGH (melt pieces)	2 to 2-1/2 minutes		
TIME AT HIGH (milk added)	11 to 13 minutes		
TIME AT HIGH (marshmallows)	2 to 2-1/2 minutes		

In a 3-quart casserole, combine condensed milk and chocolate pieces. Microwave at full power (HIGH) 2 to 2-1/2 minutes or until pieces are melted, stirring twice. Stir to blend well. Gradually whisk in milk, cinnamon and cloves; cover. Microwave at full power (HIGH) 11 to 13 minutes or until heated through, whisking three times. Ladle into mugs. Top each with a marshmallow. Arrange mugs in a circle in microwave oven. Microwave at full power (HIGH) 2 to 2-1/2 minutes or until marshmallows are puffed.

Variation

Make-Ahead Hot Chocolate: Melt chocolate pieces with condensed milk as above. Spoon into a refrigerator container. Cover and refrigerate. At serving time, spoon 1/4 cup chocolate mixture into each 10-ounce mug. Microwave at full power (HIGH) for time in chart below to heat syrup. Gradually whisk 3/4 cup milk into each mug, blending thoroughly. Microwave at full power (HIGH) for time in chart below or until heated through. If using 4 mugs, rearrange once. Stir well. Top each mug with a marshmallow. Microwave at full power (HIGH) for time in chart below or until marshmallows are puffed.

SERVINGS	4	2	1
TIME AT HIGH (syrup)	1 to 1-1/2 minutes	30 to 45 seconds	20 to 30 seconds
TIME AT HIGH (milk added)	7 minutes	3 minutes	1-1/2 minutes
TIME AT HIGH (marshmallows)	1 to 1-1/4 minutes	30 to 45 seconds	20 to 30 seconds

Tip

- To heat milk, pour into 10-ounce mugs. Microwave at full power (HIGH) 7 to 8 minutes for 4 mugs, 4 to 4-1/2 minutes for 2 mugs and 2 to 2-1/2 minutes for 1 mug. Rearrange mugs once during heating time. Use to make instant drinks or soups.

How to Prepare Make-Ahead Hot Chocolate

Measure 1/4 cup refrigerated chocolate mixture into each mug. Microwave chocolate mixture until syrupy. Very slowly whisk milk into each mug to blend with the chocolate.

Microwave the chocolate milk mixture until heated through. Top each serving with a marshmallow and microwave until marshmallows puff as shown above.

Traditional Hot Cocoa

SERVINGS	6 to 8	3 or 4	2
INGREDIENTS			
unsweetened cocoa powder	1/2 cup	1/4 cup	2 tablespoons
sugar	1/2 cup	1/4 cup	2 tablespoons
hot water	1/2 cup	1/4 cup	2 tablespoons
milk	7 cups	3-1/2 cups	1-3/4 cups
vanilla extract	1 teaspoon	1/2 teaspoon	1/4 teaspoon
large marshmallows	6 to 8	3 or 4	2
BAKING DISH	deep 3-qt. casserole	deep 1-1/2 qt. casserole	deep 1-qt. casserole
MUGS	6 to 8	3 or 4	2
TIME AT HIGH (water mixture)	3 minutes	2 minutes	1 minute
TIME AT HIGH (milk added)	13 to 15 minutes	7-1/2 to 8-1/2 minutes	3-1/2 to 4-1/2 minutes
TIME AT HIGH (marshmallows)	2 to 2-1/2 minutes	1-1/2 to 2 minutes	1 minute

In a casserole, see size in chart above, thoroughly blend together cocoa powder and sugar. Whisk in hot water until blended. Cover and microwave at full power (HIGH) for time in chart above. Gradually whisk in milk. Cover. Microwave at full power (HIGH) for time in chart above or until heated through, whisking three times. Whisk in vanilla. Ladle cocoa into mugs, see number in chart above. Top each serving with a marshmallow. Arrange mugs in a circle in microwave oven. Microwave at full power (HIGH) for time in chart above or until marshmallows are puffed.

Eggnog Amandine

SERVINGS	4	2
INGREDIENTS		
refrigerated, canned or dairy eggnog	4 cups	2 cups
dried ground orange peel	1 teaspoon	1/2 teaspoon
orange extract	1/2 teaspoon	1/4 teaspoon
Amaretto liqueur	1/2 cup	1/4 cup
whipped topping, toasted slivered almonds, freshly grated orange peel	to garnish	to garnish
BAKING DISH	deep 2-qt. casserole	deep 1-qt. casserole
TIME AT HIGH (eggnog)	8 to 9 minutes	3 to 3-1/2 minutes
TIME AT HIGH (liqueur added)	1 to 2 minutes	30 to 45 seconds

In a casserole, see size in chart above, combine cold eggnog, dried orange peel and orange extract. Mix well. Cover and microwave at full power (HIGH) for time in chart above or until heated through. Do not boil. Stir in Amaretto liqueur. Cover. Microwave at full power (HIGH) for time in chart above or until heated through. Serve in mugs topped with whipped topping. Sprinkle with toasted almonds and fresh orange peel.

Tomato Tang   Photo on page 13.

SERVINGS	4	2
INGREDIENTS		
vegetable-tomato juice cocktail	2 (12-oz.) cans (3 cups)	1 (12-oz.) can (1-1/2 cups)
beef broth	1 (14-1/2-oz.) can	1/2 (14-1/2-oz.) can
lemon juice	1 tablespoon	1 teaspoon
Worcestershire sauce	1 teaspoon	1/2 teaspoon
prepared horseradish	1 teaspoon	1/2 teaspoon
bottled hot pepper sauce	dash	dash
thin lemon slices, halved, with tiny sprig of parsley on each	6	3
BAKING DISH	deep 2-qt. casserole	deep 1-qt. casserole
TIME AT HIGH	8 to 10 minutes	4 to 5 minutes
TIME AT 30%	10 to 12 minutes	5 to 6 minutes

In a casserole, see size in chart above, combine vegetable-tomato juice cocktail, beef broth, lemon juice, Worcestershire sauce, horseradish and hot pepper sauce. Cover. Microwave at full power (HIGH) for time in chart above or until mixture is boiling. Stir well. Cover. Microwave at 30% (MEDIUM LOW) for time in chart above to blend flavors, stirring once. Serve garnished with lemon slices topped with parsley sprigs.

Tips

- It's best to heat large volumes of punch on top of the range—this will be much faster than in the microwave oven.
- There are attractive heatproof glass and ceramic serving bowls available for heating smaller amounts of punch in the microwave.

Mulled Apple Cider

SERVINGS	6 or 7	3
INGREDIENTS		
apple cider	4 cups	2 cups
carbonated apple wine or cider	2 cups	1 cup
brown sugar	2 tablespoons	1 tablespoon
orange, cut in wedges	1	1/2
cinnamon sticks	6 inches in total	3 inches in total
whole cloves	6	3
whole allspice	6	3
apple brandy	1/2 cup	1/4 cup
BAKING DISH	deep 3-qt. casserole	deep 1-1/2-qt. casserole
TIME AT HIGH (cider)	13 to 15 minutes	7 to 8 minutes
TIME AT HIGH (brandy added)	3 minutes	1 to 1-1/2 minutes

In a casserole, see size in chart above, combine cider, wine, brown sugar and orange wedges. Mix well. Tie cinnamon sticks, cloves and allspice in cheesecloth. Add to cider mixture. Cover. Microwave at full power (HIGH) for time in chart above or until boiling. Remove spices. Stir in brandy. Cover. Microwave at full power (HIGH) for time in chart above or until heated through.

Hot Toddies

SERVINGS	4	2
INGREDIENTS		
frozen lemonade concentrate	8 tablespoons	4 tablespoons
water	3 cups	1-1/2 cups
long cinnamon sticks	4 sticks	2 sticks
bourbon	8 tablespoons	4 tablespoons
lemon slices, halved	2	1
MUGS	4 (10-oz.) mugs	2 (10-oz.) mugs
TIME AT HIGH (lemonade)	7 to 8 minutes	4 to 4-1/2 minutes
TIME AT HIGH (bourbon added)	1 to 1-1/2 minutes	45 to 60 seconds

In each mug, see number in chart above, combine 2 tablespoons frozen lemonade concentrate and 3/4 cup water. Add a cinnamon stick stirrer. Microwave at full power (HIGH) for time in chart above or until almost boiling. Stir 2 tablespoons bourbon into each mug. Float a half slice of lemon on top. Microwave at full power (HIGH) for time in chart above or until heated through.

Tip

- If your microwave oven has a temperature probe, place the probe in the beverage and heat to 170F (75C). Stir the beverage once or twice to distribute heat evenly. The temperature will vary slightly from mug to mug, so rearrange mugs once during the cooking time to achieve a more even temperature in all the mugs.

How to Make Merry Christmas Grog

Pierce pears with a large fork. Wrap the pears in squares of waxed paper, twisting the ends to seal. Microwave until tender.

Float the pears in the spiced cranberry-wine punch. Ladle the hot punch into mugs and garnish with fresh cranberries and pear slices.

Merry Christmas Grog

SERVINGS	8	4
INGREDIENTS		
firm ripe pears	5 (1-3/4 lbs.)	3 (1 lb.)
cranberry juice cocktail	4 cups	2 cups
dry red wine	3 cups	1-1/2 cups
sugar	1/2 cup	1/4 cup
golden raisins	1/4 cup	2 tablespoons
cinnamon sticks	6 inches in total	3 inches in total
whole nutmeg	1	1
whole cloves	6	3
cranberry liqueur	1/2 cup	1/4 cup
BAKING DISH	deep 3-qt. casserole	deep 1-1/2-qt. casserole
TIME AT HIGH (pears)	4 minutes	3 minutes
TIME AT HIGH (grog)	13 to 15 minutes	8 to 9 minutes
TIME AT HIGH (liqueur added)	2 to 3 minutes	1 to 1-1/2 minutes

Pierce pears twice with a large fork. Wrap each pear in a small square of waxed paper, twisting ends to seal. Place in a circle in microwave oven. Microwave at full power (HIGH) for time in chart above or until tender, rearranging once. Leave pears wrapped and set aside. In a casserole, see size in chart above, combine cranberry juice, wine, sugar and raisins. Tie cinnamon sticks, nutmeg and cloves in cheesecloth. Add to cranberry mixture. Cover and microwave at full power (HIGH) for time in chart above or until boiling. Stir well. Stir in cranberry liqueur. Microwave at full power (HIGH) for time in chart above or until heated through. Remove spice bag. To serve, unwrap baked pears and float in grog. If desired, garnish grog with pear slices and cranberries.

Honey Spiced Tea

SERVINGS	6	3
INGREDIENTS		
water	6 cups	3 cups
frozen lemonade concentrate, thawed	1/2 (6-oz.) can (1/3 cup)	3 tablespoons
honey	1/2 cup	1/4 cup
cinnamon sticks	3 inches in total	2 inches in total
mint	3 sprigs	2 sprigs
tea bags	4	2
lemon slices	6 to 8	3 or 4
BAKING DISH	deep 3-qt. casserole	deep 1-1/2-qt. casserole
TIME AT HIGH	15 to 16 minutes	6 to 7 minutes
TIME AT 30%	10 minutes	5 minutes
STANDING TIME	3 to 4 minutes	3 to 4 minutes

In a casserole, see size in chart above, combine water, lemonade concentrate and honey. Tie cinnamon sticks and mint in cheesecloth. Add to lemonade mixture. Cover. Microwave at full power (HIGH) for time in chart above or until boiling. Stir. Cover and microwave at 30% (MEDIUM LOW) for time in chart above to blend flavors. Stir. Add tea bags. Cover. Let stand 3 to 4 minutes to steep tea. Discard spice bag and tea bags. Serve in mugs garnished with lemon slices.

Reheating Refrigerated Hot Drinks

SERVINGS	2	1
INGREDIENTS		
refrigerated drink	2 cups	1 cup
MUGS	2 (10-oz.) mugs	1 (10-oz.) mug
TIME AT HIGH	3-1/2 to 4-1/2 minutes	2 to 3 minutes

Pour refrigerated drink into mugs, see number in chart above. Microwave at full power (HIGH) for time in chart above or until heated through.

Reheating Room-Temperature Coffee

SERVINGS	4	2	1
INGREDIENTS			
room-temperature coffee	4 cups	2 cups	1 cup
MUGS	4 (10-oz.) mugs	2 (10-oz.) mugs	1 (10-oz.) mug
TIME AT HIGH	7 to 8 minutes	3 to 3-1/2 minutes	1-1/2 to 2 minutes

Pour room-temperature coffee into mugs, see number in chart above. Microwave at full power (HIGH) for time in chart above or until heated through, rearranging mugs once.

Boiling Water in Mugs

SERVINGS	4	2	1
INGREDIENTS cool water	4 cups	2 cups	1 cup
MUGS	4 (10-oz.) mugs	2 (10-oz.) mugs	1 (10-oz.) mug
TIME AT HIGH	9 to 10 minutes	4-1/2 to 5-1/2 minutes	2-1/2 to 3 minutes

Pour cool water into mugs, see number in chart above. Microwave at full power (HIGH) for time in chart above or until boiling, rearranging mugs once. Use to make instant hot drinks or soups.

Boiling Water in Bulk

YIELD	6 cups	5 cups	4 cups
INGREDIENTS cool water	6 cups	5 cups	4 cups
GLASS MEASURING CUP	2-qt.	2-qt.	2-qt.
TIME AT HIGH	16 to 16-1/2 minutes	12 to 13 minutes	10-1/2 to 11-1/2 minutes

YIELD	3 cups	2 cups	1 cup
INGREDIENTS cool water	3 cups	2 cups	1 cup
GLASS MEASURING CUP	1-qt.	1 qt.	2-cup
TIME AT HIGH	7 to 8 minutes	5 to 6 minutes	2-1/2 to 3 minutes

Pour cool water into a glass measuring cup, see size in chart above. Microwave at full power (HIGH) for time in chart above or until boiling. Use to make instant hot drinks or soups. Boiling water on top of your range may be faster than in the microwave oven, but not as convenient. Microwaving water can be done in the container used for food preparation and requires no watching.

Tips

Try these ideas for special coffees in your microwave oven:

● Stir 1/2 jigger coffee-flavored liqueur and 1/2 jigger creme de cacao into each mug of room-temperature coffee. Heat according to directions for reheating coffee, opposite. Top with a scoop of coffee ice cream and a sprinkling of chocolate-shot candies.

● Stir 1 jigger bourbon liqueur into each mug of room-temperature coffee. Heat according to directions for reheating coffee, opposite. Top with a swirl of whipped topping and a sprinkling of ground cinnamon.

● Stir 1/2 jigger almond-flavored liqueur and 1/2 jigger orange-flavored liqueur into each mug of room temperature coffee. Heat according to directions for reheating coffee. Top with a half slice of orange.

Oriental Chicken Soup

SERVINGS	4 to 6	2 or 3
INGREDIENTS		
uncooked chicken breast	1 (1-lb.) breast	1/2 (1-lb.) breast
chicken broth	2 (14-1/2-oz.) cans	1 (14-1/2-oz.) can
thinly sliced celery	1/4 cup	2 tablespoons
thinly sliced green onion	1/4 cup	2 tablespoons
dry sherry	2 tablespoons	1 tablespoon
snipped watercress leaves	1/2 cup	1/4 cup
BAKING DISH	deep 2-qt. casserole	deep 1-qt. casserole
TIME AT HIGH (broth)	8 to 10 minutes	5 to 6 minutes
TIME AT HIGH (chicken added)	3 to 4 minutes	2 to 3 minutes
TIME AT HIGH (vegetables added)	3 to 5 minutes	3 to 4 minutes

Remove skin and bone from chicken breast. Cut chicken into 1-inch slivers. Pour broth into a casserole, see size in chart above. Cover. Microwave at full power (HIGH) for time in chart above or until boiling. Add chicken. Cover. Microwave at full power (HIGH) for time in chart above or until chicken is almost done. Add celery slices, green onion slices and sherry. Microwave at full power (HIGH) for time in chart above or until vegetables are crisp-tender. Divide watercress leaves among soup cups. Pour in hot soup.

Herbed Tomato Cocktail Soup

SERVINGS	6	3
INGREDIENTS		
tomato juice	4 cups	2 cups
onion, sliced	1/2 medium	1/4 medium
parsley sprigs	2	1
celery stalk, cut up	1	1/2
carrot, cut up	1 small	1/2 small
lemon slices	4	2
dried leaf basil	1 teaspoon	1/2 teaspoon
peppercorns	4	2
bay leaf	1 small	1/2 small
dry white wine	1/2 cup	1/4 cup
BAKING DISH	deep 2-qt. casserole	deep 1-qt. casserole
TIME AT HIGH	8 to 10 minutes	4 to 5 minutes
TIME AT 30%	12 to 15 minutes	6 to 7 minutes

In a casserole, see size in chart above, combine tomato juice, onion, parsley, celery, carrot, lemon slices, basil, peppercorns and bay leaf. Cover. Microwave at full power (HIGH) for time in chart above or until boiling. Stir in wine. Cover. Microwave at 30% (MEDIUM LOW) for time in chart above to blend flavors, stirring once. Strain soup and serve.

Heating Canned Consommé & Soup

To heat canned soups, see page 416.

How to Make Oriental Chicken Soup

Use a small, sharp knife to cut a boneless chicken breast into 1-inch slivers. Add chicken to boiling broth, and microwave until chicken is no longer pink. Then add vegetables.

Place snipped watercress leaves in the bottom of small soup bowls. Ladle the hot soup over the watercress. These Oriental soup bowls have gold trim and cannot be used in the microwave oven—the gold trim could cause arcing.

Greek Lemon Soup

SERVINGS	4	2
INGREDIENTS		
chicken broth	2 (14-1/2-oz.) cans	1 (14-1/2-oz.) can
Minute rice	1/3 cup	3 tablespoons
dried grated lemon peel	1/2 teaspoon	1/4 teaspoon
egg yolks	2	1
lemon juice	2 tablespoons	1 tablespoon
BAKING DISH	deep 2-qt. casserole	deep 1-qt. casserole
TIME AT HIGH (broth)	12 to 13 minutes	7 to 9 minutes
TIME AT 30% (egg yolk added)	3 to 4 minutes	2 to 3 minutes

In a casserole, see size in chart above, combine chicken broth, rice and lemon peel. Cover. Microwave at full power (HIGH) for time in chart above or until rice is tender. In a small bowl, beat together egg yolks and lemon juice until frothy. Whisk in 1/2 cup hot broth. Add egg yolk mixture to hot broth in casserole, whisking constantly. Microwave, uncovered, at 30% (MEDIUM LOW) for time in chart above or until mixture is heated through, whisking four times. Do not boil.

Piquant Shrimp Dip

YIELD	2 cups	3/4 cup
INGREDIENTS		
Basic Hot Dip, opposite	large recipe	small recipe
bottled seafood cocktail sauce	1/4 cup	2 tablespoons
tiny shrimp, rinsed, drained	1 (6-oz.) can	1/2 (6-oz.) can
chopped green pepper	1/4 cup	2 tablespoons
snipped parsley	to garnish	to garnish

Prepare Basic Hot Dip. Stir seafood cocktail sauce, shrimp and green pepper into dip. Heat and serve, using directions for Basic Hot Dip. Garnish with snipped parsley.

Dilly Ham Dip Photo on page 13.

YIELD	2 cups	3/4 cup
INGREDIENTS		
Basic Hot Dip, opposite	large recipe	small recipe
bottled sandwich spread	3 tablespoons	1 tablespoon
finely chopped cooked ham	1 cup	1/3 cup
chopped dill pickle, drained	3 tablespoons	1 tablespoon
prepared mustard	2 teaspoons	1/2 teaspoon
green and red pepper strips, parsley sprig	to garnish	to garnish

Prepare Basic Hot Dip. Stir sandwich spread, ham, pickle and mustard into dip. Heat and serve, using directions for Basic Hot Dip. Garnish with pepper strips and parsley.

Marinated Artichoke Dip

YIELD	1-2/3 cups	3/4 cup
INGREDIENTS		
Basic Hot Dip, opposite	large recipe	small recipe
plain yogurt	3 tablespoons	1 tablespoon
marinated artichokes, drained, chopped	1 (6-oz.) jar	1/2 (6-oz.) jar
grated Parmesan cheese	1/3 cup	3 tablespoons
chopped green onion	to garnish	to garnish

Prepare Basic Hot Dip. Stir yogurt, artichokes and Parmesan cheese into dip. Heat and serve, using directions for Basic Hot Dip. Garnish with chopped green onion.

How to Make Piquant Shrimp Dip

To Basic Hot Dip, add seafood cocktail sauce, shrimp and chopped green pepper. Stir to blend ingredients.

The creamy shrimp mixture is spooned into a pie plate, then microwaved until warm. Garnish with snipped parsley. Serve with assorted fresh vegetables and crackers.

Basic Hot Dip

YIELD	large recipe	small recipe
INGREDIENTS		
cream cheese	1 (8-oz.) pkg.	1 (3-oz.) pkg.
milk	1 tablespoon	1 teaspoon
Worcestershire sauce	1 teaspoon	1/2 teaspoon
chopped green onion	2 tablespoons	1 tablespoon
freshly ground pepper	dash	dash
Dilly Ham Dip, Marinated Artichoke Dip or Piquant Shrimp Dip, opposite		
BOWL	1-1/2-qt. bowl	1-qt. bowl
PLATE	9-inch pie plate	7-inch pie plate
TIME AT 10%	1-1/2 to 2 minutes	45 seconds
TIME AT 70%	3 to 3-1/2 minutes	2 to 2-1/2 minutes

Unwrap cream cheese and place in a bowl, see size in chart above. Microwave at 10% (LOW) for time in chart above or until softened. Add milk, Worcestershire sauce, green onion and pepper. Beat with an electric mixer on medium speed until blended. Stir in ingredients, except garnishes, for Piquant Shrimp Dip, Dilly Ham Dip or Marinated Artichoke Dip. Spoon into a pie plate, see size in chart above. Cover with vented plastic wrap. Microwave at 70% (MEDIUM HIGH) for time in chart above or until heated through, stirring twice. Serve warm with fresh vegetables or crackers as dippers. Garnish according to dip recipes.

Easy Bean Dip

YIELD	2-2/3 cups	1-1/3 cups
INGREDIENTS		
condensed bean with bacon soup	1 (11-1/2-oz.) can	1/2 (11-1/2-oz.) can
process cheese spread with bacon	1 (5-oz.) jar	1/2 (5-oz.) jar
brown sugar	2 tablespoons	1 tablespoon
Worcestershire sauce	1 tablespoon	2 teaspoons
prepared mustard	1 tablespoon	1 teaspoon
instant minced onion	2 teaspoons	1 teaspoon
bottled hot pepper sauce	1/4 teaspoon	1/8 teaspoon
dairy sour cream	1 cup	1/2 cup
BAKING DISH	deep 1-qt. casserole	deep 1-qt. casserole
TIME AT HIGH	4 to 5 minutes	2-1/2 to 3 minutes
TIME AT 30%	2 minutes	1 minute

In a deep 1-quart casserole, combine soup, cheese, brown sugar, Worcestershire sauce, mustard, onion and hot pepper sauce. Cover. Microwave at full power (HIGH) for time in chart above or until cheese melts, stirring twice. Stir 1/2 cup bean mixture into sour cream. Stir sour cream mixture into bean mixture in casserole. Cover. Microwave at 30% (MEDIUM LOW) for time in chart above or until heated through, stirring once. Serve hot with vegetable dippers and chips.

Hearty Pizza Dip

YIELD	4-1/2 cups	2-1/3 cups
INGREDIENTS		
bulk pork sausage	1 lb.	8 oz.
sliced green onion	1/4 cup	2 tablespoons
chopped green pepper	1/4 cup	2 tablespoons
pizza sauce	1 (16-oz.) jar	1 (8-oz.) can
fennel seed	1 teaspoon	1/2 teaspoon
dried leaf oregano	1 teaspoon	1/2 teaspoon
dried leaf basil	1 teaspoon	1/2 teaspoon
shredded process American cheese	4 cups (1 lb.)	2 cups (8 oz.)
BAKING DISH	deep 2-qt. casserole	deep 1-qt. casserole
TIME AT HIGH (sausage)	5-1/2 to 6-1/2 minutes	3 to 4 minutes
TIME AT HIGH (sauce added)	3 minutes	2 minutes
TIME AT 30%	15 to 20 minutes	8 to 10 minutes

In a casserole, see size in chart above, combine sausage, green onion and green pepper. Microwave at full power (HIGH) for time in chart above or until sausage is browned and vegetables are tender, stirring twice. Drain well. Stir in pizza sauce, fennel seed, oregano and basil. Microwave at full power (HIGH) for time in chart above or until boiling. Stir in cheese in 2 batches. When all cheese has been added, cover. Microwave at 30% (MEDIUM LOW) for time in chart above or until cheese is melted and mixture is heated through, stirring three times. Serve hot with crackers as dippers.

Defrosting: To defrost frozen dip, see page 15.

Swiss Topping

YIELD	large recipe	medium recipe	small recipe
INGREDIENTS			
shredded Swiss cheese	3/4 cup (3 oz.)	1/3 cup (1-1/2 oz.)	3 tablespoons
grated Parmesan cheese	3 tablespoons	4 teaspoons	2 teaspoons
mayonnaise	3 tablespoons	4 teaspoons	2 teaspoons
snipped chives	4 teaspoons	2 teaspoons	1 teaspoon
dry white wine	2 teaspoons	1 teaspoon	1/2 teaspoon
ground nutmeg	1/8 teaspoon	dash	dash
pepper	1/8 teaspoon	dash	dash

In a small bowl, combine Swiss cheese, Parmesan cheese, mayonnaise, chives, wine, nutmeg and pepper. Mix well. Use as a topping for Cracker Melts, opposite. Garnish each cracker with paprika, if desired.

Bacon-Olive Topping   Photo on page 13.

YIELD	large recipe	medium recipe	small recipe
INGREDIENTS			
process cheese spread	1 (5-oz.) jar	1/2 (5-oz.) jar	1/4 (5-oz.) jar
chopped pimiento-stuffed green olives	1/4 cup	2 tablespoons	1 tablespoon
bacon, cooked, crumbled	3 slices	2 slices	1 slice
cayenne pepper	dash	dash	dash
BOWL	1-qt. bowl	2-cup bowl	2-cup bowl
TIME AT 10%	1 minute	45 seconds	30 seconds

Place cheese spread in a bowl, see size in chart above. Microwave at 10% (LOW) for time in chart above or until soft. Stir in olives, crumbled bacon and cayenne. Use as a topping for Cracker Melts, opposite. Garnish each cracker with an olive slice, if desired.

Creamy Oyster Topping

YIELD	large recipe	medium recipe	small recipe
INGREDIENTS			
cream cheese	1 (3-oz.) pkg.	1/2 (3-oz.) pkg.	1/4 (3-oz.) pkg.
snipped chives	1 tablespoon	2 teaspoons	1 teaspoon
drained capers	1 tablespoon	2 teaspoons	1 teaspoon
Worcestershire sauce	1 teaspoon	1/2 teaspoon	1/4 teaspoon
smoked oysters, drained, halved	1 (3-2/3-oz.) can	1/2 (3-2/3-oz.) can	1/4 (3-2/3-oz.) can
BOWL	1-qt. bowl	2-cup bowl	2-cup bowl
TIME AT 10%	45 to 60 seconds	30 seconds	15 seconds

Unwrap cream cheese and place in a bowl, see size in chart above. Microwave at 10% (LOW) for time in chart above or until softened. Stir chives, capers and Worcestershire sauce into cheese; mix well. Use as a topping for Cracker Melts, opposite. Garnish each cracker with a piece of smoked oyster.

How to Make Cracker Melts with Swiss Topping

Try Cracker Melts with Swiss, oyster, or bacon-olive toppings. For Swiss topping, grate fresh nutmeg into a mixture of Swiss cheese, Parmesan cheese, mayonnaise, snipped chives and white wine.

Place assorted crackers on a paper-towel-lined plate so the crackers won't become soggy. Place a generous spoonful of topping on each cracker. Sprinkle with paprika and microwave until melted.

Cracker Melts   Photo on page 13.

YIELD	24 crackers	12 crackers	6 crackers
INGREDIENTS Swiss Topping, Bacon-Olive Topping, or Creamy Oyster Topping, opposite	large recipe	medium recipe	small recipe
Melba-toast rounds or crackers	24	12	6
PLATE	12-inch microwave pizza plate	12-inch microwave pizza plate	9-inch pie plate
TIME AT HIGH (Bacon-Olive)	45 to 60 seconds	20 to 25 seconds	15 to 20 seconds
TIME AT 30% (Swiss or Creamy Oyster)	1-3/4 to 2 minutes	1-1/4 to 1-1/2 minutes	45 seconds

Prepare topping. Place Melba toast or crackers on a paper-towel-lined plate, see size in chart above. Spread about 1 teaspoon topping on each cracker. Garnish according to topping recipe. Microwave at full power (HIGH) for time in chart above for Bacon-Olive Topping or at 30% (MEDIUM LOW) for time in chart above for Swiss Topping and Creamy Oyster Topping. Microwave crackers until warm or cheese melts, giving plate a half turn once.

Deviled Cocktail Tidbits

YIELD	4-1/2 cups	2-1/4 cups	1 cup
INGREDIENTS			
cooked Basic Cocktail Meatballs, opposite, and/or cocktail franks	60	30	15
currant jelly	2 (10-oz.) jars	1 (10-oz.) jar	1/2 (10-oz.) jar
crème de cassis	1/4 cup	2 tablespoons	1 tablespoon
prepared mustard	1/4 cup	2 tablespoons	1 tablespoon
prepared horseradish	2 tablespoons	1 tablespoon	2 teaspoons
cornstarch	3 tablespoons	4 teaspoons	2 teaspoons
cold water	3 tablespoons	2 tablespoons	1 tablespoon
BAKING DISH	deep 2-qt. casserole	deep 1-1/2-qt. casserole	deep 1-qt. casserole
TIME AT HIGH (sauce)	8 to 9 minutes	4 to 5 minutes	1-1/2 to 2 minutes
TIME AT HIGH (thicken sauce)	3 to 4 minutes	2 minutes	1 to 1-1/2 minutes
TIME AT HIGH (meat added)	8 to 10 minutes	4 to 5 minutes	1 to 1-1/2 minutes

Prepare Basic Cocktail Meatballs, if using. In a casserole, see size in chart above, combine currant jelly, crème de cassis, mustard and horseradish. Mix well. Cover. Microwave at full power (HIGH) for time in chart above or until melted, stirring twice. In small bowl, blend cornstarch and cold water. Stir into casserole. Microwave at full power (HIGH) for time in chart above or until thick and bubbly, stirring three times. Mixture should be thick and smooth. Stir in meatballs or franks. Cover. Microwave at full power (HIGH) for time in chart above or until heated through, stirring once or twice. Serve with cocktail picks.

Reheating Refrigerated Cocktail Tidbits

YIELD	3 cups	2 cups	1 cup
INGREDIENTS			
cooked Cocktail Tidbits and sauce	3 cups	2 cups	1 cup
BAKING DISH	1-1/2-qt. casserole	1-qt. casserole	1-qt. casserole
TIME AT 70%	10 to 12 minutes	6 to 8 minutes	5 to 6 minutes

To chill: Spoon cooled Cocktail Tidbits and sauce into a casserole, see size in chart above. Cover tightly with lid or plastic wrap; refrigerate.

To reheat: Vent plastic wrap, if using. Microwave, covered, at 70% (MEDIUM HIGH) for time in chart above or until heated through, stirring twice.

How to Make Deviled Cocktail Tidbits

Microwave currant jelly, crème de cassis, mustard and horseradish until jelly melts. Blend together cornstarch and cold water, then whisk into hot jelly mixture.

Microwave jelly mixture until thickened and clear, stirring often to prevent lumps in the sauce. Microwave meatballs and cocktail franks in the sauce and serve with cocktail picks.

Basic Cocktail Meatballs

YIELD	60 balls	30 balls	15 balls
INGREDIENTS			
ground beef chuck	1 lb.	8 oz.	4 oz.
quick-cooking oats	1/4 cup	3 tablespoons	1 tablespoon
ketchup	2 tablespoons	1 tablespoon	2 teaspoons
egg	1	1	1 egg yolk
instant minced onion	2 teaspoons	1 teaspoon	1/2 teaspoon
dried parsley flakes	1 teaspoon	1/2 teaspoon	1/4 teaspoon
celery salt	1/2 teaspoon	1/4 teaspoon	1/8 teaspoon
BAKING DISH	12-inch square microwave baker	12" x 7" baking dish	8-inch square baking dish
TIME AT HIGH	4 minutes	2 minutes	2 minutes
TIME AT 30%	3 to 4 minutes	3 to 4 minutes	2 to 3 minutes

In a medium bowl, combine ground beef, oats, ketchup, egg or egg yolk, onion, parsley flakes and celery salt; mix thoroughly. Shape into 3/4-inch balls, see number in chart above, using about 1/2 tablespoon for each meatball. Place in a baking dish, see size in chart above. Cover with vented plastic wrap. Microwave at full power (HIGH) for time in chart above. Turn meatballs over and rearrange in baking dish; cover. Microwave at 30% (MEDIUM LOW) for time in chart above or until done when cut in center. Drain.

Mexicali Cocktail Tidbits

YIELD	6 cups	3 cups	1-1/2 cups
INGREDIENTS			
cooked Basic Cocktail Meatballs, page 33, and/or cocktail franks	60	30	15
chili sauce	2 cups	1 cup	1/2 cup
water	1 cup	1/2 cup	1/4 cup
chopped canned green chilies	1/2 cup	1/4 cup	2 tablespoons
chopped green onion	1/3 cup	3 tablespoons	2 tablespoons
taco seasoning mix	1/3 cup	3 tablespoons	4 teaspoons
shredded process American cheese	1 cup (4 oz.)	1/2 cup (2 oz.)	1/4 cup (1 oz.)
BAKING DISH	deep 3-qt. casserole	deep 1-1/2-qt. casserole	deep 1-qt. casserole
TIME AT HIGH (sauce)	6 to 8 minutes	3 minutes	1-1/2 to 2 minutes
TIME AT HIGH (meat added)	9 to 10 minutes	5 to 6 minutes	2 to 3 minutes
TIME AT HIGH (cheese added)	1-1/2 to 2 minutes	1 to 1-1/2 minutes	1 minute

Prepare Basic Cocktail Meatballs, if using. In a casserole, see size in chart above, combine chili sauce, water, chilies, green onion and taco seasoning. Mix well. Cover. Microwave at full power (HIGH) for time in chart above or until boiling, stirring once. Stir in meatballs or franks. Cover. Microwave at full power (HIGH) for time in chart above or until heated through, stirring once. Top with shredded cheese. Microwave, uncovered, at full power (HIGH) for time in chart above or until cheese has melted. Serve with cocktail picks.

Sweet & Sour Cocktail Tidbits

YIELD	4 cups	2 cups
INGREDIENTS		
cooked Basic Cocktail Meatballs, page 33, and/or cocktail franks	30	15
sauce from Sweet & Sour Ham Balls, page 120	large recipe	small recipe
pineapple chunks, drained	1 (8-oz.) can	1/2 (8-oz.) can
BAKING DISH	deep 2-qt. casserole	deep 1-qt. casserole
TIME AT HIGH	5 minutes	2 to 3 minutes

Prepare Basic Cocktail Meatballs, if using. Prepare sauce from Sweet & Sour Ham Balls in a casserole, see size in chart above. Stir in pineapple and meatballs or franks. Cover. Microwave at full power (HIGH) for time in chart above or until heated through, stirring once. Serve with cocktail picks.

Chicken Liver & Bacon Appetizers (Rumaki)

Photo on page 13.

YIELD	18 pieces
INGREDIENTS	
chicken livers	4 oz.
soy sauce	2 tablespoons
dry sherry	1 tablespoon
garlic, minced	1 clove
grated fresh gingerroot	1 teaspoon
water chestnuts, drained	1/2 (8-oz.) can
bacon	9 slices
BAKING DISH	12-inch square microwave baker with microwave rack
TIME AT HIGH (bacon)	4 minutes
TIME AT HIGH (Rumaki)	5-1/2 to 6-1/2 minutes

Cut chicken livers in 1-inch pieces. Pierce with a large fork. In a medium bowl, combine soy sauce, sherry, garlic and gingerroot. Mix well. Place chicken livers in marinade. Cover and marinate at room temperature 30 minutes. Cut water chestnuts in half. Cut bacon slices in half crosswise. Remove chicken livers from marinade. Place bacon on a rack in a 12-inch square microwave baker. Cover with white paper towels. Microwave at full power (HIGH) 4 minutes or until bacon begins to brown. Place 1 piece of water chestnut and 1 piece of chicken liver on 1 half-slice of bacon. Roll up and secure with a wooden pick. Place on rack in same baker. Repeat with remaining water chestnuts, chicken livers and bacon. Microwave at full power (HIGH) 5-1/2 to 6-1/2 minutes or until bacon is crisp and liver is slightly pink. Turn livers over and rearrange once during cooking.

Note: To cook 8 ounces of chicken livers, cook in 2 batches using directions above. Do not attempt to microwave 36 Rumaki at once.

Defrosting Chicken Livers

YIELD	1 lb.	8 oz.
INGREDIENTS		
frozen chicken livers	2 (8-oz.) blocks	1 (8-oz.) block
BAKING DISH	12" x 7" baking dish with microwave rack	round, 8-inch baking dish with microwave rack
TIME AT 30%	4 minutes	3 minutes
TIME AT 10%	5 minutes	3 minutes
STANDING TIME	5 minutes	3 minutes

Remove chicken livers from package. Place frozen chicken livers on a microwave rack in a baking dish, see size in chart above. Cover with waxed paper. Microwave at 30% (MEDIUM LOW) for time in chart above, turning livers over once halfway through defrosting time. Separate pieces as soon as possible, placing the more-frozen livers to outside of dish. Cover with waxed paper. Microwave at 10% (LOW) for time in chart above. Let stand, covered, same number of minutes as livers defrosted at 10%. Livers should be cool to the touch but completely defrosted after standing time. Chicken livers must be completely defrosted before cooking.

Chicken Liver Pâté

YIELD	2 cups
INGREDIENTS	
chicken livers	1 lb.
chicken broth	2 cups
chopped onion	2 tablespoons
butter or margarine, softened	1/4 cup
mayonnaise or salad dressing	2 tablespoons
brandy	2 tablespoons
celery salt	1 teaspoon
dry mustard	1/2 teaspoon
ground thyme	1/4 teaspoon
ground allspice	1/4 teaspoon
bay leaves	4
cranberry-orange relish, drained	1/4 cup
watercress, cranberry-orange relish	to garnish
BAKING DISH	deep 2-qt. casserole
TIME AT HIGH	6 to 8 minutes
TIME AT 30%	2 to 3 minutes

Oil a 2-1/2-cup mold or small bowl; set aside. Pierce chicken livers with a large fork. I[n] a deep 2-quart casserole, combine chicken broth, chicken livers and onion. Cover. Mi[cro]crowave at full power (HIGH) 6 to 8 minutes or until boiling. Stir well. Cover. Micro[wave at 30% (MEDIUM LOW) 2 to 3 minutes or until livers are only slightly pink i[n] center. Drain. Using a food processor fitted with a steel blade, process liver mixtur[e] until smooth. Add butter or margarine, mayonnaise or salad dressing, brandy, celer[y] salt, dry mustard, thyme and allspice to liver mixture. Process until smooth. Cover an[d] refrigerate 1 hour. Arrange bay leaves in the bottom of oiled mold or bowl. Pack hal[f] the liver mixture in mold. Make a 1/4-inch hollow in pâté in mold. Spread first amoun[t] of cranberry relish in hollow. Top with remaining liver mixture. Cover mold with foi[l.] Refrigerate several hours or overnight. Dip mold in hot water. Turn mixture out o[f] mold onto platter. Garnish with watercress and additional cranberry-orange relis[h.] Serve with assorted crackers.

Reheating Refrigerated Rumaki

SERVINGS	2	1
INGREDIENTS		
cooked Rumaki, page 35	8	4
PLATE	plate	plate
TIME AT 70%	1-1/4 minutes	40 to 45 seconds

To chill: Place cooled Rumaki on a plate. Cover with plastic wrap; refrigerate.

To reheat: Place a white paper towel under Rumaki on plate. Cover with anothe[r] white paper towel. Microwave at 70% (MEDIUM HIGH) for time in chart above o[r] until heated through.

How to Make Chicken Liver Pâté

il a 2-1/2-cup mold, then line the bottom of the old with whole bay leaves. Oiling the mold elps the chilled pâté slip out of the mold more asily.

Pierce the chicken livers with a large fork to puncture the membrane. If the membrane is not punctured, the livers may burst during microwave cooking.

ombine the cooked livers with butter, mayonaise, brandy, celery salt, dry mustard, thyme d allspice in a processor fitted with a steel ade. Process until mixture is smooth. Refrigere at least 1 hour.

Spoon half of the chilled pâté into the mold. Make a hollow about 1/4 inch deep in the center. Spoon drained cranberry-orange relish into the hollow. Spread the remaining pâté over the relish layer. Refrigerate until firm.

Curried Chicken Filling Photo on page 13.

YIELD	large recipe (2 cups)	small recipe (1 cup)
INGREDIENTS		
finely diced cooked chicken	1 cup	1/2 cup
finely chopped apple	1/2 cup	1/4 cup
raisins	1/4 cup	2 tablespoons
chopped celery	2 tablespoons	1 tablespoon
chopped green onion	2 tablespoons	1 tablespoon
chopped peanuts	2 tablespoons	1 tablespoon
mayonnaise or mayonnaise-style salad dressing	2 tablespoons	1 tablespoon
plain yogurt	2 tablespoons	1 tablespoon
curry powder	1 teaspoon	1/2 teaspoon
apple slices	to garnish	to garnish

In a medium bowl, combine chicken, chopped apple, raisins, celery, green onion and peanuts. In a small bowl, mix together mayonnaise or salad dressing, yogurt and curry powder. Combine chicken mixture and mayonnaise mixture; toss lightly to mix well. Use in recipe for Basic Snack Sandwiches, opposite. Garnish with apple slices.

Tuna Salad Filling

YIELD	large recipe (2 cups)	small recipe (1 cup)
INGREDIENTS		
crushed pineapple	1 (8-oz.) can	1/2 (8-oz.) can
pineapple juice	1 tablespoon	2 teaspoons
tuna, drained, flaked	1 (7-oz.) can	1 (3-1/2-oz.) can
shredded cabbage	1 cup	1/2 cup
chopped green onion	2 tablespoons	1 tablespoon
chopped pimiento-stuffed green olives	2 tablespoons	1 tablespoon
mayonnaise or mayonnaise-style salad dressing	3 tablespoons	2 tablespoons
celery salt	dash	dash
pepper	dash	dash
chopped hard-cooked egg, avocado slices, paprika	to garnish	to garnish

Drain pineapple, reserving amount of juice listed in chart above. In a medium bowl combine tuna, cabbage, green onion, olives and pineapple. In a small bowl, combine mayonnaise or salad dressing, pineapple juice, celery salt and pepper. Mix well. Combine tuna mixture and mayonnaise mixture. Toss lightly to mix well. Use in recipe for Basic Snack Sandwiches, opposite. Garnish with chopped hard-cooked egg and avocado slices. Sprinkle with paprika.

Tip

- Stir cooked ham cut in julienne strips into your favorite barbecue sauce. Microwave at full power (HIGH) until heated through. Spoon into small pita bread halves. Microwave using Basic Snack Sandwiches, opposite, as a guideline.

How to Make Basic Snack Sandwiches

Spoon Tuna Salad Filling or Curried Chicken Filling into small pita bread halves. Place on a plate on top of a napkin. Microwave until warm.

Garnish the tuna salad sandwiches with chopped hard-cooked egg and avocado slices. Sprinkle with paprika. A mug of soup makes the perfect sandwich accompaniment.

Basic Snack Sandwiches   Photo on page 13.

SERVINGS	5 or 6	2 or 3
INGREDIENTS		
Curried Chicken Filling or Tuna Salad Filling, opposite	large recipe	small recipe
pita bread, split crosswise OR	5 or 6 (4-inch diameter)	2 or 3 (4-inch diameter)
party rye bread or Melba toast	12 to 14 slices	6 or 7 slices
PLATE	12-inch microwave pizza plate	10-inch plate
TIME AT HIGH	2-1/2 to 3 minutes	1-1/2 to 2 minutes

Prepare filling. Spoon into pita bread halves or spread on party rye bread or Melba toast. Place on a paper-towel-lined plate, see size in chart above. Microwave at full power (HIGH) for time in chart above or until filling is heated through, giving plate a half turn once. For garnishing ideas, refer to recipes for fillings.

Basic Appetizer Oysters

SERVINGS	4	2
INGREDIENTS		
Savory Cheese Stuffing, page 42, Easy Spinach Stuffing, below, or Bacon-Nut Stuffing, page 44	medium recipe	small recipe
butter or margarine	1 tablespoon	2 teaspoons
lemon juice	1/2 teaspoon	1/4 teaspoon
fresh shucked oysters, drained	8	4
APPETIZER OR OYSTER SHELLS	8	4
PLATE	12-inch microwave pizza plate	7-inch pie plate
TIME AT HIGH	45 seconds	30 seconds
TIME AT 50%	4 to 5 minutes	2 to 3 minutes
STANDING TIME (spinach-stuffed oysters)	1 minute	1 minute

Prepare stuffing. Place butter or margarine in a custard cup. Microwave at full power (HIGH) for time in chart above or until melted. Stir in lemon juice. Pat oysters dry on paper towels. Pierce with a large fork. Dip oysters in melted butter or margarine mixture and place in shells. Top oysters with prepared stuffing. Drizzle with any remaining butter or margarine mixture. Arrange in a circle on a plate, see size in chart above. Garnish as directed in stuffing recipe. Microwave at 50% (MEDIUM) for time in chart above or until heated through and oysters are tender, giving plate a half turn once. Let spinach-stuffed oysters stand 1 minute before serving.

Easy Spinach Stuffing

YIELD	large recipe (2 cups)	medium recipe (1 cup)	small recipe (1/2 cup)
INGREDIENTS			
frozen spinach soufflé	1 (12-oz.) pkg.	1/2 (12-oz.) pkg.	1/4 (12-oz.) pkg.
seasoned dry breadcrumbs	1/3 cup	3 tablespoons	2 tablespoons
grated Parmesan cheese	1/3 cup	3 tablespoons	2 tablespoons
pimiento strips	to garnish	to garnish	to garnish
BOWL	1-qt. bowl	1-qt. bowl	2-cup bowl
TIME AT 30%	6 to 7 minutes	3 minutes	2 minutes
STANDING TIME	3 minutes	3 minutes	3 minutes

Remove frozen soufflé from package. If necessary, cut amount to be used with a sharp knife. Return any remaining soufflé to the freezer. Place frozen soufflé in a bowl, see size in chart above. Microwave at 30% (MEDIUM LOW) for time in chart above or until thawed, breaking up with a fork once. Let stand 3 minutes. Stir breadcrumbs and Parmesan cheese into soufflé. Use as directed in recipes for Basic Stuffed Mushrooms, page 45, Basic Stuffed Artichokes, page 42, and Basic Appetizer Oysters, above. Garnish with pimiento strips.

How to Make Basic Appetizer Oysters

Pierce the oysters with a large fork to break the membrane. This helps prevent the oysters from bursting during microwaving.

Dip the oysters in a mixture of melted butter and lemon juice. Place the butter-dipped oysters either in small appetizer shells or rinse and reuse the oyster shells.

Place the shells in a circle in a baking dish. Top each oyster with a spoonful of cheese, spinach or other stuffing of your choice.

Garnish each mound of stuffing with a swirl of pimiento or other garnish. Microwave at 50% (MEDIUM) to keep oysters tender.

Basic Stuffed Artichokes

SERVINGS	6	3
INGREDIENTS		
Savory Cheese Stuffing, below, Easy Spinach Stuffing, page 40, or Bacon-Nut Stuffing, page 44	large recipe	medium recipe
artichoke bottoms, drained	2 (14-oz.) cans (about 12 bottoms)	1 (14-oz.) can (about 6 bottoms)
butter or margarine	3 tablespoons	2 tablespoons
lemon juice	1 teaspoon	1/2 teaspoon
BAKING DISH	12-inch square microwave baker	12-inch microwave pizza plate
TIME AT HIGH (butter)	45 to 60 seconds	30 seconds
TIME AT HIGH (artichokes)	5 to 7 minutes	3 to 5 minutes
STANDING TIME (spinach-stuffed artichokes)	1 minute	1 minute

Prepare stuffing. Rinse artichoke bottoms and pat dry with paper towels. Place butter or margarine in a 1-1/2-cup bowl. Microwave at full power (HIGH) for time in chart above or until melted. Stir in lemon juice. Dip artichokes in butter or margarine mixture. Top artichokes with prepared stuffing. Arrange in a circle in a baking dish, see size in chart above. Drizzle with any remaining butter or margarine mixture. Garnish as directed in stuffing recipe. Microwave at full power (HIGH) for time in chart above or until heated through, giving dish a half turn once. Let spinach-stuffed artichokes stand 1 minute before serving.

Savory Cheese Stuffing

YIELD	large recipe (3 cups)	medium recipe (1-1/2 cups)	small recipe (3/4 cup)
INGREDIENTS			
herb-seasoned stuffing mix	1 cup	1/2 cup	1/4 cup
shredded Swiss cheese	1 cup	1/2 cup	1/4 cup
snipped parsley	1/2 cup	1/4 cup	2 tablespoons
finely chopped water chestnuts	1/2 cup	1/4 cup	2 tablespoons
chopped pimiento	1/4 cup	2 tablespoons	1 tablespoon
water	1/3 cup	3 tablespoons	1 tablespoon
chicken bouillon granules	1 teaspoon	1/2 teaspoon	1/4 teaspoon
pimiento strips	to garnish	to garnish	to garnish
GLASS MEASURING CUP	1-cup	1-cup	1-cup
TIME AT HIGH	45 to 60 seconds	30 seconds	15 seconds

In a medium bowl, combine stuffing mix, Swiss cheese, parsley, water chestnuts and chopped pimiento. In a 1-cup glass measuring cup, combine water and chicken bouillon granules. Microwave at full power (HIGH) for time in chart above or until water boils and granules have dissolved, stirring once. Add bouillon to stuffing mixture. Toss with a fork until mixed well. Use as directed in recipes for Basic Stuffed Mushrooms, page 45, Basic Stuffed Artichokes, above, and Basic Appetizer Oysters, page 40. Garnish with pimiento strips.

Starting at the top, Basic Stuffed Mushrooms, page 45, with Savory Cheese Stuffing; Basic Stuffed Artichokes with Bacon-Nut Stuffing, page 44; and Basic Appetizer Oysters, page 40, with Easy Spinach Stuffing, page 40.

Bacon-Nut Stuffing

YIELD	large recipe (2 cups)	medium recipe (1 cup)	small recipe (1/2 cup)
INGREDIENTS			
bacon	8 slices	4 slices	2 slices
bacon drippings	1/4 cup	2 tablespoons	1 tablespoon
chopped onion	1/2 cup	1/4 cup	2 tablespoons
chopped pecans, toasted	1/2 cup	1/4 cup	2 tablespoons
seasoned dry breadcrumbs	2/3 cup	1/3 cup	3 tablespoons
dry white wine	2 tablespoons	1 tablespoon	2 teaspoons
pecan halves	to garnish	to garnish	to garnish
BAKING DISH	12-inch square microwave baker with microwave rack	12" x 7" baking dish with microwave rack	round, 8-inch baking dish with microwave rack
TIME AT HIGH (bacon)	7 to 9 minutes	4 minutes	2 to 2-1/2 minutes
TIME AT HIGH (onion)	3 to 4 minutes	2 minutes	1 minute

Place bacon on a microwave rack in a baking dish, see size in chart above. Cover bacon with white paper towel. Microwave at full power (HIGH) for time in chart above or until crisp, giving dish a half turn once. Remove bacon. Drain on paper towels, then crumble. Remove rack from baking dish. Drain off all but amount of drippings listed in chart above. Add onion to baking dish. Microwave at full power (HIGH) for time in chart above or until tender, stirring once. Add chopped pecans, breadcrumbs, wine and crumbled bacon. Toss lightly to mix well. Use as directed in recipes for Basic Stuffed Mushrooms, opposite, Basic Stuffed Artichokes, page 42, and Basic Appetizer Oysters, page 40. Garnish with pecan halves.

Toasting Nuts

YIELD	1 cup	1/2 cup
INGREDIENTS		
slivered almonds or pecan pieces	1 cup	1/2 cup
PLATE	9-inch pie plate	7-inch pie plate
TIME AT HIGH	4 to 5 minutes	3 to 4 minutes

Spread nuts in a pie plate, see size in chart above. Microwave at full power (HIGH) for time in chart above or until lightly toasted, stirring three times. Nuts will continue to darken after they are removed from microwave oven.

Basic Stuffed Mushrooms

SERVINGS	4	2
INGREDIENTS		
Savory Cheese Stuffing, page 42, Easy Spinach Stuffing, page 40, or Bacon-Nut Stuffing, opposite	medium recipe	small recipe
fresh mushrooms, 1-1/2 inches in diameter	12	6
butter or margarine	2 tablespoons	1 tablespoon
BAKING DISH	12-inch microwave pizza plate	9-inch pie plate
TIME AT HIGH (butter)	45 seconds	30 seconds
TIME AT HIGH (mushrooms)	4 to 5 minutes	2 to 3 minutes
STANDING TIME (spinach-stuffed mushrooms)	1 minute	1 minute

Prepare stuffing. Remove stems from mushrooms and reserve for another use. Wash mushrooms and pat dry on paper towels. Place butter or margarine in a custard cup. Microwave at full power (HIGH) for time in chart above or until melted. Dip mushrooms in butter or margarine. Fill mushrooms with prepared stuffing. Arrange mushrooms in a circle in a baking dish, see size in chart above, propping mushrooms up along edge of dish. Drizzle with any remaining butter or margarine. Garnish as directed in stuffing recipe. Microwave at full power (HIGH) for time in chart above or until heated through, giving dish a half turn once. Remove any smaller mushrooms as soon as they are cooked and continue microwaving remaining mushrooms. Let spinach-stuffed mushrooms stand 1 minute before serving.

Toasting Seeds

YIELD	1/4 cup	2 tablespoons
INGREDIENTS		
sesame seeds or sunflower kernels	1/4 cup	2 tablespoons
PLATE	7-inch pie plate	7-inch pie plate
TIME AT HIGH	3 to 5 minutes	2 to 4 minutes

Spread seeds in a 7-inch pie plate. Microwave at full power (HIGH) for time in chart above or until lightly toasted, stirring twice. Seeds will continue to darken after they are removed from microwave oven.

Fruity Popcorn Treat

YIELD	12 cups	6 cups
INGREDIENTS		
popcorn, popped	2 qts.	1 qt.
salted peanuts	1 cup	1/2 cup
sunflower kernels	1 cup	1/2 cup
shredded coconut	2/3 cup	1/3 cup
sugar	1/2 cup	1/4 cup
butter or margarine	1/4 cup	2 tablespoons
ground cinnamon	1 teaspoon	1/2 teaspoon
salt	1 teaspoon	1/2 teaspoon
honey	1/2 cup	1/4 cup
golden raisins	1 cup	1/2 cup
snipped dried apricots or peaches	1 cup	1/2 cup
BAKING DISH	12-inch square microwave baker	12" x 7" baking dish
GLASS MEASURING CUP	1-qt.	2-cup
TIME AT HIGH	2 minutes	1 minute
TIME AT 30% (syrup)	5 minutes	3 minutes
TIME AT 30% (popcorn mixture)	5 minutes	3 minutes

In a baking dish, see size in chart above, combine popcorn, peanuts, sunflower kernels and coconut. Toss to mix well. Set aside. In a glass measuring cup, see size in chart above, combine sugar, butter or margarine, cinnamon and salt. Drizzle honey into sugar mixture. Microwave at full power (HIGH) for time in chart above or until boiling, stirring once. Stir well. Microwave at 30% (MEDIUM LOW) for time in chart above, stirring once. Pour over popcorn mixture. Mix with 2 forks, coating all pieces with syrup. Microwave at 30% (MEDIUM LOW) for time in chart above or until heated through, stirring once. Stir in raisins and apricots or peaches. Cool completely. Store in a tightly covered container.

Toasting Coconut

YIELD	1 cup	1/2 cup
INGREDIENTS		
flaked coconut	1 cup	1/2 cup
PLATE	9-inch pie plate	7-inch pie plate
TIME AT HIGH	3 to 3-1/2 minutes	2 to 2-1/2 minutes

Spread coconut in a pie plate, see size in chart above. Microwave at full power (HIGH) for time in chart above or until lightly toasted, stirring four times. **Watch coconut closely; it burns easily.** Coconut will continue to darken after it is removed from microwave oven.

Microwave Caution

Trying to pop popcorn in the microwave without the proper equipment can be dangerous and even result in fire! Do not attempt to pop popcorn in your microwave unless you have a popcorn popper specifically designed for use in microwave ovens. You should not pop popcorn in a paper bag or in oil in a regular casserole.

How to Make Fruity Popcorn Treat

Drizzle honey into a mixture of sugar, butter or margarine, cinnamon and salt in a glass measuring cup. Microwave honey mixture until boiling.

Pour the syrup mixture over popcorn, peanuts, sunflower kernels and coconut. Mix with forks, coating all pieces with syrup. Microwave until warm. Add raisins and snipped dried apricots.

TV Mix Italiano

YIELD	8 cups	4 cups
INGREDIENTS		
dry roasted mixed nuts with sesame sticks	2 cups	1 cup
chow mein noodles	1 (3-oz.) can (2 cups)	1/2 (3-oz.) can (1 cup)
corn cereal squares	2 cups	1 cup
pretzel twists	2 cups	1 cup
butter or margarine	1/4 cup	2 tablespoons
dry spaghetti sauce mix	2 tablespoons	1 tablespoon
grated Parmesan cheese	2 tablespoons	1 tablespoon
Italian herbs	1 teaspoon	1/2 teaspoon
BAKING DISH	12-inch square microwave baker	12" x 7" baking dish
GLASS MEASURING CUP	1-cup	1-cup
TIME AT HIGH	45 seconds	30 seconds
TIME AT 30%	7 to 8 minutes	4 minutes

In a baking dish, see size in chart above, toss together nuts, chow mein noodles, cereal squares and pretzels. Set aside. In a 1-cup glass measuring cup, combine butter or margarine and spaghetti sauce mix. Microwave at full power (HIGH) for time in chart above, or until butter or margarine has melted. Mix well. Pour over nut mixture, tossing to coat evenly. Microwave at 30% (MEDIUM LOW) for time in chart above or until mixture is toasted and heated through, stirring twice. Sprinkle with Parmesan cheese and Italian herbs. Cool completely. Store in a plastic bag or airtight container.

Nut Nibblers

YIELD	6 cups	3 cups
INGREDIENTS		
butter or margarine	1/4 cup	2 tablespoons
celery salt	2 teaspoons	1 teaspoon
chili powder	2 teaspoons	1 teaspoon
onion powder	2 teaspoons	1 teaspoon
mixture of pecan halves, cashews, whole almonds	7 cups (26 oz.)	3-1/2 cups (13 oz.)
GLASS MEASURING CUP	1-cup	1-cup
BAKING DISH	12-inch square microwave baker	12" x 7" baking dish
TIME AT HIGH	45 seconds	30 seconds
TIME AT 30%	40 to 45 minutes	20 minutes

In a 1-cup glass measuring cup, combine butter or margarine, celery salt, chili powder and onion powder. Microwave at full power (HIGH) for time in chart above or until butter or margarine has melted. Place nuts in a baking dish, see size in chart above. Stir butter or margarine mixture; pour over nuts. Toss until coated thoroughly. Microwave at 30% (MEDIUM LOW) for time in chart above or until toasted, stirring three times. Cool completely. Store in a plastic bag or airtight container.

Nachos

YIELD	24 chips	12 chips	6 chips
INGREDIENTS			
tortilla chips	24	12	6
chopped canned green chilies	to taste	to taste	to taste
shredded Cheddar cheese	1-1/3 cups	2/3 cup	1/3 cup
taco seasoning mix	to garnish	to garnish	to garnish
PLATE	12-inch microwave pizza plate	12-inch microwave pizza plate	9-inch pie plate
TIME AT HIGH	1 to 1-1/4 minutes	30 to 45 seconds	25 to 30 seconds

Place tortilla chips in a circle on a paper-towel-lined plate, see size in chart above. Top each chip with a few chopped green chilies. Top with shredded cheese. Sprinkle cheese with taco seasoning mix. Microwave at full power (HIGH) for time in chart above or until cheese melts, giving plate a half turn once.

Tips

- For a fast snack, melt cheese of various kinds on assorted crackers. Use a paper-towel-lined plate so crackers remain crisp. Follow the timings for Bacon-Olive Topping on Cracker Melts, page 31, as a guideline.
- For creamy cheese toppings with cream cheese, sour cream or yogurt, follow the timings for Swiss Topping on Cracker Melts, page 31, as a guideline.

Meats

Meats

New defrosting techniques mean you no longer have to remember in the morning to take meat out of the freezer for the evening meal. Complete instructions tell you how to bring meats from freezer to table in less time than you thought possible.

Q. What are the advantages of cooking meat in the microwave?

A. Most meats can be cooked in the microwave with a good time saving. In addition, there are fewer preparation dishes and no baked-on mess to clean up.

Q. What are the disadvantages of cooking meat in the microwave?

A. A few meats, such as pot roast, take almost as long to cook in the microwave as they would conventionally. In addition, these meats usually require more attention from the cook when the microwave is used. Unless the microwave is the only cooking device available, it may be less trouble to cook these recipes conventionally. Roasts may be cooked considerably faster in the microwave. But they also require more attention and should be a uniform and compact shape. When considering cost, time and convenience, many cooks may feel more comfortable cooking them conventionally.

Q. Which meats do not cook satisfactorily in the microwave?

A. Meats cannot be deep-fried in the microwave. Extra-large roasts and pot roasts are difficult to cook in the microwave because it is not easy to achieve an even doneness. Tips are given on how to select roasts that will give you the best possible results.

Q. How are meats cooked in the microwave?

A. Generally, meats are divided into the same two categories used in conventional cooking—meats requiring *moist-heat* cooking and those using *dry-heat* cooking. Most meats requiring moist heat in conventional cooking also require moist heat in microwave cooking. The same holds true for dry-heat microwave cooking. Ham is the most notable exception. It is cooked with moist heat in the microwave to prevent it from drying out.

Q. How do you know when meat is done?

A. Doneness tests are given with each type of basic meat recipe. A microwave meat thermometer is especially helpful when checking the doneness of roasts. Pot roasts should be fork-tender, just as they are when cooked conventionally. A small slit in the center of a chop will reveal if the meat is pink. Meat, and all foods, continue cooking during the standing time given in the recipe.

Q. How can I make meat cooked in the microwave look brown?

A. This is really only a problem for small, thin cuts, such as chops, which cook quickly. You can use a sauce or crumb coating to cover the meat. Or, sprinkle it sparingly with one of the color-enhancing products available. Or, use a flavoring such as paprika. The browning skillet has eliminated this problem with steaks, burgers and chops. With cuts requiring longer cooking, the opposite problem arises. You have to be careful to avoid overbrowning. Follow the cooking times given in the recipes. If the meat is cooked in liquid, be sure it is under the liquid throughout cooking. Meat cooked in the microwave darkens quickly after cooking. Keep meat closely covered after taking it from the oven. This includes sliced meat.

Q. How can favorite conventional recipes be converted for microwave cooking?

A. Throughout the chapter there are tips on how to adapt recipes to microwave techniques. Check the basic recipe given for the specific type of recipe you wish to make. Most recipes can be converted successfully for microwave cooking.

Q. What about cooking main-dish convenience foods in the microwave?

A. Many convenience foods can be microwaved. Check the packages for the manufacturers' instructions. The packaging material of frozen foods is changing rapidly to enable more foods to be cooked in original packaging in the microwave.

Q. How do you defrost meat in the microwave?

A. Microwave defrosting can be extremely successful if you use two power levels. Start defrosting at 30% (MEDIUM LOW) then use 10% (LOW) to finish the process. You will find complete directions for each type of meat in this section.

Q. Are there any special utensils needed to cook meats in the microwave?

A. Many meats requiring dry-heat cooking, such as roasts and chops, are cooked on a microwave rack in a baking dish. The rack holds the meat out of the juices so it will not stew. Most microwave racks are made from special plastic or ceramic. Inverted saucers can be used to simulate a rack. A browning skillet is essential for searing cuts like steaks or chops that cook in a short time.

How to Cook a Roast in the Microwave

After taking roast out of the microwave, insert a microwave meat thermometer into center of largest muscle of roast. The thermometer should not rest on bone or in fat. Most microwave thermometers register more accurately if they are not left in the roasts during cooking.

Place small pieces of foil on the roast and secure with wooden picks to shield areas that are overcooking. After cooking the roast, cover with a tent of foil. Roast will finish cooking during the standing time.

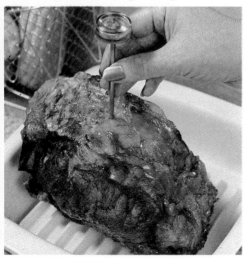
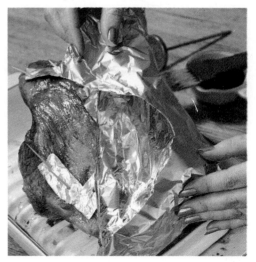

Defrosting Beef Rib Roast

SERVINGS	8	6
INGREDIENTS beef rib roast, 3-3/4 to 4-1/4 lbs.	boneless rolled-rib roast, 5-1/2 inches in diameter, 4-1/2 inches long	bone-in standing-rib roast, cut from small end, ribs 11 and 12, 5 to 5-1/2 inches high, 6 to 7 inches long
BAKING DISH	12" x 7" baking dish with microwave rack	12" x 7" baking dish with microwave rack
TIME AT 30%	20 minutes	20 minutes
TIME AT 10%	20 to 40 minutes	20 to 40 minutes
STANDING TIME	20 to 40 minutes	20 to 40 minutes

Place prepackaged meat, Styrofoam tray side down, on a microwave rack or inverted saucer in a shallow 12" x 7" baking dish. Microwave at 30% (MEDIUM LOW) for time in chart, removing packaging as soon as possible and covering meat loosely with waxed paper. After half the time, turn meat over on rack or saucer. Shield edges and warm fat areas with small pieces of foil. For a leg of lamb roast, shield shank end and shank bone, if present, with foil. Secure with wooden picks, if necessary. Cover loosely with waxed paper. After defrosting at 30%, turn roast over. Shield any warm edges or areas with more small pieces of foil. Cover loosely with waxed paper. Microwave at 10% (LOW) for minimum time in chart, turning roast over once. Let roast stand for same number of minutes as it defrosted at 10%. Insert a metal skewer into center of meat. If skewer can be inserted easily, begin cooking time. If skewer cannot be inserted easily, microwave at 10% (LOW) for remaining time in chart, turning roast over once. Let roast stand again same number of minutes as it defrosted the second time at 10%. Meat should be cool to the touch but completely defrosted before cooking.

Defrosting Leg of Lamb

SERVINGS	8 to 10	4 or 5
INGREDIENTS leg of lamb	whole*, 5 to 7 lbs.	sirloin half or shank half*, 3-1/2 to 4 lbs.
BAKING DISH	12" x 7" baking dish with microwave rack	12" x 7" baking dish with microwave rack
TIME AT 30%	28 minutes	18 minutes
TIME AT 10%	28 to 42 minutes	18 to 36 minutes
STANDING TIME	28 to 42 minutes	18 to 36 minutes

See directions for Defrosting Beef Rib Roast, above.

*Ask the butcher to hinge the shank bone so roast can be bent to fit the baking dish. Or have shank bone removed and meat skewered back to roast with wooden skewers. If shank bone is removed, do not cap the shank end with foil.

How to Defrost Pork Loin Roast

Halfway through the 30% (MEDIUM LOW) defrosting time, shield the edges of the roast with strips of foil. Secure the strips of foil with wooden picks to hold them tightly against the roast. This helps prevent the edges from starting to cook during defrosting time.

After the standing time, insert a metal skewer into the thickest portion of the roast. The skewer should slide in easily with little pressure. If the skewer cannot be inserted easily, continue defrosting the roast at 10% (LOW). Let the roast stand the same number of extra minutes it was defrosted at 10% (LOW).

Defrosting Pork Loin Roast

SERVINGS	8	6
INGREDIENTS pork loin roast, about 4 lbs.	boneless roast, 3 to 4 inches in diameter, 9-1/2 to 10 inches long	bone-in roast, 3 to 4 inches in diameter, 6-1/2 inches long
BAKING DISH	12" x 7" baking dish with microwave rack	12" x 7" baking dish with microwave rack
TIME AT 30%	20 minutes	20 minutes
TIME AT 10%	20 to 40 minutes	20 to 40 minutes
STANDING TIME	20 to 40 minutes	20 to 40 minutes

See directions for Defrosting Beef Rib Roast, opposite.

How to Defrost Beef Chuck Roast

When roast is halfway through the 30% (MEDIUM LOW) defrosting time, slash the fat edges of the roast at about 1-inch intervals so the roast will stay flat during cooking. Fat edges are difficult to slash when warm.

To make paper-thin slices of roast for stir-frying, cut the slices with a sharp knife when the roast is partway through the 10% (LOW) defrosting time. It's easier to cut the meat into thin slices while it is still partially frozen.

Defrosting Beef or Veal Chuck Roast

SERVINGS	6	4	2
INGREDIENTS beef or veal chuck roast, 1-1/2 to 2 inches thick	3 lbs.	2 lbs.	1 lb.
BAKING DISH	12" x 7" baking dish with microwave rack	12" x 7" baking dish with microwave rack	8-inch round or square baking dish with microwave rack
TIME AT 30%	15 minutes	10 minutes	5 minutes
TIME AT 10%	15 to 30 minutes	10 to 20 minutes	5 to 10 minutes
STANDING TIME	15 to 30 minutes	10 to 20 minutes	5 to 10 minutes

Place prepackaged meat, Styrofoam tray side down, on a microwave rack or inverted saucer in a shallow baking dish, see size in chart above. Microwave at 30% (MEDIUM LOW) for time in chart above, removing packaging as soon as possible and covering with waxed paper. Halfway through defrosting at 30%, slash fat edges of roast at 1-inch intervals. Microwave for remaining time at 30%. Turn roast over on rack or saucer. Shield edges with small pieces of foil. Secure with wooden picks, if necessary. Cover loosely with waxed paper. Microwave at 10% (LOW) for minimum time in chart above, turning roast over once. Let roast stand, covered, for same number of minutes as it defrosted at 10%. Insert a metal skewer into center of meat. If skewer can be inserted easily, begin cooking time. If skewer cannot be inserted easily, turn roast over and microwave at 10% (LOW) for remaining time in chart above. Let roast stand again same number of minutes as it defrosted the second time at 10%. Meat should be cool to the touch but completely defrosted before cooking.

Defrosting Beef Ribs

SERVINGS	3 or 4	2

INGREDIENTS
beef short ribs,
  2-1/2 inches long,
  1/2 to 1 inch thick
	3 to 3-1/2 lbs.	1-1/2 lbs.

BAKING DISH	12-inch square microwave baker with microwave rack	12" x 7" baking dish with microwave rack
TIME AT 30%	10 minutes	5 minutes
TIME AT 10%	10 to 15 minutes	7 to 10 minutes
STANDING TIME	10 to 15 minutes	7 to 10 minutes

Place prepackaged meat, Styrofoam tray side down, on a microwave rack or inverted saucer in a shallow baking dish, see size in chart above. Microwave at 30% (MEDIUM LOW) for time in chart, removing packaging as soon as possible and covering loosely with waxed paper. After defrosting at 30%, separate ribs and lay flat. Place the more frosty ribs toward outside of dish. For pork ribs, shield all edges with small strips of foil. Secure with wooden picks, if necessary. For beef ribs, the ribs along the outside edge of the dish will become warm before ribs in center of dish are thawed. Shield outside edges of outer ribs with small pieces of foil. Cover loosely with waxed paper. Microwave at 10% (LOW) for minimum time in chart. Remove any defrosted ribs. If some ribs are still icy, microwave at 10% (LOW) for remaining time in chart. Let stand same number of minutes as meat defrosted at 10%. Meat should be cool to the touch but completely defrosted before cooking.

Defrosting Pork Ribs

SERVINGS	3 or 4	2 or 3	1 or 2
INGREDIENTS pork loin back ribs	3-1/2 lbs.	2 lbs.	1 lb.
BAKING DISH	12-inch square microwave baker with microwave rack	12" x 7" baking dish with microwave rack	12" x 7" baking dish with microwave rack
TIME AT 30%	11 minutes	6 minutes	3 minutes
TIME AT 10%	5-1/2 to 11 minutes	4 to 8 minutes	2 to 4 minutes
STANDING TIME	5-1/2 to 11 minutes	4 to 8 minutes	2 to 4 minutes

See directions for Defrosting Beef Ribs, above.

Tips

- Shield any warm areas of meat with foil during defrosting. Areas that become warm will continue to get warmer than the rest of the meat and may start cooking.

Defrosting Beef Rib-Eye Steaks

SERVINGS	2	1
INGREDIENTS beef rib-eye steaks, 3/4 to 1 inch thick	2 (11-oz.) steaks	1 (11-oz.) steak
BAKING DISH	12" x 7" baking dish with microwave rack	8-inch round or square baking dish with microwave rack
TIME AT 30%	6 minutes	4 minutes
TIME AT 10%	7 to 10 minutes	3 to 5 minutes
STANDING TIME	7 to 10 minutes	3 to 5 minutes

Place prepackaged meat, Styrofoam tray side down, on a microwave rack or inverted saucer in a shallow baking dish, see size in chart above. Microwave at 30% (MEDIUM LOW) for time in chart, removing packaging as soon as possible and covering loosely with waxed paper. After defrosting at 30%, turn meat over on rack or saucer. Separate steaks, if possible. Shield edges with small pieces of foil. Secure with wooden picks, if necessary. Cover loosely with waxed paper. Microwave at 10% (LOW) for minimum time in chart, turning meat over once. If meat is still icy, continue defrosting at 10% (LOW) for remaining time in chart, turning steaks over once. Let steaks stand same number of minutes as they defrosted at 10%. Meat should be cool to the touch but completely defrosted before cooking.

Defrosting Beef T-Bone Steaks

SERVINGS	2	1	2	1
INGREDIENTS beef T-bone steaks	2 (1-1/4- to 1-1/2-lb.) steaks, 1-1/2 inches thick	1 (1-1/4- to 1-1/2-lb.) steak, 1-1/2 inches thick	2 (3/4-lb.) steaks, 1 inch thick	1 (3/4-lb.) steak, 1 inch thick
BAKING DISH	12" x 7" baking dish with microwave rack	8-inch round or square baking dish with microwave rack	12" x 7" baking dish with microwave rack	8-inch round or square baking dish with microwave rack
TIME AT 30%	8 minutes	5 minutes	5 minutes	4 minutes
TIME AT 10%	15 to 20 minutes	7 to 10 minutes	5 to 8 minutes	4 to 7 minutes
STANDING TIME	15 to 20 minutes	7 to 10 minutes	5 to 8 minutes	4 to 7 minutes

See directions for Defrosting Beef Rib-Eye Steaks, above.

Tip

- Slash the fat edges of steaks and chops before meat is completely defrosted. It's difficult to slash fat once it warms up during defrosting.
- Standing times after defrosting at 10% (LOW) are very important to help the meat defrost evenly.

Defrosting Beef Sirloin Steak

SERVINGS	4	2
INGREDIENTS beef sirloin steak	2 lbs., 1 to 1-1/4 inches thick	1 lb., 1/2 to 3/4 inch thick
BAKING DISH	12-inch square microwave baker with microwave rack	12" x 7" baking dish with microwave rack
TIME AT 30%	10 minutes	5 minutes
TIME AT 10%	15 to 20 minutes	7 to 12 minutes
STANDING TIME	15 to 20 minutes	7 to 12 minutes

Place prepackaged meat, Styrofoam tray side down, on a microwave rack or inverted saucer in a shallow baking dish, see size in chart above. Microwave at 30% (MEDIUM LOW) for time in chart, removing packaging as soon as possible and covering loosely with waxed paper. After defrosting at 30%, turn meat over on rack or saucer. Shield edges with small pieces of foil. Secure with wooden picks, if necessary. Cover loosely with waxed paper. Microwave at 10% (LOW) for minimum time in chart, turning meat over once. If meat is still icy, continue defrosting at 10% (LOW) for remaining time in chart. Let steak stand same number of minutes as it defrosted at 10%. Meat should be cool to the touch but completely defrosted before cooking.

Defrosting Beef or Veal Round Steak

SERVINGS	5 or 6	3 or 4	2
INGREDIENTS beef or veal round steak, 1/2 inch thick	1-1/2 lbs.	1 lb.	8 oz.
BAKING DISH	12-inch square microwave baker with microwave rack	12" x 7" baking dish with microwave rack	8-inch round or square baking dish with microwave rack
TIME AT 30%	7-1/2 minutes	5 minutes	2-1/2 minutes
TIME AT 10%	10 to 15 minutes	5 to 10 minutes	4 to 7 minutes
STANDING TIME	10 to 15 minutes	5 to 10 minutes	4 to 7 minutes

See directions for Defrosting Beef Sirloin Steak, above.

Tips

● Check the meat and move the most frosty pieces toward the outside of the dish to speed up defrosting.

● Always defrost steaks, chops and roasts on a microwave rack to hold the meat out of any juices. Otherwise, the meat will stew in its own juice as it defrosts.

● Cover meat loosely with waxed paper during defrosting to keep it from drying out.

● Always cook defrosted meat as soon as possible.

● Do not refreeze meat unless ice crystals still remain in the meat. Even so, the meat will be less juicy after a second defrosting.

Defrosting Pork or Lamb Blade Steaks

SERVINGS	4	2	1

INGREDIENTS
pork or lamb
  blade steaks,
  1/2 to 5/8 inch
  thick
	4 (6-oz.) steaks	2 (6-oz.) steaks	1 (6-oz.) steak

BAKING DISH	12" x 7" baking dish with microwave rack	12" x 7" baking dish with microwave rack	8-inch round or square baking dish with microwave rack
TIME AT 30%	7-1/2 minutes	3-1/2 minutes	2-1/2 minutes
TIME AT 10%	7-1/2 to 10 minutes	3-1/2 to 5 minutes	2-1/2 to 4 minutes
STANDING TIME	7-1/2 to 10 minutes	3-1/2 to 5 minutes	2-1/2 to 4 minutes

See directions for Defrosting Beef Rib-Eye Steaks, page 56.

Defrosting Lamb Loin or Rib Chops

SERVINGS	3	2	1
INGREDIENTS lamb loin or rib chops, 1 to 1-1/4 inches thick	6 (4-oz.) chops	4 (4-oz.) chops	2 (4-oz.) chops
BAKING DISH	12" x 7" baking dish with microwave rack	8-inch square baking dish with microwave rack	9-inch pie plate with microwave rack
TIME AT 30%	7 minutes	4 minutes	3 minutes
TIME AT 10%	4 to 6 minutes	2 to 3 minutes	2 to 3 minutes
STANDING TIME	4 to 6 minutes	2 to 3 minutes	2 to 3 minutes

See directions for Defrosting Thick Pork Chops, opposite.

Defrosting Thin Pork or Veal Chops

SERVINGS	4	2	1
INGREDIENTS veal or pork chops, about 1/2 inch thick	4 (4-oz.) chops	2 (4-oz.) chops	1 (4-oz.) chop
BAKING DISH	12" x 7" baking dish with microwave rack	8-inch square baking dish with microwave rack	9-inch pie plate with microwave rack
TIME AT 30%	5 minutes	2-1/2 minutes	1-1/4 minutes
TIME AT 10%	3 to 5 minutes	2-1/2 to 3-1/2 minutes	1-1/4 to 2 minutes
STANDING TIME	3 to 5 minutes	2-1/2 to 3-1/2 minutes	1-1/4 to 2 minutes

See directions for Defrosting Thick Pork Chops, opposite.

How to Defrost Thick Pork Chops

Shield all edges of chops with small strips of foil before defrosting. Otherwise, the edges will become warm very quickly during defrosting and may start to cook. Secure the strips of foil with wooden picks.

If the chops are to be stuffed, it's easier to cut the pockets for the stuffing after the chops have defrosted for the 30% (MEDIUM LOW) time. Shield edges again with foil and defrost for 10% (LOW) time.

Defrosting Thick Pork Chops

SERVINGS	4	2	1
INGREDIENTS pork chops, about 1 inch thick	4 (8- or 9-oz.) chops	2 (8- or 9-oz.) chops	1 (8- or 9-oz.) chop
BAKING DISH	12" x 7" baking dish with microwave rack	8-inch square baking dish with microwave rack	9-inch pie plate with microwave rack
TIME AT 30%	10 minutes	5 minutes	2-1/2 minutes
TIME AT 10%	10 to 20 minutes	8 to 12 minutes	4 to 6 minutes
STANDING TIME	10 to 20 minutes	8 to 12 minutes	4 to 6 minutes

Place prepackaged meat, Styrofoam tray side down, on a microwave rack or inverted saucer in a shallow baking dish, see size in chart. Or, if possible, remove packaging and shield all edges with small pieces of foil, then cover loosely with waxed paper. Microwave at 30% (MEDIUM LOW) for time in chart, removing packaging and separating chops as soon as possible. Shield all edges with small pieces of foil. Secure with wooden picks, if necessary. After defrosting at 30%, place frosty chops toward outside of dish. Cover chops loosely with waxed paper. Microwave at 10% (LOW) for minimum time in chart, turning chops over once. If chops are still icy, microwave at 10% (LOW) for remaining time in chart. Let stand same number of minutes as chops defrosted at 10%. Meat should be cool to the touch but completely defrosted before cooking.

Defrosting Bulk Ground Meat

SERVINGS	4	2
INGREDIENTS bulk ground beef, pork or lamb	1 lb.	8 oz.
BAKING DISH	8-inch round or square baking dish with microwave rack	8-inch round or square baking dish with microwave rack
TIME AT 30%	5 minutes	2-1/2 minutes
TIME AT 10%	5 to 10 minutes	2-1/2 to 5 minutes
STANDING TIME	5 to 10 minutes	2-1/2 to 5 minutes

Place prepackaged meat, Styrofoam tray side down, on a microwave rack or inverted saucer in a shallow 8-inch round or square baking dish. Microwave at 30% (MEDIUM LOW) for time in chart above, removing packaging as soon as possible and covering loosely with waxed paper. After defrosting at 30%, turn meat over on rack or saucer. Shield warm edges with small pieces of foil. Secure with wooden picks, if necessary. Cover loosely with waxed paper. Microwave at 10% (LOW) for minimum time in chart above, turning meat over once. Insert a metal skewer into center of meat. If skewer cannot be inserted easily, microwave at 10% (LOW) for remaining time in chart above, turning meat over once. Test again with metal skewer. If skewer can be inserted easily, let meat stand covered same number of minutes as it defrosted at 10%. Meat should be cool to the touch but completely defrosted before cooking.

Defrosting Ground-Meat Patties

SERVINGS	4	2	1

INGREDIENTS
ground-meat patties,
  4 inches in diameter,
  1/2 inch thick
	4 (4-oz.) patties	2 (4-oz.) patties	1 (4-oz.) patty

BAKING DISH	12" x 7" baking dish	9-inch pie plate	9-inch pie plate
TIME AT 30%	4 minutes	2 minutes	1-1/4 minutes
TIME AT 10%	3 to 4 minutes	2-1/2 to 3-1/2 minutes	2-1/2 to 3-1/2 minutes
STANDING TIME	3 to 4 minutes	2-1/2 to 3-1/2 minutes	2-1/2 to 3-1/2 minutes

Place patties in a shallow baking dish, see size in chart above. Remove packaging, if possible, and cover loosely with waxed paper. Microwave at 30% (MEDIUM LOW) for time in chart above. Remove packaging and turn patties over. Cover loosely with waxed paper. Microwave at 10% (LOW) for minimum time in chart above, turning patties over once. If patties are still icy, microwave at 10% (LOW) for remaining time in chart above. Let stand same number of minutes as meat defrosted at 10%. Meat should be cool to the touch but completely defrosted before cooking.

How to Defrost Stew Meat

As soon as possible, remove the meat from the Styrofoam tray and place it on a microwave rack. The Styrofoam tray will slow down defrosting.

To speed up defrosting, use a large fork to separate the cubes of meat as soon as possible. Place the icy pieces of meat toward the outside of the dish.

Defrosting Stew Meat

SERVINGS	3 or 4	2 or 3

INGREDIENTS
beef chuck, or lamb,
  pork or veal shoulder,
  cut in 1-inch cubes
	1 lb.	8 oz.

BAKING DISH	8-inch round or square baking dish with microwave rack	8-inch round or square baking dish with microwave rack
TIME AT 30%	5 minutes	2-1/2 minutes
TIME AT 10%	5 to 10 minutes	4 to 6 minutes
STANDING TIME	5 to 10 minutes	4 to 6 minutes

Place prepackaged meat, Styrofoam tray side down, on a microwave rack or inverted saucer in a shallow 8-inch round or square baking dish. Microwave at 30% (MEDIUM LOW) for time in chart above, removing packaging as soon as possible and covering loosely with waxed paper. After defrosting at 30%, turn meat over and break apart, if possible. Spread out meat on rack. Shield any warm edges with small pieces of foil. Secure with wooden picks, if necessary. Cover loosely with waxed paper. Microwave at 10% (LOW) for minimum time in chart above. If meat is still icy, rearrange on rack with frosty pieces toward outside of dish. Microwave at 10% (LOW) for remaining time in chart above. Let stand same number of minutes as meat defrosted at 10%. Meat should be cool to the touch but completely defrosted before cooking.

Speedy Stew

SERVINGS	3 or 4	2 or 3
INGREDIENTS		
beef chuck, or lamb, pork or veal shoulder, cut in 1-inch cubes	1 lb.	8 oz.
water	2-2/3 cups	1-1/3 cups
seasoning mix for stew	1 (1.5-oz.) envelope	1/2 (1.5-oz.) envelope
frozen stew vegetables	1 (24-oz.) pkg.	1/2 (24-oz.) pkg.
frozen peas	1 cup	1/2 cup
all-purpose flour	3 tablespoons	
cold water	1/3 cup	
BAKING DISH	deep 3-qt. casserole	deep 1-1/2-qt. casserole
TIME AT HIGH (meat)	10 minutes	10 minutes
TIME AT 30% (meat)	30 minutes	20 minutes
TIME AT 30% (stew vegetables added)	45 minutes	45 minutes
TIME AT 30% (peas added)	15 minutes	10 minutes
STANDING TIME	10 minutes	10 minutes
TIME AT HIGH (gravy)	2 to 3 minutes	

Pierce meat deeply on all sides with a large fork. Place meat in a casserole, see size in chart above. Add first amount of water and stew seasoning. Mix well, making sure meat is covered by liquid. Cover. Microwave at full power (HIGH) 10 minutes. Microwave at 30% (MEDIUM LOW) for time in chart above. Stir in frozen stew vegetables, making sure meat is still covered by liquid. Cover. Microwave at 30% (MEDIUM LOW) 45 minutes or until meat and vegetables are almost tender. Stir in peas; mix well. Cover. Microwave at 30% (MEDIUM LOW) for time in chart above or until meat and vegetables are tender. Let stand, covered, 10 minutes. If using larger recipe, shake together flour and cold water in a screw-top jar. Stir into stew. Microwave, uncovered, at full power (HIGH) 2 to 3 minutes or until thickened and bubbly, stirring three times.

Doneness Test: Meat is done when it can be shredded with a fork. Vegetables should be tender when pierced with a fork.

Defrosting: To defrost stew meat, see page 61.

How to Make Speedy Stew

Pierce the meat deeply on all sides with a large fork. This makes the meat more tender and juicy. Cut the meat into 1-inch cubes so pieces will be done at the same time.

When meat purchased is already cut in cubes, it is still important to pierce the cubes all over with a large fork. Place the cubes in a deep casserole and add stew-seasoning mix and water. All meat should be covered by liquid.

Partway through the cooking time, add the frozen stew vegetables. Make sure the meat cubes are still covered by liquid to prevent the meat from darkening. Frozen peas are added later so they won't overcook.

The stew is ready when the meat can be shredded with a fork and the vegetables are tender. Serve the stew in bowls either with its juices or with thickened gravy. The standing time after cooking is essential for maximum tenderness.

Basic Stew

SERVINGS	3 or 4	2 or 3
INGREDIENTS		
beef chuck, or lamb, pork or veal shoulder, cut in 1-inch cubes	1 lb.	8 oz.
vegetable-tomato juice cocktail	1 (12-oz.) can (1-1/2 cups)	1/2 (12-oz.) can (3/4 cup)
beef broth	1 (14-1/2-oz.) can	1 cup
bay leaf	1 large	1 small
Worcestershire sauce	1 tablespoon	2 teaspoons
dried leaf basil	1/2 teaspoon	1/4 teaspoon
potatoes, cut up	2 small	1 small
carrots, cut up	3 medium	2 small
onion, cut up	1 large	1 small
all-purpose flour	3 tablespoons	2 tablespoons
cold water	1/3 cup	1/4 cup
BAKING DISH	deep 3-qt. casserole	deep 1-1/2-qt. casserole
TIME AT HIGH	10 minutes	10 minutes
TIME AT 30%	80 to 90 minutes	50 to 60 minutes
STANDING TIME	10 minutes	10 minutes
TIME AT HIGH (gravy)	3 minutes	2 to 3 minutes

Pierce meat deeply on all sides with a large fork. In a casserole, see size in chart above combine meat, juice, broth, bay leaf, Worcestershire sauce and basil. Add vegetables Mix well, making sure meat is covered by liquid. Cover and microwave at full power (HIGH) 10 minutes. Microwave at 30% (MEDIUM LOW) for time in chart above o until meat and vegetables are tender, stirring once. Let stand, covered, 10 minutes. In a screw-top jar, shake together flour and cold water. Stir into stew. Microwave, uncovered, at full power (HIGH) for time in chart above or until thickened and bubbly, stirring three times.

Doneness Test: Meat is done when it can be shredded with a fork. Vegetables should be tender when pierced with a fork.

Tips

- It's easier to pierce partially frozen meat than meat that is completely thawed.
- Save time by piercing meat in a large piece with a fork, then cubing the meat for stew.
- Be sure meat is covered by liquid during cooking to prevent darkening.

Reheating Refrigerated Stew

SERVINGS	2	1
INGREDIENTS cooked stew	2 cups	1 cup
BAKING DISH	1-qt. casserole	2-cup casserole
TIME AT 70%	7 to 8 minutes	4-1/2 to 5 minutes
STANDING TIME	1 minute	1 minute

To chill: Place cooled stew in a casserole, see size in chart above. Cover with plastic wrap or lid; refrigerate.

To reheat: Vent plastic wrap, if using. Microwave, covered, at 70% (MEDIUM HIGH) for time in chart above or until heated through, stirring once. Let casserole stand, covered, 1 minute.

Reheating Frozen Stew

SERVINGS	3 or 4	2
INGREDIENTS cooked stew	1 qt.	2 cups
BAKING DISH	1-1/2-qt. casserole	1-qt. casserole
TIME AT 30%	30 to 35 minutes	20 minutes
TIME AT 70%	4 minutes	3 to 4 minutes
STANDING TIME	1 minute	1 minute

To freeze: Spoon cooled stew into a freezer container, leaving 1/2 inch headspace. Cover tightly and freeze.

To reheat: Dip freezer container in hot water to loosen stew. Place block of frozen stew in a casserole, see size in chart above. Cover. Microwave at 30% (MEDIUM LOW) for time in chart above. Break stew apart twice with a large fork, being careful not to break vegetable pieces. Cover. Microwave at 70% (MEDIUM HIGH) for time in chart above or until heated through, stirring once. Let stand, covered, 1 minute.

Adapting Stew Recipes for Microwave Oven

- Use the recipe for Basic Stew, opposite, as a guideline for the amount of meat, vegetables and liquid to use.
- Pierce meat deeply on all sides with a large fork, then cut into 1-inch cubes.
- Increase liquid, if necessary, until meat is completely covered.
- Cut vegetables into 1-inch pieces and add at the beginning of cooking time.
- Use a deep 3-quart casserole for 1 pound of stew meat, a deep 1-1/2-quart casserole for 1/2 pound of stew meat.
- Cover and microwave 1 pound of stew meat at full power (HIGH) for 10 minutes, then at 30% (MEDIUM LOW) for 80 to 90 minutes. Cover and microwave 1/2 pound of stew meat at full power (HIGH) for 10 minutes, then at 30% (MEDIUM LOW) for 50 to 60 minutes. Let stand, covered, 10 minutes.
- Meat is done when it can be shredded with a fork. Vegetables should be tender when pierced with a fork. If stew is not done, continue microwaving at 30% (MEDIUM LOW).

Easy Beef & Noodles

SERVINGS	4 or 5	2 or 3
INGREDIENTS		
beef chuck, cut in 1-inch cubes	1 lb.	8 oz.
condensed onion soup	2 (10-1/2-oz.) cans	1 (10-1/2-oz.) can
water	1 soup can	1/2 soup can
dry white wine	1/3 cup	3 tablespoons
Worcestershire sauce	1 tablespoon	2 teaspoons
frozen noodles	1 (8-oz.) pkg. (3 cups)	1/2 (8-oz.) pkg. (1-1/2 cups)
BAKING DISH	deep 3-qt. casserole	deep 2-qt. casserole
TIME AT HIGH	10 minutes	10 minutes
TIME AT 30% (meat, liquid)	45 minutes	30 minutes
TIME AT 30% (noodles added)	45 minutes	30 minutes
STANDING TIME	10 minutes	10 minutes

Pierce meat deeply on all sides with a large fork. Place meat in a casserole, see size in chart above. Add onion soup, water, wine and Worcestershire sauce. Mix well, making sure meat is covered by liquid. Cover and microwave at full power (HIGH) 10 minutes. Microwave at 30% (MEDIUM LOW) for time in chart above. Stir in frozen noodles; cover. Microwave at 30% (MEDIUM LOW) for time in chart above or until meat is tender, stirring once or twice. When meat is tender, stir mixture. Let stand, covered, 10 minutes.

Doneness Test: Meat is done when it can be shredded with a fork. Noodles should be fully hydrated and tender.

Reheating Refrigerated Easy Beef & Noodles

To chill: Place 1-1/2 cups cooled Easy Beef & Noodles in a 2-cup casserole. Cover with plastic wrap or lid; refrigerate.

To reheat: Vent plastic wrap, if using. Microwave, covered, at 70% (MEDIUM HIGH) 7 minutes or until heated through, stirring twice. Let casserole stand, covered, 1 minute.

Reheating Frozen Easy Beef & Noodles

To freeze: Place 1-1/2 cups cooled Easy Beef & Noodles in a 2-cup freezer-to-oven casserole. Cover tightly and freeze.

To reheat: Microwave, covered, at 30% (MEDIUM LOW) 10 minutes. Break apart edges with a large fork, being careful not to break up noodles. Microwave, covered, at 30% (MEDIUM LOW) 5 minutes more. Stir. Microwave, covered, at 70% (MEDIUM HIGH) 1 to 2 minutes more or until heated through. Let stand, covered, 1 minute.

Basic Pot Roast with Vegetables

SERVINGS	6	4	2
INGREDIENTS			
beef chuck roast, about 1-1/4 to 1-1/2 inches thick	3 lbs. (cut in 6 pieces)	2 lbs. (cut in 4 pieces)	1 lb. (cut in 2 pieces)
dried leaf thyme	1 teaspoon	1 teaspoon	1/2 teaspoon
apple juice	2 cups	1 cup	1 cup
beef broth	1 to 2 cups	1 to 1-1/2 cups	1 to 1-1/2 cups
vinegar	2 tablespoons	2 tablespoons	1 tablespoon
potatoes, cut up	3 (3 cups)	2 (2 cups)	1 (1 cup)
carrots, cut up	6 (3 cups)	4 (2 cups)	2 (1 cup)
onion, cut up	3 medium	2 medium	1 medium
BAKING DISH	deep 4-qt. casserole	deep 3-qt. casserole	deep 2-qt. casserole
TIME AT HIGH	10 minutes	10 minutes	10 minutes
TIME AT 30% (without vegetables)	30 minutes	30 minutes	30 minutes
TIME AT 30% (vegetables added)	80 to 90 minutes	60 to 75 minutes	40 to 50 minutes
STANDING TIME	20 minutes	20 minutes	20 minutes

Trim off any large outside fat edges from roast. Slash fat edges of roast at 1-inch intervals. Pierce roast deeply all over on both sides with a large fork. Cut in serving pieces see number in chart above. Place in a casserole, see size in chart above; roast should lie flat. Sprinkle with thyme. Combine apple juice, beef broth and vinegar in a medium bowl or glass measuring cup. Pour over roast. Roast must be completely covered with liquid to cook evenly. Add additional broth to cover, if necessary. If time permits, cover meat and let marinate several hours or overnight in the refrigerator. This gives added tenderness. Cover roast with lid. Microwave at full power (HIGH) 10 minutes. Microwave at 30% (MEDIUM LOW) 30 minutes. Turn pieces of roast over. Give dish a half turn. Add vegetables and cover. Other vegetables can be substituted such as turnips celery, rutabaga and parsnips. Microwave at 30% (MEDIUM LOW) for time in chart above or until meat and vegetables are tender. Turn top vegetables over in broth. Let stand, covered, 20 minutes. Standing time is very important; do not omit this step. Serve with Gravy for Pot Roast, page 70, if desired.

Doneness Test: Meat is done when it can be shredded with a fork. Vegetables should be tender when pierced with a fork.

Reheating Refrigerated Pot Roast

To chill: Place 1 serving (5 ounces) cooled pot roast in a 2-cup casserole. Cover with 1/ cup gravy. This helps prevent drying and overbrowning. Cover with plastic wrap or lid refrigerate.

To reheat: Vent plastic wrap, if using. Microwave, covered, at 70% (MEDIUM HIGH 3-1/2 minutes or until heated through, turning meat over once during cooking. Let stand, covered, 1 minute.

How to Make Basic Pot Roast with Vegetables

Slash the fat edges of the roast with a sharp knife—this helps to keep the meat flat during cooking. Cut the roast in serving-size pieces. This makes the meat easier to arrange in the casserole, and helps the meat cook more evenly.

Pierce the roast deeply all over with a large fork. Then turn the roast over and pierce the other side. This has the same effect as pounding other cuts of meat. It makes the pot roast more tender and juicy.

Arrange the pot roast pieces in a deep casserole. Pour in the cooking liquid until the roast is *completely covered.* This is extremely important because it keeps the top surface of the meat from turning dark.

For gravy, shake flour and water together in a covered jar. Stir into juices. Whisk the gravy occasionally during microwaving to prevent lumping. While making gravy, keep roast closely covered to prevent meat from darkening.

Gravy for Pot Roast

YIELD	2-3/4 cups	1-1/3 cups
INGREDIENTS		
pan juices	2 cups	1 cup
all-purpose flour	1/3 cup	3 tablespoons
cold water	2/3 cup	1/3 cup
Kitchen Bouquet	1 teaspoon	1/2 teaspoon
salt and pepper	to taste	to taste
GLASS MEASURING CUP	4-cup	4-cup
TIME AT HIGH	3 minutes	2 minutes

Keep meat closely covered with plastic wrap while making gravy. Measure pan juices into a 4-cup glass measuring cup. In a screw-top jar, shake together flour and cold water. Stir flour mixture and Kitchen Bouquet into meat juices. Microwave at full power (HIGH) for time in chart above or until thickened and bubbly, whisking three times. Season to taste with salt and pepper.

Adapting Pot Roast Recipes for Microwave Oven

- Select flat, evenly shaped roasts. It's difficult to keep a rolled roast completely covered by liquid.
- Cut the meat in serving-size pieces before cooking.
- Slash the fat edges so meat will lie flat during cooking. Pierce the meat deeply all over on both sides with a large fork.
- Increase the amount of liquid so meat is completely covered during cooking.
- Use red potatoes—they will hold their shape better than baking potatoes.
- Add vegetables partway through cooking time.
- Use Basic Pot Roast with Vegetables, page 68, as a guideline for cooking times for different-size pot roasts.
- Meat is done when it can be shredded with a fork. Vegetables should be tender when pierced with a fork. If roast is not done, continue microwaving at 30% (MEDIUM LOW).
- Let stand 20 minutes before serving.
- Not much time is saved by cooking a pot roast in the microwave oven. It takes long, slow cooking for the roast to be tender. But for cool summer cooking, or if the microwave oven is the only cooking appliance available, this method produces a flavorful, tender roast.

Reheating Frozen Pot Roast

To freeze: Place 1 serving (5 ounces) cooled pot roast in a small dish. Cover with 1/2 cup gravy. Cover tightly and freeze.

To reheat: Cover with vented plastic wrap. Microwave at 30% (MEDIUM LOW) 10 minutes. Turn meat over. Microwave at 30% (MEDIUM LOW) 2 minutes more. Microwave at 70% (MEDIUM HIGH) 1-1/2 minutes or until heated through. Let stand, covered, 1 minute. Turn meat over in gravy and spoon some gravy over meat.

Reheating Refrigerated Roast & Vegetables

To chill: Place 1 serving (5 ounces) cooled Roast & Vegetables, page 68, in a 2-cup casserole. Add enough vegetables to make 1 serving. Cover with 1/2 cup gravy. Cover with plastic wrap or lid; refrigerate.

To reheat: Vent plastic wrap, if using. Microwave, covered, at 70% (MEDIUM HIGH) 6 minutes or until heated through. Turn meat over once and stir vegetables twice during cooking. Let stand, covered, 1 minute.

Reheating Refrigerated Gravy

To chill: Place 1 cup cooled gravy in a 2-cup glass measuring cup. Cover with plastic wrap and refrigerate.

To reheat: Vent plastic wrap. Microwave at full power (HIGH) 4 to 4-1/2 minutes, stirring once.

Chili Pot Roast   Photo on page 49.

SERVINGS	3 or 4	2
INGREDIENTS		
Beef chuck roast, about 1-3/4 inches thick	2 lbs. (cut in 3 or 4 pieces)	1 lb. (cut in 2 pieces)
Condensed tomato soup	1 (10-3/4-oz.) can	1/2 (10-3/4-oz.) can
Beer	1/2 soup can	1/2 soup can
Beef bouillon granules	2 teaspoons	1 teaspoon
Dried leaf oregano, crushed	2 teaspoons	1 teaspoon
Chili powder	1 teaspoon	1/2 teaspoon
Onion, sliced, separated in rings	1 medium	1/2 medium
Green or red pepper, thinly sliced	1 medium	1/2 medium
Bay leaf	1 large	1 small
Red beans, drained, rinsed	1 (15-oz.) can	1/2 (15-oz.) can
BAKING DISH	deep 3-qt. casserole	deep 2-qt. casserole
TIME AT HIGH	10 minutes	10 minutes
TIME AT 30% (without beans)	30 minutes	30 minutes
TIME AT 30% (beans added)	60 minutes	30 minutes
STANDING TIME	20 minutes	20 minutes

Trim off any large outside fat edges from roast. Slash fat edges of roast at 1-inch intervals. Pierce meat deeply all over on both sides with a large fork. Cut in serving pieces, see number in chart above. Place in a casserole, see size in chart above; roast should lie flat. In a medium bowl, combine tomato soup, beer, beef bouillon granules, oregano and chili powder. Whisk until well blended. Place onion, green pepper and bay leaf on roast. Pour soup mixture over meat, covering completely. Cover and microwave at full power (HIGH) 10 minutes. Microwave at 30% (MEDIUM LOW) 30 minutes. Add beans. Turn roast over. Spoon vegetables over roast to cover it completely. Give casserole a half turn. Microwave at 30% (MEDIUM LOW) for time in chart above or until meat is tender. Turn roast over. Spoon vegetables over roast. Let stand, covered, 20 minutes. Serve pan juices with roast and vegetables.

Doneness Test: Meat is done when it can be shredded with a fork.

Defrosting: To defrost chuck roasts, see page 54.

Basic Swiss Steak & Rice

SERVINGS	5 or 6	3 or 4	2
INGREDIENTS			
veal or beef round steak, 1/2 inch thick	1-1/2 lbs. (cut in 5 or 6 pieces)	1 lb. (cut in 3 or 4 pieces)	8 oz. (cut in 2 pieces)
all-purpose flour	2 to 3 tablespoons	2 tablespoons	1 tablespoon
dry mustard	2 teaspoons	1-1/2 teaspoons	1/2 teaspoon
chopped onion	1/2 cup	1/3 cup	2 tablespoons
chopped green pepper	1/4 cup	2 tablespoons	1 tablespoon
beef bouillon granules	2 teaspoons	1-1/2 teaspoons	1 teaspoon
tomatoes, cut up	1 (28-oz.) can	1 (16-oz.) can	1 (8-oz.) can
Worcestershire sauce	1 tablespoon	2 teaspoons	1 teaspoon
Minute rice	1 cup	2/3 cup	1/3 cup
BAKING DISH	deep 3-qt. casserole	deep 2-qt. casserole	deep 1-qt. casserole
TIME AT HIGH	10 minutes	10 minutes	5 minutes
TIME AT 30%	30 minutes	25 minutes	15 minutes
TIME AT 30% (rice added)	20 minutes	20 minutes	20 minutes
STANDING TIME	10 minutes	10 minutes	10 minutes

For extra tenderness, ask the butcher to put steak through a meat tenderizer. Cut mea
in serving pieces, see number in chart above. Slash fat edges of meat. In a small bow
mix flour and dry mustard. Coat meat with flour mixture. With a meat mallet, poun
meat on both sides until it is 1/4 inch thick. Place in a casserole, see size in chart abov
Sprinkle with onion, green pepper and bouillon granules. Combine tomatoes and Wor
cestershire sauce. Pour over steak pieces, covering them completely. Cover and micro
wave at full power (HIGH) for time in chart above. Microwave at 30% (MEDIUM
LOW) for time in chart above. Turn steak over and give dish a half turn. Add rice. Sti
until all rice is moistened; cover. Microwave at 30% (MEDIUM LOW) 20 minutes o
until meat is tender and rice is done. Let stand, covered, 10 minutes.

Doneness Test: Meat is done when it can be shredded with a fork. Rice should be full
hydrated and tender.

Defrosting: To defrost round steak, see page 57.

Reheating Refrigerated Swiss Steak

To chill: Place 1 serving (5 ounces) cooled Swiss steak in a small dish. Cover with 1/
cup rice and sauce. Cover with plastic wrap; refrigerate.

To reheat: Vent plastic wrap. Microwave at 70% (MEDIUM HIGH) 4 minutes or unti
heated through. Let stand, covered, 1 minute.

Reheating Frozen Swiss Steak

To freeze: Place 1 serving (5 ounces) cooled Swiss steak in a small dish. Cover with 1/
cup rice and sauce. Cover tightly; freeze.

To reheat: Cover with vented plastic wrap. Microwave at 30% (MEDIUM LOW) 1
minutes. Stir. Microwave at 70% (MEDIUM HIGH) 2 to 2-1/2 minutes or until heate
through, stirring once. Let stand, covered, 1 minute.

How to Make Basic Swiss Steak & Rice

Cut meat in serving-size pieces. Slash fat edges of meat. Coat meat on both sides with seasoned flour. Pound both sides with a meat mallet until 1/4 inch thick. Pounding makes meat more tender.

Place meat in deep casserole. Sprinkle meat with chopped onion, green pepper and bouillon granules. Cut up the tomatoes with kitchen shears. Stir Worcestershire sauce into the tomatoes before pouring over meat. Make sure meat is covered with tomato mixture.

Partway through cooking time, stir quick-cooking rice into the casserole until all rice is moistened. Rice kernels not mixed with sauce will remain hard after cooking.

Let the casserole stand, covered, for 10 minutes after cooking. This makes the meat more tender and the rice more fluffy. Serve the rice mixture over the steaks.

Pizza Swiss Steak

SERVINGS	6 or 7	4 or 5	2
INGREDIENTS			
beef or veal round steak, 1/2 inch thick	1-1/2 lbs. (cut in 6 or 7 pieces)	1 lb. (cut in 4 or 5 pieces)	8 oz. (cut in 2 pieces)
bulk pork sausage	12 oz.	8 oz.	4 oz.
fresh mushroom slices	1-1/2 cups	1 cup	1/2 cup
chopped onion	3/4 cup	1/2 cup	1/4 cup
fennel seed	1-1/2 teaspoons	1 teaspoon	1/2 teaspoon
bottled Italian cooking sauce	1-1/2 cups	1 cup	3/4 cup
all-purpose flour	3 tablespoons	2 tablespoons	1 tablespoon
cold water	1/3 cup	1/4 cup	2 tablespoons
shredded mozzarella cheese	1-1/2 cups (6 oz.)	1 cup (4 oz.)	1/2 cup (2 oz.)
BAKING DISH	deep 3-qt. casserole	deep 2-qt. casserole	deep 1-qt. casserole
TIME AT HIGH (sausage, mushrooms, onion)	6 minutes	4 minutes	3 minutes
TIME AT HIGH (steak added)	10 minutes	10 minutes	5 minutes
TIME AT 30% (before thickening sauce)	30 minutes	10 minutes	10 minutes
TIME AT HIGH (to thicken sauce)	3 minutes	3 minutes	3 minutes
TIME AT 30% (after thickening sauce)	20 minutes	15 minutes	10 minutes
STANDING TIME	10 minutes	10 minutes	10 minutes

For extra tenderness, ask the butcher to put steak through a meat tenderizer. Cut meat in serving pieces, see number in chart above. Slash fat edges of meat. With a meat mallet, pound meat until it is 1/4 inch thick. Set aside. In a casserole, see size in chart above, combine sausage, mushrooms and onion. Microwave at full power (HIGH) for time in chart above, stirring three times. Drain. Stir in fennel seed and Italian cooking sauce. Add steak pieces to sauce in same casserole, making sure all meat is covered by sauce. Cover and microwave at full power (HIGH) for time in chart above. Microwave at 30% (MEDIUM LOW) for time in chart above. Remove steak from casserole; skim off excess fat from sauce. In a screw-top jar, shake together flour and cold water. Stir into sauce in casserole. Microwave at full power (HIGH) 3 minutes or until thickened and bubbly, stirring twice. Add steaks to sauce, making sure meat is covered by sauce. Cover. Microwave at 30% (MEDIUM LOW) for time in chart above or until meat is tender. Sprinkle with cheese. Let stand, covered, 10 minutes.

Doneness Test: Meat is done when it can be shredded with a fork.

Pork or Lamb Chops Creole

SERVINGS	4	2	1
INGREDIENTS			
pork or lamb shoulder or blade chops, 1/2 to 5/8 inch thick	4 (6-oz.)chops	2 (6-oz.) chops	1 (6-oz.)chop
all-purpose flour	3 tablespoons	2 tablespoons	1 tablespoon
dry mustard	2 teaspoons	1 teaspoon	1/2 teaspoon
chopped onion	1/2 cup	1/4 cup	2 tablespoons
chopped green pepper	1/4 cup	2 tablespoons	1 tablespoon
beef bouillon granules	2 teaspoons	1-1/2 teaspoons	1 teaspoon
tomatoes, cut up	1 (28-oz.) can	1 (16-oz.) can	1 (8-oz.) can
Worcestershire sauce	1 tablespoon	2 teaspoons	1 teaspoon
BAKING DISH	deep 3-qt. casserole	deep 2-qt. casserole	deep 1-qt. casserole
TIME AT HIGH	10 minutes	10 minutes	10 minutes
TIME AT 30%	30 minutes	15 minutes	10 minutes
TIME AT 30% (after turning chops)	30 minutes	15 minutes	10 minutes
STANDING TIME	10 minutes	10 minutes	10 minutes

Slash fat edges of meat. Pierce chops deeply all over on both sides with a large fork. In small bowl, mix flour and dry mustard. Coat meat with flour mixture. Place in casserole, see size in chart above. Top with onion, green pepper and bouillon granules. Combine tomatoes and Worcestershire sauce. Pour over chops. Cover and microwave at full power (HIGH) 10 minutes. Microwave at 30% (MEDIUM LOW) for time in chart above. Turn chops over. Spoon sauce over top of chops. Give dish a half turn. Microwave at 30% (MEDIUM LOW) for time in chart above or until chops are tender. Let stand, covered, 10 minutes. Skim off excess fat. If desired, see Gravy for Pot Roast, page 70, to make gravy from pan juices.

Defrosting: To defrost shoulder or blade chops or steaks, see page 58.

Adapting Swiss-Steak Recipes for Microwave Oven

- Select beef or veal round steak that the butcher has put through the meat tenderizer. Lamb and pork shoulder steaks have bones so cannot go through the meat tenderizer.

- Slash fat edges of meat to prevent curling during cooking. Pierce lamb or pork steaks on all sides with a large fork. Coat beef or veal with flour and seasonings, then pound.

- Increase the amount of sauce mixture, if necessary, so meat is completely covered during cooking. Keep steaks covered with sauce to prevent darkening.

- Turn steaks over partway through cooking time.

- Use the recipes for Basic Swiss Steak & Rice, page 72, and Pork or Lamb Chops Creole above, as guidelines for amount of meat, cooking times and casserole sizes.

- Meat is done when it can be shredded with a fork. If meat is not done, continue microwaving at 30% (MEDIUM LOW).

Easy Swiss Steak

SERVINGS	5 or 6
INGREDIENTS	
beef round steak, 1/2 inch thick	1-1/2 lbs. (cut in 5 or 6 pieces)
all-purpose flour	3 tablespoons
tomato sauce	1 (8-oz.) can
water	1 cup
swiss-steak seasoning mix	1 (1-oz.) envelope
BAKING DISH	deep 3-qt. casserole
STANDING TIME	10 minutes
TIME AT HIGH	10 minutes
TIME AT 30%	30 minutes
TIME AT 30% (after turning steaks)	20 minutes
STANDING TIME	10 minutes

For extra tenderness, ask the butcher to put steak through a meat tenderizer. Cut meat in 5 or 6 pieces. Slash fat edges of meat. Coat meat with flour. With a meat mallet, pound meat until it is 1/4 inch thick. In a 3-quart casserole, mix tomato sauce, water and Swiss-steak seasoning mix. Add steak pieces, making sure all meat is covered by liquid. Cover and let stand 10 minutes. Microwave at full power (HIGH) 10 minutes. Microwave at 30% (MEDIUM LOW) 30 minutes. Turn steak over and give casserole a half turn. Microwave at 30% (MEDIUM LOW) 20 minutes or until meat is tender. Let stand, covered, 10 minutes.

Reheating Refrigerated Beef Short Ribs

To chill: Place 4 cooled ribs (11 to 12 ounces) in a 1-quart bowl. Cover with 3 to 4 table-spoons sauce. Cover tightly with plastic wrap; refrigerate.

To reheat: Vent plastic wrap. Microwave at 70% (MEDIUM HIGH) 7 to 8 minutes or until heated through, rearranging once. Let stand, covered, 1 minute.

Reheating Frozen Beef Short Ribs

To freeze: Place 4 cooled ribs (11 to 12 ounces) in a 1-quart freezer-to-oven casserole. Cover with 3 to 4 tablespoons sauce. Cover tightly with plastic wrap or lid; freeze.

To reheat: Vent plastic wrap, if using. Microwave, covered, at 30% (MEDIUM LOW) 15 minutes or until thawed, breaking apart with a large fork. Microwave, covered, at 70% (MEDIUM HIGH) 2 minutes or until heated through. Let stand, covered, 1 minute.

Simmered Barbecued Ribs

SERVINGS	3 or 4	1 or 2
INGREDIENTS		
pork loin back ribs	3 to 3-1/2 lbs.	1-1/2 lbs.
OR		
beef short ribs,		
2-1/2 inches long,		
1/2 to 1 inch thick		
onion, sliced, separated	1 large	1 small
in rings		
bay leaf	1 large	1 small
beer, room temperature	2 (12-oz.) cans	1 (12-oz.) can
Worcestershire sauce	2 tablespoons	1 tablespoon
bottled barbecue sauce	2-1/2 cups	1 cup
BAKING DISH	deep 4-qt. casserole	deep 2- or 3-qt. casserole
TIME AT HIGH	10 minutes	10 minutes
TIME AT 30%	30 minutes	30 minutes
TIME AT 30% (after rearranging)	60 to 75 minutes	30 to 40 minutes
STANDING TIME	20 minutes	10 minutes
TIME AT 30% (sauce added)	10 minutes	5 minutes

Cut pork ribs into 2-rib portions. Cut thick beef short ribs in half lengthwise. Pierce rib all over with a large fork. Place, bone side up, in a casserole, see size in chart above. Add onion and bay leaf. Pour in beer and Worcestershire sauce. Cover and microwave at full power (HIGH) 10 minutes. Microwave at 30% (MEDIUM LOW) 30 minutes. Rearrange ribs, bringing ribs in center of casserole to outside edge. Be sure ribs are bone side up and meaty side is under liquid. Cover. Microwave at 30% (MEDIUM LOW) for time in chart above or until tender. Let ribs stand, covered, for time in chart above. Pour off pan juices from casserole. Turn ribs meaty side up. Pour bottled barbecue sauce over ribs, coating well. Cover. Microwave at 30% (MEDIUM LOW) for time in chart above or until heated through. Serve ribs with onion and sauce.

Savory Simmered Beef Ribs

SERVINGS	3 or 4	1 or 2
INGREDIENTS		
beef short ribs,	3 to 3-1/2 lbs.	1-1/2 lbs.
2-1/2 inches long,		
1/2 to 1 inch thick		
Same ingredients as for Simmered Barbecued Ribs, above, but replace bottled barbecue sauce with:		
packed brown sugar	1/4 cup	2 tablespoons
all-purpose flour	1/4 cup	2 tablespoons
pan juices	2 cups	1 cup
TIME AT HIGH (to thicken sauce)	3 minutes	2 to 2-1/2 minutes

Following directions for Simmered Barbecued Ribs, above, cook beef short ribs and let stand, covered. Do not pour off pan juices. Remove ribs to a warm platter and cover tightly with plastic wrap. Pour pan juices into a large glass measuring cup. With a slotted spoon, return onion to casserole. Stir brown sugar and flour into onion. Skim fat from pan juices. Measure pan juices, see amount in chart above. Return pan juices to casserole; mix well. Microwave at full power (HIGH) for time in chart above or until thickened and bubbly, stirring twice. Serve over ribs.

How to Make Savory Simmered Beef Ribs

Pierce ribs all over with a large fork. This is essential for maximum tenderness and juiciness in beef ribs. Place ribs, bone side up, in a deep casserole.

Add onion rings and a bay leaf to casserole. Pour in beer, completely covering ribs. Meaty side of ribs should be under cooking liquid.

When ribs are fork-tender, remove ribs to serving platter and cover tightly with plastic wrap. Strain onion from pan juices, then toss onion in casserole with brown sugar and flour.

Whisk pan juices into the onion mixture, then microwave to thicken the gravy. Stir several times during cooking to prevent lumping. Ladle the gravy over ribs and mashed potatoes.

Sweet & Sour Beef Ribs

SERVINGS	3 or 4	1 or 2
INGREDIENTS		
crushed pineapple, juice-packed	1 (8-oz.) can	1 (8-oz.) can
beef short ribs, 2-1/2 inches long, 1/2 to 1 inch thick	3 lbs.	1-1/2 lbs.
onion, sliced, separated in rings	1 large	1 small
pineapple juice	2 (12-oz.) cans (3 cups)	1 (12-oz.) can (1-1/2 cups)
soy sauce	1/3 cup	3 tablespoons
honey	1/4 cup	2 tablespoons
ground ginger	1 teaspoon	1/2 teaspoon
garlic powder	1/4 teaspoon	1/8 teaspoon
pineapple rings, quartered	to garnish	to garnish
BAKING DISH	deep 4-qt. casserole	deep 2-qt. casserole
TIME AT HIGH	10 minutes	10 minutes
TIME AT 30%	30 minutes	30 minutes
TIME AT 30% (after rearranging)	60 minutes	30 minutes
STANDING TIME	20 minutes	10 minutes
TIME AT 30% (sauce added)	10 minutes	7 minutes

Drain pineapple, reserving juice; set pineapple aside. Cut thick ribs in half lengthwise. Pierce ribs all over with a large fork. Place, bone side up, in a casserole, see size in chart above. Top with onions. Pour in pineapple juice and juice drained from fruit. Cover and microwave at full power (HIGH) 10 minutes. Microwave at 30% (MEDIUM LOW) 30 minutes. Rearrange ribs, bringing ribs in center of casserole to outside edge. Be sure meaty sides of ribs are under liquid. Cover. Microwave at 30% (MEDIUM LOW) for time in chart above or until tender. Let stand, covered, for time in chart above. While ribs are standing, combine drained pineapple, soy sauce, honey, ginger and garlic powder in a small bowl. Pour off pan juices from casserole and remove onions. Turn ribs meaty side up. Pour pineapple mixture over ribs. Cover. Microwave at 30% (MEDIUM LOW) for time in chart above or until heated through. Garnish with quartered pineapple rings.

Defrosting: To defrost beef or pork ribs, see page 55.

Adapting Rib Recipes for Microwave Oven

- Cut pork ribs in 2-rib portions for quicker cooking. Halve thick beef ribs lengthwise.
- Pierce ribs on all sides with a large fork.
- For ribs that become so tender they fall off the bone, use Simmered Barbecued Ribs page 78, as a guideline for amounts of meat, baking dish sizes and cooking times. These ribs are simmered in liquid until tender, then drained and heated with barbecue sauce. For ribs with meat that clings to the bone after cooking, use Baked Barbecued Pork Ribs, page 82, as a guideline for amounts of meat, baking dish sizes and cooking times. This method is only suitable for pork ribs. Beef ribs need to be simmered to be tender.
- Rearrange the ribs in the baking dish during cooking time for more even cooking.

Sweet & Sour Beef Ribs

Baked Barbecued Pork Ribs

SERVINGS	3 or 4	2 or 3	1 or 2
INGREDIENTS			
Tangy Barbecue Sauce, see below, or bottled barbecue sauce	2 cups	1-1/3 cups	2/3 cup
pork loin back ribs	3-1/2 lbs.	2 lbs.	1 lb.
dry mustard	1-1/2 teaspoons	1 teaspoon	1/2 teaspoon
celery seed	3/4 teaspoon	1/2 teaspoon	1/4 teaspoon
garlic powder	1/4 teaspoon	1/4 teaspoon	1/8 teaspoon
onion, thinly sliced, separated in rings	1 large	1 medium	1 small
lemon, thinly sliced	1	1/2	1/4
BAKING DISH	12-inch square microwave baker with microwave rack	12" x 7" baking dish with microwave rack	12" x 7" baking dish with microwave rack
TIME AT HIGH	15 minutes	10 minutes	5 minutes
TIME AT 30% (without sauce)	30 to 40 minutes	30 to 40 minutes	20 to 25 minutes
TIME AT 30% (sauce added)	10 minutes	10 minutes	10 minutes
STANDING TIME	10 minutes	10 minutes	10 minutes

Prepare Tangy Barbecue Sauce, if using; set aside. Cut ribs into 2-rib portions. Arrange, bone side down, on a rack in a baking dish, see size in chart above. Overlap ribs slightly, if necessary. In a small bowl, combine dry mustard, celery seed and garlic powder. Rub over ribs. Arrange onion and lemon slices over ribs. Cover with vented plastic wrap. Microwave at full power (HIGH) for time in chart above, giving dish a half turn once. Rearrange ribs. Microwave at 30% (MEDIUM LOW) for time in chart above or until tender, rearranging ribs once. Push onion and lemon slices to center of casserole. Pour Tangy Barbecue Sauce or bottled barbecue sauce over ribs. Cover with vented plastic wrap. Microwave at 30% (MEDIUM LOW) 10 minutes or until heated through. Let stand, covered, 10 minutes.

Doneness Test: Ribs are done when they are fork-tender and have no pink color when cut in center.

Tangy Barbecue Sauce

YIELD	2-1/2 cups (for 3 to 3-1/2 lbs. of ribs)	1-1/4 cups (for 1 to 2 lbs. of ribs)
INGREDIENTS		
chili sauce	1 (12-oz.) bottle	1/2 (12-oz.) bottle
orange marmalade	1 (10-oz.) jar	1/2 (10-oz.) jar
vinegar	1/3 cup	3 tablespoons
Worcestershire sauce	1 tablespoon	2 teaspoons
celery seed	1 teaspoon	1/2 teaspoon
dry mustard	1 teaspoon	1/2 teaspoon
liquid smoke	1/2 teaspoon	1/4 teaspoon

In a medium bowl, combine chili sauce, marmalade, vinegar, Worcestershire sauce, celery seed, dry mustard and liquid smoke. Mix well. Use with ribs or chicken.

How to Make Baked Barbecued Pork Ribs

Cut loin back ribs between every 2 ribs to make serving-size portions.

Arrange ribs, bone side down, in baking dish. Rub a mixture of dry mustard, celery seed and garlic powder over ribs, coating all sides well.

Top ribs with onion rings and fresh lemon slices. Cover with plastic wrap and turn back a corner to vent. The onion and lemon provide moisture for the ribs during cooking.

Push lemon and onion slices to center of dish when ribs are almost done. Pour barbecue sauce over ribs, making sure all surfaces of ribs are well-coated. Microwave to heat sauce.

Creamy Onion-Smothered Chops

SERVINGS	4	2	1
INGREDIENTS			
veal or pork loin chops, 1/2 inch thick	4 (4- to 6-oz.) chops	2 (4- to 6-oz.) chops	1 (4- to 6-oz.) chop
all-purpose flour	3 tablespoons	1 tablespoon	2 teaspoons
ground marjoram for veal, ground sage for pork	1 teaspoon	1/2 teaspoon	1/4 teaspoon
onion, sliced, separated in rings	1 large	1 small	1/2 small
condensed cream of onion soup	1 (10-1/2-oz.) can	1/2 (10-1/2-oz.) can	1/3 cup
milk	1/2 soup can	1/3 cup	3 tablespoons
beef bouillon granules	2 teaspoons	1 teaspoon	1/2 teaspoon
bottled steak sauce	2 tablespoons	1 tablespoon	2 teaspoons
snipped parsley	to garnish	to garnish	to garnish
BAKING DISH	deep 2-qt. casserole	deep 1-qt. casserole	2-cup casserole
Cooking time for veal:			
TIME AT HIGH	10 minutes	5 minutes	2 minutes
TIME AT 30%	30 minutes	15 minutes	8 to 9 minutes
STANDING TIME	10 minutes	10 minutes	5 minutes
Cooking time for pork:			
TIME AT 30%	30 minutes	20 minutes	8 minutes
STANDING TIME	10 minutes	5 minutes	5 minutes

Slash fat edges of chops. Mix flour and marjoram or sage. Coat meat with flour mixture. Place in a casserole, see size in chart above, with tenderloin section toward inside of dish. Top with onion. In a medium bowl, whisk together until smooth, soup, milk, bouillon granules, steak sauce and any remaining flour mixture. Pour mixture over chops being sure to coat all chops. Cover and microwave according to times in chart above. Halfway through cooking time, turn chops over and rearrange; push chops under liquid. Cover and microwave for remaining time or until tender. Let stand, covered, according to time in chart above. Skim off fat. Serve pan juices over chops and mashed potatoes, if desired. Garnish with snipped parsley.

Doneness Test: Chops are done when they have no pink color when cut in center.

Reheating Refrigerated Chops

To chill: Place 2 cooled chops in a 3-cup casserole. Cover with 2/3 cup onion sauce or other sauce. Or, place 1 chop in a 2-cup casserole. Cover with 1/3 cup sauce. Cover with plastic wrap or lid; refrigerate.

To reheat: Vent plastic wrap, if using. Microwave 2 chops, covered, at 70% (MEDIUM HIGH) 7 minutes or until heated through, rearranging once. Microwave 1 chop, covered, at 70% (MEDIUM HIGH) 4 minutes or until heated through. Let chops stand, covered, 1 minute.

How to Make Creamy Onion-Smothered Chops

Place coated chops in a deep casserole. Whisk together onion soup, milk, bouillon granules, steak sauce and any remaining flour mixture.

Top chops with onion rings. Arrange chops in the casserole so the small tenderloin portion is toward the center of the casserole. The thicker loin portion is to the outside of the casserole because it takes longer to cook.

Pour onion soup sauce over chops and onion. Make sure all chops are coated with soup sauce. Partway through cooking time, chops are turned over and pushed back under sauce.

After cooking and standing, chops should be tender when pierced with a fork. Serve chops and pan gravy over mashed potatoes, noodles or rice. Garnish with snipped parsley.

Fruit-Glazed Chops

SERVINGS	4	2	1
INGREDIENTS			
pork loin chops, 1/2 inch thick	4 (6-oz.) chops	2 (6-oz.) chops	1 (4- to 5-oz.) chop
white catawba grape juice	1-1/2 cups	3/4 cup	1/2 cup
cream sherry or marsala wine	1/2 cup	1/4 cup	3 tablespoons
dry mustard	1/2 teaspoon	1/4 teaspoon	1/8 teaspoon
ground ginger	1/2 teaspoon	1/4 teaspoon	1/8 teaspoon
dried mixed fruit	1 (8-oz.) pkg. (about 2 cups)	1/2 (8-oz.) pkg. (about 1 cup)	1/4 (8-oz.) pkg. (about 1/2 cup)
cornstarch	1 tablespoon	2 teaspoons	2 teaspoons
cold water	2 tablespoons	1 tablespoon	1 tablespoon
pan juices	1 cup	1/2 cup	1/2 cup
BAKING DISH	deep 2-qt. casserole	deep 1-1/2-qt. casserole	deep 2-cup casserole
TIME AT HIGH (4 chops)	5 minutes	none	none
TIME AT 30%	30 minutes	20 minutes	8 to 9 minutes
STANDING TIME	10 minutes	10 minutes	5 minutes
TIME AT HIGH (sauce)	2 to 3 minutes	1 to 1-1/2 minutes	1 to 1-1/2 minutes

Slash fat edges of chops. Arrange chops with meaty side out in a casserole, see size in chart above. In a 2-cup measure, whisk together grape juice, sherry or marsala, dry mustard and ginger; pour over chops. Add dried fruits, pushing fruits down into liquid. If cooking 4 chops, cover and microwave at full power (HIGH) for time in chart above. Microwave all chops, covered, at 30% (MEDIUM LOW) for time in chart above or until tender, giving dish a half turn once. Let stand, covered, for time in chart above. Remove chops and fruit to a warm platter. Cover tightly with plastic wrap. In a screw-top jar shake together cornstarch and cold water. Stir into measured pan juices, see amount in chart above. Microwave at full power (HIGH) for time in chart above or until thickened and bubbly, stirring three times. Pass fruit sauce with chops.

Doneness Test: Chops are done when they have no pink color when cut in center.

Defrosting: To defrost chops, see pages 58 and 59.

Adapting Chop Recipes for Microwave Oven

- Determine the basic cooking method desired. To cook chops in sauce, use Creamy Onion-Smothered Chops, page 84, as a guideline for baking dish sizes and cooking times. To cook breaded chops, see Crumb-Coated Pork Chops, page 88. For stuffed thick chops, use Basic Stuffed Pork Chops, page 90, as a guideline.

- Select the baking dishes and cooking times according to the number of chops to be cooked.

- Slash fat edges of chops to prevent curling during cooking.

- Chops are done when they have no pink color when cut in center.

Fruit-Glazed Chops

Crumb-Coated Pork Chops

SERVINGS	6	4	2	1
INGREDIENTS				
pork loin chops, 1/2 inch thick	6 (5-oz.) chops	4 (5-oz.) chops	2 (5-oz.) chops	1 (5-oz.) chop
water or milk	to moisten	to moisten	to moisten	to moisten
seasoned coating mix for pork	3/4 envelope from 4-3/4-oz. pkg. (6 tablespoons)	1/2 envelope from 4-3/4-oz. pkg. (1/4 cup)	2 tablespoons	1 tablespoon
BAKING DISH	12-inch square microwave baker with microwave rack	12" x 7" baking dish with micro-wave rack	12" x 7" baking dish with micro-wave rack	9-inch pie plate with microwave rack
TIME AT 30%	22 to 25 minutes	18 minutes	11 minutes	6 minutes

Slash fat edges of chops. Moisten chops with water or milk and shake in coating mix according to package directions. Place with meaty side toward outside of dish, on a rack in a baking dish, see size in chart above. Cover with vented plastic wrap. Microwave at 30% (MEDIUM LOW) for time in chart above or until tender. Halfway through cooking time, give dish a half turn. The coating on the chops will not be crisp.

Doneness Test: Chops are done when they have no pink color when cut in center.

Easy Stuffing

YIELD	4 cups (for 4 to 6 chops)	2 cups (for 1 or 2 chops)
INGREDIENTS		
stuffing mix for pork, saucepan-style	1 (6-oz.) pkg.	1/2 (6-oz.) pkg. (2 to 3 tablespoons vegetable seasoning and 1-1/4 cups stuffing crumbs)
water	1-1/2 cups	3/4 cup
butter or margarine	1/4 cup	2 tablespoons
chopped apple	1/2 cup	1/4 cup
BOWL	1-1/2-qt. bowl	1-qt. bowl
TIME AT HIGH	8 minutes	5 minutes
STANDING TIME	5 minutes	5 minutes

In a bowl, see size in chart above, combine appropriate amount vegetable seasoning from stuffing mix and water. Add butter or margarine. Cover and microwave at full power (HIGH) for time in chart above. Add appropriate amount crumbs from stuffing mix and stir to moisten. Let stand, covered, 5 minutes. Fluff stuffing with a fork and stir in chopped apple. Serve with pork chops or use to stuff pork chops.

How to Make Crumb-Coated Pork Chops

Slash fat edges of chops with a sharp knife to prevent chops from curling during cooking.

Dip chops in milk or water, then place in coating crumbs in a plastic bag. Shake chops until well-coated.

Place chops on microwave rack in baking dish. Cover with plastic wrap, turning back one corner of wrap to vent steam.

Chops are done when they are fork-tender and have no pink color when cut in center. Coating on chops will be moist, not crisp.

Basic Stuffed Pork Chops

SERVINGS	6	4	2	1
INGREDIENTS				
Easy Stuffing, page 88	4 cups	4 cups	2 cups	2 cups
pork loin chops, 1 inch thick	6 (6- to 8-oz.) chops	4 (6- to 8-oz.) chops	2 (6- to 8-oz.) chops	1 (6- to 8-oz.) chop
salt and pepper	to taste	to taste	to taste	to taste
thin apple slices	6	4	2	1
gravy mix for pork	2 (3/4-oz.) envelopes	1 (3/4-oz.) envelope	1 (3/4-oz.) envelope	1/2 (3/4-oz.) envelope (about 2 tablespoons)
water	2 cups	1 cup	1 cup	1/2 cup
BAKING DISH	12-inch square microwave baker with microwave rack	12" x 7" baking dish with microwave rack	10" x 6" baking dish with inverted saucers	1-qt. casserole with inverted saucer
TIME AT HIGH	5 minutes	5 minutes	5 minutes	5 minutes
TIME AT 30% (chops)	45 minutes	35 minutes	18 minutes	10 minutes
TIME AT 30% (stuffing added)	3 minutes	3 minutes	2 minutes	2 minutes
TIME AT HIGH (gravy)	3 minutes	2 to 3 minutes	2 to 3 minutes	1-1/2 to 2-1/2 minutes

Prepare Easy Stuffing; set aside. Cut pockets in pork chops, starting from fat side. Season pockets of chops with salt and pepper. Stuff pockets with some of the stuffing; reserve remaining stuffing. Place chops, with meaty side toward outside of dish, on a rack or inverted saucers in a baking dish, see size in chart above. Cover with vented plastic wrap. Microwave at full power (HIGH) 5 minutes. Microwave at 30% (MEDIUM LOW) for time in chart above or until chops are tender. Give dish a half turn halfway through cooking time. Spoon a mound of remaining stuffing on top of each chop. Top each mound with an apple slice. Cover with vented plastic wrap. Microwave at 30% (MEDIUM LOW) for time in chart above or until heated through. Remove chops to a warm platter and cover tightly with plastic wrap. Remove rack or saucer from baking dish. Stir gravy mix and water into pan drippings. Microwave at full power (HIGH) for time in chart above or until thickened and bubbly, stirring three times. Serve gravy with chops.

Doneness Test: Chops are done when they have no pink color when cut in center.

Reheating Refrigerated Stuffed Pork Chops

To chill: Place 2 cooled Stuffed Pork Chops in a 1-quart casserole. Cover with 1/3 cup gravy. Or, place 1 Stuffed Pork Chop in a 1-1/2-cup casserole. Cover with 1/3 cup gravy. Cover with plastic wrap or lid; refrigerate.

To reheat: Vent plastic wrap, if using. Microwave 2 chops, covered, at 70% (MEDIUM HIGH) 7 minutes or until heated through, giving dish a half turn once. Microwave 1 chop, covered, at 70% (MEDIUM HIGH) 5 minutes or until heated through. Let chops stand, covered, 1 minute.

How to Make Basic Stuffed Pork Chops

Prepare stuffing from a mix, adding water and butter or margarine. After stuffing stands, covered, for 5 minutes, fluff with a fork and add chopped fresh apple.

Stand pork chops on edge; cut pockets starting at the fat edge of the loin. Cut pockets through to the bone and season with salt and pepper. Fill pockets with stuffing mixture.

Before the end of cooking time, spoon extra stuffing on top of the chops. Garnish with an apple slice. Then microwave for a short time.

Cover the chops tightly with foil or plastic wrap after cooking. Stir gravy mix and water into the pan drippings to make a quick and tasty gravy.

Grilled Steak & Onion Rings

SERVINGS	2	1
INGREDIENTS		
beef New York strip or rib-eye steaks, 1 inch thick	2 (8- to 10-oz.) steaks	1 (8- to 10-oz.) steak
Kitchen Bouquet		
frozen French-fried onion rings	6	3
vegetable oil for dipping rings	1/4 cup	1/4 cup
vegetable oil for grilling rings	2 tablespoons	1 tablespoon
BROWNING SKILLET	10-inch microwave browning skillet	10-inch microwave browning skillet
TIME AT HIGH (preheat skillet for onions)	6 minutes	6 minutes
TIME AT HIGH (first side)	45 seconds	45 seconds
TIME AT HIGH (second side)	1 minute	45 seconds
TIME AT HIGH (preheat skillet for steak)	3 minutes	3 minutes

Slash fat edges of steaks. Brush fat edges lightly with Kitchen Bouquet; set aside. Pre heat a 10-inch browning skillet, uncovered, at microwave full power (HIGH) 6 min utes. Dip frozen onion rings in first amount of oil in a small bowl. Let stand on a plate Add second amount of oil to hot browning skillet. Using hot pads, tilt skillet to coa evenly with oil. Quickly add onion rings. Microwave at full power (HIGH) 45 second or until browned. Turn and rearrange. Microwave at full power (HIGH) for time i chart above or until browned. Remove onion rings and place on a white paper towel o a cookie sheet. Keep warm in a slow oven while grilling steak. Wipe out browning skil let with paper towel. Preheat browning skillet, uncovered, at microwave full powe (HIGH) 3 minutes. Grill steak according to directions given for Basic Grilled Rib-Ey Steak, page 95. Remove steak to a warm platter. Top with onion rings.

Adapting Steak Recipes for Microwave Oven

- Slash fat edges of steaks to prevent curling during cooking. Brush fat edges and an large fat areas of steak lightly with Kitchen Bouquet.

- Preheat a 10-inch browning skillet, uncovered, at full power (HIGH) 6 minutes. The smal round browning skillet does not work well for 1 small steak because the edges of the steak tend to burn.

- In the large browning skillet, the maximum per batch is 2 rib-eye or strip steaks, pieces of sirloin or 1 T-bone. Two T-bones are a difficult fit and do not brown well.

- Use the timings for the various kinds of Basic Grilled Steaks, pages 94 and 95, as guideline. These timings are for medium-done steaks.

- To check doneness of a steak, make a tiny cut in center of steak with a sharp knife. Re center indicates rare; pink indicates medium; gray means steak is well-done. Microwav steaks until a little more rare than you'd like because they will continue to cook afte removing from the microwave oven.

- Wipe out the browning skillet with a paper towel, and preheat skillet between cookin each steak after the first one. It takes half as long to preheat the browning skillet afte the first preheating.

How to Make Grilled Steak & Onion Rings

Slash fat edges. Brush the fat edges and any large portions of fat on the steak with Kitchen Bouquet. This improves the color of the fat after cooking.

Dip each frozen French-fried onion ring in a small dish of vegetable oil. Add measured oil to the preheated browning skillet and quickly cook the onion rings. Keep warm in a slow oven.

Wipe out the browning skillet and preheat. Add vegetable oil, tilting skillet to coat evenly. When steaks are browned on the first side, turn with tongs or a spatula to retain all the juices.

Test steaks for doneness by making a small slit near the center of the steak. Serve steaks with French-fried onion rings. Garnish with cherry tomatoes and sweet woodruff, if available.

Basic Grilled T-Bone Steak

SERVINGS	2	1
INGREDIENTS		
beef T-bone steak, 1 inch thick		1 (12-oz.) steak
OR		
beef T-bone steak, 1-1/2 inches thick	1 (22-oz.) steak	
Kitchen Bouquet		
vegetable oil	1 tablespoon	1 tablespoon
BROWNING SKILLET	10-inch microwave browning skillet	10-inch microwave browning skillet
TIME AT HIGH (preheat skillet)	6 minutes	6 minutes
TIME AT HIGH (first side)	2 minutes	2 minutes
TIME AT HIGH (second side)	5 to 6 minutes	1-1/4 to 1-3/4 minutes

See directions for Basic Grilled Sirloin Steak, below.

Basic Grilled Sirloin Steak

SERVINGS	4	2
INGREDIENTS		
beef sirloin steak, 1/2 to 3/4 inch thick		1 (1-lb.) steak, cut in 2 pieces
OR		
beef sirloin steak, 1-1/4 inches thick	1 (2-lb.) steak, cut in 4 pieces	
Kitchen Bouquet		
vegetable oil	1 tablespoon	1 tablespoon
BROWNING SKILLET	10-inch microwave browning skillet	10-inch microwave browning skillet
TIME AT HIGH (preheat skillet)	6 minutes	6 minutes
TIME AT HIGH (first side)	3 minutes	2-1/2 minutes
TIME AT HIGH (second side)	5 to 6 minutes	3 to 4 minutes

Slash fat edges of steaks. Brush fat edges lightly with Kitchen Bouquet. Preheat a 10-inch browning skillet, uncovered, at microwave full power (HIGH) 6 minutes. Add oil to hot browning skillet. Using hot pads, tilt skillet to coat evenly with oil. Quickly add steaks. Microwave at full power (HIGH) for time in chart. Turn steaks and if cooking 2 steaks, rearrange. Microwave at full power (HIGH) for time in chart or until done to your liking. These timings are for medium-done steaks. It is best to cook steaks slightly underdone because they will continue to cook after removing from microwave.

Doneness Test: Make a tiny cut in center of steak with a sharp knife. Red center indicates rare; pink indicates medium; gray means steak is well-done.

Basic Grilled Rib-Eye or Strip Steaks

SERVINGS	2	1
INGREDIENTS		
beef New York strip or rib-eye steaks, 1 inch thick	2 (8- to 10-oz.) steaks	1 (8- to 10-oz.) steak
OR		
beef New York strip or rib-eye steaks, 1-1/2 inches thick	2 (1-lb.) steaks	1 (1-lb.) steak
Kitchen Bouquet vegetable oil	1 tablespoon	1 tablespoon
BROWNING SKILLET	10-inch microwave browning skillet	10-inch microwave browning skillet
TIME AT HIGH (preheat skillet)	6 minutes	6 minutes
Cooking time for 8- to 10-oz. steaks:		
TIME AT HIGH (first side)	2 minutes	1-1/2 minutes
TIME AT HIGH (second side)	1-1/2 to 2 minutes	1-1/2 minutes
Cooking time for 1-lb. steaks:		
TIME AT HIGH (first side)	3-1/2 minutes	2-1/2 to 3 minutes
TIME AT HIGH (second side)	3-1/2 to 4 minutes	3-1/2 to 4 minutes

See directions for Basic Grilled Sirloin Steak, opposite.

Basic Grilled Frozen Rib-Eye Steaks

SERVINGS	2	1
INGREDIENTS		
frozen beef rib-eye steaks, 3/4 inch thick	2 (8- to 10-oz.) steaks	1 (8- to 10-oz.) steak
vegetable oil	1 tablespoon	1 tablespoon
BROWNING SKILLET	10-inch microwave browning skillet	10-inch microwave browning skillet
TIME AT HIGH (preheat skillet)	6 minutes	6 minutes
TIME AT HIGH (first side)	3 minutes	3 minutes
TIME AT HIGH (second side)	4-1/2 to 5 minutes	4-1/2 to 5 minutes

See directions for Basic Grilled Sirloin Steak, opposite.

Defrosting: To defrost steaks, see pages 56 and 57.

Creamy Lamb Chops au Poivre

SERVINGS	3	2	1
INGREDIENTS			
lamb loin chops, 1 inch thick	6 (4-oz.) chops	4 (4-oz.) chops	2 (4-oz.) chops
tomato wedges	6	4	2
semi-soft natural cheese with pepper	3/4 (4-oz.) container	1/2 (4-oz.) container	1/4 (4-oz.) container
snipped parsley or watercress	to garnish	to garnish	to garnish

Prepare lamb chops and cook on the first side according to Basic Grilled Lamb Chops below. Turn chops over after cooking first side. Top each chop with a tomato wedge and a small mound of cheese. Continue cooking second side according to Basic Grilled Lamb Chops. Sprinkle with parsley or watercress before serving.

Defrosting: To defrost chops, see pages 58 and 59.

Basic Grilled Lamb Chops

SERVINGS	3	2	1
INGREDIENTS			
lamb loin or rib chops, 1 inch thick	6 (4- to 5-oz.) chops	4 (4- to 5-oz.) chops	2 (4- to 5-oz.) chops
Kitchen Bouquet			
vegetable oil	1 tablespoon	1 tablespoon	1 tablespoon
BROWNING SKILLET	10-inch microwave browning skillet	10-inch microwave browning skillet	10-inch microwave browning skillet
TIME AT HIGH (preheat skillet)	6 minutes	6 minutes	6 minutes
TIME AT HIGH (first side)	3 minutes	2-1/2 minutes	2 minutes
TIME AT HIGH (second side)	3 to 4 minutes	1-1/2 minutes	1 minute

Preheat a 10-inch browning skillet, uncovered, at microwave full power (HIGH) 6 minutes. Trim fat edges of chops close to meat. Slash fat edges of chops. Brush fat edges lightly with Kitchen Bouquet. Add oil to hot browning skillet. Using hot pads, tilt skillet to coat evenly with oil. Quickly add chops. Microwave at full power (HIGH) for time in chart above. Turn chops over. Rearrange chops and give dish a half turn. Microwave at full power (HIGH) for time in chart above or until done to your liking. The timings are for medium-done chops. It is best to undercook chops slightly because they continue cooking after removing from microwave oven.

Doneness Test: Make a tiny cut in center of chop with a sharp knife. Pink indicates medium; gray means chop is well-done.

Adapting Lamb Chop Recipes for Microwave Oven

See information under Adapting Steak Recipes for Microwave Oven, page 92.

How to Make Creamy Lamb Chops au Poivre

Add oil to preheated browning skillet. Using hot pads, tilt skillet to coat with oil. Add lamb chops and microwave on first side. Turn lamb chops over with tongs or spatula to retain juices.

Top each chop with a tomato wedge and a small mound of semi-soft natural cheese with pepper. Microwave chops on second side until done to your liking and cheese has started to melt. Garnish with snipped parsley or watercress.

Deviled Onion Steak Sauce

SERVINGS	2	1
INGREDIENTS		
butter or margarine	2 tablespoons	1 tablespoon
onion, thinly sliced, separated in rings	1/2 medium	1/4 medium
prepared horseradish	2 teaspoons	1 teaspoon
Dijon-style mustard	2 teaspoons	1 teaspoon
Worcestershire sauce	2 teaspoons	1 teaspoon
all-purpose flour	1 teaspoon	1/2 teaspoon
dry red wine	1/4 cup	2 tablespoons
paprika, snipped parsley	to garnish	to garnish
BAKING DISH	1-qt. casserole	3- to 4-cup casserole
TIME AT HIGH (butter)	30 to 60 seconds	30 seconds
TIME AT HIGH (onion added)	5 minutes	3 minutes
TIME AT HIGH (seasonings added)	1-1/2 minutes	1 minute

Place butter or margarine in a casserole, see size in chart above. Microwave at full power (HIGH) for time in chart above or until melted. Add onion. Cover. Microwave at full power (HIGH) for time in chart above or until tender. Stir in horseradish, mustard, Worcestershire sauce and flour. Add wine and mix well. Cover. Microwave at full power (HIGH) for time in chart above or until thickened and bubbly, stirring twice. Spoon over grilled steaks or chops. Sprinkle with paprika and parsley.

Basic Pork or Veal Cutlets

SERVINGS	4	2	1
INGREDIENTS			
egg	1	1	1
water	1 tablespoon	1 tablespoon	1 tablespoon
all-purpose flour	2 tablespoons	1 tablespoon	2 teaspoons
dry seasoned breadcrumbs	3/4 cup	1/3 cup	3 tablespoons
dried leaf marjoram	1/2 teaspoon	1/4 teaspoon	1/8 teaspoon
dried parsley flakes	1 tablespoon	2 teaspoons	1 teaspoon
pork or veal cutlets	4 (4- to 5-oz.) cutlets	2 (4- to 5-oz.) cutlets	1 (4- to 5-oz.) cutlet
vegetable oil	3 tablespoons	3 tablespoons	2 teaspoons
BROWNING SKILLET	10-inch microwave browning skillet	10-inch microwave browning skillet	6-1/2-inch microwave browning skillet
TIME AT HIGH (preheat skillet)	6 minutes	6 minutes	2 minutes
TIME AT HIGH (first side)	3-1/2 minutes	2 minutes	1-1/4 minutes
TIME AT HIGH (second side)	3-1/2 minutes	1-3/4 minutes	1-1/2 minutes

In a pie plate, whisk egg and water until frothy. Place flour in a pie plate or on waxed paper. In another pie plate or on waxed paper, mix breadcrumbs, marjoram and parsley flakes. Coat cutlets on both sides with flour. Dip both sides in egg mixture, then in crumb mixture, coating generously. Preheat a browning skillet, see size in chart above, uncovered, at microwave full power (HIGH) for time in chart above. Add oil to hot browning skillet. Using hot pads, tilt skillet to coat evenly with oil. Quickly add cutlets. Microwave at full power (HIGH) for time in chart above. Turn cutlets over and give skillet a half turn. Microwave at full power (HIGH) for time in chart above or until done.

Doneness Test: Cutlets should be browned. Center of cutlets should be gray when cut.

Reheating Refrigerated Cutlets

To chill: Place 2 cooled cutlets with sauce in a 1-1/2-quart casserole. Or, place 1 cutlet and sauce in a 2- to 3-cup casserole. Cover with plastic wrap or lid; refrigerate.

To reheat: Vent plastic wrap, if using. Microwave 2 cutlets, covered, at 70% (MEDIUM HIGH) 11 minutes or until heated through. Give dish a half turn and rearrange cutlets once during cooking. Microwave 1 cutlet, covered, at 70% (MEDIUM HIGH) 7 minutes or until heated through. Let cutlets stand, covered, 1 minute.

How to Make Instant Cutlets Parmigiana

Top cooked, breaded cutlets in the browning skillet with a spoonful of canned sliced mushrooms. Pour Italian cooking sauce over mushrooms, then heat briefly in the microwave.

Sprinkle the cutlets with Parmesan cheese, then mozzarella cheese. Microwave to melt the cheese. Then serve on top of hot spaghetti tossed with butter or margarine and grated Parmesan cheese.

Instant Cutlets Parmigiana

SERVINGS	4	2	1
INGREDIENTS			
Cooked pork or veal cutlets, see Basic Pork or Veal Cutlets, opposite	4	2	1
Sliced mushrooms, drained	1 (2-1/2-oz.) jar	2 to 3 tablespoons	1 tablespoon
Bottled Italian cooking sauce	1 (16-oz.) jar	1 cup	1/2 cup
Grated Parmesan cheese	1/4 cup (1 oz.)	2 tablespoons	1 tablespoon
Shredded mozzarella cheese	1 cup (4 oz.)	1/2 cup (2 oz.)	1/4 cup (1 oz.)
BROWNING SKILLET	10-inch microwave browning skillet	10-inch microwave browning skillet	6-1/2-inch microwave browning skillet
TIME AT HIGH	2 minutes	1 minute	1 minute
TIME AT HIGH (cheese added)	1-1/2 minutes	30 to 45 seconds	30 seconds

Cook Basic Pork or Veal Cutlets and drain oil from browning skillet. Arrange mushrooms on top of cooked cutlets. Pour Italian cooking sauce over cutlets. Cover and microwave at full power (HIGH) for time in chart above. Top with Parmesan cheese, then mozzarella cheese. Cover. Microwave at full power (HIGH) for time in chart above or until cheese is melted. Serve with spaghetti tossed with additional Parmesan cheese and butter or margarine.

Cutlets Cordon Bleu

SERVINGS	4	2	1
INGREDIENTS			
beef cubed steaks	4 (4- to 5-oz.) steaks	2 (4- to 5-oz.) steaks	1 (4- to 5-oz.) steak
semi-soft natural cheese with garlic and herbs	1 (4-oz.) container	1/2 (4-oz.) container	1/4 (4-oz.) container
thin ham slices	4	2	1
asparagus or broccoli spears, cooked, drained	12 spears	6 spears	3 spears
Swiss cheese	1 slice, quartered	1/2 slice, halved	1/4 slice
BAKING DISH	12" x 7" baking dish	10" x 6" baking dish	flat 2-cup casserole
TIME AT HIGH	5 minutes	2-1/2 minutes	2 minutes
TIME AT 30%	5 minutes	3 to 4 minutes	2 minutes
STANDING TIME	5 minutes	5 minutes	5 minutes

Spread cubed steaks with some of the semi-soft cheese. Top each steak with a ham slice and spread with remaining semi-soft cheese. Place asparagus or broccoli spears in center of ham-topped steak. Top with Swiss cheese. Fold over sides and secure with wooden picks. Place steaks, seam side up, in a baking dish, see size in chart above. Cover with vented plastic wrap or lid. Microwave at full power (HIGH) for time in chart above. Rearrange steaks. Cover. Microwave at 30% (MEDIUM LOW) for time in chart above or until meat is done. Let stand, covered, 5 minutes.

Doneness Test: Meat should be slightly pink when cut in center.

Adapting Cutlet Recipes for Microwave Oven

- Use beef, veal or pork cutlets—thin flat steaks that the butcher has put through the meat tenderizer.

- Dip pork or veal cutlets in flour before dipping in egg and crumbs. This prevents grease from soaking in during cooking.

- Cook the pork or veal cutlets using Basic Pork or Veal Cutlets, page 98, as a guideline.

- Cook beef minute or cubed steaks without breading, using Basic Beef Cubed Steaks opposite, as a guideline.

- Breaded cutlets will have a crisp crumb coating if you use the browning skillet.

- Pork and veal cutlets are done when they show no pink when cut in center. Medium done beef minute steaks should be pink when cut in center. Increase cooking time a few seconds for well-done beef; decrease cooking time a few seconds for rare beef.

- Always use vegetable oil to brown cutlets in the browning skillet. Butter and margarine will burn in the hot skillet.

- After you finish cooking, clean the browning skillet with one of the special cleaning products available in stores.

How to Make Cutlets Cordon Bleu

Spread beef cubed steaks, sometimes called *minute steaks,* with herbed, semi-soft natural cheese. Top with a ham slice and spread with more cheese. Top either broccoli or asparagus spears with a slice of Swiss cheese.

Bring two opposite corners of the steaks to the center to form bundles. Secure the bundles by threading wooden picks through the steak and ham. If not secured, the bundles will open during cooking.

Basic Beef Cubed Steaks (Minute Steaks)

SERVINGS	4	2	1
INGREDIENTS			
vegetable oil	2 tablespoons	1 tablespoon	1 tablespoon
beef cubed steaks	4 (4- to 5-oz.) steaks	2 (4- to 5-oz.) steaks	1 (4- to 5-oz.) steak
butter or margarine	4 teaspoons	2 teaspoons	1 teaspoon
BROWNING SKILLET	10-inch microwave browning skillet	10-inch microwave browning skillet	10-inch microwave browning skillet
TIME AT HIGH (preheat skillet)	6 minutes	6 minutes	6 minutes
TIME AT HIGH (first side)	2 minutes	1 minute	45 seconds
TIME AT HIGH (second side)	30 seconds	30 seconds	15 to 30 seconds

Preheat a 10-inch browning skillet, uncovered, at microwave full power (HIGH) 6 minutes. Add oil to hot skillet. Using hot pads, tilt skillet to coat evenly with oil. Quickly add steaks. Microwave at full power (HIGH) for time in chart above. Pour off pan juices. Turn steaks. Top each steak with butter or margarine. Microwave at full power (HIGH) for time in chart above or until done to your liking.

Doneness Test: For medium steaks, meat should be pink when cut in center.

Basic Simmered Corned Beef

	TYPE OF CORNED BEEF		
INGREDIENTS 1 (2-1/2- to 3-lb.) boneless corned beef brisket or round	flat brisket, 1-1/2 inches thick	round brisket, 3-1/2 inches thick	corned beef round, 3 inches thick
ginger ale	4 cups	4 cups	3 to 4 cups
ROASTING BAG	16" x 10" bag	16" x 10" bag	23" x 19" bag
BAKING DISH	deep 3-qt. casserole or bowl	deep 2-qt. casserole or bowl	deep 3-qt. casserole or bowl
TIME AT HIGH	10 minutes	10 minutes	10 minutes
TIME AT 30% (fat side down)	30 minutes	30 minutes	30 minutes
TIME AT 30% (after turning roast)	1 hour	1-1/2 hours	1-1/2 to 2 hours
STANDING TIME	20 minutes	20 minutes	20 minutes

Slash fat edges of roast. Score fat on top and bottom of roast. Place roast, fat side down in a floured roasting bag set in a baking dish, see size in chart above. Choose the size roasting bag and baking dish that allows the meat to be as totally immersed in liquid as possible. Add spices from corned beef package, if any. Add ginger ale to cover roast. Tie roasting bag with string, leaving a 2-inch opening to vent steam. Microwave at full power (HIGH) 10 minutes. Microwave at 30% (MEDIUM LOW) 30 minutes. Open roasting bag and let steam escape. Turn roast over. Give dish a half turn. Tie roasting bag, leaving a 2-inch opening. Microwave at 30% (MEDIUM LOW) for time in chart above or until meat is tender. **Allow steam to escape before testing for doneness.** When meat is tender, tie bag tightly. Let roast stand 20 minutes. To serve, carve meat in thin slices diagonally across the grain. Allow 3 servings per pound. For added tenderness, refrigerate roast in cooking liquid. When cold, slice thinly diagonally across the grain.

Doneness Test: Meat is done when it can be shredded with a fork.

Adapting Corned Beef Recipes for Microwave Oven

- Select flat-shaped briskets. It's more difficult to keep round-shaped briskets under cooking liquid.
- Place meat in a floured roasting bag set in a baking dish that closely conforms to shape of meat. When tying bag with string, leave a 2-inch opening for steam to escape. Do not use metal twist ties.
- Follow Basic Simmered Corned Beef, above, as a cooking guideline.
- Adding vegetables to corned beef, as in the New England Boiled Dinner, page 104, will increase cooking time slightly.
- Each muscle of corned beef should be sliced diagonally across the grain. This means corned beef brisket needs to be carved from several different directions depending on the muscles.
- Meat is done when it can be shredded with a fork.

How to Make Basic Simmered Corned Beef

Slash fat edges of corned beef, then score fat covering with a sharp knife. Choose a roasting bag and deep casserole that conform as closely as possible to shape and size of meat.

Place corned beef, fat side down, in floured roasting bag. Add any spice packets that may come in the corned beef package. Pour in ginger ale to cover beef as much as possible.

To vent the roasting bag, leave a 2-inch opening when the bag is tied with string. Do not use metal twist ties in the microwave oven. Twist ties will cause arcing. Some roasting bags have ties developed especially for use in the microwave oven.

For added tenderness, refrigerate cooked roast overnight in roasting liquid. To serve hot, microwave the meat following directions for Peach-Glazed Corned Beef, page 126. Or, serve chilled for sandwiches. Carve corned beef in thin slices diagonally across the grain.

New England Boiled Dinner

SERVINGS	4	2 to 3
INGREDIENTS		
boneless corned beef brisket	2-1/2 to 3 lbs.	2 lbs.
ginger ale	4 cups	3 cups
potatoes, cut up	2 (2 cups)	1 (1 cup)
onions, cut up	2 medium	1 medium
carrots, cut up	2 medium	1 medium
rutabaga, peeled, cubed	1/2 large	1/2 medium
cabbage, in wedges	1/2 small head (4 wedges)	1/4 small head (2 wedges)
ROASTING BAG	23" x 19"	16" x 10"
BAKING DISH	deep 4-qt. casserole or bowl	deep 3-qt. casserole or bowl
TIME AT HIGH	10 minutes	10 minutes
TIME AT 30% (meat)	30 minutes	30 minutes
TIME AT 30% (vegetables added)	60 minutes	45 minutes
TIME AT 30% (cabbage added)	30 minutes	20 minutes
STANDING TIME	20 minutes	20 minutes

Slash fat edges of roast. Score fat on top and bottom of roast. Place roast, fat side down in a floured roasting bag set in a baking dish, see size in chart above. Choose the size roasting bag and baking dish that allow the meat to be as totally immersed in liquid as possible. Add spices from corned beef package, if any. Add ginger ale to cover roast. Tie roasting bag with string, leaving a 2-inch opening to vent steam. Microwave at full power (HIGH) 10 minutes. Microwave at 30% (MEDIUM LOW) 30 minutes. Open roasting bag and let steam escape. Turn roast over. Give dish a half turn. Add potatoes, onions, carrots and rutabaga. Tie bag, leaving a 2-inch opening. Microwave at 30% (MEDIUM LOW) for time in chart above or until meat is almost tender. Open roasting bag and let steam escape. Add cabbage wedges. Tie roasting bag, leaving a 2-inch opening. Microwave at 30% (MEDIUM LOW) for time in chart above or until meat is tender and vegetables are done. **Allow steam to escape before testing for doneness.** When meat and vegetables are done, tie bag tightly. Let stand 20 minutes. Carve meat in thin slices diagonally across the grain. Arrange on warm serving platter with vegetables. Refrigerate any leftover corned beef in cooking liquid.

Doneness Test: Meat is done when it can be shredded with a fork.

Tips

- For a quick dinner, buy thick-sliced deli corned beef to make Peach-Glazed Corned Beef, page 126.
- For extra tender corned beef, refrigerate meat in cooking liquid in tightly closed roasting bag overnight after cooking.

How to Make Basic Thick Ham Slice

Slash the fat edges of a thick ham slice to prevent curling. Microwave the ham slice for part of the cooking time. Then turn the slice over and spread with prepared mustard.

After spreading with mustard, sprinkle the ham slice with brown sugar and cinnamon. Spread the whole slice with apricot or peach pie filling and finish microwaving.

Basic Thick Ham Slice

SERVINGS	5 or 6	2 or 3	1
INGREDIENTS			
fully cooked center-cut ham slice, 1 inch thick	1 slice (2-1/4 to 2-1/2 lbs.)	1/2 slice (1 to 1-1/4 lbs.)	1/4 slice (about 8 oz.)
prepared mustard	2 tablespoons	1 tablespoon	2 teaspoons
brown sugar	2 tablespoons	1 tablespoon	2 teaspoons
ground cinnamon	1/2 teaspoon	1/4 teaspoon	1/8 teaspoon
apricot or peach pie filling	1 cup	1/2 cup	1/4 cup
BAKING DISH	12" x 7" baking dish	10" x 6" baking dish	2-cup casserole
TIME AT HIGH	5 minutes	5 minutes	3 minutes
TIME AT 30%	15 minutes	6 minutes	3 minutes
STANDING TIME	5 minutes	5 minutes	5 minutes

Slash fat edges of ham at 1-inch intervals to prevent curling during cooking Place ham in a baking dish, see size in chart above. Cover with vented plastic wrap or lid. Microwave at full power (HIGH) for time in chart above. Turn ham slice over. Spread with mustard. Sprinkle with brown sugar and cinnamon. Spread with pie filling. Cover with vented plastic wrap or lid. Microwave at 30% (MEDIUM LOW) for time in chart above or until heated through. Cover tightly and let stand 5 minutes.

How to Make Basic Thin Ham Slices

To heat a fully cooked ham half quickly, slice it before microwaving. It will heat faster and more evenly. Overlap the slices in a baking dish. Spoon pineapple and orange marmalade over slices.

Keep the slices moist during cooking by completely coating the slices with the marmalade sauce. Grate fresh nutmeg over the slices. Cover the baking dish with vented plastic wrap.

Basic Thin Ham Slices

SERVINGS	6	4	2	1
INGREDIENTS				
fully cooked ham slices, 1/4 inch thick	6 (3-oz.) slices	4 (3-oz.) slices	2 (3-oz.) slices	1 (3-oz.) slice
canned crushed pineapple, drained	1 (8-oz.) can	1/2 (8-oz.) can (1/3 cup)	1/4 cup	2 tablespoons
orange marmalade or apricot preserves	1/2 cup	1/4 cup	2 tablespoons	1 tablespoon
freshly grated nutmeg	to taste	to taste	to taste	to taste
BAKING DISH	12" x 7" baking dish	8-inch square baking dish	9-inch pie plate	flat 2-cup casserole
TIME AT HIGH	3 minutes	2 minutes	1 minute	1 minute
TIME AT 30%	10 to 12 minutes	5 minutes	3 minutes	1 minute

Arrange ham slices in a baking dish, see size in chart above, overlapping to fit dish. In a small bowl, mix pineapple and marmalade or preserves. Spread mixture over ham slices, being sure to cover all slices completely. Top with grated nutmeg. Cover with vented plastic wrap or lid. Microwave at full power (HIGH) for time in chart above. Give dish a half turn. Microwave at 30% (MEDIUM LOW) for time in chart above or until heated through.

Glazed Ham & Squash

SERVINGS	2 or 3	1 or 2
INGREDIENTS		
butter or margarine	3 tablespoons	1 tablespoon
maple syrup	1/2 cup	1/4 cup
ground cinnamon	1/4 teaspoon	1/8 teaspoon
ground cloves	1/4 teaspoon	1/8 teaspoon
acorn squash	1 (1-1/2 lb.) squash, use 6 rings	1 (1-1/2 lb.) squash, use 3 rings
fully cooked center-cut ham slice, 1 inch thick	1/2 slice (1 to 1-1/4 lbs.)	1/4 slice (about 8 oz.)
orange juice	1/2 cup	1/4 cup
bananas, halved crosswise	2	1
orange slices	to garnish	to garnish
BAKING DISH	12" x 7" baking dish	8-inch square baking dish
TIME AT HIGH (butter)	30 to 45 seconds	30 seconds
TIME AT HIGH (squash)	2 minutes plus 5 to 6 minutes	2 minutes plus 5 to 6 minutes
TIME AT HIGH (ham)	5 minutes	3 minutes
TIME AT 30% (ham)	4 minutes	2 minutes
TIME AT 30% (ham, squash, bananas)	6 minutes	5 minutes

Place butter or margarine in a 2-cup glass measuring cup. Microwave butter or marga rine at full power (HIGH) for time in chart above or until melted. Whisk in syrup an spices; set aside. Place whole squash in a baking dish, see size in chart above. Micro wave at full power (HIGH) 2 minutes. Pierce in several places with a large fork an turn squash over. Microwave at full power (HIGH) 5 to 6 minutes or until tender, turn ing squash over once. Slice squash into six 1/2-inch rings and remove seeds; set squas aside. Slash fat edges of ham at 1-inch intervals to prevent curling during cooking Place ham in same baking dish. Pour orange juice over ham. Cover with vented plasti wrap. Microwave at full power (HIGH) for time in chart above. Turn ham slice ove Microwave, covered, at 30% (MEDIUM LOW) for time in chart above. Pour off pa juices. Add squash rings and bananas to baking dish. Drizzle with syrup mixture. Cove with vented plastic wrap. Microwave at 30% (MEDIUM LOW) for time in chart abov or until heated through. Garnish with orange slices.

Reheating Refrigerated Thick Ham Slice

To chill: Place 1/2 of a cooled thick ham slice in a flat casserole or pie plate to fit. Cove with plastic wrap or lid; refrigerate.

To reheat: Vent plastic wrap, if using. Microwave casserole or pie plate, covered, a 70% (MEDIUM HIGH) 7 minutes or until heated through. Let stand, covered, 1 minute.

Fully Cooked Ham Halves

SERVINGS	8 to 10	6 to 8
INGREDIENTS		
boneless fully cooked smoked half ham	1 (4-lb.) ham	1 (3-lb.) ham
pineapple juice	1 (12-oz.) can (1-1/2 cups)	1 (12-oz.) can (1-1/2 cups)
Cherry Glaze, below, Old Southern Glaze, or Currant Glaze, page 112	large recipe	large recipe
BAKING DISH	deep 3-qt. casserole	deep 3-qt. casserole
TIME AT HIGH (ham)	5 minutes	5 minutes
TIME AT 30%	30 minutes	30 minutes
TIME AT 30% (after capping)	40 minutes	30 minutes
TIME AT 30% (glaze added)	see glaze recipe	
STANDING TIME	10 minutes	10 minutes

Place ham fat side down in a 3-quart casserole. Pour pineapple juice over ham. Cover and microwave at full power (HIGH) 5 minutes. Turn ham fat side up. Cover. Microwave at 30% (MEDIUM LOW) 30 minutes. Remove ham from microwave oven. Cap front edge with foil and secure with wooden picks. Give dish a half turn; cover. Microwave at 30% (MEDIUM LOW) for time in chart above or until a microwave meat thermometer inserted in center of ham registers 130F (55C). Prepare glaze. When ham is done, drain liquid from casserole. Spread glaze over ham. Cover and microwave as directed in glaze recipe. Let ham stand, covered, 10 minutes before slicing. Internal temperature will rise about 10F (5C) during standing time.

Doneness Test: Ham is done when microwave meat thermometer inserted in center registers 140F (60C).

Cherry Glaze

YIELD	1-1/4 cups (for 3-, 4- or 5-lb. ham)	2/3 cup (for 1- to 1-1/2-lb. ham)
INGREDIENTS		
golden raisins	2 tablespoons	1 tablespoon
dry white wine or pan juices	2 tablespoons	1 tablespoon
cherry pie filling	1 cup	1/2 cup
ground cinnamon	1/8 teaspoon	dash
ground cloves	1/8 teaspoon	dash
TIME AT 30% (glazed ham)	5 minutes	3 to 5 minutes
STANDING TIME (ham)	10 minutes	10 minutes

If time permits, combine golden raisins and wine and let stand 15 to 30 minutes. In a medium bowl, combine raisins, wine or pan juices, cherry pie filling, cinnamon and cloves. Mix well. When ham is done, drain liquid from casserole. Spread glaze over ham. Cover. Microwave at 30% (MEDIUM LOW) for time in chart above. Let ham stand, covered, 10 minutes before slicing.

How to Microwave Fully Cooked Ham Halves

Place fully cooked ham half, fat side down, in a deep casserole that most closely conforms to shape of ham. Pour pineapple juice over ham. Cover and microwave for part of cooking time.

Using several thicknesses of paper towels to protect hands, turn ham fat side up in casserole. Avoid turning with a large fork because this pierces the ham, allowing juices to escape.

Cap the front edge of the ham down to the juice line with a small strip of foil. Secure the foil tightly against the ham with wooden picks. Also shield any overcooked spots on top of ham.

After center of the ham has reached 130F (55C), spoon Cherry Glaze or a favorite glaze over ham. Microwave briefly to heat the glaze, then let stand, covered, before carving.

Old Southern Glaze

YIELD	2/3 cup (for 3-, 4- or 5-lb. ham)	1/3 cup (for 1- to 1-1/2-lb. ham)
INGREDIENTS		
packed brown sugar	1/2 cup	1/4 cup
dry mustard	1 teaspoon	1/2 teaspoon
ground ginger	1/2 teaspoon	1/4 teaspoon
bourbon	2 tablespoons	1 tablespoon
sliced peaches, drained	1 (8-oz.) can	1/2 (8-oz.) can
TIME AT 30% (glazed ham)	3 minutes	2 to 3 minutes
STANDING TIME (ham)	10 minutes	10 minutes

In a small bowl, combine brown sugar, dry mustard and ginger; mix well. Stir in bourbon until all sugar is moistened. When ham is done, drain liquid from casserole. Spread glaze over ham. Arrange peach slices on top. Cover and microwave at 30% (MEDIUM LOW) for time in chart above. Let ham stand, covered, 10 minutes before slicing.

Currant Glaze

YIELD	3/4 cup (for 3-, 4- or 5-lb. ham)	1/3 cup (for 1- to 1-1/2-lb. ham)
INGREDIENTS		
red or black currant jelly	1/2 cup	1/4 cup
crème de cassis	1/4 cup	2 tablespoons
GLASS MEASURING CUP	2-cup	1-cup
TIME AT HIGH (heat glaze)	1 minute	45 to 60 seconds
TIME AT 30% (glazed ham)	5 minutes	3 to 5 minutes
STANDING TIME (ham)	10 minutes	10 minutes

In a glass measuring cup, see size in chart above, mix currant jelly and crème de cassis. Microwave at full power (HIGH) for time in chart above, stirring once. When ham is done, drain liquid from casserole. Spread glaze over ham. Cover and microwave at 30% (MEDIUM LOW) for time in chart above. Let ham stand, covered, 10 minutes before slicing. Spoon juices over ham slices.

Adapting Baked Ham Recipes for Microwave Oven

- Heat smoked ham halves or canned ham in a covered casserole with a little liquid to prevent ham from drying out.
- Shield edges of ham with small strips of foil secured with wooden picks to keep edges from overcooking.
- For quicker, more even heating, slice ham before cooking. Use the directions for Basic Thin Ham Slices, page 107, as a guideline.
- Glaze ham only during the last 3 to 5 minutes cooking time. Adding a sugary glaze any sooner results in overcooking of the outside layer of ham.
- Hams over 5 pounds tend to dry out and overbrown before they are heated through in the microwave oven.

Canned Ham

SERVINGS	12 to 15	6 to 8	3 or 4	2 or 3
INGREDIENTS				
canned ham	1 (5-lb.) ham	1 (3-lb.) ham	1 (1-1/2-lb.) ham	1 (1-lb.) ham
pineapple juice or orange juice	1-1/2 cups	1 cup	1/2 cup	1/2 cup
Cherry Glaze, page 110, Old Southern Glaze, or Currant Glaze, opposite	large recipe	large recipe	small recipe	small recipe
BAKING DISH	deep 4-qt. casserole	deep 2-qt. casserole	deep 1-1/2-qt. casserole	deep 1-qt. casserole
TIME AT HIGH (ham)	10 minutes	5 minutes	5 minutes	5 minutes
TIME AT 30%	65 to 70 minutes	40 to 45 minutes	20 to 22 minutes	13 to 15 minutes
TIME AT 30% (glaze)	see glaze recipe			
STANDING TIME	10 minutes	10 minutes	10 minutes	10 minutes

Place ham, fat side down, in a casserole, see size in chart above. Pour pineapple juice over ham. Cover and microwave at full power (HIGH) for time in chart above. Turn ham fat side up. Cover all edges down to juice line with small strips of foil; secure with wooden picks. Cover. Microwave at 30% (MEDIUM LOW) for time in chart above or until microwave meat thermometer inserted in center of ham registers 130F (55C). Give dish a half turn once during time at 30%. Prepare glaze. When ham is done, drain liquid from casserole. Spread glaze over ham. Cover and microwave as directed in glaze recipe. Let ham stand, covered, 10 minutes before slicing. Internal temperature will rise about 10F (5C) during standing time.

Doneness Test: Ham is done when microwave meat thermometer inserted in center registers 140F (60C).

Smoked Pork-Shoulder Roll

SERVINGS	8 to 10	4 to 6
INGREDIENTS		
smoked pork-shoulder roll	1 (2-1/2-lb.) roll	1 (1-1/2-lb.) roll
ginger ale	2-1/2 to 3 cups	2-1/2 to 3 cups
ROASTING BAG	16" x 10" bag	16" x 10" bag
LOAF DISH	9" x 5" loaf dish	9" x 5" loaf dish
TIME AT HIGH	15 minutes	7 to 8 minutes
TIME AT 30%	90 minutes	60 minutes

If necessary, remove casing from roll, see directions on package. Place roll in floured 16" x 10" roasting bag set in a 9" x 5" loaf dish. Pour in enough ginger ale to cover meat. Pull bag up around meat. Tie roasting bag loosely with string, leaving a 2-inch opening to vent steam. Microwave at full power (HIGH) for time in chart above or until liquid is boiling. Microwave at 30% (MEDIUM LOW) for time in chart above or until meat is tender and heated through, giving dish a half turn once.

Doneness Test: Center of roll should be tender when pierced with a large fork.

Easy Scalloped Potatoes & Ham

SERVINGS	6	3
INGREDIENTS		
butter or margarine	1 tablespoon	1 tablespoon
cheese or poppy-seed cracker crumbs	1/2 cup	1/2 cup
butter or margarine	2 tablespoons	1 tablespoon
chopped celery	1/2 cup	1/4 cup
chopped onion	1/4 cup	2 tablespoons
frozen creamed peas and potatoes	2 (10-oz.) pkgs.	1 (10-oz.) pkg.
milk	1-1/2 cups	3/4 cup
chopped pimiento	1/4 cup	2 tablespoons
prepared mustard	2 teaspoons	1 teaspoon
cooked ham, cut in 1/2-inch cubes	2 cups (8 oz.)	1 cup (4 oz.)
watercress	to garnish	to garnish
BAKING DISH	2-qt. casserole	1-1/2-qt. casserole
TIME AT HIGH (butter)	30 seconds	30 seconds
TIME AT HIGH (butter, celery, onion)	3 minutes	2 to 3 minutes
TIME AT HIGH (peas and potatoes added)	6 minutes	3 minutes
TIME AT HIGH (ham added)	6 to 7 minutes	3 to 4 minutes

In a small bowl, melt first amount of butter or margarine at full power (HIGH) 30 seconds. Stir in cracker crumbs and set aside. In a casserole, see size in chart above, combine second amount of butter or margarine, celery and onion. Cover. Microwave at full power (HIGH) for time in chart above, stirring once. Add frozen creamed peas and potatoes, milk, pimiento and mustard. Cover. Microwave at full power (HIGH) for time in chart above. Stir until sauce is smooth. Stir in ham. Cover. Microwave at full power (HIGH) for time in chart above or until heated through. Stir. Sprinkle buttered crumbs around edge of dish. Garnish with watercress.

Canadian-Style Bacon

SERVINGS	3	2	1
INGREDIENTS			
Canadian-style bacon slices, 1/4 inch thick	6 slices	4 slices	2 slices
PLATE	paper plate	paper plate	paper plate
TIME AT HIGH	2 minutes	1-1/4 to 1-1/2 minutes	45 seconds

Line paper plate with white paper towel. Place Canadian-style bacon on paper plate. Cover with another white paper towel. Microwave at full power (HIGH) for time in chart above or until heated through. Remove cooked bacon from towel immediately to prevent sticking.

Saucy Scalloped Corn & Chops

SERVINGS	4	2	1
INGREDIENTS			
butter or margarine	2 tablespoons	1 tablespoon	2 teaspoons
chopped onion	1/2 cup	1/4 cup	2 tablespoons
chopped green pepper	1/4 cup	2 tablespoons	1 tablespoon
cream-style corn	1 (16-oz.) can	1 (8-3/4-oz.) can	1/2 (8-3/4-oz.) can
whole-kernel corn, drained	1 (16-oz.) can	1 (8-3/4-oz.) can	1/2 (8-3/4-oz.) can
chopped pimiento	1/4 cup	2 tablespoons	1 tablespoon
dried leaf thyme, crushed	1/2 teaspoon	1/4 teaspoon	1/8 teaspoon
fully cooked smoked pork chops, 1/2 inch thick	4 (5-oz.) chops	2 (5-oz.) chops	1 (5-oz.) chop
BAKING DISH	12" x 7" baking dish	10" x 6" baking dish	2-cup casserole
TIME AT HIGH (butter)	1 minute	1 minute	45 seconds
TIME AT HIGH (onion, green pepper)	3 minutes	3 minutes	2 minutes
TIME AT HIGH (corn added)	5 minutes	3 minutes	2 minutes
TIME AT HIGH (chops added)	5 minutes	3 minutes	2 minutes
TIME AT 30%	10 to 15 minutes	8 minutes	4 minutes

Place butter or margarine in a baking dish, see size in chart above. Microwave at full power (HIGH) for time in chart above or until melted. Stir in onion and green pepper. Cover. Microwave at full power (HIGH) for time in chart above or until tender, stirring once. Stir in cream-style corn, whole-kernel corn, pimiento and thyme; mix well. Cover with vented plastic wrap or lid. Microwave at full power (HIGH) for time in chart above. Stir corn mixture. Slash fat edges of pork chops. Place on top of corn mixture. Cover. Microwave at full power (HIGH) for time in chart above. Rearrange chops if cooking 4. Give dish a half turn. Cover. Microwave at 30% (MEDIUM LOW) for time in chart above or until heated through.

Doneness Test: Chops are done when they are hot when cut in center.

Adapting Smoked Pork Chop Recipes for Microwave Oven

- Slash fat edges of chops to prevent curling during cooking.
- Use the number of chops, amount of liquid, casserole sizes and cooking times for Basic Smoked Pork Chops, opposite, as guidelines.
- For casseroles, microwave the casserole mixture until heated through, then add the fully cooked smoked chops. Microwave until heated through. This prevents the chops from drying out and overcooking.
- Fully cooked smoked chops are done when they are hot when cut in center.

How to Make Saucy Scalloped Corn & Chops

After cooking onion and green pepper with a little butter in a baking dish, stir in corn, pimiento and thyme. Microwave the corn mixture until heated through.

Slash the fat edges of fully cooked smoked pork chops, then place the chops on top of the warm corn mixture. Cover with vented plastic wrap and microwave until chops are hot in center.

Basic Smoked Pork Chops

SERVINGS	6	4	2	1
INGREDIENTS				
fully cooked smoked pork chops, 1/2 inch thick	6 (5- to 6-oz.) chops	4 (5- to 6-oz.) chops	2 (5- to 6-oz.) chops	1 (5- to 6-oz.) chop
apricot nectar	1 (6-oz.) can (3/4 cup)	1 (6-oz.) can (3/4 cup)	1/2 (6-oz.) can (1/3 cup)	1/2 (6-oz.) can (1/3 cup)
orange slices	6	4	2	1
BAKING DISH	13" x 9" baking dish	12" x 7" baking dish	10" x 6" baking dish	2-cup casserole
TIME AT HIGH	5 minutes	5 minutes	3 minutes	2 minutes
TIME AT 30%	10 minutes	5 minutes	4 minutes	4 minutes

Slash fat edges of chops. Place chops in a baking dish, see size in chart above, with tenderloins toward center of dish. Pour apricot nectar over, coating all chops well. Top with orange slices. Cover with vented plastic wrap or lid. Microwave at full power (HIGH) for time in chart above. Give dish a half turn. Microwave at 30% (MEDIUM LOW) for time in chart above or until heated through.

Basic Ham Loaf or Ring

SERVINGS	6	4	2
INGREDIENTS			
ground ham	12 oz.	8 oz.	4 oz.
ground pork	12 oz.	8 oz.	4 oz.
eggs	2	1	1
quick-cooking oats	1/3 cup	1/4 cup	2 tablespoons
chili sauce	1/3 cup	1/4 cup	2 tablespoons
chopped onion	3 tablespoons	2 tablespoons	1 tablespoon
chopped green pepper	3 tablespoons	2 tablespoons	1 tablespoon
dry mustard	3/4 teaspoon	1/2 teaspoon	1/4 teaspoon
chili sauce	1/2 cup	1/4 cup	2 tablespoons
brown sugar	2 tablespoons	1 tablespoon	2 teaspoons
dry mustard	1/2 teaspoon	1/4 teaspoon	1/8 teaspoon
Meat in loaf shape:			
BAKING DISH	9" x 5" loaf dish	9" x 5" loaf dish	10-inch pie plate
TIME AT HIGH	5 minutes	5 minutes	3 minutes
TIME AT 30%	30 to 35 minutes	15 to 18 minutes	11 to 13 minutes
STANDING TIME	5 minutes	5 minutes	5 minutes
Meat in ring shape:			
BAKING DISH	10-inch pie plate	10-inch pie plate	
TIME AT HIGH	5 minutes	5 minutes	
TIME AT 30%	25 to 30 minutes	9 to 10 minutes	
STANDING TIME	5 minutes	5 minutes	

In a medium bowl, thoroughly mix ham, pork, eggs, oats, first amount of chili sauce, onion, green pepper and first amount of dry mustard. Press into a loaf or ring in a loaf dish or pie plate, see size in chart above. Shape ring around custard cup in center of pie plate. Shape either loaf or ring so meat does not touch sides of dish. Cover with waxed paper. Microwave at full power (HIGH) for time in chart above. Combine remaining chili sauce, brown sugar and remaining mustard. Spread over loaf or ring, coating entire top and sides. Give dish a half turn. Microwave at 30% (MEDIUM LOW) for time in chart above or until a microwave meat thermometer inserted in center of loaf or ring registers 170F (75C). Cover with foil and let stand 5 minutes.

Reheating Refrigerated Meat or Ham Loaf

To chill: Wrap cooled meat loaf or ham loaf in plastic wrap; refrigerate.

To reheat: Slice loaf. Place 2 slices (7 to 8 ounces) on a luncheon plate. Or, place 1 slice (4 ounces) on a saucer. Cover with vented plastic wrap. Microwave 2 slices at 70% (MEDIUM HIGH) 3 minutes or until heated through. Microwave 1 slice at 70% (MEDIUM HIGH) 2 minutes or until heated through. Let stand, covered, 1 minute.

How to Make Basic Ham Loaf or Ring

Place a custard cup in center of 10-inch pie plate. Form the ham loaf mixture into a ring shape around the cup. Be sure to smooth out any cracks where sections of the ring are joined.

Unmold the ring onto a serving platter and fill the center with one of the frozen mixed vegetable combinations. Garnish a loaf shape with green pepper rings during the last 5 minutes of microwaving, if desired.

Basic Ham Patties

SERVINGS	4 (4 patties)	2 (2 patties)
INGREDIENTS		
ground ham	8 oz.	4 oz.
ground pork	8 oz.	4 oz.
egg, beaten	1	1/2
quick-cooking oats	1/4 cup	2 tablespoons
ketchup	1/4 cup	2 tablespoons
BAKING DISH	13" x 9" baking dish	10" x 6" baking dish
TIME AT HIGH	4 minutes	3 minutes
TIME AT 30%	10 to 11 minutes	6 to 7 minutes
STANDING TIME	1 minute	1 minute

In a medium bowl, thoroughly mix ham, pork, egg, oats and ketchup. Shape into patties about 1/2 inch thick and 4-1/2 to 5 inches in diameter. Place in a baking dish, see size in chart above. Cover with waxed paper. Microwave at full power (HIGH) for time in chart above. Carefully turn patties over and rearrange in dish. Give dish a half turn. Cover. Microwave at 30% (MEDIUM LOW) for time in chart above or until done in center. Let stand, covered with waxed paper, 1 minute.

Note: Microwave 1 patty at full power (HIGH) 2 minutes, then 3 to 4 minutes at 30% (MEDIUM LOW). Let stand as above.

Sweet & Sour Ham Balls

SERVINGS	4 to 6	2 or 3
INGREDIENTS		
tomato sauce	1 (8-oz.) can	1/2 (8-oz.) can
packed brown sugar	1/2 cup	1/4 cup
red wine vinegar	1/2 cup	1/4 cup
chopped onion	1/4 cup	2 tablespoons
chopped green pepper	1/4 cup	2 tablespoons
cornstarch	2 tablespoons	1 tablespoon
cold water	2 tablespoons	1 tablespoon
pineapple chunks, drained	1 (8-oz.) can	1/2 (8-oz.) can
chilled, cooked Basic Ham Balls, below	24	12
rice noodles or hot cooked rice		
BAKING DISH	deep 2-qt. casserole	deep 1-qt. casserole
TIME AT HIGH (sauce)	5 minutes	4 minutes
TIME AT HIGH (cornstarch added)	3 minutes	2 minutes
TIME AT 30%	10 minutes	6 to 7 minutes

In a casserole, see size in chart above, mix tomato sauce, brown sugar, wine vinegar, onion and green pepper. Cover. Microwave at full power (HIGH) for time in chart above, stirring once. Stir together cornstarch and cold water. Stir into casserole. Microwave, uncovered, at full power (HIGH) for time in chart above or until thickened and bubbly, stirring three times. Stir in pineapple and ham balls. Cover. Microwave at 30% (MEDIUM LOW) for time in chart above or until heated through, stirring once. Serve over rice noodles or hot cooked rice.

Basic Ham Balls

SERVINGS	6 to 8 (36 balls)	4 to 6 (24 balls)	2 or 3 (12 balls)
INGREDIENTS			
ground pork	12 oz.	8 oz.	4 oz.
ground ham	12 oz.	8 oz.	4 oz.
quick-cooking oats	1/3 cup	1/4 cup	3 tablespoons
ketchup	3 tablespoons	2 tablespoons	1 tablespoon
egg	1	1	1
instant minced onion	1 tablespoon	2 teaspoons	1 teaspoon
dried parsley flakes	1-1/2 teaspoons	1 teaspoon	1/2 teaspoon
dry mustard	1-1/2 teaspoons	1 teaspoon	1/2 teaspoon
BAKING DISH	13" x 9" baking dish	12" x 7" baking dish	10" x 6" baking dish
TIME AT HIGH	5 minutes	4 minutes	2 minutes
TIME AT 30%	5 to 6 minutes	4 to 5 minutes	3 minutes

In a medium bowl, throughly mix pork, ham, oats, ketchup, egg, onion, parsley and dry mustard. Shape into 1-inch balls, see number in chart above. Place in a baking dish, see size in chart above. Cover with vented plastic wrap. Microwave at full power (HIGH) for time in chart above. Turn meatballs over and rearrange meatballs in center of dish to outside edge. Cover with vented plastic wrap. Microwave at 30% (MEDIUM LOW) for time in chart above or until meat is done when cut in center.

Savory Stuffed Pork Roast

SERVINGS	6		
INGREDIENTS			
bone-in center-cut pork loin roast, chine bone cracked	4-lbs. (6 ribs)		
bulk pork sausage	8 oz.		
chopped celery	3/4 cup		
chopped onion	1/2 cup		
corn-bread stuffing mix	2 cups		
chopped apple	1 cup		
chicken broth	1 cup		
garlic salt	1/4 teaspoon		
dried rosemary, crushed	1/2 teaspoon		
Kitchen Bouquet			
BAKING DISH	1-1/2-qt. casserole		
BAKING DISH	12" x 7" baking dish with microwave rack		
TIME AT HIGH (sausage)	5 minutes		
TIME AT HIGH (first side)	7 minutes		
TIME AT HIGH (second side)	7 minutes		
TIME AT 30%	45 to 60 minutes		
STANDING TIME	15 minutes		
TIME AT HIGH (reheat stuffing)	3 minutes		

Starting from fat side, cut 5 or 6 pockets in roast, corresponding to rib bones. Crumble pork sausage into a 1-1/2-quart casserole. Add celery and onion. Cover. Microwave at full power (HIGH) 5 minutes or until sausage is browned, stirring three times. Pour off liquid. Add stuffing mix, apple, broth, garlic salt and rosemary; mix well. Stuff about 1/4 cup stuffing mixture into each pocket of roast. Cover and refrigerate remaining stuffing in casserole. Tie roast securely with string to hold in stuffing. Place roast, bone side up, on a microwave rack in a 12" x 7" baking dish. Cover with a tent of waxed paper. Microwave at full power (HIGH) 7 minutes. Turn roast bone side down. Cover again with waxed paper. Microwave at full power (HIGH) 7 minutes. Cap any over-brown bone ends or edges of roast with small pieces of foil. Secure with wooden picks. Cover with waxed paper. Microwave at 30% (MEDIUM LOW) 45 to 60 minutes or until a microwave meat thermometer inserted in largest muscle registers 170F (75C). Give dish a half turn twice during cooking. Twenty minutes before end of cooking time, lightly brush any pale fat areas with Kitchen Bouquet. When roast is done, cover with a tent of foil and let stand 15 minutes. Internal temperature must register at least 170F (75C) after standing time. Microwave remaining stuffing in same casserole at full power (HIGH) 3 minutes or until heated through. Slice and serve roast, cutting between ribs so each person gets a stuffed chop. Cover any remaining meat tightly with foil to prevent darkening and drying out.

Doneness Test: After removing meat from microwave oven, insert microwave meat thermometer in roast, placing bulb or tip in the center of the largest muscle. The tip should not touch bone or rest in fat. After the standing time, thermometer must register at least 170F (75C) in several places, including the area of the roast along the bone. Meat should not have pinkish coloring. If temperature of roast is not 170F (75C), continue cooking at 30% (MEDIUM LOW) until you get this reading.

Defrosting: To defrost pork roasts, see page 53.

How to Make Savory Stuffed Pork Roast

Have the butcher crack the chine bone on a pork loin roast. This will allow easy carving at the table. Be sure the roast has as many rib bones as the number of servings.

Position a sharp knife over the rib bones. Cut deep pockets down to the rib bone. There will usually be 6 rib bones on a 4-pound roast, making 6 pockets for stuffing.

After stuffing each pocket with apple stuffing, tie the roast securely end to end with string. This helps hold the stuffing in place and helps the roast hold its shape during cooking.

Garnish with frosted grapes and herbs. Lemon balm is herb used here. To serve, carve between the ribs so each guest has a stuffed chop. Serve any extra stuffing with the roast.

Bone-in Pork Loin Roast

SERVINGS	6

INGREDIENTS
bone-in loin roast, center
  or end cut, 3 to 5 inches in
  diameter, 7 to 8 inches long
Kitchen Bouquet
	3-1/2 to 4 lbs.

BAKING DISH	12" x 7" baking dish with microwave rack
TIME AT HIGH (first side)	7 minutes
TIME AT HIGH (second side)	7 minutes
TIME AT 30%	45 to 55 minutes
STANDING TIME	15 minutes

Place roast, fat side down, on a microwave rack in a 12" x 7" baking dish. Cover with a tent of waxed paper. Microwave at full power (HIGH) 7 minutes. Turn roast fat side up. Give dish a half turn. Cover again with waxed paper. Microwave at full power (HIGH) 7 minutes. Cap edges at end of roast with small pieces of foil. Secure with wooden picks. Cover with waxed paper. Microwave at 30% (MEDIUM LOW) 45 to 55 minutes or until microwave meat thermometer inserted in largest muscle registers 170F (75C). Give dish a half turn twice during cooking. Turn roast over once during cooking if cooking unevenly. Twenty minutes before end of cooking time, lightly brush any pale fat areas with Kitchen Bouquet. When roast is done, cover with a tent of foil and let stand 15 minutes. Internal temperature must register at least 170F (75C) after standing time. Slice and serve. Cover any remaining meat tightly with foil to prevent darkening and drying out.

Doneness Test: After removing meat from microwave oven, insert microwave meat thermometer in roast, placing bulb or tip in the center of the largest muscle. The tip should not touch bone or rest in fat. After the standing time, thermometer must register at least 170F (75C) in several places, including the area of the roast along the bone. Meat should not have pinkish coloring. If temperature of roast is not 170F (75C), continue cooking at 30% (MEDIUM LOW) until you get this reading.

Gravy for Roasts

YIELD	1-1/2 cups	1 cup
INGREDIENTS all-purpose flour pan juices from meat water or broth Kitchen Bouquet salt and pepper	3 tablespoons 1-1/2 cups to taste	2 tablespoons 1 cup to taste
BAKING DISH	12" x 7" baking dish	12" x 7" baking dish
TIME AT HIGH	4 minutes	3 minutes

After cooking roast, remove microwave rack from baking dish. Stir flour into pan juices in baking dish. Use melted butter if there are no pan juices. Blend well. Stir in broth or water. Add Kitchen Bouquet as needed for color. Microwave at full power (HIGH) for time in chart above or until thickened and bubbly, stirring twice. Season to taste with salt and pepper.

Boneless Pork Loin Roast

SERVINGS	8 to 12
INGREDIENTS	
boneless pork loin roast, 3 to 4 inches in diameter, 9-1/2 to 10 inches long	4 to 4-1/2 lbs.
Kitchen Bouquet	
BAKING DISH	12" x 7" baking dish with microwave rack
TIME AT HIGH (first side)	7 minutes
TIME AT HIGH (second side)	7 minutes
TIME AT 30%	50 to 60 minutes
STANDING TIME	15 minutes

Place roast, fat side down, on a microwave rack in a 12" x 7" baking dish. Cover with a tent of waxed paper. Microwave at full power (HIGH) 7 minutes. Turn roast fat side up. Give dish a half turn. Cover again with waxed paper. Microwave at full power (HIGH) 7 minutes. Cap edges at end of roast with small pieces of foil. Secure with wooden picks. Cover with waxed paper. Microwave at 30% (MEDIUM LOW) 50 to 60 minutes or until microwave meat thermometer registers 170F (75C). Give dish a half turn twice during cooking. Turn roast over once during cooking if cooking unevenly. Twenty minutes before end of cooking time, lightly brush any pale fat areas with Kitchen Bouquet. When roast is done, cover with a tent of foil and let stand 15 minutes. Internal temperature must register at least 170F (75C) after standing time. Slice and serve. Cover any remaining meat tightly with foil to prevent darkening and drying out.

Doneness Test: After removing meat from microwave oven, insert microwave meat thermometer in roast, placing bulb or tip in the center of the largest muscle. The tip should not rest in fat. After the standing time, thermometer must register at least 170F (75C) in several places. Meat should not have pinkish coloring. If temperature of roast is not 170F (75C), continue cooking at 30% (MEDIUM LOW) until you get this reading.

Adapting Pork Loin Recipes for Microwave Oven

- Pork loins cooked to 170F (75C) should not have a pinkish cast. For more well-done pork, increase the cooking time at 30% (MEDIUM LOW).
- Check the temperature at several places in the roast to be sure whole roast is done.
- Select a uniformly shaped roast. Roasts that are about the same diameter at each end will cook more evenly in the microwave oven.
- Have the butcher crack the chine bone on a bone-in loin roast to make carving easier.
- The boneless loin roast is really two pork loins tied together to form a round roast.
- To make gravy, see Gravy for Roasts, opposite.

Easy Paella

SERVINGS	4 to 6	2 or 3
INGREDIENTS		
bacon	4 slices	2 slices
frozen Spanish-style rice	2 (10-oz.) pkgs.	1 (10-oz.) pkg.
water	6 tablespoons	3 tablespoons
cubed, cooked pork or ham	1 cup (4 oz.)	1/2 cup (2 oz.)
large shrimp, drained	1 (4-1/2-oz.) can	1/2 (4-1/2-oz.) can
tomato, cut in wedges	1 large	1 small
BAKING DISH	2-qt. casserole	1-1/2-qt. casserole
TIME AT HIGH (bacon)	4 minutes	3 minutes
TIME AT HIGH (rice)	6 minutes	3 minutes
TIME AT HIGH (meat added)	8 minutes	4 minutes

Place bacon in a casserole, see size in chart above. Cover with white paper towels. Microwave at full power (HIGH) for time in chart above or until crisp. Remove bacon from casserole, leaving drippings in casserole. Crumble bacon; set aside. Stir contents of seasoning pouch from rice into reserved bacon drippings. Stir in water. Add frozen rice. Cover. Microwave at full power (HIGH) for time in chart above. Stir in pork or ham, shrimp and tomato wedges; cover. Microwave at full power (HIGH) for time in chart above or until rice is tender and meat is heated through. Top with crumbled bacon.

Peach-Glazed Corned Beef

SERVINGS	3 or 4	2
INGREDIENTS		
chilled, cooked corned beef slices, about 1/4 inch thick	1 lb. (about 6 slices)	8 oz. (about 3 slices)
sliced peaches	1 (8-oz.) can	1/2 (8-oz.) can
peach jam	1/4 cup	2 tablespoons
packed brown sugar	2 tablespoons	1 tablespoon
lemon juice	2 teaspoons	1 teaspoon
dry mustard	1/4 teaspoon	1/8 teaspoon
ground cinnamon	1/4 teaspoon	1/8 teaspoon
reserved peach syrup	1 tablespoon	1 tablespoon
BAKING DISH	10" x 6" baking dish	9-inch pie plate
TIME AT 70%	10 minutes	5 minutes

Overlap corned beef slices in a baking dish, see size in chart above. Drain peaches, reserving 1 tablespoon syrup. Arrange peach slices on top of corned beef. In a small bowl, combine peach jam, brown sugar, lemon juice, dry mustard, cinnamon and reserved peach syrup; mix well. Spoon peach glaze over corned beef and peaches. Cover with vented plastic wrap. Microwave at 70% (MEDIUM HIGH) for time in chart above or until meat is heated through. Glaze will heat much more quickly than meat so be sure to check meat.

Leg of Lamb

SERVINGS	8 to 10	4 or 5
INGREDIENTS leg of lamb	whole, 7 to 8 lbs.	sirloin half or shank half, 3-1/2 to 4 lbs.
Kitchen Bouquet		
BAKING DISH	12" x 7" baking dish with microwave rack	12" x 7" baking dish with microwave rack
TIME AT HIGH (first side)	15 minutes	7 minutes
TIME AT HIGH (second side)	15 minutes	7 minutes
TIME AT 30%	60 to 75 minutes	45 minutes
STANDING TIME	15 minutes	15 minutes

Place roast, fat side down, on a microwave rack in a 12" x 7" baking dish. If using a shank half or a whole leg, cap shank end of leg with foil and secure with wooden picks. Cover roast with a tent of waxed paper. Microwave at full power (HIGH) for time in chart above. Turn roast fat side up. Give dish a half turn. Cover again with waxed paper. Microwave at full power (HIGH) for time in chart above. Give dish a half turn. Microwave at 30% (MEDIUM LOW) for time in chart above or until a microwave meat thermometer inserted in center of largest muscle registers 160F (70C). Give dish a half turn twice during cooking. During cooking, cap any overdone spots or edges with small pieces of foil and secure with wooden picks. Twenty minutes before end of cooking time, brush any pale fat areas with Kitchen Bouquet. When roast is done, cover with a tent of foil and let stand 15 minutes. Internal temperature will rise about 10F (5C) during standing time. Slice and serve. Cover any remaining meat tightly with foil to prevent drying and darkening.

Doneness Test: After removing meat from microwave oven, insert microwave meat thermometer in roast, placing bulb or tip in the center of the largest muscle. The tip should not touch bone or rest in fat. After the standing time, thermometer should register 170F (75C).

Note: If using a whole leg or a shank half, ask the butcher to hinge the shank bone so roast will fit the baking dish. Or, have shank bone removed and meat skewered back to roast with wooden skewers. If shank bone is removed, omit capping the shank end with foil.

Defrosting: To defrost a leg of lamb, see page 52.

Easy Stew for Two

In a 1-quart casserole, combine 1-1/3 cups beef broth, 1/2 teaspoon dried basil leaves, 1/4 teaspoon celery salt and 2 teaspoons Worcestershire sauce. Mix well. Add 2 carrots, cut in 1-inch pieces, and 1 large onion, cut up. Cover and microwave at full power (HIGH) 10 minutes or until vegetables are almost tender. Stir in 1-1/2 to 2 cups cubed cooked beef, lamb or pork. Cover and microwave at full power (HIGH) 2 minutes or until heated through.

How to Microwave Leg of Lamb

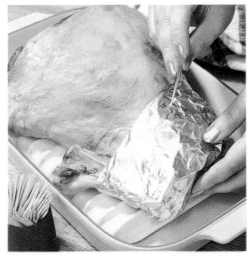

The sirloin half of the leg of lamb is in the baking dish. The butcher has hinged the shank bone of the leg of lamb so it will fit into the baking dish. It is essential to have this done if you are cooking the whole leg of lamb.

To prevent the small shank end from overcooking, cap it with foil and secure with wooden picks. After capping with foil, this roast will be turned over so the fat side is down for the initial cooking time. The sirloin half will also be turned over during the first cooking time.

Some areas of the roast may start to overbrown during cooking. Cover these areas with small pieces of foil and secure with wooden picks. To even out the browning, brush any pale fat areas with Kitchen Bouquet near the end of the roasting time.

Let the roast stand covered with foil for 15 minutes before carving. This evens out the temperature of the roast and makes carving easier. The end of the roast has a pinkish tinge even though it is done. Don't let this color deceive you into overcooking the roast.

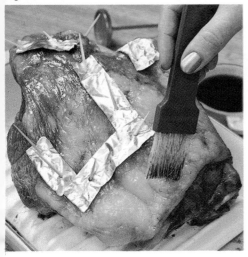

Shepherd's Pie

SERVINGS	6	3
INGREDIENTS		
sliced green onion	1/4 cup	2 tablespoons
butter or margarine	3 tablespoons	2 tablespoons
all-purpose flour	1/4 cup	2 tablespoons
celery salt	1/2 teaspoon	1/4 teaspoon
dried dillweed	1/4 teaspoon	1/8 teaspoon
milk	1 cup	1/2 cup
condensed beef broth	1 (10-1/2-oz.) can	1/2 cup
Kitchen Bouquet	1/2 teaspoon	1/4 teaspoon
whole baby carrots, drained	1 (16-oz.) jar	1/2 (16-oz.) jar
cubed, cooked lamb	2 cups	1 cup
sliced mushrooms, drained	1 (2-1/2-oz.) jar	1/2 (2-1/2-oz.) jar
water	1-1/3 cups	2/3 cup
milk	1/3 cup	2 tablespoons
butter or margarine	3 tablespoons	1 tablespoon
salt	1/2 teaspoon	1/4 teaspoon
instant mashed potato buds	1-1/3 cups	2/3 cup
snipped dill or parsley, paprika	to garnish	to garnish
BAKING DISH (meat mixture)	2-qt. casserole	1-qt. casserole
BAKING DISH (mashed potatoes)	1-1/2-qt. casserole	1-qt. casserole
TIME AT HIGH (green onion)	2 minutes	1 to 1-1/2 minutes
TIME AT HIGH (gravy)	5 to 6 minutes	4 to 5 minutes
TIME AT HIGH (water-milk mixture for potatoes)	3 minutes	2 minutes
TIME AT HIGH (meat mixture)	6 minutes	3 to 4 minutes
TIME AT 30%	12 to 15 minutes	7 to 8 minutes

In a casserole, see size in chart above, combine green onion and first amount of butter or margarine. Microwave at full power (HIGH) for time in chart above or until green onion is tender. Stir in flour, celery salt and dillweed; mix well. Stir in first amount of milk, broth and Kitchen Bouquet. Microwave at full power (HIGH) for time in chart above or until thickened and bubbly, stirring twice. Gently stir in carrots, lamb cubes and mushrooms; set aside. In a second casserole, see size in chart above, combine water, second amount of milk, second amount of butter or margarine and salt. Microwave at full power (HIGH) for time in chart above or until liquid begins to boil. With a fork, beat in potato buds until blended and fluffy. Cover and set aside. Microwave lamb mixture, covered, at full power (HIGH) for time in chart above or until boiling, stirring once. Drop potato in mounds on top of lamb mixture around edge of casserole or pipe through a pastry tube. Cover and microwave at 30% (MEDIUM LOW) for time in chart above or until heated through. Give dish a half turn once during cooking. Sprinkle with dill or parsley and paprika.

Doneness Test: Casserole is ready to serve when microwave meat thermometer inserted in center registers 170F to 180F (75C to 80C).

Shepherd's Pie

Beef Standing-Rib Roast

SERVINGS	6 to 8

INGREDIENTS
beef standing-rib roast, cut from
  small end, 4 to 5-1/2 inches high,
  7 to 8-1/2 inches wide
Kitchen Bouquet
	4 to 4-1/2 lbs., ribs 11 and 12

BAKING DISH	12" x 7" baking dish with microwave rack
TIME AT HIGH	5 minutes
TIME AT 30% (fat side down)	30 to 40 minutes
TIME AT 30% (fat side up)	20 to 25 minutes
STANDING TIME	15 minutes

Place roast, fat side down, on a microwave rack in a 12" x 7" baking dish. Cover with a tent of waxed paper. Microwave at full power (HIGH) 5 minutes. Microwave at 30% (MEDIUM LOW) for time in chart or until a microwave meat thermometer inserted in center of roast registers 90F (30C). Turn roast fat side up. Cap any overdone spots or edges with small pieces of foil; secure with wooden picks. Cover again with waxed paper. Give dish a half turn. Microwave at 30% (MEDIUM LOW) for time in chart or until microwave meat thermometer inserted in center registers 130F (55C). Twenty minutes before end of cooking time, lightly brush any pale fat areas with Kitchen Bouquet. When roast is done, cover with a tent of foil and let stand 15 minutes. Internal temperature will rise about 10F (5C) during standing time. Slice and serve. Cover any remaining meat tightly with foil to prevent darkening and drying out.

Doneness Test: After removing meat from microwave oven, insert microwave meat thermometer in roast, placing bulb or tip in the center of the largest muscle. The tip should not touch bone or rest in fat. After the standing time, thermometer should register 140F (60C). These timings are for medium-done roasts. Roasts cooked to well-done in the microwave will have an overcooked section around outside of roast.

Beef Rolled-Rib Roast

SERVINGS	8 to 10

INGREDIENTS
boneless beef rolled-rib roast,
  4-1/2 to 5-1/2 inches in diameter,
  4-1/2 to 5 inches long
Kitchen Bouquet
	3-1/2 to 4 lbs.

BAKING DISH	12" x 7" baking dish with microwave rack
TIME AT HIGH	5 minutes
TIME AT 30% (fat side down)	30 minutes
TIME AT 30% (fat side up)	25 to 30 minutes
STANDING TIME	15 minutes

See directions for Beef Standing-Rib Roast, above.

Defrosting: To defrost beef rib roasts, see page 52.

How to Microwave Beef Standing-Rib Roast

Select the most desirably shaped roast for microwave cooking. The roast in the background is a rib roast cut from the large end of the roast with a long tail portion. A more compact roast from the small end of the rib section cooks more evenly in the microwave oven. The diameter of the roast in the foreground is about 4-1/2 inches and it has almost no tail portion.

Place the roast on a microwave rack set in a baking dish so meat is kept above the juices. Cover the roast with waxed paper to prevent excessive spattering. Tuck the waxed paper down along ends of roast so the waxed paper will not blow off in the microwave oven. Before this roast is microwaved for the first cooking time, it will be turned so the bone side is up.

Check the roast occasionally to see if any spots are overcooking. Place small pieces of foil over these areas and secure with wooden picks to hold the foil firmly against the meat.

To insert a microwave meat thermometer, first measure the distance to the center of the largest muscle using the thermometer. Insert the thermometer to this depth in the center of the roast.

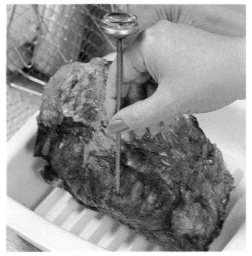

Meat Paprikash

SERVINGS	4 to 6	2 or 3
INGREDIENTS		
chopped green onion	1/2 cup	1/4 cup
chopped celery	1/2 cup	1/4 cup
butter or margarine	1 tablespoon	1 tablespoon
cubed, cooked beef or lamb	2 cups	1 cup
red beans or kidney beans, drained, rinsed	1 (15-oz.) can	1 (8-oz.) can
tomatoes, cut up	1 (16-oz.) can	1 (8-oz.) can
paprika	1 teaspoon	1/2 teaspoon
all-purpose flour	1 tablespoon	2 teaspoons
dairy sour cream	1 cup	1/2 cup
hot cooked noodles		
snipped parsley	to garnish	to garnish
BAKING DISH	2-qt. casserole	1-qt. casserole
TIME AT HIGH (onion, celery, butter)	3 to 5 minutes	2 to 3 minutes
TIME AT HIGH (meat, beans, tomatoes, paprika added)	5 minutes	4 minutes
TIME AT 30% (meat mixture)	12 to 15 minutes	6 to 8 minutes
TIME AT 30% (sour cream added)	2 to 3 minutes	2 minutes

In a casserole, see size in chart above, combine green onion, celery and butter or margarine. Microwave at full power (HIGH) for time in chart above or until tender. Stir in meat, beans, tomatoes and paprika; cover. Microwave at full power (HIGH) for time in chart above or until boiling around edges; stir well. Cover. Microwave at 30% (MEDIUM LOW) for time in chart above or until heated through. In a small bowl, stir flour into sour cream until blended. Stir 1/4 to 1/2 cup hot casserole liquid into sour cream mixture. Stir into casserole. Microwave at 30% (MEDIUM LOW) for time in chart above or until heated through, stirring twice. Do not boil. Serve over hot noodles. Garnish with snipped parsley.

Reheating Frozen Barbecued Beef

To freeze: Spoon 4 servings cooled Barbecued-Beef mixture into a 2-cup freezer container, leaving 1/2 inch headspace. Cover and freeze.

To reheat: Dip freezer container in hot water to loosen beef mixture. Place block of frozen beef in a glass bowl. Cover with vented plastic wrap. Microwave at 30% (MEDIUM LOW) 10 minutes, breaking mixture apart twice with a large fork. Stir well and cover. Microwave at 70% (MEDIUM HIGH) 2 minutes or until heated through, stirring once.

Tip

- It's a good idea to remove the frozen barbecued beef from the plastic freezer carton and reheat the mixture in a glass bowl. Some plastic containers may melt or distort during microwave cooking.

How to Make Barbecued-Beef Sandwiches

Turn frozen beef mixture into bowl. Twice during the defrosting time, break apart the semi-frozen mixture with a large fork to speed up thawing.

Spoon the hot beef onto hamburger buns and top with shredded cheese. Crisp carrot sticks and green onions make good relish partners. Keep these tasty sandwiches in mind to use up leftover beef roast.

Barbecued-Beef Sandwiches

SERVINGS	8	4
INGREDIENTS		
chili sauce	1 cup	1/2 cup
packed brown sugar	1/4 cup	2 tablespoons
instant minced onion	2 teaspoons	1 teaspoon
steak sauce	1 tablespoon	2 teaspoons
vinegar	1 tablespoon	2 teaspoons
Worcestershire sauce	2 teaspoons	1 teaspoon
prepared mustard	2 teaspoons	1 teaspoon
cooked beef, cut in strips	1 lb.	8 oz.
hamburger buns, split	8	4
shredded Cheddar cheese	1 cup (4 oz.)	1/2 cup (2 oz.)
BAKING DISH	2-qt. casserole	1-1/2-qt. casserole
TIME AT HIGH	1-1/2 to 2 minutes	1 minute
TIME AT 70%	6 to 7 minutes	4 minutes

In a casserole, see size in chart above, thoroughly mix chili sauce, brown sugar, onion, steak sauce, vinegar, Worcestershire sauce and mustard. Cover and microwave at full power (HIGH) for time in chart above. Stir in beef and cover. Microwave at 70% (MEDIUM HIGH) for time in chart above or until heated through, stirring once. Serve on hamburger buns topped with shredded cheese.

Hot Dogs (regular size)

SERVINGS	6	4	2	1

INGREDIENTS
hot dogs, 10 per
  12-oz. pkg.,
  3/4 inch in
  diameter, 5 inches
  long
	6	4	2	1

PLATE	9-inch plate or pie plate	8-inch plate or pie plate	8-inch plate or pie plate	8-inch plate or pie plate
TIME AT HIGH (not in buns)	2 minutes	1-1/4 minutes	45 seconds	30 seconds
TIME AT HIGH (in buns)	3 minutes	2 minutes	1 minute	40 seconds

Place hot dogs between white paper towels on a plate, see size in chart. Microwave at full power (HIGH) for time in chart. Or, place hot dogs in buns on a plate lined with white paper towel. Place another paper towel over hot dogs and buns. Or, place hot dogs in buns and wrap individually in white paper towels or napkins. Microwave at full power (HIGH) for time in chart. If cooking 4 or 6 hot dogs, rearrange them once during cooking.

Doneness Test: Hot dogs should be hot in center. A microwave meat thermometer inserted in center should register 180F (80C).

Hot Dogs (smoked)

SERVINGS	6	4	2	1

INGREDIENTS
smoked beef or pork
  hot dogs, 8 per lb.,
  7/8 inch in diameter,
  5 inches long
	6	4	2	1

PLATE	9-inch plate or pie plate	8-inch plate or pie plate	8-inch plate or pie plate	8-inch plate or pie plate
TIME AT HIGH (not in buns)	3 minutes	2 minutes	1-1/4 minutes	50 seconds
TIME AT HIGH (in buns)		2-3/4 minutes	1-1/2 to 1-3/4 minutes	1 minute

See directions for Hot Dogs (regular size), above.

Note: To cook extra large beef hot dogs (4 per pound), place them on a pie plate without buns. Microwave 4 hot dogs at full power (HIGH) 4 minutes, 2 hot dogs for 3 minutes and 1 hot dog for 1 minute.

How to Make Chili Dogs

Place hot dogs in buns on a paper-towel-lined plate. The paper towel absorbs the moisture so the buns won't get soggy. Cover the hot dogs with another paper towel to prevent spattering.

Spoon the warm chili mixture on each hot dog, then top with shredded cheese. Microwave just long enough to melt the cheese. Serve with tortilla chips and cold drinks.

Chili Dogs

	4	2
INGREDIENTS		
chili with beans	1 (7-1/2-oz.) can	1/2 (7-1/2-oz.) can
ketchup	1 tablespoon	2 teaspoons
Worcestershire sauce	1 teaspoon	1/2 teaspoon
instant minced onion	1/4 teaspoon	1/8 teaspoon
prepared mustard	1/4 teaspoon	1/8 teaspoon
smoked beef hot dogs	4	2
hot-dog buns, split	4	2
shredded process American cheese	1/2 cup (2 oz.)	1/4 cup (1 oz.)
BOWL	1-qt. bowl	2-cup bowl
PLATE	dinner plate	luncheon plate
TIME AT HIGH (chili)	2 minutes	1 minute
TIME AT HIGH (chili, hot dogs)	3-1/2 to 4 minutes	2 minutes
TIME AT HIGH (cheese added)	1 minute	30 seconds

In a bowl, see size in chart above, combine chili, ketchup, Worcestershire sauce, onion and mustard. Mix well. Cover with vented plastic wrap. Microwave at full power (HIGH) for time in chart above. Place a white paper towel on a plate, see size in chart above. Place hot dogs in buns on plate. Top with a second paper towel. Move chili to back corner of microwave oven. Place plate with hot dogs in microwave oven. Microwave chili and hot dogs at full power (HIGH) for time in chart above or until heated through. Remove paper towels. Spoon chili mixture onto hot dogs on serving plate. Top with cheese. Microwave at full power (HIGH) for time in chart above or until cheese melts.

Fresh Pork Sausage Patties

SERVINGS	4	3	2	1

INGREDIENTS
fresh pork
  sausage patties,
  2-1/4 inches in
  diameter, 3/4 inch
  thick
	8 (1-3/4-oz.)
	patties
		6 (1-3/4-oz.)
		patties
			4 (1-3/4-oz.)
			patties
				2 (1-3/4-oz.)
				patties

BROWNING SKILLET	10-inch microwave browning skillet	10-inch microwave browning skillet	10-inch microwave browning skillet	6-1/2-inch microwave browning skillet
TIME AT HIGH (preheat skillet)	6 minutes	6 minutes	6 minutes	2 minutes
TIME AT HIGH (first side)	2-1/2 minutes	2-1/4 minutes	2 minutes	1 minute
TIME AT HIGH (second side)	2-1/2 minutes	2-1/4 minutes	2-1/4 minutes	1-1/2 minutes

Preheat a browning skillet, see size in chart above, uncovered, at microwave full power (HIGH) for time in chart above. Quickly place patties in a circle in hot browning skillet. Microwave on first side at full power (HIGH) for time in chart above. Turn patties over and give skillet a half turn. Microwave on second side at full power (HIGH) for time in chart above or until done. Remove from browning skillet. Drain on white paper towels.

Doneness Test: Patties should be well-browned on first side and not be pink when cut in center.

Fresh Pork Link Sausage

SERVINGS	6	4	2
INGREDIENTS fresh pork link sausage	12 (1-oz.) links	8 (1-oz.) links	4 (1-oz.) links
BROWNING SKILLET	10-inch microwave browning skillet	10-inch microwave browning skillet	6-1/2-inch microwave browning skillet
TIME AT HIGH (preheat skillet)	6 minutes	6 minutes	2 minutes
TIME AT HIGH (first side)	2 minutes	1-1/2 minutes	1 minute
TIME AT HIGH (second side)	2 to 2-1/4 minutes	2 minutes	1 minute

Preheat a browning skillet, see size in chart above, uncovered, at microwave full power (HIGH) for time in chart above. If links have casings, pierce each link several times with a large fork. Quickly place links in a spoke pattern in hot browning skillet. Microwave on first side at full power (HIGH) for time in chart above. Turn links over. Microwave on second side at full power (HIGH) for time in chart above or until done. Remove from browning skillet. Drain on white paper towels.

Doneness Test: Links should be browned. Center of links should be hot with no pink remaining.

How to Microwave Sausage in a Browning Skillet

Place sausages in preheated browning skillet. All of these types of sausage cook satisfactorily in the browning skillet, clockwise from left: pork sausage patties, Brown 'n Serve beef sausage links, fresh skinless pork sausage links and fresh pork sausage links in casings.

To prevent overcooking, remove any patties or links that are done before the others. Drain sausage on paper towels. It's a good idea to cook more than you need for a meal and refrigerate or freeze the rest. Cooked sausages can be reheated quickly. See directions on page 140.

Brown 'n Serve Pork or Beef Sausage Links

SERVINGS	5	2	1
INGREDIENTS Brown 'n Serve pork or beef sausage links	1 (8-oz.) pkg. (10 links)	4 links	2 links
BROWNING SKILLET	10-inch microwave browning skillet	6-1/2-inch microwave browning skillet	6-1/2-inch microwave browning skillet
TIME AT HIGH **(preheat skillet)**	6 minutes	2 minutes	2 minutes
TIME AT HIGH **(first side)**	1 minute	45 seconds	15 to 30 seconds
TIME AT HIGH **(second side)**	1 minute	45 seconds	45 seconds

Preheat a browning skillet, see size in chart above, uncovered, at microwave full power (HIGH) for time in chart above. Quickly place links in hot browning skillet. Microwave on first side at full power (HIGH) for time in chart above. Turn links over. Give skillet a half turn. Microwave on second side at full power (HIGH) for time in chart above, or until done. Remove from browning skillet. Drain on paper towels.

Doneness Test: Links should be browned. Center of links should be hot with no pink remaining.

Reheating Sausage Links or Patties

SERVINGS	2	1	2	1
INGREDIENTS				
frozen cooked sausage links or patties	4 links or patties	2 links or patties		
OR				
refrigerated cooked sausage links or patties			4 links or patties	2 links or patties
PLATE	8-inch plate	8-inch plate	8-inch plate	8-inch plate
TIME AT 70% (links)	1-1/2 minutes	45 seconds	1 minute	30 seconds
TIME AT 70% (patties)	2 to 2-1/4 minutes	1-1/4 to 1-1/2 minutes	1-3/4 to 2 minutes	45 to 60 seconds

Place frozen or refrigerated cooked sausage links or patties on an 8-inch plate lined with white paper towel. Cover with another white paper towel. Microwave at 70% (MEDIUM HIGH) for time in chart above or until heated through.

Microwave Caution

Do not attempt to cook 2 links in a small browning skillet. The links will overcook on the ends before the center is done and there will be a dangerous amount of smoke.

Bacon (regular thickness)

SLICES	6	4	2	1
INGREDIENTS				
bacon, regular thickness, 22 to 25 slices per lb.	6 slices	4 slices	2 slices	1 slice
BAKING DISH	see suggestions in method opposite			
TIME AT HIGH	3-1/2 to 4-1/2 minutes	2-1/2 to 3-1/2 minutes	1-1/2 to 2 minutes	1 minute

See directions for Beef Strips or Extra-Lean Pork Strips, opposite.

Bacon (thick-sliced)

SLICES	6	4	2	1
INGREDIENTS				
bacon, thick-sliced, 11 to 12 slices per lb.	6 slices	4 slices	2 slices	1 slice
BAKING DISH	flat baking dish with microwave rack			
TIME AT HIGH	7-1/2 minutes	5-1/2 minutes	3 minutes	1-3/4 minutes

See directions for Beef Strips or Extra-Lean Pork Strips, opposite.

w to Microwave Bacon

ok a few slices of bacon, line a paper plate
white paper towels. Colored towels may dye
acon! Place the bacon on the towel-lined
and cover with another white paper towel
event spattering. Remove cooked bacon
kly so it doesn't stick to the towels.

To reserve drippings from bacon for cooking,
cook the bacon on a microwave bacon rack or
rack set in a baking dish. Besides regular bacon,
the extra-lean beef strips, at left, and extra-lean
pork strips, foreground, may be cooked in the
same manner.

---

ef Strips or Extra-Lean Pork Strips

ES	6	4	2	1
REDIENTS or pork akfast strips, ed, chopped, ned	6 slices	4 slices	2 slices	1 slice
ING DISH	see suggestions in method below			
E AT HIGH	4-1/2 to 5 minutes	3- to 3-1/2 minutes	1-1/2 to 2 minutes	1 minute

oking less than 6 slices bacon, place bacon on a microwave rack, microwave bacon
ker, or on a paper plate or baking dish lined with white paper towels. Cover with
te paper towels to prevent spattering. If cooking 6 slices bacon, use rack, cooker, or
ing dish; do not use paper plate. Microwave at full power (HIGH) for time in chart
ve. Remove paper towels and serve at once. If cooking 6 slices, some end slices may
k more rapidly than center slices. If done, remove end slices and continue cooking
aining slices.

e: Cooking times vary with brands and thickness of bacon. Use times given as a
le for cooking each type of bacon.

Vegetable Burgers Deluxe

SERVINGS	4 (4 patties)	2 (2 patties)	1 (1 patty)
INGREDIENTS			
ground beef chuck	1 lb.	8 oz.	4 oz.
cucumber sour cream dip	1/4 cup	2 tablespoons	1 tablespoon
onion salt	1/2 teaspoon	1/4 teaspoon	1/8 teaspoon
pared, seeded chopped cucumber	1/4 cup	2 tablespoons	1 tablespoon
chopped green onion	1 tablespoon	2 teaspoons	1 teaspoon
celery seed	1/4 teaspoon	1/8 teaspoon	dash
cucumber sour cream dip	1/2 cup	1/4 cup	2 tablespoons
leaf lettuce	4 leaves	2 leaves	1 leaf
hamburger buns, split	4	2	1
tomato slices	4	2	1
green-pepper rings	4	2	1
BAKING DISH	12" x 7" baking dish	9-inch pie plate	9-inch pie plate
TIME AT HIGH	3 minutes	1-1/2 minutes	1 minute
TIME AT 30%	5-1/2 minutes	3-1/2 minutes	3 minutes
STANDING TIME	1 minute	1 minute	1 minute

In a medium bowl, combine ground chuck, first amount of cucumber dip and onion salt; mix well. Shape into patties about 4 inches in diameter and 1/2 inch thick. Place in a baking dish, see size in chart above. Cover with waxed paper. Microwave at full power (HIGH) for time in chart above. Turn patties over and rearrange. Give dish a half turn. Microwave at 30% (MEDIUM LOW) for time in chart above or until almost done. These timings are for medium-done burgers. For well-done burgers, increase the cooking time at 30% (MEDIUM LOW) by a few seconds. Let stand, covered, 1 minute. In a small bowl, combine cucumber, onion, celery seed and second amount of cucumber dip; mix well. Serve burgers on lettuce-lined buns. Top with tomato slices, green pepper rings and a dollop of cucumber dip mixture.

Doneness Test: Burgers may still appear slightly pink in the center when done. This pink portion should be firm to the touch.

Defrosting: To defrost hamburger patties, see page 60.

Tips

- Cook extra burgers, then wrap and freeze them. Reheat the burgers in the microwave oven using the timings in Reheating Frozen Hamburgers, page 145, as guidelines.
- When burgers are served on buns with toppings, and a browned look is not important, cook the burgers in the microwave oven in a baking dish. For a browned look, cook the burgers in the browning skillet.
- Preheat browning skillet without the lid for time listed in recipes. The hot skillet will have a yellowish cast inside.

Hamburgers

SERVINGS	4	2	1
INGREDIENTS ground beef-chuck patties, 4 inches in diameter, 1/2 inch thick	4 (4-oz.) patties	2 (4-oz.) patties	1 (4-oz.) patty
BAKING DISH	12" x 7" baking dish	9-inch pie plate	9-inch pie plate
TIME AT HIGH	3 minutes	1-1/2 minutes	1 minute
TIME AT 30%	4 to 4-1/2 minutes	3 to 3-1/2 minutes	2 to 2-1/2 minutes
STANDING TIME	1 minute	1 minute	1 minute

Place patties in a baking dish, see size in chart above. Cover with waxed paper. Microwave at full power (HIGH) for time in chart above. Turn patties over and rearrange. Give dish a half turn. Cover with waxed paper. Microwave at 30% (MEDIUM LOW) for time in chart above or until almost done. These timings are for medium-done hamburgers. For well-done burgers, increase the cooking time at 30% (MEDIUM LOW) by a few seconds. Let stand, covered, 1 minute.

Doneness Test: Burgers may still appear slightly pink in the center when done. The pink portion should be firm to the touch.

Grilled Hamburgers

SERVINGS	4	2	1
INGREDIENTS ground beef-chuck patties, 4 inches in diameter, 1/2 inch thick	4 (4-oz.) patties	2 (4-oz.) patties	1 (4-oz.) patty
BROWNING SKILLET	10-inch microwave browning skillet	10-inch microwave browning skillet	6-1/2-inch microwave browning skillet
TIME AT HIGH (preheat skillet)	6 minutes	6 minutes	2 minutes
TIME AT HIGH (first side)	2 minutes	1-1/2 minutes	1-1/2 minutes
TIME AT HIGH (second side)	1-1/2 to 1-3/4 minutes	1 to 1-1/4 minutes	30 to 60 seconds
STANDING TIME	1 minute	1 minute	1 minute

Preheat a browning skillet, see size in chart above, uncovered, at microwave full power (HIGH) for time in chart above. Quickly add patties to hot browning skillet. Microwave at full power (HIGH) for time in chart above. Turn patties over. Microwave at full power (HIGH) for time in chart above or until done to your liking. These timings are for medium-done hamburgers. For well-done burgers, increase cooking time by a few seconds. Let stand, uncovered, 1 minute.

Doneness Test: Burgers should be browned on the outside and slightly pink in the center when done.

Reheating Refrigerated Hamburgers

SERVINGS	4	2	1
INGREDIENTS			
cooked hamburgers	4 patties	2 patties	1 patty
PLATE	dinner plate	luncheon plate	saucer
TIME AT 70%	3 minutes	2 minutes	1 minute

To chill: Wrap cooled burgers in plastic wrap; refrigerate.

To reheat: Unwrap burgers and place on a plate, see size in chart above. Cover with vented plastic wrap. Microwave at 70% (MEDIUM HIGH) for time in chart above or until heated through.

Reheating Frozen Hamburgers

SERVINGS	4	2	1
INGREDIENTS			
cooked hamburgers	4 patties	2 patties	1 patty
PLATE	dinner plate	luncheon plate	saucer
TIME AT 30%	6 to 7 minutes	4 to 5 minutes	2 to 3 minutes
TIME AT 70%	3 minutes	1-1/2 minutes	1 minute

To freeze: Wrap cooled burgers in plastic wrap; freeze. When frozen, store in a plastic bag.

To reheat: Unwrap patties and place on a plate, see size in chart above. Cover with vented plastic wrap. Microwave at 30% (MEDIUM LOW) for time in chart above or until thawed. Microwave at 70% (MEDIUM HIGH) for time in chart above or until heated through.

Reheating Refrigerated Stroganoff Meatballs

SERVINGS	2 or 3	2	1
INGREDIENTS cooked Stroganoff Meatballs, page 146	12 meatballs with sauce	8 meatballs with sauce	4 meatballs with sauce
BAKING DISH	1-1/2-qt. casserole	1-qt. casserole	1-1/2-cup casserole
TIME AT 70%	8 to 8-1/2 minutes	5 to 5-1/2 minutes	3 to 3-1/2 minutes
STANDING TIME	1 minute	1 minute	1 minute

To chill: Spoon cooled meatballs and sauce into a casserole, see size in chart above. Cover with plastic wrap or lid; refrigerate.

To reheat: Vent plastic wrap, if using. Microwave, covered, at 70% (MEDIUM HIGH) for time in chart above or until heated through, stirring once. Stir again before serving. Let stand, covered, 1 minute.

Basic Beef Meatballs

SERVINGS	6 to 8 (36 balls)	4 to 6 (24 balls)	2 or 3 (12 balls)
INGREDIENTS			
ground beef chuck	1-1/2 lbs.	1 lb.	8 oz.
quick-cooking oats	1/3 cup	1/4 cup	3 tablespoons
ketchup	3 tablespoons	2 tablespoons	1 tablespoon
egg	1	1	1
instant minced onion	1 tablespoon	2 teaspoons	1 teaspoon
dried parsley flakes	1-1/2 teaspoons	1 teaspoon	1/2 teaspoon
celery salt	3/4 teaspoon	1/2 teaspoon	1/4 teaspoon
BAKING DISH	13" x 9" baking dish	12" x 7" baking dish	8-inch square baking dish
TIME AT HIGH	4 minutes	4 minutes	2 minutes
TIME AT 30%	5 to 6 minutes	3 to 4 minutes	2 minutes

In a medium bowl, thoroughly mix ground chuck, oats, ketchup, egg, onion, parsley and celery salt. Shape into 1-inch meatballs, see number in chart above. Place in a baking dish, see size in chart above. Cover with vented plastic wrap. Microwave at full power (HIGH) for time in chart above. Turn meatballs over. Rearrange meatballs in center of dish to outside edge. Cover with vented plastic wrap. Microwave at 30% (MEDIUM LOW) for time in chart above or until meat is done when cut in center. Drain. Use meatballs for Stroganoff Meatballs, below, or in one of your favorite recipes.

Stroganoff Meatballs

SERVINGS	4 to 6	2 or 3	2 or 3
INGREDIENTS			
semi-soft natural cheese with garlic and herbs	1 (4-oz.) container	1/2 (4-oz.) container	1/2 (4-oz.) container
condensed cream of mushroom soup	1 (10-1/2-oz.) can	1/2 (10-1/2-oz.) can	1/2 (10-1/2-oz.) can
milk	3/4 cup	1/3 cup	1/3 cup
tomato paste	2 tablespoons	1 tablespoon	1 tablespoon
Basic Beef Meatballs, above	24 chilled	12 hot	12 frozen
sliced mushrooms, drained	1 (2-1/2-oz.) jar	1/2 (2-1/2-oz.) jar	1/2 (2-1/2-oz.) jar
hot cooked green noodles			
paprika	to garnish	to garnish	to garnish
BAKING DISH	deep 2-qt. casserole	deep 1-1/2-qt. casserole	deep 1-1/2-qt. casserole
TIME AT HIGH	5 minutes	3 minutes	3 minutes
TIME AT 30%	20 minutes	5 minutes	15 minutes

In a casserole, see size in chart above, combine cheese, soup, milk and tomato paste. Whisk until mixture is smooth. Cover. Microwave at full power (HIGH) for time in chart above or until boiling, stirring once. Stir in meatballs and mushrooms. Cover. Microwave at 30% (MEDIUM LOW) for time in chart above or until heated through, stirring once. Serve over green noodles. Sprinkle with paprika.

Defrosting: To defrost ground beef, see page 60.

How to Make Stroganoff Meatballs

Thoroughly combine ground beef and seasonings. Pat meat mixture evenly into bowl. Using a table knife, divide the meat mixture in four pie-shape wedges.

Divide the total number of meatballs to be made by four. Then, using wet hands, shape each wedge of meat mixture into one-fourth the total number of meatballs.

After cooking Basic Beef Meatballs at full power (HIGH), turn the meatballs over and rearrange center meatballs to outside edge and vice versa. This promotes more even cooking.

Stroganoff Meatballs can start three ways—chilled, frozen or hot cooked. After heating the mushroom sauce, the meatballs are added and heated. Serve over green noodles.

Basic Meat Loaf or Ring

SERVINGS	6	4	2
INGREDIENTS			
ground beef chuck	1-1/2 lbs.	1 lb.	8 oz.
eggs	2	1	omit
quick-cooking oats	1/3 cup	1/4 cup	2 tablespoons
chopped onion	3 tablespoons	2 tablespoons	1 tablespoon
tomato sauce	1 (8-oz.) can	1 (8-oz.) can	1/2 (8-oz.) can
dried leaf thyme	1/2 teaspoon	1/4 teaspoon	1/8 teaspoon
dried leaf marjoram	1/2 teaspoon	1/4 teaspoon	1/8 teaspoon
celery salt	3/4 teaspoon	1/2 teaspoon	1/4 teaspoon
brown sugar	1 tablespoon	1 tablespoon	2 teaspoons
Worcestershire sauce	1 teaspoon	1 teaspoon	1/2 teaspoon
prepared mustard	1 teaspoon	1 teaspoon	1/2 teaspoon
Meat in loaf shape:			
BAKING DISH	9" x 5" loaf dish	9" x 5" loaf dish	9-inch pie plate
TIME AT HIGH	5 minutes	5 minutes	3 minutes
TIME AT 30%	35 to 40 minutes	17 to 20 minutes	8 to 10 minutes
STANDING TIME	5 minutes	5 minutes	5 minutes
Meat in ring shape:			
PLATE	9-inch pie plate	9-inch pie plate	
TIME AT HIGH	5 minutes	5 minutes	
TIME AT 30%	18 to 20 minutes	8 to 9 minutes	
STANDING TIME	5 minutes	5 minutes	

In a medium bowl, thoroughly combine meat, eggs, oats, onion, half the tomato sauce, thyme, marjoram and celery salt. Shape into a loaf or ring in a loaf dish or pie plate, see size in chart above. Shape ring around custard cup in center of pie plate. Shape loaf or ring so meat does not touch sides of dish. Cover with waxed paper. Microwave at full power (HIGH) for time in chart above. Pour off juices. Stir brown sugar, Worcestershire sauce and mustard into remaining tomato sauce. Spoon tomato glaze over loaf or ring, coating entire top and sides. Give dish a half turn. Cover with waxed paper. Microwave at 30% (MEDIUM LOW) for time in chart above or until a microwave meat thermometer inserted in center of loaf or ring registers 170F (75C). Cover with foil and let stand 5 minutes. Temperature will rise about 10F (5C) during standing time.

Adapting Meat Loaf Recipes for Microwave Oven

- Use directions in Basic Meat Loaf or Ring, above, as a guideline for amount of meat, baking dish sizes and cooking times.

- Shape the meat mixture in a loaf or ring shape, leaving space around edges of meat for juices to drain during cooking. If you're in a hurry, the ring-shape loaf cooks in a much shorter time than the traditional loaf shape.

- Cover with waxed paper and microwave at full power (HIGH) for time listed in the basic recipe. Pour off juices.

- Spoon barbecue sauce, ketchup or any sauce over loaf. The sauce helps keep the meat from overbrowning during the remaining cooking time. Give the dish a half turn to ensure more even cooking. Cover with waxed paper and microwave at 30% (MEDIUM LOW) for time in basic recipe.

- Loaf or ring is done when a microwave meat thermometer inserted in center registers 170F (75C).

How to Make Basic Meat Loaf

In a mixing bowl, make a well in center of ground beef. Add oats, eggs, onion, half the tomato sauce and herbs to well. Mix the beef gently but thoroughly with the other ingredients.

Gently shape the meat mixture into a loaf shape in baking dish, smoothing out any cracks that appear in the loaf. Leave space around loaf for juices to drain during cooking.

After microwaving at full power (HIGH), drain the juices from the loaf. Again, smooth out any cracks that may have formed in the loaf, because they will widen during cooking.

Spoon the glaze over the loaf, coating entire top surface and sides. The glaze prevents the loaf from overbrowning during cooking. Slice the loaf with a serrated knife after the standing time.

Chinese Tacos

SERVINGS	5 or 6	2 or 3
INGREDIENTS		
ground beef or pork	1 lb.	8 oz.
chopped green onion	1/4 cup	2 tablespoons
chopped water chestnuts	1/4 cup	2 tablespoons
cornstarch	2 teaspoons	1 teaspoon
soy sauce	2 tablespoons	1 tablespoon
vinegar	1 teaspoon	1/2 teaspoon
dry mustard	1/2 teaspoon	1/4 teaspoon
ground ginger	1/2 teaspoon	1/4 teaspoon
beef bouillon granules	1/2 teaspoon	1/4 teaspoon
water	1/3 cup	3 tablespoons
large crisp iceberg lettuce leaves	5 or 6	2 or 3
canned fried rice noodles or chow mein noodles	1 (3-oz.) can	1/2 (3-oz.) can
BAKING DISH	deep 2-qt. casserole	deep 1-qt. casserole
TIME AT HIGH (meat)	5 minutes	3 minutes
TIME AT HIGH (cornstarch)	3 minutes	1-1/2 minutes

Crumble meat into a casserole, see size in chart above. Add green onion. Cover with waxed paper. Microwave at full power (HIGH) for time in chart above or until meat is browned, stirring twice. Pour off juices. Add water chestnuts. In a small bowl, mix cornstarch, soy sauce and vinegar. Stir in dry mustard and ginger until smooth. Stir into meat mixture; mix well. Add bouillon granules and water, stirring until well mixed. Cover. Microwave at full power (HIGH) for time in chart above or until thickened and bubbly, stirring once. To serve, spoon meat mixture into center of lettuce leaves. Top with noodles. Fold up envelope-style to eat. Serve with additional soy sauce.

Defrosting: To defrost ground beef, see page 60.

Reheating Refrigerated Chinese Taco Filling

SERVINGS	2	1
INGREDIENTS		
cooked Chinese Taco filling	2/3 cup	1/3 cup
BAKING DISH	2-cup bowl	5-oz. custard cup
TIME AT 70%	2 minutes	1 minute

To chill: Spoon cooled Chinese Taco filling into a small bowl or custard cup, see size in chart above. Cover with plastic wrap; refrigerate.

To reheat: Vent plastic wrap. Microwave at 70% (MEDIUM HIGH) for time in chart above or until heated through.

Spaghetti & Meat Sauce

SERVINGS	4	2
INGREDIENTS		
ground beef chuck	1 lb.	8 oz.
chopped onion	1 cup	1/2 cup
chopped green pepper	1/2 cup	1/4 cup
tomatoes, cut up	1 (16-oz.) can	1 (8-oz.) can
tomato sauce	1 (8-oz.) can	1/2 (8-oz.) can
tomato paste	1 (6-oz.) can	1/2 (6-oz.) can
water	1/4 cup	2 tablespoons
bay leaf	1	1
dried leaf oregano	2 teaspoons	1 teaspoon
dried leaf basil	1 teaspoon	1/2 teaspoon
Worcestershire sauce	1 tablespoon	2 teaspoons
hot cooked spaghetti		
grated Parmesan cheese		
BAKING DISH	deep 3-qt. casserole	deep 2-qt. casserole
TIME AT HIGH (meat)	5 to 6 minutes	3 to 4 minutes
TIME AT HIGH (tomatoes, herbs added)	10 minutes	5 minutes
TIME AT 30%	45 minutes	30 minutes

Crumble meat into a casserole, see size in chart above. Add onion and green pepper. Cover with waxed paper. Microwave at full power (HIGH) for time in chart above or until meat is browned, stirring twice. Pour off juices. Stir in tomatoes, tomato sauce, tomato paste, water, bay leaf, oregano, basil and Worcestershire sauce. Cover. Microwave at full power (HIGH) for time in chart above or until boiling. Stir well. Microwave at 30% (MEDIUM LOW) for time in chart above or until sauce reaches desired consistency, stirring occasionally. Serve over hot cooked spaghetti. Sprinkle with Parmesan cheese.

Reheating Frozen Meat Sauce for Spaghetti

SERVINGS	2	1
INGREDIENTS		
cooked meat sauce for spaghetti	2 cups	1 cup
BAKING DISH	1-qt. casserole	2-cup casserole
TIME AT 30%	16 to 18 minutes	10 minutes
TIME AT 70%	5 to 5-1/2 minutes	3 to 3-1/2 minutes
STANDING TIME	1 minute	1 minute

To freeze: Spoon cooled meat sauce into a freezer container, leaving 1/2 inch headspace. Cover tightly and freeze.

To reheat: Dip freezer container in hot water to loosen sauce. Place block of frozen sauce in a casserole, see size in chart above. Cover with vented plastic wrap or lid. Microwave at 30% (MEDIUM LOW) for time in chart above, breaking apart edges of sauce with a large fork partway through cooking time. Stir well; cover with vented plastic wrap or lid. Microwave at 70% (MEDIUM HIGH) for time in chart above or until heated through. Let stand, covered, 1 minute. Stir before serving.

How to Make Spaghetti & Meat Sauce

Crumble ground beef into a casserole. Add chopped onion and green pepper. Use this method for browning ground beef and vegetables for other casseroles.

Partway through the cooking time, stir the meat mixture so the cooked portions along the edge are moved to the center of the casserole. Stir the uncooked center portions toward the edge.

Pour off the juices after browning the ground beef, then stir in the tomatoes and seasonings. Cut whole tomatoes into large pieces. Bring the mixture to a boil at full power (HIGH), then simmer at 30% (MEDIUM LOW) until thick.

When sauce is desired consistency, ladle over hot cooked spaghetti. Sprinkle freshly grated Parmesan cheese over each serving. Freeze any extra sauce to reheat later in the microwave oven.

Old-Fashioned Chili

SERVINGS	4	2
INGREDIENTS		
ground beef chuck	1 lb.	8 oz.
chopped onion	1/2 cup	1/4 cup
chopped green pepper	1/4 cup	2 tablespoons
tomatoes, cut up	1 (16-oz.) can	1 (8-oz.) can
tomato sauce	1 (8-oz.) can	1/2 (8-oz.) can
dried leaf oregano	1 teaspoon	1/2 teaspoon
bay leaf	1 large	1 small
chili powder	1 teaspoon	1/2 teaspoon
salt	1/2 teaspoon	1/4 teaspoon
kidney beans, drained, rinsed	1 (16-oz.) can	1 (8-oz.) can
shredded Cheddar cheese	to garnish	to garnish
BAKING DISH	deep 3-qt. casserole	deep 1-1/2-qt. casserole
TIME AT HIGH (meat)	5 minutes	3 minutes
TIME AT HIGH (beans added)	7 minutes	4 minutes
TIME AT 30%	25 to 30 minutes	15 to 18 minutes

Crumble meat into a casserole, see size in chart above. Add onion and green pepper. Cover with waxed paper. Microwave at full power (HIGH) for time in chart above or until meat is browned, stirring twice. Pour off juices. Stir in tomatoes, tomato sauce, oregano, bay leaf, chili powder and salt. Mix well. Gently fold in beans. Cover. Microwave at full power (HIGH) for time in chart above or until boiling. Stir well. Cover. Microwave at 30% (MEDIUM LOW) for time in chart above or until vegetables are tender and flavors blended, stirring once. Serve in bowls and garnish with shredded Cheddar cheese.

Reheating Frozen Chili

SERVINGS	4	2	1
INGREDIENTS			
cooked chili	1 qt.	2 cups	1 cup
BAKING DISH	1-1/2-qt. casserole	1-qt. casserole	2-cup casserole
TIME AT 30%	30 minutes	17 minutes	10 minutes
TIME AT 70%	10 minutes	6 minutes	4 to 4-1/2 minutes
STANDING TIME	1 minute	1 minute	1 minute

To freeze: Spoon cooled chili into a freezer container, leaving 1/2 inch headspace. Cover tightly and freeze.

To reheat: Dip freezer container in hot water to loosen chili. Place block of frozen chili in a casserole, see size in chart above. Cover with vented plastic wrap or lid. Microwave at 30% (MEDIUM LOW) for time in chart above, breaking apart edges of chili with a large fork partway through cooking time. Stir gently. Cover and microwave at 70% (MEDIUM HIGH) for time in chart above or until heated through. Let casserole stand, covered, 1 minute. Stir before serving.

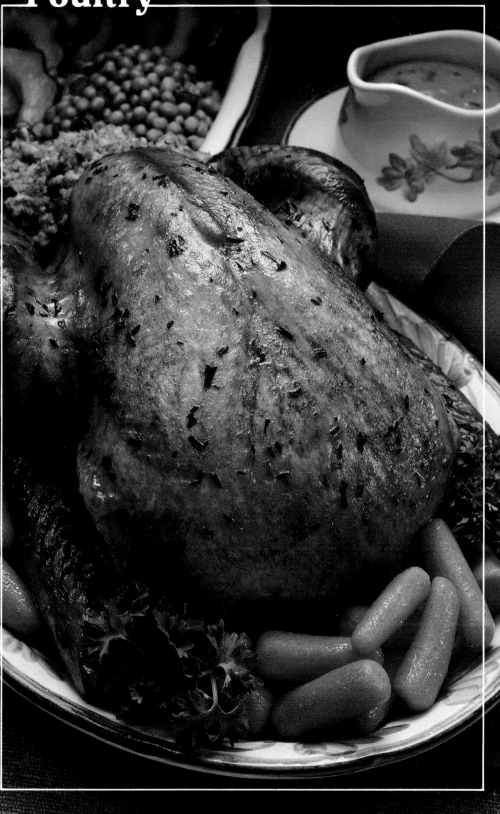

Poultry

The natural tenderness of poultry makes it ideal for fast microwave cooking. For a quick and easy dish for guests, try delicious Chicken Cacciatore—it takes little more than 30 minutes to prepare and cook.

Q. How is poultry cooked in the microwave?

A. Most poultry can be cooked at full power (HIGH) because it is already tender meat. Larger whole poultry, such as turkeys, require a quick start at microwave full power (HIGH) and then additional cooking at 50% (MEDIUM) to cook through evenly.

Q. Which poultry recipes do not cook satisfactorily in the microwave?

A. Deep-fried chicken cannot be cooked in the microwave. Turkeys over 12 pounds are difficult to cook evenly. Smaller whole turkeys weighing between 6 and 10 pounds can be cooked successfully in the microwave. Frozen, stuffed, whole turkeys should not be microwaved.

Q. How do you know when poultry is done?

A. Whole poultry is done when a microwave meat thermometer inserted between the leg and thigh registers 185F (85C). The temperature will rise very little, if any, during the standing time. For this reason, it is best to cook the poultry until it is done. As an additional test for doneness, the juices should run clear when whole poultry is cut between the leg and thigh, or when chicken or turkey pieces are pierced with a meat fork.

Q. How do you reheat poultry dishes in the microwave?

A. Easy-to-follow instructions are in each section of the chapter. They include reheating fried chicken, chicken pieces in sauce, casseroles and sliced turkey in gravy.

Q. Are any recipes given for using leftover turkey and chicken?

A. Try Chicken Aloha Crepes, Chicken à la King or Herbed Chicken Pot Pies. These and other delicious recipes use cooked turkey or chicken.

Q. Can poultry convenience foods be successfully cooked in the microwave?

A. Yes. Included in this chapter are instructions for cooking convenience foods such as frozen chicken pies. Many other frozen convenience foods, such as TV dinners or frozen chicken entrees in pouches, have microwave instructions on the package.

Q. Why do you rearrange chicken pieces during microwave cooking?

A. Chicken pieces are rearranged to promote even cooking. Move the center pieces of chicken to the outside of the dish and the ones from the outside edges to the center. Whole birds are turned over partway through the cooking time for the same reason.

Q. Will poultry brown in the microwave?

A. Poultry cooks so quickly in the microwave that the browning often needs a little assistance. Sauces and glazes enhance the appearance of whole birds. Chicken pieces can be cooked in sauce or crumbs for color.

Q. Is it safe to stuff whole birds that will be cooked in the microwave?

A. Stuffing must be cooked until its center reaches a temperature of 165F (75C). This may mean overcooking the bird to reach this temperature. One way to overcome this problem is to select one of the airy bread stuffings given here rather than a heavy one using corn bread, for example. Do not pack the stuffing tightly into the bird. Always check the temperature of the stuffing before serving it.

Q. How much stuffing and glaze are needed for different birds?

A. There is a complete guide to stuffing and glaze amounts for each type of poultry on the following pages.

Q. How can favorite conventional recipes be converted for microwave cooking?

A. Most poultry recipes can be adapted easily for microwave cooking. Look for the special sections in the chapter giving tips for converting recipes. Study the basic recipe that most closely resembles the recipe you are trying to adapt.

Q. How do you defrost poultry in the microwave?

A. It is essential to place poultry on a microwave rack for defrosting so the bottom of the poultry does not start to cook in the juices. Poultry is defrosted first at 30% (MEDIUM LOW) and then at 10% (LOW). Finally, the poultry stands in cold water until it is completely defrosted. Full directions are in this section.

Q. Are any special utensils needed for cooking poultry in the microwave?

A. Although you can use inverted saucers in the bottom of a baking dish to form a makeshift rack, it is handy to have a microwave rack. A microwave meat thermometer is useful to test doneness of whole birds and turkey pieces.

How to Cook Whole Poultry

Brush whole birds with a sauce or glaze before, during and after microwave cooking. This Plum-Good Glaze, page 190, gives roast duckling a pretty, rosy color. Self-basting turkeys usually brown better than turkeys that have not been injected with a basting sauce.

Shielding with pieces of foil will prevent small areas of the whole bird from overcooking. Foil reflects the microwaves away from the item being cooked. Look for areas that are browner than the rest of the bird. These will often be the wings, drumsticks and top of the breast.

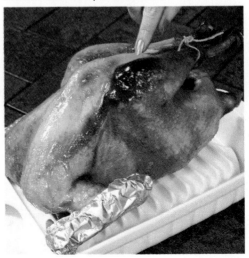

Defrosting Chicken Drumsticks

SERVINGS	4	2	1
INGREDIENTS frozen chicken drumsticks	8 (4-oz.) drumsticks	4 (4-oz.) drumsticks	2 (4-oz.) drumsticks
BAKING DISH	12" x 7" baking dish with microwave rack	8-inch round or square baking dish with microwave rack	8-inch round or square baking dish with microwave rack
TIME AT 30% (4 minutes per lb.)	8 minutes	4 minutes	2 minutes
TIME AT 10% (5 minutes per lb.)	10 minutes	5 minutes	2-1/2 minutes
STANDING TIME IN COLD WATER	10 minutes	5 minutes	2-1/2 minutes

Place chicken pieces, Styrofoam tray side down, on a microwave rack or inverted saucer in a baking dish, see size in chart. Microwave at 30% (MEDIUM LOW) for time in chart, removing packaging as soon as possible and covering loosely with waxed paper. Separate chicken pieces as soon as possible. Turn skin side up on rack with meaty portions toward outside of dish. After defrosting at 30%, shield any warm spots with small pieces of foil; secure with wooden picks. Cover loosely with waxed paper. Microwave at 10% (LOW) for time in chart. Immediately plunge chicken pieces into cold water. Let stand in water same number of minutes as they defrosted at 10%. Chicken should be cool to the touch but completely defrosted after standing time in cold water. To check, insert a metal skewer into thickest part. If skewer can be inserted easily, begin cooking. If skewer cannot be inserted easily, repeat defrosting at 10% (LOW) and standing time in cold water. Chicken must be completely defrosted before cooking.

Defrosting Chicken Thighs

SERVINGS	2	1
INGREDIENTS frozen chicken thighs	4 (4-oz.) thighs	2 (4-oz.) thighs
BAKING DISH	8-inch round or square baking dish with microwave rack	8-inch round or square baking dish with microwave rack
TIME AT 30% (4 minutes per lb.)	4 minutes	2 minutes
TIME AT 10% (5 minutes per lb.)	5 minutes	2-1/2 minutes
STANDING TIME IN COLD WATER	5 minutes	2-1/2 minutes

See directions for Defrosting Chicken Drumsticks, above.

How to Defrost Chicken Drumsticks

During defrosting, use a large fork to separate the drumsticks as soon as possible. This helps the drumsticks defrost more evenly.

Finish defrosting the drumsticks in a bowl of cold water. They are ready to cook when a skewer can be easily inserted into the thickest part of the drumstick.

Defrosting Chicken Wings

SERVINGS	4	2	1
INGREDIENTS frozen chicken wings	8 (3-1/2-oz.) wings	4 (3-1/2-oz.) wings	2 (3-1/2-oz.) wings
BAKING DISH	12" x 7" baking dish with microwave rack	8-inch round or square baking dish with microwave rack	8-inch round or square baking dish with microwave rack
TIME AT 30% (4 minutes per lb.)	7 minutes	3-1/2 minutes	2 minutes
TIME AT 10% (5 minutes per lb.)	8-1/2 minutes	4 minutes	2-1/2 minutes
STANDING TIME IN COLD WATER	8-1/2 minutes	4 minutes	2-1/2 minutes

See directions for Defrosting Chicken Drumsticks, opposite.

Note: To defrost 2 (8-ounce) chicken legs with thighs attached, use a 12" x 7" baking dish with microwave rack and follow directions for 4 chicken thighs, opposite. To defrost 1 (8-ounce) chicken leg with thigh attached, follow directions for 2 thighs.

Defrosting Cut-Up Broiler-Fryer Chicken

SERVINGS	3 or 4	1 or 2
INGREDIENTS frozen cut-up broiler-fryer chicken	1 (3-lb.) chicken	1/2 (3-lb.) chicken
BAKING DISH	12" x 7" baking dish with microwave rack	12" x 7" baking dish with microwave rack
TIME AT 30% (4 minutes per lb.)	12 minutes	6 minutes
TIME AT 10% (5 minutes per lb.)	15 minutes	7-1/2 minutes
STANDING TIME IN COLD WATER	15 minutes	7-1/2 minutes

Place chicken pieces, Styrofoam tray side down, on a microwave rack or inverted saucer in a baking dish, see size in chart. Microwave at 30% (MEDIUM LOW) for time in chart, removing packaging as soon as possible and covering loosely with waxed paper. Separate chicken pieces as soon as possible. Turn skin side up on rack with meaty portions toward outside of dish. After defrosting at 30%, shield any warm spots with small pieces of foil; secure with wooden picks. Cover loosely with waxed paper. Microwave at 10% (LOW) for time in chart. Immediately plunge chicken pieces into cold water. Let stand in water for the same number of minutes as they defrosted at 10%. Chicken should be cool to the touch but completely defrosted after standing time in cold water. To check, insert a metal skewer into thickest part. If skewer can be inserted easily, begin cooking. If skewer cannot be inserted easily, repeat defrosting at 10% (LOW) and standing time in cold water. Chicken must be completely defrosted before cooking.

Defrosting Chicken Breasts

SERVINGS	4	2
INGREDIENTS frozen whole chicken breasts	2 (1-lb.) breasts	1 (1-lb.) breast
BAKING DISH	8-inch round or square baking dish with micro- wave rack	8-inch round or square baking dish with micro- wave rack
TIME AT 30% (4 minutes per lb.)	8 minutes	4 minutes
TIME AT 10% (5 minutes per lb.)	10 minutes	5 minutes
STANDING TIME IN COLD WATER	10 minutes	5 minutes

See directions for Defrosting Cut-up Broiler-Fryer Chicken, above.

Note: To defrost 2 pounds of chicken backs, follow directions for 2 (1-pound) chicken breasts, above.

Defrosting Whole Broiler-Fryer Chicken

SERVINGS	3 or 4
INGREDIENTS frozen whole broiler-fryer chicken, weight as purchased	3 to 3-1/2 lbs.
BAKING DISH	12" x 7" baking dish with microwave rack
TIME AT 30% (4 minutes per lb.)	12 to 14 minutes
TIME AT 10% (5 minutes per lb.)	15 to 17-1/2 minutes
STANDING TIME IN COLD WATER	15 to 17-1/2 minutes

Remove packaging, including metal clip on package from frozen bird. For chickens and other birds frozen at home, remove metal twist ties, then remove wrapping as soon as possible during defrosting. Place frozen bird, breast side up, on a microwave rack or inverted saucer in a 12" x 7" baking dish. Cover loosely with waxed paper. Microwave at 30% (MEDIUM LOW) for time in chart, removing any remaining packaging as soon as possible and covering loosely with waxed paper. After half the time at 30% (MEDIUM LOW), turn bird breast side down. Shield wings, drumsticks and any warm spots with small pieces of foil; secure with wooden picks. Cover loosely with waxed paper. After defrosting at 30% (MEDIUM LOW), turn bird breast side up. Shield any additional warm spots with small pieces of foil; secure with wooden picks. Cover loosely with waxed paper. Microwave at 10% (LOW) for time in chart. Immediately plunge bird into cold water. Let stand in water same number of minutes as it defrosted at 10%. Remove giblets and gravy packet, if present. Bird should be cool to the touch but completely defrosted in the cavity after standing time in cold water. To check, insert a metal skewer into thickest part of thigh. If skewer can be inserted easily, begin cooking. If skewer cannot be inserted easily, repeat defrosting time at 10% (LOW) and standing time in cold water. Bird must be completely defrosted before cooking.

Defrosting Whole Capon

SERVINGS	8
INGREDIENTS frozen whole capon, weight as purchased	7-1/4 to 7-3/4 lbs.
BAKING DISH	12" x 7" baking dish with microwave rack
TIME AT 30% (4 minutes per lb.)	29 to 31 minutes
TIME AT 10% (5 minutes per lb.)	36-1/2 to 39 minutes
STANDING TIME IN COLD WATER	36-1/2 to 39 minutes

See directions for Defrosting Whole Broiler-Fryer Chicken, above.

Tips

- Remove the Styrofoam tray packaging as soon as possible. The tray insulates the poultry and slows down the defrosting.

- Shield any warm areas with small pieces of foil. Otherwise, these areas defrost faster than the rest of the bird and eventually start to cook. Hold the foil tightly against the warm areas by using wooden picks.

- On whole birds, the wings, drumsticks and highest portion of the breast are most likely to need shielding.

Defrosting Whole Turkey

SERVINGS	10 to 12	8 to 10	6 to 8
INGREDIENTS frozen whole turkey, self-basting-type, weight as purchased	9 to 10 lbs.	7 to 8 lbs.	5-1/2 to 6-1/2 lbs.
BAKING DISH	12" x 7" baking dish with microwave rack	12" x 7" baking dish with microwave rack	12" x 7" baking dish with microwave rack
TIME AT 30% **(4 minutes per lb.)**	36 to 40 minutes	28 to 32 minutes	22 to 26 minutes
TIME AT 10% **(5 minutes per lb.)**	45 to 50 minutes	35 to 40 minutes	27-1/2 to 32-1/2 minutes
STANDING TIME **IN COLD WATER**	45 to 50 minutes	35 to 40 minutes	27-1/2 to 32-1/2 minutes

Remove packaging, including metal clip on package, from frozen bird. Place frozen bird, breast side up, on a microwave rack or inverted saucer in a baking dish, see size in chart. Cover loosely with waxed paper. Microwave at 30% (MEDIUM LOW) for time in chart, removing any remaining packaging as soon as possible and covering loosely with waxed paper. Follow manufacturer's directions concerning removal of metal clip around drumstick. After half the time at 30% (MEDIUM LOW), turn bird breast side down. Shield wings, drumsticks and any warm spots with small pieces of foil; secure with wooden picks. Cover loosely with waxed paper. After defrosting at 30% (MEDIUM LOW), turn bird breast side up. Shield any additional warm spots with small pieces of foil; cover loosely with waxed paper. Microwave at 10% (LOW) for time in chart. Immediately plunge bird into cold water. Let stand in water same number of minutes as it defrosted at 10%. Remove giblets and gravy packet, if present. Bird should be cool to the touch but completely defrosted in the cavity after standing time in cold water. To check, insert a metal skewer into thickest part of thigh. If skewer can be inserted easily, begin cooking. If skewer cannot be inserted easily, repeat defrosting time at 10% (LOW) and standing time in cold water. Bird must be completely defrosted before cooking.

Defrosting Whole Duckling

SERVINGS	2
INGREDIENTS frozen domestic duckling, weight as purchased	4-1/2 to 5 lbs.
BAKING DISH	12"x 7" baking dish with microwave rack
TIME AT 30% (4 minutes per lb.)	18 to 20 minutes
TIME AT 10% (5 minutes per lb.)	22-1/2 to 25 minutes
STANDING TIME IN COLD WATER	22-1/2 to 25 minutes

See directions for Defrosting Whole Turkey, above.

How to Defrost Whole Turkey

During defrosting, shield any warm areas or areas that are starting to brown with small pieces of foil. Secure the foil with wooden picks. This usually means shielding the wings, drumstick ends and top of breast.

Check the thawed turkey after the standing time in cold water. Insert a skewer between the leg and thigh into the thickest part of the thigh. Skewer can be inserted easily if turkey is fully thawed.

Defrosting Whole Cornish Hens

SERVINGS	4	2	1
INGREDIENTS frozen Cornish hens, weight as purchased	4 (20-oz.) hens	2 (20-oz.) hens	1 (20-oz.) hen
BAKING DISH	12" x 7" baking dish with microwave rack	8-inch round or square baking dish with microwave rack	8-inch round or square baking dish with microwave rack
TIME AT 30%	14 minutes	10 minutes	7 minutes
TIME AT 10%	16 minutes	10 minutes	6 minutes
STANDING TIME IN COLD WATER	16 minutes	10 minutes	6 minutes

See directions for Defrosting Whole Turkey, opposite.

Tips

- Be sure to use a microwave rack or inverted saucer for defrosting. Otherwise the portion of the bird at the bottom of the dish will get too warm and cook in the juice.

- Some poultry processors and microwave oven manufacturers say the metal clip that holds the drumsticks in place may be left on the turkey during defrosting; others say to remove it. Follow package directions and consult the use-and-care guide for your microwave oven.

- Turkeys larger than 10 pounds should be defrosted and cooked conventionally. They tend to defrost and cook unevenly in the microwave oven. Many microwave ovens cannot accommodate the larger baking dish necessary to hold larger birds.

Defrosting Turkey Wings

SERVINGS	2
INGREDIENTS frozen turkey wings	2 (1-1/4-lb.) wings
BAKING DISH	12" x 7" baking dish with microwave rack
TIME AT 30% (5 minutes per lb.)	12-1/2 minutes
TIME AT 10% (7 minutes per lb.)	17-1/2 minutes
STANDING TIME IN COLD WATER	17-1/2 minutes

Remove packaging, including metal clip on package, from frozen turkey pieces. For pieces frozen at home, remove metal twist ties, then remove wrapping as soon as possible during defrosting. Place frozen turkey pieces on a microwave rack in a 12" x 7" baking dish. Cover loosely with waxed paper. Microwave at 30% (MEDIUM LOW) for time in chart. After defrosting at 30%, shield wing tips, drumstick ends and any warm spots with small pieces of foil; secure with wooden picks. Turn turkey pieces over. Give dish a half turn. Cover loosely with waxed paper. Microwave at 10% (LOW) for time in chart. Immediately plunge turkey pieces into cold water. Let stand in water same number of minutes as they defrosted at 10%. Turkey pieces should be cool to the touch but completely defrosted after standing time in cold water. To check, insert a metal skewer into thickest part. If skewer can be inserted easily, begin cooking. If skewer cannot be inserted easily, repeat defrosting time at 10% (LOW) and standing time in cold water. Turkey must be completely defrosted before cooking.

Defrosting Turkey Drumsticks

SERVINGS	2	1
INGREDIENTS frozen turkey drumsticks	2 (1-1/4- to 1-1/2-lb.) drumsticks	1 (1-1/4- to 1-1/2-lb.) drumstick
BAKING DISH	12" x 7" baking dish with microwave rack	12" x 7" baking dish with microwave rack
TIME AT 30% (4 minutes per lb.)	10 to 12 minutes	5 to 6 minutes
TIME AT 10% (5 minutes per lb.)	12-1/2 to 15 minutes	6 to 7-1/2 minutes
STANDING TIME IN COLD WATER	12-1/2 to 15 minutes	6 to 7-1/2 minutes

See directions for Defrosting Turkey Wings, above.

Defrosting Turkey Hindquarter

SERVINGS	2
INGREDIENTS	
frozen turkey hindquarter	about 2 lbs.
BAKING DISH	12" x 7" baking dish with microwave rack
TIME AT 30% (5 minutes per lb.)	10 minutes
TIME AT 10% (7 minutes per lb.)	14 minutes
STANDING TIME IN COLD WATER	14 minutes

See directions for Defrosting Turkey Wings, opposite.

Defrosting Turkey Breast

SERVINGS	6 to 8	3 or 4
INGREDIENTS		
frozen whole turkey breast	6 to 7 lbs.	3-1/2 to 4-1/2 lbs.
BAKING DISH	12" x 7" baking dish with microwave rack	12" x 7" baking dish with microwave rack
TIME AT 30% (4 minutes per lb.)	24 to 28 minutes	14 to 18 minutes
TIME AT 10% (5 to 10 minutes per lb.)	30 to 70 minutes	17-1/2 to 45 minutes
STANDING TIME IN COLD WATER	30 to 70 minutes	17-1/2 to 45 minutes

Remove packaging, including metal clip on package, from frozen turkey breast. Place frozen breast, skin side up, on a microwave rack in a 12" x 7" baking dish. Cover loosely with waxed paper. Microwave at 30% (MEDIUM LOW) for time in chart above. After half the cooking time at 30%, turn breast skin side down. Shield warm spots and wing tips, if present, with small pieces of foil; secure with wooden picks. Cover with a tent of waxed paper. After defrosting at 30%, turn breast skin side up. Microwave at 10% (LOW) for minimum time in chart above. Immediately plunge bird into cold water. Let stand in water same number of minutes as breast defrosted at 10%. Breast should be cool to the touch but completely defrosted after standing time. To check, insert a metal skewer into thickest part. If skewer can be inserted easily, begin cooking. If skewer cannot be inserted easily, defrost for remaining time at 10%. Let stand in cold water for same number of minutes as breast defrosted the second time at 10%. Turkey must be completely defrosted before cooking.

Chicken Cacciatore

SERVINGS	3 or 4	1 or 2
INGREDIENTS		
butter or margarine	2 tablespoons	1 tablespoon
onion, sliced, separated in rings	1 medium	1/2 medium
garlic clove, minced	1 medium	1 small
dried leaf oregano	1 teaspoon	1/2 teaspoon
broiler-fryer chicken, cut up, not using backs	1 (3-lb.) chicken	1/2 (3-lb.) chicken
bottled Italian cooking sauce	1 (16-oz.) jar	1 cup
hot cooked spaghetti		
grated Parmesan cheese		
BAKING DISH	12" x 7" baking dish	round, 8-inch baking dish
TIME AT HIGH (butter, onion)	5 minutes	3 minutes
TIME AT HIGH (first side)	12 minutes	7 minutes
TIME AT HIGH (second side)	12 to 14 minutes	8 to 9 minutes
STANDING TIME	5 minutes	5 minutes

In a baking dish, see size in chart above, combine butter or margarine, onion, garlic and oregano. Cover with vented plastic wrap. Microwave at full power (HIGH) for time in chart above or until tender, stirring once. Turn chicken pieces over in butter or margarine mixture to coat. Arrange chicken skin side down with meaty pieces toward outside of dish. Spoon cooking sauce over chicken, coating completely. Cover with vented plastic wrap. Microwave at full power (HIGH) for time in chart above. Turn chicken skin side up. Spoon sauce over chicken. Cover with vented plastic wrap. Microwave at full power (HIGH) for time in chart above or until tender. Let stand, covered, 5 minutes. Serve chicken and sauce over hot cooked spaghetti. Sprinkle with Parmesan cheese.

Reheating Refrigerated Chicken Cacciatore

SERVINGS	2	1
INGREDIENTS		
cooked Chicken Cacciatore, above	4 pieces chicken and 1 cup sauce	2 pieces chicken and 1/2 cup sauce
BAKING DISH	1-qt. casserole	1-qt. casserole
TIME AT 70%	9 to 10 minutes	6 to 7 minutes

To chill: Place cooled chicken pieces in a 1-quart casserole. Spoon sauce over chicken. Cover and refrigerate.

To reheat: Microwave, covered, at 70% (MEDIUM HIGH) for time in chart above or until heated through, stirring once.

Defrosting: To defrost a cut-up chicken, chicken wings, drumsticks, thighs or breasts, see pages 158 to 160.

How to Make Chicken Cacciatore

Cook onions in butter with garlic and oregano until tender. Turn the chicken pieces over in the onion mixture, being sure to coat chicken on all sides.

Arrange the chicken pieces skin side down with the thickest portion of each piece toward the outside of the dish. Pour Italian cooking sauce over the chicken.

Halfway through the cooking time, turn the chicken pieces skin side up. Keep the thickest portion of each piece toward the outside of the dish. Spoon the sauce over the chicken, coating completely with sauce.

After cooking, chicken should be tender when pierced with a fork and juices should run clear. Serve the chicken over hot cooked spaghetti. Spoon sauce over the chicken and pasta. Top with freshly grated Parmesan cheese.

Sherried Chicken Rolls

SERVINGS	6	3
INGREDIENTS		
butter or margarine	1/4 cup	2 tablespoons
sliced mushrooms, drained	1 (2-1/2-oz.) jar	1/2 (2-1/2-oz.) jar
shredded Swiss cheese	1/2 cup (2 oz.)	1/4 cup (1 oz.)
snipped parsley	2 tablespoons	1 tablespoon
dried rubbed sage	1 teaspoon	1/2 teaspoon
whole chicken breasts, skinned and boned	6 (2-1/2 to 3 lbs. after boning)	3 (1-1/2 lbs. after boning)
onions, sliced, separated in rings	2	1
condensed creamy chicken-mushroom soup	2 (10-3/4-oz.) cans	1 (10-3/4-oz.) can
dry sherry	1 cup	1/2 cup
hot cooked rice		
BAKING DISH	12" x 7" baking dish	9" x 5" loaf dish
TIME AT HIGH (butter)	1 minute	30 seconds
TIME AT HIGH (chicken)	10 minutes	5 minutes
TIME AT 30%	40 minutes	25 to 30 minutes
STANDING TIME	5 minutes	5 minutes

Place butter or margarine in a baking dish, see size in chart above. Microwave at full power (HIGH) for time in chart above, or until melted. In a small bowl, toss together mushrooms, Swiss cheese, parsley and sage. Spoon mushroom mixture over chicken breasts. Roll up or fold over. Secure with wooden picks. Place in baking dish. Turn chicken pieces over in butter or margarine to coat. Top with sliced onion. In a medium bowl, whisk together soup and sherry. Pour over chicken, coating completely. Cover with vented plastic wrap. Microwave at full power (HIGH) for time in chart above. Give dish a half turn and rearrange chicken rolls. Microwave at 30% (MEDIUM LOW) for time in chart above or until tender. Let stand, covered, 5 minutes. Stir sauce well and spoon some over chicken. Serve chicken and sauce with hot cooked rice.

Adapting Chicken with Sauce Recipes for Microwave Oven

- Delicate egg or sour cream sauces tend to curdle with fast microwave cooking. It's best to select recipes with more hearty, stable sauces, such as Chicken Cacciatore, page 166.

- Microwave any chopped vegetables for the sauce in the same baking dish you intend to use for the chicken.

- Stir the flour or cornstarch used to thicken the sauce into melted butter or sautéed vegetables. Cook the flour mixture at full power (HIGH) for 30 seconds before blending in the liquid. Whisk the liquid into the flour mixture and microwave at full power (HIGH) for about 2-1/2 minutes per cup of sauce. Whisk the sauce often during cooking to prevent lumping.

- Microwave the chicken pieces skin side down in the sauce for the first half of the cooking time. Turn the chicken pieces over in the sauce and microwave for the remaining time.

- Use directions for Chicken Cacciatore, page 166, as guidelines for cooking times for cut-up broiler-fryer chickens. For wings and drumsticks, refer to Saucy Barbecued Drumsticks & Wings, page 170. Microwave the chicken in sauce covered with vented plastic wrap. This promotes more even cooking.

Saucy Barbecued Drumsticks & Wings

SERVINGS	4	2	1
INGREDIENTS			
butter or margarine	2 tablespoons	1 tablespoon	2 teaspoons
chicken drumsticks and/or wings	8 (3-1/2- to 4-oz.) pieces	4 (3-1/2- to 4-oz.) pieces	2 (3-1/2- to 4-oz.) pieces
bottled barbecue sauce	1 cup	1/2 cup	1/4 cup
thin lemon slices, halved	4	2	1
thin onion slices, separated in rings	4	2	1
BAKING DISH	12" x 7" baking dish	round, 8-inch baking dish	round, 8-inch baking dish
TIME AT HIGH (butter)	40 seconds	30 seconds	20 seconds
TIME AT HIGH (first side)	10 minutes	5 minutes	3 minutes
TIME AT HIGH (second side)	8 to 11 minutes	4 to 5 minutes	2 to 4 minutes

Place butter or margarine in a baking dish, see size in chart above. Microwave at full power (HIGH) for time in chart above or until melted. Turn chicken pieces over in butter or margarine to coat. Arrange chicken, skin side down, in baking dish with meaty pieces toward outside of dish. Spoon barbecue sauce over chicken, coating completely. Cover loosely with waxed paper. Microwave at full power (HIGH) for time in chart above. Turn chicken skin side up. When cooking 8 drumsticks, rearrange so center drumsticks are toward outside of dish. Top with lemon slices and onion rings. Spoon sauce over chicken. Cover with waxed paper. Microwave at full power (HIGH) for time in chart above or until chicken is tender. If cooking 8 drumsticks, stir sauce during this cooking time. Spoon sauce over chicken pieces before serving.

Roasting Bag Chicken

SERVINGS	3 or 4
INGREDIENTS	
broiler-fryer chicken, cut up	1 (2-1/2- to 3-lb.) chicken
seasoning mix and roasting bag for chicken	1 (1.37-oz.) envelope
BAKING DISH	12" x 7" baking dish
TIME AT HIGH	25 to 30 minutes
STANDING TIME	5 minutes

Make a small slit in the skin on each piece of chicken. Roll pieces in seasoning mix according to package directions. Place chicken pieces, skin side up, in a single layer in the roasting bag included with mix. Place in a 12" x 7" baking dish. Tie bag with string, leaving a 1-inch opening for steam to escape. Cut 4 small slits in top of bag. Microwave at full power (HIGH) 25 to 30 minutes, or until tender, giving dish a half turn once. Let stand in closed roasting bag 5 minutes.

Basic Easy Oven Chicken

SERVINGS	3 or 4	1 or 2
INGREDIENTS		
Broiler-fryer chicken, cut up, not using backs	1 (3-lb.) chicken	1/2 (3-lb.) chicken
Water or milk	to moisten	to moisten
Seasoned coating mix for chicken	1 (2-3/8-oz.) envelope	1/2 (2-3/8-oz.) envelope
BAKING DISH	12" x 7" baking dish with microwave rack	round, 8-inch baking dish with microwave rack
TIME AT HIGH	19 to 21 minutes	12 minutes

Make a small slit in skin on each piece of chicken. Dip chicken pieces in milk or water; shake off excess liquid. Following package directions, shake in coating mix in shaker bag provided. Place chicken, skin side up, on a microwave rack in a baking dish, see size in chart above. Arrange meaty portions toward outside of dish. Microwave, uncovered, at full power (HIGH) for time in chart above, or until tender and juices run clear when chicken is pierced with a fork. Rearrange chicken pieces once during cooking. Check for doneness toward end of cooking time; remove any done pieces. Continue cooking remaining pieces.

Adapting Crumb-Coated Baked Chicken Recipes for Microwave

● Microwave crumb-coated chicken pieces on a microwave rack so the chicken doesn't stew in the pan juices.

It's best not to turn the chicken pieces over during cooking because some of the crumbs will fall off and stick to the rack.

● Arrange the meaty portions of the chicken toward the outside of the baking dish.

● Microwave the chicken uncovered so the crumbs won't be as soggy. Most crumb-coated chicken cooked in the microwave will not have as crisp a coating as conventionally baked chicken.

● Follow the timings for chicken wings, thighs, drumsticks, breasts and cut-up broiler-fryer chicken on this page and page 172 as a guideline for your favorite recipe.

● If you prefer, make your own coating mix rather than using a prepared mix.

● Chicken is done when it is tender and the juices run clear when chicken is pierced with a fork.

Defrosting: To defrost a cut-up chicken, chicken wings, drumsticks, thighs or breasts, see pages 158 to 160.

Basic Easy Oven Chicken Drumsticks, Wings, Thighs & Breasts

SERVINGS	4	2	1
INGREDIENTS			
chicken drumsticks and/or wings and/or thighs OR	8 (4-oz.) pieces	4 (4-oz.) pieces	2 (4-oz.) pieces
chicken breasts, split lengthwise	2 (1-lb.) breasts	1 (1-lb.) breast	1/2 (1-lb.) breast
water or milk	to moisten	to moisten	to moisten
seasoned coating mix for chicken	1 (2-3/8-oz.) envelope	1/2 (2-3/8-oz.) envelope	1/4 (2-3/8-oz.) envelope
BAKING DISH	12" x 7" baking dish with microwave rack	round, 8-inch baking dish with microwave rack	round, 8-inch baking dish with microwave rack
TIME AT HIGH	20 to 24 minutes	10 to 12 minutes	7 to 9 minutes

Make a small slit in skin on each piece of chicken. Dip chicken pieces in milk or water shake off excess liquid. Following package directions, shake chicken in coating mix in shaker bag provided. Place chicken, skin side up, on a microwave rack in a baking dish see size in chart above. Arrange meaty portions toward outside of dish. Microwave uncovered, at full power (HIGH) for time in chart above or until tender and juices run clear when chicken is pierced with a fork. Rearrange chicken pieces once during cooking. Check for doneness toward end of cooking time; remove any done pieces. Continue cooking remaining pieces.

Reheating Fried Chicken

SERVINGS	3	2	1
INGREDIENTS			
cooked fried chicken	6 pieces	4 pieces	2 pieces
BAKING DISH	12" x 7" baking dish	round, 8-inch baking dish	medium plate
TIME AT 70%	8 to 9 minutes	6 to 7 minutes	4 to 5 minutes

To chill: Place cooled fried chicken, skin side up, in a baking dish or on a plate, see size in chart above. Cover tightly with plastic wrap; refrigerate.

To reheat: Remove plastic wrap. Microwave chicken, uncovered, at 70% (MEDIUM HIGH) for time in chart above or until heated through. Coating will not be crisp.

Tip

- Frozen Fried Chicken: Many brands of frozen fried chicken have microwave instructions on the package. It's best to follow the manufacturer's directions for reheating fried chicken in the microwave.

How to Make Basic Easy Oven Chicken Drumsticks

Shake excess milk or water off drumsticks before placing in bag of crumbs that comes with the mix. Coat 2 or 3 drumsticks at a time.

Arrange the drumsticks on a rack in baking dish. This baking dish has a built-in rack. Place the meatiest portion of the drumsticks toward the outside of the dish.

Don't turn the drumsticks over during cooking or some of the coating will fall off. Drumsticks are done when the juices run clear when chicken is pierced with a fork.

Dress up the drumsticks with paper pants or make your own with colored paper and scissors. Garnish the serving tray with parsley and cherry tomatoes, if desired.

Basic Crisp Pan-Fried Chicken Drumsticks, Thighs, Wings & Breasts

SERVINGS	4	2	1
INGREDIENTS			
chicken drumsticks and/or thighs and/or wings OR	8 (3-1/2-to 4-oz.) pieces	4 (3-1/2- to 4-oz.) pieces	2 (3-1/2- to 4-oz.) pieces
chicken breasts, split lengthwise	2 (1-lb.) breasts	1 (1-lb.) breast	1/2 (1-lb.) breast
egg	1	1	1
water	1 tablespoon	1 tablespoon	1 tablespoon
seasoned crumb coating for chicken	1 (4.2-oz.) pkg.	1/2 (4.2-oz.) pkg.	1/4 (4.2-oz.)pkg.
vegetable oil	2 tablespoons	2 tablespoons	2 teaspoons
BROWNING SKILLET	10-inch microwave browning skillet	10-inch microwave browning skillet	6-1/2-inch microwave browning skillet
TIME AT HIGH (preheat skillet)	5 minutes	4 minutes	1 minute
TIME AT HIGH (first side)	6 minutes (breasts) 4 minutes (all others)	3 to 4 minutes	2 minutes
TIME AT HIGH (second side)	5 to 6 minutes	4 minutes	2 to 3 minutes

Preheat a browning skillet, see size in chart above, uncovered, at microwave full power (HIGH) for time in chart above. Make a small slit in skin on each piece of chicken. In a pie plate, whisk together egg and water. Dip chicken pieces in egg mixture, then in coating mix according to package directions. Add oil to hot browning skillet. Using hot pads, tilt skillet to coat evenly with oil. Quickly add chicken pieces, skin side down and with meaty portions toward outside of skillet. Microwave at full power (HIGH) for time in chart above. Turn chicken pieces over. Microwave at full power (HIGH) for time in chart above or until tender and juices run clear when chicken is pierced with a fork. Check for doneness toward end of cooking time; remove any done pieces. Continue cooking remaining pieces.

Microwave Caution

Do not attempt to deep-fat-fry chicken in the microwave oven. Deep hot fat reaches dangerous temperatures in this appliance. This can result in a large amount of smoke or a fire.

Defrosting: To defrost a cut-up chicken, chicken wings, drumsticks, thighs or breasts, see pages 158 to 160.

How to Make Basic Crisp Pan-Fried Chicken Wings

Make a small slit in the skin of each chicken wing. Chicken cooks so quickly in the microwave that the skin may burst with a loud popping sound. Slitting the skin helps prevent this.

Whisk together egg and water in a pie plate. Dip each chicken wing in the egg mixture and then in crumbs. Press the crumbs firmly onto the wings.

Using hot pads, remove the preheated skillet from the microwave oven and set it on a trivet. Add oil to the preheated browning skillet. Tilt the skillet to coat evenly with oil.

Halfway through the cooking time, carefully turn the chicken pieces over. Microwave for remaining cooking time. Chicken should be tender and juices should run clear when chicken is done.

Basic Crisp Pan-Fried Chicken

SERVINGS	3 or 4	1 or 2
INGREDIENTS		
broiler-fryer chicken, cut up, not using backs	1 (3-lb.) chicken	1/2 (3-lb.) chicken
egg	1	1
water	1 tablespoon	1 tablespoon
seasoned crumb coating for chicken	1 (4.2-oz.) pkg.	1/2 (4.2-oz.) pkg.
vegetable oil	2 tablespoons	2 tablespoons
BROWNING SKILLET	10-inch microwave browning skillet	10-inch microwave browning skillet
TIME AT HIGH (preheat skillet)	6 minutes	5 minutes
TIME AT HIGH (first side)	6 minutes	4 minutes
TIME AT HIGH (second side)	6 to 8 minutes	4 to 5 minutes

Preheat a 10-inch browning skillet, uncovered, at microwave full power (HIGH) fo
time in chart above. Make a small slit in skin on each piece of chicken. In a pie plate
whisk together egg and water. Dip chicken pieces in egg mixture, then in coating mi×
according to package directions. Add oil to hot browning skillet. Using hot pads, tilt skil
let to coat evenly with oil. Quickly add chicken pieces, skin side down and with meaty
portions toward outside of skillet. Microwave at full power (HIGH) for time in char
above. Turn chicken pieces over. Microwave at full power (HIGH) for time in char
above or until tender and juices run clear when chicken is pierced with a fork. Check
for doneness toward end of cooking time; remove any done pieces. Continue cooking
remaining pieces.

Gravy for Basic Crisp Pan-Fried Chicken

YIELD	1-2/3 cups	1-1/4 cups
INGREDIENTS		
drippings from Basic Crisp Pan-Fried Chicken, above	from 1 (3-lb.) fryer	from 1/2 (3-lb.) fryer
butter or margarine	3 tablespoons	2 tablespoons
all-purpose flour	3 tablespoons	2 tablespoons
milk	1-1/2 cups	1 cup
chicken bouillon granules	2 teaspoons	1-1/2 teaspoons
poultry seasoning	1/8 teaspoon	dash
BROWNING SKILLET	10-inch microwave browning skillet	10-inch microwave browning skillet
TIME AT HIGH (butter)	1-1/4 minutes	1-1/4 minutes
TIME AT HIGH (flour added)	30 seconds	30 seconds
TIME AT HIGH (milk added)	6 minutes	4-1/2 to 5 minutes

Remove chicken pieces from browning skillet. Keep warm. Remove any dark crumbs
from skillet. Add butter or margarine to drippings in skillet. Microwave at full power
(HIGH) 1-1/4 minutes or until melted. Stir in flour. Microwave at full power (HIGH) 30
seconds. Stir in milk, chicken bouillon granules and poultry seasoning. Microwave at
full power (HIGH) for time in chart above or until thickened and bubbly, stirring three
times.

Basic Oven-Fried Chicken Drumsticks, Thighs, Wings & Breasts

SERVINGS	4	2	1
INGREDIENTS			
butter or margarine	2 tablespoons	1 tablespoon	2 teaspoons
chicken drumsticks and/or thighs and/or wings	8 (4-oz.) pieces	4 (4-oz.) pieces	2 (4-oz.) pieces
OR			
chicken breasts, split lengthwise	2 (1-lb.) breasts	1 (1-lb.) breast	1/2 (1-lb.) breast
egg	1	1	1
water	1 tablespoon	1 tablespoon	1 tablespoon
seasoned crumb coating for chicken	1 (4.2-oz.) pkg.	1/2 (4.2-oz.) pkg.	1/4 (4.2-oz.) pkg.
BAKING DISH	12" x 7" baking dish	round, 8-inch baking dish	round, 8-inch baking dish
TIME AT HIGH (butter)	30 seconds	20 to 30 seconds	20 seconds
TIME AT HIGH (first side)	10 minutes	5 to 6 minutes	3 minutes
TIME AT HIGH (second side)	9 to 12 minutes	4 to 5 minutes	2 to 4 minutes

Place butter or margarine in a baking dish, see size in chart above. Microwave at full power (HIGH) for time in chart above or until melted. Set aside. Make a small slit in skin on each piece of chicken. In a pie plate, whisk together egg and water. Dip chicken pieces in egg mixture, then in coating mix according to package directions. Place chicken, skin side down, in butter or margarine with meaty portions toward outside of dish. Microwave at full power (HIGH) for time in chart above. Turn chicken pieces over. Microwave at full power (HIGH) for time in chart above, or until tender and juices run clear when chicken is pierced with a fork. Check for doneness toward end of cooking time; remove any done pieces. Continue cooking remaining pieces.

Defrosting: To defrost a cut-up chicken, chicken wings, drumsticks, thighs or breasts, see pages 158 to 160.

Adapting Recipes for Crumb-Coated Oven-Fried Chicken

- A recipe for crumb-coated chicken cooked in butter using a conventional oven will give almost the same result in the microwave oven.

- Melt the butter in the microwave, then add the crumb-coated chicken, skin side down, to the butter in the baking dish.

- Microwave the crumb-coated chicken for half the cooking time. Carefully turn the pieces over and microwave for the remaining cooking time.

- The timings for Basic Oven-Fried Chicken Drumsticks, Thighs, Wings & Breasts, above and page 178, will serve as good guidelines. Microwave the chicken uncovered so the crumbs will stay as crisp as possible.

Basic Oven-Fried Chicken

SERVINGS	3 or 4	1 or 2
INGREDIENTS		
butter or margarine	2 tablespoons	1 tablespoon
broiler-fryer chicken, cut up, not using backs	1 (3-lb.) chicken	1/2 (3-lb.) chicken
egg	1	1
water	1 tablespoon	1 tablespoon
seasoned crumb coating for chicken	1 (4.2-oz.) pkg.	1/2 (4.2-oz.) pkg.
BAKING DISH	12" x 7" baking dish	round, 8-inch baking dish
TIME AT HIGH (butter)	30 seconds	20 to 30 seconds
TIME AT HIGH (first side)	12 minutes	7 minutes
TIME AT HIGH (second side)	10 to 11 minutes	5 to 6 minutes

Place butter or margarine in a baking dish, see size in chart above. Microwave at full power (HIGH) for time in chart above or until melted. Set aside. Make a small slit in skin on each piece of chicken. In a pie plate, whisk together egg and water. Dip chicken pieces in egg mixture, then in coating mix according to package directions. Place chicken, skin side down, in butter or margarine with meaty portions toward outside of dish. Microwave at full power (HIGH) for time in chart above. Turn chicken pieces over. Microwave at full power (HIGH) for time in chart above, or until tender and juices run clear when chicken is pierced with fork. Check for doneness toward end of cooking time; remove any done pieces. Continue cooking remaining pieces.

Gravy for Basic Oven-Fried Chicken

YIELD	1-1/2 cups	1 cup
INGREDIENTS		
drippings from Basic Oven-Fried Chicken, above	from 1 (3-lb.) fryer	from 1/2 (3-lb.) fryer
butter or margarine	3 tablespoons	2 tablespoons
all-purpose flour	3 tablespoons	2 tablespoons
milk	1-1/2 cups	1 cup
chicken bouillon granules	2 teaspoons	1-1/2 teaspoons
poultry seasoning	1/8 teaspoon	dash
Kitchen Bouquet	4 to 6 drops	2 to 3 drops
BAKING DISH	12" x 7" baking dish	round, 8-inch baking dish
TIME AT HIGH (butter)	30 to 60 seconds	30 to 60 seconds
TIME AT HIGH (flour added)	30 seconds	30 seconds
TIME AT HIGH (milk added)	7 minutes	4 minutes

Remove chicken pieces from baking dish. Keep warm. Remove any dark crumbs from baking dish. Add butter or margarine to drippings in baking dish. Microwave at full power (HIGH) 30 to 60 seconds or until melted. Stir in flour. Microwave at full power (HIGH) 30 seconds. Stir in milk, chicken bouillon granules and poultry seasoning. Microwave at full power (HIGH) for time in chart above or until thickened and bubbly, stirring three times. Stir in Kitchen Bouquet.

Basic Poached Chicken Breasts

SERVINGS	6	4	2
INGREDIENTS			
whole chicken breasts	3 (1-lb.) breasts	2 (1-lb.) breasts	1 (1-lb.) breast
celery, cut up	2 stalks	1 stalk	1/2 stalk
carrot, cut up	2 small	1 medium	1 small
onion, cut up	1 medium	1 small	1/2 small
fresh parsley	3 sprigs	2 sprigs	1 sprig
water or chicken broth	3/4 cup	1/2 cup	1/4 cup
BAKING DISH	deep 3-qt. casserole	deep 2-qt. casserole	deep 1-qt. casserole
TIME AT HIGH	22 to 25 minutes	15 to 17 minutes	10 to 11 minutes
STANDING TIME	5 minutes	5 minutes	5 minutes
YIELD	3 cups cubed chicken, 2-1/2 cups broth	2 cups cubed chicken, 1-3/4 cups broth	1 cup cubed chicken, 3/4 cup broth

See directions for Basic Poached Chicken, below.

Note: To poach 2 pounds chicken backs (7 backs), follow directions for 2 pounds chicken breasts, above.

Basic Poached Chicken

SERVINGS	3 or 4
INGREDIENTS	
broiler-fryer chicken, cut up	1 (3-lb.) chicken
celery, cut up	2 stalks
carrot, cut up	2 small
onion, cut up	1 medium
fresh parsley	3 sprigs
water or chicken broth	3/4 cup
BAKING DISH	deep 3-qt. casserole
TIME AT HIGH	24 to 26 minutes
STANDING TIME	5 minutes

In a casserole, see size in chart, arrange chicken pieces with meaty portions toward outside of dish. Add celery, carrot, onion and parsley. Add water or broth; cover. Microwave at full power (HIGH) for time in chart, or until chicken is tender, turning pieces over once. Keep chicken under liquid as much as possible during cooking. If giblets are included, slash thoroughly on all sides with a sharp knife. Make sure gizzard and heart are under liquid. Place liver on top of chicken in center of dish; remove liver when done. When chicken is tender, let chicken and broth stand, covered, 5 minutes.

To chill chicken: Remove chicken from broth. Remove skin and bones. Cover chicken closely or wrap with plastic wrap; refrigerate. When needed, cube chicken. Strain broth; cover. Refrigerate until required. Makes 2 cups cubed chicken and 2-1/3 cups broth.

Defrosting: To defrost cut up chicken, chicken breasts or backs, see pages 158 to 160.

How to Make Basic Poached Chicken Breasts

Place meatiest portions of chicken breasts to the outside of the baking dish. Add cut up celery, carrot, onion and parsley sprigs to give the broth flavor.

When chicken is cooked, remove the skin and bones while hot. If you don't need to use the chicken right away, cover closely and refrigerate. Cooled chicken can be sliced or cubed more evenly than hot chicken.

Poached Turkey or Chicken Giblets

SERVINGS	from 1 turkey	from 1 chicken
INGREDIENTS		
giblets, including neck	8 oz. giblets from 1 (6- to 7-lb.) turkey	5 oz. giblets from 1 (3-lb.) chicken
celery, cut up	1 stalk	1 stalk
carrot, cut up	1 medium	1 medium
onion, cut up	1 small	1 small
fresh parsley	2 sprigs	2 sprigs
water or chicken broth	about 1-1/2 cups	about 1-1/2 cups
BAKING DISH	1-qt. casserole	1-qt. casserole
TIME AT HIGH	7 to 8 minutes	5 to 6 minutes
TIME AT 30%	1 hour	30 to 35 minutes

Remove skin from neck. Slash giblets thoroughly on all sides with a sharp knife. Set liver aside. Place neck, heart and gizzard in a 1-quart casserole. Add celery, carrot, onion and parsley. Add water or broth to cover. Cover and microwave at full power (HIGH) for time in chart above or until boiling. Stir and cover. Microwave at 30% (MEDIUM LOW) for time in chart above or until tender. Add liver during last 5 minutes of cooking time.

Chicken Aloha Crepes

SERVINGS	4 to 6	2 or 3
INGREDIENTS		
cubed cooked chicken or turkey	3 cups	1-1/2 cups
pineapple chunks, drained	1 (8-oz.) can	1/2 (8-oz.) can
chopped macadamia nuts	1/2 cup	1/4 cup
chopped celery	1/2 cup	1/4 cup
chopped green onion	1/4 cup	2 tablespoons
celery salt	1/2 teaspoon	1/4 teaspoon
pineapple-flavored yogurt	3/4 cup	1/3 cup
mayonnaise or mayonnaise-style salad dressing	3/4 cup	1/3 cup
dry white wine	2 tablespoons	1 tablespoon
Dijon-style mustard	1 teaspoon	1/2 teaspoon
6-inch crepes	8 to 10	4 to 5
toasted chopped macadamia nuts, toasted coconut	to garnish	to garnish
BAKING DISH	12-inch square microwave baker	8-inch square baking dish
TIME AT HIGH	7 to 8 minutes	4 to 5 minutes

In a large bowl, combine chicken or turkey, pineapple, first amount of macadamia nuts, celery, green onion and celery salt; mix gently. In a small bowl, combine yogurt, mayonnaise, white wine and mustard; mix well. Reserve about 1/3 of yogurt mixture; set aside. Fold remaining yogurt mixture into chicken mixture. Spoon about 1/2 cup chicken filling down center of each crepe; roll up. Place, seam side up, in a baking dish, see size in chart above. Cover with vented plastic wrap. Microwave at full power (HIGH) for time in chart above or until heated through, giving dish a half turn once. Top each crepe with a dollop of reserved yogurt mixture, then sprinkle with toasted macadamia nuts and toasted coconut.

Sweet & Sour Chicken

SERVINGS	4 to 6	2 or 3
INGREDIENTS		
sauce from Sweet & Sour Ham Balls, page 120	large recipe	small recipe
pineapple chunks, drained	1 (8-oz.) can	1/2 (8-oz.) can
cubed cooked chicken or turkey	3 cups	1-1/2 cups
hot cooked rice		
BAKING DISH	deep 2-qt. casserole	deep 1-qt. casserole
TIME AT 30%	10 minutes	6 to 7 minutes

Prepare sauce in a casserole, see size in chart above. Stir in pineapple and chicken or turkey. Cover. Microwave at 30% (MEDIUM LOW) for time in chart above or until heated through. Serve over rice.

Creamy Stuffed Pasta Shells

SERVINGS	4	2
INGREDIENTS		
bulk pork sausage	6 oz.	3 oz.
finely chopped green onion	1/4 cup	2 tablespoons
finely diced cooked chicken or turkey	1 cup	1/2 cup
chopped mushrooms, drained	1 (3-oz.) can	1/2 (3-oz.) can
coarsely crushed saltine cracker crumbs	1/2 cup	1/4 cup
snipped parsley	2 tablespoons	1 tablespoon
dry white wine	2 tablespoons	1 tablespoon
celery salt	1/2 teaspoon	1/4 teaspoon
conchiglioni (jumbo macaroni shells), cooked, drained, rinsed	16 (about 5 oz.)	8 (about 2-1/2 oz.)
Mornay Sauce, below	3-1/2 cups	1-3/4 cups
BAKING DISH (filling)	1-qt. casserole	1-qt. casserole
BAKING DISHES (stuffed shells)	4 (2-cup) au gratin dishes	2 (2-cup) au gratin dishes
TIME AT HIGH (sausage)	3 to 4 minutes	1-1/2 to 2 minutes
TIME AT HIGH (stuffed shells)	7 to 8 minutes	4 to 5 minutes

Crumble sausage into a 1-quart casserole. Add green onion. Microwave at full power (HIGH) for time in chart above or until sausage is browned, stirring twice. Pour off fat. Stir in chicken or turkey, mushrooms, crumbs, parsley, wine and celery salt. Mix well. Stuff 2 heaping tablespoons filling into each pasta shell. Place 4 stuffed shells, filling side up, in each au gratin dish, see number in chart above. Pour Mornay Sauce over shells, coating pasta completely. Cover with vented plastic wrap. Microwave at full power (HIGH) for time in chart above or until heated through, giving dishes a half turn once. Spoon sauce over pasta before serving. Sprinkle with Parmesan cheese, snipped parsley and paprika, if desired.

Mornay Sauce

YIELD	3-1/2 cups	1-3/4 cups
INGREDIENTS		
butter or margarine	6 tablespoons	3 tablespoons
all-purpose flour	6 tablespoons	3 tablespoons
salt	1/4 teaspoon	1/8 teaspoon
chicken broth	1-1/2 cups	3/4 cup
milk	1-1/2 cups	3/4 cup
grated Parmesan cheese	1/4 cup	2 tablespoons
BAKING DISH	deep 1-1/2-qt. casserole	1-qt. glass measuring cup
TIME AT HIGH (butter)	1 to 1-1/4 minutes	30 seconds
TIME AT HIGH (flour added)	30 seconds	30 seconds
TIME AT HIGH (sauce)	8 minutes	5 minutes

Place butter or margarine in a casserole or measuring cup, see size in chart above. Microwave at full power (HIGH) for time in chart above or until melted. Stir in flour. Microwave at full power (HIGH) 30 seconds. Stir in salt, chicken broth, milk and Parmesan cheese; mix well. Microwave at full power (HIGH) for time in chart above or until thickened and bubbly, stirring four times. Mixture should be thick and smooth.

How to Make Creamy Stuffed Pasta Shells

Stir wine, chicken, mushrooms, cracker crumbs, celery salt and parsley into the cooked sausage and green-onion mixture to make the stuffing.

Hold the pasta shells open, being careful not to tear them. Spoon the chicken stuffing into the shells.

Spoon Mornay Sauce over the stuffed shells, being sure to coat each shell completely to prevent drying out during cooking.

Spoon the sauce over the pasta again before serving. Garnish each dish with a sprinkling of Parmesan cheese, snipped parsley and paprika.

Chicken à la King

SERVINGS	4 (4 cups)	2 (2 cups)
INGREDIENTS		
butter or margarine	1/4 cup	2 tablespoons
shredded carrot	1/4 cup	2 tablespoons
chopped celery	1/4 cup	2 tablespoons
chopped onion	1/4 cup	2 tablespoons
all-purpose flour	1/4 cup	2 tablespoons
salt	1/2 teaspoon	1/4 teaspoon
chicken broth	1 cup	1/2 cup
half and half	1 cup	1/2 cup
cubed cooked chicken or turkey	2 cups	1 cup
sliced mushrooms, drained	1 (2-1/2-oz.) jar	1/2 (2-1/2-oz.) jar
chopped pimiento	1/4 cup	2 tablespoons
patty shells, toast triangles or mashed potatoes		
BAKING DISH	deep 2-qt. casserole	deep 1-qt. casserole
TIME AT HIGH (butter, vegetables)	5 minutes	3 minutes
TIME AT HIGH (flour added)	30 seconds	30 seconds
TIME AT HIGH (broth, half and half added)	4 to 5 minutes	2-1/2 to 3-1/2 minutes
TIME AT HIGH (chicken added)	3 minutes	2 minutes

In a casserole, see size in chart above, combine butter or margarine, carrot, celery and onion. Microwave at full power (HIGH) for time in chart above or until vegetables are tender, stirring twice. Blend in flour and salt. Microwave at full power (HIGH) 30 seconds. Stir in broth and half and half. Microwave at full power (HIGH) for time in chart above or until thickened and bubbly, stirring three times. Mixture should be thick and smooth. Stir in chicken or turkey, mushrooms and pimiento; cover. Microwave at full power (HIGH) for time in chart above or until heated through. Stir before serving in patty shells, or over toast triangles or mashed potatoes. For reheating, see page 188.

Frozen Individual Chicken or Turkey Pies

SERVINGS	3	2	1
INGREDIENTS			
frozen individual chicken or turkey pies	3 (8-oz.) pies	2 (8-oz.) pies	1 (8-oz.) pie
BAKING DISHES	3 (2-cup) casseroles	2 (2-cup) casseroles	1 (2-cup) casserole
TIME AT HIGH	10 to 12 minutes	8 to 10 minutes	5 to 5-1/2 minutes
TIME IN CONVENTIONAL OVEN AT 450F (230C)	12 minutes	12 minutes	8 to 10 minutes

Preheat conventional oven to 450F (230C). Remove pies from original containers. Place in 2-cup casseroles, see number in chart above. Microwave at full power (HIGH) for time in chart above or until filling is bubbling. Place on a baking sheet and bake in pre-heated conventional oven for time in chart above or until crust is brown.

How to Make Herbed Chicken Pot Pies

Prepare Chicken à la King, then stir thawed frozen peas, thyme and sage into the hot creamed mixture.

Spoon the creamed mixture into individual casseroles; heat through. Top each with a pastry round; then heat briefly in the microwave.

Herbed Chicken Pot Pies

SERVINGS	4	2
INGREDIENTS		
pie-crust mix	2 sticks	1 stick
frozen peas, thawed	1 cup	1/2 cup
dried leaf thyme	1/2 teaspoon	1/4 teaspoon
dried rubbed sage	1/2 teaspoon	1/4 teaspoon
hot Chicken à la King, opposite	4 cups	2 cups
BAKING DISH (pie crust)	12-inch microwave pizza plate	12-inch microwave pizza plate
BAKING DISHES (pies)	4 (1-1/2-cup) casseroles	2 (1-1/2-cup) casseroles
TIME AT 70%	7-1/2 to 8 minutes	3-1/2 minutes
TIME AT HIGH (filling)	6 to 7 minutes	3 to 3-1/2 minutes
TIME AT HIGH (pies)	2 minutes	1 minute

Prepare pie-crust mix according to package directions. Roll out pastry on a lightly floured board. Cut in circles slightly larger than the tops of the individual casseroles, see number and sizes in chart above. Fold under edges of pastry rounds and flute so pastry will fit inside tops of casseroles. Pierce pastry with a fork or use a cookie cutter to make a chicken-shape cutout in center of each round. Place pastry rounds on a 12-inch pizza plate. Microwave at 70% (MEDIUM HIGH) for time in chart above, or until just starting to brown, giving dish a half turn once. Remove any rounds that start to overbrown. Cool pastry rounds on a wire rack. Stir peas, thyme and sage into hot Chicken à la King. Spoon hot chicken mixture into individual casseroles. Cover with vented plastic wrap. Microwave at full power (HIGH) for time in chart above or until heated through, rearranging once. Uncover casseroles and stir fillings. Top each casserole with a pastry round. Microwave, uncovered, at full power (HIGH) for time in chart above or until pastry is warm.

Chicken Tetrazzini

SERVINGS	5	3
INGREDIENTS		
bacon	6 slices	4 slices
bacon drippings	6 tablespoons	1/4 cup
sliced fresh mushrooms	3/4 cup	1/2 cup
chopped onion	1/3 cup	1/4 cup
all-purpose flour	6 tablespoons	1/4 cup
salt	3/4 teaspoon	1/2 teaspoon
white pepper	1/4 teaspoon	1/8 teaspoon
chicken broth	1-1/2 cups	1 cup
half and half	1-1/2 cups	1 cup
dry sherry	3 tablespoons	2 tablespoons
spaghetti, cooked, drained	8 oz. (3-1/4 cups cooked)	5 oz. (2 cups cooked)
cubed cooked chicken or turkey	2 cups	1-1/2 cups
grated Parmesan cheese	6 tablespoons	1/4 cup
snipped parsley	to garnish	to garnish
BAKING DISH	12" x 7" baking dish with microwave rack	8-inch square baking dish with microwave rack
TIME AT HIGH (bacon)	6 to 7 minutes	4 to 5 minutes
TIME AT HIGH (mushrooms, onion)	4 to 5 minutes	3 minutes
TIME AT HIGH (flour added)	30 seconds	30 seconds
TIME AT HIGH (sauce)	9 to 10 minutes	5 to 6 minutes
TIME AT HIGH (complete casserole)	13 to 15 minutes	8 to 9 minutes

Place bacon on a microwave rack in a baking dish, see size in chart above. Cover with white paper towel. Microwave at full power (HIGH) for time in chart above or until crisp. Crumble bacon and set aside. Remove rack from baking dish. Measure bacon drippings, see amount in chart above, into same baking dish. If necessary, add melted butter to make enough drippings. Add mushrooms and onion to bacon drippings. Microwave at full power (HIGH) for time in chart above or until onion is tender, stirring once. Stir in flour, salt and pepper. Microwave at full power (HIGH) 30 seconds. Add broth and half and half. Mix well. Microwave at full power (HIGH) for time in chart above or until thickened and bubbly, stirring five times. Stir in sherry. Stir in spaghetti, chicken or turkey, crumbled bacon and Parmesan cheese. Mix well. Cover with vented plastic wrap. Microwave at full power (HIGH) for time in chart above or until heated through, stirring well once. Stir before serving. Garnish with parsley.

Reheating Chicken à la King

To chill: Spoon 2 cups Chicken à la King, page 186, into a 1-quart casserole. Cover tightly and refrigerate.

To reheat: Microwave, covered, at 70% (MEDIUM HIGH) 10 to 12 minutes or until heated through, stirring once.

Golden Soy Glaze

YIELD	about 1 cup	about 1/2 cup
INGREDIENTS		
cornstarch	2 teaspoons	1 teaspoon
soy sauce	1/4 cup	2 tablespoons
water	2/3 cup	1/3 cup
BOWL	small bowl	small bowl
TIME AT HIGH	2-1/2 to 3 minutes	1-1/2 to 2 minutes

Combine cornstarch and soy sauce in a small bowl. Stir until blended. Stir in water. Microwave at full power (HIGH) for time in chart above or until thickened, stirring three times. Brush soy glaze on poultry. Grease waxed paper. Place waxed paper, greased side down, over glazed poultry, forming a tent.

Plum-Good Glaze

YIELD	1 cup	1/2 cup
INGREDIENTS		
plum-with-tapioca baby food	1 (7-3/4-oz.) jar	1 (4-3/4-oz.) jar
corn syrup	3 tablespoons	2 tablespoons
lemon juice	2 teaspoons	1 teaspoon
ground cinnamon	1/2 teaspoon	1/4 teaspoon
dried ground lemon peel	1/4 teaspoon	1/8 teaspoon
BOWL	small bowl	small bowl
TIME AT HIGH	2 to 2-1/2 minutes	1-1/2 to 2 minutes

In a small bowl, combine plum baby food, corn syrup, lemon juice, cinnamon and lemon peel. Mix well. Microwave at full power (HIGH) for time in chart above or until warm, stirring once. Brush glaze on poultry. Grease waxed paper. Place waxed paper, greased side down, over glazed poultry, forming a tent.

Herb-Butter Turkey-Basting Sauce

YIELD	1/2 cup	1/4 cup
INGREDIENTS		
butter or margarine	1/2 cup	1/4 cup
dried leaf rosemary	2 teaspoons	1 teaspoon
dried parsley flakes	2 teaspoons	1 teaspoon
dried leaf thyme	2 teaspoons	1 teaspoon
dried rubbed sage	2 teaspoons	1 teaspoon
Kitchen Bouquet	1 teaspoon	1/2 teaspoon
BOWL	small bowl	small bowl
TIME AT HIGH	1 to 1-1/2 minutes	45 seconds

Place butter or margarine in a small bowl. Microwave at full power (HIGH) for time in chart above or until melted. Stir in rosemary, parsley, thyme, sage and Kitchen Bouquet. Mix well. Stir well just before brushing on poultry.

How to Use Poultry Glaze

For small birds, such as chicken and Cornish hens, select Golden Soy Glaze; it gives the bird some brown coloring. Small birds cook too fast to achieve natural browning.

Large birds, such as turkeys, cook long enough to become brown. Browning is enhanced by flavorful butter sauces such as Herb-Butter Turkey-Basting Sauce.

Plum-Good Glaze enhances the appearance of roast duckling. When using this or other sweet glazes, be sure to grease the waxed paper before tenting it over the bird. Otherwise the waxed paper will stick to the bird.

Brush all birds generously with glaze or basting sauce before cooking, and again when you turn them over partway through the cooking time. For the most attractive bird, brush with sauce after cooking and before tenting with foil.

Ruby Cranberry Basting Sauce

YIELD	1-1/3 cups	2/3 cup
INGREDIENTS		
packed brown sugar	1/4 cup	2 tablespoons
cornstarch	2 tablespoons	1 tablespoon
ground nutmeg	1/2 teaspoon	1/4 teaspoon
cranberry juice cocktail	1 cup	1/2 cup
cranberry liqueur	1/4 cup	2 tablespoons
GLASS MEASURING CUP	1-qt.	2-cup
TIME AT HIGH	3 to 3-1/2 minutes	1-1/2 to 2 minutes

In a glass measuring cup, see size in chart above, combine brown sugar, cornstarch and
nutmeg. Mix well. Stir in cranberry juice and liqueur. Microwave at full power (HIGH)
for time in chart above or until thickened and bubbly, stirring twice. Brush sauce on
poultry. Grease waxed paper. Place waxed paper, greased side down, over poultry
forming a tent.

Crabapple Basting Sauce

YIELD	1 cup	1/2 cup
INGREDIENTS		
cornstarch	4 teaspoons	2 teaspoons
syrup from canned spiced crabapples	1 cup	1/2 cup
Kitchen Bouquet	2 teaspoons	1 teaspoon
BOWL	small bowl	small bowl
TIME AT HIGH	2-1/2 to 3 minutes	1-1/2 minutes

In a small bowl, combine cornstarch and a little crabapple syrup until mixture is
smooth. Stir in remaining crabapple syrup and Kitchen Bouquet. Mix well. Microwave
at full power (HIGH) for time in chart above or until thickened and bubbly, whisking
twice. Brush sauce on poultry. Grease waxed paper. Place waxed paper, greased side
down, over poultry, forming a tent.

Wine Basting Sauce

YIELD	1 cup	1/2 cup
INGREDIENTS		
cornstarch	2 tablespoons	1 tablespoon
dry red wine	1 cup	1/2 cup
Kitchen Bouquet	1 teaspoon	1/2 teaspoon
BOWL	small bowl	small bowl
TIME AT HIGH	2-1/2 to 3 minutes	1-1/2 to 2 minutes

In a small bowl, combine cornstarch and a little wine until mixture is smooth. Stir in remaining wine and Kitchen Bouquet. Mix well. Microwave at full power (HIGH) for
time in chart above or until thickened and bubbly, whisking twice. Brush sauce on poultry. Grease waxed paper. Place waxed paper, greased side down, over poultry, forming
a tent.

Rosy Currant Glaze

YIELD	2/3 cup	1/3 cup
INGREDIENTS		
red currant jelly	1/2 cup	1/4 cup
crème de cassis	2 tablespoons	1 tablespoon
ground allspice	1/4 teaspoon	1/8 teaspoon
GLASS MEASURING CUP	1-cup	1-cup
TIME AT HIGH	1-1/2 to 2 minutes	45 to 60 seconds

In a 1-cup glass measuring cup, combine jelly, crème de cassis and allspice. Microwave at full power (HIGH) for time in chart above or until jelly melts, stirring twice. Brush sauce on poultry. Grease waxed paper. Place waxed paper, greased side down, over glazed poultry, forming a tent.

Apricot Basting Sauce

YIELD	1-1/3 cups	2/3 cup
INGREDIENTS		
butter or margarine	1/2 cup	1/4 cup
apricot jam	2/3 cup	1/3 cup
orange liqueur	2 tablespoons	1 tablespoon
Kitchen Bouquet	1/2 teaspoon	1/4 teaspoon
ground mace	1/4 teaspoon	1/8 teaspoon
GLASS MEASURING CUP	1-qt.	2-cup
TIME AT HIGH (butter)	45 to 60 seconds	30 seconds
TIME AT HIGH (sauce)	1-1/2 to 2 minutes	45 to 60 seconds

Place butter or margarine in a glass measuring cup, see size in chart above. Microwave at full power (HIGH) for time in chart above or until melted. Stir in apricot jam, orange liqueur, Kitchen Bouquet and mace. Mix well. Microwave at full power (HIGH) for time in chart above or until heated through. Stir well. Brush sauce on poultry. Grease waxed paper. Place waxed paper, greased side down, over poultry, forming a tent.

Food Processor Basting Sauce

YIELD	1-1/4 cups	1/3 cup
INGREDIENTS		
paprika	3 tablespoons	1 tablespoon
Kitchen Bouquet	1 tablespoon	1 teaspoon
water	1/4 cup	2 tablespoons
vegetable oil	3/4 cup	1/4 cup

In a food processor fitted with a steel cutting blade or in a blender container, combine paprika, Kitchen Bouquet and water. Cover and process until blended. With motor running, gradually pour in oil through feeder tube or hole in lid, blending constantly until smooth. Stir before brushing on poultry.

Seasoned-Butter Basting Sauce

YIELD	2/3 cup	1/3 cup
INGREDIENTS		
butter or margarine	1/2 cup	1/4 cup
paprika	2 tablespoons	1 tablespoon
salad seasoning	2 tablespoons	1 tablespoon
BOWL	small bowl	custard cup
TIME AT HIGH	1 to 1-1/2 minutes	45 seconds

Place butter or margarine in a bowl or custard cup. Microwave at full power (HIGH) for time in chart above or until melted. Stir in paprika and salad seasoning. Stir befor brushing over poultry.

Tarragon-Butter Basting Sauce

YIELD	1/2 cup	1/4 cup
INGREDIENTS		
butter or margarine	1/2 cup	1/4 cup
dried leaf tarragon	2 teaspoons	1 teaspoon
celery salt	1/2 teaspoon	1/4 teaspoon
onion salt	1/2 teaspoon	1/4 teaspoon
Kitchen Bouquet	1 teaspoon	1/2 teaspoon
BOWL	small bowl	small bowl
TIME AT HIGH	45 to 60 seconds	30 seconds

Place butter or margarine in a small bowl. Microwave at full power (HIGH) for time i chart above or until melted. Stir in tarragon, celery salt, onion salt and Kitchen Bouque Mix well. Stir well just before brushing on poultry.

Spicy Orange Sauce

YIELD	2/3 cup
INGREDIENTS	
orange marmalade	1/2 cup
dry sherry	2 tablespoons
ground ginger	1/4 teaspoon
GLASS MEASURING CUP	1-cup
TIME AT HIGH	1 minute

In a 1-cup glass measuring cup, combine orange marmalade, sherry and ginger; mix well. Microwave at full power (HIGH) 1 minute or until warm, stirring once. Serve with roast duckling or other roast poultry.

How to Make Old-Fashioned Cranberry Sauce

Microwave sugar, water and cranberry liqueur until sugar dissolves and a clear syrup forms. Add fresh or thawed frozen whole cranberries.

Microwave the cranberries at full power (HIGH) until the skins pop. Then simmer the sauce at 30% (MEDIUM LOW) until desired consistency.

Old-Fashioned Cranberry Sauce

YIELD	2 cups	1 cup
INGREDIENTS		
sugar	1 cup	1/2 cup
water	1/2 cup	1/4 cup
cranberry liqueur	1/2 cup	1/4 cup
fresh or thawed frozen cranberries	2 cups	1 cup
BAKING DISH	deep 2-qt. casserole	deep 1-qt. casserole
TIME AT HIGH (syrup)	4 to 5 minutes	3 to 3-1/2 minutes
TIME AT HIGH (cranberries added)	5 minutes	3 minutes
TIME AT 30%	15 minutes	10 minutes

In a casserole, see size in chart above, combine sugar, water and cranberry liqueur. Microwave, uncovered, at full power (HIGH) for time in chart above or until boiling, stirring once or twice to dissolve sugar. Syrup should be clear. Stir in cranberries. Cover loosely with waxed paper. Microwave at full power (HIGH) for time in chart above or until skins on cranberries pop, stirring once. Uncover and microwave at 30% (MEDIUM LOW) for time in chart above, or until thickened to desired consistency, stirring once. Cover and refrigerate.

Basic Turkey Gravy

YIELD	2 cups	1-1/2 cups
INGREDIENTS		
turkey drippings	1/2 cup	1/3 cup
all-purpose flour	1/2 cup	1/3 cup
cooking liquid from Poached Turkey or Chicken Giblets, page 181, chicken broth or water	1-1/2 cups	1 cup
salt and pepper	to taste	to taste
Kitchen Bouquet, if desired		
BAKING DISH	12" x 7" baking dish	12" x 7" baking dish
TIME AT HIGH (flour)	30 seconds	30 seconds
TIME AT HIGH (gravy)	4 to 5 minutes	3 to 3-1/2 minutes

Remove rack from the 12" x 7" baking dish in which turkey was roasted. Skim off excess fat. Measure drippings and return amount in chart above to same baking dish. Whisk flour into drippings, blending well. Microwave at full power (HIGH) 30 seconds. Whisk in cooking liquid, broth or water until blended. Microwave at full power (HIGH) for time in chart above or until thickened and bubbly, whisking three times. Season to taste with salt and pepper. Stir in a few drops of Kitchen Bouquet for color, if desired.

Variations

For thinner gravy, use 1/3 cup drippings, 1/3 cup flour and 1-1/3 cups liquid. Microwave as for larger recipe above.

For giblet gravy, add chopped cooked giblets, page 181, with the liquid in recipe above.

Easy Turkey Gravy

YIELD	2-3/4 cups	1-1/4 cups
INGREDIENTS		
turkey drippings	1/2 cup	1/4 cup
condensed cream of chicken soup	2 (10-3/4-oz.) cans	1 (10-3/4-oz.) can
poultry seasoning	1 teaspoon	1/2 teaspoon
water	1/2 cup	1/4 cup
Kitchen Bouquet	1/2 to 1 teaspoon	1/4 to 1/2 teaspoon
BAKING DISH	12" x 7" baking dish	12" x 7" baking dish
TIME AT HIGH	16 to 17 minutes	10 to 11 minutes

Remove rack from the 12" x 7" baking dish in which turkey was roasted. Skim off excess fat. Measure drippings and return amount in chart above to same baking dish. Whisk in soup and poultry seasoning. Gradually whisk in water until smooth. Add Kitchen Bouquet, if necessary, for color. Microwave at full power (HIGH) for time in chart above or until heated through, stirring occasionally.

To cook turkey or chicken giblets, see page 181.

Basic Stuffing Mix

YIELD	4 cups	2 cups	1 cup
INGREDIENTS			
butter or margarine*	1/2 cup	1/3 cup	3 tablespoons
chopped onion	1/2 cup	1/4 cup	2 tablespoons
chopped celery	1/2 cup	1/4 cup	2 tablespoons
water or broth*	1 cup	2/3 cup	1/3 cup
herb-seasoned stuffing mix*	1 (8-oz.) bag (4 cups)	1/2 (8-oz.) bag (2 cups)	1 cup
BAKING DISH	deep 2-qt. casserole	deep 1-1/2-qt. casserole	deep 1-qt. casserole
TIME AT HIGH (vegetables)	4 to 5 minutes	3 minutes	2 minutes
TIME AT HIGH (water added)	2-1/2 to 3 minutes	1-1/2 minutes	45 to 60 seconds

*See stuffing package directions for exact amounts of butter, water and stuffing mix.

In a casserole, see size in chart above, combine butter or margarine, onion and celery. Microwave at full power (HIGH) for time in chart above or until tender, stirring once. Stir in water or broth. Microwave at full power (HIGH) for time in chart above or until boiling. Add stuffing mix. Toss lightly with a fork until moist and blended. Use 4 cups to stuff an 8- to 10-pound turkey, 1-1/2 to 2 cups to stuff a 3- to 4-pound chicken, and 1/2 cup to stuff 1 Cornish hen.

Variations
For each cup of stuffing, add one of the following: 1/3 cup drained, canned mushrooms, 1/3 cup drained, crumbled, cooked sausage, 1/4 cup chopped, cooked oysters, 3 tablespoons chopped, toasted almonds.

Casserole Stuffing

YIELD	4 cups	2 cups	1 cup
INGREDIENTS			
prepared stuffing	4 cups	2 cups	1 cup
BAKING DISH	see stuffing recipe		
TIME AT HIGH	2 to 3 minutes	1-1/2 to 2-1/2 minutes	1 to 1-1/2 minutes

Prepare stuffing of your choice. Heat stuffing in the same casserole instead of stuffing a bird. Cover with vented plastic wrap or lid. Microwave at full power (HIGH) for time in chart above or until heated through, stirring once.

Adapting Stuffing Recipes for Microwave Oven

- Stuffings that are fairly moist and loosely mixed work best. Do not use compact, heavy stuffing, such as corn bread.

- It's convenient to microwave chopped vegetables, such as celery and onion, in the butter or liquid called for in the recipe. Add other ingredients to the same baking dish.

- Refer to the Glaze & Stuffing Guides in this section to estimate how much stuffing is needed for each type of bird.

- To heat stuffing in a casserole instead of stuffing a bird, see Casserole Stuffing, above, for guidelines on amounts and cooking times.

Fruited Bacon Stuffing

YIELD	4 cups	2 cups
INGREDIENTS		
bacon	4 to 5 slices	2 to 3 slices
bacon drippings	1/4 cup	2 tablespoons
chopped green onion	1/4 cup	2 tablespoons
broth or water	2/3 cup	1/3 cup
raisins	1/4 cup	2 tablespoons
herb-seasoned croutons for stuffing	1/2 (7-oz.) pkg. (3-1/2 cups)	1-1/2 cups
finely chopped unpared apple	1/2 cup	1/4 cup
BAKING DISH (bacon)	12" x 7" baking dish with microwave rack	12" x 7" baking dish with microwave rack
BAKING DISH (stuffing)	deep 1-1/2-qt. casserole	deep 1-qt. casserole
TIME AT HIGH (bacon)	4 to 5 minutes	3 to 4 minutes
TIME AT HIGH (onion)	2 to 3 minutes	1-1/2 to 2 minutes
TIME AT HIGH (broth, raisins added)	2 to 3 minutes	1-1/2 to 2 minutes

Place bacon on a microwave rack in a 12" x 7" baking dish. Cover with white paper towel. Microwave at full power (HIGH) for time in chart above or until bacon is crisp. Remove bacon; drain on paper towel. Crumble bacon and set aside. Measure amount of drippings shown in chart above into a baking dish for stuffing, see size in chart above. If necessary, add melted butter or margarine, to make enough drippings. Add onion to dish. Microwave at full power (HIGH) for time in chart above or until tender. Stir in broth or water and raisins. Microwave at full power (HIGH) for time in chart above or until liquid boils and raisins are plumped. Add croutons, apple and reserved bacon. Toss lightly with a fork until all are moistened. Use 4 cups to stuff an 8- to 10-pound turkey, 1-1/2 to 2 cups to stuff a 3- to 4-pound chicken, and 1/2 cup to stuff 1 Cornish hen.

Stuffing Mix, Saucepan-Style

YIELD	4 cups	2 cups
INGREDIENTS		
stuffing mix for chicken, saucepan-style	1 (6-oz.) pkg.	1/2 (6-oz.) pkg. (2 to 3 tablespoons vegetable seasoning, 1-1/4 cups stuffing crumbs)
water	1-1/2 cups	3/4 cup
butter or margarine	1/4 cup	2 tablespoons
sliced mushrooms, drained	1 (2-1/2-oz.) jar	1/2 (2-1/2-oz.) jar
BOWL	1-1/2-qt. bowl	1-qt. bowl
TIME AT HIGH	8 minutes	5 minutes
STANDING TIME	5 minutes	5 minutes

Prepare as for Easy Stuffing, page 88, omitting apple. Add sliced mushrooms along with stuffing crumbs. Let stand and fluff as directed. Serve with chicken or turkey.

How to Make Orange Rice Stuffing

Here's an easy way to stuff the bird—stand the bird at an angle in a bowl, then spoon the stuffing into the body cavity.

To keep the stuffing from falling out when the bird is turned over during cooking, secure the opening closed with a wooden pick.

Orange Rice Stuffing

YIELD	4 cups	2-2/3 cups	1-1/2 cups
INGREDIENTS			
Butter or margarine	6 tablespoons	1/4 cup	2 tablespoons
Chopped celery	1/3 cup	1/4 cup	2 tablespoons
Chopped onion	1/3 cup	1/4 cup	2 tablespoons
Chopped pecans	1/3 cup	1/4 cup	2 tablespoons
Orange juice	1/3 cup	1/4 cup	2 tablespoons
Chicken bouillon granules	1 tablespoon	2 teaspoons	1 teaspoon
Cooked rice	3 cups	2 cups	1 cup
Chopped orange sections	1 cup	2/3 cup	1/3 cup
Dried ground orange peel	3/4 teaspoon	1/2 teaspoon	1/4 teaspoon
BAKING DISH	deep 2-qt. casserole	deep 2-qt. casserole	deep 1-qt. casserole
TIME AT HIGH (vegetables, nuts)	4 minutes	3 to 4 minutes	2 to 2-1/2 minutes
TIME AT HIGH (orange juice, bouillon granules added)	1-1/2 minutes	1-1/2 minutes	1 minute

In a casserole, see size in chart above, combine butter or margarine, celery, onion and pecans. Microwave at full power (HIGH) for time in chart above or until vegetables are tender. Stir in orange juice and chicken bouillon granules. Microwave at full power (HIGH) for time in chart above or until granules dissolve. Add rice, orange sections and dried peel; mix lightly to blend. Use 4 cups to stuff a 7-pound capon, 1-1/2 to 2 cups to stuff a 3- to 4-pound chicken, and 1/2 cup to stuff 1 Cornish hen. See Glaze & Stuffing Guides throughout this section.

Basic Roast Capon

SERVINGS	8
INGREDIENTS	
basting sauce, see pages 190 to 194	2/3 cup
frozen capon, thawed	
(with giblets)	7-1/4 to 7-3/4 lbs.
(without giblets)	6-1/4 to 6-3/4 lbs.
BAKING DISH	12" x 7" baking dish with microwave rack
TIME AT HIGH	18 minutes
TIME AT 50%	65 to 70 minutes
STANDING TIME	5 minutes

Prepare basting sauce of your choice. Remove giblets from capon. Twist wings behind back. Tie legs together tightly with string. Make a small slit in back skin for release of steam. Brush whole capon with basting sauce. Place capon, breast side down, on a microwave rack in a 12" x 7" baking dish. Cover with a tent of greased waxed paper. Microwave at full power (HIGH) 18 minutes. Turn capon breast side up. Brush with more basting sauce. Give dish a half turn. Shield wings, ends of drumsticks and top of breast with small pieces of foil if these areas are browning faster than the rest of the bird. Secure foil with wooden picks, if necessary. Cover with tent of waxed paper. Microwave at 50% (MEDIUM) 65 to 70 minutes or until juices run clear when capon is pierced with a fork. A microwave meat thermometer inserted between leg and thigh should register 185F (85C). Give dish a half turn once during 50% cooking time. When done, brush capon with more basting sauce. Cover tightly with foil. Let stand 5 minutes.

Variation

Stuffed Capon: Lightly pack 2-3/4 to 3 cups stuffing of your choice, pages 197 to 199 into body cavity and 3/4 cup stuffing into neck cavity. Skewer openings closed with wooden picks. Microwave as above. Stuffed capon may need up to 5 minutes longer cooking time at 50% (MEDIUM). A microwave meat thermometer inserted in center of stuffing must register 165F (75C). If not, continue cooking until this temperature is reached.

Glaze & Stuffing Guide for Capon

capon (with giblets)	7-1/4 to 7-3/4 lbs.
glaze	2/3 cup
stuffing	4 cups

Recommended Glazes: Rosy Currant Glaze, Apricot Basting Sauce, Ruby Cranberry Basting Sauce, pages 192 and 193.

Defrosting: To defrost capon, see page 161.

Basic Roast Capon with Orange Rice Stuffing page 199, and Apricot Basting Sauce, page 193

Basic Roast Broiler-Fryer Chicken

SERVINGS	3 or 4
INGREDIENTS	
basting sauce, see pages 190 to 194	1/3 to 1/2 cup
whole broiler-fryer chicken	
(with giblets)	3 to 3-1/4 lbs.
(without giblets)	2-3/4 to 3 lbs.
BAKING DISH	12" x 7" baking dish with microwave rack
TIME AT HIGH (first side)	10 minutes
TIME AT HIGH (second side)	12 to 14 minutes
STANDING TIME	3 to 5 minutes

Prepare basting sauce of your choice. Remove giblets from chicken. Twist wing tips behind back. Tie legs together tightly with string. Make a small slit in back skin for release of steam. Brush whole chicken with basting sauce. Place chicken, breast side down, on a microwave rack in a 12" x 7" baking dish. Cover with a tent of greased waxed paper. Microwave at full power (HIGH) 10 minutes. Turn chicken breast side up. Brush with more basting sauce. Give dish a half turn. Cover with tent of waxed paper. Microwave at full power (HIGH) 12 to 14 minutes or until juices run clear when chicken is pierced with a fork between leg and thigh. A microwave meat thermometer inserted between leg and thigh should register 185F (85C). When done, brush chicken with more basting sauce. Cover tightly with foil and let stand 3 to 5 minutes.

Variations

Stuffed Broiler-Fryer Chicken: Lightly pack 1-1/4 to 1-1/2 cups stuffing of your choice, pages 197 to 199, into body and neck cavities. Skewer openings closed with wooden picks. Microwave as above. Stuffed chicken may need up to 2 minutes longer cooking time. A microwave meat thermometer inserted in center of stuffing must register 165F (75C). If not, continue cooking until this temperature is reached.

Roasting Chicken: A 3-1/2- to 3-3/4-pound roasting chicken without giblets will need about 2 minutes longer microwave cooking time than the unstuffed broiler-fryer chicken in the chart above. If you want to stuff the chicken, use 2 cups stuffing. Microwave stuffed roasting chicken as above, increasing cooking time to 15 minutes on the first side and to 15 to 20 minutes on the second side. A microwave meat thermometer inserted in center of stuffing must register 165F (75C). If not, continue cooking until this temperature is reached.

Chicken in a Clay Pot: See page 210.

Glaze & Stuffing Guide for Chicken

chicken (with giblets)	3 to 4 lbs.
glaze	1/3 to 1/2 cup
stuffing	1-1/2 to 2 cups

Recommended Glaze: Golden Soy Glaze, Seasoned Butter Basting Sauce, Food Processor Basting Sauce, Wine Basting Sauce, pages 190 to 194.

Defrosting: To defrost whole chickens, see page 161.

How to Make Stuffed Broiler-Fryer Chicken

Twist wing tips behind back of chicken. Make a small slit in back skin. Stuff the neck and body cavities with Basic Stuffing Mix or your favorite stuffing. Skewer the skin over stuffing with a wooden pick.

Tie the legs of the stuffed chicken together tightly with string. Brush the chicken all over with Golden Soy Glaze or other glaze.

Halfway through the cooking time, turn the chicken breast side up, using paper towels to protect your hands. If you turn the chicken over with a meat fork, it will lose some of the juices. Brush the chicken with more basting sauce and microwave for remaining cooking time.

To test for doneness, insert a microwave meat thermometer between both legs and thighs. Insert the thermometer in several places. The thermometer should register 185F (85C). The temperature of the stuffing must be 165F (75C).

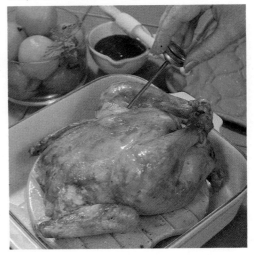

Basic Roast Duckling

SERVINGS	2
INGREDIENTS	
basting sauce, see pages 190 to 194	1/3 cup
frozen domestic duckling, thawed	
(with giblets)	4-1/2 to 5 lbs.
(without giblets)	3-3/4 to 4-1/4 lbs.
Spicy Orange Sauce, page 194, if desired	
BAKING DISH	12" x 7" baking dish with microwave rack
TIME AT HIGH (first side)	12 minutes
TIME AT HIGH (second side)	12 to 13 minutes
STANDING TIME	5 minutes

Prepare basting sauce of your choice. Remove giblets from duckling. Pierce skin all over with the tip of a sharp knife. Twist wing tips behind back. Skewer neck skin to back, covering wing tips. Use wooden picks for skewers. Tie legs together tightly with string. Brush whole duck with basting sauce. Place duck, breast side down, on a microwave rack in a 12" x 7" baking dish. Cover with a tent of greased waxed paper. Microwave at full power (HIGH) 12 minutes. Turn duck breast side up. Drain off fat from baking dish and give dish a half turn. Brush duck with more basting sauce. Cover with tent of waxed paper. Microwave at full power (HIGH) 12 to 13 minutes or until juices run clear when duck is pierced with a fork between leg and thigh. A microwave meat thermometer inserted between leg and thigh should register 185F (85C). When done, brush duckling with more basting sauce. Cover tightly with foil and let stand 5 minutes. Serve with Spicy Orange Sauce, if desired.

Note: To crisp duck skin, split duck in half lengthwise after microwave cooking. Place skin side up on conventional broiler pan. Shield wings with foil. Broil in preheated broiler about 4 inches from the heat for 2 to 3 minutes.

Glaze & Stuffing Guide for Duckling

duckling (with giblets)	4-1/2 to 5 lbs.
glaze	1/3 cup
stuffing	do not stuff

Recommended Glazes: Rosy Currant Glaze, Plum-Good Glaze, Wine Basting Sauce, pages 190 to 193.

Defrosting: To defrost duckling, see page 162.

How to Make Basic Roast Duckling

Use the tip of a small sharp knife to pierce duck skin all over at about 1-inch intervals. This allows the fat to escape from beneath the skin during cooking.

Twist wing tips behind back, then skewer the neck skin over the wing tips with a wooden pick. Brush the duck all over with Plum-Good Glaze or other glaze.

Halfway through the cooking time, turn the duck breast side up. Drain off the excess fat from the baking dish using a baster. Brush the duck with more glaze.

If you prefer crisp skin on duck, split the cooked duck in half lengthwise with poultry shears. Place on conventional broiler pan and broil in conventional oven until crisp.

Basic Roast Cornish Hens

SERVINGS	4	2	1
INGREDIENTS			
basting sauce, see pages 190 to 194	1 cup	1/2 cup	1/4 cup
frozen Cornish hens, thawed			
(as purchased)	4 (20-oz.) hens	2 (20-oz.) hens	1 (20-oz.) hen
(without giblets)	4 (16-oz.) hens	2 (16-oz.) hens	1 (16-oz.) hen
BAKING DISH	12-inch square microwave baker with microwave rack	8-inch square baking dish with microwave rack	round, 8-inch baking dish with microwave rack
TIME AT HIGH (first side)	16 minutes	8 minutes	4 minutes
TIME AT HIGH (second side)	16 to 18 minutes	6 to 8 minutes	4 to 5 minutes
STANDING TIME	3 to 5 minutes	3 to 5 minutes	3 to 5 minutes

Prepare basting sauce of your choice. Remove giblets from Cornish hens. Twist wing tips behind backs. Tie legs together tightly with string. Make a small slit in back skin of each hen for release of steam. Brush hens with basting sauce. Place hens, breast side down, on a microwave rack in a baking dish, see size in chart above. Cover with a tent of greased waxed paper. Microwave at full power (HIGH) for time in chart above. Turn breast side up and give each hen a half turn in baking dish. Brush with more basting sauce and give dish a half turn. Cover with tent of waxed paper. Microwave at full power (HIGH) for time in chart above, basting with sauce once. Hens are done when juices run clear when hens are pierced with a fork between leg and thigh. A microwave meat thermometer inserted between leg and thigh should register 185F (85C). When done, brush Cornish hens with more basting sauce. Cover tightly with foil and let stand 3 to 5 minutes.

Variation

Stuffed Cornish Hens: Lightly pack 1/2 cup stuffing, of your choice, pages 197 to 199, into each hen. Skewer skin across body cavity with wooden picks to hold in stuffing. Microwave as above. Stuffed hens may need 1 to 2 minutes longer cooking time *per hen*. A microwave meat thermometer inserted in center of stuffing must register 165F (75C). If not, continue cooking until this temperature is reached.

Glaze & Stuffing Guide for Cornish Hens

Cornish hens (with giblets)	4 (20-oz.) hens	2 (20-oz.) hens	1 (20-oz.) hen
glaze	1 cup	1/2 cup	1/4 cup
stuffing	2 cups	1 cup	1/2 cup

Recommended Glazes: Crabapple Basting Sauce; Ruby Cranberry Basting Sauce; Apricot Basting Sauce; Rosy Currant Glaze, pages 192 and 193.

Defrosting: To defrost Cornish Hens, see page 163.

Basic Roast Cornish Hens with Fruited Bacon Stuffing, page 198, and Rosy Currant Glaze, page 193.

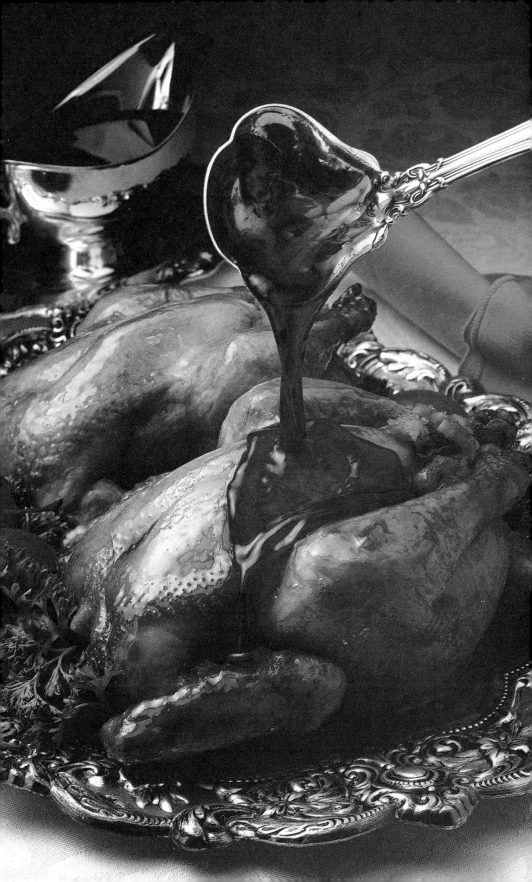

Basic Roast Turkey   Photo on page 155.

SERVINGS	10 to 12	8 to 10	6 to 8
INGREDIENTS basting sauce, see pages 190 to 194	1/2 to 1 cup	1/2 to 1 cup	1/2 to 3/4 cup
frozen whole self-basting turkey, thawed (with giblets and gravy package, if present)	9 to 10 lbs.	7 to 8 lbs.	5-1/2 to 6-1/2 lbs.
(without giblets and gravy package)	7-3/4 to 9-1/4 lbs.	6 to 7-1/4 lbs.	4-3/4 to 5-3/4 lbs.
BAKING DISH	12" x 7" baking dish with micro- wave rack	12" x 7" baking dish with micro- wave rack	12" x 7" baking dish with micro- wave rack
TIME AT HIGH (2 minutes per lb. without giblets)	15 to 19 minutes	12 to 15 minutes	9 to 11-1/2 minutes
TIME AT 50%	70 to 90 minutes	65 to 75 minutes	45 to 60 minutes
STANDING TIME	5 to 10 minutes	5 to 10 minutes	5 to 10 minutes

Prepare basting sauce of your choice. Remove giblets from turkey. Twist wing tips behind back. Tie legs together tightly with string or replace under band of skin, if present. Make a small slit in back skin for release of steam. Brush whole turkey with basting sauce. Place turkey, breast side down, on a microwave rack in a 12" x 7" baking dish. Cover with a tent of greased waxed paper. Microwave at full power (HIGH) for time in chart above. Turn turkey breast side up. Brush with more basting sauce. Give dish a half turn. Shield wings, ends of drumsticks and top of breast with small pieces of foil if these areas are browning faster than the rest of the bird. Secure foil with wooden picks if necessary. Cover with tent of waxed paper. Microwave at 50% (MEDIUM) for time in chart above or until juices run clear when turkey is pierced with a fork between leg and thigh. A microwave meat thermometer should register 185F (85C) between leg and thigh and at thickest part of breast meat. Give dish a half turn twice during 50% cooking time. When done, brush turkey with more sauce and cover tightly with foil. Let stand 5 to 10 minutes.

Variation

Roast Stuffed Turkey: Lightly pack 2-1/2 to 3 cups stuffing, see pages 197 to 199, into body cavity and 3/4 to 1-1/4 cups into neck cavity. Skewer openings closed with wooden picks. Microwave as above. For larger stuffed turkey, cooking time will be about the same. Smaller stuffed turkey may need up to 3 to 5 minutes longer cooking time at 50% (MEDIUM). A microwave meat thermometer inserted in center of stuffing must register 165F (75C). If not, continue microwaving until this temperature is reached.

Defrosting: To defrost whole turkeys, see page 162.

How to Make Basic Roast Turkey

Microwave the turkey, breast side down, on a microwave rack. Turn the bird breast side up partway through the cooking time. Shield any areas that are overbrowning with small pieces of foil and secure with wooden picks.

Use a microwave meat thermometer to test the stuffing temperature when turkey is done. Insert it into the thickest part of the stuffing. The thermometer must register at least 165F (75C). Continue cooking the turkey until this temperature is reached.

Glaze & Stuffing Guide for Turkey

turkey (with giblets)	7 to 10 lbs.	5-1/2 to 6-1/2 lbs.
glaze	1/2 to 1 cup	1/2 to 3/4 cup
stuffing	4 cups	3 cups

Recommended Glazes: Herb-Butter Turkey-Basting Sauce, page 190, Tarragon-Butter Basting Sauce, page 194.

Tip

- The purpose of the initial cooking time at full power (HIGH) is to heat the turkey quickly. Figure the weight of your turkey without the giblets, which weigh about 12 ounces. If your turkey has a gravy packet or other similar item, the weight of this should be subtracted and not counted as part of the turkey weight. To figure the minutes at full power (HIGH) for your turkey, multiply the **corrected** weight of the turkey by 2. This gives you the number of minutes at full power (HIGH). In testing, it was found that minutes-per-pound was not accurate for the second cooking period at 50% (MEDIUM). Times given for cooking at 50% (MEDIUM) in the chart, opposite, are a guide; check turkey for doneness toward end of minimum cooking time. To be sure of getting an accurate temperature reading, insert the microwave meat thermometer in more than one section of the bird. For an additional test, cut between leg and thigh to be certain that juices run clear.

Turkey Breast in a Clay Pot

SERVINGS	4
INGREDIENTS	
chopped celery	1/2 cup
chopped onion	1/2 cup
chopped carrot	1/2 cup
dry white wine	1/2 cup
frozen whole turkey breast, thawed	1 (4-lb.) breast
fresh lemon balm, if available	2 sprigs
sage	2 sprigs fresh sage or 1/2 teaspoon dried rubbed sage
thyme	2 sprigs fresh thyme or 1/2 teaspoon dried leaf thyme
butter or margarine	1/4 cup
Kitchen Bouquet	1/4 teaspoon
garlic powder	1/4 teaspoon
onion powder	1/4 teaspoon
CLAY POT	2-1/2-qt. unglazed clay pot with lid
BOWL (butter)	small bowl
TIME AT HIGH (butter)	45 seconds
TIME AT HIGH (turkey)	10 minutes
TIME AT 50%	45 to 50 minutes
STANDING TIME	5 minutes

Soak a 2-1/2-quart clay pot and its lid in cold water 20 minutes or according to manufacturer's directions. Line clay pot with parchment paper, if desired. In bottom of pot combine celery, onion and carrot. Add wine. Fold back rib portion of turkey breast Stuff with fresh lemon balm, sage and thyme. Fold rib portion back over ribs and tie with string. Place breast, skin side up, over vegetables in pot. Microwave butter or margarine in a small bowl at full power (HIGH) 45 seconds or until melted. Stir in Kitchen Bouquet, garlic powder and onion powder. Brush butter or margarine mixture over turkey breast. Place lid on clay pot. Microwave at full power (HIGH) 10 minutes. Give pot a half turn. Microwave at 50% (MEDIUM) 45 to 50 minutes or until a microwave meat thermometer inserted in thickest part of breast registers 185F (85C). Brush again with butter or margarine mixture. Cover tightly with foil and let stand 5 minutes. Serve pan juices and vegetables with turkey.

Defrosting: To defrost turkey breast, see page 165.

How to Make Turkey Breast in a Clay Pot

Stuff the rib-cage cavity of the turkey breast with fresh sage, lemon balm and thyme. If you don't have fresh herbs, substitute dried ones. Tie the cavity shut with string.

Soak the clay pot in water. Add chopped celery, carrot and onion to the bottom of the pot. Pour in a little wine and place the breast, skin side up, over the vegetables in pot. Brush the breast with seasoned butter.

Basic Roast Turkey Breast

SERVINGS	6 to 8	3 or 4

INGREDIENTS
basting sauce, see
  pages 190 to 194
frozen whole turkey
  breast, thawed
	1/2 cup
	
	6 to 7-lb. breast
		1/4 cup
		
		3-1/2- to 4-lb. breast

BAKING DISH	12" x 7" baking dish with microwave rack	12" x 7" baking dish with microwave rack
TIME AT HIGH	16 to 18 minutes	9 to 11 minutes
TIME AT 50%	60 to 65 minutes	42 to 45 minutes
STANDING TIME	3 to 5 minutes	3 to 5 minutes

Prepare basting sauce of your choice. Tie wing portions to body if they are still attached to breast. Tie back section together, if necessary. Skewer neck skin to back with wooden picks. Brush breast with basting sauce. Place breast, skin side down, on a microwave rack in a 12" x 7" baking dish. Cover with a tent of greased waxed paper. Microwave at full power (HIGH) for time in chart above. Give dish a half turn. Brush again with basting sauce. Shield top of breast and wing edges with small pieces of foil, if they are browning faster than the rest of the bird. Secure foil with wooden picks, if necessary. Cover with tent of waxed paper. Microwave at 50% (MEDIUM) for time in chart above or until juices run clear when turkey is pierced with a fork. Halfway through cooking time at 50%, turn skin side up, brush with basting sauce and give dish a half turn. When done, a microwave meat thermometer should register 185F (85C) when inserted into thickest part of breast. Brush again with basting sauce. Cover tightly with foil and let stand 3 to 5 minutes.

Basic Roast Turkey Wings

SERVINGS	2
INGREDIENTS	
basting sauce, see pages 190 to 194	1/4 cup
frozen turkey wings, thawed	2 (1-1/4-lb.) wings
BAKING DISH	12" x 7" baking dish with microwave rack
TIME AT HIGH	5 minutes
TIME AT 50%	35 to 37 minutes
STANDING TIME	5 minutes

Prepare basting sauce of your choice. Make a small slit in skin of each wing for release of steam. Brush with basting sauce. Place wings, skin side down, on a microwave rack in a 12" x 7" baking dish. Cover with a tent of greased waxed paper. Microwave at full power (HIGH) 5 minutes. Turn skin side up. Give dish a half turn. Shield wing tips with small pieces of foil, if they are browning faster than the rest of the wings. Secure foil with wooden picks, if necessary. Cover with tent of waxed paper. Microwave at 50% (MEDIUM) 35 to 37 minutes or until juices run clear when turkey is pierced with a fork. When done, a microwave meat thermometer should register 185F (85C) when inserted into thickest part. Brush with basting sauce. Cover tightly with foil and let stand 5 minutes.

Basic Roast Turkey Drumsticks

SERVINGS	2	1
INGREDIENTS		
basting sauce, see pages 190 to 194	1/2 cup	1/4 cup
frozen turkey drumsticks, thawed	2 (1-lb. 6-oz.) drumsticks	1 (1-lb. 6-oz.) drumstick
BAKING DISH	12" x 7" baking dish with microwave rack	12" x 7" baking dish with microwave rack
TIME AT HIGH	6 minutes	2-1/2 minutes
TIME AT 50%	45 to 50 minutes	26 to 28 minutes
STANDING TIME	5 minutes	5 minutes

Prepare basting sauce of your choice. Make 2 small slits in skin on each drumstick for release of steam. Brush each drumstick with basting sauce. Place on a microwave rack in a 12" x 7" baking dish. Cover with a tent of greased waxed paper. Microwave at full power (HIGH) for time in chart above. Turn drumsticks over. Brush with basting sauce. Give dish a half turn. Shield edges and ends of drumsticks with small pieces of foil, if these areas are browning faster than the rest of the drumsticks. Secure foil with wooden picks, if necessary. Cover with tent of waxed paper. Microwave at 50% (MEDIUM) for time in chart above or until juices run clear when turkey is pierced with a fork. Turn drumsticks over and give dish a half turn halfway through cooking time at 50%. When done, a microwave meat thermometer should register 185F (85C) when inserted into thickest part. Brush with more basting sauce. Cover tightly with foil and let stand 5 minutes.

How to Make Basic Roast Turkey Hindquarter

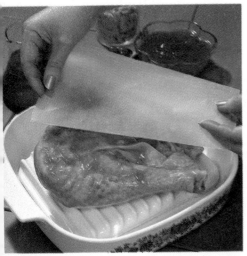 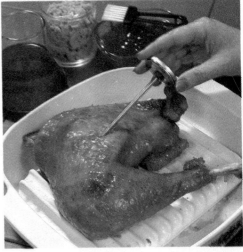

Make a small slit in turkey skin and place meaty side down on microwave rack. Brush with Ruby Cranberry Basting Sauce or other glaze, then tent loosely with greased waxed paper.	To test for doneness, insert a microwave meat thermometer at an angle into the thickest part of the thigh. When turkey is done, the thermometer should register 185F (85C).

Basic Roast Turkey Hindquarter

SERVINGS	2
INGREDIENTS	
basting sauce, see pages 190 to 194	1/4 cup
frozen turkey hindquarter, thawed	1 (2-lb.) hindquarter
BAKING DISH	12" x 7" baking dish with microwave rack
TIME AT HIGH	4-1/2 minutes
TIME AT 50%	28 to 30 minutes
STANDING TIME	5 minutes

Prepare basting sauce of your choice. Make a small slit in skin for release of steam. Brush with basting sauce. Place turkey, skin side down, on a microwave rack in a 12" x 7" baking dish. Cover with a tent of greased waxed paper. Microwave at full power (HIGH) 4-1/2 minutes. Turn skin side up. Give dish a half turn. Shield edges with small pieces of foil if these areas are browning faster than the rest of the hindquarter. Secure with wooden picks, if necessary. Cover with tent of waxed paper. Microwave at 50% (MEDIUM) 28 to 30 minutes or until juices run clear when turkey is pierced with a fork. When done, a microwave meat thermometer should register 185F (85C) when inserted into thickest part. Brush with more basting sauce. Cover tightly with foil and let stand 5 minutes.

Defrosting: To defrost turkey wings, drumsticks and hindquarters, see pages 164 and 165.

Reheating Refrigerated Stuffing

SERVINGS	2	1
INGREDIENTS cooked stuffing	1 cup	1/2 cup
BAKING DISH	1-1/2-cup casserole	1-1/2-cup casserole
TIME AT 70%	4 to 4-1/2 minutes	2 to 2-1/2 minutes
STANDING TIME	1 minute	1 minute

To chill: Spoon cooled stuffing into a 1-1/2-cup casserole. Cover with plastic wrap or lid; refrigerate.

To reheat: Vent plastic wrap, if using. Microwave, covered, at 70% (MEDIUM HIGH) for time in chart above or until heated through, stirring once. Let stand, covered, 1 minute.

Doneness Test: Reheated stuffing is ready to serve when thermometer inserted in center of mixture registers 175F to 180F (80C).

Reheating Sliced Turkey & Gravy

SERVINGS	2	1
INGREDIENTS turkey slices gravy	4 (1-oz.) slices 1 cup	2 (1-oz.) slices 1/2 cup
BAKING DISH	2-cup casserole	1-1/2-cup casserole
TIME AT 70%	6 to 7 minutes	4 to 5 minutes

To chill: Place turkey slices in a casserole, see size in chart above. Spoon gravy over turkey, coating slices well. Cover tightly with lid or plastic wrap; refrigerate.

To reheat: Vent plastic wrap, if using. Microwave, covered, at 70% (MEDIUM HIGH) for time in chart above or until heated through. Stir before serving.

Reheating Turkey Gravy

To chill: Spoon 1 cup cooled gravy into a 2-cup glass measuring cup. Cover with plastic wrap; refrigerate.

To reheat: Vent plastic wrap. Microwave at full power (HIGH) 4 to 4-1/2 minutes, or until bubbly, stirring once.

Seafood

Fish & Seafood

Use the microwave oven to produce delicious summer dishes without heating up your kitchen. Serve Ginger-Lime Salmon Steaks or Crabmeat Crepes for an elegant patio dinner.

Q. How is fish cooked in the microwave?

A. Because fish is already tender, most varieties cook very satisfactorily at full power (HIGH) in the microwave.

Q. What are the disadvantages of cooking fish in the microwave?

A. Shellfish becomes tough if overcooked in the microwave. Watch shellfish carefully and test for doneness before the end of the cooking time.

Q. Can fish be pan-fried in the microwave?

A. Breaded fish can be cooked quickly and successfully in the microwave with special microwave browning skillets. The opposite is true for batter-coated fish which tends to get soggy when cooked in the browning skillet. Frozen fish portions and fish sticks that are breaded give particularly good results.

Q. Which fish or seafood dishes do not cook satisfactorily in the microwave?

A. Fish cannot be deep-fried in the microwave. Whole live lobsters require a large kettle of boiling water and this takes too long in the microwave. And, a kettle holding enough water for more than one or two lobsters is too large for this appliance.

Q. How do you know when fish is done?

A. Using the tines of a fork, gently lift up the flesh in the center of the fish. The flesh should be beginning to flake. It will continue cooking during the standing time. Shellfish usually turns from translucent in its raw state to opaque when cooked.

Q. Can fish be reheated in the microwave?

A. This is not recommended unless the fish is heated in a sauce. Fish overcooks quickly. The reheating time is often equal to the original cooking time and the fish will become tough from overcooking.

Q. How do you adapt conventional fish recipes to the microwave?

A. There are tips throughout the chapter for converting many kinds of conventional fish recipes for the microwave. These include tips for whole fish and tuna casseroles.

Q. How do you defrost fish in the microwave?

A. Fish is easy to defrost in the microwave. Start with a 30% (MEDIUM LOW) defrosting time, then a 10% (LOW) defrosting time, plus standing time in cold water. See the complete directions in this chapter.

Q. Are any special utensils needed to cook fish in the microwave?

A. If you often cook whole fish, a large microwave fish-baking dish can be very useful. It's difficult to find other baking dishes big enough to accommodate a large whole fish.

How to Defrost Block Fish Fillets

Place the block of frozen fillets on a microwave rack in a baking dish. After defrosting at 30% (MEDIUM LOW) and the first time at 10% (LOW), gently separate fillets with a fork.

After defrosting the fish for the second time at 10% (LOW), plunge it into a bowl of cold water and let stand for the same number of minutes as the second time at 10% (LOW) to finish thawing.

Defrosting Block Fish Fillets

SERVINGS	6 to 8	3 or 4
INGREDIENTS frozen packaged block fish fillets	2 (1-lb.) pkgs.	1 (1-lb.) pkg.
BAKING DISH	12" x 7" baking dish with microwave rack	12" x 7" baking dish with microwave rack
TIME AT 30%	10 minutes	5 minutes
TIME AT 10%	3 minutes	3 minutes
TIME AT 10% (after removing any thawed fillets)	3 minutes	3 minutes
STANDING TIME IN COLD WATER	3 minutes	3 minutes

Remove frozen fish from box. Place fish on a microwave rack or inverted saucer in a 12" x 7" baking dish. Cover with a tent of waxed paper. Microwave at 30% (MEDIUM LOW) for time in chart above. Give dish a half turn and turn fish over. Cover with waxed-paper tent. Microwave at 10% (LOW) 3 minutes. Gently separate any defrosted fillets from frozen block and set aside. These fillets may still be frosty. Turn remaining block of fillets over. Give dish a half turn. Cover with waxed-paper tent. Microwave frozen fish at 10% (LOW) 3 minutes. Immediately plunge all fish into cold water. Let stand in water 3 minutes. Drain well. Fish should be cool to the touch but completely defrosted after standing time in cold water. To check, insert a metal skewer into thickest part of fish. If skewer can be inserted easily, begin cooking. If skewer cannot be inserted easily, repeat second defrosting time at 10% (LOW) and standing time in cold water. Drain well. Fish must be completely defrosted before cooking.

Defrosting Individually Frozen Fish Fillets

SERVINGS	6 to 8	4 or 5
INGREDIENTS individually frozen fish fillets	10 (3-oz.) fillets	6 (3-oz.) fillets
BAKING DISH	12-inch square microwave baker with microwave rack	12" x 7" baking dish with microwave rack
TIME AT 30%	8 minutes	4 minutes
TIME AT 10%	8 minutes	4 minutes
STANDING TIME IN COLD WATER	4 minutes	2 minutes

Place fish, Styrofoam tray side down, on a microwave rack or inverted saucer in a baking dish, see size in chart. Microwave at 30% (MEDIUM LOW) for time in chart, removing packaging as soon as possible and covering with tent of waxed paper. Separate fillets as soon as possible. After defrosting time at 30% (MEDIUM LOW), shield any warm spots with small pieces of foil. Give dish a half turn; turn fish over. Remove any fish that is nearly defrosted; set aside. Cover still-frozen fish with waxed-paper tent. Microwave at 10% (LOW) for time in chart. Immediately plunge all fish into cold water and let stand in water for time in chart. Drain well. Fish should be cool to the touch but completely defrosted after standing time in cold water. To check, insert a metal skewer into thickest part of fish. If skewer can be inserted easily, begin cooking. If skewer cannot be inserted easily, repeat the defrosting at 10% (LOW) and standing in cold water. Drain well. Fish must be completely defrosted before cooking.

Defrosting Fish Steaks

SERVINGS	4	2
INGREDIENTS frozen fish steaks	4 (6-oz.) steaks	2 (6-oz.) steaks
BAKING DISH	12" x 7" baking dish with microwave rack	8-inch square baking dish with microwave rack
TIME AT 30%	8 minutes	4 minutes
TIME AT 10%	4 minutes	2 minutes
STANDING TIME IN COLD WATER	4 minutes	2 minutes

See directions for Defrosting Individually Frozen Fish Fillets, above.

Tips

- Fish structure is very delicate. Be gentle when separating fillets from the partially defrosted block of fish.
- Fish will still seem partially frozen when it is plunged into cold water for the standing time. Standing in cold water will finish defrosting the fish without cooking it.
- Make sure whole fish is completely defrosted before cooking. Check for ice crystals in the cavities. The last part to thaw is usually the thickest portion along the backbone.

Defrosting Whole Small Fish

SERVINGS	4	2
INGREDIENTS frozen rainbow trout	4 (10-oz.) trout	2 (10-oz.) trout
BAKING DISH	12-inch square microwave baker with microwave rack	12" x 7" baking dish with microwave rack
TIME AT 30% **(3 minutes per lb.)**	7-1/2 minutes	3-3/4 minutes
TIME AT 10% **(3 minutes per lb.)**	7-1/2 minutes	3-3/4 minutes
STANDING TIME IN **COLD WATER** **(6 minutes per lb.)**	15 minutes	7-1/2 minutes

Remove packaging from fish. Place fish on a microwave rack or inverted saucer in a baking dish, see size in chart. Cover with a tent of waxed paper. Microwave at 30% (MEDIUM LOW) for time in chart. During time at 30% (MEDIUM LOW), shield any warm spots with small pieces of foil. After defrosting at 30% (MEDIUM LOW), turn fish over and shield any warm spots with foil. Cover with waxed-paper tent. Microwave at 10% (LOW) for time in chart. Immediately plunge fish into cold water and let stand in water for time in chart. Drain well. Fish should be cool to the touch but completely defrosted after standing time in cold water. To check, insert a metal skewer into thickest part of fish. If skewer can be inserted easily, begin cooking. If skewer cannot be inserted easily, repeat defrosting time at 10% (LOW) and standing time in cold water. Drain well. Fish must be completely defrosted before cooking.

Defrosting Whole Large Fish

SERVINGS	6	4	2
INGREDIENTS frozen whole fish	1 (3-lb.) fish	1 (2-lb.) fish	1 (1-lb.) fish
BAKING DISH	12-inch square microwave baker with microwave rack	12-inch square microwave baker with microwave rack	12" x 7" baking dish with microwave rack
TIME AT 30% **(4 minutes per lb.)**	12 minutes	8 minutes	4 minutes
TIME AT 10% **(6 minutes per lb.)**	18 minutes	12 minutes	6 minutes
STANDING TIME IN **COLD WATER** **(6 minutes per lb.)**	18 minutes	12 minutes	6 minutes

See directions for Defrosting Whole Small Fish, above.

Tips

- Fish that is properly wrapped for freezing will keep 6 to 9 months in the freezer.
- The thin parts of the fish and outside edges are the most likely areas to feel warm to the touch. Shield them with small pieces of foil.

Defrosting Scallops

SERVINGS	4 or 5	2
INGREDIENTS individually frozen scallops	2 lbs.	1 lb.
BAKING DISH	12-inch square microwave baker with microwave rack	12" x 7" baking dish with microwave rack
TIME AT 30%	8 minutes	5 minutes
TIME AT 10%	4 minutes	2 minutes
STANDING TIME IN COLD WATER	4 minutes	2 minutes

Remove packaging from scallops. Place scallops on a microwave rack or inverted saucer in a baking dish, see size in chart above. Cover with a tent of waxed paper. Microwave at 30% (MEDIUM LOW) for time in chart above, rearranging once. Separate scallops as soon as possible. After defrosting at 30% (MEDIUM LOW), rearrange scallops. Remove any scallops that are nearly defrosted; set aside. Cover still-frozen scallops with waxed-paper tent. Microwave at 10% (LOW) for time in chart above. Immediately plunge all scallops into cold water and let stand in water for the same number of minutes as they defrosted at 10% (LOW). Drain well. Scallops should be cool to the touch but completely defrosted after standing time in cold water. To check, insert a metal skewer into several scallops. If skewer can be inserted easily, begin cooking. If skewer cannot be inserted easily, repeat defrosting time at 10% (LOW) and standing time in cold water. Drain well. Scallops must be completely defrosted before cooking.

Defrosting Shucked Oysters

YIELD	1 quart	1 pint
INGREDIENTS frozen shucked oysters in oyster liquor	1 qt. (2 lbs.)	1 pt. (1 lb.)
BAKING DISH	deep 2-qt. casserole	deep 1-qt. casserole
TIME AT 30%	15 minutes	8 minutes
TIME AT 10%	8 minutes	6 minutes
STANDING TIME	8 minutes	6 minutes

Dip freezer container in hot water to loosen oysters. Place block of frozen oysters in a casserole, see size in chart above. Cover. Microwave at 30% (MEDIUM LOW) for time in chart above, breaking oysters apart two or three times with a large fork. Microwave, covered, at 10% (LOW) for time in chart above, stirring twice. Let stand, covered, same number of minutes as oysters defrosted at 10% (LOW) or until thawed. Oysters should be cool to the touch but completely defrosted after standing time. If not completely thawed, repeat defrosting time at 10% (LOW) and standing time. Oysters must be completely defrosted before cooking.

How to Defrost Lobster Tails

After microwaving the frozen lobster tails at 30% (MEDIUM LOW), check to see if there are any warm spots. Shield any warm spots, such as the thin tail fins, with small pieces of foil.

Microwave the lobster tails at 10% (LOW) and then plunge into a bowl of cold water to stand. Insert a skewer into the thickest part to check that the tails are thawed.

Defrosting Lobster Tails

SERVINGS	2	1
INGREDIENTS frozen lobster tails	2 (8-oz.) tails	1 (8-oz.) tail
BAKING DISH	8-inch square baking dish with microwave rack	8-inch square baking dish with microwave rack
TIME AT 30% **(8 minutes per lb.)**	8 minutes	4 minutes
TIME AT 10% **(4 minutes per lb.)**	4 minutes	2 minutes
STANDING TIME IN **COLD WATER** **(4 minutes per lb.)**	4 minutes	2 minutes

Remove packaging from frozen lobster tails. Place, hard shell side down, on a micro-wave rack or inverted saucer in an 8-inch square baking dish. Cover loosely with a tent of waxed paper. Microwave at 30% (MEDIUM LOW) for time in chart above. Turn lob-ster hard shell side up and give dish a half turn. Shield any warm spots with small pieces of foil. Cover with waxed-paper tent. Microwave at 10% (LOW) for time in chart above. Immediately plunge lobster tails into cold water and let stand in water for same number of minutes as they defrosted at 10% (LOW). Drain. Lobster should be cool to the touch but completely defrosted after standing time in cold water. To check, insert a metal skewer into thickest part of lobster tail. If skewer can be inserted easily, begin cooking. If skewer cannot be inserted easily, repeat defrosting time at 10% (LOW) and stand in cold water. Drain. Lobster must be completely defrosted before cooking.

Basic Fish Fillets Amandine

SERVINGS	4	2	1
INGREDIENTS			
butter or margarine	1/4 cup	2 tablespoons	1 tablespoon
dried leaf thyme	dash	dash	dash
onion salt	dash	dash	dash
fish fillets, 1/4 inch thick	8 (2-oz.) fillets	4 (2-oz.) fillets	2 (2-oz.) fillets
snipped parsley	about 2 tablespoons	about 1 tablespoon	about 2 teaspoons
paprika	to taste	to taste	to taste
toasted slivered almonds	1/4 cup	2 tablespoons	1 tablespoon
parsley sprigs	to garnish	to garnish	to garnish
BOWL	1-qt. bowl	2-cup bowl	6-oz. custard cup
BAKING DISH	12" x 7" baking dish	8-inch square baking dish	round, 8-inch baking dish
TIME AT 10%	1 minute	30 seconds	20 seconds
TIME AT HIGH	5 to 6 minutes	3-1/2 to 4 minutes	2 to 2-1/2 minutes

Place butter or margarine in a bowl, see size in chart above. Microwave at 10% (LOW) for time in chart above or until softened. Stir in thyme and onion salt; mix well. Place fish fillets flat in a baking dish, see size in chart above. Spread butter or margarine mixture on fillets. Sprinkle with snipped parsley and paprika. Cover with vented plastic wrap. Microwave at full power (HIGH) for time in chart above or until center of fish is beginning to flake when tested with a fork. Give dish a half turn once during cooking time. Sprinkle with toasted almonds and garnish with parsley before serving.

Defrosting: To defrost fish fillets, see pages 217 and 218.

Adapting Fish Fillet and Steak Recipes for Microwave Oven

- Use directions for Basic Fish Fillets Amandine, above, and Basic Ginger-Lime Salmon Steaks, page 225, as a guideline for cooking times.

- Butter-baked fish dishes are the most successful in the microwave oven. Fish cooked in a sauce tends to produce juices that dilute the sauce.

- If you are using a recipe for fish baked in sauce, increase the microwave cooking time in the guideline recipe a minute or so. Remove cooked fish to a warm platter and cover with foil. Thicken sauce remaining in baking dish with 1 tablespoon cornstarch mixed with 1 tablespoon cold water for each cup of sauce. Microwave at full power (HIGH) until mixture thickens and bubbles, whisking three times.

- Fish steaks and fillets poach rapidly in the microwave oven. Fish finishes cooking during the standing time. After the minimum cooking time, check the thickest part of the fish with a fork to see if it is beginning to flake. If fish overcooks, it will be tough. Use the directions for Basic Poached Fish Fillets, page 228, and Basic Poached Fish Steaks, page 229, as guidelines for amount of liquid, baking dish size and cooking times.

How to Make Basic Fish Fillets Amandine

Skin fillets to prevent them from curling during cooking. Lay each fillet, skin side down, on a board. Holding one end of the skin firmly against the board, run the blade of a sharp knife at an angle between the fillet and the skin.

Turn the fillets over so the former skin side is up. Often some of the skin membrane will remain. Using a sharp knife, lightly score the fillet with diagonal cuts. This helps the fillet stay flat during cooking.

Spread the fillets with herb butter, then use scissors to snip parsley over the top. Sprinkle with paprika.

After microwaving, sprinkle the fillets with toasted slivered almonds and use sprigs of parsley for garnish.

How to Make Easy Herbed-Halibut Steaks

Arrange halibut steaks with thickest portions toward outside of baking dish, then spread generously with cheese mixture.

Serve the herbed-halibut steaks with buttered green beans, canned spiced peaches and hot blueberry muffins.

Slaw Fillet Roll-Ups

SERVINGS	4	2
INGREDIENTS		
dairy sour cream	1/2 cup	1/4 cup
prepared mustard	1 teaspoon	1/2 teaspoon
prepared horseradish	1/2 teaspoon	1/4 teaspoon
celery seed	1/4 teaspoon	1/8 teaspoon
fish fillets, 1/4 inch thick	4 (4-oz.) fillets	2 (4-oz.) fillets
deli coleslaw, well-drained	2/3 cup	1/3 cup
CUSTARD CUP	6-oz. custard cup	6-oz. custard cup
BAKING DISH	12" x 7" baking dish with microwave rack	9-inch pie plate with microwave rack
TIME AT HIGH	5-1/2 to 6-1/2 minutes	4-1/2 to 5 minutes
STANDING TIME	5 minutes	5 minutes
TIME AT 50%	30 seconds	20 seconds

In a 6-ounce custard cup, combine sour cream, mustard, horseradish and celery seed. Pat fillets dry with paper towels. Spread about 1 teaspoon sour-cream mixture on 1 side of each fillet. Set aside remaining sour cream mixture. Top each fillet with about 2 tablespoons drained coleslaw. Spread evenly on fillets. Roll up, jelly-roll fashion, starting at narrow end. Secure with wooden picks. Place fillet rolls on a microwave rack in a baking dish, see size in chart above. Cover with vented plastic wrap. Microwave at full power (HIGH) for time in chart above or until center of fish is beginning to flake when tested with a fork. Give dish a half turn once during cooking time. Let stand, covered, 5 minutes. Microwave remaining sour-cream mixture at 50% (MEDIUM) for time in chart above. Spoon over fillets. Garnish with paprika and watercress, if desired.

Easy Herbed-Halibut Steaks

SERVINGS	4	2	1
INGREDIENTS			
semi-soft natural cheese with garlic and herbs	1/2 (4-oz.) carton	1/4 (4-oz.) carton	2 tablespoons
bottled tartar sauce	1/4 cup	2 tablespoons	1 tablespoon
halibut steaks, 3/4 inch thick	4 (6-oz.) steaks	2 (6-oz.) steaks	1 (6-oz.) steak
cucumber slices	12	6	3
shredded Cheddar cheese	1/2 cup (2 oz.)	1/4 cup (1 oz.)	2 tablespoons
snipped chives	1 tablespoon	2 teaspoons	1 teaspoon
BAKING DISH	12" x 7" baking dish	round, 8-inch baking dish	7-inch pie plate
TIME AT HIGH (fish)	7 to 8 minutes	4 to 5 minutes	3 to 4 minutes
TIME AT HIGH (Cheddar cheese)	2-1/2 minutes	1-1/2 minutes	1-1/4 minutes
STANDING TIME	5 minutes	4 minutes	3 minutes

In a small bowl, whisk together semi-soft cheese and tartar sauce. Arrange halibut steaks in a baking dish, see size in chart above, placing larger pieces and thicker portions toward outside of dish. Spread steaks with cheese mixture. Cover with vented plastic wrap. Microwave at full power (HIGH) for time in chart above or until center of fish is beginning to flake when tested with a fork. Give dish a half turn once during cooking time. Top steaks with cucumber slices. Sprinkle with Cheddar cheese and snipped chives. Microwave, uncovered, at full power (HIGH) for time in chart above or until cheese melts. Let stand, covered, for time in chart above.

Basic Ginger-Lime Salmon Steaks

SERVINGS	4	2	1
INGREDIENTS			
butter or margarine	1/2 cup	1/2 cup	1/2 cup
fresh gingerroot, pared, cut up	3" x 1-1/2" piece	3" x 1-1/2" piece	3" x 1-1/2" piece
salmon steaks, about 1 inch thick	4 (4- to 5-oz.) steaks	2 (4- to 5-oz.) steaks	1 (4- to 5-oz.) steak
lime slices	8	4	2
BAKING DISH	10" x 6" baking dish	round, 8-inch baking dish	7-inch pie plate
TIME AT HIGH	5-1/2 to 6-1/2 minutes	3 to 4 minutes	1-1/2 to 2-1/2 minutes
STANDING TIME	5 minutes	5 minutes	3 minutes

In a food processor fitted with a steel blade, process butter or margarine and gingerroot until smooth and creamy, scraping down sides of processor often. Place salmon steaks in a baking dish, see size in chart above, arranging thicker portions toward outside of dish. Spread each steak with about 1 tablespoon butter or margarine mixture. Top with lime slices. Cover with vented plastic wrap. Microwave at full power (HIGH) for time in chart above or until center of fish is beginning to flake when tested with a fork. Give dish a half turn once during cooking time. Let stand, covered, for time in chart above. Serve with lime wedges, if desired, and additional ginger-butter mixture. Cover and refrigerate any remaining ginger-butter mixture.

Halibut Steaks with Corn-Bread Topping

SERVINGS	4	2
INGREDIENTS		
bacon	4 slices	2 slices
bacon drippings	2 tablespoons	1 tablespoon
chopped green onion	1/2 cup	1/4 cup
crushed pineapple	1 (8-oz.) can	1/2 (8-oz.) can
reserved pineapple syrup	1/2 cup	1/4 cup
coarse corn-bread crumbs	2 cups	1 cup
fruited granola	2 cups	1 cup
dried leaf thyme	1/2 teaspoon	1/4 teaspoon
halibut steaks, 1 inch thick	4 (6-oz.) steaks	2 (6-oz.) steaks
pineapple slices, halved crosswise	2	1
BAKING DISH	12" x 7" baking dish with microwave rack	round, 8-inch baking dish with microwave rac
TIME AT HIGH (bacon)	3-1/2 to 4 minutes	1-1/2 to 2 minutes
TIME AT HIGH (onion)	4 minutes	2 minutes
TIME AT HIGH (fish)	10 to 11 minutes	5 to 6 minutes
TIME AT HIGH (pineapple ring)	2 minutes	1-1/2 minutes
STANDING TIME	5 minutes	5 minutes

Place bacon on a microwave rack in a baking dish, see size in chart above. Cover with white paper towels. Microwave at full power (HIGH) for time in chart above or until crisp. Drain bacon, reserving drippings in dish, see amount in chart above. Crumble bacon; set aside. Remove microwave rack from baking dish. Add green onion to reserved bacon drippings in dish. Microwave at full power (HIGH) for time in chart above or until onion is tender. Drain pineapple, reserving syrup, see amount in chart above. Stir corn-bread crumbs, granola, crushed pineapple, bacon and thyme into onion mixture. Add reserved pineapple syrup. Stir until mixture is moistened. Remove corn-bread mixture; set aside. Place halibut steaks in same baking dish, arranging thickest portions toward outside of dish. Top each steak with a mound of corn-bread mixture. Cover with vented plastic wrap. Microwave at full power (HIGH) for time in chart above or until center of fish is beginning to flake when tested with a fork. Give dish a half turn once during cooking time. Top each corn-bread mound with a half slice of pineapple. Microwave, uncovered, at full power (HIGH) for time in chart above or until heated through. Let stand, covered, 5 minutes.

Continental Fish Steaks in a Clay Pot

See page 242.

Defrosting: To defrost fish steaks, see page 218.

Basic Poaching Liquid for Fish

YIELD	large recipe (2-3/4 cups stock)	medium recipe (1-2/3 cups stock)	small recipe (2/3 cup stock)
INGREDIENTS			
water	2 cups	1 cup	1/2 cup
dry white wine	1 cup	1/2 cup	1/4 cup
chopped carrot	1/2 cup	1/4 cup	2 tablespoons
chopped celery	1/2 cup	1/4 cup	2 tablespoons
chopped onion	1/2 cup	1/4 cup	2 tablespoons
parsley	6 sprigs	3 sprigs	1 sprig
lemon slices	4	2	1
bay leaf	1 large	1 small	1/2 small
peppercorns	16	8	4
salt	1/2 teaspoon	1/4 teaspoon	1/8 teaspoon
BAKING DISH	deep 3- or 4-qt. casserole	deep 1- or 2-qt. casserole	deep 1-qt. casserole
TIME AT HIGH	8 to 10 minutes	5 to 6 minutes	2-1/2 to 3 minutes

In a casserole, see size in chart above, combine water, wine, carrot, celery, onion, parsley, lemon, bay leaf, peppercorns and salt. Cover. Microwave at full power (HIGH) for time in chart above or until boiling. Use poaching liquid in recipes for Basic Poached Fish Fillets, below, Basic Poached Fish Steaks, opposite, Basic Poached Whole Fish, page 241, and Basic Poached Scallops, page 254.

Basic Poached Fish Fillets

SERVINGS	6 to 8	3 or 4	1 or 2
INGREDIENTS			
Basic Poaching Liquid for Fish, above	large recipe	medium recipe	small recipe
fish fillets, 1/4 to 1/2 inch thick	8 (4-oz.) fillets	4 (4-oz.) fillets	2 (4-oz.) fillets
TIME AT HIGH	3 to 4 minutes	2-1/2 to 3 minutes	1-1/4 to 1-1/2 minutes
STANDING TIME	5 minutes	5 minutes	5 minutes

Prepare Basic Poaching Liquid for Fish. Add fillets or steaks to hot poaching liquid. Cover. Microwave at full power (HIGH) for time in chart or until center of fish is beginning to flake when tested with a fork. Give dish a half turn once during cooking time. Let stand, covered, 5 minutes. Remove fish from liquid with a slotted spoon. Serve poached fish with Tangy Tartar Sauce, page 235, or Creamy Caper Sauce, page 232. Or use as cooked fish in recipes. Strain poaching liquid through cheesecloth to use as stock.

How to Make Basic Poached Fish Steaks

Bring water, wine, carrot, celery, onion, parsley, lemon and seasonings to a boil. Add fish steaks to the poaching liquid.

Fish steaks will finish cooking during the standing time. Strain the stock through cheesecloth to use in soups and sauces.

Basic Poached Fish Steaks

SERVINGS	6	3	2
INGREDIENTS Basic Poaching Liquid for Fish, opposite	large recipe	medium recipe	small recipe
fish steaks, 3/4 to 1 inch thick	6 (5-oz.) steaks	3 (5-oz.) steaks	2 (4- or 5-oz.) steaks
TIME AT HIGH	4 to 5 minutes	3 to 4 minutes	2 to 3 minutes
STANDING TIME	5 minutes	5 minutes	5 minutes

See directions for Basic Poached Fish Fillets, opposite.

Basic Poached Whole Fish

See page 241.

Luncheon Seashells

SERVINGS	4

INGREDIENTS	
butter or margarine	1 tablespoon
dry breadcrumbs	3 tablespoons
grated Parmesan cheese	3 tablespoons
snipped parsley	1 tablespoon
butter or margarine	3 tablespoons
all-purpose flour	3 tablespoons
dried leaf thyme	1/2 teaspoon
celery salt	1/4 teaspoon
pepper	1/8 teaspoon
strained fish stock or chicken broth	1 cup
half and half	1/2 cup
fish or scallops, poached, cubed	1 lb. (2-1/4 cups cubed)
artichoke hearts, drained, quartered	1 (14-oz.) can
sliced mushrooms, drained	1 (2-1/2-oz.) jar

BOWL	2-cup bowl

GLASS MEASURING CUP	1-qt.

BAKING SHELLS	4 shells (5-1/2 inch diameter, 3/4 inch deep)

TIME AT HIGH (butter for crumbs)	30 seconds
TIME AT HIGH (butter for sauce)	1 minute
TIME AT HIGH (flour added)	30 seconds
TIME AT HIGH (sauce)	3 to 4 minutes
TIME AT HIGH (shells)	6 to 8 minutes

Place 1 tablespoon butter or margarine in a 2-cup bowl. Microwave at full power (HIGH) 30 seconds or until melted. Stir in breadcrumbs, Parmesan cheese and parsley; set aside. Place 3 tablespoons butter or margarine in a 1-quart glass measuring cup. Microwave at full power (HIGH) 1 minute or until melted. Stir in flour, thyme, celery salt and pepper. Microwave at full power (HIGH) 30 seconds. Stir in fish stock or chicken broth and half and half. Microwave at full power (HIGH) 3 to 4 minutes or until thickened and bubbly, stirring three times. Mixture should be thick and smooth. Fold in fish or scallops, artichoke hearts and mushrooms. Spoon into 4 shells, see size in chart above. Microwave at full power (HIGH) 6 to 8 minutes or until heated through, rearranging shells once. Sprinkle with crumb mixture.

How to Make Salmon Divan en Papillote

Butter squares of parchment paper. Layer cooked broccoli spears, pimiento and poached salmon steaks in 1 corner of the buttered side of the paper. Spoon sauce over fish, then sprinkle with parsley and paprika.

Fold the other half of the paper square over fish, forming a triangle. Fold the edges together twice to seal all the way around the triangle. To make packets ahead of time, refrigerate, then microwave 2 minutes longer than times in recipe.

Salmon Divan en Papillote

SERVINGS	6	3
INGREDIENTS		
frozen broccoli spears, cooked, drained	2 (10-oz.) pkgs.	1 (10-oz.) pkg.
chopped pimiento	1/4 cup	2 tablespoons
salmon steaks, poached	6 (5-oz.) steaks	3 (5-oz.) steaks
condensed cream of onion soup	2 (10-3/4-oz.) cans	1 (10-3/4-oz.) can
bottled tartar sauce	2/3 cup	1/3 cup
all-purpose flour	2 tablespoons	1 tablespoon
dried dillweed	1/2 teaspoon	1/4 teaspoon
lemon juice	1 tablespoon	2 teaspoons
paprika, snipped parsley	to taste	to taste
BAKING PARCHMENT	6 (12-inch) squares	3 (12-inch) squares
BAKING DISH	12-inch square microwave baker	12" x 7" baking dish
TIME AT HIGH	12 to 14 minutes	6 to 8 minutes
STANDING TIME	2 minutes	2 minutes

Butter 1 side of each baking parchment square, see number in chart above. Place squares buttered side up. Place broccoli spears and pimiento in 1 corner of each square. Top with fish. In a medium bowl, whisk together soup, tartar sauce, flour, dillweed and lemon juice. Spoon over fish. Sprinkle with paprika and snipped parsley. Fold half of each parchment square over steaks to make a triangle; fold edges to seal. Place packets in a baking dish, see size in chart above. Microwave at full power (HIGH) for time in chart above or until fish is heated through, giving dish a half turn once. Let stand, covered, 2 minutes.

Hearty Fish Stew

SERVINGS	3 or 4	1 or 2
INGREDIENTS		
butter or margarine	2 tablespoons	1 tablespoon
cubed, pared rutabaga	1/2 cup	1/4 cup
chopped onion	1/4 cup	2 tablespoons
strained fish stock or chicken broth	1-1/2 cups	3/4 cup
tomatoes, peeled, quartered	2	1
corn on the cob, cut in 1-1/2-inch pieces	2 ears	1 ear
dried leaf basil	1/2 teaspoon	1/4 teaspoon
dried leaf oregano	1/2 teaspoon	1/4 teaspoon
salt	1/2 teaspoon	1/4 teaspoon
fish fillets or steaks, poached, chilled	1 lb.	8 oz.
zucchini, cut in 1-inch pieces	1 medium	1 small
BAKING DISH	deep 2-qt. casserole	deep 1-qt. casserole
TIME AT HIGH (butter mixture)	5 minutes	2-1/2 to 3 minutes
TIME AT HIGH (stock added)	18 to 20 minutes	10 to 12 minutes
TIME AT HIGH (fish added)	3 to 4 minutes	3 to 4 minutes

In a casserole, see size in chart above, combine butter or margarine, rutabaga and onion. Cover. Microwave at full power (HIGH) for time in chart above or until onion is tender. Stir in fish stock or chicken broth, tomatoes, corn, basil, oregano and salt. Cover. Microwave at full power (HIGH) for time in chart above or until vegetables are barely tender, stirring once. Break fish into chunks. Add fish to casserole with zucchini. Cover. Microwave at full power (HIGH) 3 to 4 minutes or until fish is heated through and zucchini is crisp-tender.

Creamy Caper Sauce

YIELD	1-1/3 cups	2/3 cup
INGREDIENTS		
mayonnaise or mayonnaise-style salad dressing	1/2 cup	1/4 cup
dairy sour cream	1/2 cup	1/4 cup
lemon juice	2 teaspoons	1 teaspoon
Dijon-style mustard	2 teaspoons	1 teaspoon
finely chopped celery	1/4 cup	2 tablespoons
drained capers	2 tablespoons	1 tablespoon
chopped pimiento	2 tablespoons	1 tablespoon
snipped parsley	2 tablespoons	1 tablespoon
snipped chives	1 tablespoon	2 teaspoons

In a medium bowl, combine mayonnaise or salad dressing, sour cream, lemon juice and mustard. Mix well. Fold in celery, capers, pimiento, parsley and chives. Cover and refrigerate until serving time. Serve with hot or cold fish dishes.

Cheesy Fish Stew

SERVINGS	8	4
INGREDIENTS		
butter or margarine	1/4 cup	2 tablespoons
chopped onion	1 cup	1/2 cup
chopped celery	1 cup	1/2 cup
sliced carrots, 1/4 inch thick	1 cup	1/2 cup
pared potatoes, cut in 1/4-inch cubes	3 cups	1-1/2 cups
chopped pimiento	1/2 cup	1/4 cup
strained fish stock or chicken broth	3 cups	1-1/2 cups
whipping cream	2 cups	1 cup
shredded process American cheese	4 cups (1 lb.)	2 cups (8 oz.)
fish, poached, chilled	2 lbs.	1 lb.
herb-seasoned croutons, sliced green onion	to garnish	to garnish
BAKING DISH	deep 4-qt. casserole	deep 2-qt. casserole
TIME AT HIGH (onion)	8 to 9 minutes	5 minutes
TIME AT HIGH (potato added)	23 to 25 minutes	15 minutes
TIME AT HIGH (fish added)	10 to 12 minutes	6 to 7 minutes

In a casserole, see size in chart above, combine butter or margarine, onion, celery and carrots. Cover. Microwave at full power (HIGH) for time in chart above or until onion and celery are tender. Stir in potato, pimiento and fish stock or chicken broth. Cover. Microwave at full power (HIGH) for time in chart above or until potato is tender, stirring once. Stir in cream and cheese. Break fish into chunks and add to casserole. Cover. Microwave at full power (HIGH) for time in chart above or until heated through, stirring twice. Top each serving with croutons and sliced green onion.

Reheating Cheesy Fish Stew

To chill: Pour 1 cup cooled Cheesy Fish Stew into each of 1 or 2 serving bowls. Cover tightly with plastic wrap and refrigerate.

To serve: Vent plastic wrap. Microwave at full power (HIGH) 4-1/2 to 5 minutes for bowls or 2-1/2 to 3 minutes for 1 bowl, or until heated through, stirring twice.

Basic Pan-Fried Fish Fillets

SERVINGS	3 or 4	1 or 2
INGREDIENTS		
milk	1/4 cup	2 tablespoons
yellow cornmeal	1/4 cup	2 tablespoons
packaged biscuit mix	1/4 cup	2 tablespoons
all-purpose flour	1/4 cup	2 tablespoons
sesame seeds	1 tablespoon	2 teaspoons
paprika	1/2 teaspoon	1/4 teaspoon
celery salt	1/2 teaspoon	1/4 teaspoon
onion powder	1/8 teaspoon	1/8 teaspoon
fish fillets, 1/4 to 1/2 inch thick	1 lb.	8 oz.
vegetable oil	1/4 cup	2 tablespoons
BROWNING SKILLET	10-inch microwave browning skillet	10-inch microwave browning skillet
TIME AT HIGH (preheat skillet)	6 minutes	6 minutes
TIME AT HIGH (first side)	1-1/2 minutes	1-1/2 minutes
TIME AT HIGH (second side)	1-1/2 to 2 minutes	1-1/2 minutes

Pour milk into a pie plate. In another pie plate, mix together cornmeal, biscuit mix, flour, sesame seeds, paprika, celery salt and onion powder. Dip fish fillets in milk to moisten both sides; shake off excess milk. Dip in cornmeal mixture, coating both sides. Place breaded fish on a rack; set aside. Preheat a 10-inch browning skillet, uncovered, at microwave full power (HIGH) 6 minutes. Add oil to skillet. Using hot pads, tilt skillet so entire surface is coated with oil. Quickly add fish. If fillets have skin, place skin side up. Microwave on first side at full power (HIGH) 1-1/2 minutes. Turn fish over and give dish a half turn. Microwave at full power (HIGH) for time in chart above or until browned and center of fish is beginning to flake when tested with a fork.

Variation

Pan-Fried Filleted Trout: Tie whole trout together with string. Use milk and breading mixture as above. Preheat browning skillet 6 minutes. Add 1/4 cup oil as above. Microwave 2 (8-ounce) trout at full power (HIGH) 2 minutes. Turn trout over. Microwave at full power (HIGH) 2 minutes or until center of fish is beginning to flake when tested with a fork.

Tangy Tartar Sauce

YIELD	1-1/2 cups	3/4 cup	1/3 cup
INGREDIENTS			
plain yogurt	1/2 cup	1/4 cup	2 tablespoons
mayonnaise or mayonnaise-style salad dressing	1/2 cup	1/4 cup	2 tablespoons
chopped dill pickle	1/2 cup	1/4 cup	2 tablespoons
sliced pimiento-stuffed green olives	1/2 cup	1/4 cup	2 tablespoons
onion powder	1/4 teaspoon	1/8 teaspoon	dash
freshly ground pepper	1/4 teaspoon	1/8 teaspoon	dash

In a medium bowl, combine all ingredients. Mix well. Cover and refrigerate until serving time. Serve with hot or cold fish dishes.

Basic Frozen Breaded Fish Fillets

SERVINGS	4	2	1
INGREDIENTS vegetable oil frozen breaded fish fillets	1 tablespoon 4 (3-oz.) or 7 (2-oz.) fillets	1 tablespoon 2 (3-oz.) or 4 (2-oz.) fillets	2 teaspoons 1 (3-oz.) or 2 (2-oz.) fillets
BROWNING SKILLET	10-inch microwave browning skillet	10-inch microwave browning skillet	6-1/2-inch microwave browning skillet
TIME AT HIGH (preheat skillet)	5 minutes	3 minutes	45 seconds
TIME AT HIGH (first side)	1 minute	1-1/2 to 2 minutes	1-1/2 minutes
TIME AT HIGH (second side)	4-1/2 to 6 minutes	3 minutes	1-1/2 to 2 minutes

Preheat microwave browning skillet, see size in chart, uncovered, at microwave full power (HIGH) for time in chart. Add oil. Using hot pads, tilt skillet so entire surface is coated with oil. Quickly add fish. Microwave on first side at full power (HIGH) for time in chart. Turn fish over and give skillet a half turn. Microwave at full power (HIGH) for time in chart, or until fish is browned and center is beginning to flake when tested with a fork.

Basic Frozen Breaded Fish Sticks

SERVINGS	4 to 6	2	1
INGREDIENTS vegetable oil frozen breaded fish sticks	1 tablespoon 18 (2/3-oz.) sticks	1 tablespoon 6 (2/3-oz.) sticks	2 teaspoons 3 (2/3-oz.) sticks
BROWNING SKILLET	10-inch microwave browning skillet	10-inch microwave browning skillet	6-1/2-inch microwave browning skillet
TIME AT HIGH (preheat skillet)	5 minutes	3 minutes	45 seconds
TIME AT HIGH (first side)	1 to 1-1/2 minutes	1-1/2 minutes	1-1/2 minutes
TIME AT HIGH (second side)	4 minutes	2 minutes	1 minute

See directions for Basic Frozen Breaded Fish Fillets, above.

Microwave Caution

Never attempt to deep-fat-fry fish in the microwave oven. The fat may reach dangerous temperatures and cause smoke and possibly fire.

How to Make Frozen Breaded Fish Fillets

Preheat a browning skillet in the microwave oven, then add oil and frozen breaded fish fillets. Turn fillets over partway through cooking time.

Serve the crisp fish fillets with cups of Tangy Tartar Sauce, page 235, fresh lemon wedges, red-cabbage slaw vinaigrette and cold beer.

Easy Crumb-Coated Baked Fish

SERVINGS	3 or 4	2	1
INGREDIENTS			
water			
fish fillets, about 1/4 inch thick	1 lb.	8 oz.	4 oz.
seasoned coating mix for fish	1 (2-oz.) pkg.	1/2 (2-oz.) pkg.	1/4 (2-oz.) pkg.
BAKING DISH	12-inch square microwave baker with microwave rack	12" x 7" baking dish with microwave rack	round, 8-inch baking dish with microwave rack
TIME AT HIGH	6 to 7 minutes	3-1/2 to 4 minutes	2 to 2-1/2 minutes

Pour water into a pie plate. Dip fish fillets in water to moisten both sides; shake off excess liquid. Shake fish in coating mix in package shaker bag according to package directions. Place fish, skin side down, on a microwave rack in a baking dish, see size in chart above. Arrange fish with thicker portion toward outside of dish. Microwave, uncovered, at full power (HIGH) for time in chart above or until center of fish is beginning to flake when tested with a fork. Give dish a half turn once during cooking time. Coating on fish will not be crisp.

Tips

- Select *breaded* frozen fish, not batter-coated frozen fish. Batter-coated fish becomes greasy and unappetizing when cooked in the microwave oven.

- Fish browns very quickly on the first side. It browns more slowly on the second side because the browning skillet has cooled somewhat. Watch carefully so the fish does not get too brown on the first side. Cooking a longer time on the second side allows the fish to cook through without overbrowning.

Basic Stuffed Whole Fish

SERVINGS	4	2
INGREDIENTS		
Spinach Stuffing, Rice Stuffing or Vegetable Stuffing, page 240	small recipe	small recipe
cleaned whole fish	1 (2-1/2- to 3-lb.) fish	1 (1-1/2-lb.) fish
butter or margarine	2 tablespoons	2 tablespoons
dried leaf basil	1/2 teaspoon	1/2 teaspoon
dried leaf oregano	1/2 teaspoon	1/2 teaspoon
lemon slices		
BAKING DISH	18" x 9" microwave fish baker with saucers	18" x 9" microwave fish baker with saucers
TIME AT HIGH (butter)	30 seconds	30 seconds
TIME AT HIGH (fish)	12 to 14 minutes	8 to 10 minutes
STANDING TIME	5 minutes	5 minutes

Prepare stuffing. Fill cavity of cleaned fish with stuffing. Tie fish cavity closed in several places with string so fish holds its shape. Place stuffed fish on a microwave rack or inverted saucers in baking dish, see size in chart. Place butter or margarine in a custard cup. Microwave at full power (HIGH) for time in chart or until melted. Stir in basil and oregano. Brush butter or margarine mixture over fish. Top with lemon slices. Cover with vented plastic wrap. Microwave at full power (HIGH) for time in chart, or until center of fish is beginning to flake when tested with a fork. Give dish a half turn once during cooking time. Let stand, covered, 5 minutes.

Basic Stuffed Whole Trout Photo on page 215.

SERVINGS	4	2
INGREDIENTS		
Spinach Stuffing, Rice Stuffing or Vegetable Stuffing, page 240	large recipe	small recipe
cleaned whole trout	4 (12-oz.) trout	2 (12-oz.) trout
parsley	1 bunch	1/2 bunch
butter or margarine	2 tablespoons	1 tablespoon
dried leaf basil	1/2 teaspoon	1/4 teaspoon
dried leaf oregano	1/2 teaspoon	1/4 teaspoon
lemon slices	8	4
BAKING DISH	12-inch square microwave baker with microwave rack	12" x 7" baking dish with microwave rack
TIME AT HIGH (butter)	30 seconds	20 seconds
TIME AT HIGH (fish)	12 to 14 minutes	7 to 8 minutes
STANDING TIME	5 minutes	5 minutes

Prepare, stuff and tie fish as for Basic Stuffed Whole Fish, above. Place parsley on a microwave rack in a baking dish, see size in chart above. Arrange fish along sides of baking dish with backs of fish toward outside of dish. Brush with butter or margarine mixture. Top with lemon slices. Microwave and let stand as for recipe above.

How to Make Basic Stuffed Whole Fish

Sprinkle fish cavity with garlic salt, then stuff with green-pepper rings, onion rings and tomato slices for Vegetable Stuffing, page 240.

Tie fish cavity closed in several places with string. This helps keep the Vegetable Stuffing from falling out.

Place stuffed fish on inverted saucers in a baking dish, then brush fish with herbed-butter mixture.

Cover with vented plastic wrap and microwave stuffed fish until the flesh is beginning to flake in the thickest portion when tested with a fork.

Rice Stuffing

YIELD	large recipe (2-1/2 cups)	small recipe (1-1/4 cups)
INGREDIENTS		
butter or margarine	1/4 cup	2 tablespoons
chopped onion	1/2 cup	1/4 cup
chopped celery	1/2 cup	1/4 cup
chopped carrot	1/2 cup	1/4 cup
cooked brown rice	1 cup	1/2 cup
chopped apple	1/2 cup	1/4 cup
toasted sunflower kernels	2 tablespoons	1 tablespoon
plain yogurt	1/2 cup	1/4 cup
BAKING DISH	deep 1-qt. casserole	deep 1-qt. casserole
TIME AT HIGH	5 to 6 minutes	4 to 5 minutes

In a 1-quart casserole, combine butter or margarine, onion, celery and carrot. Micro-wave at full power (HIGH) for time in chart above or until vegetables are tender. Stir in cooked rice, apple and sunflower kernels. Fold in yogurt. Use to stuff whole fish, see page 238.

Spinach Stuffing

YIELD	large recipe (3 cups)	small recipe (1-1/2 cups)
INGREDIENTS		
bulk pork sausage	8 oz.	4 oz.
chopped onion	1/4 cup	2 tablespoons
frozen chopped spinach, cooked, well-drained	1 (10-oz.) pkg.	1/2 (10-oz.) pkg.
herb-seasoned stuffing mix	3/4 cup	1/3 cup
grated Parmesan cheese	2 tablespoons	1 tablespoon
strained fish stock or chicken broth	about 1/4 cup	about 2 tablespoons
BAKING DISH	1-qt. casserole	1-qt. casserole
TIME AT HIGH	5 minutes	2-1/2 to 3 minutes

Crumble sausage into a 1-quart casserole. Add onion. Microwave at full power (HIGH) for time in chart above or until meat is brown and onion is tender, stirring once. Drain well. Stir in spinach, stuffing mix and Parmesan cheese. Stir in enough fish stock or chicken broth to moisten mixture. Use to stuff whole fish, see page 238.

Vegetable Stuffing

YIELD	large recipe	small recipe
INGREDIENTS		
garlic salt	to taste	to taste
green-pepper rings	4	2 or 3
onion rings	4	2 or 3
tomato slices	4	2 or 3

Sprinkle cavity of fish with garlic salt. Stuff cavity with green-pepper rings, onion rings and tomato slices. Use to stuff whole fish, see page 238.

Basic Poached Whole Fish

SERVINGS	4	3
INGREDIENTS		
Basic Poaching Liquid for Fish, page 228	large recipe	large recipe
cleaned whole fish (as purchased)	1 (2-3/4-lb.) fish	1 (2-lb.) fish
(head, tail removed)	2 lbs.	1-1/2 lbs.
TIME AT HIGH	10 to 11 minutes	8 to 9 minutes
STANDING TIME	5 minutes	5 minutes

Prepare Basic Poaching Liquid for Fish using a deep 4-quart casserole. Tie fish cavity closed with string so fish holds its shape. Add fish to hot poaching liquid. Cover. Microwave at full power (HIGH) for time in chart above or until center of fish is beginning to flake when tested with a fork. Turn fish over once during cooking time. Let stand, covered, 5 minutes. Remove fish from liquid with slotted spatulas. Serve with Tangy Tartar Sauce, page 235, or Creamy Caper Sauce, page 232. Strain poaching liquid through cheesecloth to use as stock.

Basic Poached Whole Trout

SERVINGS	2	1
INGREDIENTS		
Basic Poaching Liquid for Fish, page 228	medium recipe	medium recipe
cleaned whole trout	2 (12-oz.) trout	1 (12-oz.) trout
TIME AT HIGH	8 minutes	6 minutes
STANDING TIME	5 minutes	5 minutes

Prepare Basic Poaching Liquid for Fish using a deep 4-quart casserole. Wrap each trout in cheesecloth, leaving enough cheesecloth at each end of trout to use to lift trout in and out of the casserole. Lower trout into hot poaching liquid. Cover. Microwave at full power (HIGH) for time in chart above or until center of fish is beginning to flake when tested with a fork. Turn fish over once during cooking time. Let stand, covered, 5 minutes. Lift fish from poaching liquid using ends of cheesecloth. Remove cheesecloth. Serve with Tangy Tartar Sauce, page 235, or Creamy Caper Sauce, page 232. Strain poaching liquid through cheesecloth to use as stock.

Adapting Whole-Fish Recipes for Microwave Oven

- Use recipes for Basic Stuffed Whole Fish and Basic Stuffed Whole Trout, page 238, as a guideline for weights and cooking times for fish.

- Select a moist stuffing or a vegetable stuffing. Dry bread stuffings may become tough.

- For poached whole fish, follow the recipes for Basic Poached Whole Fish and Basic Poached Whole Trout, above, as a guideline for weights and cooking times for fish. Use your favorite poaching liquid in the same proportion of liquid to fish as above.

Defrosting: To defrost whole fish, see page 219.

Continental Whole Fish in a Clay Pot

SERVINGS	6
INGREDIENTS	
sorrel or spinach leaves	
cleaned whole fish	
(as purchased)	1 (3-1/2-lb.) fish
(head, tail removed)	3 lbs.
garlic salt	to taste
chopped fennel	1/4 cup
sliced leeks	1/4 cup
chopped radish	1/4 cup
butter or margarine	3 tablespoons
dry white wine	3 tablespoons
CLAY POT (unglazed)	4-qt. clay pot with microwave rack or inverted saucers
TIME AT HIGH (butter)	45 to 60 seconds
TIME AT HIGH (fish)	40 to 45 minutes

Soak clay pot and lid in cold water 20 minutes or according to manufacturer's directions. Soak sorrel or spinach leaves in hot water. Sprinkle cavity of fish with garlic salt. In a small bowl, combine fennel, leeks and radish. Stuff fennel mixture into cavity of fish. Tie fish cavity with string to hold in stuffing. Drain sorrel or spinach. Wind sorrel or spinach leaves around entire fish. Place fish on a microwave rack or inverted saucer in a 4-quart clay pot. Place butter or margarine in a custard cup. Microwave at full power (HIGH) 45 to 60 seconds or until melted. Stir in wine. Drizzle butter or margarine mixture over fish. Cover with clay-pot lid. Microwave at full power (HIGH) 40 to 45 minutes or until center of fish is beginning to flake when tested with a fork. Give clay pot a half turn once during cooking time. Serve fish with cooking juices.

Continental Fish Steaks in a Clay Pot

SERVINGS	4	2
INGREDIENTS		
fish steaks, 1 inch thick	4 (6-oz.) steaks	2 (6-oz.) steaks
garlic salt	to taste	to taste
chopped fennel	1/4 cup	2 tablespoons
sliced leeks	1/4 cup	2 tablespoons
chopped radish	1/4 cup	2 tablespoons
sorrel or spinach leaves		
butter or margarine	3 tablespoons	2 tablespoons
dry white wine	3 tablespoons	2 tablespoons
CLAY POT (unglazed)	4-qt. clay pot	2-1/2-qt. clay pot
TIME AT HIGH (butter)	45 seconds	30 seconds
TIME AT HIGH (fish)	18 to 20 minutes	14 to 15 minutes

Soak clay pot and lid, see size above, in cold water 20 minutes or according to manufacturer's directions. Sprinkle fish steaks with garlic salt. Combine fennel, leeks and radish in bottom of clay pot. Place fish steaks over vegetables. Cover steaks with sorrel or spinach leaves. Place butter or margarine in a custard cup. Microwave at full power (HIGH) for time in chart above or until melted. Stir in white wine. Drizzle butter or margarine mixture over fish. Cover with clay-pot lid. Microwave at full power (HIGH) for time in chart above or until center of fish is beginning to flake when tested with a fork. Give dish a half turn once during cooking. Serve fish with juices and vegetables.

How to Make Continental Whole Fish in a Clay Pot

Chop leeks, radishes and bulbous stalks on fennel, to use as a stuffing mixture. This two-level cutting board makes chopping easier.

Spoon the vegetable stuffing into the fish cavity. It may be necessary to remove the head and tail so the fish will fit the clay pot.

Tie the fish cavity closed with string. Soak sorrel or spinach leaves in hot water to make them pliable and easy to wind around the fish.

Place the stuffed fish on a microwave rack or inverted saucers in the clay pot, then drizzle with the wine and butter sauce.

Creamy Stuffed Manicotti

SERVINGS	4 to 6
INGREDIENTS	
Zucchini Sauce, below	
egg	1
cream-style cottage cheese	1 cup (8 oz.)
tuna, drained, flaked	1 (9-1/4-oz.) can
herb-seasoned stuffing mix	1/2 cup
chopped ripe olives	1/2 cup
grated Parmesan cheese	1/4 cup
snipped parsley	2 tablespoons
snipped chives	1 teaspoon
manicotti shells, cooked, drained	8
snipped chives	to garnish
BAKING DISH	12" x 7" baking dish
TIME AT 50%	20 to 25 minutes
STANDING TIME	5 minutes

Prepare Zucchini Sauce. Pour half the sauce into a 12" x 7" baking dish. Set aside remaining sauce. Beat egg in a medium bowl. Stir in cottage cheese, tuna, stuffing mix, olives, Parmesan cheese, parsley and first amount of chives. Mix well. Spoon about 1/2 cup cottage cheese mixture into each manicotti shell. Place manicotti on top of sauce in baking dish. Pour remaining sauce over manicotti, coating all pasta. Cover with vented plastic wrap. Microwave at 50% (MEDIUM) 20 to 25 minutes or until heated through, giving dish a half turn once. At the end of cooking time, stir sauce and spoon over manicotti shells. Let stand, covered, 5 minutes. Garnish with additional snipped chives.

Zucchini Sauce

YIELD	3-1/2 cups
INGREDIENTS	
butter or margarine	1/4 cup
coarsely chopped zucchini	2 cups
sliced green onion	1/2 cup
chopped pimiento	1/2 cup
all-purpose flour	1/4 cup
celery salt	1 teaspoon
pepper	1/4 teaspoon
milk	1-3/4 cups
BAKING DISH	deep 1-1/2-qt. casserole
TIME AT HIGH (vegetables)	3 to 5 minutes
TIME AT HIGH (flour added)	30 seconds
TIME AT HIGH (milk added)	5 to 7 minutes

In a 1-1/2-quart casserole, combine butter or margarine, zucchini and green onion. Microwave at full power (HIGH) 3 to 5 minutes or until barely tender. Stir in pimiento. Blend in flour, celery salt and pepper. Microwave at full power (HIGH) 30 seconds. Whisk in milk. Microwave at full power (HIGH) 5 to 7 minutes or until mixture thickens and bubbles, stirring three times. Mixture should be thick and smooth.

Saucy Tuna Pie

SERVINGS	5 or 6	2 or 3
INGREDIENTS		
butter or margarine	3 tablespoons	2 tablespoons
chopped onion	1/4 cup	3 tablespoons
all-purpose flour	3 tablespoons	2 tablespoons
celery salt	1/2 teaspoon	1/4 teaspoon
chicken broth	1/2 cup	1/3 cup
milk	1/2 cup	1/3 cup
dairy sour cream	1/2 cup	1/3 cup
tuna, drained, broken in chunks	1 (9-1/4-oz.) can	1 (6-1/2-oz.) can
frozen peas and carrots, cooked, drained	2 cups	1-1/2 cups
chopped pimiento	2 tablespoons	1 tablespoon
packaged instant mashed-potato buds, page 355	4 servings	2 servings
egg	1 whole	1 yolk
herb-seasoned stuffing mix	1 cup	1/2 cup
paprika	to taste	to taste
BAKING DISH	deep 2-qt. casserole	deep 1-1/2-qt. casserole
PLATE	9-inch pie plate	7-inch pie plate
TIME AT HIGH (onion)	3 to 3-1/2 minutes	2 minutes
TIME AT HIGH (flour added)	30 seconds	30 seconds
TIME AT HIGH (broth, milk)	2-1/2 to 3 minutes	2 to 2-1/4 minutes
TIME AT HIGH (tuna added)	5 to 6 minutes	3-1/2 to 4 minutes
TIME AT HIGH (pie)	4 to 5 minutes	2-1/2 to 3 minutes
STANDING TIME	5 minutes	5 minutes

In a casserole, see size in chart above, combine butter or margarine and onion. Microwave at full power (HIGH) for time in chart above or until tender. Stir in flour and celery salt. Microwave at full power (HIGH) 30 seconds. Whisk in broth and milk. Microwave at full power (HIGH) for time in chart above or until thickened and bubbly, stirring three times. Mixture should be thick and smooth. Place sour cream in a small bowl. Gradually stir half the hot sauce into sour cream. Stir mixture into remaining hot sauce in casserole. Fold in tuna, peas and carrots and pimiento. Cover and microwave at full power (HIGH) for time in chart above or until heated through, stirring once. Cover and set aside. Prepare instant mashed potatoes. Beat whole egg or egg yolk into potatoes. Fold in stuffing mix. Spoon potato mixture into a pie plate, see size in chart above. Using the back of a spoon, form potatoes into a crust, building up edge above rim of pie plate. Sprinkle with paprika. Spoon tuna mixture into crust. Cover with vented plastic wrap. Microwave at full power (HIGH) for time in chart above or until heated through, giving dish a half turn once. Let stand, covered, 5 minutes.

Adapting Tuna Casserole Recipes for Microwave Oven

- Choose casseroles with precooked ingredients. For example, if the recipe calls for rice or pasta, make sure it is cooked before it is added to the casserole.

- Use the directions for Hearty Tuna Casserole, page 248, as a guideline for amounts and cooking times.

- Watch and stir casseroles containing mayonnaise or sour cream—they tend to curdle. Microwave these casseroles only until heated through—do not overheat.

How to Make Saucy Tuna Pie

Stir half the hot white sauce into the sour cream. This warms the sour cream so it is less likely to curdle. Stir mixture into remaining sauce in casserole.

To make the pie filling, stir chunks of tuna, cooked peas and carrots and pimiento into the sour cream sauce. Cover and microwave the filling until heated through, stirring once.

Prepare instant mashed potatoes, then beat in a whole egg or egg yolk and fold in herb-seasoned stuffing. Use the back of a spoon to form the potato mixture into a crust in a pie plate.

Spoon the warm tuna filling into the potato-stuffing crust. Cover and microwave the pie until heated through. Garnish with parsley sprigs and whole cherry tomatoes.

Salmon Salad Loaf

SERVINGS	4 to 6	2 or 3
INGREDIENTS		
Creamy Caper Sauce, page 232		
salmon, drained, flaked, bones and skin removed	1 (16-oz.) can	1 (7-3/4-oz.) can
crushed saltine cracker crumbs	1 cup	1/2 cup
pickle relish	1/4 cup	2 tablespoons
eggs, slightly beaten	2	1
milk	1/3 cup	3 tablespoons
prepared mustard	1 tablespoon	2 teaspoons
lemon juice	1 tablespoon	2 teaspoons
BAKING DISH	9" x 5" loaf dish	7-inch pie plate
TIME AT HIGH	8 to 9 minutes	4 to 4-1/2 minutes
STANDING TIME	5 minutes	5 minutes

Prepare Creamy Caper Sauce. In a medium bowl, thoroughly combine salmon, cracker crumbs, relish, eggs, milk, mustard and lemon juice. In a baking dish, see size in chart above, form larger amount of salmon mixture into a 7"x 4" loaf shape or smaller amount into a 5" x 3" loaf shape. Cover with vented plastic wrap. Microwave at full power (HIGH) for time in chart above or until set and almost firm in center. Give dish a half turn once during cooking time. Let stand, covered, 5 minutes. Serve with Creamy Caper Sauce.

Hearty Tuna Casserole

SERVINGS	5 or 6	1 or 2
INGREDIENTS		
condensed creamy chicken-mushroom soup	1 (10-3/4-oz.) can	1/3 (10-3/4-oz.) can
milk	1/4 cup	1 tablespoon
chopped celery	1/2 cup	3 tablespoons
sliced green onion	1/4 cup	1 tablespoon
shoestring potatoes	1 (4-oz.) can	1 (1-1/2-oz.) can
water-pack tuna, drained, broken in chunks	1 (9-1/2-oz.) can	1 (3-1/2-oz.) can
toasted whole almonds	1/2 cup	3 tablespoons
shredded process American cheese	1 cup (4 oz.)	1/3 cup
snipped parsley	2 tablespoons	2 teaspoons
BAKING DISH	10" x 6" baking dish	2-cup casserole
TIME AT HIGH (soup mixture)	4 to 5 minutes	2 minutes
TIME AT HIGH (casserole)	5 minutes	2 minutes
TIME AT HIGH (cheese added)	2 minutes	1 minute

In a baking dish, see size in chart above, whisk together soup and milk. Stir in celery and green onion. Cover with vented plastic wrap. Microwave at full power (HIGH) for time in chart above or until boiling, stirring once. Fold in half the potatoes, reserving remaining potatoes. Fold in tuna and almonds. Cover with vented plastic wrap. Microwave at full power (HIGH) for time in chart above or until heated through, stirring once. Top with reserved potatoes. Sprinkle with cheese and parsley. Microwave, uncovered, at full power (HIGH) for time in chart above or until cheese melts.

How to Make Salmon Salad Loaf

Drain canned salmon and remove bones and skin. Thoroughly mix salmon with cracker crumbs, relish, eggs, milk, mustard and lemon juice.

In a loaf dish, shape salmon mixture into a loaf, patting the mixture firmly but gently so loaf will hold together.

Cover and microwave salmon loaf until the center is set and almost firm to the touch. Let the loaf stand 5 minutes to finish cooking.

Slice salmon loaf and serve with Creamy Caper Sauce, page 232, buttered mixed vegetables and squares of corn bread.

Stuffed Lobster Tails

SERVINGS	2
INGREDIENTS	
butter or margarine	2 tablespoons
seasoned dry breadcrumbs	1/3 cup
grated Parmesan cheese	2 tablespoons
snipped parsley	1 tablespoon
cooked lobster tails	2 (8-oz.) tails
fresh mushroom slices	1/4 cup
butter or margarine	2 tablespoons
all-purpose flour	1 tablespoon
salt	1/8 teaspoon
paprika	1/8 teaspoon
half and half	3/4 cup
lemon juice	1 tablespoon
poached scallops or shrimp, halved	1/2 cup
BOWL	2-cup bowl
BAKING DISH (sauce mixture)	deep 2-qt. casserole
BAKING DISH (stuffed tails)	8-inch square baking dish
TIME AT HIGH (butter)	30 seconds
TIME AT HIGH (mushrooms)	3 to 3-1/2 minutes
TIME AT HIGH (flour added)	30 seconds
TIME AT HIGH (half and half)	2-1/2 to 3 minutes
TIME AT HIGH (stuffed tails)	4 to 4-1/2 minutes

Place 2 tablespoons butter or margarine in a 2-cup bowl. Microwave at full power (HIGH) 30 seconds or until melted. Stir in breadcrumbs, Parmesan cheese and parsley; set aside. Remove cooked meat from lobster tails. Cut meat in chunks and reserve shells intact; set aside. In a 2-quart casserole, combine mushrooms and 2 tablespoons butter or margarine. Microwave at full power (HIGH) 3 to 3-1/2 minutes or until tender. Stir in flour, salt and paprika. Microwave at full power (HIGH) 30 seconds. Whisk in half and half. Microwave at full power (HIGH) 2-1/2 to 3 minutes or until thickened and bubbly, stirring three times. Mixture should be thick and smooth. Stir in lemon juice, lobster meat and scallops or shrimp. Spoon about 1 cup filling into each lobster shell. Set shells in an 8-inch square baking dish. Cover with vented plastic wrap. Microwave at full power (HIGH) 4 to 4-1/2 minutes or until heated through.

Defrosting: To defrost lobster tails, see page 221.

How to Make Basic Lobster Tails

Place the lobster tails, with the hard shell side down, on a board. Using sharp scissors, cut down the center of the soft shell. Fold back the soft shell, exposing the lobster meat.

Starting at the tail-fin end, insert a wooden skewer lengthwise into the lobster tails. This keeps them from curling during cooking.

Basic Lobster Tails

SERVINGS	2	1
INGREDIENTS		
butter or margarine	1/4 cup	2 tablespoons
lemon juice	2 tablespoons	1 tablespoon
garlic powder	dash	dash
cayenne pepper	dash	dash
lobster tails	2 (8-oz.) tails	1 (8-oz.) tail
BOWL	2-cup bowl	custard cup
BAKING DISH	8-inch square baking dish	9-inch pie plate
TIME AT HIGH (butter)	45 to 60 seconds	30 to 45 seconds
TIME AT HIGH (lobster)	6-1/2 to 7-1/2 minutes	3-1/2 to 4 minutes

Place butter or margarine in a bowl, see size in chart above. Microwave at full power (HIGH) for time in chart above or until melted. Stir in lemon juice, garlic powder and cayenne pepper; set aside. Using sharp scissors, split soft shell underside of lobster tails lengthwise in center. Fold back shell. Insert wooden skewer lengthwise so tails will lie flat during cooking. Place lobster tails, hard shell side down, in a baking dish, see size in chart above. Spoon some butter or margarine mixture over lobster. Cover with vented plastic wrap. Microwave at full power (HIGH) for time in chart above or until meat turns white and is no longer translucent. Give dish a quarter turn twice during cooking time. Serve with remaining butter sauce.

Creamy Crabmeat Crepes

SERVINGS	6 to 8	3 or 4
INGREDIENTS		
butter or margarine	1/4 cup	2 tablespoons
chopped green onion	1/2 cup	1/4 cup
chopped green pepper	1/2 cup	1/4 cup
thinly sliced celery	1/2 cup	1/4 cup
cream cheese	2 (3-oz.) pkgs.	1 (3-oz.) pkg.
Basic White Sauce—Thick page 428	2/3 cup	1/3 cup
crabmeat, drained, flaked, cartilage removed	2 (6-1/2-oz.) cans	1 (6-1/2-oz.) can
sliced pitted ripe olives	1 cup	1/2 cup
water chestnuts, thinly sliced	1 (8-oz.) can	1/2 (8-oz.) can
crepes	12 (6-inch) crepes	6 (6-inch) crepes
grated Parmesan cheese	1/4 cup	2 tablespoons
dry white wine	1/3 cup	3 tablespoons
dried leaf tarragon	1 teaspoon	1/2 teaspoon
Basic White Sauce—Thick	2 cups	1 cup
sliced ripe olives, sliced green onions	to garnish	to garnish
BAKING DISH (filling)	deep 3-qt. casserole	deep 1-1/2-qt. casserole
BAKING DISH (crepes)	12-inch square microwave baker	12" x 7" baking dish
TIME AT HIGH (vegetables)	4 to 5 minutes	3 to 4 minutes
TIME AT 10%	1-1/2 to 2 minutes	1 minute
TIME AT HIGH (crepes)	10 to 12 minutes	5 to 6 minutes
TIME AT HIGH (sauce added)	3 to 4 minutes	2 to 3 minutes

In a casserole, see size in chart above, combine butter or margarine, first amount of green onion, green pepper and celery. Microwave at full power (HIGH) for time in chart above or until vegetables are tender. Add cream cheese to vegetables. Microwave at 10% (LOW) for time in chart above or until cheese is softened. Stir together cream cheese and vegetables. Blend in first amount of white sauce. Stir in crabmeat, first amount of olives and water chestnuts. Mix well. Spoon about 1/3 cup filling down center of each crepe; roll up. Place, seam side up, in a baking dish, see size in chart above. Cover with vented plastic wrap. Microwave at full power (HIGH) for time in chart above or until heated through, giving dish a half turn once. Stir Parmesan cheese, wine and tarragon into second amount of white sauce. Mix well. Spoon over crepes. Cover with vented plastic wrap. Microwave at full power (HIGH) for time in chart above or until heated through, giving dish a half turn once. Garnish with additional sliced ripe olives and sliced green onions.

How to Make Creamy Crabmeat Crepes

Lay each crepe on a flat surface. Spoon about 1/3 cup of crabmeat filling down the center of each crepe and roll up.

Serve the crepes garnished with additional sauce and a sprinkling of sliced green onions and sliced ripe olives.

Basic King Crab Legs

SERVINGS	3 or 4	2 or 3
INGREDIENTS		
butter or margarine	1/2 cup	1/4 cup
lime juice	1/4 cup	2 tablespoons
Dijon-style mustard	2 teaspoons	1 teaspoon
prepared horseradish	2 teaspoons	1 teaspoon
frozen, cooked king crab legs	4 lbs. (6 legs)	2 lbs. (3 legs)
BAKING DISH	12-inch square microwave baker with microwave rack	12-inch square microwave baker with microwave rack
TIME AT HIGH (butter)	1-1/2 minutes	1 minute
TIME AT HIGH (first side)	6 minutes	3 minutes
TIME AT HIGH (second side)	18 to 20 minutes	9 to 10 minutes

Place butter or margarine in a small bowl. Microwave at full power (HIGH) for time in chart above or until melted. Whisk in lime juice, mustard and horseradish; set aside. Using paper towels to protect hands, break frozen crab legs in half at the joint. Arrange large ends of crab legs in a 12-inch square microwave baker with largest part of leg toward outside of dish. Reserve small ends of crab legs. Cover legs in baker with waxed paper. Microwave at full power (HIGH) for time in chart above. Turn legs over and place toward outside of dish. Place small ends of legs in center of dish. Cover all legs with waxed paper. Microwave at full power (HIGH) for time in chart above or until heated through, giving dish a half turn once. Serve crab legs with nut crackers and picks for opening. Pass butter or margarine mixture for dipping.

Scallops Véronique

SERVINGS	4	2
INGREDIENTS		
butter or margarine	1/4 cup	2 tablespoons
chopped shallots	1/2 cup	1/4 cup
cornstarch	1/4 cup	2 tablespoons
ground mace	1/2 teaspoon	1/4 teaspoon
strained fish stock or chicken broth	3 cups	1-1/2 cups
dry white wine	1/2 cup	1/4 cup
lemon juice	2 tablespoons	1 tablespoon
scallops, poached	2 lbs.	1 lb.
seedless green grapes, halved	2 cups	1 cup
hot cooked white and wild rice		
BAKING DISH	deep 3-qt. casserole	deep 2-qt. casserole
TIME AT HIGH (shallots)	3 minutes	2 to 2-1/2 minutes
TIME AT HIGH (cornstarch added)	30 seconds	30 seconds
TIME AT HIGH (sauce)	8 to 10 minutes	4 to 5 minutes
TIME AT HIGH (scallops added)	4 to 5 minutes	3 to 3-1/2 minutes
STANDING TIME	5 minutes	5 minutes

In a casserole, see size in chart above, combine butter or margarine and shallots. Micro wave at full power (HIGH) for time in chart above or until shallots are tender. Stir in cornstarch and mace. Microwave at full power (HIGH) 30 seconds. Whisk in fish stock or chicken broth, and wine. Microwave at full power (HIGH) for time in chart above or until thickened and bubbly, stirring three times. Mixture should be thick and smooth. Stir in lemon juice. Gently fold in scallops. Cover. Microwave at full power (HIGH) for time in chart above or until heated through. Stir in grapes. Let stand, covered, 5 minutes. Serve over hot cooked white and wild rice. Sprinkle with paprika.

Basic Poached Scallops

SERVINGS	4	2
INGREDIENTS		
Basic Poaching Liquid for Fish, page 228	large recipe	medium recipe
scallops	2 lbs.	1 lb.
TIME AT HIGH	5 minutes	3 minutes
STANDING TIME	3 minutes	3 minutes

Prepare Basic Poaching Liquid for Fish. Add scallops to hot poaching liquid. Push scallops under poaching liquid as much as possible. Cover. Microwave at full power (HIGH) for time in chart above or until scallops are opaque and firm, stirring three times. Let stand, covered, 3 minutes. Remove scallops with a slotted spoon. Serve with Tangy Tartar Sauce, page 235, or Creamy Caper Sauce, page 232, or use as cooked scallops in recipes. Strain poaching liquid through cheesecloth to use as stock.

Defrosting: To defrost scallops, see page 220.

Creamy Scalloped Oysters

SERVINGS	4	2
INGREDIENTS		
butter or margarine	1/2 cup	1/4 cup
oyster crackers, crushed	2 cups	1 cup
snipped parsley	2 tablespoons	1 tablespoon
snipped chives	1 tablespoon	2 teaspoons
paprika	1/4 teaspoon	1/8 teaspoon
shucked oysters	1 pt.	1/2 pt.
oyster liquor	2 tablespoons	1 tablespoon
whipping cream	3/4 cup	1/3 cup
bottled hot pepper sauce	1/4 teaspoon	1/8 teaspoon
freshly ground pepper	1/4 teaspoon	1/8 teaspoon
BOWL	1-1/2-qt. bowl	1-qt. bowl
BAKING DISH	round, 8-inch baking dish	2 (1-cup) casseroles
TIME AT HIGH	1-3/4 minutes	1 minute
TIME AT 50% (casserole)	9 to 10 minutes	5 to 6 minutes
TIME AT 50% (crumb topping)	1 minute	45 seconds

Place butter or margarine in a bowl, see size in chart above. Microwave at full power (HIGH) for time in chart above or until melted. Toss oyster-cracker crumbs, parsley, chives and paprika with butter or margarine. Reserve 1/3 of the cracker mixture for topping. Drain oysters, reserving amount of liquor listed in chart above. Add oysters to remaining cracker mixture. In a small bowl, combine oyster liquor, whipping cream, hot pepper sauce and pepper. Mix well. Stir into oyster mixture. Spoon into a baking dish or casseroles, see sizes in chart above. Cover with vented plastic wrap. Microwave at 50% (MEDIUM) for time in chart above or until heated through, stirring twice. Stir again and top with reserved crumb mixture. Microwave, uncovered, at 50% (MEDIUM) until crumbs are heated through.

Basic Appetizer Oysters

See page 40.

Adapting Shellfish Recipes for Microwave Oven

- Do not overcook shellfish in the microwave or the fish will become tough and rubbery.
- Use Seafood Newburg, page 261, as a guideline for adapting your favorite Newburg recipe. Add any sherry or other liquor at the end of the cooking time to prevent the sauce from breaking down.
- Use Luncheon Seashells, page 230, as a guideline for adapting your favorite en coquille recipes. Real seashells, ceramic shells and oven-glass shells all make attractive serving pieces.
- Creamy Crabmeat Crepes, page 252, can serve as a basic recipe for almost any kind of seafood-stuffed crepes.
- Refer to Stuffed Lobster Tails, page 250, as a guideline for adapting your favorite stuffed lobster tail recipe.

Defrosting: To defrost shucked oysters, see page 220.

How to Make Basic Steamed Hard-Shell Clams

Scrub clams, then soak in salt water to remove sand. Place the clams in a floured roasting bag set in a baking dish. Tie the bag loosely with string, leaving a 1-inch opening to vent steam.

As soon as the clams open, they are done. Do not cook any longer or they will be tough. If clams do not open, like the one on the spoon above, discard. They are not safe to eat.

Basic Steamed Hard-Shell Clams

SERVINGS	2 (in the shell) or 1 cup diced clams	1 (in the shell) or 1/2 cup diced clams
INGREDIENTS		
fresh cherrystone clams in shells	24 (7-1/2 lbs.)	12 (3 lbs.)
OR		
fresh quahog clams in shells	12 (5 lbs.)	6 (2-1/2 lbs.)
water	1 cup	1/2 cup
ROASTING BAG	23-1/2" x 19" bag	16" x 10" bag
BAKING DISH	12-inch square microwave baker	12" x 7" baking dish
GLASS MEASURING CUP	2-cup	1-cup
TIME AT HIGH (water)	2-1/2 to 3 minutes	1-1/2 to 2 minutes
TIME AT HIGH (clams)	10 to 12 minutes	6 to 7 minutes

Thoroughly scrub clams. Place in a sink or large bowl. Cover with salt water made in a solution of 1/3 cup salt to 1 gallon water. Let stand 15 minutes. Rinse. Repeat soaking and rinsing twice. Drain. Flour a roasting bag, see size in chart above, according to manufacturer's directions. Place bag in a baking dish, see size in chart above. Place clams in a single layer in roasting bag. Place water in a glass measuring cup, see size in chart above. Microwave water at full power (HIGH) for time in chart above or until boiling. Pour over clams in bag. Tie bag loosely with string, leaving a 1-inch opening to vent steam. Microwave at full power (HIGH) for time in chart above or until clams are opened, giving dish a half turn once. Discard any clams that do not open. Serve cherry-stone clams in shells with melted butter. Dice meat from quahog clams for chowder or casseroles.

Easy Seafood Spaghetti Sauce

SERVINGS	4	2
INGREDIENTS		
fresh steamer (soft-shell) clams in shells, or mussels	4 dozen	2 dozen
olive oil	1/4 cup	2 tablespoons
small onions, sliced, separated in rings	6	3
garlic, minced	2 cloves	1 clove
Italian cooking sauce	2 (16-oz.) jars (4 cups)	1 (16-oz.) jar (2 cups)
dried leaf oregano	2 teaspoons	1 teaspoon
hot cooked spaghetti		
BAKING DISH	deep 3-qt. casserole	deep 2-qt. casserole
TIME AT HIGH (onions)	5 to 6 minutes	3 to 4 minutes
TIME AT HIGH (sauce)	8 to 9 minutes	4 to 5 minutes
TIME AT HIGH (clams added)	6 to 7 minutes	4 to 5 minutes

Thoroughly scrub clams or mussels. Remove beard from mussels. Discard any extra heavy mussels. Place clams or mussels in a sink or large bowl. Cover with a salt water solution of 1/3 cup salt to 1 gallon water. Soak for 15 minutes. Rinse. Repeat soaking and rinsing twice. Drain. In a casserole, see size in chart above, combine olive oil, onion rings and garlic. Microwave at full power (HIGH) for time in chart above or until tender. Stir in Italian cooking sauce and oregano. Cover. Microwave at full power (HIGH) for time in chart above or until boiling, stirring once. Add clams or mussels. Cover. Microwave at full power (HIGH) for time in chart above or until clams or mussels are beginning to open, stirring twice. Discard any unopened clams or mussels. Serve sauce over hot cooked spaghetti.

Basic Frozen Breaded Clams

SERVINGS	2
INGREDIENTS	
vegetable oil	1 tablespoon
frozen breaded clams	1 (5-oz.) pkg.
BROWNING SKILLET	10-inch microwave browning skillet
TIME AT HIGH (preheat skillet)	3 minutes
TIME AT HIGH (clams)	4 minutes

Preheat a 10-inch browning skillet, uncovered, at microwave full power (HIGH) 3 minutes. Add oil. Using hot pads, tilt skillet so entire surface is coated with oil. Quickly add clams. Microwave at full power (HIGH) 4 minutes or until browned, stirring twice. Drain on paper towels.

Tips

- Hard-shell clams have round shells that are difficult to break with your hands. There is a small bluish-purple area on the inside of the white shell. The smaller clams are often called *littlenecks* or *cherrystones*. The larger clams are usually called *quahogs*.

- Soft-shell clams are oval. The shells are soft enough to be broken easily with your hands. The clams are often called *steamers*.

Hot Shrimp Luncheon Salad

SERVINGS	4	2
INGREDIENTS		
vegetable oil	1/4 cup	2 tablespoons
white-wine tarragon vinegar	3 tablespoons	4 teaspoons
Italian salad-dressing mix	2 teaspoons	1 teaspoon
cooked, shelled shrimp	2 cups	1 cup
chopped tomato	1/4 cup	2 tablespoons
chopped celery	2 tablespoons	1 tablespoon
chopped green onion	2 tablespoons	1 tablespoon
drained capers	2 teaspoons	1 teaspoon
shredded lettuce		
shredded Cheddar cheese	1/2 cup (2 oz.)	1/4 cup (1 oz.)
snipped parsley	2 tablespoons	1 tablespoon
BOWL	1-1/2-qt. bowl	1-qt. bowl
TIME AT 30%	5 to 6 minutes	3 to 4 minutes

In a screw-top jar, combine oil, wine vinegar and Italian dressing mix. Cover and shake well. In a bowl, see size in chart above, combine shrimp, tomato, celery, green onion and capers. Drizzle dressing over shrimp mixture. Toss gently. Microwave at 30% (MEDIUM LOW) for time in chart above or until warm, tossing once. Place lettuce on salad plates. Spoon shrimp mixture over lettuce. Sprinkle with cheese and parsley.

Shrimp Creole

SERVINGS	6	4
INGREDIENTS		
bacon, diced	2 slices	1-1/2 slices
chopped celery	1/3 cup	1/4 cup
chopped onion	1/3 cup	1/4 cup
garlic, minced	1 large clove	1 small clove
tomatoes, cut up	1 (28-oz.) can	1 (16-oz.) can
chili sauce	1 cup	3/4 cup
dried leaf thyme	1-1/2 teaspoons	1 teaspoon
salt	1/4 teaspoon	1/8 teaspoon
pepper	1/4 teaspoon	1/8 teaspoon
bottled hot pepper sauce	1/4 teaspoon	1/8 teaspoon
cooked, shelled shrimp	3-1/2 cups	2-1/3 cups
hot cooked rice		
BAKING DISH	deep 3-qt. casserole	deep 2-qt. casserole
TIME AT HIGH (vegetables)	5 minutes	3 to 4 minutes
TIME AT HIGH (sauce)	6 minutes	3 to 4 minutes
TIME AT 30%	20 minutes	15 minutes
TIME AT HIGH (shrimp added)	4 to 5 minutes	3 to 4 minutes

In a casserole, see size in chart above, combine bacon, celery, onion and garlic. Microwave at full power (HIGH) for time in chart above or until vegetables are tender, stirring once. Stir in tomatoes, chili sauce, thyme, salt, pepper and hot pepper sauce. Mix well. Cover. Microwave at full power (HIGH) for time in chart above or until boiling. Stir. Cover. Microwave at 30% (MEDIUM LOW) for time in chart above. Stir in shrimp. Cover. Microwave at full power (HIGH) for time in chart above or until heated through, stirring once. Serve over hot cooked rice.

Defrosting: For best results, microwave frozen shrimp without defrosting first.

How to Make Hot Shrimp Luncheon Salad

Drizzle the dressing mixture over shrimp, tomato, celery, green onion and capers. Microwave until warm.

Spoon hot shrimp mixture over shredded lettuce on salad plates. Serve a mixture of shredded cheese and snipped parsley as garnish.

Seafood Newburg

SERVINGS	4	2
INGREDIENTS		
butter or margarine	1/4 cup	2 tablespoons
all-purpose flour	1/4 cup	2 tablespoons
celery salt	1/2 teaspoon	1/4 teaspoon
paprika	1/2 teaspoon	1/4 teaspoon
onion powder	1/4 teaspoon	1/8 teaspoon
white pepper	1/4 teaspoon	1/8 teaspoon
garlic powder	1/8 teaspoon	dash
half and half	3 cups	1-1/2 cups
cooked lump crabmeat, lobster, scallops or shrimp	2 cups	1 cup
dry sherry	1/4 cup	2 tablespoons
baked patty shells	4	2
BAKING DISH	deep 2-qt. casserole	deep 1-qt. casserole
TIME AT HIGH (butter)	1 minute	30 seconds
TIME AT HIGH (flour added)	30 seconds	30 seconds
TIME AT HIGH (sauce)	7 to 8 minutes	3-1/2 to 4-1/2 minutes
TIME AT HIGH (seafood added)	3 to 4 minutes	1-1/2 to 2 minutes

Place butter or margarine in a casserole, see size in chart above. Microwave at full power (HIGH) for time in chart above or until melted. Stir in flour, celery salt, paprika, onion powder, white pepper and garlic powder. Microwave at full power (HIGH) 30 seconds. Whisk in half and half. Microwave at full power (HIGH) for time in chart above or until thickened and bubbly, stirring three times. Mixture should be thick and smooth. Stir in seafood and sherry. Mix well. Cover. Microwave at full power (HIGH) for time in chart above or until heated through, stirring once. Serve in patty shells.

Basic Frozen Shelled Shrimp

SERVINGS	4 to 6 (small shrimp)	3 or 4 (medium shrimp)
INGREDIENTS		
beer	2 (12-oz.) cans	2 (12-oz.) cans
water	1-1/2 cups	none
bay leaf	1 large	1 medium
pickling spice	1 tablespoon	2 teaspoons
frozen shelled shrimp	2 (12-oz.) pkgs.	1 (1-lb.) pkg.
BAKING DISH	deep 4-qt. casserole	deep 3-qt. casserole
TIME AT HIGH (beer mixture)	13 to 15 minutes	7 to 8 minutes
TIME AT HIGH (shrimp added)	8 minutes	6 minutes

In a casserole, see size in chart above, combine beer, water, if used, bay leaf and pickling spice. Cover. Microwave at full power (HIGH) for time in chart above or until boiling. Add frozen shrimp. Microwave, uncovered, at full power (HIGH) for time in chart above or until shrimp turn pink and are becoming opaque, stirring three or four times. Drain immediately. Rinse with cold water; drain. Cover and refrigerate. Serve as appetizer with Seafood Cocktail Sauce, below, or use in salads or casseroles.

Basic Fresh Shrimp in the Shell

SERVINGS	4 or 5	2
INGREDIENTS		
beer	2 (12-oz.) cans	1 (12-oz.) can
bay leaf	1 medium	1 small
pickling spice	2 teaspoons	1 teaspoon
fresh large shrimp in the shell, 16 to 20 shrimp per lb.	2 lbs.	1 lb.
BAKING DISH	deep 3-qt. casserole	deep 2-qt. casserole
TIME AT HIGH (beer mixture)	7 to 8 minutes	3 to 4 minutes
TIME AT HIGH (shrimp added)	7 to 8 minutes	4 to 5 minutes

In a casserole, see size in chart above, combine beer, bay leaf and pickling spice. Cover. Microwave at full power (HIGH) for time in chart above or until boiling. Add shrimp. Microwave, uncovered, at full power (HIGH) for time in chart above or until shrimp turn pink and are becoming opaque, stirring three times. Drain immediately. Serve hot in the shell with melted butter. Or, remove shell and sand vein and refrigerate shrimp. Serve as appetizer with Seafood Cocktail Sauce, below, or use in salads or casseroles.

Seafood Cocktail Sauce

YIELD	3/4 cup	1/3 cup
INGREDIENTS		
chili sauce	1/2 cup	1/4 cup
prepared horseradish	2 tablespoons	1 tablespoon
finely chopped onion	2 tablespoons	1 tablespoon
lemon juice	2 teaspoons	1 teaspoon
Worcestershire sauce	1 teaspoon	1/2 teaspoon
bottled hot pepper sauce	1/4 to 1/2 teaspoon	1/8 to 1/4 teaspoon

In a medium bowl, combine all ingredients. Mix well. Cover and refrigerate until serving time. Serve with chilled seafood dishes.

Eggs & Cheese

Eggs & Cheese

When everyone is rushing off to school or work, cooking breakfast in the microwave saves precious minutes. Send the family on their way with the lightest scrambled eggs they have ever tasted! The recipe is in this chapter.

Q. How are eggs cooked in the microwave?

A. Because eggs are already tender, most egg dishes cook well at full power (HIGH). The exceptions are quiches and layered casseroles. They are cooked at a lower power so the centers will get done without overcooking the edges.

Q. Which egg dishes do not cook satisfactorily in the microwave?

A. *Never try to cook an egg in the shell in the microwave.* The egg will explode, making a considerable mess in the oven. To cook whole eggs out of the shell, prick the yolk with a pin. The yolk has a high fat content and consequently attracts microwaves more than the white. In addition, the yolk has an outer membrane that has the same effect as the egg shell, so unpricked yolks are likely to explode. Egg dishes that rely on the puffiness of beaten egg whites are not successful in the microwave. Soufflés or puffy omelets puff beautifully while they are being cooked in the microwave, but they fall immediately when removed. Even using low power levels, the outside edges will be tough and overcooked by the time the center of the soufflé is done.

Q. Can egg substitutes be cooked in the microwave?

A. For those on a low-cholesterol diet, there are directions for using egg substitutes in scrambled eggs and a delicious quiche.

Q. How do you know when eggs are done?

A. For most egg dishes in large casseroles, a knife inserted in the center should feel hot. Cooking casseroles is deceiving—the edges will bubble vigorously before the center is even warm. That is why stirring the edges of the casserole to the center promotes more even heating.

Q. How can favorite egg and cheese recipes be adapted to the microwave?

A. Look for the basic recipes throughout the chapter. Compare your recipe to the basic recipe and conversion is easy.

Q. Can egg and cheese dishes be reheated in the microwave?

A. Wedges of quiche and servings of casseroles reheat excellently in the microwave. Other items such as scrambled eggs cook so quickly in the microwave, it's best to start over. Reheating eggs tends to overcook and toughen them.

Q. What about cooking convenience egg and cheese dishes?

A. Many frozen TV breakfasts and cheese casseroles have microwave cooking directions on the package.

Q. Are any special utensils needed to cook eggs in the microwave?

A. Browning skillets are necessary to fry eggs in the microwave. For quiches you can use the same ceramic or glass quiche dishes or pie plates that you use in a conventional oven.

Scrambled Egg Substitute

SERVINGS	2	1
INGREDIENTS		
frozen egg substitute, thawed	1 (8-1/2-oz.) carton (about 1 cup)	1 (4-oz.) carton or 1/2 cup
margarine	2 teaspoons	1 teaspoon
salt and pepper	dash	dash
BOWL	3-cup bowl	2-cup bowl
TIME AT 70%	2-3/4 to 3 minutes	1-1/4 to 1-3/4 minutes
STANDING TIME	1 minute	1 minute

Shake egg substitute in carton. Pour egg substitute into a bowl, see size in chart above. Add margarine, salt and pepper. Cover with vented plastic wrap. Microwave at 70% (MEDIUM HIGH) for time in chart above or until just set, stirring once. Let stand, covered, 1 minute.

Note: To defrost egg substitute, open an 8-1/2-ounce or 4-ounce carton to vent. Microwave opened carton at 10% (LOW) for 20 to 22 minutes for large carton, or 5 to 6 minutes for small carton, stirring three times. Let stand 5 minutes.

Low-Cholesterol Quiche

SERVINGS	6
INGREDIENTS	
unpricked baked, oil pastry shell	9-inch pastry shell
margarine	1 tablespoon
chopped onion	1/4 cup
chopped green pepper	1/4 cup
shredded pasteurized process filled cheese food made with corn oil	1-1/2 cups (6 oz.)
imitation bacon bits	1/4 cup
canned, skimmed evaporated milk	1 cup
frozen egg substitute, thawed	3/4 cup
PIE PLATE	9-inch pie plate
BOWL	2-cup bowl
TIME AT HIGH	2 to 3 minutes
TIME AT 50%	17 to 20 minutes
STANDING TIME	10 minutes

Prepare oil pastry shell in a 9-inch pie plate; set aside. In a 2-cup bowl, combine margarine, onion and green pepper. Microwave at full power (HIGH) 2 to 3 minutes or until vegetables are tender, stirring once. Drain. Sprinkle half the cheese in baked pastry shell. Layer drained vegetables and bacon bits over cheese in pastry shell. Sprinkle with remaining cheese. In a small bowl, combine evaporated milk and egg substitute; mix well. Pour over cheese in pastry shell. Microwave at 50% (MEDIUM) 17 to 20 minutes or until set, giving dish a quarter turn twice. Do not rely on testing for doneness with a knife because the consistency of the cheese will prevent the knife from coming out clean. Let stand 10 minutes.

Deviled-Egg Tostada   Photo on page 263.

SERVINGS	4	2
INGREDIENTS		
shredded lettuce	2 cups	1 cup
shredded carrot	1/4 cup	2 tablespoons
sliced green onion	1/4 cup	2 tablespoons
chopped zucchini	1/4 cup	2 tablespoons
hard-cooked eggs	8	4
mayonnaise or mayonnaise- style salad dressing	3 to 4 tablespoons	1-1/2 to 2 tablespoons
chopped, seeded, canned green chilies	2 tablespoons	1 tablespoon
celery salt	1/2 teaspoon	1/4 teaspoon
taco sauce	1 (16-oz.) jar (2 cups)	1 (8-oz.) jar (1 cup)
corn tortillas	4	2
shredded Cheddar cheese, chopped, seeded, canned green chilies, if desired	to garnish	to garnish
BAKING DISH	8-inch square baking dish	7-inch pie plate
TIME AT HIGH	2 to 3 minutes	1 to 1-1/2 minutes
TIME AT 70%	5 to 7 minutes	2 to 3 minutes
STANDING TIME	1 minute	1 minute

In a bowl, toss together lettuce, carrot, green onion and zucchini. Cover and refrigerate. Cut hard-cooked eggs in half lengthwise. Remove yolks and place in a small bowl. Mash yolks. Stir in mayonnaise or salad dressing, first amount of chilies and celery salt; mix well. Fill egg whites with yolk mixture; set aside. Pour taco sauce into a baking dish, see size in chart above. Cover with vented plastic wrap. Microwave at full power (HIGH) for time in chart above or until hot. Arrange stuffed eggs in sauce. Cover with vented plastic wrap. Microwave at 70% (MEDIUM HIGH) for time in chart above or until heated through, giving dish a half turn once. Let stand, covered, 1 minute. To serve, top tortillas with lettuce mixture. Arrange hot stuffed eggs and sauce on lettuce mixture. Sprinkle with shredded cheese and additional chilies, if desired.

Microwave Cautions

Never microwave a whole egg in the shell. The egg will explode into more parti-cles than you can imagine. Not only does this make a tremendous mess inside your microwave oven, it can be harmful if the egg explodes in your face.

Never reheat a whole hard-cooked egg in the microwave oven. Some hard-cooked eggs may explode if they are reheated whole. Always slice or quarter hard-cooked eggs before reheating.

Never microwave a poached, baked or fried egg without pricking the yolk. The egg yolk has a thin membrane over it. If this membrane is not pricked before microwaving, the yolk may explode.

How to Make Smoky Eggs à la King

Scissors make fast work of snipping smoked sliced beef into the zucchini sauce. Notice that the hard-cooked eggs have been sliced before heating in the microwave oven. Never reheat whole hard-cooked eggs in the microwave oven—they may explode.

Ladle the creamy egg sauce over warm chow-mein noodles or toast triangles. Garnish with additional hard-cooked egg slices and a sprinkling of paprika. This recipe is also good made with smoked sliced turkey or ham instead of the smoked sliced beef.

Smoky Eggs à la King

SERVINGS	6 to 8	3 or 4
INGREDIENTS		
butter or margarine	1/4 cup	2 tablespoons
chopped zucchini	1 cup	1/2 cup
chopped onion	1/3 cup	3 tablespoons
all-purpose flour	1/3 cup	2 tablespoons
milk	1 cup	1/2 cup
chicken broth	1 cup	1/2 cup
sliced smoked beef, snipped	1 (2-1/2-oz.) pkg.	1/2 (2-1/2-oz.) pkg. (1/2 cup)
hard-cooked eggs, sliced	4	2
chopped pimiento	1/4 cup	2 tablespoons
warm chow mein noodles		
BAKING DISH	deep 2-qt. casserole	deep 1-qt. casserole
TIME AT HIGH (vegetables)	4 minutes	3 minutes
TIME AT HIGH (flour added)	30 seconds	30 seconds
TIME AT HIGH (sauce)	5 to 6 minutes	2-1/2 to 3-1/2 minutes
TIME AT HIGH (meat added)	4 to 5 minutes	2 to 2-1/2 minutes

In a casserole, see size in chart above, combine butter or margarine, zucchini and onion. Microwave at full power (HIGH) for time in chart above or until vegetables are tender, stirring once. Stir in flour; mix well. Microwave at full power (HIGH) 30 seconds. Whisk in milk and broth. Microwave at full power (HIGH) for time in chart above or until thickened and bubbly, stirring three times. Mixture should be thick and smooth. Stir in beef, eggs and pimiento. Cover. Microwave at full power (HIGH) for time in chart above or until heated through, stirring once. Stir; serve over chow mein noodles.

Basic Scrambled Eggs

SERVINGS	4	2	1
INGREDIENTS			
eggs	4	2	1
milk	1/4 cup	2 tablespoons	1 tablespoon
salt	dash	dash	dash
pepper	dash	dash	dash
butter or margarine	2 teaspoons	1 teaspoon	1/2 teaspoon
BOWL	deep 1-qt. bowl	1-1/2-cup bowl	1-cup bowl
TIME AT 70%	2-1/2 minutes	1-1/2 minutes	45 seconds
TIME AT 70% (after stirring)	1-1/4 to 1-1/2 minutes	30 to 45 seconds	15 to 30 seconds
STANDING TIME	1 minute	1 minute	1 minute

In a bowl, see size in chart above, whisk together eggs, milk, salt and pepper. Add butter or margarine. Cover with vented plastic wrap. Microwave at 70% (MEDIUM HIGH) for first time in chart above or until about half set; stir. Microwave at 70% (MEDIUM HIGH) for second time in chart above or until almost set. Stir. Let stand, covered, 1 minute before serving.

Scrambled Eggs Deluxe

SERVINGS	6	4
INGREDIENTS		
butter or margarine	6 tablespoons	1/4 cup
sliced fresh mushrooms	3 cups	2 cups
chopped green onion	1/3 cup	1/4 cup
garlic, minced	1 medium clove	1 small clove
artichoke hearts, drained, halved	1 (14-oz.) can	1 (8-oz.) can
eggs, beaten	6	4
shredded Cheddar cheese	1-1/2 cups (6 oz.)	1 cup (4 oz.)
cubed, cooked ham	2-1/2 cups (13 oz.)	1-1/2 cups (8 oz.)
seasoned dry breadcrumbs	1/3 cup	1/4 cup
French-fried onions	1 (3-oz.) can	1 (3-oz.) can
BAKING DISH	12" x 7" baking dish	10" x 6" baking dish
TIME AT HIGH (vegetables)	5 to 6 minutes	3 to 4 minutes
TIME AT 70%	12 to 14 minutes	8 to 10 minutes
TIME AT HIGH (topping)	2 minutes	2 minutes

In a baking dish, see size in chart above, combine butter or margarine, mushrooms, green onion and garlic. Cover with vented plastic wrap. Microwave at full power (HIGH) for time in chart above or until onion is tender, stirring once. Stir in artichoke hearts, eggs, cheese, ham and breadcrumbs. Mix well. Cover with vented plastic wrap. Microwave at 70% (MEDIUM HIGH) for time in chart above or until eggs are set, stirring twice. Top with French-fried onions. Microwave, uncovered, at full power (HIGH) 2 minutes or until onions are warm.

How to Make Denver Sandwich Pita-Style

Stir cooked portion of eggs around the edges to the center of the dish and let the uncooked portion flow to the edge. When eggs are almost set, stir in the yogurt. Yogurt will curdle if added too soon.

Split pita bread crosswise so each half forms a pocket. Gently open pocket and spoon egg mixture into pita-bread halves. Garnish the sandwiches with chopped tomato, alfalfa sprouts and shredded Monterey Jack cheese.

Denver Sandwich Pita-Style

SERVINGS	2 or 4	1 or 2
INGREDIENTS		
butter or margarine	2 tablespoons	1 tablespoon
chopped onion	2 tablespoons	1 tablespoon
chopped green pepper	2 tablespoons	1 tablespoon
chopped celery	2 tablespoons	1 tablespoon
eggs, slightly beaten	4	2
salt	1/4 teaspoon	1/8 teaspoon
plain yogurt	1/4 cup	2 tablespoons
pita bread, split crosswise	2 (4 halves)	1 (2 halves)
chopped tomato		
alfalfa sprouts		
shredded Monterey Jack cheese		
BAKING DISH	10" x 6" baking dish	9" x 5" loaf dish
TIME AT HIGH	2 to 3 minutes	1-1/2 to 2 minutes
TIME AT 70% (eggs added)	3-1/2 to 4 minutes	1-1/2 to 2 minutes
TIME AT 70% (yogurt added)	1 minute	30 to 45 seconds

In a baking dish, see size in chart above, combine butter or margarine, onion, green pepper and celery. Microwave, uncovered, at full power (HIGH) for time in chart above or until vegetables are tender. Stir in eggs and salt. Cover with vented plastic wrap. Microwave at 70% (MEDIUM HIGH) for time in chart above or until eggs are almost set, stirring twice. Stir yogurt into egg mixture. Microwave, covered, at 70% (MEDIUM HIGH) for time in chart above or until heated through. Spoon egg mixture into pita bread. Top with tomato, alfalfa sprouts and Monterey Jack cheese.

Overnight Brunch Casserole

SERVINGS	8	4
INGREDIENTS		
butter or margarine	2 tablespoons	1 tablespoon
all-purpose flour	2 tablespoons	1 tablespoon
milk	1-1/4 cups	2/3 cup
semi-soft natural cheese with garlic and herbs	1 (4-oz.) carton	1/2 (4-oz.) carton
bulk pork sausage	8 oz.	4 oz.
chopped green onion	1/4 cup	2 tablespoons
chopped, stuffed green olives	1/4 cup	2 tablespoons
drained, cooked corn or peas	1 cup	1/2 cup
eggs, slightly beaten	12	6
tomato wedges, snipped parsley	to garnish	to garnish
GLASS MEASURING CUP	1-qt.	2-cup
BAKING DISH	12" x 7" baking dish	9" x 5" loaf dish
TIME AT HIGH (butter)	45 seconds	30 seconds
TIME AT HIGH (flour added)	30 seconds	30 seconds
TIME AT HIGH (milk added)	2-1/2 to 3 minutes	2 to 2-1/2 minutes
TIME AT HIGH (cheese added)	1 minute	30 seconds
TIME AT HIGH (sausage)	5 minutes	3-1/2 minutes
TIME AT 70% (eggs added)	8 minutes	4 minutes
TIME AT 70% (chilled casserole)	8 to 10 minutes	6 to 7 minutes
TIME AT 70% (tomato added)	2 to 3 minutes	2 to 3 minutes

Place butter or margarine in a glass measuring cup, see size in chart above. Microwave at full power (HIGH) for time in chart above or until melted. Stir in flour. Microwave at full power (HIGH) 30 seconds. Whisk in milk. Microwave at full power (HIGH) for time in chart above or until mixture thickens and bubbles, stirring three times. Mixture should be thick and smooth. Stir in cheese. Microwave at full power (HIGH) for time in chart above or until cheese melts. Stir until smooth; set aside. In a baking dish, see size in chart above, combine sausage and green onion. Microwave at full power (HIGH) for time in chart above or until sausage is browned and done, stirring twice. Drain well. Stir in olives, corn or peas, and eggs. Cover with vented plastic wrap. Microwave at 70% (MEDIUM HIGH) for time in chart above or until eggs are just set, stirring three times. Fold in cheese sauce. Cover with plastic wrap; refrigerate overnight. To serve, vent plastic wrap. Microwave at 70% (MEDIUM HIGH) for time in chart above or until heated through, stirring twice. Top with tomato wedges. Microwave at 70% (MEDIUM HIGH) for time in chart above or until tomatoes are warmed. Sprinkle with parsley.

Tip

- Soufflés are light, airy mixtures that never set satisfactorily when cooked in the microwave. Even at a low cooking power, the egg mixture tends to toughen and the outside overcooks before the center is done. It's best to cook soufflés conventionally. The same is true for puffy omelets.

Basic French Omelet

SERVINGS	2	1
INGREDIENTS		
Bacon Omelet Filling, below, or Sunshine Omelet Filling, opposite	2/3 cup	1/3 cup
butter or margarine	1 tablespoon	2 teaspoons
eggs	3	2
milk	3 tablespoons	2 tablespoons
salt and pepper	dash	dash
PIE PLATE	9-inch pie plate	7-inch pie plate
TIME AT HIGH	30 seconds	20 to 30 seconds
TIME AT 70%	1-1/2 minutes	1 minute
TIME AT 70% (after stirring)	1-1/4 to 1-3/4 minutes	1 to 1-1/4 minutes
STANDING TIME	1 minute	1 minute

Prepare filling for omelet; set aside. Place butter or margarine in a pie plate, see size in chart above. Microwave at full power (HIGH) for time in chart above or until melted. Beat together eggs, milk, salt and pepper. Add to pie plate. Cover completely with plastic wrap; do not vent. Microwave at 70% (MEDIUM HIGH) for first time in chart above. Gently lift cooked egg edges, allowing uncooked egg to flow underneath. Cover completely with unvented plastic wrap. Microwave at 70% (MEDIUM HIGH) for time in chart above or until set. Let stand, covered, 1 minute. Fill with prepared filling. Fold over and serve immediately. Garnish according to filling recipe.

Bacon Omelet Filling

YIELD	1 cup	2/3 cup	1/3 cup
INGREDIENTS			
bacon	6 slices	4 slices	2 slices
bacon drippings	2 tablespoons	4 teaspoons	1 tablespoon
thin onion slices, separated in rings	6 slices	4 slices	2 slices
green-pepper rings	6 rings	4 rings	2 rings
dried leaf Italian herbs	3/4 teaspoon	1/2 teaspoon	1/4 teaspoon
BAKING DISH	12" x 7" baking dish with microwave rack	12" x 7" baking dish with microwave rack	8-inch round or square baking dish with microwave rack
TIME AT HIGH (bacon)	4-1/2 to 5 minutes	3-1/2 to 4 minutes	1-1/2 to 2 minutes
TIME AT HIGH (onion)	4-1/2 to 5 minutes	3-1/2 to 4-1/2 minutes	2 to 3 minutes

Place bacon on a microwave rack in a baking dish, see size in chart above. Cover with white paper towel. Microwave at full power (HIGH) for time in chart above or until crisp. Drain bacon, reserving pan drippings. Crumble bacon; set aside. Remove microwave rack. Measure amount of bacon drippings listed in chart above into same baking dish. Stir in onion, green-pepper rings and Italian herbs. Microwave, uncovered, at full power (HIGH) for time in chart above or until tender, stirring once. Drain off excess drippings. Stir in crumbled bacon. Reserve 1 to 2 tablespoons mixture for topping each omelet; use remaining mixture as filling for Basic French Omelet, above.

How to Make Basic French Omelet

Pour beaten egg mixture into melted butter in a pie plate. Cover the pie plate tightly with plastic wrap. Do not vent the plastic wrap or portions of the omelet will not cook. Microwave at 70% for first time in chart.

Gently lift the cooked edges and let the uncooked egg flow underneath. Cover with unvented plastic wrap and continue microwaving. Fill with Sunshine Omelet Filling, below.

Sunshine Omelet Filling

YIELD	1-1/3 cups	2/3 cup	1/3 cup
INGREDIENTS			
butter or margarine	1 tablespoon	2 teaspoons	1 teaspoon
chopped zucchini	1 cup	1/2 cup	1/4 cup
shredded carrot	1/4 cup	2 tablespoons	1 tablespoon
chopped green onion	1/4 cup	2 tablespoons	1 tablespoon
dried leaf basil	1/2 teaspoon	1/4 teaspoon	1/8 teaspoon
cherry tomatoes, halved	12	6	3
sunflower kernels	1 tablespoon	2 teaspoons	1 teaspoon
BAKING DISH	1-qt. casserole	1-qt. casserole	2-cup casserole
TIME AT HIGH (zucchini)	3-1/2 to 4 minutes	2-1/2 to 3 minutes	1-1/2 to 2 minutes
TIME AT HIGH (tomatoes added)	1 minute	45 to 60 seconds	20 to 30 seconds

In a casserole, see size in chart above, combine butter or margarine, zucchini, carrot, green onion and basil. Microwave, uncovered, at full power (HIGH) for time in chart above or until vegetables are tender, stirring once. Add tomatoes. Microwave at full power (HIGH) for time in chart above or until heated through. Stir in sunflower kernels. Reserve 1 to 2 tablespoons mixture for topping each omelet; use remaining mixture as filling for Basic French Omelet, opposite.

Eggs Florentine au Poivre

SERVINGS	4	2
INGREDIENTS		
frozen chopped spinach	1 (10-oz.) pkg.	1/2 (10-oz.) pkg.
semi-soft natural cheese with pepper	1 (4-oz.) carton	1/2 (4-oz.) carton
chopped pimiento	1/4 cup	2 tablespoons
hot toasted English-muffin halves	4	2
hot Basic Poached Eggs, below	4	2
rolled anchovy fillets	4	2
BAKING DISH	deep 1-qt. casserole	deep 1-qt. casserole
TIME AT HIGH (spinach)	7 to 8 minutes	3 to 4 minutes
TIME AT HIGH (cheese added)	1 to 2 minutes	1 minute

Place spinach in a 1-quart casserole. Cover. Microwave at full power (HIGH) for time in chart above or until tender, stirring twice. Drain thoroughly. Stir in cheese until melted. Stir in pimiento. Cover. Microwave at full power (HIGH) for time in chart above or until heated through, stirring once. Spoon a scant 1/2 cup spinach mixture on top of each English-muffin half. Top each mound with a poached egg. Garnish with an anchovy fillet.

Basic Poached Eggs

SERVINGS	2	1
INGREDIENTS		
hot water	1 cup	1/2 cup
vinegar	1/4 teaspoon	1/4 teaspoon
eggs	2	1
BAKING DISH	2-cup casserole	1-1/2-cup casserole
TIME AT HIGH	2 to 2-1/2 minutes	1 to 1-1/2 minutes
TIME AT 70%	1-1/2 to 1-3/4 minutes	40 to 50 seconds
STANDING TIME	1 minute	1 minute

In a casserole, see size in chart above, combine hot water and vinegar. Cover. Microwave at full power (HIGH) for time in chart above or until boiling. Break eggs into a custard cup or saucer; prick yolks with a pin or wooden pick. Gently slip eggs, one at a time, into hot water mixture. Cover. Microwave at 70% (MEDIUM HIGH) for time in chart above or until almost set. Let stand, covered, 1 minute. Remove eggs from water with a slotted spoon.

Note: To poach 4 eggs, it is best to cook 2 eggs at a time for more even doneness.

Serving Ideas

- To make Eggs Benedict: Microwave Canadian-bacon slices, page 114, and place on toasted English-muffin halves. Top with poached eggs. Ladle No-Fail Hollandaise Sauce, page 422, over the poached eggs.
- To make Huevos Rancheros: Serve poached eggs on heated tortillas with warmed taco sauce or salsa. Top with shredded Cheddar cheese and green chilies.

How to Make Eggs Florentine au Poivre

Thoroughly drain cooked, frozen, chopped spinach in a colander. Then stir semi-soft cheese with pepper into the hot spinach until melted.

Prick egg yolks with a pin, wooden pick or bamboo skewer before poaching in the microwave oven. This prevents yolks from exploding.

Gently slip the eggs into boiling water and vinegar mixture. The vinegar helps set the whites so they don't spread too far. Microwave the eggs for the minimum time for soft yolks, maximum time for firm yolks.

Remove the poached eggs from the water with a slotted spoon. Serve the eggs on toasted English muffins on a bed of spinach-and-cheese mixture. Garnish with a rolled anchovy fillet. This makes a special breakfast or an easy supper dish.

Basic Quiche

SERVINGS	8	4 to 6	2
INGREDIENTS			
shredded cheese*	2 cups (8 oz.)	1-1/2 cups (6 oz.)	3/4 cup (3 oz.)
baked, unpricked pastry shell	10-inch quiche shell	9-inch pie shell or 4 (5-inch) individual quiche shells	2 (5-inch) individual quiche shells
Chicken, Ham or Sausage Quiche Filling, page 278	1-1/3 cups	1 cup	1/2 cup
half and half	2 cups	1-1/2 cups	3/4 cup
salt	1/4 teaspoon	1/4 teaspoon	1/8 teaspoon
seasonings*	1/2 teaspoon	1/2 teaspoon	1/4 teaspoon
eggs, beaten	5	4	2
BAKING DISH	10-inch quiche dish (6 cup)	9-inch pie plate or 4 (5-inch) individual quiche dishes	2 (5-inch) individual quiche dishes
GLASS MEASURING CUP	1-qt.	1-qt.	2-cup
TIME AT HIGH	2-1/2 to 3-1/2 minutes	2-1/2 to 3 minutes	1-1/4 to 1-3/4 minutes
TIME AT 50%	17 to 19 minutes	pie plate: 14 to 16 minutes individual quiches: 17 to 19 minutes	9 to 11 minutes
STANDING TIME	10 minutes	10 minutes	10 minutes

*Note: Suggested cheeses and seasonings are listed at the end of the Chicken, Ham and Sausage Quiche Filling recipes, page 278.

Sprinkle shredded cheese into baked quiche shells, see sizes in chart above. Add well drained filling; set aside. In a glass measuring cup, see size in chart above, combine half and half, salt and seasonings. Microwave at full power (HIGH) for time in chart above or until almost boiling. Gradually stir half-and-half mixture into eggs. Pour into quiche shells. Microwave, uncovered, at 50% (MEDIUM) for time in chart above or until a knife inserted off-center comes out clean. Give large dishes quarter turns twice during time at 50% (MEDIUM); rearrange individual quiche dishes once. Remove any individual quiches that are done and continue cooking remaining quiches until done. Center should appear set when quiche is done. Let stand 10 minutes.

Reheating Refrigerated Quiches

To chill individual quiches: Cover quiches tightly with plastic wrap; refrigerate.
To reheat individual quiches: Vent plastic wrap. Microwave at 70% (MEDIUM HIGH) 3 to 3-1/2 minutes for 1 quiche or 6 to 7 minutes for 2 quiches, giving dishes a half turn once.

To chill a large quiche: Cover cooled quiche tightly with plastic wrap; refrigerate.
To reheat a large quiche: Place individual servings on serving plates. Cover with vented plastic wrap. Microwave at 70% (MEDIUM HIGH) 1-1/2 to 2 minutes for 1 serving or 3-1/2 to 4 minutes for 2 servings, giving plates a half turn once.

How to Make Basic Quiche with Ham Filling

Do not prick the pastry shells before baking. Layer the shredded cheese, then the well-drained filling into the baked pastry shells.

To help the quiche cook more evenly in the microwave oven, heat the half-and-half mixture before whisking it slowly into the beaten eggs.

Use 50% (MEDIUM) to microwave quiche. This allows slower, more even cooking. When done, a knife inserted off-center in quiche should come out clean.

Garnish the individual quiches with shredded lettuce, chopped tomatoes and a spoonful of Thousand Island dressing. This makes a chef's salad in a quiche!

Chicken Quiche Filling

YIELD	1-1/3 cups	1 cup	1/2 cup
INGREDIENTS			
butter or margarine	1 tablespoon	2 teaspoons	1 teaspoon
cubed, cooked chicken	1 cup	3/4 cup	1/3 cup
chopped green onion	1/4 cup	3 tablespoons	2 tablespoons
cooked, drained corn	1/3 cup	1/4 cup	2 tablespoons
BAKING DISH	1-qt. casserole	1-qt. casserole	2-cup casserole
TIME AT HIGH	2 to 3 minutes	1-1/2 to 2 minutes	1 to 1-1/2 minutes

In a casserole, see size in chart above, combine butter or margarine, chicken, green onion and corn. Cover with waxed paper. Microwave at full power (HIGH) for time in chart above or until onion is tender. Drain very well. Use in Basic Quiche, page 276.

Suggested Cheese: Gruyère.
Suggested Seasonings: dried rubbed sage and dried leaf thyme.

Ham Quiche Filling

YIELD	1-1/3 cups	1 cup	1/2 cup
INGREDIENTS			
butter or margarine	1 tablespoon	2 teaspoons	1 teaspoon
cubed, cooked ham	1 cup	3/4 cup	1/3 cup
chopped green pepper	1/4 cup	3 tablespoons	2 tablespoons
chopped pimiento	1/4 cup	3 tablespoons	1 tablespoon
BAKING DISH	1-qt. casserole	1-qt. casserole	2-cup casserole
TIME AT HIGH	2 to 3 minutes	1-1/2 to 2 minutes	1 to 1-1/2 minutes

In a casserole, see size in chart above, combine butter or margarine, ham, green pepper and pimiento. Cover. Microwave at full power (HIGH) for time in chart above or until green pepper is tender. Drain very well. Use in Basic Quiche, page 276.

Suggested Cheese: Cheddar or Colby.
Suggested Seasonings: nutmeg, oregano or fennel.

Sausage Quiche Filling

YIELD	1-1/3 cups	1 cup	1/2 cup
INGREDIENTS			
bulk pork sausage	8 oz.	6 oz.	3 oz.
chopped onion	1/4 cup	3 tablespoons	2 tablespoons
chopped green pepper	1/4 cup	3 tablespoons	2 tablespoons
BAKING DISH	1-qt. casserole	1-qt. casserole	2-cup casserole
TIME AT HIGH	5 to 6 minutes	4 to 5 minutes	3 minutes

In a casserole, see size in chart above, combine sausage, onion and green pepper. Cover with waxed paper. Microwave at full power (HIGH) for time in chart above or until meat is browned. Drain very well. Use in Basic Quiche, page 276.

Suggested Cheese: Swiss or Monterey Jack.
Suggested Seasonings: marjoram, basil, thyme or taco seasoning.

Basic Quiche, page 276, with Chicken Quiche Filling

Pizza Egg Cups

SERVINGS	4	2	1
INGREDIENTS			
salami slices, halved	8 slices	4 slices	2 slices
pizza sauce	1/2 cup	1/4 cup	2 tablespoons
eggs	4	2	1
shredded mozzarella cheese	1/4 cup	2 tablespoons	1 tablespoon
dried leaf Italian herbs	1/2 teaspoon	1/4 teaspoon	1/8 teaspoon
fresh oregano or parsley	to garnish	to garnish	to garnish
CUSTARD CUPS	4 (6-oz.) custard cups	2 (6-oz.) custard cups	1 (6-oz.) custard cup
TIME AT 70%	8 to 10 minutes	3-1/2 to 4 minutes	2-1/2 to 3 minutes
STANDING TIME	1 minute	1 minute	1 minute

Place 3 half slices of salami around edge of each 6-ounce custard cup, see number in chart above, forming a scalloped edge at the top. Place another half slice on bottom of each cup. Spoon half the pizza sauce into salami-lined cups. Gently slip 1 egg into each cup. Prick yolks with a pin or wooden pick. Top with remaining pizza sauce. Sprinkle with mozzarella cheese and Italian herbs. Cover each cup with vented plastic wrap. Microwave at 70% (MEDIUM HIGH) for time in chart above or until eggs are just set, rearranging cups once and giving them a half turn once. Let stand, covered, 1 minute. Garnish with fresh oregano or parsley.

Basic Shirred (Baked) Eggs

SERVINGS	4	2	1
INGREDIENTS			
butter or margarine	4 teaspoons	2 teaspoons	1 teaspoon
eggs	4	2	1
seasoned salt	dash	dash	dash
shredded Cheddar cheese	1/4 cup	2 tablespoons	1 tablespoon
snipped parsley	to garnish	to garnish	to garnish
CUSTARD CUPS	4 (6-oz.) custard cups	2 (6-oz.) custard cups	1 (6-oz.) custard cup
TIME AT HIGH	20 seconds	20 seconds	15 seconds
TIME AT 70%	3 to 3-1/2 minutes	2 to 2-1/2 minutes	1 to 1-1/2 minutes
STANDING TIME	1 minute	1 minute	1 minute

Butter insides of 6-ounce custard cups, see number in chart above. Place 1 teaspoon butter or margarine in bottom of each cup. Microwave at full power (HIGH) for time in chart above or until melted. Gently slip 1 egg into each custard cup. Prick yolks with a pin or wooden pick. Sprinkle with seasoned salt, cheese and snipped parsley. Cover each cup with vented plastic wrap. Microwave at 70% (MEDIUM HIGH) for time in chart above or until eggs are just set, rearranging cups once and giving them a half turn once. Let stand, covered, 1 minute.

How to Make Pizza Egg Cups

Halve 2 salami slices for each custard cup. Overlap 3 half slices around the edge of the custard cup, then place the other half on the bottom of the cup.

Add a spoonful of pizza sauce to each cup, then slip an egg into each cup. Prick the membrane of the yolk with a pin or wooden pick to prevent the yolk from exploding during cooking.

Top each egg with another spoonful of pizza sauce, some shredded mozzarella cheese and a sprinkling of dried Italian herbs. Cover each cup with vented plastic wrap before microwaving.

Microwave the eggs until the yolks are just set. The eggs will finish cooking during the standing time. Garnish each egg cup with a sprig of fresh oregano or parsley and serve with toast.

Canadian Bacon & Eggs

SERVINGS	2	1
INGREDIENTS		
butter or margarine	1 tablespoon	2 teaspoons
Canadian-bacon slices, 1/4 inch thick	2 slices	1 slice, halved
eggs	2	1
BROWNING SKILLET	10-inch microwave browning skillet	6-1/2-inch microwave browning skillet
TIME AT HIGH (preheat skillet)	3 minutes	1 minute
TIME AT HIGH (Canadian bacon)	30 seconds	30 seconds
TIME AT HIGH (eggs added)	2 to 2-1/2 minutes	45 to 60 seconds
STANDING TIME	1 minute	1 minute

See directions for Bacon & Eggs, opposite.

Sausage Links & Eggs

SERVINGS	2	1
INGREDIENTS		
butter or margarine	1 tablespoon	2 teaspoons
fully cooked Brown 'n Serve sausage links	4 links	2 links
eggs	2	1
BROWNING SKILLET	10-inch microwave browning skillet	6-1/2-inch microwave browning skillet
TIME AT HIGH (preheat skillet)	3 minutes	1 minute
TIME AT HIGH (sausage links)	45 seconds	45 seconds
TIME AT HIGH (eggs added)	1-1/4 to 1-3/4 minutes	45 to 60 seconds
STANDING TIME	1 minute	1 minute

See directions for Bacon & Eggs, opposite.

Sausage Patties & Eggs

SERVINGS	2	1
INGREDIENTS		
sausage patties, 3/4 inch thick	2 (1-3/4-oz.) patties	1 (1-3/4-oz.) patty
eggs	2	1
BROWNING SKILLET	10-inch microwave browning skillet	6-1/2-inch microwave browning skillet
TIME AT HIGH (preheat skillet)	3 minutes	45 seconds
TIME AT HIGH (sausage)	3 minutes	2 minutes
TIME AT HIGH (eggs added)	1-1/4 to 1-3/4 minutes	45 to 75 seconds
STANDING TIME	1 minute	1 minute

See directions for Bacon & Eggs, opposite.

How to Make Bacon & Eggs

Place bacon in a preheated microwave browning skillet. Microwave. Turn the bacon over and add eggs to browning skillet. Prick egg yolks with a pin or wooden pick.

Microwave the bacon and eggs for the minimum time for soft yolks or for the maximum time for firmer yolks. Cover the browning skillet for 1 minute before serving the eggs.

Bacon & Eggs

SERVINGS	2	1
INGREDIENTS		
bacon	2 slices, halved	1 slice, halved
eggs	2	1
BROWNING SKILLET	10-inch microwave browning skillet	6-1/2-inch microwave browning skillet
TIME AT HIGH (preheat skillet)	3 minutes	1 minute
TIME AT HIGH (bacon)	30 to 60 seconds	45 to 60 seconds
TIME AT HIGH (eggs added)	1-1/2 to 2 minutes	45 to 60 seconds
STANDING TIME	1 minute	1 minute

Preheat a browning skillet, see size in chart, uncovered, at microwave full power (HIGH) for time in chart. For sausage links and Canadian bacon, add butter or margarine. Using hot pads, tilt skillet to coat evenly with butter or margarine. Quickly add meat at 1 end of skillet. Microwave, uncovered, at full power (HIGH) for time in chart. Turn meat over. Using hot pads, tilt skillet to coat with drippings. Break eggs into a custard cup. Gently add eggs to other end of skillet. Prick yolks with a pin or wooden pick. Give skillet a half turn. Microwave, uncovered, at full power (HIGH) for time in chart or until eggs are done as desired. Let stand, covered, 1 minute.

Old-Fashioned Cheese Rarebit

SERVINGS	4 or 5 (2-1/2 cups)	2 (1-1/4 cups)
INGREDIENTS		
half and half	1-1/2 cups	3/4 cup
shredded process American cheese	1 cup (4 oz.)	1/2 cup (2 oz.)
shredded process Swiss cheese	1 cup (4 oz.)	1/2 cup (2 oz.)
all-purpose flour	2 tablespoons	1 tablespoon
dry mustard	1 teaspoon	1/2 teaspoon
Worcestershire sauce	2 teaspoons	1 teaspoon
egg yolks, beaten	2	1
BOWL	1-1/2-qt. bowl	1-qt. bowl
TIME AT HIGH (half and half)	2-1/2 to 3 minutes	1-1/2 to 2 minutes
TIME AT HIGH (cheese added)	3 to 3-1/2 minutes	1 to 1-1/2 minutes
TIME AT HIGH (yolks added)	1 to 1-1/2 minutes	45 to 60 seconds

Pour half and half into a bowl, see size in chart above. Microwave at full power (HIGH) for time in chart above or until almost boiling. Toss together cheeses, flour and dry mustard. Gradually add cheese mixture to hot half and half, whisking well after each addition. Whisk in Worcestershire sauce. Microwave at full power (HIGH) for time in chart above or until cheeses are melted, stirring three times. Whisk until smooth. Gradually stir half the hot sauce into egg yolks; mix well. Stir yolk mixture into remaining hot sauce in bowl. Microwave at full power (HIGH) for time in chart above or until thickened and heated through, stirring twice. Serve over toasted English muffins or open-face sandwiches.

Mushroom Macaroni Bake

SERVINGS	5 or 6	3
INGREDIENTS		
butter or margarine	2 tablespoons	1 tablespoon
fresh mushroom slices	2 cups	1 cup
chopped red or green pepper	1/2 cup	1/4 cup
chopped onion	1/4 cup	2 tablespoons
condensed cream of onion soup	1 (10-3/4-oz.) can	1/2 (10-3/4-oz.) can
milk	3/4 cup	1/3 cup
dried dillweed	1/2 teaspoon	1/4 teaspoon
shredded Edam cheese	2 cups (8 oz.)	1 cup (4 oz.)
medium-shell macaroni, cooked, drained	2 cups (7 oz.)	1 cup (3-1/2 oz.)
frozen Italian green beans, cooked, drained	1 (9-oz.) pkg.	1/2 (9-oz.) pkg. (1 cup)
BAKING DISH	deep 2-qt. casserole	deep 1-qt. casserole
TIME AT HIGH (mushrooms)	4 to 5 minutes	2-1/2 to 3 minutes
TIME AT HIGH (casserole)	10 to 12 minutes	5 to 6 minutes

In a casserole, see size in chart above, combine butter or margarine, mushrooms, red or green pepper and onion. Cover. Microwave at full power (HIGH) for time in chart above or until vegetables are just tender, stirring once. Stir in soup, milk and dillweed. Mix well. Stir in cheese, macaroni and green beans. Cover. Microwave at full power (HIGH) for time in chart above or until heated through, stirring once. Stir. Sprinkle with sunflower kernels and snipped parsley before serving, if desired.

How to Make Basic Cheese Fondue

Microwave the cheese mixture until almost melted, then whisk until smooth. Add the remaining cheese and microwave, then whisk again.

To eat the fondue, dip chunks of French bread in a small dish of kirsch, then swirl bread in the creamy cheese mixture.

Basic Cheese Fondue

SERVINGS	4	2
INGREDIENTS		
process Swiss cheese slices, diced	8 oz.	4 oz.
process Gruyère cheese, diced	8 oz.	4 oz.
all-purpose flour	2 tablespoons	1 tablespoon
garlic powder	1/8 teaspoon	dash
ground nutmeg	1/8 teaspoon	dash
fresh ground pepper	1/8 teaspoon	dash
dry white wine	1-1/2 cups	3/4 cup
French bread chunks		
kirsch		
BAKING DISH	deep 2-qt. casserole	deep 1-qt. casserole
TIME AT HIGH (wine)	3 to 4 minutes	1-1/2 to 2 minutes
TIME AT HIGH (half the cheese mixture added)	2 minutes	1 minute
TIME AT HIGH (remaining cheese mixture added)	2 to 3 minutes	1 to 1-1/2 minutes

In a medium bowl, combine Swiss cheese, Gruyère cheese, flour, garlic powder, nutmeg and pepper. Toss to mix well. Pour wine into a casserole, see size in chart above. Microwave at full power (HIGH) for time in chart above or until bubbles start to appear; do not boil. Stir in half the cheese mixture, mixing well. Microwave at full power (HIGH) for time in chart above or until almost melted. Mix well. Stir in remaining cheese mixture. Microwave at full power (HIGH) for time in chart above or until almost melted. Whisk until smooth. Keep warm while serving. Dip chunks of French bread in kirsch, then in cheese mixture. If mixture becomes too thick, stir in a little more warmed wine.

Basic Macaroni & Cheese

SERVINGS	4 to 6	2 or 3
INGREDIENTS		
butter or margarine	3 tablespoons	2 tablespoons
chopped green onion	1/4 cup	2 tablespoons
all-purpose flour	3 tablespoons	4 teaspoons
celery salt	1/4 teaspoon	1/8 teaspoon
freshly ground pepper	1/4 teaspoon	1/8 teaspoon
milk	2 cups	1 cup
process American cheese slices, torn up	8 oz.	4 oz.
macaroni, cooked, drained	1-1/2 cups (6 oz.)	3/4 cup (3 oz.)
chopped pimiento	1/4 cup	2 tablespoons
snipped parsley	2 tablespoons	1 tablespoon
tomato slices	6	3
green-pepper rings	6	3
grated Parmesan cheese	1/4 cup	2 tablespoons
BAKING DISH	deep 2-qt. casserole	deep 1-qt. casserole
TIME AT HIGH (onion)	2 minutes	1 to 1-1/2 minutes
TIME AT HIGH (flour added)	30 seconds	30 seconds
TIME AT HIGH (milk added)	5 to 6 minutes	3 to 3-1/2 minutes
TIME AT HIGH (cheese added)	1 to 2 minutes	1 minute
TIME AT HIGH (macaroni added)	6 to 8 minutes	4 to 5 minutes
TIME AT HIGH (tomato, green pepper added)	2 minutes	2 minutes

In a casserole, see size in chart above, combine butter or margarine and green onion. Microwave, uncovered, at full power (HIGH) for time in chart above or until green onion is tender. Stir in flour, celery salt and pepper. Mix well. Microwave at full power (HIGH) 30 seconds. Stir in milk. Microwave at full power (HIGH) for time in chart above or until bubbly, stirring three times. Stir in cheese. Microwave at full power (HIGH) for time in chart above or until cheese melts, stirring twice. Stir in macaroni and pimiento. Cover. Microwave at full power (HIGH) for time in chart above or until heated through, stirring once. Stir in parsley. Top with tomato slices and green-pepper rings. Sprinkle with Parmesan cheese. Cover. Microwave at full power (HIGH) 2 minutes or until tomato and pepper are heated through.

Adapting Layered Casserole Recipes for Microwave Oven

- Because layered casseroles cannot be stirred to even out the microwave cooking, use the 50% (MEDIUM) power setting. This microwaves the casserole more slowly and allows the center to heat through without overcooking the edges.

- Cover casseroles to help even out the cooking and keep food moist.

- If the casserole has an egg-cheese filling, such as lasagne, let the casserole stand 5 to 10 minutes to set up before serving.

Cheese Lover's Lasagne

SERVINGS	6	3
INGREDIENTS		
egg	1	1
all-purpose flour	2 tablespoons	1 tablespoon
cottage cheese	1 cup	1/2 cup
grated Parmesan cheese	1/2 cup	1/4 cup
shredded carrot	1/4 cup	2 tablespoons
chopped celery	1/4 cup	2 tablespoons
chopped pimiento	1/4 cup	2 tablespoons
chopped green onion	1/4 cup	2 tablespoons
frozen chopped spinach, cooked, drained well	1 (10-oz.) pkg.	1/2 (10-oz.) pkg.
all-purpose flour	2 tablespoons	1 tablespoon
plain yogurt	1/2 cup	1/4 cup
condensed cream of onion soup	1 (10-3/4-oz.) can	1/2 (10-3/4-oz.) can
plain or whole-wheat lasagne noodles, cooked, drained well	6	4
sliced sharp process American cheese	8 oz.	4 oz.
BAKING DISH	12" x 7" baking dish	9" x 5" loaf dish
TIME AT 50%	25 to 30 minutes	15 to 20 minutes
STANDING TIME	10 minutes	10 minutes

Butter a baking dish, see size in chart above; set aside. In a medium bowl, beat egg. Stir in first amount of flour, cottage cheese, Parmesan cheese, carrot, celery, pimiento, green onion and well-drained spinach; set aside. In a medium bowl, whisk second amount of flour into yogurt. Whisk in soup, mixing well. In prepared baking dish, layer half the noodles, then half each of the cottage cheese mixture, sharp process cheese and yogurt sauce. Repeat layers. Cover with vented plastic wrap. Microwave at 50% (MEDIUM) for time in chart above or until hot in center, giving dish a half turn once. Let stand, uncovered, 10 minutes.

Reheating Lasagne

SERVINGS	2
INGREDIENTS	
cooked lasagne	2 (4" x 3-1/2") squares
BAKING DISH	9" x 5" loaf dish
TIME AT 70%	8 minutes

To chill: Place lasagne in a 9" x 5" loaf dish. Cover with plastic wrap and refrigerate.

To reheat: Vent plastic wrap. Microwave at 70% (MEDIUM HIGH) 8 minutes or until hot in center, giving dish a half turn once.

How to Make Cheese Lover's Lasagne

Press the cooked spinach in a sieve to remove excess moisture. Spinach must be well-drained or the filling will be watery.

Shredded carrot, chopped celery, pimiento, green onion and spinach are folded into the Parmesan-cottage-cheese filling.

Whisk flour into the yogurt, then whisk in onion soup for the sauce. The flour helps keep the yogurt from curdling.

Layer half the lasagne noodles, then cottage cheese filling, cheese slices and yogurt sauce. Repeat layers. Microwave lasagne until hot.

Asparagus Luncheon Roll-Ups

SERVINGS	4 to 8
INGREDIENTS	
frozen asparagus soufflé, thawed	1 (12-oz.) pkg.
seasoned dry breadcrumbs	1/2 cup
grated Parmesan cheese	1/2 cup
lasagne noodles, cooked, drained	8
bacon, crisp-cooked, crumbled	8 slices
Triple Cheese Sauce, page 431, prepared without salt	1-3/4 cups
paprika	to garnish
BAKING DISH	4 (9-inch) au gratin dishes
TIME AT HIGH	9 to 10 minutes

In a medium bowl, combine soufflé, breadcrumbs and Parmesan cheese. Mix well. Spread a scant 1/4 cup soufflé mixture on each flat lasagne noodle. Sprinkle with bacon. Roll up jelly-roll fashion. Place 2 roll-ups, seam side down, in each of four 9-inch au gratin dishes. Leave space between roll-ups. Prepare Triple Cheese Sauce, omitting salt. Pour hot sauce over lasagne rolls, thoroughly coating all pasta. Cover with vented plastic wrap. Microwave at full power (HIGH) 9 to 10 minutes or until heated through. Rearrange dishes once and give them a half turn once during cooking time. Stir sauce to serve. Sprinkle with paprika.

Cheesy Broccoli Stratas

SERVINGS	4	2
INGREDIENTS		
herb-seasoned croutons	1-1/2 cups	3/4 cup
shredded process American cheese	1 cup (4 oz.)	1/2 cup (2 oz.)
frozen chopped broccoli, cooked, drained	2 (10-oz.) pkgs.	1 (10-oz.) pkg.
chopped pimiento	1/4 cup	2 tablespoons
chopped green onion	1/4 cup	2 tablespoons
bottled tartar sauce	1/2 cup	1/4 cup
lemon juice	1 teaspoon	1/2 teaspoon
shredded process American cheese	1 cup (4 oz.)	1/2 cup (2 oz.)
herb-seasoned croutons	1-1/2 cups	3/4 cup
eggs, slightly beaten	4	2
evaporated milk	1 (13-oz.) can	1 (5-1/3-oz.) can
BAKING DISH	4 (2-cup) casseroles	2 (2-cup) casseroles
TIME AT 50%	25 to 30 minutes	15 to 20 minutes
STANDING TIME	5 minutes	5 minutes

Butter 2-cup casseroles, see number in chart above. Divide first amount of croutons among casseroles. Top with first amount of cheese. In a medium bowl, combine broccoli, pimiento and green onion. Fold in tartar sauce and lemon juice. Divide broccoli mixture among casseroles. Top with second amount of cheese and croutons. In a small bowl, whisk eggs and evaporated milk. Pour over croutons. Cover each casserole with plastic wrap. Refrigerate 2 to 24 hours. To serve, vent plastic wrap. Microwave at 50% (MEDIUM) for time in chart above or until set, giving dishes quarter turns twice and rearranging once. Let stand, covered, 5 minutes.

Salads

Vegetables & Salads

Vegetables are cooked to a perfect crisp-tender doneness in the microwave oven with minimum flavor and vitamin loss. They not only taste good, but also look fresh and appetizing because their natural color is retained.

Q. How are the vegetable and salad recipes organized in this chapter?

A. The vegetables are in alphabetical order from artichokes through turnips. Next you will find mixed vegetables, blanching vegetables for freezing, molded salads, hot vegetable salads and relishes. Each vegetable has basic cooking directions for fresh, frozen and canned items where appropriate. Most vegetables also have some quick serving ideas and one or more flavorful recipes.

Q. What are the advantages of cooking vegetables in the microwave?

A. Vegetables have more flavor when cooked in the microwave because they cook more quickly. They usually require little or no water that might dilute some of the flavor. Studies indicate that vegetables cooked in the microwave actually retain more vitamins and minerals.

Q. Which vegetable dishes do not cook satisfactorily in the microwave?

A. Vegetable soufflés do not work in the microwave because the egg structure cannot be set without overcooking the edges of the soufflé. Commercially frozen vegetable soufflés can be reheated in the microwave because the structure is already set.

Q. How are vegetables cooked in the microwave?

A. Most fresh, frozen and canned vegetables are cooked at full power (HIGH). Many fresh vegetables have directions for a unique method of cooking. They are blanched, or partially cooked, and then refrigerated. Shortly before serving time, the vegetables are reheated with butter in the microwave. This is an easy make-ahead method to use for entertaining. Vegetables frozen in pouches are microwaved right in the pouch after a small slit is cut on one side of the pouch. It's handy to blanch and freeze your own vegetables in family-size pouches. If you have a small family, buy frozen loose-pack vegetables in large plastic bags and follow directions in this chapter to cook the amount you need.

Q. How do you know when vegetables are done?

A. The cooking times given are for crisp-tender vegetables. When pierced with a fork, crisp-tender vegetables will still have a little resistance. Vegetables continue to cook during the standing time, so allow for that when estimating doneness. If you prefer well-done vegetables, add cooking time in 30- to 60-second amounts. Baked potatoes should be cooked until still slightly firm, then wrapped in foil for the standing time to finish cooking. Potatoes cooked until tender to the touch will be shriveled by the time they are served.

Q. How do you reheat cooked vegetables in the microwave?

A. Use the timings for the appropriate canned vegetable as a guideline. Add about a minute to the cooking time when you reheat refrigerated vegetables.

Q. Can vegetable convenience foods be cooked in the microwave?

A. Yes. Many frozen vegetable casseroles or combinations with sauces have microwave directions on the package. Many of the dry packaged vegetables, such as potatoes, also have microwave cooking directions on the package.

Q. Why do you stir or rearrange vegetables during cooking?

A. Vegetables are stirred during cooking so they will cook more evenly. If they are not moved around, the vegetables close to the edges of the dish will overcook before the vegetables in the center are done. To rearrange vegetables in a pouch, pick up the pouch and flex it several times to move the frozen vegetables in the center toward the outside of the pouch. In the case of larger vegetables that cannot be stirred, move the center pieces to the outside of the dish and the pieces from the outside to the center.

Q. Why are vegetables salted after cooking?

A. Unless the salt is dissolved in a sauce, vegetables should be salted after cooking. Otherwise, salt lying on the surface of the vegetables may cause dehydration and shriveling where it touches the vegetables.

Q. Why are two weights given on some fresh vegetable recipes?

A. The amounts as purchased are stated in typical market units, such as 1 pound. The amount after trimming is listed as a guideline to show approximately how much vegetable is going to be cooked. This is important in microwave cooking because twice as much vegetable takes almost twice as long to cook. Therefore, the final after-trimming weight is important in estimating cooking times.

How to Garnish Vegetables with a Flourish

Try simple toppings such as crumbled bacon, flavored croutons, toasted nuts or seeds, or shredded cheeses on plain vegetables. Fresh herbs, buttered cracker crumbs or canned French-fried onions turn everyday vegetables into something special.

Top hot cooked vegetables with yogurt, sour-cream dip, cheese or hollandaise sauce. Snip fresh chives over the topping. For the easiest creamed vegetables you ever made, try Quick Creamed Vegetables, page 424.

Fresh Artichokes

SERVINGS	4	2	1
INGREDIENTS			
fresh artichokes	4 (10- to 12-oz.) artichokes	2 (10- to 12-oz.) artichokes	1 (10- to 12-oz.) artichoke
lemon juice	2 tablespoons	1 tablespoon	1 tablespoon
BAKING DISH	12" x 7" baking dish	deep 1-1/2-qt. casserole	deep 1-1/2-qt. casserole
TIME AT HIGH	15 to 16 minutes	7 minutes	4 to 5 minutes
STANDING TIME	2 minutes	2 minutes	2 minutes

Wash artichokes under cold water. Cut off stem and 1 inch from top of artichoke. With scissors, snip off tips of leaves. Brush cut edges with lemon juice to prevent darkening. Place artichokes, stem end down, in a baking dish, see size in chart above. Cover with lid or vented plastic wrap. Or wrap each artichoke in waxed paper, twisting ends to seal. Microwave at full power (HIGH) for time in chart above, rearranging artichokes or giving baking dish a half turn once. Let stand, covered, 2 minutes. Serve hot with butter sauce or chill and serve with vinaigrette dressing.

Doneness Test: Artichokes are done when a leaf pulls out easily.

Dilled Artichoke Butter

SERVINGS	4	2
INGREDIENTS		
butter or margarine	1/2 cup	1/4 cup
lemon juice	2 tablespoons	1 tablespoon
dried dillweed	1/2 teaspoon	1/4 teaspoon
onion powder	1/4 teaspoon	1/8 teaspoon
celery salt	1/4 teaspoon	1/8 teaspoon
white pepper	1/8 teaspoon	dash
BOWL	3-cup bowl	2-cup bowl
TIME AT HIGH	1-1/4 minutes	45 seconds

In a bowl, see size in chart above, melt butter or margarine at full power (HIGH) for time in chart above. Stir in lemon juice, dillweed, onion powder, celery salt and white pepper. Serve warm as artichoke dipper.

Serving Ideas

- Stir dill, basil or thyme into mayonnaise for an artichoke dipper.
- Serve whole artichokes chilled as an appetizer with vinaigrette dressing.
- Roll canned artichoke hearts in smoked sliced beef before heating.

How to Cook Fresh Artichokes

Using a large sharp knife, cut off the stem and 1 inch from pointed top of each artichoke. With scissors, snip off the prickly tips of each leaf.

Brush the cut edges of each leaf with lemon juice to prevent darkening. Wrap each artichoke in a square of waxed paper; twist ends to seal.

After cooking, use a grapefruit spoon to remove the fuzzy center of the artichoke. The leaves on the artichoke at left have been folded back to show the choke. In the foreground, notice the choke attached to the artichoke bottom or heart.

To eat the artichoke, remove the leaves and dip the meaty end in butter sauce. Then pull the leaf through your teeth. After removing all the leaves, cut the round, cup-shaped bottom from the artichoke. Dip in butter sauce and enjoy!

Frozen Artichoke Hearts

SERVINGS	3
INGREDIENTS frozen artichoke hearts	1 (9-oz.) pkg.
BAKING DISH	1-qt. casserole
TIME AT HIGH	8 to 9 minutes
STANDING TIME	1 to 2 minutes

Place artichoke hearts in a 1-quart casserole. Cover. Microwave at full power (HIGH) 8 to 9 minutes or until tender, stirring once. Let stand, covered, 1 to 2 minutes.

Canned Artichoke Hearts

SERVINGS	4	2	2
INGREDIENTS plain artichoke hearts OR	1 (14-oz.) can	1 (8-1/2-oz.) can	
marinated artichoke hearts			1 (6-oz.) jar
BOWL	3- to 4-cup bowl	2- to 3-cup bowl	2- to 3-cup bowl
TIME AT HIGH	3-1/2 to 4-1/2 minutes	1-1/2 to 2-1/2 minutes	2 to 3 minutes

Drain off all but 2 tablespoons liquid from can or jar. In a bowl, see size in chart above, combine artichoke hearts and remaining liquid. Cover with vented plastic wrap. Microwave at full power (HIGH) for time in chart above or until heated through.

Frozen Asparagus Cuts or Spears

SERVINGS	4	3
INGREDIENTS frozen asparagus cuts OR	1 (10-oz.) pkg.	
frozen asparagus spears		1 (10-oz.) pkg.
BAKING DISH	1-qt. casserole	1-qt. casserole
TIME AT HIGH	7 minutes	8 minutes
STANDING TIME	1 to 2 minutes	1 to 2 minutes

Place asparagus in a 1-quart casserole. Cover. Microwave at full power (HIGH) for time in chart above or until tender, stirring once. Let stand, covered, 1 to 2 minutes.

Frozen Asparagus Spears in a Pouch

SERVINGS	3
INGREDIENTS	
frozen cut asparagus spears in butter sauce	1 (9-oz.) pkg.
TIME AT HIGH	6 to 7 minutes

With a sharp knife or scissors, cut a small "X" in center of top side of pouch. Microwave pouch at full power (HIGH) 6 to 7 minutes, flexing pouch once to rearrange asparagus.

Canned Asparagus Spears

SERVINGS	2 or 3	1 or 2
INGREDIENTS		
asparagus spears	1 (14-1/2-oz.) can	1 (8-1/4-oz.) can
BOWL	3- to 4-cup bowl	2- to 3-cup bowl
TIME AT HIGH	2-1/2 to 3 minutes	1-1/2 to 2 minutes

Drain off all but 2 tablespoons liquid from can. In a bowl, see size in chart above, combine asparagus and remaining liquid. Cover with vented plastic wrap. Microwave at full power (HIGH) for time in chart above or until heated through.

Blanched & Butter-Cooked Asparagus

SERVINGS	4 to 6	2 or 3
INGREDIENTS		
fresh asparagus spears		
(as purchased)	2 lbs.	1 lb.
(after trimming)	1 lb.	7 oz.
water	1/2 cup	1/4 cup
butter or margarine	2 tablespoons	1 tablespoon
BAKING DISH	2- to 3-qt. casserole	1-qt. casserole
TIME AT HIGH (blanching)	6 to 7 minutes	3-1/2 minutes
TIME AT HIGH (butter)	45 seconds	30 seconds
TIME AT HIGH (asparagus added)	9 to 10 minutes	4 minutes
STANDING TIME	2 minutes	2 minutes

Wash asparagus. Grasp stalk at either end and bend in a bow shape. Stalk will break where tender part of stalk starts. Discard tough part of stalk. Place spears in a casserole, see size in chart above. Add water. Cover. Microwave at full power (HIGH) for time in chart above or until starting to get tender, rearranging spears once. Drain in a colander and run cold water over asparagus. Wrap and refrigerate. At serving time, melt butter or margarine in same casserole at full power (HIGH) for time in chart above. Add asparagus, stirring to coat. Cover. Microwave at full power (HIGH) for time in chart above or until crisp-tender and heated through, stirring once. Let stand, covered, 2 minutes.

Confetti Asparagus Bake

SERVINGS	6	3
INGREDIENTS		
frozen asparagus spears	2 (10-oz.) pkgs.	1 (10-oz.) pkg.
butter or margarine	1/4 cup	2 tablespoons
seasoned dry breadcrumbs	2 tablespoons	2 tablespoons
finely chopped onion	3 tablespoons	1 tablespoon
finely chopped celery	3 tablespoons	2 tablespoons
tomato, chopped, drained	1	1/2
dried leaf basil, crushed	1/4 teaspoon	1/8 teaspoon
dried leaf thyme, crushed	1/4 teaspoon	1/8 teaspoon
grated Parmesan cheese	2 tablespoons	1 tablespoon
PLATE	12-inch microwave pizza plate	10-inch plate
TIME AT HIGH (asparagus)	3 minutes	1-1/2 minutes
TIME AT HIGH (butter)	1 minute	30 seconds
TIME AT HIGH (platter)	10 to 11 minutes	6 to 7 minutes

Loosen wrapping on asparagus packages. Place packages in microwave oven. Microwave at full power (HIGH) for time in chart above. On a plate, see size in chart above, arrange asparagus spears spoke-fashion, with tips pointing to center. In a small bowl, microwave butter or margarine at full power (HIGH) for time in chart above or until melted. Combine 1 tablespoon melted butter or margarine with breadcrumbs; set aside. Sprinkle onion, celery and tomato pieces over asparagus; drizzle with remaining melted butter or margarine. Sprinkle with basil and thyme. Cover with vented plastic wrap. Microwave at full power (HIGH) for time in chart above or until asparagus is tender, giving plate a half turn once. Sprinkle with Parmesan cheese and buttered crumbs.

Fresh Asparagus

SERVINGS	4 to 6	2 or 3
INGREDIENTS		
fresh asparagus spears		
(as purchased)	2 lbs.	1 lb.
(after trimming)	1 lb.	7 oz.
water	1/4 cup	1/4 cup
BAKING DISH	flat 1-qt. casserole	flat 1-qt. casserole
TIME AT HIGH	12 minutes	7 minutes
STANDING TIME	2 minutes	2 minutes

Wash asparagus. Grasp stalk at either end and bend in a bow shape. Stalk will break where tender part of stalk starts. Discard tough part of stalk. Place spears in a flat 1-quart casserole. Add water. Cover. Microwave at full power (HIGH) for time in chart above or until tender, rearranging spears once. Let stand, covered, 2 minutes. Drain.

Serving Ideas

- Stir curry powder and lemon juice into mayonnaise, then spoon over hot cooked asparagus spears.
- Microwave slivered almonds in butter, then pour over hot cooked asparagus spears.
- Marinate cooked asparagus spears in French dressing, then serve on a cold plate.

Succotash Scallop

SERVINGS	8	4
INGREDIENTS		
frozen baby lima beans	2 (10-oz.) pkgs.	1 (10-oz.) pkg.
water	1 cup	1 cup
butter or margarine	2 tablespoons	1 tablespoon
seasoned dry breadcrumbs	1/2 cup	1/4 cup
butter or margarine	1/4 cup	2 tablespoons
chopped onion	1/4 cup	2 tablespoons
chopped green pepper	1/4 cup	2 tablespoons
all-purpose flour	1 tablespoon	2 teaspoons
milk	1 cup	1/2 cup
shredded Monterey Jack cheese	2 cups (8 oz.)	1 cup (4 oz.)
whole-kernel corn, drained	1 (16-oz.) can	1 (8-3/4-oz.) can
water chestnuts, drained, sliced	1 (8-oz.) can	1/2 (8-oz.) can
chopped pimiento	1/4 cup	2 tablespoons
celery seed	1 teaspoon	1/2 teaspoon
BAKING DISH	deep 3-qt. casserole	deep 1-1/2-qt. casserole
TIME AT HIGH (limas)	20 minutes	11 minutes
TIME AT HIGH (butter)	45 seconds	30 seconds
TIME AT HIGH (onion mixture)	3 minutes	2-1/2 to 3 minutes
TIME AT HIGH (sauce)	3 minutes	1-1/2 to 2 minutes
TIME AT HIGH (casserole)	10 minutes	6 minutes

Combine lima beans and water in a casserole, see size in chart above. Cover and micro-wave at full power (HIGH) for time in chart above or until tender, stirring once. Drain. Cover and set aside. In a small bowl, microwave first amount of butter or margarine at full power (HIGH) for time in chart above or until melted. Stir in breadcrumbs; set aside. In same casserole, microwave second amount of butter or margarine, onion and green pepper at full power (HIGH) for time in chart above or until vegetables are tender, stirring once. Stir in flour until blended. Add milk. Microwave at full power (HIGH) for time in chart above or until thickened and bubbly, stirring three times. Gradually add cheese; stir until melted. Stir in limas, corn, water chestnuts, pimiento and celery seed. Cover. Microwave at full power (HIGH) for time in chart above or until heated through. Top with buttered crumbs.

Canned Lima Beans

SERVINGS	2 or 3	1 or 2
INGREDIENTS		
lima beans	1 (17-oz.) can	1 (8-1/2-oz.) can
BOWL	3- to 4-cup bowl	2- to 3-cup bowl
TIME AT HIGH	4-1/2 to 5-1/2 minutes	3-1/2 to 4-1/2 minutes

Drain off all but 2 tablespoons liquid from can. In a bowl, see size in chart above, com-bine beans and remaining liquid. Cover with vented plastic wrap. Microwave at full power (HIGH) for time in chart above or until heated through.

How to Make Succotash Scallop

Gradually shred Monterey Jack cheese into thickened sauce, then stir until melted.

Stir cooked lima beans, corn, pimiento, water chestnuts and celery seed into the sauce.

Frozen Baby Lima Beans

SERVINGS	6	4	2	1
INGREDIENTS				
frozen baby lima beans	4 cups	3 cups	1 (8- or 10-oz.) pkg. (2 cups)	1 cup
water	1-1/2 cups	1-1/3 cups	1 cup	1/2 cup
BAKING DISH	deep 2-qt. casserole	deep 1-1/2-qt. casserole	deep 1-1/2-qt. casserole	deep 1-qt. casserole
TIME AT HIGH	15 to 16 minutes	13 to 14 minutes	10 to 11 minutes	8 to 9 minutes
STANDING TIME	1 to 2 minutes	1 to 2 minutes	1 to 2 minutes	1 to 2 minutes

In a casserole, see size in chart above, combine lima beans and water. Cover. Microwave at full power (HIGH) for time in chart above or until tender, stirring once. Let stand, covered, 1 to 2 minutes. Drain.

Serving Ideas

- Toss hot cooked green beans with hot bacon drippings and crumbled bacon.
- Add cubed ham or salt pork, finely chopped onion and marjoram to green beans before cooking.
- Stir chili sauce, instant minced onion and pickle relish into hot cooked green beans.
- Toss hot cooked lima beans with butter, chopped pimiento, thyme and cheese croutons.

Frozen French-Style Green Beans

SERVINGS	5	2 or 3
INGREDIENTS		
frozen French-style green beans	5 cups	1 (8- or 9-oz.) pkg. (2-1/2 cups)
water	1/4 cup	2 tablespoons
BAKING DISH	2-qt. casserole	1-qt. casserole
TIME AT HIGH	12 minutes	6 minutes
STANDING TIME	1 to 2 minutes	1 to 2 minutes

In a casserole, see size in chart above, combine beans and water. Cover. Microwave at full power (HIGH) for time in chart above or until tender, stirring twice. Let stand, covered, 1 to 2 minutes. Drain.

Frozen French-Style Green Beans in a Pouch

SERVINGS	3
INGREDIENTS	
frozen French-style green beans in butter sauce	1 (9-oz.) pkg.
TIME AT HIGH	6 to 7 minutes

With a sharp knife or scissors, cut a small "X" in center of top side of pouch. Microwave pouch at full power (HIGH) 6 to 7 minutes, flexing pouch once to rearrange beans.

Frozen Whole or Italian Green Beans

SERVINGS	3
INGREDIENTS	
frozen whole or Italian green beans	1 (9-oz.) pkg.
water	2 tablespoons
BAKING DISH	1-qt. casserole
TIME AT HIGH	7 minutes
STANDING TIME	1 to 2 minutes

Combine beans and water in a 1-quart casserole. Cover. Microwave at full power (HIGH) 7 minutes or until tender, stirring once. Let stand, covered, 1 to 2 minutes. Drain.

Frozen Cut Green Beans

SERVINGS	6	4	2	1
INGREDIENTS				
frozen cut green beans	4 cups	3 cups	1 (8- or 9-oz.) pkg. (2 cups)	1 cup
water	2/3 cup	1/2 cup	1/2 cup	1/3 cup
BAKING DISH	2-qt. casserole	1-1/2 qt. casserole	1-1/2-qt. casserole	1-qt. casserole
TIME AT HIGH	16 to 17 minutes	14 to 15 minutes	12 to 13 minutes	10 to 11 minutes
STANDING TIME	1 to 2 minutes	1 to 2 minutes	1 to 2 minutes	1 to 2 minutes

In a casserole, see size in chart above, combine beans and water. Cover. Microwave at full power (HIGH) for time in chart above or until tender, stirring once. Let stand, covered, 1 to 2 minutes. Drain.

Frozen Cut Green Beans in a Pouch

SERVINGS	3
INGREDIENTS	
frozen cut green beans in butter sauce	1 (9-oz.) pkg.
TIME AT HIGH	5 to 6 minutes

With a sharp knife or scissors, cut a small "X" in center of top side of pouch. Microwave pouch at full power (HIGH) 5 to 6 minutes, flexing pouch once to rearrange beans.

Fresh Green or Wax Beans

SERVINGS	6 to 8	3 or 4	1 or 2
INGREDIENTS			
fresh green or wax beans	1 lb. (4 cups)	8 oz. (2 cups)	4 oz. (1 cup)
hot water	2 cups	1-1/2 cups	1 cup
BAKING DISH	deep 2-qt. casserole	deep 1-qt. casserole	deep 1-qt. casserole
TIME AT HIGH	21 to 23 minutes	16 to 18 minutes	12 to 14 minutes
STANDING TIME	2 minutes	2 minutes	2 minutes

Wash beans and remove ends. Cut in 1- to 2-inch pieces or leave whole. In a casserole, see size in chart above, combine beans and hot water to cover. Cover. Microwave at full power (HIGH) for time in chart above or until tender, stirring once. Let stand, covered, 2 minutes. Drain.

Green Beans Italiano

SERVINGS	6 to 8	3 or 4
INGREDIENTS		
frozen Italian green beans	2 (9-oz.) pkgs.	1 (9-oz.) pkg.
water	1/4 cup	2 tablespoons
garbanzo beans, drained	1 (16-oz.) can	1/2 (16-oz.) can
chopped pimiento	1/4 cup	2 tablespoons
pitted ripe olive slices	1/4 cup	2 tablespoons
chopped pepperoni	1/4 cup	2 tablespoons
olive oil	1/4 cup	2 tablespoons
dried leaf oregano, crushed	1 teaspoon	1/2 teaspoon
garlic powder	1/4 teaspoon	1/8 teaspoon
BAKING DISH	deep 2-qt. casserole	deep 1-1/2-qt. casserole
TIME AT HIGH (beans)	12 to 14 minutes	7 minutes
TIME AT HIGH (casserole)	3 to 4 minutes	2 minutes

In a casserole, see size in chart above, combine Italian beans and water. Cover. Micro
wave at full power (HIGH) for time in chart above or until tender, stirring once. Drain
well. Add garbanzo beans, pimiento, olives, pepperoni, olive oil, oregano and garlic
powder; mix well. Cover. Microwave at full power (HIGH) for time in chart above or
until heated through, stirring once.

Canned Green Beans

SERVINGS	2 or 3	1 or 2
INGREDIENTS		
cut green or Italian green beans	1 (16-oz.) can	1 (8-1/2-oz.) can
BOWL	3- to 4-cup bowl	2- to 3-cup bowl
TIME AT HIGH	2-1/2 to 3 minutes	1-1/2 to 2-1/2 minutes

Drain off all but 2 tablespoons liquid from can. In a bowl, see size in chart above, combine beans and remaining liquid. Cover with vented plastic wrap. Microwave at full
power (HIGH) for time in chart above or until heated through.

Canned Pork & Beans in Tomato Sauce

SERVINGS	2 or 3	1 or 2
INGREDIENTS		
pork and beans in tomato sauce	1 (16-oz.) can	1 (8-oz.) can
BOWL	3- to 4-cup bowl	2- to 3-cup bowl
TIME AT HIGH	4 to 5 minutes	2-1/2 to 3-1/2 minutes

Place beans and liquid in a bowl, see size in chart above. Cover with vented plastic
wrap. Microwave at full power (HIGH) for time in chart above or until heated through
stirring once.

Maple Baked Beans

SERVINGS	6 to 8	3 or 4
INGREDIENTS		
dried pea beans	1 lb. (2 cups)	8 oz. (1 cup)
water	2 qts.	1 qt.
baking soda	1/4 teaspoon	1/8 teaspoon
water	6 cups	3 cups
salt	1 teaspoon	1/2 teaspoon
bacon, cooked, crumbled	8 slices	4 slices
packed brown sugar	1/2 cup	1/4 cup
maple-flavored syrup	1/2 cup	1/4 cup
instant minced onion	2 teaspoons	1 teaspoon
Worcestershire sauce	2 teaspoons	1 teaspoon
ground cinnamon	1 teaspoon	1/2 teaspoon
reserved cooking liquid	1 cup	1/2 cup
apples, cored, sliced	2	1
BAKING DISH	deep 4-qt. casserole	deep 2-qt. casserole
TIME AT HIGH	18 to 20 minutes	10 minutes
TIME AT 30% (beans)	60 to 70 minutes	45 to 50 minutes
TIME AT 30% (bacon added)	80 to 90 minutes	45 minutes
TIME AT 30% (apples added)	15 to 20 minutes	10 minutes

Sort and rinse beans. In a casserole, see size in chart above, combine beans and first amount of water. Stir in baking soda. Cover and let stand overnight. Drain and rinse beans. Return beans to casserole. Add second amount of water and salt. Cover and microwave at full power (HIGH) for time in chart above or until boiling. Stir. Cover and microwave at 30% (MEDIUM LOW) for time in chart above or until beans are tender, stirring occasionally. Drain, reserving liquid. Stir bacon, brown sugar, maple-flavored syrup, onion, Worcestershire sauce and cinnamon into beans. Add measured reserved cooking liquid, see amount in chart above. Cover. Microwave at 30% (MEDIUM LOW) for time in chart above or until beans are very tender and flavors blend, stirring occasionally. Add more reserved cooking liquid, if necessary. Top with a ring of apple slices. Cover. Microwave at 30% (MEDIUM LOW) for time in chart above or until apples are tender, giving dish a half turn once.

Reheating Maple Baked or Refried Beans

SERVINGS	2	1
INGREDIENTS		
Maple Baked Beans, above OR refried beans	2 cups	1 cup
BAKING DISH	2-cup casserole	1-1/2-cup casserole
TIME AT 70%	6 to 7 minutes	4 to 5 minutes

Spoon beans into a casserole, see size in chart above. Cover with a lid or vented plastic wrap. Microwave at 70% (MEDIUM HIGH) for time in chart above or until heated through. Stir in a few tablespoons hot water, if necessary. Stir before serving.

How to Make Maple Baked Beans

For maximum tenderness, soak dried beans overnight in a solution of water and baking soda. Drain and rinse beans before cooking.

After cooking beans in water until tender, mix drained beans with bacon, brown sugar and maple syrup. Garnish beans with a ring of rosy red apple slices.

Dried Beans

SERVINGS	8	4
INGREDIENTS		
dried kidney, baby lima, pinto or navy beans	1 lb. (about 3 cups)	8 oz. (about 1-1/2 cups)
water	2 qts.	1 qt.
baking soda	1/4 teaspoon	1/8 teaspoon
water	6 cups	3 cups
salt	1 teaspoon	1/2 teaspoon
BAKING DISH	deep 4-qt. casserole	deep 2-qt. casserole
TIME AT HIGH	20 minutes	10 minutes
TIME AT 30%	55 to 65 minutes	40 to 45 minutes
STANDING TIME	10 minutes	10 minutes

In a casserole, see size in chart above, combine dried beans, first amount of water and baking soda. Stir. Cover and let stand overnight. Drain and rinse beans. Return to casserole. Add second amount of water and salt. Cover. Microwave at full power (HIGH) for time in chart above or until boiling. Stir. Cover and microwave at 30% (MEDIUM LOW) for time in chart above or until beans are tender, stirring twice. Let stand, covered, 10 minutes.

Fresh Beets

SERVINGS	6 to 8	3 or 4	1 or 2
INGREDIENTS small beets OR		1 lb. 6 oz. (10 beets)	11 oz. (5 beets)
medium beets	3 lbs. (11 beets)	1-1/2 lbs. (6 beets)	
water	4 cups	3 cups	2 cups
BAKING DISH	deep 5-qt. casserole	deep 2-qt. casserole	deep 1-1/2-qt. casserole
TIME AT HIGH	25 to 27 minutes	16 to 18 minutes (small beets) 19 to 20 minutes (medium beets)	12 minutes
STANDING TIME	2 minutes	2 minutes	2 minutes

Select small or medium beets. Wash beets. Cut off all but 1 inch of stem and root. Do not pare. In a casserole, see size in chart above, combine either whole medium or small beets with water. Cover. Microwave at full power (HIGH) for time in chart above or until tender, stirring once. Let stand, covered, 2 minutes. Drain. Peel and slice or dice, or serve small beets whole.

Fresh Beet Greens

SERVINGS	4 to 6	2 or 3	1
INGREDIENTS fresh beet greens	1 lb. (12 cups)	8 oz. (6 cups)	4 oz. (3 cups)
BAKING DISH	deep 5-qt. casserole	deep 2-qt. casserole	deep 1-1/2-qt. casserole
TIME AT HIGH	14 to 15 minutes	8 to 9 minutes	6 to 7 minutes

Wash greens. Place greens with water that clings to leaves in a casserole, see size in chart above. Cover. Microwave at full power (HIGH) for time in chart above or until tender, stirring once.

Canned Beets

SERVINGS	2 or 3	1 or 2
INGREDIENTS small whole, sliced, or diced beets	1 (16-oz.) can	1 (8-oz.) can
BOWL	3- to 4-cup bowl	2- to 3-cup bowl
TIME AT HIGH	3 to 4 minutes	2 to 3 minutes

Drain off all but 2 tablespoons liquid from can. In a bowl, see size in chart above, combine beets and remaining liquid. Cover with vented plastic wrap. Microwave at full power (HIGH) for time in chart above or until heated through.

How to Make Glazed Beets

Vinegar and horseradish are combined with cranberry juice cocktail for this tasty sauce. After thickening, stir in either canned or thawed, frozen cranberry-orange relish.

Pour cranberry sauce over beets in the casserole dish. Mix gently until all beets are coated. A quick heating in the microwave finishes this attractive dish.

Glazed Beets

SERVINGS	6	3
INGREDIENTS		
whole tiny beets, drained	2 (16-oz.) cans	1 (16-oz.) can
packed brown sugar	2 tablespoons	1 tablespoon
cornstarch	2 teaspoons	1 teaspoon
cranberry juice cocktail	2/3 cup	1/3 cup
white vinegar	2 tablespoons	1 tablespoon
prepared horseradish	1 teaspoon	1/2 teaspoon
cranberry-orange relish	1/4 cup	2 tablespoons
BAKING DISH	2-qt. casserole	1-qt. casserole
GLASS MEASURING CUP	2-cup	2-cup
TIME AT HIGH (sauce)	2 to 2-1/2 minutes	1 to 1-1/2 minutes
TIME AT HIGH (beets added)	7 minutes	3 to 4 minutes

Place beets in a casserole, see size in chart above; set aside. In a 2-cup glass measuring cup, mix brown sugar and cornstarch until well combined. Stir in cranberry juice cocktail, vinegar and horseradish. Microwave at full power (HIGH) for time in chart above or until mixture thickens and bubbles, stirring twice. Stir in cranberry-orange relish. Gently mix sauce into beets. Cover. Microwave at full power (HIGH) for time in chart above or until heated through.

Serving Ideas

● Glaze whole tiny beets with orange marmalade mixed with a little lemon juice.
● Drizzle hot beets with wine vinegar, then sprinkle with chopped hard-cooked eggs.
● For easy pickled beets, heat whole tiny beets in leftover pickle juice, then refrigerate.

Fresh Broccoli

SERVINGS	4	2	1
INGREDIENTS			
fresh broccoli			
(as purchased)	1 lb. 6 oz.	10 oz.	5 oz.
(after trimming)	12 oz.	7 oz.	3 oz.
water	1/4 cup	1/4 cup	1/4 cup
BAKING DISH	flat 1-qt. casserole	round, 8-inch baking dish	round, 8-inch baking dish
TIME AT HIGH	9 to 10 minutes	7 to 8 minutes	6 to 7 minutes
STANDING TIME	2 minutes	2 minutes	2 minutes

Wash broccoli. Cut into flowerets leaving 2 inches of stalk. Place in a baking dish, see size in chart above, with stems toward outside of dish. Add water. Cover with lid or vented plastic wrap. Microwave at full power (HIGH) for time in chart above, or until tender, rearranging once. Let stand, covered, 2 minutes. Drain.

Blanched & Butter-Cooked Broccoli

SERVINGS	4	2	1
INGREDIENTS			
fresh broccoli			
(as purchased)	1 lb. 6 oz.	10 oz.	5 oz.
(after trimming)	12 oz.	7 oz.	3 oz.
water	1/4 cup	2 tablespoons	1 tablespoon
butter or margarine	1 tablespoon	2 teaspoons	1 teaspoon
BAKING DISH	1-qt. casserole	1-qt. casserole	2-cup casserole
TIME AT HIGH (blanching)	6 to 7 minutes	4 to 5 minutes	3 to 4 minutes
TIME AT HIGH (butter)	45 seconds	45 seconds	30 seconds
TIME AT HIGH (broccoli added)	4 to 5 minutes	3 to 4 minutes	3 to 4 minutes
STANDING TIME	2 minutes	2 minutes	2 minutes

Wash broccoli and cut into flowerets leaving 1 to 2 inches of stalk. Place in a casserole, see size in chart above, with stems toward outside of dish. Add water. Cover. Microwave at full power (HIGH) for time in chart above or until starting to get tender. Drain in a colander and run cold water over broccoli. Wrap and refrigerate. At serving time, melt butter or margarine in same casserole at full power (HIGH) for time in chart above. Add broccoli, stirring to coat. Cover. Microwave at full power (HIGH) for time in chart above or until tender and heated through, stirring once. Let stand, covered, 2 minutes.

How to Make Curried Broccoli Deluxe

In a flat baking dish, arrange cooked broccoli spears so the stalks alternate toward the edge of the dish. Tuck in slices of hard-cooked egg.

Drizzle the curry sauce evenly over casserole. Microwave, then sprinkle with crumbs *after* heating so crumbs do not become tough.

Curried Broccoli Deluxe

SERVINGS	6	2 or 3
INGREDIENTS		
butter or margarine	2 tablespoons	1 tablespoon
seasoned dry breadcrumbs	1/2 cup	1/4 cup
snipped parsley	2 tablespoons	1 tablespoon
frozen broccoli spears, cooked, drained	2 (10-oz.) pkgs.	1 (10-oz.) pkg.
hard-cooked eggs, sliced	4	2
condensed cream of onion soup	1 (10-1/2-oz.) can	1/2 (10-1/2-oz.) can
dry white wine	1/4 cup	2 tablespoons
mayonnaise or salad dressing	1/4 cup	2 tablespoons
curry powder	1 teaspoon	1/2 teaspoon
BAKING DISH	12" x 7" baking dish	2 small dishes
TIME AT HIGH (butter)	30 seconds	30 seconds
TIME AT HIGH (sauce)	4 minutes	2 minutes
TIME AT HIGH (casserole)	4 minutes	3 minutes

In a small bowl, microwave butter or margarine at full power (HIGH) 30 seconds or until melted. Stir in breadcrumbs and parsley; set aside. In a baking dish, see size in chart above, arrange broccoli spears and egg slices. In a medium bowl, whisk together onion soup, wine, mayonnaise or salad dressing and curry powder. Cover with vented plastic wrap. Microwave at full power (HIGH) for time in chart above or until hot, stirring twice. Spoon sauce over broccoli and eggs. Cover with waxed paper. Microwave at full power (HIGH) for time in chart above or until heated through, giving dish a half turn once. Sprinkle with reserved buttered breadcrumbs.

Frozen Broccoli Spears

SERVINGS	3
INGREDIENTS frozen broccoli spears	1 (10-oz.) pkg.
BAKING DISH	1-qt. casserole
TIME AT HIGH	7 to 8 minutes
STANDING TIME	1 to 2 minutes

Place broccoli in a 1-quart casserole. Cover. Microwave at full power (HIGH) 7 to 8 minutes or until tender, rearranging once. Let stand, covered, 1 to 2 minutes.

Frozen Broccoli Cuts

SERVINGS	6	4	2	1
INGREDIENTS frozen broccoli cuts	4 cups	3 cups	2 cups*	1 cup
BAKING DISH	2-qt. casserole	1-1/2-qt. casserole	1-1/2-qt. casserole	1-qt. casserole
TIME AT HIGH	10 to 11 minutes	8 to 9 minutes	5 to 6 minutes	3 to 4 minutes
STANDING TIME	1 to 2 minutes	1 to 2 minutes	1 to 2 minutes	1 to 2 minutes

Place broccoli in a casserole, see size in chart above. Cover and microwave at full power (HIGH) for time in chart above or until tender. Let stand, covered, 1 to 2 minutes.

*Or microwave 1 (10-oz.) package frozen chopped broccoli with 2 tablespoons water at full power (HIGH) 9 to 10 minutes or until tender.

Frozen Broccoli Spears in a Pouch

SERVINGS	3
INGREDIENTS frozen broccoli spears in butter sauce	1 (10-oz.) pkg.
TIME AT HIGH	6 to 7 minutes

With a sharp knife or scissors, cut a small "X" in center of top side of pouch. Microwave pouch at full power (HIGH) 6 to 7 minutes, flexing pouch once to rearrange broccoli.

Serving Ideas

- Toss chopped broccoli with sesame seeds and almonds toasted in butter.
- Ladle No-Fail Hollandaise Sauce, page 422, over hot cooked broccoli, then sprinkle with paprika and grated lemon peel.
- Sprinkle shredded Cheddar cheese and basil over hot cooked broccoli.

Fresh Brussels Sprouts

SERVINGS	6	4	2

INGREDIENTS
brussels sprouts
  (as purchased)
  (after trimming)
water
	
	1-1/2 lbs.
	1 lb.
	1/4 cup
		
		1 lb.
		12 oz.
		1/4 cup
			
			8 oz.
			6 oz.
			1/4 cup

BAKING DISH	1-1/2-qt. casserole	1-qt. casserole	1-qt. casserole
TIME AT HIGH	10 to 11 minutes	8 to 9 minutes	5 to 6 minutes
STANDING TIME	2 minutes	2 minutes	2 minutes

Trim off wilted outer leaves and excess stem from brussels sprouts. Wash sprouts. Halve any large sprouts. In a casserole, see size in chart above, combine sprouts and water. Cover. Microwave at full power (HIGH) for time in chart above or until tender, stirring once. Let stand, covered, 2 minutes. Drain.

Frozen Brussels Sprouts

SERVINGS	6	4	2	1
INGREDIENTS frozen brussels sprouts	4 cups	3 cups	1 (10-oz.) pkg. (2 cups)	1 cup
BAKING DISH	2-qt. casserole	1-1/2-qt. casserole	1-1/2-qt. casserole	1-qt. casserole
TIME AT HIGH	10 to 12 minutes	8 to 10 minutes	6 to 8 minutes	3 to 5 minutes
STANDING TIME	1 to 2 minutes	1 to 2 minutes	1 to 2 minutes	1 to 2 minutes

Place brussels sprouts in a casserole, see size in chart above. Cover. Microwave at full power (HIGH) for time in chart above or until tender, stirring once. Let stand, covered, 1 to 2 minutes.

Serving Ideas

- Sprinkle hot cooked sprouts with crumbled bleu cheese.
- Drizzle hot cooked sprouts with lemon juice, then top with buttered crumbs and snipped parsley.
- Cook sprouts in leftover dill-pickle juice, then refrigerate in liquid to serve as a relish.

How to Make Zesty Brussels Sprouts

Brussels sprouts, green onion, celery and carrots are microwaved until starting to get tender. Gently fold in tomatoes and microwave briefly.

Keep vegetables warm by covering with foil. Quickly prepare yogurt sauce. Spoon warmed sauce over vegetables before serving.

Zesty Brussels Sprouts

SERVINGS	6 to 8	3 or 4
INGREDIENTS		
frozen brussels sprouts	2 (10-oz.) pkgs.	1 (10-oz.) pkg.
chopped green onion	1/2 cup	1/4 cup
chopped celery	1/2 cup	1/4 cup
chopped carrots	1/2 cup	1/4 cup
water	1/4 cup	2 tablespoons
butter or margarine	1/4 cup	2 tablespoons
cherry tomatoes	2 cups	1 cup
plain yogurt	1 cup	1/2 cup
all-purpose flour	2 tablespoons	1 tablespoon
Dijon-style mustard	4 teaspoons	2 teaspoons
prepared horseradish	2 teaspoons	1 teaspoon
BAKING DISH	deep 3-qt. casserole	deep 1-1/2-qt. casserole
TIME AT HIGH (sprout mixture)	15 minutes	8 minutes
TIME AT HIGH (tomatoes added)	3 minutes	2 to 3 minutes
TIME AT 30%	6 minutes	3 minutes

In a casserole, see size in chart above, combine brussels sprouts, green onion, celery, carrots and water. Cover. Microwave at full power (HIGH) for time in chart above or until tender, stirring once. Drain well. Stir in butter or margarine. Add cherry tomatoes. Cover. Microwave at full power (HIGH) for time in chart above or until heated through. Let stand, covered, while making sauce. In a small bowl, combine yogurt, flour, mustard and horseradish; whisk to mix well. Microwave at 30% (MEDIUM LOW) for time in chart above or until hot and thickened, stirring three times. Stir sauce and spoon over vegetables.

Fresh Cabbage Wedges

SERVINGS	4	2	1
INGREDIENTS fresh cabbage 　(as purchased) 　(after trimming) water	 1 lb. (1/2 head) 13 oz. 1/4 cup	 8 oz. (1/4 head) 7 oz. 2 tablespoons	 4 oz. (1/8 head) 3 oz. 1 tablespoon
BAKING DISH	1-qt. casserole	2-cup casserole	1-1/2-cup casserole
TIME AT HIGH	10 minutes	7 minutes	4 minutes
STANDING TIME	2 minutes	2 minutes	2 minutes

Cut cabbage in wedges, allowing 1 wedge per serving. Remove outer leaves and core. In a casserole, see size in chart above, place wedges with core end to inside of dish. Add water. Cover. Microwave at full power (HIGH) for time in chart above or until tender, turning wedges over and rearranging halfway through cooking time. Let stand, covered, 2 minutes. Drain.

Fresh Shredded Cabbage

SERVINGS	3 or 4	2	1
INGREDIENTS shredded cabbage water	 4 cups (10 oz.) 1/3 cup	 2 cups (5 oz.) 1/3 cup	 1 cup (2-1/2 oz.) 1/3 cup
BAKING DISH	2-qt. casserole	1-qt. casserole	1-qt. casserole
TIME AT HIGH	12 to 14 minutes	10 to 12 minutes	8 to 10 minutes

In a casserole, see size in chart above, combine cabbage and water. Cover. Microwave at full power (HIGH) for time in chart above or until tender, stirring once. Drain.

Canned Sauerkraut

SERVINGS	2 or 3	1 or 2
INGREDIENTS sauerkraut	 1 (16-oz.) can	 1 (8-oz.) can
BOWL	3- to 4-cup bowl	2- to 3-cup bowl
TIME AT HIGH	4 to 5 minutes	3 to 4 minutes

Place sauerkraut and juice in a bowl, see size in chart above. Cover with vented plastic wrap. Microwave at full power (HIGH) for time in chart above or until heated through.

Hot Slaw Mexicana

SERVINGS	6 to 8	3 or 4
INGREDIENTS		
cabbage	1/4 medium head	1/8 medium head
carrot	1 medium	1/2 medium
green pepper	1/2 medium	1/4 medium
cherry tomatoes	1 cup	1/2 cup
pitted ripe olives	1/2 cup	1/4 cup
whole-kernel corn, cooked, drained	1/2 cup	1/4 cup
shredded process pepper cheese or sharp process cheese	1 cup (4 oz.)	1/2 cup (2 oz.)
milk	2 tablespoons	1 tablespoon
celery seed	1 teaspoon	1/2 teaspoon
dry mustard	1/4 teaspoon	1/8 teaspoon
avocado, pared, seeded, sliced	1	1/2
BOWL	deep 4-qt. bowl	deep 2-qt. bowl
TIME AT 30%	2-1/2 to 3 minutes	2 to 2-1/2 minutes
TIME AT HIGH	4 minutes	2 to 3 minutes

Using thin slicing blade on a food processor, slice cabbage, carrot, green pepper, cherry tomatoes and olives. Or slice finely by hand. Toss with corn in a bowl, see size in chart above; set aside. In a medium bowl, combine cheese, milk, celery seed and dry mustard. Microwave at 30% (MEDIUM LOW) for time in chart above or until cheese has melted, stirring twice. Stir until smooth. Pour cheese dressing over cabbage mixture. Toss gently. Cover with vented plastic wrap. Microwave at full power (HIGH) for time in chart above or until heated through, stirring once. Garnish with avocado slices. Serve salad hot.

Serving Ideas

- Toss hot carrot slices with a little pineapple jam and dry white wine.
- Serve whole tiny cooked carrots tossed with butter, snipped parsley, snipped chives and snipped dillweed.
- Toss thinly sliced carrots with butter, brown sugar and nutmeg.
- Serve hot Horseradish-Mustard Sauce, page 431, over hot cooked cabbage wedges, then sprinkle with snipped chives.
- Ladle hot canned mushroom-flavored spaghetti sauce over hot cooked cabbage wedges, then sprinkle with grated Parmesan cheese and dried Italian herbs.
- Toss hot shredded cabbage with caraway seeds, sweet-sour salad dressing and pineapple chunks.

Carrot Coins

SERVINGS	4	2	1
INGREDIENTS			
carrots	1 lb. (3 cups, sliced)	8 oz. (1-1/2 cups, sliced)	4 oz. (3/4 cup, sliced)
water	1/4 cup	1/4 cup	2 tablespoons
BAKING DISH	1-qt. casserole	1-qt. casserole	2-cup casserole
TIME AT HIGH	11 to 12 minutes	8 to 9 minutes	5 to 6 minutes
STANDING TIME	2 minutes	2 minutes	2 minutes

Wash, trim and pare carrots. Halve thick portion of carrots lengthwise. Slice 1/2 inch thick. In a casserole, see size in chart above, combine carrots and water. Cover. Microwave at full power (HIGH) for time in chart above or until tender, stirring once. Let stand, covered, 2 minutes. Drain.

Food Processor Carrots

SERVINGS	4	2	1
INGREDIENTS			
carrots	1 lb. (3-1/2 cups, sliced)	8 oz. (1-3/4 cups, sliced)	3 oz. (3/4 cup, sliced)
beef broth	1/4 cup	2 tablespoons	1 tablespoon
butter or margarine	1 tablespoon	2 teaspoons	1 teaspoon
snipped chives	1 teaspoon	1/2 teaspoon	1/4 teaspoon
dried leaf tarragon	1/2 teaspoon	1/4 teaspoon	1/8 teaspoon
celery salt	dash	dash	dash
BAKING DISH	1-qt. casserole	1-qt. casserole	1-qt. casserole
TIME AT HIGH	7 minutes	6 minutes	5 minutes
STANDING TIME	2 minutes	2 minutes	2 minutes

Wash, trim and pare carrots. Using thin slicing blade on a food processor, slice carrots. In a 1-quart casserole, combine carrots and broth. Cover. Microwave at full power (HIGH) for time in chart above or until tender, stirring once. Let stand, covered, 2 minutes. Do not drain. Stir in butter or margarine, chives, tarragon and celery salt.

Whole Tiny Carrots

SERVINGS	6	3
INGREDIENTS		
whole tiny carrots	1-1/2 lbs. (4 cups)	12 oz. (2 cups)
water	1/4 cup	1/4 cup
BAKING DISH	2-qt. casserole	1-qt. casserole
TIME AT HIGH	14 minutes	10 minutes
STANDING TIME	2 minutes	2 minutes

Wash, trim and pare carrots. Halve thick carrots lengthwise. In a casserole, see size in chart above, combine carrots and water. Cover. Microwave at full power (HIGH) for time in chart above or until tender, stirring once. Let stand, covered, 2 minutes. Drain.

How to Make Honey-Glazed Carrots

Pare carrots and cut into 1/2-inch pieces. A waffle cutter gives carrot slices a fancy look with little effort!

Cook carrots until crisp-tender when tested with a fork. Drizzle carrots with honey. Chopped pecans make the perfect garnish.

Honey-Glazed Carrots

SERVINGS	4	2	1
INGREDIENTS			
carrots	1 lb. (3 cups, sliced)	8 oz. (1-1/2 cups, sliced)	4 oz. (3/4 cup, sliced)
water	1/4 cup	1/4 cup	2 tablespoons
butter or margarine	1 tablespoon	2 teaspoons	1 teaspoon
ground cinnamon	dash	dash	dash
honey	1 tablespoon	2 teaspoons	1 teaspoon
chopped pecans	2 tablespoons	1 tablespoon	2 teaspoons
BAKING DISH	1-qt. casserole	1-qt. casserole	2-cup casserole
TIME AT HIGH (carrots)	10 to 12 minutes	8 to 9 minutes	5 to 6 minutes
STANDING TIME	2 minutes	2 minutes	2 minutes
TIME AT HIGH (glaze added)	30 seconds	30 seconds	15 seconds

Wash, trim and pare carrots. Slice carrots 1/2 inch thick. In a casserole, see size in chart above, combine carrots and water. Cover. Microwave at full power (HIGH) for time in chart above or until tender, stirring once. Let stand, covered, 2 minutes. Drain carrots and return to casserole. Stir in butter or margarine and cinnamon. Drizzle with honey. Mix gently. Cover and microwave at full power (HIGH) for time in chart above. Sprinkle with pecans.

Blanched & Butter-Cooked Carrots

SERVINGS	4	2	1
INGREDIENTS			
carrots	1 lb.	8 oz.	4 oz.
	(3 cups, sliced)	(1-1/2 cups, sliced)	(3/4 cup, sliced)
water	1/4 cup	2 tablespoons	1 tablespoon
butter or margarine	1 tablespoon	2 teaspoons	1 teaspoon
dried dillweed	1/4 teaspoon	1/8 teaspoon	dash
BAKING DISH	1-qt. casserole	1-qt. casserole	1-qt. casserole
TIME AT HIGH (blanching)	5 minutes	4 minutes	3 minutes
TIME AT HIGH (butter)	45 seconds	45 seconds	30 seconds
TIME AT HIGH (carrots added)	6 minutes	5 minutes	3 minutes
STANDING TIME	2 minutes	2 minutes	2 minutes

Wash, trim and pare carrots. Slice diagonally, 1/2 inch thick. In a 1-quart casserole, combine carrots and water. Cover. Microwave at full power (HIGH) for time in chart above or until starting to get tender, stirring once. Drain in a colander and run cold water over carrots. Refrigerate in a plastic bag. At serving time, melt butter or margarine in same casserole at full power (HIGH) for time in chart above. Stir in carrots and dillweed until coated. Cover. Microwave at full power (HIGH) for time in chart above or until tender, stirring once. Let stand, covered, 2 minutes.

Frozen Carrots in a Pouch

SERVINGS	3
INGREDIENTS	
frozen carrots in butter sauce	1 (10-oz.) pkg.
TIME AT HIGH	6 to 7 minutes

With a sharp knife or scissors, cut a small "X" in center of top side of pouch. Microwave pouch at full power (HIGH) 6 to 7 minutes, flexing pouch once to rearrange carrots.

Canned Carrots

SERVINGS	2 or 3	1 or 2
INGREDIENTS		
sliced carrots	1 (16-oz.) can	1 (8-oz.) can
BOWL	3- to 4-cup bowl	2- to 3-cup bowl
TIME AT HIGH	3 to 4 minutes	2 to 3 minutes

Drain off all but 2 tablespoons liquid from can. In a bowl, see size in chart above, combine carrots and remaining liquid. Cover with vented plastic wrap. Microwave at full power (HIGH) for time in chart above or until heated through.

Fresh Cauliflowerets

SERVINGS	5 or 6	2 or 3	1 or 2
INGREDIENTS			
whole cauliflower	1 head	1/2 head	1/4 head
(as purchased)	1-1/2 lbs.	12 oz.	7 oz.
(after trimming)	1 lb. 2 oz.	8 oz.	5 oz.
water	1/4 cup	2 tablespoons	1 tablespoon
BAKING DISH	1-1/2-qt. casserole	1-qt. casserole	2-cup casserole
TIME AT HIGH	7 to 8 minutes	4 to 5 minutes	2 to 2-1/2 minutes
STANDING TIME	2 minutes	2 minutes	2 minutes

Wash and trim cauliflower. Cut into flowerets. Place in a casserole, see size in chart above, with stems toward outside of dish. Add water; cover. Microwave at full power (HIGH) for time in chart above or until tender, stirring once. Let stand, covered, 2 minutes. Drain.

Blanched & Butter-Cooked Cauliflower

SERVINGS	5 or 6	2 or 3	1 or 2
INGREDIENTS			
whole cauliflower	1 head	1/2 head	1/4 head
(as purchased)	1-1/2 lbs.	12 oz.	7 oz.
(after trimming)	1 lb. 2 oz.	8 oz.	5 oz.
water	1/4 cup	2 tablespoons	1 tablespoon
butter or margarine	1 tablespoon	2 teaspoons	1 teaspoon
BAKING DISH	1-1/2-qt. casserole	1-qt. casserole	2-cup casserole
TIME AT HIGH (blanching)	4 minutes	3 minutes	2 minutes
TIME AT HIGH (butter)	30 seconds	30 seconds	30 seconds
TIME AT HIGH (cauliflower added)	5 to 6 minutes	4 to 5 minutes	2 to 3 minutes
STANDING TIME	2 minutes	2 minutes	2 minutes

Wash and trim cauliflower. Cut into flowerets. Place in a casserole, see size in chart above, with stems toward outside of dish. Add water. Cover. Microwave at full power (HIGH) for time in chart above or until starting to get tender, stirrring once. Drain in colander and run cold water over cauliflower. Wrap and refrigerate. At serving time, melt butter or margarine in same casserole at full power (HIGH) 30 seconds. Add cauliflower, stirring to coat; cover. Microwave at full power (HIGH) for time in chart above or until tender and heated through, stirring once. Let stand, covered, 2 minutes.

Serving Ideas

- Toss hot cooked cauliflowerets with creamy onion dressing. Refrigerate and marinate for a salad tossed with croutons and grated Parmesan cheese.
- Toss hot cooked cauliflowerets with chopped pimiento, chopped green onion and chopped green pepper sautéed in butter.

How to Make Frosted Cauliflower

After cooking the whole head of cauliflower, frost with sour cream and chive dip, or any other favorite dip. This makes a star attraction for a beautiful vegetable platter.

Sprinkle the frosted cauliflower with shredded Cheddar cheese, then sprinkle generously with salad seasoning. Microwave the frosted head to warm the sauce and melt the cheese.

Frosted Cauliflower

SERVINGS	6	3
INGREDIENTS		
whole cauliflower	1 head	1/2 head
(as purchased)	1-1/2 lbs.	12 oz.
(after trimming)	1 lb. 2 oz.	8 oz.
water	1/4 cup	2 tablespoons
sour cream and chive dip	1/2 cup	1/4 cup
dry mustard	1/2 teaspoon	1/4 teaspoon
celery seed	1/4 teaspoon	1/8 teaspoon
shredded Cheddar cheese	1 cup (4 oz.)	1/2 cup (2 oz.)
salad seasoning		
BAKING DISH	deep 2-qt. casserole	deep 1-qt. casserole
TIME AT HIGH (cauliflower)	8 to 9 minutes	5 to 6 minutes
STANDING TIME	2 minutes	2 minutes
TIME AT HIGH (frosted)	2 minutes	1 to 1-1/4 minutes

Wash and core cauliflower, leaving head intact. Remove excess leaves. Place cauliflower, stem end down, in a casserole, see size in chart above. Add water. Cover. Microwave at full power (HIGH) for time in chart above or until tender, giving dish a half turn once. Let stand, covered, 2 minutes. Drain. In a small bowl, mix dip, dry mustard and celery seed. Spread over hot cauliflower in casserole. Sprinkle with Cheddar cheese, then sprinkle generously with salad seasoning. Microwave, uncovered, at full power (HIGH) for time in chart above or until cheese melts, giving dish a half turn once.

Fresh Whole Cauliflower

SERVINGS	6	3
INGREDIENTS		
whole cauliflower		
(as purchased)	1 head	1/2 head
	1-1/2 lbs.	12 oz.
(after trimming)	1 lb. 2 oz.	8 oz.
water	1/4 cup	2 tablespoons
BAKING DISH	deep 2-qt. casserole	deep 1-qt. casserole
TIME AT HIGH	8 to 9 minutes	5 to 6 minutes
STANDING TIME	2 minutes	2 minutes

Wash and core cauliflower, leaving head intact. Remove excess leaves. Place cauliflower, stem end down, in a casserole, see size in chart above. Add water. Cover. Microwave at full power (HIGH) for time in chart above or until tender, giving dish a half turn once. Let stand, covered, 2 minutes. Drain.

Frozen Cauliflower

SERVINGS	6	4	2	1
INGREDIENTS				
frozen cauliflower	4 cups	3 cups	1 (10-oz.) pkg. (2 cups)	1 cup
BAKING DISH	2-qt. casserole	1-1/2-qt. casserole	1-1/2-qt. casserole	1-qt. casserole
TIME AT HIGH	12 to 14 minutes	9 to 11 minutes	6 to 8 minutes	4 to 6 minutes
STANDING TIME	1 to 2 minutes	1 to 2 minutes	1 to 2 minutes	1 to 2 minutes

Place cauliflower in a casserole, see size in chart above. Cover. Microwave at full power (HIGH) for time in chart above or until tender, stirring once. Let stand, covered, 1 to 2 minutes.

Fresh Celery

YIELD	1-1/2 cups	2/3 cup	1/3 cup
INGREDIENTS			
celery	2-1/2 stalks (2 cups, sliced)	1-1/4 stalks (1 cup, sliced)	2/3 stalk (1/2 cup, sliced)
water	2 tablespoons	1 tablespoon	1 tablespoon
BAKING DISH	1-qt. casserole	2-cup casserole	1-cup casserole
TIME AT HIGH	8 to 9 minutes	5 to 6 minutes	3 to 4 minutes

Wash and trim celery. Slice 1/4 to 1/2 inch thick. In a casserole, see size in chart above, combine celery and water. Cover. Microwave at full power (HIGH) for time in chart above or until tender, stirring once.

Quick Sweet & Sour Greens

SERVINGS	6	3
INGREDIENTS		
red onion, sliced, separated in rings	1 medium	1/2 medium
salad dressing with garlic and herbs	1/2 cup	1/4 cup
small cooked ham cubes	1/2 cup	1/4 cup
hot, cooked, drained greens	2-1/2 to 3 cups	1-1/4 to 1-1/2 cups
BAKING DISH	1-qt. casserole	1-qt. casserole
TIME AT HIGH (onion)	4 to 5 minutes	3 to 4 minutes
TIME AT HIGH (greens added)	3 minutes	2 minutes

Mix onion rings and salad dressing in a 1-quart casserole. Microwave at full power (HIGH) for time in chart above or until tender, stirring once. Stir in ham cubes. Toss cooked, drained greens with dressing mixture. Cover. Microwave at full power (HIGH) for time in chart above or until heated through, stirring once.

Frozen Chopped Collard Greens or Kale

SERVINGS	3	3
INGREDIENTS		
frozen chopped collard greens OR	1 (10-oz.) pkg.	
frozen chopped kale		1 (10-oz.) pkg.
hot water	2-1/4 cups	1-1/4 cups
BAKING DISH	deep 1-1/2-qt. casserole	deep 1-1/2-qt. casserole
TIME AT HIGH	28 minutes	13 minutes
STANDING TIME	1 to 2 minutes	1 to 2 minutes

In a 1-1/2-quart casserole, combine collards or kale and hot water. Cover. Microwave at full power (HIGH) for time in chart above or until tender, stirring twice. Let stand, covered, 1 to 2 minutes. Drain.

Fresh Chard

SERVINGS	6	3	1
INGREDIENTS			
Swiss chard	1 lb. (16 cups)	8 oz. (8 cups)	4 oz. (4 cups)
BAKING DISH	deep 5-qt. casserole	deep 2-qt. casserole	deep 1-1/2-qt. casserole
TIME AT HIGH	17 to 18 minutes	11 to 12 minutes	8 to 9 minutes

Wash and trim chard. Cut stems in 2-inch lengths. Place chard with water that clings to leaves in a casserole, see size in chart above. Cover. Microwave at full power (HIGH) for time in chart above or until tender, stirring twice.

How to Make Quick Sweet & Sour Greens

To cut greens with large leaves—roll up several leaves at a time, then cut across the roll. The lighter green crinkly leaves to the left in the colander are mustard greens and the small dark green leaves in the colander are turnip greens. The leaves being sliced are collards.

Red onion slices are separated into rings and then cooked in a salad dressing containing garlic and herbs. Cooked, drained collards, mustard greens, turnip greens, chard or kale are then tossed with the onion mixture along with cubes of ham.

Fresh Collards

SERVINGS	4	2
INGREDIENTS		
fresh collards		
(as purchased)	1-1/2 lbs.	12 oz.
(after trimming)	14 oz. (12 cups, shredded)	7 oz. (6 cups, shredded)
bacon, diced	4 slices	2 slices
water	1/3 cup	3 tablespoons
thin lemon slices	6 to 8	3 to 4
BAKING DISH	deep 3-qt. casserole	deep 2-qt. casserole
TIME AT HIGH (bacon)	3 to 3-1/2 minutes	2 to 2-1/2 minutes
TIME AT HIGH (collards added)	15 to 18 minutes	10 to 11 minutes
TIME AT HIGH (lemon added)	1 to 2 minutes	1 minute

Wash and trim collards, discarding yellow leaves. Shred collards into thin slices. Set aside. In a casserole, see size in chart above, microwave bacon at full power (HIGH) for time in chart above, stirring twice. Stir in collards and water. Cover. Microwave at full power (HIGH) for time in chart above or until tender, stirring twice. Add lemon slices. Cover and microwave at full power (HIGH) for time in chart above.

Fresh Corn on the Cob

SERVINGS	6	4	2	1
INGREDIENTS fresh corn on the cob melted butter or margarine, if desired	6 ears	4 ears	2 ears	1 ear
TIME AT HIGH	12 to 13 minutes	9 minutes	5 minutes	2-1/2 minutes

To cook in waxed paper: Cut squares of waxed paper. Husk corn and remove silks. Wash corn. Roll each ear with water that clings to kernels in waxed paper. Brush with melted butter or margarine before rolling up in waxed paper, if desired. Twist ends of waxed paper to seal. Place spoke-fashion in microwave oven. Microwave at full power (HIGH) for time in chart above or until kernels are tender, rearranging ears once.

To cook in the husks: Carefully pull husks down ear far enough to remove silks but still keep husks intact. Brush corn with melted butter or margarine, if desired. Pull husks back over corn. Quickly run husks under cold water to add moisture for cooking. Place spoke-fashion in microwave oven. Microwave at full power (HIGH) for time in chart above or until kernels are tender, rearranging ears once.

Creamy Buttered Corn

SERVINGS	4	2
INGREDIENTS corn on the cob milk butter or margarine	6 ears 1/4 cup 2 tablespoons	3 ears 2 tablespoons 1 tablespoon
BAKING DISH	2-qt. casserole	1-qt. casserole
TIME AT HIGH	11 to 12 minutes	5 to 6 minutes
STANDING TIME	2 minutes	2 minutes

Cut corn off cobs. In a casserole, see size in chart above, combine corn, milk and butter or margarine. Cover. Microwave at full power (HIGH) for time in chart above or until tender, stirring once. Let stand, covered, 2 minutes.

Serving Ideas

- Whip prepared mustard and horseradish into butter to serve with corn on the cob.
- Add spices, herbs, sliced fresh mushrooms, chopped celery and chopped green onion to clear French dressing. Pour over hot cooked corn and toss gently. Chill and serve for a salad.
- Top hot cooked corn with shredded Swiss cheese, snipped parsley and paprika.

How to Cook Fresh Corn on the Cob

Here are two good ways to cook fresh corn on the cob—either in the husk or out. If you wish to husk the corn, brush the ears with butter, but do not salt. Wrap the ears in squares of waxed paper, twisting the ends to seal.

To cook corn in the husks, strip the husks down the cob. Be careful to leave the husks attached at the bottom of the cob. Remove the corn silks. Brush the ears with butter but do not salt. Pull the husks back up over the corn.

To keep second helpings warm, combine 1 cup hot water and 1/2 cup milk in an 8-inch square baking dish. Add hot corn, turning ears over to coat with milk. Cover tightly with unvented plastic wrap. Microwave at 10% (LOW) up to 30 minutes, turning ears in milk occasionally.

To serve corn piping hot, keep it wrapped in a large napkin or cloth towel in the serving bowl. Salt corn *after* cooking to prevent dehydration of the kernels where they are in contact with the salt. Serve with softened butter mixed with prepared horseradish and mustard or chives and dried dillweed.

Frozen Half Ears of Corn on the Cob

SERVINGS	3	2	1
INGREDIENTS frozen half ears corn on the cob	6 ears	4 ears	2 ears
BAKING DISH	12" x 7" baking dish	10" x 6" baking dish	9-inch pie plate
TIME AT HIGH	10 to 10-1/2 minutes	7 to 7-1/2 minutes	5 to 5-1/2 minutes

Place corn on the cob in a baking dish, see size in chart above. Cover with vented plastic wrap. Microwave at full power (HIGH) for time in chart above or until tender, rearranging once.

Frozen Whole Ears of Corn on the Cob

SERVINGS	4	3	2	1
INGREDIENTS frozen whole ears corn on the cob	4 ears	3 ears	2 ears	1 ear
BAKING DISH	12" x 7" baking dish	10" x 6" baking dish	10" x 6" baking dish	9-inch pie plate
TIME AT HIGH	10 to 12 minutes	8 to 10 minutes	6 to 8 minutes	4 to 5 minutes

Place corn on the cob in a baking dish, see size in chart above. Cover with lid or vented plastic wrap. Microwave at full power (HIGH) for time in chart above or until tender, rearranging once.

Frozen Whole-Kernel Corn

SERVINGS	6	4	2	1
INGREDIENTS frozen whole-kernel corn	4 cups	3 cups	1 (8- or 10-oz.) pkg. (2 cups)	1 cup
water	5 tablespoons	1/4 cup	3 tablespoons	2 tablespoons
BAKING DISH	2-qt. casserole	1-1/2-qt. casserole	1-1/2-qt. casserole	1-qt. casserole
TIME AT HIGH	10 to 11 minutes	8 to 9 minutes	5 to 6 minutes	3 to 4 minutes
STANDING TIME	1 to 2 minutes	1 to 2 minutes	1 to 2 minutes	1 to 2 minutes

In a casserole, see size in chart above, combine corn and water. Cover. Microwave at full power (HIGH) for time in chart above or until tender, stirring once. Let stand, covered, 1 to 2 minutes. Drain.

Frozen Corn in a Pouch

SERVINGS	3	
INGREDIENTS frozen corn in butter sauce	1 (10-oz.) pkg.	
TIME AT HIGH	6 to 7 minutes	

With a sharp knife or scissors, cut a small "X" in center of top side of pouch. Microwave pouch at full power (HIGH) 6 to 7 minutes, flexing pouch once to rearrange corn.

Canned Whole-Kernel Corn

SERVINGS	2 or 3	1 or 2
INGREDIENTS whole-kernel corn	1 (16-oz.) can	1 (8-oz.) can
BOWL	3- to 4-cup bowl	2- to 3-cup bowl
TIME AT HIGH	3 to 4 minutes	2 to 3 minutes

Drain off all but 2 tablespoons liquid from can. In a bowl, see size in chart above, combine corn and remaining liquid. Cover with vented plastic wrap. Microwave at full power (HIGH) for time in chart above or until heated through.

Canned Cream-Style Corn

SERVINGS	2 or 3	1 or 2
INGREDIENTS cream-style corn	1 (17-oz.) can	1 (8-3/4-oz.) can
BOWL	3- to 4-cup bowl	2- to 3-cup bowl
TIME AT HIGH	3-1/2 to 4-1/2 minutes	2-1/2 to 3-1/2 minutes

Place cream-style corn in a bowl, see size in chart above. Cover with vented plastic wrap. Microwave at full power (HIGH) for time in chart above or until heated through, stirring once.

Canned Hominy

SERVINGS	2 or 3
INGREDIENTS hominy	1 (15-oz.) can
BAKING DISH	1-qt. casserole
TIME AT HIGH	4 to 5 minutes

Drain off all but 2 tablespoons liquid from can. Combine hominy and remaining liquid in a 1-quart casserole. Cover. Microwave at full power (HIGH) 4 to 5 minutes or until heated through.

Crisp Fried Eggplant

SERVINGS	6 (slices)	4 (sticks)
INGREDIENTS		
fresh eggplant	1/2 medium (8 oz.)	1/3 medium (5 oz.)
all-purpose flour	1/2 cup	1/2 cup
milk	1/2 cup	1/2 cup
egg white	1	1
onion salt	1/4 teaspoon	1/4 teaspoon
seasoned dry breadcrumbs	to coat	to coat
vegetable oil	9 tablespoons	1/4 cup
BROWNING SKILLET	10-inch microwave browning skillet	10-inch microwave browning skillet
TIME AT HIGH (first preheat for skillet)	6 minutes	6 minutes
TIME AT HIGH (first side for each batch)	1 minute	2 minutes
TIME AT HIGH (second side for each batch)	30 seconds	2 minutes
TIME AT HIGH (preheat skillet before each additional batch)	3 minutes	

To make sliced eggplant: Cut eggplant into 12 to 14 thin slices, about 1/8 inch thick Set aside. Preheat a 10-inch microwave browning skillet, uncovered, at microwave full power (HIGH) 6 minutes. In a small bowl, beat together flour, milk, egg white and onion salt. Place breadcrumbs in a pie plate. Dip eggplant in batter, then in breadcrumbs coating well. Place crumb-coated slices on a wire rack over waxed paper. Add 3 tablespoons oil to preheated browning skillet. Quickly add 4 to 5 eggplant slices in a single layer. Microwave, uncovered, at full power (HIGH) for time in chart above. Turn slices over and microwave at full power (HIGH) for time in chart above or until tender Keep warm in a 200F (95C) oven while preparing remaining slices. Wipe out browning skillet with paper towels, being careful not to touch hot skillet. Preheat browning skillet at full power (HIGH) 3 minutes. Add 3 tablespoons oil. Quickly add 4 to 5 more crumb-coated slices and microwave as before. Repeat with remaining slices and oil, wiping out and preheating browning skillet as before.

To make eggplant sticks: Cut eggplant into 22 to 24 sticks, about 1/2" x 1/2" x 4". Place sticks in a large bowl. In a small bowl, beat together flour, milk, egg white and onion salt. Pour over sticks and toss to coat evenly. Place breadcrumbs in plastic bag. Add half the sticks at a time to crumbs in bag. Turn over in bag to coat evenly with crumbs. Place crumb-coated sticks on a wire rack over waxed paper. Repeat, coating remaining sticks with crumbs. Preheat a 10-inch browning skillet, uncovered, at microwave full power (HIGH) 6 minutes. Add 1/4 cup oil to preheated skillet. Quickly add sticks in a single layer. Microwave, uncovered, at full power (HIGH) for time in chart above. Turn sticks over carefully. Microwave at full power (HIGH) for time in chart above or until tender Drain on paper towels.

How to Make Crisp Fried Eggplant

Dip thin eggplant slices into the batter. Then coat each slice with seasoned dry breadcrumbs. Let the slices dry on a wire rack before cooking in the microwave.

After preheating the browning skillet, add a measured amount of vegetable oil. Quickly add the crumb-coated eggplant slices to the hot skillet. Turn slices over once during the cooking time.

Fresh Eggplant Cubes

SERVINGS	2	1
INGREDIENTS		
fresh eggplant	7 oz. (2 cups, cubed)	4 oz. (1 cup, cubed)
water	2 tablespoons	1 tablespoon
BAKING DISH	1-qt. casserole	2-cup casserole
TIME AT HIGH	4 to 5 minutes	3 to 3-1/2 minutes

Trim, pare and cube eggplant. In a casserole, see size in chart above, combine eggplant and water. Cover. Microwave at full power (HIGH) for time in chart above or until tender, stirring once.

Serving Ideas

- Toss hot eggplant cubes, fresh tomato wedges and hot zucchini slices with butter, oregano and basil.
- Sprinkle hot Crisp Fried Eggplant sticks with Parmesan cheese and dried dillweed.
- Top Crisp Fried Eggplant slices with canned spaghetti sauce and shredded mozzarella cheese. Microwave briefly until heated through.

Fresh Fennel

SERVINGS	4 to 6	4 to 6	2 or 3
INGREDIENTS			
fresh fennel			
(as purchased)	1 (2-1/2-lb.) fennel	4 (12-oz.) fennel	2 (12-oz.) fennel
(after trimming)	1 (1-lb.) heart	4 (3-oz.) hearts	2 (3-oz.) hearts
water	1/2 cup	1/4 cup	2 tablespoons
BAKING DISH	1-1/2-qt. casserole	1-qt. casserole	2-cup casserole
TIME AT HIGH	10 to 12 minutes	7 to 8 minutes	4 to 5 minutes
STANDING TIME	2 minutes	2 minutes	2 minutes

Cut tops off fennel. Reserve a few feathery leaves for garnish. Cut off bottoms. If using 1 large fennel, quarter it lengthwise. Halve smaller fennel bulbs lengthwise. Remove tough outer portion, leaving just the heart. Arrange hearts, cut side up, with bottom halves toward outside of casserole, see size in chart above. Add water. Cover. Microwave at full power (HIGH) for time in chart above or until tender, turning hearts cut side down halfway through cooking time. Let stand, covered, 2 minutes. Drain. Garnish with feathery tops.

Kohlrabi Oriental-Style

SERVINGS	5 or 6	2 or 3
INGREDIENTS		
kohlrabies, peeled,	2 (8-oz.) kohlrabies	1 (8-oz.) kohlrabi
thinly sliced	(2-1/2 cups, sliced)	(1-1/2 cups, sliced)
fresh gingerroot, finely chopped	2 teaspoons	1 teaspoon
vegetable oil	2 tablespoons	1 tablespoon
frozen pea pods, thawed	1 (6-oz.) pkg.	1/2 (6-oz.) pkg.
red pepper, cut in strips	1 small	1/2 small
chopped onion	1/4 cup	2 tablespoons
soy sauce	2 teaspoons	1 teaspoon
white vinegar	2 teaspoons	1 teaspoon
BAKING DISH	2-qt. casserole	1-qt. casserole
TIME AT HIGH (kohlrabi)	7 to 8 minutes	3 to 4 minutes
TIME AT HIGH (other vegetables added)	4 minutes	3 minutes

In a casserole, see size in chart above, combine kohlrabi, gingerroot and oil. Cover and microwave at full power (HIGH) for time in chart above, stirring once. Stir in pea pods, red pepper and onion. Sprinkle with soy sauce and vinegar; toss well. Cover. Microwave at full power (HIGH) for time in chart above or until vegetables are crisp-tender, stirring twice. Serve with additional soy sauce, if desired.

How to Make Kohlrabi Oriental-Style

are the large bulb end of the kohlrabi and dis-
ard the tops. Slice the kohlrabi crosswise into
nin slices. Pare the brown, knobby gingerroot
nd cut the fibrous interior into very fine pieces.
tore any leftover gingerroot unpared in a jar
lled with dry sherry.

After precooking the kohlrabi and gingerroot in
vegetable oil, the quicker cooking Chinese pea
pods or snow peas, red pepper strips and onion
are tossed gently with the kohlrabi. The mixture
is seasoned with soy sauce and white vinegar
before microwaving until crisp-tender.

Fresh Leeks

SERVINGS	3 or 4	1 or 2
INGREDIENTS		
Fresh leeks		
(as purchased)	11 oz.	8 oz.
(after trimming)	7 oz. (2 cups, sliced)	4 oz. (1 cup, sliced)
water	1/4 cup	2 tablespoons
BAKING DISH	1-qt. casserole	1-qt. casserole
TIME AT HIGH	6 to 7 minutes	4 to 5 minutes

Cut off tops from leeks to within 1 to 2 inches of white part. Remove outer leaves and
discard. Wash leeks. Slice 1/4 inch thick. Cut large leeks lengthwise, then in 1/4-inch
slices. Combine leeks and water in a 1-quart casserole. Cover. Microwave at full power
(HIGH) for time in chart above or until tender, stirring once. Drain.

Marinated Vegetable Kabobs

SERVINGS	4	2
INGREDIENTS		
green pepper, cut in wedges	1/2 medium	1/4 medium
red pepper, cut in wedges	1/2 medium	1/4 medium
onion, cut in wedges	1 small	1/2 small
water	1/3 cup	3 tablespoons
salad dressing with herbs and spices	1 cup	1/2 cup
dry white wine	1/4 cup	2 tablespoons
Worcestershire sauce	1 tablespoon	2 teaspoons
dried leaf tarragon	1/2 teaspoon	1/4 teaspoon
fresh mushrooms	8	4
artichoke hearts, drained	1 (14-1/2-oz.) can	1/2 (14-1/2-oz.) can
cherry tomatoes	8	4
BOWL	large bowl	medium bowl
BAKING DISH	12" x 7" baking dish	10" x 6" baking dish
TIME AT HIGH (green pepper, onion)	5 minutes	3 minutes
TIME AT HIGH (marinade)	3-1/2 minutes	1-1/2 to 2 minutes
TIME AT HIGH (kabobs)	5 minutes	3 minutes
STANDING TIME	2 minutes	2 minutes

In a bowl, see size in chart above, combine green and red peppers, onion and water.
Cover. Microwave at full power (HIGH) for time in chart above or until crisp-tender.
Remove vegetables with a slotted spoon, reserving juices in bowl. Set vegetables aside.
To vegetable juice in bowl, add salad dressing, wine, Worcestershire sauce and tarragon; whisk until combined. Microwave at full power (HIGH) for time in chart above or
until boiling. Add pepper and onion wedges, mushrooms and artichoke hearts. Cover
and marinate at room temperature 30 minutes, gently stirring occasionally. At serving
time, drain vegetables, reserving marinade. Thread marinated vegetables and tomatoes
alternately on 12-inch bamboo skewers. Place in a baking dish, see size in chart above.
Drizzle with some of the reserved marinade. Cover with vented plastic wrap. Microwave at full power (HIGH) for time in chart above or until heated through, drizzling
once with reserved marinade. Let stand, covered, 2 minutes.

Stuffed Mushrooms

To make stuffed mushrooms, see page 45.

Serving Ideas

- Stir a little flour and dry red wine into sautéed mushrooms, then microwave until thick-
  ened. Serve over steak.
- Add chopped shallots, thyme and marjoram to mushrooms while sautéeing.
- Pour steak sauce into large mushroom caps, then microwave briefly. Serve with chops.

Fresh Mushroom Slices

SERVINGS	2	1
INGREDIENTS		
butter or margarine	2 tablespoons	1 tablespoon
mushrooms, sliced	2 cups (5 oz.)	1 cup (2-1/2 oz.)
BAKING DISH	1-qt. casserole	1-qt. casserole
TIME AT HIGH (butter)	45 seconds	30 seconds
TIME AT HIGH (mushrooms added)	3 to 4 minutes	2 to 3 minutes

Place butter or margarine in a 1-quart casserole. Microwave at full power (HIGH) for time in chart above or until melted. Add mushrooms. Toss to coat. Cover. Microwave at full power (HIGH) for time in chart above or until tender, stirring once.

Canned Mushroom Buttons in Butter Sauce

SERVINGS	4	2
INGREDIENTS		
whole button mushrooms in butter sauce	1 (6-oz.) can	1 (3-oz.) can
BAKING DISH	2-cup casserole	1-cup casserole
TIME AT HIGH	2 to 3 minutes	1 to 2 minutes

Place mushrooms and butter sauce in a casserole, see size in chart above. Cover. Microwave at full power (HIGH) for time in chart above or until heated through.

Fresh Mustard Greens

SERVINGS	4	2
INGREDIENTS		
fresh mustard greens		
(as purchased)	2 lbs. (16 cups)	1 lb. (8 cups)
(after trimming)	18 oz.	10 oz.
BAKING DISH	deep 4-qt. casserole	deep 2-qt. casserole
TIME AT HIGH	25 to 28 minutes	14 to 16 minutes

Wash and trim greens. Place mustard greens with water that clings to leaves in a casserole, see size in chart above. Cover. Microwave at full power (HIGH) for time in chart above or until tender, stirring three times.

Frozen Mustard Greens

SERVINGS	3
INGREDIENTS	
frozen chopped mustard greens	1 (10-oz.) pkg.
hot water	1-1/2 cups
BAKING DISH	deep 1-1/2-qt. casserole
TIME AT HIGH	20 minutes
STANDING TIME	1 to 2 minutes

Combine mustard greens and hot water in a 1-1/2-quart casserole. Cover. Microwave at full power (HIGH) 20 minutes or until tender, stirring twice. Let stand, covered, 1 to 2 minutes. Drain.

Serving Ideas

- Drizzle hot cooked mustard greens with red wine vinegar, then top with chopped hard-cooked eggs and paprika.
- Drizzle hot cooked mustard greens with Cheese Sauce, page 431, then top with canned French-fried onions.
- Stir sour-cream dip with bacon and horseradish into hot cooked mustard greens, then top with seasoned stuffing crumbs.

Canned Cut Okra

SERVINGS	2 or 3
INGREDIENTS	
cut okra	1 (14-1/2-oz.) can
BOWL	3- to 4-cup bowl
TIME AT HIGH	2-1/2 to 3 minutes

Drain off all but 2 tablespoons liquid from can. Combine okra and remaining liquid in a 3- to 4-cup bowl. Cover with vented plastic wrap. Microwave at full power (HIGH) 2-1/2 to 3 minutes or until heated through.

Calico Okra Bake

SERVINGS	6	3
INGREDIENTS		
bacon slices	6	3
chopped onion	1/2 cup	1/4 cup
chopped green pepper	1/4 cup	2 tablespoons
chili powder	1/2 teaspoon	1/4 teaspoon
sliced okra, cooked, drained	3 cups	1-1/2 cups
tomatoes, cut in wedges	2	1
sliced ripe olives	1/2 cup	1/4 cup
grated Parmesan cheese	2 tablespoons	1 tablespoon
BAKING DISH	deep 2-qt. casserole	deep 1-qt. casserole
TIME AT HIGH (bacon)	4 to 5 minutes	3 minutes
TIME AT HIGH (onion, green pepper)	3 minutes	2 minutes
TIME AT HIGH (okra, tomato, olives added)	6 minutes	3 minutes
TIME AT HIGH (cheese added)	1 minute	30 seconds

Dice bacon. In a casserole, see size in chart above, cover bacon closely with white paper towel. Microwave at full power (HIGH) for time in chart above or until crisp. Remove bacon with a slotted spoon; set aside. Add onion and green pepper to drippings in casserole. Microwave at full power (HIGH) for time in chart above or until vegetables are tender. Stir in chili powder. Gently stir in okra, tomato and olives. Cover. Microwave at full power (HIGH) for time in chart above or until heated through, stirring once. Sprinkle with Parmesan cheese and bacon. Microwave, uncovered, at full power (HIGH) for time in chart above.

Fresh Okra Slices

SERVINGS	4 (3 cups)	2 (1-1/2 cups)
INGREDIENTS		
fresh okra		
(as purchased)	1 lb.	8 oz.
(after trimming)	12 oz. (4 cups, sliced)	7 oz. (2 cups, sliced)
water	1/2 cup	1/4 cup
BAKING DISH	2-qt. casserole	1-qt. casserole
TIME AT HIGH	9 minutes	5 minutes

Wash okra and trim ends. Cut in 1/2-inch slices. In a casserole, see size in chart above, combine okra and water. Cover. Microwave at full power (HIGH) for time in chart above or until tender, stirring once. Drain.

How to Make Calico Okra Bake

With scissors, dice bacon by snipping several slices in small pieces directly into the casserole. Cover the bacon closely with a paper towel during cooking to promote crisping.

Okra, tomato wedges and ripe olive slices are dressed with a bacon-flavor dressing and a generous dash of chili powder. Fresh Parmesan cheese is grated over the hot casserole. Bacon is added before serving.

Frozen Cut or Whole Okra

SERVINGS	4	2	3 or 4
INGREDIENTS			
frozen cut okra	4 cups	2 cups	
OR			
frozen whole okra			1 (10-oz.) pkg.
hot water	1/2 cup	1/4 cup	1/4 cup
BAKING DISH	1-1/2-qt. casserole	1-qt. casserole	1-qt. casserole
TIME AT HIGH	12 minutes	8 minutes	9 minutes
STANDING TIME	1 to 2 minutes	1 to 2 minutes	1 to 2 minutes

In a casserole, see size in chart above, combine okra and hot water. Cover. Microwave at full power (HIGH) for time in chart above or until tender, stirring once. Let stand, covered, 1 to 2 minutes. Drain.

Whole Tiny Fresh Onions

SERVINGS	4	2
INGREDIENTS		
whole tiny onions	1 lb. (4 cups)	8 oz. (2 cups)
water	1/4 cup	2 tablespoons
BAKING DISH	2-qt. casserole	1-qt. casserole
TIME AT HIGH	10 to 12 minutes	7 to 9 minutes
STANDING TIME	2 minutes	2 minutes

Peel onions. In a casserole, see size in chart above, combine onions and water. Cover. Microwave at full power (HIGH) for time in chart above or until tender, stirring once. Let stand, covered, 2 minutes. Drain.

Fresh Chopped Onion

YIELD	2/3 cup	1/3 cup
INGREDIENTS		
chopped onion	1 cup (5 oz.)	1/2 cup (2-1/2 oz.)
water	2 tablespoons	2 tablespoons
BAKING DISH	1-qt. casserole	2-cup casserole
TIME AT HIGH	6 to 8 minutes	4-1/2 to 5-1/2 minutes
STANDING TIME	2 minutes	2 minutes

In a casserole, see size in chart above, combine onions and water. Cover. Microwave a full power (HIGH) for time in chart above or until tender, stirring once. Let stand, covered, 2 minutes.

Fresh Onion Rings

YIELD	1-3/4 cups	1 cup
INGREDIENTS		
onions	2 medium	1 medium
(after trimming)	9 oz. (4 cups rings)	4-1/2 oz. (2 cups rings)
water	2 tablespoons	2 tablespoons
BAKING DISH	1-qt. casserole	1-qt. casserole
TIME AT HIGH	8 to 10 minutes	6 to 7 minutes
STANDING TIME	2 minutes	2 minutes

Peel onions and slice 1/4 inch thick. Separate onion into rings. Combine onion rings and water in a 1-quart casserole. Cover. Microwave at full power (HIGH) for time in chart above or until tender, stirring once. Let stand, covered, 2 minutes.

How to Make Baked Onions with Herb Butter

Cut a slice from the top and bottom of each onion. This keeps the inside of the onions from exploding during cooking. For the same reason, pierce each onion several times with a large fork. Wrap each onion in a square of waxed paper, twisting ends to seal.

Let the herb butter mellow at room temperature before serving over the piping hot onions. These onions make a tasty and attractive garnish for a steak or roast platter.

Baked Onions with Herb Butter

SERVINGS	4	2	1
INGREDIENTS			
butter or margarine	1/2 cup	1/4 cup	2 tablespoons
celery salt	1/2 teaspoon	1/4 teaspoon	1/8 teaspoon
parsley flakes	1/2 teaspoon	1/4 teaspoon	1/8 teaspoon
dried leaf tarragon	1/2 teaspoon	1/4 teaspoon	1/8 teaspoon
medium onions	4 (5-oz.) onions	2 (5-oz.) onions	1 (5-oz.) onion
TIME AT 10%	1 minute	30 seconds	15 seconds
TIME AT HIGH	9 to 11 minutes	5 to 7 minutes	3-1/2 to 4 minutes
STANDING TIME	2 minutes	2 minutes	2 minutes

Place butter or margarine in a small bowl. Microwave at 10% (LOW) for time in chart above or until softened. Add celery salt, parsley and tarragon; mix well. Set butter or margarine mixture aside at room temperature. Wash onions, leaving outer skin intact. Trim top and bottom off each onion. Pierce onions deeply several times with a large fork. Wrap each onion in waxed paper, twisting ends loosely to seal. Microwave at full power (HIGH) for time in chart above or until tender, turning onions over and rearranging once. Let stand, wrapped, 2 minutes. To serve, top onions with herb-butter mixture.

To use large onions (8 ounces each): Prepare and wrap in waxed paper as above. Microwave onions at full power (HIGH) 5 minutes for 1 large onion, 10 to 12 minutes for 2 large onions, or 13 to 15 minutes for 4 large onions. Let stand, wrapped, 2 minutes. Cut onions in half to serve.

Frozen Chopped Onions

YIELD	2/3 cup
INGREDIENTS frozen chopped onions	1 cup
BAKING DISH	1-qt. casserole
TIME AT HIGH	1-1/2 minutes

Place onions in a 1-quart casserole. Cover. Microwave at full power (HIGH) 1-1/2 minutes or until tender, stirring twice.

Canned Whole Onions

SERVINGS	2 or 3	1 or 2
INGREDIENTS whole onions	1 (16-oz.) can	1 (8-oz.) can
BOWL	3- to 4-cup bowl	2- to 3-cup bowl
TIME AT HIGH	3-1/2 to 4-1/2 minutes	2-1/2 to 3-1/2 minutes

Drain off all but 2 tablespoons liquid from can. In a bowl, see size in chart above, combine onions and remaining liquid. Cover with vented plastic wrap. Microwave at full power (HIGH) for time in chart above or until heated through.

Frozen French-Fried Onion Rings

See directions for Grilled Steak & Onion Rings, page 92, to microwave a few onion rings in a microwave browning skillet. Never attempt to deep-fat-fry onion rings in the microwave oven.

Serving Ideas

- Add butter, snipped parsley, oregano and savory to hot cooked onion rings, then serve over green beans.
- Stir steak sauce mixed with a little sour cream into hot cooked onion rings, then serve over steak.
- Fold whole tiny cooked fresh or canned onions into Basic White Sauce, page 430. Reheat briefly in the microwave oven and garnish with chopped salted peanuts.

Fresh Sliced Parsnips

SERVINGS	8	4	2
INGREDIENTS			
fresh parsnips			
(as purchased)	2 lbs.	1 lb.	8 oz.
(after trimming)	1 lb. 11 oz. (7 cups, sliced)	14 oz. (3-1/2 cups, sliced)	6 oz. (1-1/2 cups, sliced)
orange juice	1 cup	1/2 cup	1/4 cup
all-purpose flour	2 tablespoons	1 tablespoon	2 teaspoons
orange juice	1/2 cup	1/4 cup	1/4 cup
BAKING DISH	2-qt. casserole	2-qt. casserole	2-qt. casserole
TIME AT HIGH (parsnips)	11 to 12 minutes	8 to 9 minutes	5 to 6 minutes
TIME AT HIGH (sauce added)	2-1/2 minutes	2-1/2 minutes	2-1/2 minutes
STANDING TIME	2 minutes	2 minutes	2 minutes

Wash, trim and pare parsnips. Cut thick portion of parsnips in half lengthwise. Slice 1/2 inch thick. In a 2-quart casserole, combine parsnips and first amount of orange juice. Cover. Microwave at full power (HIGH) for time in chart above or until tender, stirring once. In a screw-top jar, shake together flour and second amount of orange juice. Stir into parsnips and juices. Cover. Microwave at full power (HIGH) 2-1/2 minutes or until thickened and bubbly, stirring once. Let stand, covered, 2 minutes.

Fresh Quartered Parsnips

SERVINGS	8	4	2
INGREDIENTS			
fresh parsnips			
(as purchased)	2 lbs. (10 medium)	1 lb. (5 medium)	8 oz. (2 medium)
(after trimming)	1 lb. 10 oz.	12 oz.	6 oz.
orange juice	1 cup	1/2 cup	1/4 cup
all-purpose flour	2 tablespoons	1 tablespoon	2 teaspoons
orange juice	1/2 cup	1/4 cup	1/4 cup
BAKING DISH	2-qt. casserole	2-qt. casserole	2-qt. casserole
TIME AT HIGH (parsnips)	12 to 14 minutes	9 minutes	5 to 6 minutes
TIME AT HIGH (sauce added)	2-1/2 minutes	2-1/2 minutes	2-1/2 minutes
STANDING TIME	2 minutes	2 minutes	2 minutes

Wash, trim and pare parsnips. Cut into fourths. In a 2-quart casserole, combine parsnips and first amount of orange juice. Cover. Microwave at full power (HIGH) for time in chart above or until tender, stirring once. In a screw-top jar, shake together flour and second amount of orange juice. Stir into parsnips and juices. Cover. Microwave at full power (HIGH) 2-1/2 minutes or until thickened and bubbly, stirring once. Let stand, covered, 2 minutes.

Fresh Peas

SERVINGS	3 or 4	2	1
INGREDIENTS fresh peas	2 lbs. (2-1/3 cups, shelled)	1 lb. (1-1/3 cups, shelled)	8 oz. (2/3 cup, shelled)
water	1/4 cup	1/4 cup	1/4 cup
BAKING DISH	1-qt. casserole	2-cup casserole	1-1/2-cup casserole
TIME AT HIGH	7 to 8 minutes	5 to 6 minutes	4 to 5 minutes
STANDING TIME	2 minutes	2 minutes	2 minutes

Shell peas; wash. In a casserole, see size in chart above, combine peas and water. Cover. Microwave at full power (HIGH) for time in chart above or until tender, stirring once. Let stand, covered, 2 minutes. Drain.

Frozen Peas

SERVINGS	6	4	2	1
INGREDIENTS frozen peas	4 cups	3 cups	1 (8- or 10-oz.) pkg. (2 cups)	1 cup
water	2/3 cup	1/2 cup	1/3 cup	1/4 cup
BAKING DISH	2-qt. casserole	1-1/2-qt. casserole	1-1/2-qt. casserole	1-qt. casserole
TIME AT HIGH	13 to 14 minutes	11 to 12 minutes	7 to 9 minutes	4 to 6 minutes
STANDING TIME	1 to 2 minutes	1 to 2 minutes	1 to 2 minutes	1 to 2 minutes

In a casserole, see size in chart above, combine peas and water. Cover. Microwave at full power (HIGH) for time in chart above or until tender, stirring once. Let stand, covered, 1 to 2 minutes. Drain.

Frozen Peas in a Pouch

SERVINGS	3
INGREDIENTS frozen peas in butter sauce	1 (10-oz.) pkg.
TIME AT HIGH	6 to 7 minutes

With a sharp knife or scissors, cut a small "X" in center of top side of pouch. Microwave pouch at full power (HIGH) 6 to 7 minutes, flexing pouch once to rearrange peas.

How to Make Peas à la Française

Line a casserole or serving bowl with large iceberg lettuce leaves. Gently combine frozen peas and onions, shredded lettuce, butter and sugar in the lettuce leaves. The leaves provide moisture for cooking the peas.

Serve the peas with dollops of sour cream for a delightful sweet and sour flavor. For a garnish, sprinkle fresh, frozen or freeze-dried chives over the sour cream.

Peas à la Française

SERVINGS	6	3
INGREDIENTS		
large iceberg lettuce leaves	several	several
frozen peas and onions	2 (10-oz.) pkgs.	1 (10-oz.) pkg.
shredded iceberg lettuce	2 cups	1 cup
sugar	2 tablespoons	1 tablespoon
butter or margarine	1/4 cup	2 tablespoons
dairy sour cream, snipped chives	to garnish	to garnish
BAKING DISH	deep 2-qt. casserole	deep 1-qt. casserole
TIME AT HIGH	10 minutes	6 minutes
STANDING TIME	2 minutes	2 minutes

Line a casserole, see size in chart above, with large lettuce leaves. Break apart peas and onions. In lettuce-lined casserole, gently combine peas and onions, shredded lettuce, sugar and butter or margarine. Cover. Microwave at full power (HIGH) for time in chart above or until peas are tender, tossing gently once. Let stand, covered, 2 minutes. Serve topped with a dollop of sour cream and sprinkling of snipped chives.

Frozen Chinese Pea Pods

SERVINGS	6	3
INGREDIENTS frozen Chinese pea pods	2 (6-oz.) pkgs.	1 (6-oz.) pkg.
BAKING DISH	1-qt. casserole	1-qt. casserole
TIME AT HIGH	7 to 8 minutes	5 to 6 minutes

Place pea pods in a 1-quart casserole. Cover. Microwave at full power (HIGH) for tim in chart above or until crisp-tender, stirring once.

Frozen Peas & Carrots

SERVINGS	3 or 4
INGREDIENTS frozen peas and carrots water	1 (10-oz.) pkg. 1 tablespoon
BAKING DISH	1-qt. casserole
TIME AT HIGH	6 to 7 minutes
STANDING TIME	1 to 2 minutes

Combine peas and carrots and water in a 1-quart casserole. Cover. Microwave at ful power (HIGH) 6 to 7 minutes or until tender, stirring once. Let stand, covered, 1 to minutes.

Canned Peas

SERVINGS	2 or 3	1 or 2
INGREDIENTS peas	1 (17-oz.) can	1 (8-1/2-oz.) can
BOWL	3- to 4-cup bowl	2- to 3-cup bowl
TIME AT HIGH	2-1/2 to 3 minutes	1-1/2 to 2-1/2 minutes

Drain off all but 2 tablespoons liquid from can. In a bowl, see size in chart above, com bine peas and remaining liquid. Cover with vented plastic wrap. Microwave at ful power (HIGH) for time in chart above or until heated through.

Serving Ideas

- Toss hot cooked peas with butter, chopped pimiento, dillweed and drained, canned mushrooms.
- Toss hot cooked pea pods with vinegar, oil, soy sauce and finely chopped fresh ginger-root, then refrigerate for salad.
- Mix hot cooked peas with buttermilk dressing, then refrigerate to marinate. Toss with croutons, hard-cooked egg slices and cubed cheese to serve.

Dried Black-Eyed Peas

SERVINGS	8	4
INGREDIENTS		
dried black-eyed peas	1 lb. (about 3 cups)	8 oz. (about 1-1/2 cups)
water	2 qts.	1 qt.
baking soda	1/4 teaspoon	1/8 teaspoon
water	6 cups	3 cups
salt	1 teaspoon	1/2 teaspoon
BAKING DISH	deep 4-qt. casserole	deep 2-qt. casserole
TIME AT HIGH	20 minutes	10 minutes
TIME AT 30%	55 to 60 minutes	40 to 45 minutes
STANDING TIME	10 minutes	10 minutes

In a casserole, see size in chart above, combine dried black-eyed peas and first amount of water. Stir in baking soda. Cover and let stand overnight. Drain and rinse peas. Return to casserole. Add second amount of water and salt. Cover. Microwave at full power (HIGH) for time in chart above or until boiling. Stir. Cover. Microwave at 30% (MEDIUM LOW) for time in chart above or until peas are tender, stirring twice. Let stand, covered, 10 minutes.

Frozen Black-Eyed Peas

SERVINGS	3 or 4
INGREDIENTS	
frozen black-eyed peas	1 (10-oz.) pkg.
hot water	2-1/4 cups
BAKING DISH	deep 2-qt. casserole
TIME AT HIGH	29 minutes
STANDING TIME	1 to 2 minutes

Combine black-eyed peas and hot water in a 2-quart casserole. Cover. Microwave at full power (HIGH) 29 minutes or until tender, stirring twice. Let stand, covered, 1 to 2 minutes. Drain.

Canned Black-Eyed Peas

SERVINGS	2 or 3	1 or 2
INGREDIENTS		
black-eyed peas	1 (15-oz.) can	1 (7-1/2-oz.) can
BOWL	3- to 4-cup bowl	2- to 3-cup bowl
TIME AT HIGH	4 to 5 minutes	3 to 4 minutes

Drain off all but 2 tablespoons liquid from can. In a bowl, see size in chart above, combine black-eyed peas and remaining liquid. Cover with vented plastic wrap. Microwave at full power (HIGH) for time in chart above or until heated through, stirring once.

Confetti-Stuffed Peppers

SERVINGS	8	4
INGREDIENTS		
butter or margarine	2 tablespoons	1 tablespoon
cheese cracker crumbs	1/2 cup	1/4 cup
frozen mixed vegetables with onion sauce	2 (8-oz.) pkgs.	1 (8-oz.) pkg.
milk	1 cup	1/2 cup
butter or margarine	2 tablespoons	1 tablespoon
Minute rice	1/2 cup	1/4 cup
chopped pimiento	1/4 cup	2 tablespoons
dried leaf thyme, crushed	1/2 teaspoon	1/4 teaspoon
medium green peppers, halved lengthwise	4 (5-oz.) peppers	2 (5-oz.) peppers
BAKING DISH (filling)	1-1/2-qt. casserole	1-1/2-qt. casserole
BAKING DISH (peppers)	12" x 7" baking dish	8-inch square baking dish
TIME AT HIGH (butter)	30 seconds	30 seconds
TIME AT HIGH (vegetables)	10 minutes	6 minutes
STANDING TIME (rice added)	5 minutes	5 minutes
TIME AT HIGH (unstuffed peppers)	7 minutes	5 minutes
TIME AT HIGH (stuffed peppers)	5 minutes	4 minutes

Place first amount of butter or margarine in a small bowl. Microwave at full power (HIGH) 30 seconds or until melted. Stir in cracker crumbs and set aside. In a 1-1/2-quart casserole, combine frozen vegetables, milk and second amount of butter or margarine. Cover and microwave at full power (HIGH) for time in chart above. Halfway through the cooking time, stir sauce until it is smooth. When vegetables are tender, quickly stir in rice, pimiento and thyme. Let stand, covered, 5 minutes. Arrange peppers, cut side down, in a baking dish, see size in chart above. Cover with vented plastic wrap. Microwave at full power (HIGH) for time in chart above. Turn peppers cut side up and drain off juices. Spoon creamed vegetables into peppers. Cover dish with vented plastic wrap. Microwave at full power (HIGH) for time in chart above or until heated through. Sprinkle with buttered cracker crumbs.

Chopped Green Pepper

YIELD	2/3 cup	1/3 cup
INGREDIENTS		
chopped green pepper	1 cup	1/2 cup
water	1 tablespoon	1 tablespoon
BAKING DISH	1-cup casserole	1-cup casserole
TIME AT HIGH	4 to 5 minutes	2 to 3 minutes

Combine green pepper and water in a 1-cup casserole. Cover. Microwave at full power (HIGH) for time in chart above or until tender, stirring once.

How to Make Confetti-Stuffed Peppers

For precooking, pepper halves are placed cut side down against the baking dish to capture the steam and speed cooking. Turn the shells cut side up and drain before filling with creamed vegetable and rice combination.

Cook the peppers until they are crisp-tender and the filling is heated through. Slip a silver knife into the center of the filling to check if it is hot. Sprinkle with cracker crumbs after cooking; this prevents the crumbs from getting soggy.

Crispy Bacon Topper

YIELD	for 3 potatoes	for 1 or 2 potatoes
INGREDIENTS		
bacon, crisp-cooked	4 slices	2 slices
egg, hard-cooked	1	1/2
snipped chives	1 teaspoon	1/2 teaspoon
paprika	1 teaspoon	1/2 teaspoon

Crumble cooked bacon slices. Chop hard-cooked eggs. In a small bowl, combine all ingredients. Sprinkle over cooked potatoes. Microwave as directed in Fast & Fancy Baked Potatoes, page 350.

Italiano Topper

YIELD	for 2 or 3 potatoes	for 1 potato
INGREDIENTS		
chopped olives	2 tablespoons	1 tablespoon
chopped canned mushrooms	2 tablespoons	1 tablespoon
grated Parmesan cheese	1 tablespoon	2 teaspoons
dried leaf oregano	1/2 teaspoon	1/4 teaspoon

In a small bowl, combine all ingredients. Sprinkle over cooked potatoes. Microwave as directed in Fast & Fancy Baked Potatoes, page 350.

Fast & Fancy Baked Potatoes

SERVINGS	6	4	2
INGREDIENTS			
Onion Crunch, Golden Cheese, Italiano or Crispy Bacon Toppers, see below and page 349	6 tablespoons	4 tablespoons	2 tablespoons
baking potatoes	3 (8-oz.) potatoes	2 (8-oz.) potatoes	1 (8-oz.) potato
butter or margarine	3 tablespoons	2 tablespoons	1 tablespoon
BAKING DISH	12" x 7" baking dish	10" x 6" baking dish	9-inch pie plate
TIME AT HIGH (butter)	60 seconds	45 seconds	45 seconds
TIME AT HIGH (potatoes)	10 to 12 minutes	8 to 10 minutes	4 to 5 minutes
TIME AT HIGH (toppings added)	2 minutes	1 minute	1 minute

Prepare topping. Pare potatoes and halve lengthwise. Score flat side of each potato half about 1/4 inch deep at 1-inch intervals, both crosswise and lengthwise. Place butter or margarine in a baking dish, see size in chart above. Microwave at full power (HIGH) for time in chart above or until melted. Turn potatoes over in butter or margarine and place flat side down in dish. Cover with vented plastic wrap. Microwave at full power (HIGH) for time in chart above or until tender. Halfway through cooking time, rearrange potatoes and turn flat side up; give dish a half turn. When potatoes are tender, sprinkle each half with about 1 tablespoon topping. Microwave, uncovered, at full power (HIGH) for time in chart above or until topping is heated through.

Golden Cheese Topper

YIELD	for 2 or 3 potatoes	for 1 potato
INGREDIENTS		
shredded carrot	2 tablespoons	1 tablespoon
shredded American cheese	2 tablespoons	1 tablespoon
chopped green onion	1 tablespoon	2 teaspoons
salad seasoning	1/2 teaspoon	1/4 teaspoon

In a small bowl, combine all ingredients. Sprinkle over cooked potatoes. Microwave as directed in Fast & Fancy Baked Potatoes, above.

Onion Crunch Topper

YIELD	for 3 potatoes	for 1 or 2 potatoes
INGREDIENTS		
chopped pecans	2 tablespoons	1 tablespoon
chopped celery	2 tablespoons	1 tablespoon
dry onion soup mix	2 tablespoons	1 tablespoon
snipped parsley	1 tablespoon	2 teaspoons

In a small bowl, combine all ingredients. Sprinkle over cooked potatoes. Microwave as directed in Fast & Fancy Baked Potatoes, above.

How to Make Dill-Buttered New Potatoes

Pare a small strip of skin around the center of each tiny red potato to prevent the skins from breaking during cooking.

Hot water gives potatoes a faster start in microwave cooking. Drain potatoes and toss with butter and snipped fresh dill or dried dillweed.

Dill-Buttered New Potatoes

SERVINGS	4	2	1
INGREDIENTS			
tiny new potatoes	2 lbs. (about 13 potatoes)	1 lb. (about 7 potatoes)	8 oz. (about 4 potatoes)
hot water	3-1/2 cups	2-1/2 cups	2 cups
butter or margarine	3 tablespoons	2 tablespoons	1 tablespoon
dried dillweed	1 teaspoon	1/2 teaspoon	1/4 teaspoon
BAKING DISH	deep 3-qt. casserole	deep 2-qt. casserole	deep 1-1/2-qt. casserole
TIME AT HIGH	20 to 22 minutes	15 to 17 minutes	10 to 12 minutes
STANDING TIME	2 minutes	2 minutes	2 minutes

Wash potatoes. Halve any large potatoes so all potatoes are about the same size. Pare a small strip of skin around center of whole potatoes. In a casserole, see size in chart above, combine potatoes and hot water to cover. Cover. Microwave at full power (HIGH) for time in chart above or until potatoes are fork-tender, stirring once. Let stand, covered, 2 minutes. Drain. Add butter or margarine and dillweed; toss until all potatoes are well coated.

Serving Ideas

- Using an electric mixer, whip butter and sharp process-cheese spread with bacon until fluffy. Serve on baked potatoes.
- Fold tiny new potatoes and hot cooked peas into Basic White Sauce, page 430. Sprinkle with chives.
- Marinate hot cubed potatoes in your favorite salad dressing. At serving time, toss with lettuce, chopped celery, chopped green pepper and chopped pimiento.

Baked Russet Potatoes

SERVINGS	6	4	2	1
INGREDIENTS russet potatoes	6 (6- to 8-oz.) potatoes	4 (6- to 8-oz.) potatoes	2 (6- to 8-oz.) potatoes	1 (6- to 8-oz.) potato
TIME AT HIGH	14 to 16 minutes	10 to 12 minutes	5 to 7 minutes	3 to 5 minutes
STANDING TIME	5 minutes	5 minutes	5 minutes	5 minutes

Wash potatoes. Pierce each potato several times with a large fork to allow steam to escape. Arrange potatoes spoke-fashion in a circle in microwave oven. Microwave at full power (HIGH) for time in chart above or until almost tender in centers, turning potatoes over and rearranging once. Wrap in foil and let stand 5 minutes.

Fresh Cubed Potatoes

SERVINGS	4 or 5	2 or 3
INGREDIENTS fresh potatoes, pared, cut in 3/4-inch cubes	4 cups	2 cups
hot water	2-1/2 cups	1-1/2 cups
BAKING DISH	deep 2-qt. casserole	deep 1-1/2-qt. casserole
TIME AT HIGH	14 to 15 minutes	9 to 10 minutes
STANDING TIME	2 minutes	2 minutes

In a casserole, see size in chart above, combine potatoes and hot water to cover. Cover. Microwave at full power (HIGH) for time in chart above or until tender, stirring once. Let stand, covered, 2 minutes.

Boiled Red Potato Halves

SERVINGS	3	2	1
INGREDIENTS red potatoes	3 (5- to 7-oz.) potatoes	2 (5- to 7-oz.) potatoes	1 (5- to 7-oz.) potato
hot water	3 cups	2-1/2 cups	2 cups
BAKING DISH	deep 2-qt. casserole	deep 2-qt. casserole	deep 1-qt. casserole
TIME AT HIGH	14 to 16 minutes	12 to 14 minutes	9 to 11 minutes
STANDING TIME	2 minutes	2 minutes	2 minutes

Wash and halve potatoes. Pare if desired. In a casserole, see size in chart above, combine potatoes and hot water to cover. Cover. Microwave at full power (HIGH) for time in chart above or until tender, stirring once. Let stand, covered, 2 minutes. Drain.

Busy-Day Scalloped Potatoes

SERVINGS	6	3
INGREDIENTS		
frozen hashed brown potatoes O'Brien	1-1/2 lbs. (6 cups)	12 oz. (3 cups)
half and half	1 cup	1/2 cup
cubed process American cheese	1-1/2 cups (6 oz.)	3/4 cup (3 oz.)
butter or margarine, cut up	1/2 cup	1/4 cup
shredded Cheddar cheese	1 cup (4 oz.)	1/2 cup (2 oz.)
snipped parsley, paprika	to garnish	to garnish
BAKING DISH	12" x 7" baking dish	10" x 6" baking dish
GLASS MEASURING CUP	4-cup	4-cup
TIME AT 30% (defrosting)	5 minutes	3 minutes
TIME AT HIGH (sauce)	3 to 4 minutes	1-1/2 to 2 minutes
TIME AT HIGH (potatoes, sauce)	5 minutes	5 minutes
TIME AT 30% (potatoes, sauce)	30 minutes	10 minutes
TIME AT 30% (cheese added)	15 minutes	3 minutes

Place frozen potatoes in a baking dish, see size in chart above. Microwave at 30% (MEDIUM LOW) for time in chart above. Let stand while preparing sauce. In a 4-cup glass measuring cup, combine half and half, cubed process American cheese and butter or margarine. Microwave at full power (HIGH) for time in chart above, stirring often until cheese and butter or margarine melt. Stir until smooth. Spread defrosted potatoes evenly in baking dish. Pour cheese sauce over potatoes; stir gently. Cover with vented plastic wrap. Microwave at full power (HIGH) 5 minutes; stir well. Cover with vented plastic wrap. Microwave at 30% (MEDIUM LOW) for time in chart above. Sprinkle potato mixture with shredded Cheddar cheese, parsley and paprika. Microwave, uncovered, at 30% (MEDIUM LOW) for time in chart above or until potatoes are tender.

Frozen Potatoes

Tater Tots: Even the browning skillet doesn't help crisp these frozen potato nuggets. They warm through but remain soggy and unappetizing. It's best to cook them conventionally.

Hashed Brown Potatoes: The frozen potatoes are so icy cold that even hot butter in the browning skillet isn't enough to make them crisp and brown on the outside. Frozen hashed browns are best cooked conventionally.

French-Fried Potatoes: Deep-fat-frying should never be attempted in the microwave. Without deep-fat-frying, these frozen fries remain limp and pale, even when cooked with a small amount of oil in the browning skillet. Cook French fries conventionally.

How to Make Busy-Day Scalloped Potatoes

Spread thawed hashed brown potatoes O'Brien in a baking dish. Pour melted cheese mixture over the potatoes. These hashed browns include chopped onions and peppers.

After the potatoes are partially baked, sprinkle shredded Cheddar cheese, paprika and snipped parsley on top. Microwave until cheese is melted and potatoes are tender. Be sure to check the potatoes in the center of the baking dish for doneness as they will be done last.

Instant Mashed Potatoes

SERVINGS	4	2
INGREDIENTS		
water		
milk		
salt		
butter or margarine		
instant mashed potato buds	4 servings	2 servings
BOWL	deep 1-1/2-qt. bowl	deep 1-qt. bowl
TIME AT HIGH	4 to 5 minutes	2-1/2 to 3 minutes

In a bowl, see size in chart above, combine water, milk, salt and butter or margarine according to directions on instant-potato package. Microwave at full power (HIGH) for time in chart above or until boiling. Stir in potatoes. Mix with a fork until smooth.

Dry Packaged Potatoes

Many dried potato products can be successfully cooked in the microwave oven. Follow the manufacturer's package directions.

Twice-Baked Sweet Potatoes

SERVINGS	4	2	1
INGREDIENTS			
hot baked sweet potatoes or yams	4	2	1
caramel or butter-scotch ice-cream topping	1/2 cup	1/4 cup	2 tablespoons
butter or margarine	1/4 cup	2 tablespoons	1 tablespoon
ground cinnamon	1/4 teaspoon	1/8 teaspoon	dash
ground nutmeg	1/8 teaspoon	dash	dash
caramel or butterscotch ice-cream topping	1/4 cup	2 tablespoons	1 tablespoon
toasted chopped pecans, if desired	4 teaspoons	2 teaspoons	1 teaspoon
PLATE	serving plate	serving plate	serving plate
TIME AT HIGH	5 to 7 minutes	3 to 4 minutes	1-1/2 to 2 minutes

Cut top off hot baked sweet potatoes. Quickly scoop out hot potato pulp with a spoon, being careful to keep shells intact. Set shells aside. In a mixing bowl, combine hot potato pulp, first amount of ice-cream topping, butter or margarine, cinnamon and nutmeg. Beat with electric mixer on high speed until fluffy. Spoon mixture into potato shells. Place on a serving plate. Cover with vented plastic wrap. Microwave at full power (HIGH) for time in chart above or until heated through. Top with additional topping and sprinkle with chopped pecans, if desired.

Baked Sweet Potatoes or Yams

SERVINGS	4	2	1
INGREDIENTS			
sweet potatoes or yams	4 (6- to 8-oz.) potatoes or yams	2 (6- to 8-oz.) potatoes or yams	1 (6- to 8-oz.) potato or yam
TIME AT HIGH	11 to 14 minutes	6 to 7 minutes	4 to 5 minutes
STANDING TIME	5 minutes	5 minutes	5 minutes

Wash potatoes. Pierce each potato several times with a large fork to allow steam to escape. Arrange potatoes spoke-fashion in a circle in microwave oven. Microwave at full power (HIGH) for time in chart above, turning potatoes over and rearranging once. When done, potatoes should be almost tender in center when pierced with a fork. Wrap in foil. Let stand 5 minutes.

Canned Sweet Potatoes or Yams

SERVINGS	3 or 4	1 or 2
INGREDIENTS whole sweet potatoes in syrup or yams	1 (23-oz.) can	1 (9-oz.) can
BOWL	3- to 4-cup bowl	2- to 3-cup bowl
TIME AT HIGH	4-1/2 to 5-1/2 minutes	3 to 4 minutes

Drain off all but about 1/4 cup syrup from can. In a bowl, see size in chart above, com
bine sweet potatoes or yams and remaining liquid. Cover with vented plastic wrap. Mi
crowave at full power (HIGH) for time in chart above or until heated through, stirring
once.

Serving Ideas

- Toss hot sweet potatoes or yams with peach jam, drained canned sliced peaches and a
little lemon juice. Top with chopped cashews.
- Drizzle hot sweet potatoes or yams with maple syrup, then sprinkle with nutmeg or all
spice.
- Fold cooked whole-kernel corn, sliced ripe olives, chopped canned green chilies and
cherry tomatoes into cubed potatoes. Toss with vinegar and oil dressing seasoned with
taco seasoning mix. Microwave until heated through.
- Marinate hot cooked cubed potatoes in French dressing. Toss with zucchini chunks, red
onion rings, radish slices and herbed croutons just before serving.
- Substitute potato salad for the artichoke stuffing in Tomato Stars, page 368.
- Substitute canned German potato salad for the vegetable stuffing in Confetti-Stuffed
Peppers, page 348.
- Stir crisp-cooked, crumbled bacon, chopped celery, sliced green olives and sliced
green onion into canned potato salad. Microwave until heated through. Top with shred
ded Cheddar cheese.

Fresh Cubed Rutabaga

SERVINGS	6	3	1

INGREDIENTS
fresh rutabaga
  (as purchased)
  (after trimming)
 	
water
	
	1 lb. 13 oz.
	1-1/2 lbs.
	(4 cups, cubed)
	1/2 cup
		
		13 oz.
		10 oz.
		(2 cups, cubed)
		1/4 cup
			
			7 oz.
			5 oz.
			(1 cup, cubed)
			2 tablespoons

BAKING DISH	2-qt. casserole	1-qt. casserole	1-qt. casserole
TIME AT HIGH	10 to 14 minutes	8 to 10 minutes	4 to 6 minutes
STANDING TIME	2 minutes	2 minutes	2 minutes

Wash, trim and pare rutabaga. Cut into cubes. In a casserole, see size in chart above
combine rutabaga and water. Cover. Microwave at full power (HIGH) for time in char
above or until tender, stirring once. Let stand, covered, 2 minutes. Drain.

How to Make Ruby Rutabaga Bake

Prepare the rutabaga and cut into cubes. Try to cut the cubes about the same size for more even cooking in the microwave oven.

Top the cooked rutabaga with a row of apple slices. Then spoon sugared cranberries on top and sprinkle with brown sugar and cinnamon.

Ruby Rutabaga Bake

SERVINGS	6	3
INGREDIENTS		
rutabaga, pared, cubed	4 cups	2 cups
apple juice or water	1/2 cup	1/4 cup
fresh cranberries	1/2 cup	1/4 cup
granulated sugar	1/4 cup	2 tablespoons
apples, cored, sliced	2	1
packed brown sugar	1/2 cup	1/4 cup
ground cinnamon	1/2 teaspoon	1/4 teaspoon
butter or margarine	2 tablespoons	1 tablespoon
BAKING DISH	deep 2-qt. casserole	deep 1-qt. casserole
TIME AT HIGH (rutabaga)	10 to 14 minutes	8 to 10 minutes
TIME AT HIGH (fruit added)	5 to 6 minutes	3 minutes

In a casserole, see size in chart above, combine rutabaga and apple juice or water. Cover. Microwave at full power (HIGH) for time in chart above or until almost tender, stirring twice. While rutabaga is in the microwave, combine cranberries and granulated sugar in a small bowl. Stir well and let stand while rutabaga cooks. Drain cooked rutabaga; top with apple slices. Spoon cranberry mixture over apple. Mix together brown sugar and cinnamon; sprinkle over fruit. Dot with butter or margarine. Cover. Microwave at full power (HIGH) for time in chart above or until fruit is tender, giving dish a half turn once. Serve in small bowls with juice.

Savory Spinach Mounds

SERVINGS	8	4
INGREDIENTS		
No-Fail Hollandaise Sauce, page 422	1/2 cup	1/4 cup
frozen chopped spinach, cooked	2 (10-oz.) pkgs.	1 (10-oz.) pkg.
cream cheese, softened	1 (3-oz.) pkg.	1/2 (3-oz.) pkg.
butter or margarine	2 tablespoons	1 tablespoon
dry onion soup mix	2 tablespoons	1 tablespoon
lemon juice	1 teaspoon	1/2 teaspoon
canned artichoke bottoms or thick tomato slices	8 or 9	4 or 5
BAKING DISH	10" x 6" baking dish	9-inch pie plate
TIME AT HIGH	6 minutes	3 minutes

Prepare No-Fail Hollandaise Sauce; keep warm in water bath. Drain spinach well in sieve. Press out as much liquid as possible from spinach. In a bowl, combine hot spinach, cream cheese, butter or margarine, onion soup mix and lemon juice. Mix well. Rinse artichoke bottoms; pat dry. Place artichoke bottoms or tomato slices in a baking dish, see size in chart above. Using a 1/4-cup ice-cream scoop, mound spinach mixture on artichoke bottoms or tomato slices. Cover with vented plastic wrap. Microwave at full power (HIGH) for time in chart above or until heated through. Top with warm hollandaise sauce.

Fresh Spinach

SERVINGS	4	2	1
INGREDIENTS			
fresh spinach	1 lb. (12 cups)	8 oz. (6 cups)	4 oz. (3 cups)
BAKING DISH	deep 5-qt. casserole	deep 1-1/2-qt. casserole	1-qt. casserole
TIME AT HIGH	9 to 10 minutes	4 to 5 minutes	3 to 4 minutes

Wash and drain spinach. Trim off tough stem ends. Place spinach with water that clings to leaves in a casserole, see size in chart above. Cover. Microwave at full power (HIGH) for time in chart above or until tender, stirring once.

Frozen Chopped or Leaf Spinach

SERVINGS	2 or 3	2 or 3
INGREDIENTS		
frozen chopped spinach	1 (10-oz.) pkg.	
OR		
frozen leaf spinach		1 (10-oz.) pkg.
BAKING DISH	1-qt. casserole	1-qt. casserole
TIME AT HIGH	7 to 8 minutes	9 to 10 minutes
STANDING TIME	1 to 2 minutes	1 to 2 minutes

Place spinach in a 1-quart casserole. Cover. Microwave at full power (HIGH) for time in chart above or until tender, stirring once. Let stand, covered, 1 to 2 minutes.

How to Make Savory Spinach Mounds

With an ice-cream scoop, mound onion-spinach mixture into artichoke bottoms or on thick slices of tomato.

Complete this dish by spooning warm hollandaise sauce over the mounds of spinach.

Frozen Spinach in a Pouch

SERVINGS	3
INGREDIENTS	
Frozen spinach in butter sauce	1 (10-oz.) pkg.
TIME AT HIGH	6-1/2 to 7-1/2 minutes

With a sharp knife or scissors, cut a small "X" in center of top side of pouch. Microwave pouch at full power (HIGH) 6-1/2 to 7-1/2 minutes, flexing pouch once to rearrange spinach.

Canned Spinach

SERVINGS	2 or 3	1 or 2
INGREDIENTS		
Spinach	1 (15-oz.) can	1 (7-3/4-oz.) can
BOWL	3- to 4-cup bowl	2- to 3-cup bowl
TIME AT HIGH	3-1/2 to 4 minutes	3 to 3-1/2 minutes

Drain off all but 2 tablespoons liquid from can. In a bowl, see size in chart above, combine spinach and remaining liquid. Cover with vented plastic wrap. Microwave at full power (HIGH) for time in chart above or until heated through.

Fresh Summer Pickles

YIELD	2 qts.	1 qt.
INGREDIENTS		
zucchini	2 medium	1 medium
yellow crookneck squash	2 medium	1 medium
unwaxed cucumbers	2 medium	1 medium
pattypan squash	1 medium	1/2 medium
green pepper, cut in strips	1 medium	1/2 medium
red pepper, cut in strips	1 medium	1/2 medium
onion, sliced, separated in rings	1 medium	1/2 medium
fennel seed	1 tablespoon	2 teaspoons
cracked ice		
white wine tarragon vinegar	1 cup	1/2 cup
water	1 cup	1/2 cup
pickling salt	2 tablespoons	1 tablespoon
sugar	2 tablespoons	1 tablespoon
celery seed	1 teaspoon	1/2 teaspoon
mustard seed	1 teaspoon	1/2 teaspoon
hot pepper sauce	1/4 teaspoon	1/8 teaspoon
garlic powder	1/8 teaspoon	dash
BAKING DISH	14" x 10" baking dish	12" x 7" baking dish
GLASS MEASURING CUP	4-cup	4-cup
TIME AT HIGH	5 to 6 minutes	2-1/2 to 3-1/2 minutes

Cut zucchini, crookneck squash, cucumbers and pattypan squash in half crosswise. Cut again lengthwise in sixths or eighths to form serving-size spears. In a baking dish, see size in chart above, combine spears, green and red peppers, onion, fennel seed and some cracked ice. Mix well. Add enough ice to cover mixture. Let stand 3 hours. Drain. In a 4-cup glass measuring cup, combine vinegar, water, pickling salt, sugar, celery seed, mustard seed, hot pepper sauce and garlic powder. Microwave at full power (HIGH) for time in chart above or until sugar and salt have dissolved, stirring twice. Pour vinegar mixture over zucchini mixture. Cover and refrigerate at least 2 days or up to several weeks, stirring occasionally.

Frozen Summer or Zucchini Squash

SERVINGS	3
INGREDIENTS	
frozen sliced summer squash (yellow crookneck) or frozen zucchini squash	1 (10-oz.) pkg.
BAKING DISH	1-qt. casserole
TIME AT HIGH	6 to 7 minutes
STANDING TIME	1 to 2 minutes

Place squash in a 1-quart casserole. Cover. Microwave at full power (HIGH) 6 to 7 minutes or until tender, stirring once. Let stand, covered, 1 to 2 minutes.

How to Make Fresh Summer Pickles

Cut serving-size spears of crookneck squash, zucchini and pattypan squash. Add onion rings and strips of red and green pepper. To crisp the vegetables, mix them with ice.

Drain the vegetables and remove any ice particles. Pour the hot pickling brine over the mixture and refrigerate at least 2 days or up to several weeks. Stir occasionally to distribute the brine.

Sliced Fresh Zucchini

SERVINGS	4	3	2	1
INGREDIENTS				
Zucchini	1 lb.	12 oz.	8 oz.	4 oz.
	(4 cups, sliced)	(3 cups, sliced)	(2 cups, sliced)	(1 cup, sliced)
Water	1/4 cup	1/4 cup	1/4 cup	1/4 cup
BAKING DISH	2-qt.	2-qt.	1-1/2-qt.	3-cup
	casserole	casserole	casserole	casserole
TIME AT HIGH	8 to 9	7 to 8	4 to 5	3 to 4
	minutes	minutes	minutes	minutes

Wash zucchini. Cut in 1/4-inch slices. In a casserole, see size in chart above, combine zucchini and water. Cover. Microwave at full power (HIGH) for time in chart above or until tender, stirring once. Drain.

Variation:

Slice zucchini with the thin slicing blade of a food processor. Cook as above, allowing 1 or 2 minutes less cooking time when cooking 1 pound or 12 ounces. When cooking 8 ounces or 4 ounces, the times are approximately the same as those in the chart above.

Canned Zucchini in Italian Tomato Sauce

SERVINGS	2 or 3	1 or 2
INGREDIENTS zucchini squash in Italian tomato sauce	1 (16-oz.) can	1 (8-oz.) can
BOWL	3- to 4-cup bowl	2- to 3-cup bowl
TIME AT HIGH	4 to 5 minutes	3 to 4 minutes

Place zucchini and sauce in a bowl, see size in chart above. Cover with vented plas
wrap. Microwave at full power (HIGH) for time in chart above or until heated throug
stirring once.

Fresh Spaghetti Squash

SERVINGS	6	3
INGREDIENTS fresh spaghetti squash water	1 (4-1/4-lb.) squash 1/3 cup	1 (2-1/4-lb.) squash 1/3 cup
BAKING DISH	13" x 9" baking dish	12" x 7" baking dish
TIME AT HIGH (whole squash)	10 minutes	6 minutes
TIME AT HIGH (halves)	12 minutes	10 to 12 minutes
STANDING TIME	2 minutes	2 minutes

Place whole squash in a baking dish, see size in chart above. Microwave at full pow
(HIGH) for time in chart above. Halve squash lengthwise. Remove seeds and me
brane. Place squash, cut side up, in same baking dish. Add water. Cover with vent
plastic wrap. Microwave at full power (HIGH) for time in chart above or until tenc
giving dish a half turn once. Let stand, covered, 2 minutes.

Doneness Test: Squash should feel tender when pierced with a large fork and strar
of squash should start to pull away from the shell.

Serving Ideas

- Top hot cooked zucchini slices with shredded Cheddar cheese, croutons and snipp
  parsley.
- Toss yellow crookneck squash with bacon drippings, chopped celery and sage. T
  with crumbled bacon and snipped parsley.
- Whip hot cooked acorn squash with butter, ground cinnamon and maple syrup.

How to Make Spaghetti Squash Straw & Hay

The cooked flesh of the squash will come away in spaghetti-like strands when pulled gently with a fork. Carefully pull all the squash flesh into these strands, being sure to reserve one squash shell intact.

Spaghetti squash is mixed with ham, peas and mushrooms, then sauced with a mixture of egg yolks, whipping cream and Parmesan cheese. This makes a delightful vegetable or appetizer. Serve larger portions and make it a meal.

Spaghetti Squash Straw & Hay

SERVINGS	6	3
INGREDIENTS		
butter or margarine	1/4 cup	2 tablespoons
hot cooked spaghetti squash	6 cups	3 cups
sliced cooked ham strips	3/4 cup	1/3 cup
cooked peas	1/2 cup	1/4 cup
sliced mushrooms, drained	1 (2-1/2-oz.) jar	1/2 (2-1/2-oz.) jar
egg yolks, beaten	2	1
whipping cream	1 cup	1/2 cup
grated Parmesan cheese	1 cup (4 oz.)	1/2 cup (2 oz.)
spaghetti squash shell	1	1
BAKING DISH	13" x 9" baking dish	12" x 7" baking dish
TIME AT HIGH	7 to 10 minutes	3 to 5 minutes

In a large bowl, stir butter or margarine into hot squash until melted. Fold in ham, peas and mushrooms. In a small bowl, whisk egg yolks and cream until foamy. Slowly add cream mixture to squash mixture; mix well. Stir in half the Parmesan cheese. Drain juices from baking dish used to cook squash. Mound squash mixture into one of the squash shells in baking dish. Cover with vented plastic wrap. Microwave at full power (HIGH) for time in chart above or until heated through and sauce has thickened, tossing twice. Serve topped with remaining Parmesan cheese.

Whole Acorn Squash

SERVINGS	4	2
INGREDIENTS fresh acorn squash	2 (1-1/4-lb.) squash	1 (1-1/4-lb.) squash
TIME AT HIGH (before piercing)	2 minutes	2 minutes
TIME AT HIGH (after piercing)	10 to 12 minutes	5 to 6 minutes
STANDING TIME	5 minutes	5 minutes

Place whole squash in microwave oven. Microwave at full power (HIGH) 2 minutes. Pierce skin deeply several times with a large fork. Microwave at full power (HIGH) for time in chart above or until tender, turning squash over and rearranging twice. Wrap in foil and let stand 5 minutes. Cut in halves or rings. Remove seeds and membranes.

Acorn Squash Halves

SERVINGS	4	2
INGREDIENTS fresh acorn squash brown sugar butter or margarine	2 (1-1/4-lb.) squash to taste 1/4 cup	1 (1-1/4-lb.) squash to taste 2 tablespoons
BAKING DISH	12" x 7" baking dish	10" x 6" baking dish
TIME AT HIGH (whole squash)	3 minutes	2 minutes
TIME AT HIGH (halves)	5 minutes	3 minutes
TIME AT HIGH (sugar, butter added)	5 to 6 minutes	3 to 4 minutes

Place whole squash in a baking dish, see size in chart above. Microwave at full power (HIGH) for time in chart above. Halve squash and remove seeds and membrane. Place squash, cut side down, in same baking dish. Microwave at full power (HIGH) for time in chart above. Turn squash cut side up and rearrange. Spoon a little brown sugar and butter or margarine into centers of squash. Cover with waxed paper. Microwave at full power (HIGH) for time in chart above or until tender.

Tips

- Microwave whole winter squash for a few minutes at full power (HIGH) before piercing with a large fork. This will soften the hard shell enough to make piercing much easier.
- Microwave whole pierced winter squash until almost tender before cutting into rings. Partial cooking makes the shell soft enough to cut easily into even rings. Glaze the rings with butter or margarine and maple syrup. Microwave until tender.

Butternut Squash Halves

SERVINGS	6	4	2
INGREDIENTS fresh butternut squash	1 (2-1/4-lb.) squash	2 (13-oz.) squash	1 (13-oz.) squash
BAKING DISH	12" x 7" baking dish	12" x 7" baking dish	9-inch pie plate
TIME AT HIGH (whole squash)	2 minutes	2 minutes	2 minutes
TIME AT HIGH (cut side down)	6 minutes	5 minutes	3 minutes
TIME AT HIGH (cut side up)	6 minutes	3 minutes	2 minutes

Place whole squash in a baking dish, see size in chart above. Microwave at full power (HIGH) 2 minutes. Cut off stem end. Halve squash lengthwise. Remove seeds and membrane. Place squash, cut side down, in same baking dish or pie plate. Microwave at full power (HIGH) for time in chart above. Turn squash cut side up and rearrange. Cover with waxed paper. Microwave at full power (HIGH) for time in chart above or until tender.

Frozen Cooked Winter Squash

SERVINGS	2 or 3
INGREDIENTS frozen cooked winter squash butter or margarine	1 (12-oz.) pkg. 2 tablespoons
BAKING DISH	1-qt. casserole
TIME AT HIGH	6 to 7 minutes
STANDING TIME	1 to 2 minutes

Combine squash and butter or margarine in a 1-quart casserole. Cover. Microwave at full power (HIGH) 6 to 7 minutes or until heated through, stirring once. Let stand, covered, 1 to 2 minutes. Whip or stir before serving.

Canned Stewed Tomatoes

SERVINGS	2 or 3	1 or 2
INGREDIENTS stewed tomatoes	1 (16-oz.) can	1 (8-oz.) can
BOWL	3- to 4-cup bowl	2- to 3-cup bowl
TIME AT HIGH	6 to 7 minutes	4 to 5 minutes

Place tomatoes and juice in a bowl, see size in chart above. Cover with vented plastic wrap. Microwave at full power (HIGH) for time in chart above or until heated through, stirring once.

Tomato Stars

SERVINGS	4	2
INGREDIENTS		
tomatoes	4 large	2 large
celery salt	to taste	to taste
grated Parmesan cheese	1/2 cup (2 oz.)	1/4 cup (1 oz.)
mayonnaise or mayonnaise-style salad dressing	1/2 cup	1/4 cup
artichokes, drained, chopped	1 (8-oz.) can	1/2 (8-oz.) can
snipped watercress	2 tablespoons	1 tablespoon
drained capers	2 teaspoons	1 teaspoon
capers, paprika, if desired	to garnish	to garnish
BAKING DISH	8-inch square baking dish	10" x 6" baking dish
TIME AT HIGH	5 to 6 minutes	3 to 4 minutes
STANDING TIME	2 minutes	2 minutes

Place uncored tomatoes, stem end down, on a cutting board. Cut in 6 to 8 wedges, cutting to but not through bottom of tomato to form stars. Place tomatoes in a baking dish, see size in chart above. Sprinkle inside of tomatoes with celery salt; set aside. In a medium bowl, combine Parmesan cheese, mayonnaise or salad dressing, artichokes, watercress and drained capers; mix well. Spoon artichoke mixture into tomatoes, using about 1/3 cup for each. Cover with vented plastic wrap. Microwave at full power (HIGH) for time in chart above or until warmed through, giving dish a half turn once. Let stand, covered, 2 minutes. Garnish with additional capers and paprika, if desired.

Baked Whole Tomatoes

SERVINGS	6	4	2	1
INGREDIENTS				
fresh tomatoes	6 (4- to 5-oz.) tomatoes	4 (4- to 5-oz.) tomatoes	2 (4- to 5-oz.) tomatoes	1 (4- to 5-oz.) tomato
BAKING DISH	9-inch pie plate	9-inch pie plate	9-inch pie plate	1-cup casserole
TIME AT HIGH	5 to 6 minutes	3 to 4 minutes	1-1/2 to 2-1/2 minutes	1 to 1-1/2 minutes

Wash tomatoes. Core tomatoes and cut off tops. Arrange tomatoes in a circle in a baking dish, see size in chart above. Leave 1 inch between tomatoes. Microwave, uncovered, at full power (HIGH) for time in chart above or until heated through, giving dish a half turn once.

Serving Ideas

- Top hot cooked tomato halves with shredded mozzarella cheese, chopped pepperoni and oregano.
- Substitute drained chopped asparagus for the artichokes in Tomato Stars, above.
- Top hot stewed tomatoes with rye croutons, basil and snipped chives.

Fresh Cubed Turnips

SERVINGS	4 (2-1/2 cups)	2 (1-1/4 cups)
INGREDIENTS		
fresh turnips		
(as purchased)	1 lb.	8 oz.
(after trimming)	10 oz. (3 cups, cubed)	5 oz. (1-1/2 cups, cubed)
water	1/4 cup	3 tablespoons
BAKING DISH	1-1/2-qt. casserole	1-qt. casserole
TIME AT HIGH	8 to 9 minutes	4 to 5 minutes
STANDING TIME	2 minutes	2 minutes

Wash, trim and pare turnips. Cut into cubes. In a casserole, see size in chart above, combine turnips and water. Cover. Microwave at full power (HIGH) for time in chart above or until tender, stirring twice. Let stand, covered, 2 minutes. Drain.

Fresh Turnip Greens

SERVINGS	4	2
INGREDIENTS		
turnip greens		
(as purchased)	2 lbs.	1 lb.
(after trimming)	15 oz. (16 cups)	9 oz. (7 to 8 cups)
water	4 cups	2 cups
BAKING DISH	deep 4-qt. casserole	deep 2-qt. casserole
TIME AT HIGH	50 to 55 minutes	25 to 30 minutes

Wash greens and remove stems. Tear greens directly into a casserole, see size in chart above. Add water. Cover. Microwave at full power (HIGH) for time in chart above or until tender, stirring often to keep greens on top of casserole from turning brown. Drain.

Frozen Turnip Greens

SERVINGS	3
INGREDIENTS	
frozen chopped turnip greens or frozen chopped turnip greens with diced turnips	1 (10-oz.) pkg.
hot water	1-1/4 cups
BAKING DISH	deep 1-qt. casserole
TIME AT HIGH	14 minutes
STANDING TIME	1 to 2 minutes

Combine turnip greens and hot water in a 1-quart casserole. Cover. Microwave at full power (HIGH) 14 minutes or until tender, stirring twice. Let stand, covered, 1 to 2 minutes. Drain.

How to Make Marinated Turnip Salad

Drizzle hot cooked turnips with salad dressing, then sprinkle with snipped fresh dill or dried dillweed. Carefully fold the dressing mixture into the turnips, keeping the turnip cubes as whole as possible.

Marinate the turnips in the refrigerator for at least 2 hours or overnight. At serving time, toss the turnips with peas, cheese, green onion, radishes and parsley. Add extra dressing as needed to moisten the salad.

Marinated Turnip Salad

SERVINGS	6	3
INGREDIENTS		
Hot cooked cubed turnips	2-1/2 cups (1 lb.)	1-1/4 cups (8 oz.)
Creamy onion and chive salad dressing	1/2 cup	1/4 cup
Dried dillweed	1/2 teaspoon	1/4 teaspoon
Salt	1/4 teaspoon	1/8 teaspoon
Frozen peas, thawed	1 cup	1/2 cup
Cubed process American cheese	1/2 cup (2 oz.)	1/4 cup (1 oz.)
Sliced green onion	1/4 cup	2 tablespoons
Sliced radishes	1/4 cup	2 tablespoons
Snipped parsley	2 tablespoons	1 tablespoon
BOWL	medium bowl	medium bowl
TIME AT HIGH	2 minutes	1 minute

In a medium bowl, toss hot turnips, half the dressing, dillweed and salt. Cover with vented plastic wrap. Microwave at full power (HIGH) for time in chart above. Leave covered and refrigerate at least 2 hours or overnight. At serving time, toss turnip mixture with peas, cheese, green onion, radishes, parsley and enough remaining dressing to moisten. Serve in lettuce or cabbage cups, if desired.

Frozen Mixed Vegetables

SERVINGS	6	4	2	1
INGREDIENTS frozen mixed vegetables	4 cups	3 cups	1 (8- or 10-oz.) pkg. (2 cups)	1 cup
water	6 tablespoons	5 tablespoons	1/4 cup	2 tablespoons
BAKING DISH	2-qt. casserole	1-1/2-qt. casserole	1-1/2-qt. casserole	1-qt. casserole
TIME AT HIGH	12 to 13 minutes	10 to 11 minutes	8 to 9 minutes	5 to 6 minutes
STANDING TIME	1 to 2 minutes	1 to 2 minutes	1 to 2 minutes	1 to 2 minutes

In a casserole, see size in chart above, combine mixed vegetables and water. Cover. Microwave at full power (HIGH) for time in chart above or until tender, stirring once. Let stand, covered, 1 to 2 minutes. Drain.

Frozen Mixed Vegetables in a Pouch

SERVINGS	3
INGREDIENTS frozen mixed vegetables in butter sauce	1 (10-oz.) pkg.
TIME AT HIGH	6 to 7 minutes

With a sharp knife or scissors, cut a small "X" in center of top side of pouch. Microwave pouch at full power (HIGH) 6 to 7 minutes, flexing pouch once to rearrange vegetables.

Canned Mixed Vegetables

SERVINGS	2 or 3	1 or 2
INGREDIENTS mixed vegetables	1 (16-oz.) can	1 (8-oz.) can
BOWL	3- to 4-cup bowl	2- to 3-cup bowl
TIME AT HIGH	2-1/2 to 3-1/2 minutes	1-1/2 to 2-1/2 minutes

Drain off all but 2 tablespoons liquid from can. In a bowl, see size in chart above, combine mixed vegetables and remaining liquid. Cover. Microwave at full power (HIGH) for time in chart above or until heated through.

lanked Vegetables Deluxe Photo on page 291.

RVINGS	4	2
GREDIENTS		
ter		
lk		
tter or margarine		
stant mashed potato buds	enough for 4 servings plus 1/3 cup more	enough for 2 servings plus 3 tablespoons more
g yolks	2	1
ion salt	1/2 teaspoon	1/4 teaspoon
ied leaf thyme	1/2 teaspoon	1/4 teaspoon
ozen peas and onions	1 (10-oz.) pkg.	1/2 (10-oz.) pkg.
tter or margarine	1 tablespoon	2 teaspoons
iced mushrooms, drained	1 (2-1/2-oz.) jar	1/2 (2-1/2-oz.) jar
matoes, halved	2	1
ench dressing	2 tablespoons	1 tablespoon
ocess American cheese iangles	4	2
lad seasoning	to taste	to taste
XER BOWL	1-1/2-qt. bowl	1-1/2-qt. bowl
AKING DISH	1-qt. casserole	1-qt. casserole
OODEN BOARD	9" x 7" non-lacquered	6" x 4" non-lacquered
ME AT HIGH (milk mixture)	4 to 5 minutes	2-1/2 to 3 minutes
ME AT HIGH (peas and onions)	6 minutes	3 minutes
ME AT HIGH completed plank)	7 to 8 minutes	4 to 5 minutes
ME AT HIGH heese added)	1 minute	45 to 60 seconds

a 1-1/2-quart mixer bowl, combine water, milk and butter or margarine according to rections on instant-potato package for 4 or 2 servings. Omit salt called for on package. Iicrowave at full power (HIGH) for time in chart above or until boiling. Stir in potato ds with a fork until smooth. Beat in egg yolks, onion salt and thyme with electric ixer on medium speed until blended. Cover closely with plastic wrap; set aside. In a -quart casserole, combine peas and onions and second amount of butter or margarine. over and microwave at full power (HIGH) for time in chart above, stirring once. rain. Stir in mushrooms. Cover and set aside. Brush a wooden board, see size in chart ove, with vegetable oil. Place tomatoes in center of board. Spoon French dressing ver tomatoes. Using a pastry tube, pipe potato mixture around edge of board, making a igh rim and 2 wells to hold pea mixture. With a slotted spoon, scoop pea mixture into ells. Cover with plastic wrap. Microwave at full power (HIGH) for time in chart bove or until heated through. Uncover. Top tomatoes with cheese triangles and sprin- le with salad seasoning. Microwave at full power (HIGH) for time in chart above or ntil cheese melts.

How to Blanch Green Beans for Freezing

Notice the bright even green color throughout the beans that have just been blanched. The beans are plunged into ice water to stop the cooking process as quickly as possible. Leave the beans in the ice water until beans are thoroughly chilled.

Pat the chilled beans dry with paper towels, then spoon into freezer weight plastic bags. Package vegetables in a convenient serving size for your family. Press out as much air as possible from the bag before sealing. Label with contents and date.

Blanching Vegetables for Freezing

- Pare, slice or dice vegetables as usual for cooking.
- Blanch only 1 pound or 1 quart of vegetables at a time.
- Add water according to the directions for each vegetable. Spinach does not need additional water other than the water that clings to the leaves.
- Do not add salt—it may cause spotty dehydration on the vegetables.
- Microwave in a covered casserole at full power (HIGH) for time specified for each vegetable.
- Stir vegetables about halfway through the cooking time.
- When done, vegetables should be evenly bright throughout, evenly heated through and still have some crisp texture.
- Drain vegetables in a colander, then plunge immediately into ice water. Hold in ice water until vegetables are completely chilled.
- Drain vegetables and pat dry on paper towels.
- Package in moisture-vaporproof wrap.
- Seal bags air-tight using bag manufacturer's directions.
- Freeze at 0F (20C) or below. Spread packages out in the freezer to speed the freezing process. Stack packages after freezing.
- Store for up to 8 to 12 months.
- Cook using directions for frozen vegetables.

Blanching Asparagus for Freezing

INGREDIENTS	
fresh asparagus, cut in 1- or 2-inch pieces	1 lb.
water	1/4 cup
BAKING DISH	2-qt. casserole
TIME AT HIGH	2-1/2 to 3-1/2 minutes

Combine asparagus and water in a 2-quart casserole. Cover. Microwave at full power (HIGH) 2-1/2 to 3-1/2 minutes, stirring once. Drain in a colander. Plunge asparagus into ice water. When cool, drain and pat dry with paper towels. Seal in moisture-vaporproof bags. Label and freeze.

Blanching Green or Wax Beans for Freezing

INGREDIENTS	
fresh green or wax beans, whole or in 1-inch pieces	1 lb.
water	1/2 cup
BAKING DISH	1-1/2-qt. casserole
TIME AT HIGH	3-1/2 to 5-1/2 minutes

Combine beans and water in a 1-1/2-quart casserole. Cover. Microwave at full power (HIGH) 3-1/2 to 5-1/2 minutes, stirring once. Drain in a colander. Plunge beans into ice water. When cool, drain and pat dry with paper towels. Seal in moisture-vaporproof bags. Label and freeze.

Blanching Broccoli for Freezing

INGREDIENTS	
fresh broccoli, cut into 1-inch pieces	1-1/4 to 1-1/2 lbs.
water	1/2 cup
BAKING DISH	2-qt. casserole
TIME AT HIGH	3 to 5 minutes

Combine broccoli and water in a 2-quart casserole. Cover. Microwave at full power (HIGH) 3 to 5 minutes, stirring once. Drain in a colander. Plunge broccoli into ice water. When cool, drain and pat dry with paper towels. Seal in moisture-vaporproof bags. Label and freeze.

Blanching Carrots for Freezing

INGREDIENTS	
fresh carrots, pared, cut in 1/2-inch pieces	1 lb.
water	1/4 cup
BAKING DISH	1-1/2-qt. casserole
TIME AT HIGH	3-1/2 to 5-1/2 minutes

Combine carrots and water in a 1-1/2-quart casserole. Cover. Microwave at full pow
(HIGH) 3-1/2 to 5-1/2 minutes, stirring once. Drain in a colander. Plunge carrots into i
water. When cool, drain and pat dry with paper towels. Seal in moisture-vaporpro
bags. Label and freeze.

Blanching Cauliflower for Freezing

INGREDIENTS	
fresh cauliflower, cut in flowerets	1 (1-1/4- to 1-1/2-lb.) head
water	1/2 cup
BAKING DISH	2-qt. casserole
TIME AT HIGH	3 to 5 minutes

Combine cauliflowerets and water in a 2-quart casserole. Cover. Microwave at fu
power (HIGH) 3 to 5 minutes, stirring once. Drain in a colander. Plunge cauliflowere
into ice water. When cool, drain and pat dry with paper towels. Seal in moistur
vaporproof bags. Label and freeze.

Blanching Corn for Freezing

INGREDIENTS	
fresh corn, cut off the cob	4 ears
water	1/4 cup
BAKING DISH	1-qt. casserole
TIME AT HIGH	4 to 5 minutes

Combine corn and water in a 1-quart casserole. Cover. Microwave at full powe
(HIGH) 4 to 5 minutes, stirring once. Drain in a colander. Plunge corn into ice wate
When cool, drain and pat dry with paper towels. Seal in moisture-vaporproof bag
Label and freeze.

Blanching Peas for Freezing

INGREDIENTS	
fresh peas, shelled	2 lbs.
water	1/4 cup
BAKING DISH	1-qt. casserole
TIME AT HIGH	3 to 4-1/2 minutes

Combine peas and water in a 1-quart casserole. Cover. Microwave at full power (HIGH) 3 to 4-1/2 minutes, stirring once. Drain in a colander. Plunge peas into ice water. When cool, drain and pat dry with paper towels. Seal in moisture-vaporproof bags. Label and freeze.

Blanching Spinach for Freezing

INGREDIENTS	
fresh spinach, washed, stems removed	1 lb.
BAKING DISH	2-qt. casserole
TIME AT HIGH	2 to 3 minutes

Place spinach in a 2-quart casserole. Cover. Microwave at full power (HIGH) 2 to 3 minutes, stirring once. Drain in a colander. Plunge spinach into ice water. When cool, drain and pat dry with paper towels. Seal in moisture-vaporproof bags. Label and freeze.

Blanching Summer Squash for Freezing

INGREDIENTS	
fresh zucchini or yellow crookneck squash, sliced or cubed	1 lb.
water	1/4 cup
BAKING DISH	1-1/2-qt. casserole
TIME AT HIGH	2-1/2 to 4 minutes

Combine squash and water in a 1-1/2-quart casserole. Cover. Microwave at full power (HIGH) 2-1/2 to 4 minutes, stirring once. Drain in a colander. Plunge squash into ice water. When cool, drain and pat dry with paper towels. Seal in moisture-vaporproof bags. Label and freeze.

Piña Colada Salad Mold

SERVINGS	8	4
INGREDIENTS		
pineapple chunks, juice-packed	2 (8-oz.) cans	1 (8-oz.) can
lemon-flavored gelatin	2 (3-oz.) pkgs.	1 (3-oz.) pkg.
non-alcoholic Piña Colada drink mix	1 cup	1/2 cup
rum	1/2 cup	1/4 cup
lemon juice	1/4 cup	2 tablespoons
shredded coconut	1/2 cup	1/4 cup
chopped macadamia nuts	1/2 cup	1/4 cup
lettuce leaves, lime slices	to garnish	to garnish
BOWL	3-qt. bowl	1-1/2-qt. bowl
MOLD	6-cup mold	3-cup mold
TIME AT HIGH	5-1/2 minutes	2-1/2 minutes

Drain pineapple, reserving juice. For 8 servings, add water to juice to make 2 cups; for servings, add water to juice to make 1 cup. In a bowl, see size in chart above, microwav juice mixture at full power (HIGH) for time in chart above or until boiling. Stir in gela tin until completely dissolved. Stir in Piña Colada mix, rum and lemon juice. Refriger ate until almost set. Fold in pineapple, coconut and nuts. Pour into a lightly oiled mold see size in chart above. Refrigerate until firm. Unmold on lettuce leaves and garnis with lime slices.

Basic Fruit-Flavored Molded Salad

SERVINGS	8	4
INGREDIENTS		
water	2 cups	1 cup
fruit-flavored gelatin	2 (3-oz.) pkgs.	1 (3-oz.) pkg.
water or juice	2 cups	1 cup
drained fruit, chopped vegetables, nuts, coconut, marshmallows	up to 3 cups	up to 1-1/2 cups
BOWL	3-qt. bowl	1-1/2-qt. bowl
MOLD	6- to 8-cup mold	3- to 4-cup mold
TIME AT HIGH	5 to 5-1/2 minutes	2-1/2 to 3 minutes

Place first amount of water in a bowl, see size in chart above. Microwave at full powe (HIGH) for time in chart above or until boiling. Stir in gelatin until completely dis solved. Stir in second amount of water or juice. Refrigerate until almost set. Fold ir fruit or other ingredients. Turn into a lightly oiled mold, see size in chart above, or fla baking dish. Refrigerate until firm.

How to Make Piña Colada Salad Mold

Refrigerate the gelatin mixture. Fold in the pineapple and coconut when the gelatin mixture is nearly set. This keeps the fruit from sinking in the mold.

To unmold the salad, dip the mold almost up to the rim in a bowl or sink filled with warm water. Be careful not to have the water too hot or the outside of the salad will melt.

When the warm water has loosened the salad from the mold, use a knife or small spatula to slide down the outside edge of the mold to release the vacuum.

Place a wet serving plate on top of the mold. Hold firmly together and invert. If salad does not slip out, repeat these steps. The wet plate allows you to move the salad on the plate.

French Tossed Salad Mold

SERVINGS	8	4
INGREDIENTS		
unflavored gelatin	2 envelopes	1 envelope
cold water	1 cup	1/2 cup
hot water	2 cups	1 cup
sweet red French dressing	1 cup	1/2 cup
finely chopped lettuce	1 cup	1/2 cup
shredded carrot	1/4 cup	2 tablespoons
chopped green pepper	1/4 cup	2 tablespoons
chopped celery	1/4 cup	2 tablespoons
sliced ripe olives	1/4 cup	2 tablespoons
sliced green onion	1/4 cup	2 tablespoons
cherry tomatoes, whole ripe olives, celery leaves	to garnish	to garnish
BOWL	2-qt. bowl	1-qt. bowl
RING MOLD	4-1/2- to 5-cup mold	2-1/2-cup mold
TIME AT HIGH	2-1/2 to 3 minutes	1-1/2 to 2 minutes

In a bowl, see size in chart above, soften gelatin in cold water. Stir in hot water. Microwave at full power (HIGH) for time in chart above or until gelatin has dissolved, stirring three times. Stir in French dressing. Refrigerate until almost set. Fold in lettuce, carrot, green pepper, celery, sliced olives and green onion. Turn into a lightly oiled ring mold, see size in chart above. Refrigerate until set. Unmold on a platter. Garnish with cherry tomatoes, whole ripe olives and celery leaves.

Basic Unflavored Gelatin–Salad Mold

SERVINGS	8	4
INGREDIENTS		
unflavored gelatin	2 envelopes	1 envelope
cold water	1/2 cup	1/4 cup
hot water	1 cup	1/2 cup
cold juice, broth, carbonated beverage or other liquid	2-1/2 cups	1-1/4 cups
drained fruit, chopped vegetables, nuts, coconut, marshmallows	up to 3 cups	up to 1-1/2 cups
BOWL	2-qt. bowl	1-qt. bowl
MOLD	6- to 8-cup mold	3- to 4-cup mold
TIME AT HIGH	1-1/2 to 2 minutes	1- to 1-1/2 minutes

In a bowl, see size in chart above, soften gelatin in cold water. Stir in hot water. Microwave at full power (HIGH) for time in chart above or until gelatin has dissolved, stirring three times. Stir in additional cold liquid. Refrigerate until almost set. Fold in fruit or other ingredients, if desired. Turn into a lightly oiled mold, see size in chart above, or flat baking dish. Refrigerate until firm.

Greek Isle Potato Salad

SERVINGS	6 to 8	3 or 4
INGREDIENTS		
vegetable oil	2 tablespoons	1 tablespoon
chopped green onion	1/4 cup	2 tablespoons
chopped green pepper	1/4 cup	2 tablespoons
white wine vinegar	1/3 cup	2 tablespoons
dried leaf oregano, crushed	1 teaspoon	1/2 teaspoon
garlic powder	dash	dash
vegetable oil	1/3 cup	3 tablespoons
cubed cooked or canned potatoes	4 cups	2 cups
sliced ripe olives	1/4 cup	2 tablespoons
cherry tomatoes, halved	1 cup	1/2 cup
torn spinach or lettuce	2 to 3 cups	1 to 1-1/2 cups
crumbled feta cheese	1/4 cup	2 tablespoons
BAKING DISH	deep 2-qt. casserole	deep 2-qt. casserole
TIME AT HIGH (onion, pepper)	3 minutes	1-1/2 minutes
TIME AT HIGH (salad)	6 to 8 minutes	3 to 4 minutes

In a 2-quart casserole, mix first amount of oil, green onion and green pepper. Microwave at full power (HIGH) for time in chart above or until vegetables are tender. Stir in vinegar, oregano and garlic powder. Whisk in remaining oil until well combined. Toss potatoes in oil mixture. Cover. Microwave at full power (HIGH) for time in chart above or until potatoes are heated through. Toss olives, tomatoes and spinach or lettuce with potato mixture. Top with feta cheese before serving.

Herbed Vegetable Marinade

SERVINGS	4 or 5	2 or 3
INGREDIENTS		
tarragon wine vinegar	1/4 cup	2 tablespoons
lemon juice	1/4 cup	2 tablespoons
garlic, minced	1 large clove	1 small clove
dried leaf basil	1/2 teaspoon	1/4 teaspoon
fennel seed	1/2 teaspoon	1/4 teaspoon
celery salt	1/4 teaspoon	1/8 teaspoon
coarsely ground pepper	1/4 teaspoon	1/8 teaspoon
vegetable oil	1/2 cup	1/4 cup
any combination of:	4 cups	2 cups
sliced mushrooms, onion rings, halved cherry tomatoes, halved canned artichoke hearts		
snipped parsley	1/4 cup	2 tablespoons
BAKING DISH	deep 2-qt. casserole	deep 1-qt. casserole
TIME AT HIGH (marinade)	1-1/2 to 2 minutes	45 to 60 seconds
TIME AT HIGH (vegetables added)	2 minutes	1 minute

In a casserole, see size in chart above, combine vinegar, lemon juice, garlic, basil, fennel seed, celery salt and pepper. Gradually whisk in oil. Microwave at full power (HIGH) for time in chart above or until boiling. Add vegetables. Toss until coated well. Microwave at full power (HIGH) for time in chart above or until warm. Cover and refrigerate 3 to 4 hours, stirring twice. Stir in snipped parsley before serving.

How to Make Greek Isle Potato Salad

To use fresh oregano, snip it into the sautéed vegetables. Use three times as much fresh as dried.

Use a whisk and beat constantly while adding the oil to the vinegar-and-herb mixture for the salad dressing.

After heating the cubed potatoes in the dressing, toss with fresh spinach, cherry tomatoes and ripe olives.

Top each serving with feta cheese. This Greek goat cheese is available in cheese shops and gourmet cheese sections of grocery stores.

Hot Bacon Dressing

SERVINGS	4 or 5	2 or 3
INGREDIENTS		
bacon	8 slices	4 slices
bacon drippings	1/4 cup	2 tablespoons
sliced green onion	1/4 cup	2 tablespoons
all-purpose flour	4 teaspoons	2 teaspoons
celery salt	1/2 teaspoon	1/4 teaspoon
water	1/2 cup	1/4 cup
lemon juice	3 tablespoons	4 teaspoons
prepared horseradish	1 tablespoon	1-1/2 teaspoons
Worcestershire sauce	1 tablespoon	1-1/2 teaspoons
torn leaf lettuce	8 cups	4 cups
BAKING DISH	12" x 7" baking dish with microwave rack	12" x 7" baking dish with microwave rack
GLASS MEASURING CUP	2-cup	1-cup
TIME AT HIGH (bacon)	7 to 8 minutes	3 to 4 minutes
TIME AT HIGH (onion)	2 minutes	1-1/2 minutes
TIME AT HIGH (flour added)	30 seconds	30 seconds
TIME AT HIGH (water added)	1-1/2 to 2 minutes	45 to 60 seconds

Place bacon on a microwave rack in a 12" x 7" baking dish. Cover with white paper towel and microwave at full power (HIGH) for time in chart above or until crisp. Crumble bacon and set aside. Measure drippings, see amount in chart above, into glass measuring cup, see size in chart above. Add green onion. Microwave at full power (HIGH) for time in chart above or until tender. Stir in flour. Microwave at full power (HIGH) 30 seconds. Stir in celery salt, water, lemon juice, horseradish and Worcestershire sauce. Microwave at full power (HIGH) for time in chart above or until thickened and bubbly, stirring twice. Pour over lettuce in a salad bowl. Toss and serve at once. Garnish with crumbled bacon.

Adapting Hot Bacon Dressings for Microwave Oven

- Place bacon slices on a microwave rack set in a baking dish. Cover with white paper towel. Microwave at full power (HIGH) for about 1 minute per slice. Measure the desired amount of drippings into a 1-quart glass measuring cup.

- Stir flour or cornstarch into the drippings and microwave at full power (HIGH) for about 30 seconds.

- Stir in the water or other liquid ingredients. Microwave at full power (HIGH) for about 2-1/2 minutes per cup of liquid, stirring several times to prevent lumping.

- Pour the hot dressing over spinach or leaf lettuce, radish slices and hard-cooked egg slices. Microwave at full power (HIGH) for 1 to 2 minutes to wilt lettuce. Top with crumbled bacon.

How to Make Hot Oriental Salad Toss

Use a sharp knife to cut the Chinese cabbage or Napa crosswise into shreds. Discard the tough white part of the leaves. If fresh bean sprouts are not available, use drained, canned sprouts.

At serving time, heat the soy dressing mixture in the microwave oven. Toss dressing with cabbage, pea pods, bean sprouts, mushrooms and radishes. Then microwave to wilt the salad.

Hot Oriental Salad Toss

SERVINGS	6 to 8	3 or 4
INGREDIENTS		
shredded Chinese cabbage	4 to 6 cups	2 to 3 cups
frozen Chinese pea pods, thawed	1/2 (6-oz.) pkg.	1/4 (6-oz.) pkg.
bean sprouts	1 cup	1/2 cup
sliced fresh mushrooms	1 cup	1/2 cup
sliced radishes	1/4 cup	2 tablespoons
sliced green onion	1/4 cup	2 tablespoons
sesame oil or vegetable oil	1/3 cup	3 tablespoons
white vinegar	2 tablespoons	1 tablespoon
soy sauce	2 tablespoons	1 tablespoon
sesame crisps	1/4 cup	2 tablespoons
BOWL	4-qt. bowl	2-qt. bowl
GLASS MEASURING CUP	2-cup	1-cup
TIME AT HIGH (dressing)	30 seconds	15 to 20 seconds
TIME AT HIGH (salad)	1 minute	30 seconds

In a bowl, see size in chart above, combine cabbage, pea pods, bean sprouts, mushrooms, radishes and green onion. Cover and refrigerate. At serving time, combine oil, vinegar and soy sauce in a glass measuring cup, see size in chart above. Whisk until combined. Microwave at full power (HIGH) for time in chart above or until boiling. Pour over vegetables and toss. Microwave salad at full power (HIGH) for time in chart above or until wilted. Toss with sesame crisps. Pass extra soy sauce, if desired.

Creamy Wilted Lettuce

SERVINGS	6 to 8	3 or 4
INGREDIENTS		
herb dressing mix containing buttermilk	1 envelope	1/2 envelope
milk	1 cup	1/2 cup
mayonnaise or mayonnaise-style salad dressing	1 cup	1/2 cup
sugar	1 tablespoon	1 teaspoon
celery seed	1 teaspoon	1/2 teaspoon
dry mustard	1 teaspoon	1/2 teaspoon
torn leaf lettuce	8 cups	4 cups
cottage cheese, drained	1 cup	1/2 cup
alfalfa sprouts	1/2 cup	1/4 cup
mandarin oranges, drained	1 (11-oz.) can	1/2 (11-oz.) can
red onion, thinly sliced, separated in rings	1 small	1/2 small
hard-cooked eggs, sliced	4	2
fresh mushroom slices	1/2 cup	1/4 cup
rye croutons	1 cup	1/2 cup
BOWL (dressing)	1-qt. bowl	1-qt. bowl
BOWL (salad)	4-qt. bowl	2-qt. bowl
TIME AT HIGH (dressing)	3 to 4 minutes	2 minutes
TIME AT HIGH (salad)	2 to 3 minutes	1-1/2 to 2 minutes

In a 1-quart bowl, combine dressing mix, milk, mayonnaise or salad dressing, sugar, celery seed and dry mustard. Whisk until smooth and creamy, about 1-1/2 minutes. Set aside. Place lettuce in a bowl, see size in chart above. Spoon cottage cheese over lettuce. Arrange sprouts, mandarin oranges, red onion, eggs and mushrooms over cottage cheese. Microwave dressing at full power (HIGH) for time in chart above or until hot, stirring once. Pour some dressing over salad. Toss and microwave at full power (HIGH) for time in chart above or until wilted. Serve at once sprinkled with croutons. Refrigerate remaining dressing to use another time.

Serving Ideas

- Stir sliced hard-cooked eggs, chopped green onion, chopped sweet pickle and shredded process American cheese into canned kidney-bean salad. Microwave until heated through.
- Stir canned marinated garbanzo beans, canned sliced mushrooms, chopped pimiento and chopped canned green chilies into canned three-bean salad. Microwave until heated through. Top with crushed corn chips and shredded Monterey Jack cheese.
- Microwave sweet vinaigrette dressing until boiling. Whisk in celery seed. Pour over shredded cabbage, chopped carrot, chopped celery, chopped green pepper and chopped green onion. Microwave until heated through, tossing twice.
- Toss crisp fresh chard or spinach with small onion rings, tiny yellow plum tomatoes and nasturtium blossoms. Pour Hot Bacon Dressing, page 384, over the salad. Microwave a few minutes until just wilted.

Taco Salad

SERVINGS	6	3
INGREDIENTS		
mixed torn salad greens	6 cups	3 cups
red beans, drained, rinsed	1 (15-oz.) can	1 (8-oz.) can
avocado, peeled, sliced	1	1/2
tomatoes, cut in wedges	2	1
sliced ripe olives	1/2 cup	1/4 cup
ground beef	1 lb.	8 oz.
chopped green onion	1/4 cup	2 tablespoons
canned diced green chilies	2 to 4 tablespoons	1 to 2 tablespoons
bottled taco sauce	1 cup	1/2 cup
shredded Cheddar cheese	1 cup (4 oz.)	1/2 cup (2 oz.)
corn chips	to garnish	to garnish
SALAD BOWL	4-qt. bowl	2-qt. bowl
BAKING DISH	deep 1-1/2-qt. casserole	deep 1-qt. casserole
TIME AT HIGH (meat)	4 to 5 minutes	3 to 4 minutes
TIME AT HIGH (sauce added)	3 to 4 minutes	2 to 3 minutes

In a salad bowl, see size in chart above, arrange greens, beans, avocado, tomatoes and olives. Cover and refrigerate until serving time. At serving time, crumble ground beef into a casserole, see size in chart above. Stir in green onion. Microwave at full power (HIGH) for time in chart above or until meat is browned and onion is tender, stirring twice. Drain. Stir in chilies and taco sauce. Microwave at full power (HIGH) for time in chart above or until boiling. Pour over salad. Toss and serve at once, garnished with cheese and corn chips.

Chicken Salad Bake

SERVINGS	5 or 6	2 or 3
INGREDIENTS		
pecan halves	1/2 cup	1/4 cup
cubed cooked chicken	3 cups	1-1/2 cups
chopped celery	1 cup	1/2 cup
chopped fresh pears	1 cup	1/2 cup
chopped green onion	1/4 cup	2 tablespoons
mayonnaise	3/4 cup	1/3 cup
lemon juice	2 tablespoons	1 tablespoon
shredded Cheddar cheese	1 cup (4 oz.)	1/2 cup (2 oz.)
sesame sticks, crushed	1/2 cup	1/4 cup
PLATE (pecans)	9-inch pie plate	9-inch pie plate
BAKING DISH (salad)	8-inch square baking dish	9" x 5" loaf dish
TIME AT HIGH (pecans)	3 minutes	2 to 3 minutes
TIME AT HIGH (complete dish)	6 to 7 minutes	4 to 5 minutes

Spread pecans in a 9-inch pie plate. Microwave at full power (HIGH) for time in chart above or until toasted, stirring twice. In a baking dish, see size in chart above, combine chicken, celery, pears, pecans and green onion. In a small bowl, mix mayonnaise and lemon juice. Fold in cheese. Fold into chicken mixture. Cover with vented plastic wrap. Microwave at full power (HIGH) for time in chart above or until heated through. Top with crushed sesame sticks.

How to Make Taco Salad

Brown ground beef and onion in the microwave oven, then stir in chilies and taco sauce. Mix together and heat.

Spoon hot meat mixture over the crisp green salad topped with avocado, tomatoes, ripe olives and red beans. Top with cheese and corn chips.

Oriental Vegetable Marinade

SERVINGS	4 or 5	2 or 3
INGREDIENTS		
vegetable oil	1/4 cup	2 tablespoons
chopped green pepper	1/4 cup	2 tablespoons
chopped green onion	2 tablespoons	1 tablespoon
chopped fresh gingerroot	2 teaspoons	1 teaspoon
white wine vinegar	1/4 cup	2 tablespoons
soy sauce	2 tablespoons	1 tablespoon
sugar	1 teaspoon	1/2 teaspoon
dry mustard	1/2 teaspoon	1/4 teaspoon
garlic powder	dash	dash
any combination of: Chinese pea pods, cauliflowerets, zucchini sticks	4 cups	2 cups
radish slices	1/4 cup	2 tablespoons
BAKING DISH	deep 2-qt. casserole	deep 1-qt. casserole
TIME AT HIGH (green pepper)	2 minutes	1-1/2 minutes
TIME AT HIGH (marinade added)	1 minute	30 seconds
TIME AT HIGH (vegetables added)	2 minutes	1-1/2 minutes

In a casserole, see size in chart above, combine oil, green pepper, green onion and gingerroot. Microwave at full power (HIGH) for time in chart above or until vegetables are tender. Whisk in vinegar, soy sauce, sugar, dry mustard and garlic powder. Mix well. Microwave at full power (HIGH) for time in chart above or until boiling. Add vegetables. Toss until coated well. Microwave at full power (HIGH) for time in chart above or until warm. Cover and refrigerate 3 to 4 hours, stirring twice. Stir in radishes just before serving. Sprinkle with toasted sesame seeds, if desired.

Cinnamon Apple Rings

YIELD	15 rings	9 rings
INGREDIENTS		
sugar	2 cups	1 cup
apple juice	1 cup	1/2 cup
cinnamon red-hot candies	1/2 cup	1/4 cup
tart apples	5	3
ascorbic acid or lemon juice	1 tablespoon	1 tablespoon
water	1 cup	1 cup
BAKING DISH	12" x 7" baking dish	round, 8-inch baking dish
TIME AT HIGH	18 to 20 minutes	11 minutes
TIME AT 30% (first batch of apple slices)	25 to 28 minutes	12 to 14 minutes
TIME AT 30% (second batch of apple slices)	25 to 28 minutes	12 to 14 minutes

In a baking dish, see size in chart above, combine sugar, apple juice and candies. Micro wave at full power (HIGH) for time in chart above or until sugar and candies have dis solved, stirring several times. Meanwhile, wash, core and peel apples. Slice crosswis into thirds, making 3/4- to 1-inch thick rings. In a medium bowl, combine ascorbic aci or lemon juice and water. Dip apple rings in mixture to prevent darkening. Pierce eac apple ring twice with a large fork. Place half the apple rings in hot syrup. Microwave 30% (MEDIUM LOW) for time in chart above or until apples are tender and beginnin to look transparent. Turn apples about every 5 minutes during cooking so all side become evenly red in color. Remove apple rings from syrup as they are done and plac in a shallow dish. Using the same syrup, cook remaining apple slices at 30% (MEDIUM LOW) for time in chart above. Place apple rings in same shallow dish. Pour syrup ove apples. Cover and refrigerate. Turn apples over in syrup once or twice during chillin and again before serving. To serve, drain and serve as a garnish or arrange on lettuc leaves and garnish with cream cheese.

Relish Ideas

- Microwave frozen whole-kernel corn; drain. Stir in chopped onion, chopped gree pepper, chopped pimiento and celery seed. Moisten with sweet French dressing. Re frigerate.

- Microwave frozen artichoke hearts; drain. Drizzle hot artichoke hearts with Italian sala dressing. Fold in red pepper strips, fresh mushroom caps and chopped pepperoni, the refrigerate.

How to Make Cinnamon Apple Rings

o make syrup, combine apple juice, sugar and ed-hot cinnamon candies in a baking dish. Microwave, stirring occasionally, until candies ave completely dissolved.

Pare tart apples and cut in thick slices. Immediately dip the slices in ascorbic acid or lemon-juice mixture. Pierce each slice twice with a fork to keep the slices from splitting during cooking.

urn apple slices over frequently—about every ive minutes—during microwave cooking. This vill help the slices soak up the syrup more evenly and give a more uniform color.

Chill apple slices in cinnamon syrup, turning the slices over occasionally to help maintain uniform color. Top with cream cheese and serve on lettuce leaves or use as a meat garnish.

Spicy Cranberry Sauce

YIELD	3 cups	1-1/2 cups
INGREDIENTS		
sugar	1-3/4 cups	3/4 cup
orange juice	1/2 cup	1/4 cup
vinegar	1/4 cup	2 tablespoons
crème de cassis	1/4 cup	2 tablespoons
fresh cranberries	2 cups (8 oz.)	1 cup (4 oz.)
snipped dried apricots	1 cup	1/2 cup
golden raisins	3/4 cup	1/3 cup
dried ground orange peel	1/2 teaspoon	1/4 teaspoon
ground cinnamon	1/2 teaspoon	1/4 teaspoon
ground cloves	1/8 teaspoon	dash
BAKING DISH	deep 2-qt. casserole	deep 1-qt. casserole
TIME AT HIGH (sugar syrup)	6 minutes	3 minutes
TIME AT HIGH (all ingredients)	5 minutes	3 minutes
TIME AT 30% (covered)	5 minutes	2 to 3 minutes
TIME AT 30% (uncovered)	15 minutes	7 to 8 minutes

In a casserole, see size in chart above, combine sugar, orange juice and vinegar. Microwave, uncovered, at full power (HIGH) for time in chart above or until boiling, stirring once or twice to dissolve sugar. Stir in crème de cassis, cranberries, apricots, raisins, orange peel, cinnamon and cloves. Cover loosely with waxed paper. Microwave at full power (HIGH) for time in chart above or until boiling. Stir well. Cover loosely with waxed paper. Microwave at 30% (MEDIUM LOW) for time in chart above, stirring twice. Uncover. Microwave at 30% (MEDIUM LOW) for time in chart above or until mixture becomes transparent and flavors blend. Stir once or twice while cooking. Cover and refrigerate up to a month.

Sherried Prunes

YIELD	2-1/2 cups	1-1/4 cups
INGREDIENTS		
pitted dried prunes	2 cups (12 oz.)	1 cup (6 oz.)
raisins	1/4 cup	2 tablespoons
lemon, thinly sliced	1/2	1/4
cream sherry	3/4 cup	1/3 cup
apple juice	3/4 cup	1/3 cup
GLASS MEASURING CUP	2-cup	2-cup
TIME AT HIGH	2-1/2 to 3 minutes	1-1/2 minutes

Combine prunes and raisins in a 1-quart jar. Halve lemon slices; add to fruit and mix gently. In a 2-cup glass measuring cup, combine sherry and apple juice. Microwave at full power (HIGH) for time in chart above. Pour over fruit. Cover jar and shake. Let stand overnight. Store in the refrigerator up to a month. Remove lemon slices before serving prunes as a meat accompaniment, relish or fruit salad.

Marinated Carrot Relish, page 394, and Spicy Cranberry Sauce

Marinated Carrot Relish Photo on page 393.

YIELD	6 cups	3 cups
INGREDIENTS		
carrots, cut in 1/2-inch diagonal slices	5 cups (2 lbs.)	2-1/2 cups (1 lb.)
water	1/2 cup	1/4 cup
onions, sliced, separated in rings	2 small	1 small
green peppers, sliced in thin rings	2 small	1 small
condensed tomato soup	1 (10-3/4-oz.) can	1/2 (10-3/4-oz.) can
Worcestershire sauce	2 teaspoons	1 teaspoon
prepared mustard	2 teaspoons	1 teaspoon
bottled red wine vinegar and oil dressing	1-1/2 cups	3/4 cup
snipped parsley, if desired	to garnish	to garnish
BAKING DISH	deep 3-qt. casserole	deep 1-1/2-qt. casserole
TIME AT HIGH (carrots)	15 minutes	9 minutes
TIME AT HIGH (marinade)	4 minutes	3 minutes

In a baking dish, see size in chart above, combine carrots and water. Cover. Microwave at full power (HIGH) for time in chart above or until barely tender, stirring three times. Drain thoroughly. Add onions and green pepper rings. In a medium bowl, whisk together tomato soup, Worcestershire sauce, prepared mustard and dressing. Microwave at full power (HIGH) for time in chart above or until hot. Stir marinade and pour over vegetables. Toss gently. Cover and refrigerate. If desired, drain off marinade to serve. Sprinkle carrots with snipped parsley, if desired.

Curried Fruit Bake

YIELD	3 cups	1-1/2 cups
INGREDIENTS		
fruits for salad, drained	1 (16-oz.) can	1 (8-oz.) can
frozen pitted dark sweet cherries, thawed, drained	1 cup	1/2 cup
butter or margarine	3 tablespoons	2 tablespoons
French apple pie filling	1 (21-oz.) can	1/2 (21-oz.) can
packed brown sugar	1/4 cup	2 tablespoons
curry powder	1 to 1-1/2 teaspoons	1/2 to 3/4 teaspoon
lemon juice	2 teaspoons	1 teaspoon
BAKING DISH	deep 2-qt. casserole	deep 1-qt. casserole
TIME AT HIGH (butter)	30 seconds	30 seconds
TIME AT HIGH (fruit)	10 minutes	5 minutes
TIME AT 30%	15 minutes	7 to 8 minutes

In a casserole, see size in chart above, combine fruits for salad and cherries; mix gently. In a medium bowl, microwave butter or margarine at full power (HIGH) 30 seconds or until melted. Stir pie filling, brown sugar, curry powder and lemon juice into butter or margarine; spoon over fruit. Cover and microwave at full power (HIGH) for time in chart above. Stir. Microwave, covered, at 30% (MEDIUM LOW) for time in chart above or until flavors blend.

Sauces

Soups & Sauces

Serve steaming bowls of nourishing soup from the microwave without spending the whole day cooking. Sauces cooked in the microwave come out creamy smooth without constant stirring.

Q. What are the advantages of cooking soups and sauces in the microwave?

A. Individual servings of soup can be heated in moments in mugs or bowls. Big batches of soup made on top of the range can be frozen in family-size portions and reheated in the microwave. Sauces don't need to be stirred constantly as they do on top of the range. And there's an added bonus—they don't stick to the dish!

Q. Which soups or sauces do not cook satisfactorily in the microwave?

A. Dried bean and pea soups can be cooked successfully in the microwave, but not much time is saved. When a sauce depends on eggs for thickening, it is difficult to prevent it from curdling.

Q. How are soups and sauces cooked in the microwave?

A. These recipes use a range of microwave-cooking techniques. Most soups made from scratch come to boiling at full power (HIGH) and then simmer at 30% (MEDIUM LOW). Canned soups and soup mixes generally heat very quickly at full power (HIGH). For maximum thickness, the roux—butter and flour mixture—for sauces should be cooked for 30 seconds at full power (HIGH) before the liquid is added. Hollandaise sauce benefits from an ingenious hot-water bath that keeps the outside portion of the sauce from curdling before the center is warm.

Q. How do you know when soups and sauces are done?

A. Soups should be at least 170F (75C) before serving. Be sure to stir soups before serving to help equalize the temperature throughout the soup. Remember that soups bubble around the edges long before the center is hot. Thickened sauces also start to bubble at the edges partway through the cooking time. Don't stop cooking then! Stir the sauce often with a whisk to prevent lumping, and continue cooking according to the recipe until the sauce is thickened and smooth.

Q. How do you reheat soups in the microwave?

A. Look for the directions for reheating chilled and frozen soups. Bear in mind that most sauces will change thickness after standing and reheating.

Q. How do you cook convenience soups and sauces in the microwave?

A. Directions for making soup from mixes and heating canned soups are in this chapter. There are also recipes using canned soups and mixes. Many frozen soups and sauces have microwave directions on the package.

Q. Are any special utensils needed to cook soups and sauces in the microwave?

A. For many of the start-from-scratch soups, use a 4-quart casserole. This is quite large by conventional standards, but allows plenty of room for boiling and stirring. Large measuring cups in the 1- or 2-quart sizes are handy for mixing, cooking, pouring and storing sauces.

How to Reheat Frozen Soup

Place the frozen block of soup in a casserole. Cover. Microwave until the soup is partially thawed, then break apart the block of soup with the tines of a fork to hasten thawing.

After the soup is thawed, heat to serving temperature in a covered casserole. When serving Split Pea Soup, top each serving with croutons, chopped ham and snipped parsley. Frozen soup is a quick and easy meal to keep on hand.

Reheating Frozen Soup

SERVINGS	4	2
INGREDIENTS soup	1 qt.	2 cups
BAKING DISH	deep 2-qt. casserole	deep 1-qt. casserole
TIME AT 30%	12 to 15 minutes	6 to 8 minutes
TIME AT 70%	10 to 12 minutes	9 to 11 minutes

To freeze: Pour cooled soup into a 1-quart or 2-cup freezer container, leaving 1/2 inch head space. Seal and freeze.

To reheat: To loosen soup, dip freezer container in hot water or place under running hot water. Place block of frozen soup in a casserole, see size in chart above. Cover. Microwave at 30% (MEDIUM LOW) for time in chart above or until mixture is thawed. Break soup apart with a large fork twice during reheating. Cover. Microwave at 70% (MEDIUM HIGH) for time in chart above or until heated through, stirring twice.

Reheating Refrigerated Soup

To reheat refrigerated soup, see page 404.

Old-Fashioned Vegetable Soup

SERVINGS	4	2
INGREDIENTS		
beef neck bones	2 lbs.	1 lb.
onion, cut up	1 large	1 small
celery, cut up	2 stalks	1 stalk
bay leaf	1	1/2
Worcestershire sauce	1 tablespoon	2 teaspoons
vegetable-tomato juice cocktail	1 (12-oz.) can (1-1/2 cups)	3/4 cup
tomatoes, cut up	1 (28-oz.) can	1 (16-oz.) can
frozen mixed vegetables	1 (10-oz.) pkg. (2 cups)	1/2 (10-oz.) pkg. (1 cup)
BAKING DISH	4-qt. casserole	2-1/2-qt. casserole
TIME AT HIGH (bones)	15 minutes	12 to 14 minutes
TIME AT 30%	1-1/2 hours	1 hour
STANDING TIME	20 minutes	20 minutes
TIME AT HIGH (mixed vegetables added)	15 minutes	10 minutes
TIME AT HIGH (meat added)	10 minutes	3 to 5 minutes

In a casserole, see size in chart above, place neck bones meaty side down. Add onion, celery, bay leaf and Worcestershire sauce. Pour in vegetable-tomato juice cocktail and tomatoes. Cover. Microwave at full power (HIGH) for time in chart above or until boiling. Microwave at 30% (MEDIUM LOW) for time in chart above or until meat is tender, stirring twice. Let stand 20 minutes. Remove bones. Cover bones tightly and set aside. Add mixed vegetables to liquid in casserole. Break apart vegetables with a large fork. Cover. Microwave at full power (HIGH) for time in chart above or until vegetables are almost tender. While vegetables are cooking, cut meat from bones; discard bones. Stir meat into soup. Cover. Microwave at full power (HIGH) for time in chart above or until heated through. Skim off excess fat.

Adapting Beef Soup Recipes for Microwave Oven

- Have beef shank bones or neck bones cut in 2-inch-thick pieces. Choose a casserole large enough to place bones meaty side down with liquid to cover and still allow room for stirring.

- Use Old-Fashioned Vegetable Soup, above, as a guideline for size of casserole, ratio of liquid to meat and vegetables, and approximate cooking times.

- Use enough liquid to cover meat. Microwave meaty bones and seasonings, covered, at full power (HIGH) until boiling. Two pounds of bones and 5 cups of liquid in a deep 4-quart casserole will boil in about 15 minutes. Continue microwaving bones at 30% (MEDIUM LOW) for about 1-1/2 hours or until meat is tender, stirring several times. Let meat stand, covered, 20 minutes.

- Remove the bones from soup and cut meat from bones. Meanwhile, add vegetables to the stock. Cover and microwave at full power (HIGH) until vegetables are tender. Fresh cubed carrots and potatoes will cook in about 20 to 30 minutes. Frozen vegetables will be tender in about 10 to 15 minutes.

- Spaghetti, noodles or macaroni will take about 30 to 35 minutes to cook along with the vegetables. Add extra liquid to the soup if pasta is to be added later.

- When vegetables and pasta are tender, add the cut-up meat to the soup. Cover and microwave at full power (HIGH) for 5 to 10 minutes or until meat is heated through.

How to Make Old-Fashioned Vegetable Soup

Arrange beef neck bones, meaty side down, in the casserole. After adding the vegetables, the tomato liquid level rises and covers the meat so it will not turn dark during cooking.

Remove the cooked meat and bones from the soup. Add the frozen mixed vegetables and break them up with a large fork. While the vegetables cook, cut the meat off the bones.

When the frozen vegetables are tender, add the meat pieces to the soup and discard the bones. Skim off excess fat either with a spoon or with a handy miniature grease-mop.

Return the soup to the microwave oven to reheat the meat. Serve in bowls. If you like a thinner soup, add more vegetable-tomato juice cocktail at the beginning of the cooking time.

Home-Style Chicken-Noodle Soup

SERVINGS	5 or 6	2 or 3
INGREDIENTS		
broiler-fryer chicken, cut up	1 (3-lb.) chicken	1/2 (3-lb.) chicken
water	4 cups	2 cups
chopped onion	1/2 cup	1/4 cup
chopped celery	1/2 cup	1/4 cup
chopped carrot	1/2 cup	1/4 cup
chicken bouillon granules	1 tablespoon	1-1/2 teaspoons
poultry seasoning	2 teaspoons	1 teaspoon
peppercorns	16	8
medium noodles	1 cup	1/2 cup
salt	1 teaspoon	1/2 teaspoon
BAKING DISH	deep 4-qt. casserole	deep 3-qt. casserole
TIME AT HIGH (chicken)	20 minutes	10 minutes
TIME AT 30% (without noodles)	15 minutes	10 minutes
TIME AT 30% (noodles added)	30 minutes	15 minutes
TIME AT HIGH (completed soup)	5 to 6 minutes	4 to 5 minutes

In a casserole, see size in chart above, arrange chicken with bony pieces in center and meaty pieces to outer edges. Add water. Stir in onion, celery, carrot, chicken bouillon granules and poultry seasoning. Tie peppercorns in cheesecloth and add to soup. Cover. Microwave at full power (HIGH) for time in chart above or until beginning to boil. Microwave at 30% (MEDIUM LOW) for time in chart above. Rearrange chicken pieces. Stir in noodles, being sure noodles are under broth. Cover. Microwave at 30% (MEDIUM LOW) for time in chart above or until noodles and chicken are tender, stirring several times and giving dish a half turn once. Remove chicken pieces and peppercorns from soup. Skim excess fat from soup. Remove bones and skin from chicken. Discard bones and skin. Cut up chicken and return 1-1/2 cups for 6 servings or 3/4 cup for 3 servings to soup. Refrigerate remaining chicken for another use. Microwave soup at full power (HIGH) for time in chart above or until heated through.

Adapting Chicken Soup Recipes for Microwave Oven

- Use a cut-up chicken or the bones and scraps from a chicken or turkey for making stock. Place chicken or bones and scraps in a casserole large enough to hold liquid to cover the chicken and still allow room for stirring. Use Home-Style Chicken-Noodle Soup, above, as a guideline for ratio of chicken to liquid, and approximate cooking times.

- Microwave chicken, liquid and seasonings, covered, at microwave full power (HIGH) until boiling. One cut-up chicken and 4 cups of water will boil in about 20 minutes. Microwave at 30% (MEDIUM LOW) for 45 minutes or until chicken is tender.

- Remove chicken from soup. Cut meat from bones. Meanwhile, add vegetables to soup. Microwave at full power (HIGH) until tender. Fresh cubed carrots and potatoes will cook in 20 to 30 minutes. Frozen vegetables will be tender in about 10 to 15 minutes. Quick-cooking rice will cook in 5 to 10 minutes. Allow extra cooking liquid for noodles or rice.

- Add cut-up chicken meat to soup. Cover and microwave at full power (HIGH) for 5 minutes or until heated through.

French Onion Soup   Photo on page 395.

SERVINGS	4	2
INGREDIENTS		
butter or margarine	6 tablespoons	3 tablespoons
onions, thinly sliced	4 medium (4 cups)	2 medium (2 cups)
all-purpose flour	2 teaspoons	1 teaspoon
sugar	1 tablespoon	2 teaspoons
dry mustard	1 teaspoon	1/2 teaspoon
condensed chicken broth	2 (10-3/4-oz.) cans	1 (10-3/4-oz.) can
dry white wine	1/4 cup	2 tablespoons
Worcestershire sauce	2 teaspoons	1 teaspoon
croutons	1 cup	1/2 cup
shredded Parmesan cheese	1/4 cup (1 oz.)	2 tablespoons
shredded mozzarella cheese	1 cup (4 oz.)	1/2 cup (2 oz.)
BAKING DISH	deep 3-qt. casserole	deep 1-qt. casserole
SOUP BOWLS	4	2
TIME AT HIGH (butter)	1-1/2 minutes	1 minute
TIME AT HIGH (onions)	25 to 30 minutes	12 to 15 minutes
TIME AT HIGH (thickening soup mixture)	9 to 10 minutes	5 to 6 minutes
TIME AT HIGH (melt cheese)	2 to 2-1/2 minutes	1-1/2 to 2 minutes

Place butter or margarine in a casserole, see size in chart above. Microwave butter or margarine at full power (HIGH) for time in chart above or until melted. Stir in onions. Microwave at full power (HIGH) for time in chart above or until onions are browned and caramelized, stirring every 4 or 5 minutes. Stir in flour, sugar and mustard; mix well. Stir in broth, wine and Worcestershire sauce. Microwave at full power (HIGH) for time in chart above or until mixture thickens slightly and bubbles, stirring four times. Ladle into bowls. Top each serving with croutons. Sprinkle with Parmesan cheese and mozzarella cheese. Microwave at full power (HIGH) for time in chart above or until cheese melts, rearranging bowls once.

Easy Onion Soup

SERVINGS	4	2
INGREDIENTS		
condensed onion soup	2 (10-1/2-oz.) cans	1 (10-1/2-oz.) can
water	1-1/2 soup cans	3/4 soup can
dry white wine	1/2 soup can	1/4 soup can
Worcestershire sauce	2 teaspoons	1 teaspoon
sugar	1 teaspoon	1/2 teaspoon
plain rusks	4	2
shredded mozzarella cheese	1 cup (4 oz.)	1/2 cup (2 oz.)
BAKING DISH	deep 3-qt. casserole	deep 1-1/2-qt. casserole
SOUP BOWLS	4	2
TIME AT HIGH (soup)	8 to 10 minutes	4 to 5 minutes
TIME AT HIGH (melt cheese)	3 minutes	2 minutes

In a casserole, see size in chart above, combine soup, water, wine, Worcestershire sauce and sugar. Mix well. Cover. Microwave at full power (HIGH) for time in chart above or until boiling, stirring once. Ladle into soup bowls. Top with rusks. Sprinkle with mozzarella cheese. Microwave at full power (HIGH) for time in chart above or until melted.

Split Pea Soup

SERVINGS	4	2
INGREDIENTS		
dried split peas	8 oz. (about 1-1/4 cups)	4 oz. (about 2/3 cup)
bulk pork sausage	8 oz.	4 oz.
chopped onion	1/2 cup	1/4 cup
chopped celery	1/2 cup	1/4 cup
chicken broth	5 cups	3 cups
fennel seed	1 teaspoon	1/2 teaspoon
chopped ham, croutons, snipped parsley	to garnish	to garnish
BAKING DISH	deep 4-qt. casserole	deep 2-qt. casserole
TIME AT HIGH (sausage)	5 to 7 minutes	3 to 5 minutes
TIME AT HIGH (soup)	22 to 25 minutes	8 to 10 minutes
TIME AT 30%	50 to 60 minutes	50 to 60 minutes

Rinse and drain split peas. In a casserole, see size in chart above, combine sausage, onion and celery. Microwave at full power (HIGH) for time in chart above or until sausage is browned and done, stirring twice. Pour off fat. Stir in peas, broth and fennel seed; cover. Microwave at full power (HIGH) for time in chart above. Stir and cover. Microwave at 30% (MEDIUM LOW) 50 to 60 minutes or until peas are tender, stirring occasionally. Skim off excess fat. Serve garnished with chopped ham, croutons and snipped parsley.

Adapting Pea and Bean Soup Recipes for Microwave Oven

- Use Split Pea Soup, above, and Grandmother's Bean Soup, page 405, as guidelines for size of casserole, ratio of dried vegetable to water and approximate cooking times.

- Combine eight ounces of dried split peas, 5 cups of water and seasonings in a deep 4-quart casserole. Cover and microwave at full power (HIGH) for about 25 minutes. Then microwave at 30% (MEDIUM LOW) for 50 to 60 minutes or until peas are tender.

- Soak beans overnight in a mild soda solution of 1/8 teaspoon soda to 4 cups water and 8 ounces dried beans. This makes the beans more tender.

- Drain and rinse the beans. Add 5 cups of water to soaked beans in a 4-quart casserole. Add pieces of ham, a meaty ham bone or ham hocks. Cover and microwave at full power (HIGH) for 15 minutes or until boiling. Microwave at 30% (MEDIUM LOW) for 1-1/2 to 2-1/2 hours or until beans are tender, stirring occasionally.

- Remove any meat from bones and return meat to soup. Cover and microwave at full power (HIGH) for 5 minutes or until meat is heated through.

Lamb & Lentil Soup

SERVINGS	4	2
INGREDIENTS		
dried lentils	8 oz. (1-1/3 cups)	4 oz. (2/3 cup)
lamb shanks	2 (1-lb.) shanks	1 (1-lb.) shank
chopped celery	1/2 cup	1/4 cup
chopped onion	1/2 cup	1/4 cup
chopped carrot	1/2 cup	1/4 cup
water	5 cups	3 to 3-1/2 cups
Worcestershire sauce	4 teaspoons	2 teaspoons
bay leaf	1 medium	1 small
salt	1 teaspoon	1/2 teaspoon
garlic salt	1/2 teaspoon	1/4 teaspoon
dried leaf marjoram	1 teaspoon	1/2 teaspoon
dried leaf thyme	1 teaspoon	1/2 teaspoon
white pepper	1/2 teaspoon	1/4 teaspoon
sliced fresh mushrooms, chopped zucchini, snipped mint or parsley, plain yogurt	to garnish	to garnish
BAKING DISH	deep 4-qt. casserole	deep 3-qt. casserole
TIME AT HIGH (shanks)	15 minutes	12 to 14 minutes
TIME AT 30%	1-1/4 to 1-1/2 hours	1 hour
TIME AT HIGH (meat added)	3 to 5 minutes	2 to 3 minutes

Rinse and drain lentils. In a casserole, see size in chart above, combine lamb shanks, celery, onion, carrot, lentils and water. Stir in Worcestershire sauce, bay leaf, salt, garlic salt, marjoram, thyme and white pepper. Stir well. Cover. Microwave at full power (HIGH) for time in chart above or until boiling. Stir well; cover. Microwave at 30% (MEDIUM LOW) for time in chart above or until lamb and lentils are tender, stirring occasionally. Turn lamb shanks over after first 30 minutes of cooking time. When tender, remove lamb shanks from soup. Cut meat from bones and return meat to soup. Skim off excess fat; cover. Microwave at full power (HIGH) for time in chart above or until heated through. Remove bay leaf. Serve topped with mushrooms, zucchini, mint or parsley and yogurt.

Reheating Refrigerated Soup

SERVINGS	2	1
INGREDIENTS		
soup	2 cups	1 cup
SOUP BOWLS	2	1
TIME AT HIGH	6 to 7 minutes	2-1/2 to 3-1/2 minutes

To chill: Pour cooled soup into a refrigerator container. Cover and refrigerate.

To reheat: Pour soup into soup bowls. Cover with vented plastic wrap. Microwave at full power (HIGH) for time in chart above or until heated through, stirring once. Stir before serving.

How to Make Lamb & Lentil Soup

Lamb shanks are the lower part of the leg of lamb and make a delicious broth. Add chopped celery, onion and carrot to the shanks, then add the lentils and water.

Serve the steaming soup in bowls topped with zucchini, sliced mushrooms, snipped mint or parsley and a dollop of yogurt. This attractive garnish gives a Greek flair.

Grandmother's Bean Soup

SERVINGS	4 to 6	2 or 3
INGREDIENTS		
dried pea beans	8 oz. (1-1/3 cups)	4 oz. (2/3 cup)
water	4 cups	2 cups
baking soda	1/8 teaspoon	dash
smoked ham hocks, cut in 2-inch pieces	2 lbs.	1 lb.
chopped onion	1/2 cup	1/4 cup
chopped celery	1/2 cup	1/4 cup
water	5 cups	3 cups
Worcestershire sauce	1 tablespoon	2 teaspoons
snipped parsley	2 tablespoons	1 tablespoon
BAKING DISH	deep 4-qt. casserole	deep 3-qt. casserole
TIME AT HIGH (beans)	15 minutes	12 minutes
TIME AT 30%	2-1/2 hours	1-1/2 hours
TIME AT HIGH (completed soup)	5 minutes	5 minutes

Rinse and drain pea beans. In a casserole, see size in chart above, combine beans, first amount of water and baking soda. Cover and let stand overnight. Drain and rinse beans. Return to casserole. Add ham hocks, onion and celery. Stir in second amount of water and Worcestershire sauce. Cover. Microwave at full power (HIGH) for time in chart above or until boiling. Stir. Cover. Microwave at 30% (MEDIUM LOW) for time in chart above, turning hocks over in liquid and stirring occasionally. Beans should be tender. Remove ham hocks from soup. Cut meat from bone and return meat to soup. Discard bone. Skim off excess fat. Stir in parsley. Cover. Microwave at full power (HIGH) for time in chart above or until ham is heated through.

Shortcut Minestrone

SERVINGS	6	3
INGREDIENTS		
ground beef	1 lb.	8 oz.
chopped onion	1 cup	1/2 cup
chopped green pepper	1/2 cup	1/4 cup
bottled Italian cooking sauce	1 (16-oz.) jar (2 cups)	1/2 (16-oz.) jar (1 cup)
tomatoes, cut up	1 (16-oz.) can	1 (7-1/2-oz.) can
Chianti wine	1 cup	1/2 cup
chili beans in gravy	1 (15-1/2-oz.) can	1/2 (15-1/2-oz.) can
spaghetti, broken in 1-inch pieces	1/2 cup	1/4 cup
thinly sliced pepperoni	2 oz.	1 oz.
dried leaf basil	1 teaspoon	1/2 teaspoon
croutons, grated Parmesan cheese, if desired	to garnish	to garnish
BAKING DISH	deep 3-qt. casserole	deep 2-qt. casserole
TIME AT HIGH (meat)	5 to 6 minutes	3 to 4 minutes
TIME AT HIGH (all ingredients)	10 minutes	6 to 8 minutes
TIME AT 30%	35 minutes	20 to 25 minutes

In a casserole, see size in chart above, combine ground beef, onion and green pepper. Microwave at full power (HIGH) for time in chart above or until meat is browned and vegetables are tender, stirring three times. Pour off fat. Stir in cooking sauce, tomatoes, wine, beans with gravy, spaghetti, pepperoni and basil. Cover. Microwave at full power (HIGH) for time in chart above or until boiling. Stir well. Cover. Microwave at 30% (MEDIUM LOW) for time in chart above or until spaghetti is tender, stirring twice. To serve, top each serving with croutons and grated Parmesan cheese, if desired.

Pantry Minestrone

SERVINGS	6 to 8	3 or 4
INGREDIENTS		
condensed tomato bisque	2 (11-oz.) cans	1 (11-oz.) can
hot water	3 soup cans	1-1/2 soup cans
baked beans in tomato sauce	1 (16-oz.) can	1 (8-oz.) can
leftover vegetables	2 cups	1 cup
spaghetti broken in 1-inch pieces	1/2 cup	1/4 cup
BAKING DISH	deep 4-qt. casserole	deep 2-qt. casserole
TIME AT HIGH	30 minutes	25 minutes

In a casserole, see size in chart above, combine tomato bisque, water, beans with sauce, vegetables and spaghetti. Mix well. Cover. Microwave at full power (HIGH) for time in chart above or until spaghetti is tender, stirring twice.

Oyster Stew

SERVINGS	4	2
INGREDIENTS		
milk	3 cups	1-1/2 cups
oyster liquor	1/2 cup	1/4 cup
butter or margarine	1/4 cup	2 tablespoons
chopped onion	1/4 cup	2 tablespoons
celery salt	1/2 teaspoon	1/4 teaspoon
dried leaf thyme, crushed	1/2 teaspoon	1/4 teaspoon
dry mustard	1/4 teaspoon	1/8 teaspoon
freshly ground pepper	dash	dash
fresh shucked oysters	1 pint (24 oysters)	1/2 pint (12 oysters)
hot pepper sauce	dash	dash
whipping cream, whipped	1 cup	1/2 cup
GLASS MEASURING CUP	4-cup	2-cup
BAKING DISH	deep 2-qt. casserole	deep 1-qt. casserole
TIME AT HIGH (milk mixture)	5 minutes	3 minutes
TIME AT HIGH (butter)	1 minute	40 seconds
TIME AT HIGH (onion added)	3 minutes	1 to 1-1/2 minutes
TIME AT 50% (oysters added)	3 minutes	1 to 1-1/2 minutes
TIME AT 30% (milk added)	10 minutes	5 to 6 minutes
TIME AT 30% (cream added)	5 minutes	2-1/2 to 3-1/2 minutes

Place milk and oyster liquor in a glass measuring cup, see size in chart above. Microwave at full power (HIGH) for time in chart above or until hot; do not boil. Set aside. Place butter or margarine in a casserole, see size in chart above. Microwave at full power (HIGH) for time in chart above or until melted. Stir in onion. Microwave at full power (HIGH) for time in chart above or until onion is tender. Stir in celery salt, thyme, mustard and pepper until blended. Stir in oysters and hot pepper sauce. Microwave at 50% (MEDIUM) for time in chart above or until oysters are puffed and edges of a few oysters begin to curl. Do not overcook. Stir once during cooking time. Add warm milk mixture. Microwave at 30% (MEDIUM LOW) for time in chart above or until hot, stirring once. Top with whipped cream. Microwave at 30% (MEDIUM LOW) for time in chart above or until heated through, stirring once. Serve in warmed bowls.

Manhattan Clam Chowder

SERVINGS	6 to 8	3 or 4
INGREDIENTS		
condensed tomato soup	2 (10-3/4-oz.) cans	1 (10-3/4-oz.) can
hot water	1 soup can	1/2 soup can
stewed tomatoes	1 (16-oz.) can	1 (8-oz.) can
minced clams	2 (6-1/2-oz.) cans	1 (6-1/2-oz.) can
mixed vegetables	1 (16-oz.) can	1 (8-oz.) can
instant minced onion	1 teaspoon	1/2 teaspoon
BAKING DISH	deep 4-qt. casserole	deep 2-qt. casserole
TIME AT HIGH	18 to 20 minutes	8 to 9 minutes

In a casserole, see size in chart above, combine tomato soup, water and tomatoes; mix well. Stir in clams with liquid, mixed vegetables with liquid and onion. Cover. Microwave at full power (HIGH) for time in chart above or until hot, stirring once.

How to Make Oyster Stew

Microwave oysters briefly in hot butter and onion mixture until the oysters are puffed and a few edges start to curl. Stir in warm milk mixture.

After the milk and oysters are heated at 30% (MEDIUM LOW), add dollops of whipped cream and reheat briefly before serving.

Quick & Creamy Shrimp Soup

SERVINGS	7 or 8	3 or 4
INGREDIENTS		
cream of shrimp soup	2 (10-3/4-oz.) cans	1 (10-3/4-oz.) can
milk	3 soup cans	1-1/2 soup cans
frozen peas, pasta shells and mushrooms with seasoned cream-sauce cubes	2 (10-oz.) pkgs.	1 (10-oz.) pkg.
dry sherry	1/4 cup	2 tablespoons
dried dillweed	1/2 teaspoon	1/4 teaspoon
shrimp, drained	2 (4-1/4-oz.) cans	1 (4-1/4-oz.) can
grated Parmesan cheese	1/4 cup (1 oz.)	2 tablespoons
BAKING DISH	deep 4-qt. casserole	deep 2-qt. casserole
TIME AT HIGH (soup)	10 to 12 minutes	6 minutes
TIME AT HIGH (shrimp added)	18 to 22 minutes	10 to 11 minutes
STANDING TIME	2 minutes	2 minutes

In a casserole, see size in chart above, combine soup and milk; whisk until smooth. Stir in frozen vegetables with sauce cubes, sherry and dillweed. Cover. Microwave at full power (HIGH) for time in chart above. Stir well until sauce cubes dissolve. Add shrimp. Cover. Microwave at full power (HIGH) for time in chart above or until heated through, stirring once. Stir in Parmesan cheese. Cover and let stand 2 minutes. Stir before serving.

Tuna Chowder Florentine

SERVINGS	4	2
INGREDIENTS		
frozen creamed spinach in a pouch	1 (9-oz.) pkg.	1/2 (9-oz.) pkg.
milk	2 cups	1 cup
tuna, drained, broken up	1 (6-1/2-oz.) can	1 (3-1/2-oz.) can
hard-cooked eggs, chopped	2	1
chopped pimiento	2 tablespoons	1 tablespoon
snipped chives	2 teaspoons	1 teaspoon
Dijon-style mustard	2 teaspoons	1 teaspoon
lemon juice	1 teaspoon	1/2 teaspoon
sliced hard-cooked egg, paprika	to garnish	to garnish
BAKING DISH	deep 2-qt. casserole	deep 1-qt. casserole
TIME AT HIGH (spinach)	7 minutes	3-1/2 minutes
TIME AT HIGH (completed chowder)	8 minutes	4 to 5 minutes

Remove creamed spinach from pouch. Place in a casserole, see size in chart above. Cover. Microwave at full power (HIGH) for time in chart above. Stir in milk. Stir in tuna, egg, pimiento, chives, mustard and lemon juice. Cover. Microwave at full power (HIGH) for time in chart above or until hot, stirring once. Garnish with sliced hard-cooked egg and sprinkle with paprika.

New England Clam Chowder

SERVINGS	4 or 5	2
INGREDIENTS		
bacon, cut up	8 slices	4 slices
bacon drippings	1/4 cup	2 tablespoons
chopped onion	1/2 cup	1/4 cup
frozen hash brown potatoes	2 cups	1 cup
all-purpose flour	1/4 cup	2 tablespoons
salt	1/2 teaspoon	1/4 teaspoon
half and half	4 cups	2 cups
minced clams with liquid	2 (6-1/2-oz.) cans	1 (6-1/2-oz.) can
BAKING DISH	deep 3-qt. casserole	deep 2-qt. casserole
TIME AT HIGH (bacon)	6 to 8 minutes	4 to 5 minutes
TIME AT HIGH (potatoes)	7 to 8 minutes	5 minutes
TIME AT HIGH (flour added)	30 seconds	30 seconds
TIME AT HIGH (clams added)	12 to 14 minutes	7 to 8 minutes

Place bacon in a casserole, see size in chart above. Cover bacon with white paper towel. Microwave at full power (HIGH) for time in chart above or until bacon is crisp. Drain bacon, leaving amount of drippings listed in chart above in the casserole. Crumble bacon and set aside. Stir onion and potatoes into reserved drippings. Cover. Microwave at full power (HIGH) for time in chart above or until vegetables are tender. Stir in flour and salt until blended. Microwave at full power (HIGH) 30 seconds. Stir in half and half and clams with liquid. Microwave at full power (HIGH) for time in chart above or until mixture begins to boil, stirring three times. Stir before serving. Garnish each serving with crumbled bacon. Sprinkle with snipped parsley and paprika, if desired.

Smoky Cheese Soup

SERVINGS	3 or 4	1 or 2
INGREDIENTS		
butter, margarine or bacon drippings	1/4 cup	2 tablespoons
all-purpose flour	1/4 cup	2 tablespoons
paprika	1 teaspoon	1/2 teaspoon
dry mustard	1 teaspoon	1/2 teaspoon
chicken broth	1 (14-1/2-oz.) can	1/2 (14-1/2-oz.) can
milk	1 cup	1/2 cup
Worcestershire sauce	2 teaspoons	1 teaspoon
pasteurized process cheese spread	1 (8-oz.) jar	1/2 (8-oz.) jar
liquid smoke	1/2 teaspoon	1/4 teaspoon
crumbled bacon, snipped parsley	to garnish	to garnish
BAKING DISH	deep 2-qt. casserole	deep 1-qt. casserole
TIME AT HIGH (butter)	1 minute	30 seconds
TIME AT HIGH (flour added)	30 seconds	30 seconds
TIME AT HIGH (thickening soup mixture)	8 minutes	4 minutes
TIME AT 30%	10 to 12 minutes	5 to 6 minutes

Place butter, margarine or bacon drippings in a casserole, see size in chart above. Microwave at full power (HIGH) for time in chart above or until melted. Stir in flour, paprika and dry mustard; mix well. Microwave at full power (HIGH) 30 seconds. Stir in chicken broth, milk and Worcestershire sauce. Microwave at full power (HIGH) for time in chart above or until mixture thickens and bubbles, whisking three times. Stir in cheese and liquid smoke. Microwave at 30% (MEDIUM LOW) for time in chart above or until heated through. Stir before serving. Garnish each bowl with crumbled bacon and snipped parsley.

Swiss Corn Chowder

SERVINGS	8	4
INGREDIENTS		
condensed cream of onion soup	2 (10-3/4-oz.) cans	1 (10-3/4-oz.) can
milk	3 soup cans	1-1/2 soup cans
cream-style corn	1 (17-oz.) can	1 (8-3/4-oz.) can
whole-kernel corn	1 (17-oz.) can	1 (7-oz.) can
chopped pimiento	1/2 cup	1/4 cup
shredded Swiss cheese	1 cup (4 oz.)	1/2 cup (2-oz.)
BAKING DISH	deep 4-qt. casserole	deep 2-qt. casserole
TIME AT HIGH (soup)	20 to 22 minutes	10 minutes
TIME AT HIGH (cheese added)	3 minutes	2 minutes

In a casserole, see size in chart above, whisk together soup, milk and cream-style corn. Stir in whole-kernel corn with liquid and pimiento. Cover. Microwave at full power (HIGH) for time in chart above or until heated through, stirring once. Stir in cheese. Microwave, uncovered, at full power (HIGH) for time in chart above or until cheese is melted, stirring twice.

How to Make Quick & Creamy Chicken Chowder

Whisk together canned chicken soup and milk, then add frozen vegetables with sauce cubes, and sage. Partway through the cooking time, stir the soup until the sauce cubes dissolve.

Serve this colorful chowder in bowls and garnish with snipped watercress or parsley. It's also delicious with croutons, shredded cheese and a sprinkling of paprika.

Quick & Creamy Chicken Chowder

SERVINGS	7 or 8	3 or 4
INGREDIENTS		
condensed cream of chicken soup	2 (10-3/4-oz.) cans	1 (10-3/4-oz.) can
milk	3 soup cans	1-1/2 soup cans
frozen broccoli, carrots and pasta twists with lightly seasoned sauce cubes	2 (10-oz.) pkgs.	1 (10-oz.) pkg.
dried rubbed sage	1/4 teaspoon	1/8 teaspoon
diced cooked or canned chicken	2 cups	1 cup
snipped watercress or parsley	to garnish	to garnish
BAKING DISH	deep 4-qt. casserole	deep 2-qt. casserole
TIME AT HIGH (vegetables, soup, milk)	10 to 12 minutes	5 minutes
TIME AT HIGH (chicken added)	24 to 26 minutes	10 to 12 minutes
STANDING TIME	2 minutes	2 minutes

In a casserole, see size in chart above, combine soup and milk. Whisk until smooth. Stir in frozen vegetables with sauce cubes and sage. Cover. Microwave at full power (HIGH) for time in chart above. Stir until sauce cubes dissolve. Add chicken. Cover. Microwave at full power (HIGH) for time in chart above or until heated through, stirring once. Let stand, covered, 2 minutes. Stir before serving. Garnish each serving with snipped watercress or parsley.

California Corn Bisque

SERVINGS	4	2
INGREDIENTS		
whole-kernel corn, drained	1 (16-oz.) can	1 (7-oz.) can
chicken broth	1 (14-1/2-oz.) can	1/2 (14-1/2-oz.) can
butter or margarine	1/4 cup	2 tablespoons
chopped green onion	1/4 cup	2 tablespoons
all-purpose flour	3 tablespoons	2 tablespoons
celery salt	1/2 teaspoon	1/4 teaspoon
pepper	dash	dash
milk	1 cup	3/4 cup
chopped pimiento	2 tablespoons	1 tablespoon
chopped, seeded canned green chilies	2 tablespoons	1 tablespoon
shredded Monterey Jack cheese	1 cup (4-oz.)	1/2 cup (2-oz.)
avocado slices	4	2
thin tomato wedges	4	2
snipped parsley	to garnish	to garnish
BAKING DISH	deep 3-qt. casserole	deep 1-1/2-qt. casserole
TIME AT HIGH (butter)	1 minute	30 seconds
TIME AT HIGH (onion)	2-1/2 to 3 minutes	1 to 1-1/2 minutes
TIME AT HIGH (flour added)	30 seconds	30 seconds
TIME AT HIGH (thickening soup mixture)	12 to 14 minutes	6 to 8 minutes
TIME AT HIGH (cheese added)	3 minutes	2 to 3 minutes

In a blender container or food processor, combine corn and 1/2 cup chicken broth. Cover and process until smooth. Add remaining broth; set aside. Place butter or margarine in a casserole, see size in chart above. Microwave at full power (HIGH) for time in chart above or until melted. Add green onion. Microwave at full power (HIGH) for time in chart above or until tender. Stir in flour, celery salt and pepper. Microwave at full power (HIGH) 30 seconds. Whisk in corn mixture and milk. Microwave at full power (HIGH) for time in chart above or until thickened and bubbly, stirring three times. Stir in pimiento and chilies. Stir in cheese until melted. Microwave at full power (HIGH) for time in chart above or until heated through. Ladle soup into bowls. Top with avocado slices and tomato wedges. Sprinkle with snipped parsley.

Chunky Canned Soup

SERVINGS	2	1
INGREDIENTS		
chunky soup	1 (18- to 19-oz.) can	1 (10- to 11-oz.) can
GLASS MEASURING CUP OR	4-cup	2-cup
SOUP BOWLS	2	1
TIME AT HIGH	5 minutes	2-1/2 to 3 minutes

Pour soup into a glass measuring cup, see size in chart above, or into soup bowls. Do not add water. Cover with vented plastic wrap. Microwave at full power (HIGH) for time in chart above or until hot, stirring once. Stir before serving.

Condensed Canned Soup

SERVINGS	4	2
INGREDIENTS condensed canned soup water or milk	2 (10- to 11-oz.) cans 2 soup cans	1 (10- to 11-oz.) can 1 soup can
BAKING DISH	2-qt. casserole	4-cup glass measuring cup
TIME AT HIGH	8 to 9 minutes	5 to 6 minutes

Pour soup into a casserole or glass measuring cup, see size in chart above. Gradually stir or whisk in water or milk according to package directions. Cover with lid or vented plastic wrap. Microwave at full power (HIGH) for time in chart above or until hot, stirring twice. Stir before serving.

Semi-Condensed Canned Soup

SERVINGS	1
INGREDIENTS semi-condensed one-serving soup water	1 (7-oz.) can 1/2 soup can
GLASS MEASURING CUP	2-cup
TIME AT HIGH	3 to 3-1/2 minutes

Pour soup into a 2-cup glass measuring cup. Gradually stir or whisk in water. Cover with vented plastic wrap. Microwave at full power (HIGH) 3 to 3-1/2 minutes or until hot, stirring once. Stir before serving.

Dry Soup Mix

SERVINGS	4	1
INGREDIENTS hot water dry soup mix	about 4 cups 1 (4-serving-size) envelope	about 3/4 cup 1 (single-serving-size) envelope
BAKING DISH	deep 2-qt. casserole	1-cup glass measuring cup
TIME AT HIGH	6 to 8 minutes	1-1/2 to 2 minutes
TIME AT 30%	5 to 10 minutes	omit

Checking package directions for amount, measure hot water into a casserole or glass measuring cup, see size in chart above. Microwave at full power (HIGH) for time in chart above or until boiling. **For 4 servings:** Stir in dry soup mix and cover. Microwave at 30% (MEDIUM LOW) 5 to 10 minutes or until dry soup particles are fully hydrated and soup is hot; stir occasionally. **For 1 serving:** Place dry soup mix in a mug. Pour boiling water into mug while stirring constantly.

Variation

In a 1-1/2-quart casserole, combine 1 (4-serving-size) envelope dry vegetable soup mix and 3 cups hot water. Microwave at full power (HIGH) 11 to 12 minutes; stir twice.

Canned Soup Combinations

	SOUP +	SOUP +	OTHER INGREDIENTS
Spicy Tomato Soup	1 (10-3/4-oz.) can condensed tomato soup	1 (14-1/2-oz.) can ready-to-serve chicken broth	2 to 4 tablespoons mild taco sauce dash hot pepper sauce
Creamy Onion Soup	1 (10-3/4-oz.) can condensed cream of onion soup	1 (10-1/2-oz.) can condensed onion soup	1/2 soup can water 1/4 cup dry sherry
Tomato-Vegetable Soup	1 (11-oz.) can condensed tomato-rice soup	1 (10-1/2-oz.) can condensed vegetable soup	1 soup can water 1 teaspoon Worcestershire sauce
Tomato-Shrimp Bisque	1 (11-oz.) can condensed tomato bisque soup	1 (10-3/4-oz.) can condensed cream of shrimp soup	1 soup can water 2 tablespoons seafood cocktail sauce 1/4 cup dry sherry
Double-Bean Chowder	1 (11-1/2-oz.) can condensed bean with bacon soup	1 (11-1/4-oz.) can condensed chili-beef soup	1/2 soup can water 1 soup can tomato juice shredded cheese for garnish
Creamy Chicken-Rice Soup	1 (10-3/4-oz.) can condensed creamy chicken-mushroom soup	1 (10-1/2-oz.) can condensed chicken broth and rice soup	1 soup can water 1/4 to 1/2 teaspoon dried rubbed sage
Springtime Bisque	1 (10-3/4-oz.) can condensed cream of asparagus soup	1 (10-3/4-oz.) can condensed cream of celery soup	1 (14-1/2-oz.) can ready-to-serve chicken broth 1/2 teaspoon curry powder
Minute Minestrone	1 (11-oz.) can condensed Cheddar cheese soup	1 (10-1/2-oz.) can condensed minestrone	1 soup can water 3 tablespoons chopped pepperoni chopped fresh tomato for garnish
Creamy Chicken-Vegetable Soup	1 (10-3/4-oz.) can condensed golden mushroom soup	1 (10-1/2-oz.) can condensed chicken broth and vegetables	1 soup can water 1/2 teaspoon dried leaf thyme

In a deep 2-quart casserole, whisk or stir together soups and other ingredients except garnishes. Cover with vented plastic wrap or casserole lid. Microwave at full power (HIGH) 8 to 10 minutes or until soup is hot, stirring twice. A microwave thermometer held in soup should register 180F (80C). Stir before serving. Makes 3 servings.

Curried Asparagus Bisque

SERVINGS	8	4
INGREDIENTS		
butter or margarine	1/4 cup	2 tablespoons
chopped onion	1/2 cup	1/4 cup
celery salt	1 teaspoon	1/2 teaspoon
curry powder	2 teaspoons	1 teaspoon
condensed chicken broth	2 (10-3/4-oz.) cans	1 (10-3/4-oz.) can
frozen cut asparagus	2 (8-oz.) pkgs.	1 (8-oz.) pkg.
lemon juice	1 tablespoon	1-1/2 teaspoons
plain yogurt	1 cup	1/2 cup
avocado, peeled, seeded, sliced	1	1/2
plain yogurt	1/2 cup	1/4 cup
snipped chives or red caviar	to garnish	to garnish
BAKING DISH	deep 3-qt. casserole	deep 2-qt. casserole
TIME AT HIGH (butter)	1 minute	30 seconds
TIME AT HIGH (onion added)	2-1/2 to 3 minutes	2 to 2-1/2 minutes
TIME AT HIGH (asparagus added)	12 to 14 minutes	7 to 8 minutes

Place butter or margarine in a casserole, see size in chart above. Microwave at full power (HIGH) for time in chart above or until melted. Add onion. Microwave at full power (HIGH) for time in chart above or until tender. Stir in celery salt and curry powder. Stir in chicken broth. Add asparagus; cover. Microwave at full power (HIGH) for time in chart above or until tender, stirring once. Stir in lemon juice. Process mixture in a food processor or blender until smooth. Process in 2 batches if making larger amount. In same casserole, blend first amount of yogurt and a little hot soup mixture. Gradually blend in remaining hot soup. Cover and refrigerate 8 hours or overnight. Serve icy cold in small bowls or icers. Top each serving with a fan of avocado slices, a dollop of additional yogurt and a sprinkling of chives or caviar.

Asparagus Bisque Pronto

SERVINGS	8 to 12	4 to 6
INGREDIENTS		
condensed cream of asparagus soup	2 (10-3/4-oz.) cans	1 (10-3/4-oz.) can
chicken broth	2-1/2 cups	1-1/4 cups
curry powder or dried leaf tarragon, crushed	1 teaspoon	1/2 teaspoon
dairy sour cream	1 cup	1/2 cup
snipped chives	2 teaspoons	1 teaspoon
BAKING DISH	deep 3-qt. casserole	deep 1-1/2-qt. casserole
TIME AT HIGH	8 to 9 minutes	4 to 5 minutes

In a casserole, see size in chart above, whisk together soup, broth and curry powder or tarragon. Mix well. Cover. Microwave at full power (HIGH) for time in chart above or until heated through, stirring once. Slowly stir 1/2 cup hot soup into sour cream. Stir sour cream mixture back into remaining soup. Mix well. Stir in chives. Cover and refrigerate until chilled. Serve chilled in small bowls or icers.

How to Make Curried Asparagus Bisque

In the spring, substitute fresh asparagus for frozen. Microwave asparagus in chicken broth mixture. Break up the frozen block of asparagus with the tines of a large fork to speed cooking.

Pour the cooked asparagus mixture into a blender container. Squeeze in some lemon juice for tang. Cover and blend at high speed until the asparagus mixture is smooth.

Place yogurt in the same casserole the asparagus was cooked in. Stir a little of the hot pureed soup into the yogurt. This helps prevent curdling. Then blend in the remaining soup.

Serve the chilled soup in icers. Garnish each bowl with avocado slices, a dollop of yogurt and a spoonful of red caviar or a sprinkling of fresh snipped chives.

Lazy-Day Vichyssoise

SERVINGS	6 to 8	3 or 4
INGREDIENTS		
frozen small onions with cream sauce	2 (9-oz.) pkgs.	1 (9-oz.) pkg.
water	1-1/3 cups	2/3 cup
chicken bouillon granules	2 tablespoons	1 tablespoon
butter or margarine	2 tablespoons	1 tablespoon
milk	2 cups	1 cup
instant mashed potato buds	1-1/2 cups	3/4 cup
whipping cream	1 cup	1/2 cup
snipped chives	to garnish	to garnish
BAKING DISH	deep 2-qt. casserole	deep 1-qt. casserole
TIME AT HIGH (onions)	6 minutes	3 minutes
TIME AT HIGH (milk added)	8 minutes	4 minutes

In a casserole, see size in chart above, combine frozen onions, water, chicken bouillon granules and butter or margarine. Cover. Microwave at full power (HIGH) for time in chart above. Stir until sauce is smooth. Stir in milk. Cover. Microwave at full power (HIGH) for time in chart above or until onions are tender. Stir in potato buds. In a food processor or blender, process mixture until smooth. Process in 2 batches if making larger amount. Stir in whipping cream. Press mixture through a fine sieve. Cover and refrigerate 8 hours or overnight. Serve icy cold in small bowls or icers. Top with a sprinkling of chives.

Artichoke Almond Bisque

SERVINGS	8 to 12	4 to 6
INGREDIENTS		
condensed cream of chicken soup	2 (10-3/4-oz.) cans	1 (10-3/4-oz.) can
milk	2 soup cans	1 soup can
artichoke hearts, drained, cut up	1 (14-oz.) can	1 (7-oz.) can
slivered almonds	1/2 cup	1/4 cup
plain yogurt	1 cup	1/2 cup
BAKING DISH	deep 3-qt. casserole	deep 1-1/2-qt. casserole
TIME AT HIGH	8 to 9 minutes	4 to 5 minutes

In a casserole, see size in chart above, whisk together soup and milk. Mix well. Stir in artichoke hearts and almonds. Cover. Microwave at full power (HIGH) for time in chart above or until heated through, stirring once. In a food processor or blender, process mixture until smooth. Process in 2 batches if making larger amount. Stir 1/2 cup hot soup into yogurt in same casserole. Gradually stir in remaining soup. Cover and refrigerate 8 hours or overnight. Serve icy cold in small bowls or icers.

Bordelaise Sauce

YIELD	1-3/4 cups	3/4 cup
INGREDIENTS		
butter or margarine	1/4 cup	2 tablespoons
fresh mushroom slices	1 cup	1/2 cup
chopped onion	1/4 cup	2 tablespoons
dried leaf thyme, crushed	1/4 teaspoon	1/8 teaspoon
bay leaf	1 small	1/2 small
dry red wine	1/2 cup	1/4 cup
cornstarch	1 tablespoon	2 teaspoons
chicken broth	1 cup	1/2 cup
snipped parsley	to garnish	to garnish
BAKING DISH	deep 2-qt. casserole	deep 1-qt. casserole
TIME AT HIGH (butter)	45 seconds	30 seconds
TIME AT HIGH (mushrooms, onion added)	3 minutes	2 minutes
TIME AT HIGH (wine added)	5 minutes	3 minutes
TIME AT HIGH (thickening sauce)	3 minutes	2-1/2 minutes

Place butter or margarine in a casserole, see size in chart above. Microwave at full power (HIGH) for time in chart above or until melted. Stir in mushrooms and onion. Microwave at full power (HIGH) for time in chart above or until tender. Stir in thyme. Add bay leaf and wine. Microwave at full power (HIGH) for time in chart above. In a small bowl, thoroughly mix cornstarch and a little broth. Stir into mushroom mixture. Stir in remaining broth. Microwave at full power (HIGH) for time in chart above or until mixture thickens and bubbles, stirring twice. Remove bay leaf. Serve sauce over cooked beef. Garnish with snipped parsley.

Gravy Mix

YIELD	1 cup
INGREDIENTS	
gravy mix	1 (3/4- to 1-oz.) envelope
water	about 1 cup
GLASS MEASURING CUP	2-cup
TIME AT HIGH	2-1/2 to 3 minutes

Empty contents of gravy mix envelope into a 2-cup glass measuring cup. Gradually blend in amount of water listed on envelope. Microwave at full power (HIGH) 2-1/2 to 3 minutes or until gravy is thickened and bubbly, stirring three times.

Tips

- To make chicken gravy, see the recipes on pages 176 and 178. To make turkey gravy, see the recipes on page 196.
- To make gravy for roasted meat or pot roast, see the recipes on pages 70 and 124.

No-Fail Hollandaise Sauce

YIELD	1-2/3 cups	1 cup
INGREDIENTS		
egg yolks	6	3
lemon juice	1/4 cup	2 tablespoons
salt	1/8 teaspoon	dash
white pepper	1/8 teaspoon	dash
butter or margarine, cut up	1 cup	1/2 cup
dried leaf tarragon	1/2 teaspoon	1/4 teaspoon
grated fresh lemon peel	1/2 teaspoon	1/4 teaspoon
GLASS MEASURING CUP	4-cup	2-cup
TIME AT HIGH	2 minutes	1-1/2 to 2 minutes
TIME AT 30%	9 to 10 minutes	5 minutes

In a blender container, combine egg yolks, lemon juice, salt and pepper. Cover and blend at low speed until frothy. Place butter or margarine in a glass measuring cup, see size in chart above. Microwave at full power (HIGH) for time in chart above or until melted. With blender at high speed, slowly pour in melted butter or margarine, blending constantly until mixture is very thick. Stir in tarragon and lemon peel. Pour into same glass measuring cup or a sauce boat; set in bowl of hot water. The hot water should be at the same level as the sauce. Microwave at 30% (MEDIUM LOW) for time in chart above, or until warm, stirring every 2 minutes. Stir before serving. Refrigerate any leftover sauce and reheat using directions below.

Hollandaise Sauce Mix

YIELD	About 1 cup
INGREDIENTS	
hollandaise sauce mix	1 (1- to 1-1/4-oz.) envelope
water	2/3 to 3/4 cup
GLASS MEASURING CUP	4-cup
TIME AT HIGH	2 to 2-1/2 minutes

Empty contents of hollandaise sauce mix envelope into a 4-cup glass measuring cup. Gradually blend in amount of water listed on envelope. Microwave at full power (HIGH) 2 to 2-1/2 minutes or until thickened and bubbly, stirring three times.

Reheating Refrigerated Hollandaise Sauce

To chill: Pour 1 cup hollandaise sauce into a 2-cup glass measuring cup. Cover and refrigerate.

To reheat: Remove cover. Set measuring cup in a bowl of hot water. Microwave at 70% (MEDIUM HIGH) 4 to 5 minutes or until warm, stirring three times.

How to Make No-Fail Hollandaise Sauce

Pour egg yolks and lemon juice into blender container. Season with salt and white pepper, if you have it. Otherwise substitute black pepper.

Blend the egg yolks and lemon juice until frothy. Then with the blender running at high speed, slowly pour in melted butter or margarine. Blend until the sauce is thick and creamy.

Pour the sauce into a glass measuring cup or sauce boat. Set the sauce in a large bowl. Pour hot water into the bowl. This water bath helps keep the sauce from curdling.

Microwave the sauce just until warm—it will curdle if it becomes hot. Spoon the sauce over omelets, Eggs Benedict, vegetables, fish or poultry dishes.

Cheddar-Wine Sauce Stick

YIELD	6 cups sauce

INGREDIENTS	
soft-style margarine	1/2 cup
nonfat dry milk powder	1 cup
non-dairy coffee creamer	1/2 cup
all-purpose flour	1/2 cup
shredded Cheddar cheese	2 cups (8-oz.)
dried parsley flakes	1 tablespoon
dried chives	1 tablespoon
onion salt	1/2 teaspoon
dry mustard	1/2 teaspoon
dry white wine	3 tablespoons

In a medium bowl, combine all ingredients except wine; mix well. Add wine and mix until mixture holds its shape. On a piece of plastic wrap, shape cheese mixture into a stick. Use a table knife to score stick into quarters. Wrap in plastic wrap. Refrigerate up to 3 weeks.

To make Thin Cheddar-Wine Sauce:
Measure 1 cup cold water in a 4-cup glass measuring cup. Crumble in 1/4 sauce stick. Microwave at full power (HIGH) 3 to 4 minutes or until thickened and bubbly, stirring three times. Serve over vegetables, sandwiches or fish. Makes 1-1/2 cups sauce.

To make Thick Cheddar-Wine Sauce:
Follow directions for thin sauce above, except stir 1 tablespoon all-purpose flour into water along with 1/4 stick of sauce mix.

Quick Creamed Vegetables

SERVINGS	2 or 3	1 or 2
INGREDIENTS		
Cheddar-Wine Sauce Stick, above	1/4 stick	1/8 stick
water	1 cup	1/2 cup
small frozen vegetables: beans, peas, lima beans, or others	4 cups or 2 (10-oz.) pkgs.	2 cups or 1 (10-oz.) pkg.
BAKING DISH	deep 2-qt. casserole	deep 1-qt. casserole
TIME AT HIGH	Cooking time for frozen vegetable you select. See Vegetables & Salads, page 293, for cooking times.	
STANDING TIME	2 minutes	2 minutes

Crumble sauce stick into a casserole, see size in chart above. Add water and small frozen vegetables of your choice. Cover. Microwave at full power (HIGH) for time indicated for vegetables you select. Break apart vegetables with a fork as soon as possible. Stir three times during cooking. Let stand, covered, 2 minutes.

How to Make & Use Cheddar-Wine Sauce Stick

Mix soft-style tub margarine, dry milk powder, dry coffee creamer, flour, shredded Cheddar cheese, seasonings and wine. Form mixture into a stick shape. Score the stick in quarters with a knife, then wrap and refrigerate.

To use the sauce stick: Measure 1 cup cold water into a casserole. Crumble in 1/4 of the sauce stick. Microwave mixture until thickened and bubbly. Whisking during cooking keeps the sauce smooth.

To make the cheese sauce thicker, add 1 tablespoon flour to the 1 cup cold water along with the 1/4 sauce stick. Whisk to combine the flour and water. Whisk occasionally during microwaving until sauce is thickened and bubbly.

To make Quick Creamed Vegetables: Crumble 1/8 sauce stick into a casserole. Add 1/2 cup cold water and 2 cups frozen beans, peas or other small vegetables. Microwave until thickened and bubbly, stirring three times.

Spicy All-Purpose Tomato Sauce

YIELD	3 cups	1-1/2 cups
INGREDIENTS		
olive oil	3 tablespoons	2 tablespoons
chopped onion	1/3 cup	1/4 cup
chopped green pepper	1/3 cup	1/4 cup
chopped celery	1/3 cup	1/4 cup
tomatoes, drained, cut up	2 (28-oz.) cans (3-1/2 cups, drained)	2 (16-oz.) cans (1-2/3 cups, drained)
brown sugar	1 tablespoon	2 teaspoons
salt	1/2 teaspoon	1/4 teaspoon
dried leaf oregano	1/2 teaspoon	1/4 teaspoon
dried leaf basil	1/2 teaspoon	1/4 teaspoon
garlic powder	1/4 teaspoon	1/8 teaspoon
BAKING DISH	deep 2-qt. casserole	deep 1-1/2-qt. casserole
TIME AT HIGH (onion, green pepper, celery)	4 minutes	3 minutes
TIME AT HIGH (sauce)	10 to 12 minutes	5 minutes
TIME AT 30%	20 to 25 minutes	15 to 20 minutes

In a casserole, see size in chart above, combine olive oil, onion, green pepper and celery. Microwave at full power (HIGH) for time in chart above or until vegetables are tender, stirring twice. Stir in tomatoes, brown sugar, salt, oregano, basil and garlic powder. Cover. Microwave at full power (HIGH) for time in chart above or until mixture boils. Stir well; cover. Microwave at 30% (MEDIUM LOW) for time in chart above or until sauce reaches desired consistency, stirring once.

Spaghetti Sauce Mix

YIELD	2-1/2 to 3 cups
INGREDIENTS	
spaghetti sauce mix	1 (1-1/2-oz.) envelope
tomato paste	1 (6-oz.) can
water	1-3/4 to 2-1/4 cups
butter or margarine	1 to 2 tablespoons
GLASS MEASURING CUP	4-cup
TIME AT HIGH	4 to 5 minutes
TIME AT 30%	10 minutes

In a 4-cup glass measuring cup, combine spaghetti sauce mix and tomato paste. Stir in amount of water and butter or margarine listed on envelope. Cover with vented plastic wrap. Microwave at full power (HIGH) 4 to 5 minutes or until boiling. Stir; cover with vented plastic wrap. Microwave at 30% (MEDIUM LOW) 10 minutes or until flavors blend. Stir before serving.

Basic White Sauce — Thin

YIELD	2 cups	1-1/4 cups	2/3 cup
INGREDIENTS			
butter or margarine	2 tablespoons	1 tablespoon	1-1/2 teaspoons
all-purpose flour	2 tablespoons	1 tablespoon	1-1/2 teaspoons
salt	1/2 teaspoon	1/4 teaspoon	1/8 teaspoon
pepper	1/8 teaspoon	dash	dash
milk	2 cups	1 cup	1/2 cup
GLASS MEASURING CUP	4-cup	2-cup	2-cup
TIME AT HIGH (butter)	45 seconds	45 seconds	20 seconds
TIME AT HIGH (flour added)	30 seconds	30 seconds	30 seconds
TIME AT HIGH (milk added)	5-1/2 to 6 minutes	3 to 3-1/2 minutes	1-1/2 to 1-3/4 minutes

Place butter or margarine in a glass measuring cup, see size in chart. Microwave at full power (HIGH) for time in chart or until melted. Blend in flour, salt and pepper to a smooth paste. Microwave at full power (HIGH) 30 seconds. Whisk in milk. Microwave at full power (HIGH) for time in chart or until thickened and bubbly, whisking three times. Sauce should be thickened and smooth.

Basic White Sauce — Thick

YIELD	2-1/2 cups	1-1/3 cups	2/3 cup
INGREDIENTS			
butter or margarine	1/2 cup	1/4 cup	2 tablespoons
all-purpose flour	1/2 cup	1/4 cup	2 tablespoons
salt	1/2 teaspoon	1/4 teaspoon	1/8 teaspoon
pepper	1/8 teaspoon	dash	dash
milk	2 cups	1 cup	1/2 cup
GLASS MEASURING CUP	4-cup	2-cup	2-cup
TIME AT HIGH (butter)	1 minute	45 seconds	45 seconds
TIME AT HIGH (flour added)	30 seconds	30 seconds	30 seconds
TIME AT HIGH (milk added)	5 to 6 minutes	3 to 3-1/2 minutes	1-1/4 to 1-1/2 minutes

See directions for Basic White Sauce — Thin, above.

How to Make Basic White Sauce

This is the most critical step for properly thickened white sauce. Whisk flour, salt and pepper into melted butter or margarine until blended. Microwave for 30 seconds. The mixture will look foamy.

Milk is poured into the foamy butter-flour mixture, then whisked until the butter-flour mixture is well-distributed throughout the milk. The milk mixture will not be smooth.

The milk mixture must be whisked several times during microwaving to prevent lumping. When done, the white sauce should be smooth, thickened and bubbling hot.

Ladle white sauce over fresh peas and new potatoes, or use it as a base for soups or other sauces. White sauce also forms the base for creamed chicken or vegetables.

Basic White Sauce—Medium

YIELD	2-1/3 cups	1-1/4 cups	2/3 cup
INGREDIENTS			
butter or margarine	1/4 cup	2 tablespoons	1 tablespoon
all-purpose flour	1/4 cup	2 tablespoons	1 tablespoon
salt	1/2 teaspoon	1/4 teaspoon	1/8 teaspoon
pepper	1/8 teaspoon	dash	dash
milk	2 cups	1 cup	1/2 cup
GLASS MEASURING CUP	4-cup	2-cup	2-cup
TIME AT HIGH (butter)	45 seconds	45 seconds	30 seconds
TIME AT HIGH (flour added)	30 seconds	30 seconds	30 seconds
TIME AT HIGH (milk added)	5-1/2 to 6 minutes	3 to 3-1/2 minutes	1-1/2 to 1-3/4 minutes

Place butter or margarine in a glass measuring cup, see size in chart above. Microwave at full power (HIGH) for time in chart above or until melted. Blend in flour, salt and pepper to a smooth paste. Microwave at full power (HIGH) 30 seconds. Whisk in milk. Microwave at full power (HIGH) for time in chart above or until thickened and bubbly, whisking three times. Sauce should be thickened and smooth.

Adapting Cream Sauce Recipes for Microwave Oven

- Use a glass measuring cup with a capacity almost twice the amount of sauce. Melt butter, margarine or other fat in the glass measuring cup at full power (HIGH). It will take 30 to 60 seconds to melt up to 1/2 cup of fat.

- Stir flour or cornstarch and dry seasonings into melted fat until a smooth paste is formed. Microwave at full power (HIGH) for 30 seconds. This step is essential for maximum thickening. The flour mixture should look foamy.

- Whisk liquid into the fat-flour mixture. Blend well. The mixture will not be smooth.

- Microwave the liquid mixture at full power (HIGH) for about 2-1/2 minutes per cup of liquid, whisking twice each minute to prevent lumping. Microwave until mixture is thickened and bubbly. The mixture will begin to bubble in the microwave oven long before it reaches maximum thickness. Do not be deceived by this early bubbling around the edges. When done, the sauce should be thickened, smooth and bubbly throughout.

- Do not overcook starch-thickened sauces or they will curdle.

- Stir in cheese or other additions after the sauce is thickened. Microwave at full power (HIGH) for 30 to 60 seconds to melt the cheese, stirring once.

- Place plastic wrap or waxed paper directly on the surface of the sauce to keep a skin from forming.

Horseradish-Mustard Sauce

YIELD	1-1/4 cups	2/3 cup
INGREDIENTS		
Basic White Sauce—Medium, opposite	1-1/4 cups	2/3 cup
prepared or Dijon-style mustard	1 teaspoon	1/2 teaspoon
prepared horseradish	1 teaspoon	1/2 teaspoon
GLASS MEASURING CUP	2-cup	2-cup
TIME AT HIGH	30 seconds	30 seconds

Prepare medium Basic White Sauce in a 2-cup glass measuring cup. Stir mustard and horseradish into hot white sauce. Microwave at full power (HIGH) 30 seconds or until heated through.

Cheese Sauce

YIELD	1-3/4 cups	3/4 cup
INGREDIENTS		
Basic White Sauce—Medium, opposite	1-1/4 cups	2/3 cup
shredded or cubed process or natural cheese	1 cup (4-oz.)	1/2 cup (2 oz.)
GLASS MEASURING CUP	2-cup	2-cup
TIME AT HIGH	30 seconds	30 seconds

Prepare medium Basic White Sauce in a 2-cup glass measuring cup. Stir cheese into hot white sauce. Microwave at full power (HIGH) 30 seconds or until cheese melts. Stir or whisk until smooth.

Triple-Cheese Sauce

YIELD	1-3/4 cups	3/4 cup
INGREDIENTS		
Basic White Sauce—Medium, opposite	1-1/4 cups	2/3 cup
cream cheese	1/2 (3-oz.) pkg.	1/4 (3-oz.) pkg.
crumbled bleu cheese	2 tablespoons	1 tablespoon
shredded Cheddar cheese	1/2 cup (2-oz.)	1/4 cup (1 oz.)
GLASS MEASURING CUP	2-cup	2-cup
TIME AT HIGH	45 to 60 seconds	30 to 45 seconds

Prepare medium Basic White Sauce in a 2-cup measuring cup. Stir cream cheese, bleu cheese and Cheddar cheese into hot white sauce. Microwave at full power (HIGH) for time in chart above or until cheese melts. Stir or whisk until smooth.

White Sauce Mix

YIELD	1-1/3 cups
INGREDIENTS	
white sauce mix	1 (1-oz.) envelope
milk	about 1 cup
GLASS MEASURING CUP	4-cup
TIME AT HIGH	2-1/2 to 3 minutes

Empty white sauce mix into a 4-cup glass measuring cup. Gradually blend in amount of milk listed on envelope. Microwave at full power (HIGH) 2-1/2 to 3 minutes or until thickened and bubbly, stirring frequently.

Cheese Sauce Mix

YIELD	1 cup
INGREDIENTS	
cheese sauce mix	1 (1-1/4-oz.) envelope
milk	about 1 cup
GLASS MEASURING CUP	4-cup
TIME AT HIGH	3 to 3-1/2 minutes

Empty cheese sauce mix into a 4-cup glass measuring cup. Gradually blend in amount of milk listed on envelope. Microwave at full power (HIGH) 3 to 3-1/2 minutes or until thickened and bubbly, stirring three times.

Canned Spaghetti Sauce

YIELD	4 cups	2 cups
INGREDIENTS		
spaghetti sauce	1 (32-oz.) jar	1 (16-oz.) jar
BAKING DISH	deep 1-1/2-qt. casserole	deep 1-qt. casserole
TIME AT HIGH	9 to 10 minutes	5 minutes

Pour spaghetti sauce into a casserole, see size in chart above. Cover. Microwave at full power (HIGH) for time in chart above or until heated through, stirring once.

Breads, Grains, Pasta & Sandwiches

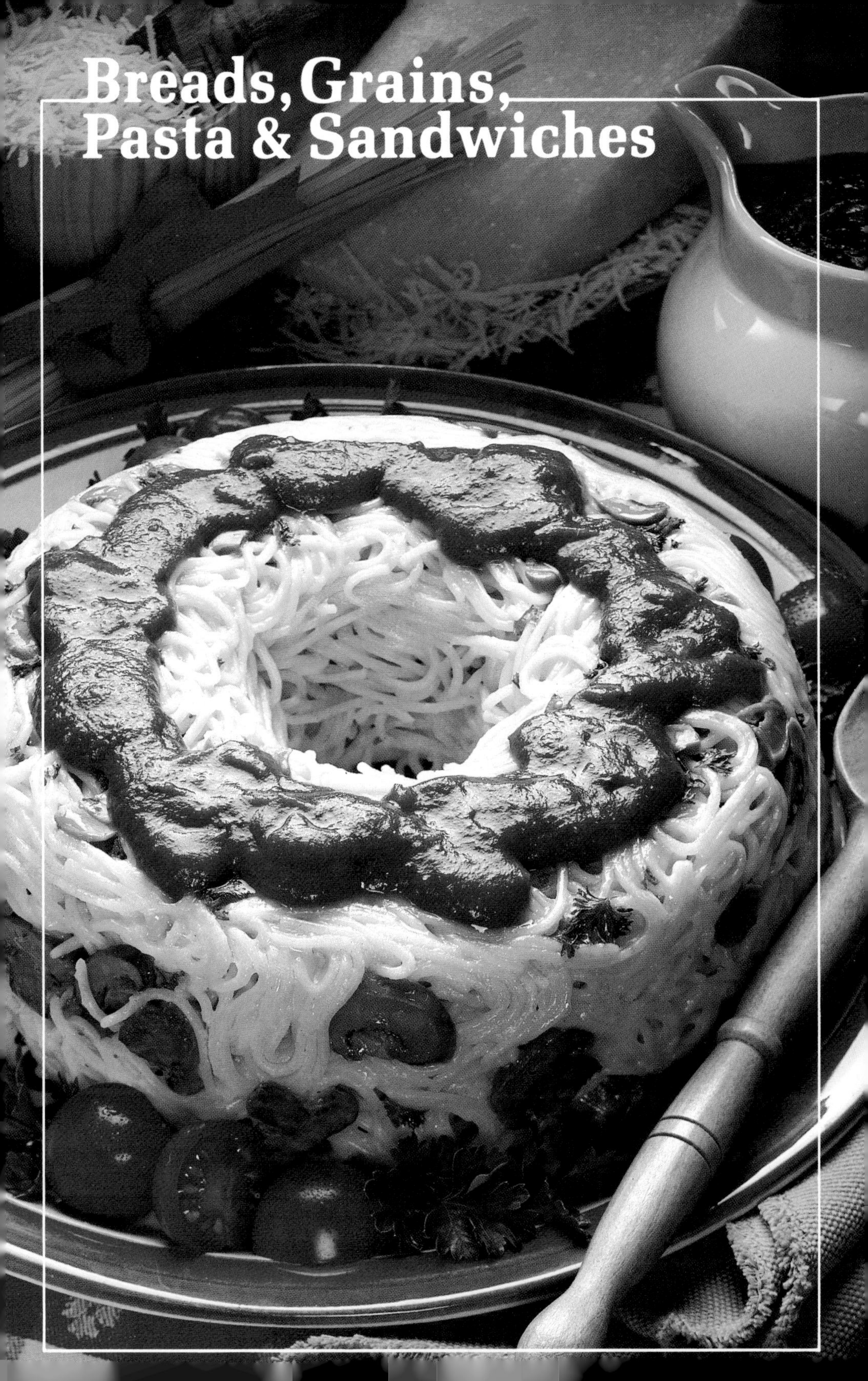

Breads, Grains, Pasta & Sandwiches

For lunch on the run, a quick, hot sandwich is a tasty solution. Try Crab Sandwiches Supreme or Snacker's Pizza for something deliciously different! Cereal can be mixed, cooked and eaten in one bowl when you use the microwave. That makes the breakfast clean-up a snap!

Q. What are the advantages of cooking breads and grains in the microwave?

A. Convenience breads defrost and heat in a matter of minutes. Keep a variety of breads and rolls on hand for sandwiches and use the microwave to defrost only the number of slices or rolls needed. You can cook and eat hot cereals right in the heat-proof serving bowls.

Q. What are the disadvantages of cooking breads and grains in the microwave?

A. Compared with conventionally baked bread, yeast breads baked in the microwave are pale, low in volume and tough. Quick breads end up pale and raise and cook unevenly. Microwaved breads do not brown, but this can be partially overcome by using toppings, frostings and dark flours. It is easy to overcook breads in the microwave. This results in a dry, tough and hard product. Although rice and pasta do not cook any faster in the microwave, they can be cooked successfully.

Q. Which breads or grains do not cook satisfactorily in the microwave?

A. Yeast breads, homemade pizza with yeast crust, refrigerated rolls, baking-powder biscuits and quick-bread loaves are much better when baked conventionally.

Q. How do you know when breads and grains are done?

A. As in conventional baking, a wooden pick inserted in the center of a quick bread, muffin or coffeecake should come out clean. Hot cereal, rice and pasta should be cooked until tender.

Q. How long do you reheat breads and grains in the microwave?

A. Follow the instructions given in this chapter for reheating rice, noodles and breads. Reheat breads on a white paper towel so the bottom won't get soggy. You can reheat breads and rolls in a straw basket if the basket has no metal parts. Anything sugary, such as raisins, jelly filling or frosting, will become hot very quickly. Baked breads, rolls and sandwiches should be heated only until warm. If they are heated beyond this point in the microwave, they will become tough and hard.

Q. What about cooking convenience breads and grains in the microwave?

A. Directions for frozen convenience breads and dough, rice mixes and hot cereal mixes are given in this chapter. Frozen rice and pasta have microwave cooking directions on the package as do many of the dry noodle mixes.

Q. How do you defrost breads in the microwave?

A. This varies with the size and number of items being defrosted. Full directions are given in this chapter.

Q. Are any special utensils needed for cooking breads and grains in the microwave?

A. It's handy to have a plastic or ceramic microwave muffin dish, but several custard cups will do. Large microwave baking sheets or pizza plates are useful for heating several sandwiches at once.

Quick Breads

There are only two quick-bread recipes in this book because such foods have better quality and taste when they are baked conventionally.

Quick-bread recipes are not easily adapted to cook in the microwave. They cook unevenly and end up pale-looking. Even when the baking dish is given a quarter turn every 2 minutes, quick-bread loaves raise unevenly.

Although some baking-mix packages include microwave instructions, do not expect totally satisfactory results.

Yeast Breads

There are no yeast-bread recipes in this book. Compared with conventionally baked bread, yeast breads baked in the microwave are pale, low in volume and tough. Frozen breads may stick to baking dishes.

The microwave can save you some time during bread making. For example, it is handy to microwave the milk-and-butter mixture to 120F (50C) before beating it into the flour-yeast mixture:

> For 2/3 cup milk and 1/4 cup butter or margarine, microwave at full power (HIGH) about 1 minute or until temperature of liquid registers 120F (50C) on a microwave thermometer. For 1-1/3 cups milk and 1/2 cup butter or margarine, microwave at full power (HIGH) 1-1/2 minutes or until liquid reaches 120F (50C). If you have a microwave temperature probe, this is an ideal time to use it. Set the end cooking temperature for 120F (50C). Stir the milk mixture a few times during heating.

RAISING YEAST DOUGH IN THE MICROWAVE

Expect only *marginal to moderate* success when you raise yeast dough in the microwave. After the dough rises, there is almost no additional rising during baking in a conventional oven. This causes heavy loaves with poor volume and a doughy, dense and uneven texture with dry spots throughout.

To raise dough in a bowl: Place dough in a greased bowl, turning over once to grease surface of dough. Place the bowl in a 12" x 7" baking dish. Pour 2 cups hot water around bowl in dish. Microwave at 10% (LOW) 15 minutes or until dough has doubled in bulk. To test if dough is ready to punch down, press your finger gently in the center. If the indentation remains and an air bubble forms to the side, it is ready.

To raise loaves of dough or rolls: Place shaped dough in greased loaf dishes set in or across a 12" x 7" baking dish, so the loaf dishes rest on the sides of the baking dish. Add 2 cups hot water to baking dish. Or, shape dough into rolls and place rolls in greased custard cups or microwave muffin pans set in or across a baking dish of hot water. Microwave at 10% (LOW) 15 minutes or until doubled in bulk.

To raise loaves of refrigerated dough or refrigerated rolls: Prepare dough as above. Microwave at 10% (LOW) 15 minutes, then leave dough in closed microwave with power off, 20 to 30 minutes or until doubled in bulk.

To raise frozen bread dough: Frozen bread dough varies in keeping quality and this affects the final product. Poor dough quality is made worse when the dough is raised in a microwave. To raise frozen bread dough in a microwave, place a loaf of frozen dough in a greased loaf dish. Position on a microwave rack set across a 2-quart casserole. Add 4 cups boiling water to the casserole. Microwave at 10% (LOW) 60 to 90 minutes or until dough has doubled in bulk. Give loaf a quarter turn every 15 minutes. During rising time, let rest several 15-minute periods with no microwave power.

Strawberry-Jam Kuchen

SERVINGS	6 to 8
INGREDIENTS	
Streusel Topping, see below	1 cup
packaged biscuit mix	2 cups
granulated sugar	2 tablespoons
egg	1
milk	2/3 cup
strawberry jam	1/2 cup
BAKING DISH	round, 8-inch baking dish
TIME AT 30%	7 minutes
TIME AT HIGH	3 minutes

Prepare Streusel Topping. Grease bottom of a round, 8-inch baking dish. In a medium bowl, combine biscuit mix, granulated sugar, egg and milk; mix well. Beat vigorously by hand 30 seconds. Spread batter in greased baking dish. Spoon jam in dollops over batter. Swirl through with a knife to marble. Sprinkle 1 cup Streusel Topping over batter. Microwave, uncovered, at 30% (MEDIUM LOW) 7 minutes, giving dish a half turn once. Microwave at full power (HIGH) 3 minutes or until a wooden pick inserted in center of cake comes out clean. Give dish a half turn once during cooking time at full power (HIGH). Cool cake on flat counter 15 minutes. Cut cake in wedges while warm. Serve sprinkled with powdered sugar and garnished with fresh strawberries, if desired.

Streusel Topping

YIELD	2-3/4 cups
INGREDIENTS	
all-purpose flour	1 cup
granulated sugar	1/2 cup
packed brown sugar	1/2 cup
ground cinnamon	2 teaspoons
butter or margarine	6 tablespoons
egg yolk	1

In a medium bowl, mix flour, granulated sugar, brown sugar and cinnamon. With a pastry blender or 2 knives, cut in butter or margarine and egg yolk until crumbly. Use as topping for Strawberry-Jam Kuchen or muffins. Cover and refrigerate leftover topping.

Frozen Coffeecakes in Foil Pans

COFFEECAKE	WEIGHT	TIME AT 30%	STANDING TIME
frozen round cake	11-1/2 oz.	5 to 5-1/2 minutes	1 to 2 minutes
frozen pull-apart rolls (9 rolls)	8-1/4 oz.	3-1/2 to 4 minutes	1 to 2 minutes
frozen Danish rolls (6 rolls)	7-3/4 oz.	3 to 3-1/2 minutes	1 to 2 minutes

Remove cover from foil pan or remove foil pan from carton. Microwave at 30% (MEDIUM LOW) for time in chart above or until warmed, giving foil pan a half turn once. Let stand 1 to 2 minutes.

How to Make Strawberry-Jam Kuchen

Spread batter in a round, 8-inch baking dish. Spoon the strawberry jam over the top of the batter. Then, with a knife, swirl through the batter to marble the jam.

For the Streusel Topping, use a pastry blender or 2 knives to cut the butter or margarine into the flour, sugar and cinnamon mixture. The topping should resemble fine crumbs.

Sprinkle the Streusel Topping evenly over the top of the batter. Refrigerate the remaining topping to use on muffins, fruit crisps or apple pie.

Garnish the cooled cake with fresh strawberries and powdered sugar. Cut in wedges and serve with hot coffee or tea.

Make-Ahead Granola-Applesauce Muffins

YIELD	60 muffins	30 muffins
INGREDIENTS		
lemon juice	1 tablespoon	2 teaspoons
milk	1-1/2 cups	3/4 cup
water	1 cup	1/2 cup
granola with fruits and nuts	3 cups	1-1/2 cups
applesauce	1 (8-oz.) can (1 cup)	1/2 cup
vegetable oil	1/2 cup	1/4 cup
eggs, beaten	2	1
all-purpose flour	2-1/2 cups	1-1/4 cups
sugar	1 cup	1/2 cup
baking powder	2 teaspoons	1 teaspoon
baking soda	2 teaspoons	1 teaspoon
salt	1 teaspoon	1/2 teaspoon
ground cinnamon	2 teaspoons	1 teaspoon
ground nutmeg	1 teaspoon	1/2 teaspoon
BOWL	4-qt. bowl	2-qt. bowl
TIME AT HIGH (water)	2-1/2 to 3 minutes	1-1/2 to 2 minutes
TIME AT HIGH (muffins)	see baking chart below	

Stir lemon juice into milk; set aside. Place water in a bowl, see size in chart above. Microwave at full power (HIGH) for time in chart above or until boiling. Sprinkle granola into boiling water. Stir until all is moistened. Stir in milk mixture, applesauce, oil and eggs; mix well. In a medium bowl, thoroughly stir together flour, sugar, baking powder, baking soda, salt, cinnamon and nutmeg. Add flour mixture to granola mixture. Stir just until moistened. Cover and refrigerate up to 3 weeks. Microwave muffins as needed.

To microwave muffins: Spoon 2 tablespoons granola batter into paper bake cups placed in a microwave muffin pan or in 5-ounce custard cups. Arrange the custard cups in a ring in the microwave oven. Microwave at full power (HIGH) for time in chart below or until a wooden pick inserted in center comes out clean. Cool on a rack. If desired, brush warm muffins with melted butter or margarine and then sprinkle with a mixture of cinnamon, sugar and grated orange peel.

Variation
Streusel-Topped Muffins: Sprinkle 2 teaspoons Streusel Topping, page 436, over each unbaked muffin. Bake as directed below.

SERVINGS	6 muffins	4 muffins	2 muffins	1 muffin
TIME AT HIGH	2-1/2 to 3 minutes	1 minute, 40 seconds	55 seconds	40 seconds

Adapting Quick Bread Recipes for Microwave Oven

● Quick breads are not easily adapted for microwave cooking, see page 435. The breads are pale and cook unevenly. Muffins with spices or dark flours look the most attractive. Use the cooking times for the Make-Ahead Granola-Applesauce Muffins, above, as a guideline. The appearance of muffins is improved if they are sprinkled with a topping before or after cooking.

● Even when the baking dish is given a quarter turn every 2 minutes, quick-bread loaves raise unevenly. Microwave directions for quick-bread mixes are available from some manufacturers. Results are not totally satisfactory.

438   Muffins

How to Make Granola-Applesauce Muffins

Sprinkle the granola into the boiling water, then stir until moistened. Stir in applesauce, milk mixture, oil, eggs, flour, sugar, leavening and spices. Cover and refrigerate for up to 3 weeks.

To bake muffins, spoon 2 tablespoonfuls of batter into each paper bake cup set in custard cups or a microwave muffin pan. The cups should be only half full.

Microwave the muffins at full power (HIGH). To test the muffins for doneness, a wooden pick should come out clean, not with batter clinging to it as shown.

To serve, brush the warm muffins with melted butter or margarine, then sprinkle with a mixture of sugar, ground cinnamon and grated orange peel. Serve with mugs of hot cider.

Defrosting & Heating Breads

TYPE OF BREAD	TIME AT HIGH TO WARM ROOM-TEMPERATURE BREAD	TIME AT HIGH TO DEFROST AND WARM FROZEN BREAD
Bagels and English muffins		
1 whole	15 seconds	25 seconds
2 whole	20 to 25 seconds	40 seconds
3 whole	30 to 35 seconds	55 seconds
French bread (1-lb. loaf)		
1 loaf	30 seconds	75 seconds
1/2 loaf	20 seconds	45 seconds
1/4 loaf	10 seconds	20 seconds
Muffins (in bake cups)		
1 muffin	10 seconds	15 seconds
2 muffins	15 seconds	25 seconds
4 muffins	20 seconds	45 seconds
Pancakes (4-inch diameter)		
3 stacked pancakes		75 seconds
2 stacks of 3 pancakes		2 minutes
Rolls (dinner rolls, sweet rolls, doughnuts, hamburger buns)		
1 roll	5 seconds	15 seconds
2 rolls	10 seconds	25 seconds
4 rolls	15 seconds	35 to 40 seconds

Place unsliced bread, bagels, muffins, pancakes or rolls on a paper-towel-lined plate. If using sliced bread, pita bread or tortillas, stack them and wrap in paper towel. Microwave at full power (HIGH) for time in chart or until warm, giving whole loaves a half turn once. Let stand 1 minute for rolls, 2 minutes for bread loaves. Tortillas do not need any standing time. Breads should be heated only until warm and not piping hot. **If breads are overheated in the microwave oven, they become tough, dry and hard.**

Defrosting Frozen Breads

TYPE OF BREAD	TIME AT HIGH TO DEFROST FROZEN BREAD
Bread loaves (1 lb.)	
1 loaf	1-1/2 minutes
1/2 loaf	50 seconds
Bread slices (from 1-lb. loaf)	
2 slices, stacked	10 seconds
4 slices, stacked	15 seconds
6 slices, stacked	25 seconds
Pita bread (6-inch diameter)	
1 pita bread	15 seconds
2 pita breads, stacked	20 seconds
3 pita breads, stacked	25 seconds
Tortillas (corn or flour)	
2 tortillas, stacked	15 seconds
4 tortillas, stacked	25 seconds
6 tortillas, stacked	30 to 35 seconds

Microwave until defrosted but not warm, using directions above.

Frozen Waffles or French Toast

SERVINGS	3 or 4	2
INGREDIENTS frozen waffles OR frozen French toast	3 squares 4 slices	2 squares 2 slices
BROWNING SKILLET	10-inch microwave browning skillet	10-inch microwave browning skillet
TIME AT HIGH (preheat skillet)	2 minutes	2 minutes
TIME AT HIGH (first side)	1 minute	1 minute
TIME AT HIGH (second side)	30 to 45 seconds	30 seconds

Preheat a 10-inch browning skillet, uncovered, at microwave full power (HIGH) 2 minutes. Quickly place waffles or French toast in hot browning skillet. Microwave at full power (HIGH) 1 minute. Turn waffles or French toast over. Microwave at full power (HIGH) for time in chart above or until heated through.

Heating Syrup

YIELD	2 cups	1 cup	1/2 cup
INGREDIENTS chilled syrup	2 cups	1 cup	1/2 cup
GLASS MEASURING CUP	4-cup	2-cup	1-cup
TIME AT HIGH	3-1/2 minutes	2-1/2 minutes	1-1/2 minutes

Pour chilled syrup into a glass measuring cup, see size in chart above. Do not heat in the syrup bottle. Microwave at full power (HIGH) for time in chart above or until hot, 180F (80C). If the syrup is already at room temperature, reduce the heating times above by 30 to 45 seconds.

Softening Butter or Margarine

YIELD	1 cup	1/2 cup	1/4 cup
INGREDIENTS butter or margarine	1 cup	1/2 cup	1/4 cup
BAKING DISH	small bowl	small bowl	small bowl
TIME AT 10%	2 minutes	1-1/4 minutes	45 seconds

Unwrap butter or margarine and place in a small bowl. Microwave at 10% (LOW) for time in chart above or until softened.

Creamy Fruited Bagels

SERVINGS	6	3
INGREDIENTS		
cream cheese	1 (3-oz.) pkg.	1/2 (3-oz.) pkg.
crushed pineapple, well-drained	1/3 cup	3 tablespoons
chopped green pepper	2 tablespoons	1 tablespoon
chopped pecans	2 tablespoons	1 tablespoon
minced green onion	2 teaspoons	1 teaspoon
bagels, split	6 halves	3 halves
BOWL	medium bowl	medium bowl
BAKING DISH	paper-towel-lined microwave pizza plate	paper-towel-lined dinner plate
TIME AT 10%	1 minute	45 seconds
TIME AT HIGH	1-1/4 minutes	30 to 45 seconds

Unwrap cream cheese and place in a medium bowl. Microwave at 10% (LOW) for time in chart above or until softened. Add crushed pineapple, green pepper, pecans and green onion; mix well. Spread on cut surfaces of bagels. Place on a paper-towel-lined plate, see size in chart above. Microwave at full power (HIGH) for time in chart above or until cheese mixture is warmed.

Sticky Rolls

SERVINGS	8 to 12
INGREDIENTS	
butter or margarine	3 tablespoons
spice cake mix	1 cup
corn syrup	3 tablespoons
chopped pecans	1/2 cup
bakery pan rolls	1 (8-inch square) pan, 12 rolls (1 lb.)
BAKING DISH	8-inch square baking dish
TIME AT HIGH (butter)	45 seconds
TIME AT HIGH (rolls)	4 minutes

Place butter or margarine in an 8-inch square baking dish. Microwave at full power (HIGH) 45 seconds or until butter or margarine has melted. Stir in dry cake mix and corn syrup. Spread evenly in dish. Sprinkle with pecans. Place rolls right side up on pecan mixture. Microwave at full power (HIGH) 4 minutes or until syrup mixture is melted. Immediately invert baking dish onto a plate. Let dish remain over rolls a few minutes. Remove dish and spoon extra topping from dish over rolls.

Herbed French Loaf

SERVINGS	8 to 12	4 to 6
INGREDIENTS		
French bread	1 (1-lb.) loaf	1 (8-oz.) loaf
butter or margarine	3/4 cup	1/2 cup
dried leaf oregano	1 tablespoon	2 teaspoons
dried leaf basil	1 tablespoon	2 teaspoons
celery seed	1-1/2 teaspoons	1 teaspoon
onion powder	3/4 teaspoon	1/2 teaspoon
sesame seeds	1 teaspoon	1/2 teaspoon
BAKING DISH	paper-towel-lined microwave pizza plate	paper-towel-lined microwave pizza plate
TIME AT 10%	2 to 2-1/4 minutes	1-1/2 to 2 minutes
TIME AT HIGH	2 to 2-1/2 minutes	1 to 1-1/2 minutes

Cut French bread in 1-inch slices, cutting to, but not quite through, bottom of loaf. If using 1-pound loaf, cut it in half crosswise, then place half loaves side by side on pizza plate to heat. In a small bowl, microwave butter or margarine at 10% (LOW) for time in chart above or until softened. Stir in oregano, basil, celery seed and onion powder. Spread between bread slices and over top of loaf. Sprinkle with sesame seeds. Place loaf on paper-towel-lined pizza plate. Microwave at full power (HIGH) for time in chart above or until warm.

Nacho French Loaf

SERVINGS	8	4
INGREDIENTS		
butter or margarine, softened	1/2 cup	1/4 cup
taco seasoning mix	2 tablespoons (1/2 envelope)	1 tablespoon (1/4 envelope)
French bread, cut in half lengthwise	1 (8-oz.) loaf	1/2 (8-oz.) loaf
crushed corn chips	1 cup	1/2 cup
chopped green chilies, drained	1 (4-oz.) can	1/2 (4-oz.) can
shredded Cheddar cheese	1-1/2 cups (6-oz.)	3/4 cup (3 oz.)
BAKING DISH	paper-towel-lined microwave pizza plate	paper-towel-lined microwave pizza plate
TIME AT HIGH	2-1/2 to 3 minutes	1-1/2 minutes

In a small bowl, beat butter or margarine and taco seasoning mix until blended. Spread on cut side of bread. Sprinkle with crushed corn chips, chilies and cheese. Place on a paper-towel-lined pizza plate. Microwave at full power (HIGH) for time in chart above or until cheese melts, giving plate a half turn once.

ABC Sandwiches

SERVINGS	8	4
INGREDIENTS		
chopped blanched almonds	1/2 cup	1/4 cup
bacon, cooked, crumbled	8 slices	4 slices
shredded sharp Cheddar cheese	1-1/2 cups (6-oz.)	3/4 cup (3-oz.)
mayonnaise or mayonnaise-style dressing	1/2 cup	1/4 cup
prepared horseradish	1 tablespoon	1-1/2 teaspoons
pepper	1/8 teaspoon	dash
French bread, cut in 1-inch slices	8 slices	4 slices
PIE PLATE	9-inch pie plate	7-inch pie plate
BAKING DISH	paper-towel-lined microwave pizza plate	paper-towel-lined dinner plate
TIME AT HIGH (almonds)	2 to 2-1/4 minutes	1-1/2 to 1-3/4 minutes
TIME AT HIGH (sandwiches)	3 minutes	1-1/2 minutes

Place almonds in a pie plate, see size in chart above. Microwave at full power (HIGH) for time in chart above or until lightly toasted. In a medium bowl, combine bacon, cheese, mayonnaise, horseradish, pepper and toasted almonds. Mix well. Spread cheese mixture on bread slices. Place on a paper-towel-lined plate, see size in chart above. Microwave at full power (HIGH) for time in chart above or until cheese melts, giving dish a half turn once.

Vegetarian Pita Sandwiches

SERVINGS	4	2
INGREDIENTS		
alfalfa sprouts	1/2 cup	1/4 cup
shredded carrot	1/2 cup	1/4 cup
chopped zucchini or cucumber	1/2 cup	1/4 cup
sunflower kernels	1/4 cup	2 tablespoons
creamy onion salad dressing	2 tablespoons	1 tablespoon
Cheddar cheese slices	4	2
pita bread, about 6 inches in diameter, halved crosswise	2	1
brick cheese slices	4	2
BAKING DISH	paper-towel-lined plate	paper-towel-lined plate
TIME AT HIGH	1-3/4 to 2 minutes	45 to 60 seconds

In a small bowl, combine alfalfa sprouts, carrot, zucchini or cucumber, sunflower kernels and onion dressing. Mix well. Place Cheddar cheese slices inside pita-bread pockets, resting on flatter side of pocket. Top with sprout mixture, then brick cheese slices. Place sandwiches on a paper-towel-lined plate. Microwave at full power (HIGH) for time in chart above or until cheese begins to melt.

Taco Hot Dogs

SERVINGS	4	2
INGREDIENTS		
bottled taco sauce	2 tablespoons	1 tablespoon
grated Cheddar cheese	1/2 cup (2 oz.)	1/4 cup (1 oz.)
chopped onion	2 tablespoons	1 tablespoon
chopped, seeded canned green chilies	2 tablespoons	1 tablespoon
hot dogs	4	2
taco shells	4	2
shredded lettuce		
marinated garbanzo beans, drained		
frozen guacamole dip, thawed		
BAKING DISH	10" x 6" baking dish	8" x 4" loaf dish
TIME AT HIGH	1-1/2 to 2 minutes	1 to 1-1/4 minutes

In medium bowl, combine taco sauce, cheese, onion and chilies. Slit the hot dogs lengthwise, but not quite through. Stuff with three-fourths of cheese mixture. Place in taco shells. Stand stuffed taco shells upright in a baking dish or loaf dish, see size in chart above. If needed, support shells with crumpled waxed paper. Spoon remaining cheese mixture over top. Microwave at full power (HIGH) for time in chart above or until heated through. To serve, top with shredded lettuce, garbanzo beans and guacamole dip.

Variation

Beef Tacos: For 4 servings, crumble 8 ounces ground beef into a 1-quart casserole. Cover loosely with waxed paper. Microwave at full power (HIGH) 4 minutes or until meat is browned, stirring once. Drain well. Stir in 1/4 cup taco sauce, 1/2 cup Cheddar cheese, 2 tablespoons chopped onion and 2 tablespoons chopped green chilies. Spoon into 4 taco shells. Microwave and serve as above.

For 2 servings, use 4 ounces ground beef in a 1-quart casserole. Microwave beef at full power (HIGH) 3 minutes. Use 2 tablespoons taco sauce and other amounts shown above for 2 servings. Microwave and serve as above.

Adapting Sandwich Recipes for Microwave Oven

- Microwave sandwiches on a paper-towel-lined plate so the bread will not get soggy. Melba toast, zwieback or rusks work well as bases for sandwiches.

- Microwave the sandwiches at full power (HIGH) only until warm, not hot. Overheating will cause the bread to become tough and dry.

- For extra wet fillings like sloppy joes, microwave the filling separately until hot, then microwave the filling and bun together until the bun is warm.

- Grilled microwave sandwiches require a microwave browning skillet. Use the recipe for Grilled Reuben Sandwiches, opposite, as a guideline. Use very firm-textured bread. Make sure any juicy filling ingredients are separated from the bread by cheese or meat.

- For cooking hot dogs and hamburgers, see pages 136 and 144.

- Pita bread makes an ideal microwave sandwich. Use the directions for Deli Pita Sandwiches on page 450 as a guideline.

How to Make Taco Hot Dogs

Cut slits in hot dogs not quite through to the other side. Spoon a mixture of taco sauce, chopped onion, grated Cheddar cheese and chopped green chilies into the hot dogs.

Microwave the hot dogs in pre-shaped taco shells. Use a piece of crumpled waxed paper in the baking dish to hold the shells upright. Top the cooked hot dogs with shredded lettuce, marinated garbanzo beans and guacamole.

Grilled Reuben Sandwiches

SERVINGS	2	1
INGREDIENTS		
rye bread	4 slices	2 slices
butter or margarine, softened	2 tablespoons	1 tablespoon
sauerkraut, drained, snipped	2/3 cup	1/3 cup
sliced corned beef	6 oz.	3 oz.
Thousand Island dressing	2 tablespoons	1 tablespoon
Swiss cheese slices	2 (2 oz.)	1 (1 oz.)
BROWNING SKILLET	10-inch microwave browning skillet	10-inch microwave browning skillet
TIME AT HIGH (preheat skillet)	4 minutes	4 minutes
TIME AT HIGH (first side)	30 seconds	30 seconds
TIME AT HIGH (second side)	30 to 60 seconds	30 to 60 seconds

Spread both sides of bread with butter or margarine. Place half the slices on a plate. Rinse sauerkraut, if desired. Layer in order on bread slices: corned beef, sauerkraut, Thousand Island dressing, cheese and remaining bread slices. Preheat browning skillet, uncovered, at microwave full power (HIGH) 4 minutes. Quickly place sandwiches in browning skillet. Microwave at full power (HIGH) 30 seconds. Turn sandwiches over. Microwave at full power (HIGH) 30 to 60 seconds or until toasted and centers are hot.

Crab Sandwiches Supreme

SERVINGS	6	3
INGREDIENTS		
Alaskan king crab, drained, flaked	1 (7-1/2-oz.) can	1/2 (7-1/2-oz.) can
diced celery	1/4 cup	2 tablespoons
semi-soft natural cheese with garlic and herbs	1/2 (4-oz.) carton (1/4 cup)	1/4 (4-oz.) carton (2 tablespoons)
minced green onion	2 tablespoons	1 tablespoon
grated Parmesan cheese	2 tablespoons	1 tablespoon
lemon juice	2 tablespoons	1 tablespoon
capers, drained	2 tablespoons	1 tablespoon
mayonnaise or mayonnaise-style salad dressing	2 tablespoons	1 tablespoon
pepper	dash	dash
hamburger buns, split	6	3
BAKING DISH	microwave pizza plate or tray	dinner plate or microwave pizza plate
TIME AT HIGH	2-3/4 minutes	1-1/2 minutes

In a medium bowl, combine crab, celery, semi-soft cheese, green onion, Parmesan cheese, lemon juice, capers, mayonnaise and pepper. Mix well. Spread mixture on hamburger buns using about 1/4 cup mixture for each. Replace tops of buns; wrap each in paper towel. Place wrapped buns on a plate, see size in chart above. Microwave at full power (HIGH) for time in chart above or until heated through, giving plate a half turn once.

Hawaiian Ham & Swiss Sandwiches

SERVINGS	4	2
INGREDIENTS		
rye toast	4 slices	2 slices
sliced ham	4 slices	2 slices
pineapple slices	4 slices	2 slices
shredded Swiss cheese	1 cup (4 oz.)	1/2 cup (2 oz.)
snipped parsley	4 teaspoons	2 teaspoons
mayonnaise or mayonnaise-style salad dressing	1/4 cup	2 tablespoons
prepared mustard	1 teaspoon	1/2 teaspoon
prepared horseradish	1 teaspoon	1/2 teaspoon
paprika	to garnish	to garnish
BAKING DISH	paper-towel-lined 12" x 7" baking dish	paper-towel-lined 8-inch square baking dish
TIME AT HIGH	2-1/2 to 3 minutes	2 to 2-1/2 minutes

Place toast in a paper-towel-lined baking dish, see size in chart above. Top each slice of toast with a ham slice, then a pineapple slice. In a small bowl, combine shredded cheese, parsley, mayonnaise, mustard and horseradish. Mix well. Spoon cheese mixture over pineapple. Sprinkle with paprika. Microwave at full power (HIGH) for time in chart above or until cheese melts and sandwiches are warm.

How to Make Snacker's Pizza

Place English-muffin halves on a paper-towel-lined plate to absorb moisture during microwaving. Spoon cooked ground beef, sausage or pepperoni on top of muffins. Add a few spoonfuls of pizza sauce, mozzarella cheese, Parmesan cheese and Italian seasoning.

Serve the piping-hot pizza snacks with mugs of frosty cold beer or another favorite beverage. Vary the snacks by using leftover chopped meats, luncheon meat or salami. Try using taco sauce or spaghetti sauce and various kinds of shredded cheese.

Snacker's Pizza

SERVINGS	3	2	1
INGREDIENTS			
English muffins	3	2	1
cooked ground beef or sausage, or sliced pepperoni			
pizza sauce			
shredded mozzarella cheese			
grated Parmesan cheese			
dried leaf Italian herbs			
BAKING DISH	paper-towel-lined microwave pizza plate	paper-towel-lined dinner plate	paper-towel-lined dinner plate
TIME AT HIGH	3-1/2 minutes	2-1/2 minutes	1-1/2 minutes

Split muffins with a fork. Place on a paper-towel-lined plate, see size in chart above. Top each half with meat of your choice. Add a spoonful or two of pizza sauce. Top generously with mozzarella cheese. Sprinkle with Parmesan cheese and a dash of Italian herbs. Microwave at full power (HIGH) for time in chart above or until heated through and cheese is melted.

Swiss Club Sandwiches

SERVINGS	4	2
INGREDIENTS		
diced cooked chicken	1 cup	1/2 cup
chopped celery	1/4 cup	2 tablespoons
sliced pimiento-stuffed olives	1/4 cup	2 tablespoons
chopped green onion	1 tablespoon	2 teaspoons
crumbled bleu cheese	2 tablespoons	1 tablespoon
mayonnaise or mayonnaise-style salad dressing	1/4 cup	2 tablespoons
plain toast zwieback, 3-1/2 x 1-1/2 inches	8 slices	4 slices
OR		
plain rusks, 3-1/2 inches in diameter	4	2
tomato slices	4	2
hot cooked asparagus spears, well-drained	12 spears	6 spears
Swiss cheese slices, halved diagonally	2	1
crisp-cooked bacon	6 slices	3 slices
BAKING DISH	12" x 7" baking dish	8-inch square baking dish
TIME AT HIGH	3-1/2 to 4 minutes	2 to 3 minutes

In a medium bowl, combine chicken, celery, olives, green onion, bleu cheese, and mayonnaise. Mix gently. Arrange 2 zwieback or 1 rusk for each serving in a baking dish, see size in chart above. Spoon chicken mixture onto zwieback or rusks. Top each with tomato slice, asparagus spears and Swiss cheese slice. Crumble bacon over each serving. Microwave at full power (HIGH) for time in chart above or until heated through.

Deli Pita Sandwiches

SERVINGS	4	2
INGREDIENTS		
pita bread, about 6 inches in diameter, halved crosswise	2	1
thin ham slices	4 (about 4 oz.)	2 (about 2 oz.)
salami	4 slices	2 slices
Cheddar cheese	4 slices (about 3 oz.)	2 slices (about 1-1/2 oz.)
thin tomato slices	8	4
cole slaw, drained	1 cup	1/2 cup
avocado slices	12 (1 avocado)	6 (1/2 avocado)
BAKING DISH	paper-towel-lined microwave pizza plate	paper-towel-lined dinner plate
TIME AT HIGH	5-1/2 to 6 minutes	2-1/2 to 3 minutes

In each pita-bread half, layer ham, salami, cheese and tomato. Top with a spoonful of cole slaw. Tuck in avocado slices. Place on a paper-towel-lined plate, see size in chart above. Microwave at full power (HIGH) for time in chart above or until heated through.

Swiss Club Sandwich

Quick-Cooking Rolled Oats

SERVINGS	4	2	1
INGREDIENTS			
hot water	3 cups	1-1/3 cups	2/3 cup
quick-cooking rolled oats	1-1/2 cups	2/3 cup	1/3 cup
salt	1/2 teaspoon	1/4 teaspoon	1/8 teaspoon
BAKING DISH	deep 2-qt. casserole	2 (16-oz.) cereal bowls	1 (16-oz.) cereal bowl
TIME AT HIGH	4-1/2 minutes	2-1/4 to 2-1/2 minutes	1 to 1-1/4 minutes

See directions for Whole-Wheat Cereal, below.

Instant Cream of Wheat

SERVINGS	4	2	1
INGREDIENTS			
hot water	2-3/4 cups	1-1/2 cups	3/4 cup
instant Cream of Wheat	2/3 cup	5 tablespoons	2-1/2 tablespoons
salt	1/2 teaspoon	1/4 teaspoon	1/8 teaspoon
BAKING DISH	deep 1-qt. casserole	2 (16-oz.) cereal bowls	1 (16-oz.) cereal bowl
TIME AT HIGH	5 to 5-1/2 minutes	3-3/4 minutes	2 minutes
STANDING TIME	1 minute	1 minute	1 minute

See directions for Whole-Wheat Cereal, below.

Whole-Wheat Cereal

SERVINGS	4	2	1
INGREDIENTS			
hot water	3 cups	1-1/2 cups	3/4 cup
instant granular whole-wheat cereal	1 cup	1/2 cup	1/4 cup
salt	1/2 teaspoon	1/4 teaspoon	1/8 teaspoon
BAKING DISH	deep 2-qt. casserole	2 (16-oz.) cereal bowls	1 (16-oz.) cereal bowl
TIME AT HIGH	9 to 10 minutes	7 to 7-1/2 minutes	3-1/2 to 4 minutes
STANDING TIME	1 minute	1 minute	1 minute

Measure hot water into a casserole or bowls, see size in chart. Stir in cereal and salt. Microwave at full power (HIGH) for time in chart or until water is nearly all absorbed. Stir well two or three times during cooking. Let stand 1 minute, if indicated in chart. Stir before serving.

How to Make Quick-Cooking Rolled Oats

Stir quick-cooking rolled oats and salt into hot water in cereal bowls. If you wish to add raisins to hot cereal, add 1 tablespoon more water and 1 tablespoon raisins to each bowl.

Stir the cereal several times during microwaving to prevent lumping. Serve with milk or cream, then top with a sprinkling of brown sugar and cinnamon or nutmeg.

Mix-in-a-Bowl Cereal

SERVINGS	2	1
INGREDIENTS		
mix-in-a-bowl cereal	2 (0.8- to 1.6-oz.) envelopes	1 (0.8- to 1.6-oz.) envelope
hot water	1 cup or 1-1/3 cups	1/2 cup or 2/3 cup
GLASS MEASURING CUP	2-cup	1-cup
TIME AT HIGH	2 to 2-1/2 minutes	1-1/2 to 1-3/4 minutes

Empty cereal into cereal bowls. Measure amount of hot water listed on cereal package into a glass measuring cup, see size in chart above. Microwave at full power (HIGH) for time in chart above or until boiling. Add to cereal; stir quickly until blended. For thinner cereal, use a little more water; for thicker cereal, use a little less water.

Tip

- Read labels carefully to select the appropriate type of hot cereal. Mix-in-a-bowl cereals usually come in individual serving packets and only require mixing with boiling water. Quick or instant hot cereals come in many versions. Look for cereals that only require a short cooking time.

Spanish Rice

SERVINGS	4 to 6	3 or 4
INGREDIENTS		
bacon	6 slices	4 slices
bacon drippings	1/4 cup	3 tablespoons
chopped onion	1/2 cup	1/3 cup
chopped green pepper	1/2 cup	1/3 cup
tomatoes, cut up	1 (28-oz.) can	1 (16-oz.) can
celery salt	1/2 teaspoon	1/4 teaspoon
long-cooking rice	3/4 cup	1/2 cup
shredded process American cheese	1/2 cup (2 oz.)	1/2 cup (2 oz.)
green-pepper rings	to garnish	to garnish
BAKING DISH (bacon)	12" x 7" baking dish with microwave rack	12" x 7" baking dish with microwave rack
BAKING DISH (rice mixture)	deep 2-qt. casserole	deep 1-1/2-qt. casserole
TIME AT HIGH (bacon)	4 to 5 minutes	3 to 4 minutes
TIME AT HIGH (onion, green pepper)	5 minutes	3 to 4 minutes
TIME AT HIGH (tomatoes added)	6 to 8 minutes	6 minutes
TIME AT 30%	25 to 30 minutes	25 to 30 minutes
TIME AT HIGH (cheese added)	1 minute	1 minute

Place bacon on a microwave rack in a 12" x 7" baking dish. Cover with white paper towel. Microwave at full power (HIGH) for time in chart above or until crisp. Measure bacon drippings into a casserole, see size in chart above. Crumble bacon; set aside. Add onion and green pepper to drippings in casserole. Microwave at full power (HIGH) for time in chart above or until tender, stirring once. Stir in tomatoes and celery salt. Cover. Microwave at full power (HIGH) for time in chart above or until boiling. Add rice. Stir until moistened. Cover. Microwave at 30% (MEDIUM LOW) 25 to 30 minutes or until rice is tender, stirring twice. Sprinkle bacon and cheese over mixture. Garnish with green-pepper rings. Microwave, uncovered, at full power (HIGH) 1 minute or until cheese is melted.

Boil-in-the-Bag Rice

SERVINGS	2 or 3 (2-1/3 cups)
INGREDIENTS	
hot water	4 cups
salt	1 teaspoon
boil-in-the-bag precooked rice	1 (3-1/2-oz.) pkg.
BAKING DISH	deep 2-qt. casserole
TIME AT HIGH (water)	6-1/2 to 7-1/2 minutes
TIME AT HIGH (rice)	15 minutes

In a 2-quart casserole, combine hot water and salt. Cover. Microwave at full power (HIGH) 6-1/2 to 7-1/2 minutes or until boiling. Remove cover and add bag of rice to boiling water. Microwave, uncovered, at full power (HIGH) 15 minutes or until rice is tender. Open bag and empty rice into a serving dish. Fluff with a fork.

How to Make Spanish Rice

Add canned tomatoes and celery salt to cooked onions and pepper and microwave until boiling. Add long-cooking rice. Stir until moistened. Cover and microwave until tender.

Top the cooked rice with shredded cheese in a ring around the casserole edge. Garnish the center with green-pepper rings. Microwave for a short time to melt the cheese.

Long-Cooking Rice

SERVINGS	4 or 5 servings (4 cups)	2 or 3 servings (2 cups)
INGREDIENTS		
hot water	2-1/4 cups	1 cup + 2 tablespoons
butter or margarine	1 tablespoon	2 teaspoons
salt	1/4 teaspoon	1/8 teaspoon
long-cooking rice	1 cup	1/2 cup
BAKING DISH	deep 2-qt. casserole	deep 1-1/2-qt. casserole
TIME AT HIGH	4 to 5 minutes	2 minutes
TIME AT 30%	20 minutes	18 to 20 minutes
STANDING TIME	5 minutes	5 minutes

In a casserole, see size in chart above, combine hot water, butter or margarine and salt. Cover. Microwave at full power (HIGH) for time in chart above or until boiling. Stir in rice; cover. Microwave at 30% (MEDIUM LOW) for time in chart above or until tender, stirring once. Let stand, covered, 5 minutes. Fluff with a fork.

Variation
Converted Rice: Follow the directions above, but use 2-1/2 cups hot water for the large recipe and 1-1/4 cups hot water for the small recipe.

Carnival Fried Rice

SERVINGS	5 or 6	2 or 3
INGREDIENTS		
butter or margarine	1 tablespoon	2 teaspoons
eggs, beaten	2	1
butter or margarine	2 tablespoons	1 tablespoon
chopped red pepper	1/4 cup	2 tablespoons
chopped green onion	1/4 cup	2 tablespoons
finely chopped gingerroot	1 teaspoon	1/2 teaspoon
garlic powder	1/4 teaspoon	1/8 teaspoon
cooked rice	3 cups	1-1/2 cups
frozen Chinese pea pods, thawed	1/2 (6-oz.) pkg.	1/4 (6-oz.) pkg.
sliced mushrooms, drained	1 (2-1/2-oz.) jar	1/2 (2-1/2-oz.) jar
fresh or drained, canned bean sprouts	1/2 cup	1/4 cup
dry sherry	2 tablespoons	1 tablespoon
soy sauce	2 tablespoons	1 tablespoon
parsley sprig	to garnish	to garnish
BAKING DISH (eggs)	9-inch pie plate	1-qt. casserole
BAKING DISH (rice)	1-1/2-qt. casserole	1-qt. casserole
TIME AT HIGH (butter)	30 seconds	30 seconds
TIME AT HIGH (eggs)	1-1/2 to 2 minutes	1 to 1-1/4 minutes
STANDING TIME (eggs)	5 minutes	5 minutes
TIME AT HIGH (pepper, onion)	2-1/2 to 3 minutes	2 to 2-1/2 minutes
TIME AT HIGH (rice added)	6 to 8 minutes	4 to 4-1/2 minutes

Place first amount of butter or margarine in a baking dish, see size in chart above. Microwave at full power (HIGH) 30 seconds or until melted. Add beaten eggs. Cover completely with plastic wrap; do not vent. Microwave at full power (HIGH) for time in chart above or until eggs are set. Let stand, covered, 5 minutes. Cut eggs into strips; set aside. Place second amount of butter or margarine, red pepper, green onion, gingerroot and garlic powder in a casserole, see size in chart above. Microwave at full power (HIGH) for time in chart above or until onion is tender. Stir in egg strips, rice, pea pods, mushrooms and bean sprouts. Toss until mixed well. Stir in sherry and soy sauce. Cover. Microwave at full power (HIGH) for time in chart above or until heated through, stirring once. Garnish with parsley. Serve with additional soy sauce, if desired.

Reheating Refrigerated Rice

To chill: Spoon cooled rice into a refrigerator container. Cover and refrigerate.

To reheat: Spoon 2 cups rice and 2 tablespoons water into a 1-quart casserole. Cover and microwave at 70% (MEDIUM HIGH) 3 to 3-1/2 minutes or until hot. Reheat 1 cup rice with 1 tablespoon water in a 1-1/2-cup casserole at 70% (MEDIUM HIGH) 2 to 2-1/2 minutes. Fluff with a fork.

Minute Rice

SERVINGS	4 or 5 (4 cups)	2 or 3 (2 cups)	1 (1 cup)
INGREDIENTS			
hot water	2 cups	1 cup	1/2 cup
salt	1/2 teaspoon	1/4 teaspoon	dash
butter or margarine	1 tablespoon	2 teaspoons	1 teaspoon
Minute rice	2 cups	1 cup	1/2 cup
BAKING DISH	1-1/2-qt. casserole	1-qt. casserole	2-cup casserole
TIME AT HIGH	9 to 10 minutes	6 to 7 minutes	3 to 4 minutes
STANDING TIME	2 to 3 minutes	2 to 3 minutes	2 to 3 minutes

In a casserole, see size in chart above, combine hot water, salt, butter or margarine and rice. Mix well. Cover. Microwave at full power (HIGH) for time in chart above or until rice is tender. Let stand, covered, 2 to 3 minutes. Fluff with a fork.

Variation

Minute Rice Mixes: Select a 6- to 7-ounce package chicken- or beef-flavored, Chinese-style fried, or long-grain and wild rice mix. In a deep 1-1/2-quart casserole, combine rice mix and seasoning envelope. Add the amount of hot water and butter or margarine listed on the package. Cover. Microwave at full power (HIGH) 6 to 8 minutes or until rice is tender. Let stand, covered, 2 to 3 minutes. Fluff with a fork.

For Spanish rice mix, add canned tomatoes with hot water and butter or margarine according to package directions. Cover. Microwave at full power (HIGH) 12 to 13 minutes or until tender.

Long- or Quick-Cooking Barley

SERVINGS	6	4
INGREDIENTS		
hot water	6 cups	3 cups
butter or margarine	1 tablespoon	1 tablespoon
salt	1/2 teaspoon	1/2 teaspoon
long-cooking medium barley	1 cup	
OR		
quick-cooking barley		1 cup
BAKING DISH	deep 3-qt. casserole	deep 2-qt. casserole
TIME AT HIGH	10 to 11 minutes	6 minutes
TIME AT 30%	60 to 70 minutes	13 to 15 minutes
STANDING TIME	5 minutes	5 minutes

In a casserole, see size in chart above, combine hot water, butter or margarine and salt. Cover. Microwave at full power (HIGH) for time in chart above or until boiling. Add barley. Stir well. Cover. Microwave at 30% (MEDIUM LOW) for time in chart above or until tender, stirring twice. Let stand, covered, 5 minutes. Drain.

Long-Cooking Brown Rice

SERVINGS	4 (3-1/2 cups)	2 (1-1/2 cups)
INGREDIENTS		
hot water	2-1/2 cups	1-1/4 cups
butter or margarine	1 tablespoon	2 teaspoons
salt	1/4 teaspoon	1/8 teaspoon
long-cooking brown rice	1 cup	1/2 cup
BAKING DISH	deep 3-qt. casserole	deep 1-1/2-qt. casserole
TIME AT HIGH	5 minutes	2-1/2 minutes
TIME AT 30%	45 minutes	30 to 35 minutes
STANDING TIME	5 minutes	5 minutes

In a casserole, see size in chart above, combine hot water, butter or margarine and salt. Cover and microwave at full power (HIGH) for time in chart above or until boiling. Stir in rice. Cover. Microwave at 30% (MEDIUM LOW) for time in chart above or until tender, stirring twice. Let stand, covered, 5 minutes. Fluff with a fork.

Variation

Quick-Cooking Brown Rice: To make 3 cups rice, combine 1-1/2 cups hot water and 1/4 teaspoon salt in deep 1-1/2-quart casserole. Cover. Microwave at full power (HIGH) 3 to 3-1/2 minutes or until boiling. Stir in 1 cup quick-cooking brown rice. Cover. Microwave at 30% (MEDIUM LOW) 15 minutes or until rice is tender, stirring once. Let stand, covered, 3 minutes. Fluff with a fork. For 1-1/2 cups of rice, use 3/4 cup hot water and 1/8 teaspoon salt in deep 1-quart casserole. Cover. Microwave at full power (HIGH) 2 to 2-1/4 minutes. Stir in 1/2 cup quick-cooking brown rice. Cover. Microwave at 30% (MEDIUM LOW) 12 minutes. Let stand, covered, 3 minutes. Fluff with a fork.

Long-Grain & Wild Rice Mix

SERVINGS	3 or 4 (3-1/3 cups)
INGREDIENTS	
hot water	2-1/3 cups
butter or margarine	1 tablespoon
long-grain and wild rice mix, long-cooking	1 (6-oz.) pkg.
BAKING DISH	deep 1-qt. casserole
TIME AT HIGH	5-1/2 to 6-1/2 minutes
TIME AT 30%	25 minutes
STANDING TIME	2 to 3 minutes

In a 1-quart casserole, combine hot water, butter or margarine, seasoning and rice packet from mix. Mix well. Microwave at full power (HIGH) 5-1/2 to 6-1/2 minutes or until boiling. Cover. Microwave at 30% (MEDIUM LOW) 25 minutes or until water is absorbed and rice is tender, stirring twice. Let stand, covered, 2 to 3 minutes. Fluff with a fork.

Spaghetti

SERVINGS	3 or 4 (3-1/2 cups)	2 (2 cups)
INGREDIENTS		
hot water	6 cups	3 cups
vegetable oil	1 tablespoon	2 teaspoons
salt	1/4 teaspoon	1/8 teaspoon
spaghetti	1 (7-oz.) pkg.	1/2 (7-oz.) pkg.
BAKING DISH	deep 3-qt. casserole	deep 2-qt. casserole
TIME AT HIGH	10 minutes	5 to 6 minutes
TIME AT 30%	12 minutes	10 to 12 minutes

In a casserole, see size in chart, combine hot water, oil and salt. Cover. Microwave at full power (HIGH) for time in chart or until boiling. Add noodles or macaroni, or ease spaghetti into water. When all spaghetti is under water, cover casserole. Microwave at 30% (MEDIUM LOW) for time in chart or until tender, stirring once. Drain and rinse with hot water before serving.

Macaroni

SERVINGS	3 or 4 (4 cups)	2 (2 cups)
INGREDIENTS		
hot water	4 cups	2 cups
vegetable oil	1 tablespoon	2 teaspoons
salt	1/4 teaspoon	1/8 teaspoon
elbow macaroni	2 cups (6 to 7 oz.)	1 cup (3 to 3-1/2 oz.)
BAKING DISH	deep 3-qt. casserole	deep 2-qt. casserole
TIME AT HIGH	6 minutes	4 minutes
TIME AT 30%	13 to 15 minutes	13 to 15 minutes

See directions for Spaghetti, above.

Medium Egg Noodles

SERVINGS	3 or 4 (2-2/3 cups)	2 (1-2/3 cups)
INGREDIENTS		
hot water	6 cups	4 cups
vegetable oil	1 tablespoon	1 tablespoon
salt	1/4 teaspoon	1/4 teaspoon
medium egg noodles	3 cups (4-1/2 oz.)	2 cups (3 oz.)
BAKING DISH	deep 4-qt. casserole	deep 3-qt. casserole
TIME AT HIGH	8 to 10 minutes	6 to 8 minutes
TIME AT 30%	12 to 14 minutes	12 to 14 minutes

See directions for Spaghetti, above.

How to Make One-Dish Macaroni & Cheese

Microwave hot water, oil and salt until boiling, then sprinkle in the macaroni. The oil helps prevent the water from boiling over during cooking. Cover. Microwave at 30% (MEDIUM LOW) until macaroni is tender.

Drain the hot macaroni. Stir in cheese spread, evaporated milk, chopped pimiento and instant minced onion. Microwave briefly until heated through. Garnish with green-pepper rings or buttered cracker crumbs.

One-Dish Macaroni & Cheese

SERVINGS	3 or 4	1 or 2
INGREDIENTS		
hot cooked Macaroni, opposite, well-drained	4 cups	2 cups
pasteurized process cheese spread	1 (8-oz.) jar	1/2 (8-oz.) jar
evaporated milk	6 tablespoons	3 tablespoons
chopped pimiento	1/4 cup	2 tablespoons
instant minced onion	1 teaspoon	1/2 teaspoon
green pepper, sliced in rings	1 small	1/2 small
BAKING DISH	deep 3-qt. casserole	deep 2-qt. casserole
TIME AT 70%	5 minutes	3 minutes
TIME AT 70% (after stirring)	5 minutes	3 minutes

In a casserole, see size in chart above, combine hot macaroni and cheese spread. Stir until cheese spread has melted. Stir in evaporated milk, pimiento and onion. Cover. Microwave at 70% (MEDIUM HIGH) for time in chart above. Stir. Top with pepper rings. Cover. Microwave at 70% (MEDIUM HIGH) for time in chart above or until heated through.

Parmesan Spaghetti Ring   Photo on page 433.

SERVINGS	8 to 10	6
INGREDIENTS		
butter or margarine	6 tablespoons	1/4 cup
spaghetti, cooked, drained	1 lb.	10 oz.
grated Parmesan cheese	1 cup	2/3 cup
eggs, beaten	4	3
chopped mushrooms, drained	1 (6-oz.) can	1 (3-1/2-oz.) can
snipped parsley	3 tablespoons	2 tablespoons
spaghetti sauce	1 (32-oz.) jar	1 (16-oz.) jar
MOLD	8-cup microwave ring mold	5-cup microwave ring mold
BAKING DISH (sauce)	1-1/2-qt. casserole	1-qt. casserole
TIME AT HIGH (ring)	6 to 7 minutes	5 minutes
TIME AT HIGH (sauce)	9 to 10 minutes	5 minutes

In a large bowl, add butter or margarine to hot, cooked spaghetti. Using 2 forks, gently lift spaghetti until butter or margarine is melted. Stir in Parmesan cheese, then eggs. Mix well. Stir in mushrooms and parsley. Turn into an oiled microwave ring mold, see size in chart above. Cover with vented plastic wrap. Microwave at full power (HIGH) for time in chart above or until set. Cover with foil; set aside. Pour spaghetti sauce into a casserole, see size in chart above. Cover. Microwave at full power (HIGH) for time in chart above or until heated through, stirring once. Slide knife around edge of mold to loosen spaghetti ring. Turn ring out onto a serving plate. Serve with spaghetti sauce.

Canned Spaghetti or Ravioli

SERVINGS	4 or 5	2 or 3
INGREDIENTS		
spaghetti in tomato sauce or ravioli in meat sauce	1 (26-1/4- to 26-1/2-oz.) can	1 (14-3/4- to 15-oz.) can
BAKING DISH	1-qt. casserole	2-cup casserole
TIME AT HIGH	6 to 7 minutes	3-1/2 to 4 minutes
STANDING TIME	2 to 3 minutes	2 to 3 minutes

Spoon spaghetti or ravioli into a baking dish, see size in chart above. Cover. Microwave at full power (HIGH) for time in chart above or until heated through, stirring once. Let stand, covered, 2 to 3 minutes. Stir before serving.

Reheating Refrigerated Noodles

To chill: Spoon cooled noodles into a refrigerator container. Cover and refrigerate.

To reheat: Spoon 2 cups noodles and 2 tablespoons water into a 1-quart casserole. Cover. Microwave at 70% (MEDIUM HIGH) 3 to 3-1/2 minutes or until hot. Heat 1 cup noodles with 1 tablespoon water in a 2-cup casserole at 70% (MEDIUM HIGH) 2-1/2 to 3 minutes. Stir before serving.

Desserts

Bake your next pie in the microwave. Not only does it cook in half the time, but the pastry is extra flaky. You won't be able to resist the fresh-fruit flavor of these fabulous desserts.

Q. Which kinds of desserts are most suitable for the microwave?

A. Puddings cooked this way are extra smooth and creamy. All fruit-based desserts have an excellent fresh flavor because of the fast cooking.

Q. Which desserts do not cook satisfactorily in the microwave?

A. Drop cookies cook so unevenly that they are not recommended. Some are burned while others are still doughy. The pastry in a two-crust pie does not cook but the filling heats rapidly. The solution is to make deep-dish pies, or microwave the pie shell first. The top crust is microwaved separately and then the pie is assembled before serving. Custard in a large pie plate and dessert soufflés overcook on the edges before the center sets. It is difficult to obtain consistently good results with cakes made from scratch. Microwave baking results are more predictable with pudding-type cake mixes. Cream puffs, angel-food cakes, chiffon cakes and meringues should not be attempted because they never give good results.

Q. Can cakes and pastries be cooked in the microwave?

A. Yes. Cakes do not brown in the microwave but they do have an excellent light, airy texture. Because cakes are usually frosted, glazed or dusted with powdered sugar, the lack of browning is easily disguised. Pastry does not brown much in the microwave. But microwave cooking makes the flakiest pastry you have ever tasted.

Q. How do you know when desserts are done?

A. A wooden pick inserted in the center of a cake should come out clean. Pudding should be thick and smooth. Pastry should be just starting to brown—it burns quickly after this point. Each recipe has a doneness test to guide you.

Q. How can favorite conventional recipes be converted for microwave cooking?

A. There are tips for converting custard, chiffon-pie, fruit-crisp and fruit-pie recipes for microwave cooking. For other desserts, compare your recipe to the basic recipe in this chapter for that type of dessert.

Q. How about cooking dessert convenience foods in the microwave?

A. Most can be cooked successfully. Follow directions for dessert mixes and frozen prepared desserts in the chapter. Many frozen desserts have microwave cooking instructions on the package.

Q. Are any special utensils needed to microwave desserts?

A. You must have a special microwave fluted tube pan in order to make tube cakes. Pans are available both in ceramic and plastic. Some care has to be taken when you select a pie plate. You will find that not all 9-inch pie plates will hold the same amount. Measure how much water your pie plate will hold, then measure how much pie filling you have. Choose a glass or ceramic pie plate that is large enough for the pie filling required in the recipe.

How to Make Basic Baked Pastry Shell

Roll out pastry on a lightly floured surface until dough is about 1/8 inch thick. Invert pie plate in center of pastry circle. Cut a circle of dough 1 inch larger than the pie plate. Dough may be pieced together to make a circle by moistening both the edges of the patch and the pastry circle.

Turn pie plate right side up. Gently fit pastry into pie plate—do not stretch the dough. Fold under and flute the edge. Prick the dough all over the bottom and sides with a fork before microwaving. This allows steam to escape and helps keep the pastry shell flat during cooking.

Basic Baked Pastry Shell

YIELD	9- or 10-inch shell	7- or 8-inch shell
INGREDIENTS		
pie-crust mix	1-1/2 sticks	1 stick
water	3 tablespoons	2 tablespoons
PIE PLATE	9- or 10-inch pie plate	7- or 8-inch pie plate
TIME AT 70%	7 to 9 minutes	6 to 7 minutes

Prepare pie-crust mix with water according to package directions. On a lightly floured surface, roll out dough 1/8 inch thick. Cut circle of dough 1 inch larger than top of pie plate, see size in chart above. Gently fit pastry in pie plate. Fold under edge and flute. Prick all over bottom and sides of pastry with a fork. Microwave at 70% (MEDIUM HIGH) for time in chart above or until brown areas begin to appear, giving dish a half turn once. If dough puffs up during cooking, gently press back against pie plate. Cool before filling.

Tips

- Pastry will not brown evenly in the microwave oven. Pastry is done as soon as brown spots *start* to appear. Cooking the pastry longer will result in burned areas.

- Pastry cooked in the microwave oven is especially flaky.

- Using amber- or dark-colored pie plates may result in more browning of the pastry.

Basic Lattice-Top Pie Crust

YIELD	1 lattice-top crust
INGREDIENTS	
pie-crust mix	1 stick
water	2 tablespoons
PLATE	12-inch microwave pizza plate
TIME AT 70%	4-1/2 to 5-1/2 minutes

Prepare pie-crust mix with water according to package directions. On a lightly floured surface, roll out dough 1 inch larger than top of casserole for deep-dish pie. Trim edge to make an even circle. With a pastry wheel or sharp knife, cut a 1-inch circular strip around edge of pastry circle. Remove a 2-inch piece from circular pastry strip. Discard the 2-inch piece. Place remaining circular strip on a 12-inch microwave pizza plate, sealing ends together. Cut remaining center circle of dough into strips, 1/2 inch wide. Twist half the strips and place 1 inch apart inside circular strip with both ends of each strip overlapping circular strip. Twist remaining strips and place at right angles across first strips, making a checkerboard pattern. Fold circular strip of dough over ends of checkerboard. Seal and flute edge. Sprinkle with a sugar-and-spice mixture, if desired. Microwave at 70% (MEDIUM HIGH) 4-1/2 to 5-1/2 minutes or until lattice begins to brown, giving dish a half turn once. Cool. Loosen edges with a spatula before transferring lattice top to pie.

Basic Baked Pastry Wedges

YIELD	8 wedges	6 wedges
INGREDIENTS		
pie-crust mix	1 stick	1/2 stick
water	2 tablespoons	1 tablespoon
PLATE	12-inch microwave pizza plate	12-inch microwave pizza plate
TIME AT 70%	4-1/2 to 5-1/2 minutes	3-1/2 to 4-1/2 minutes

Prepare pie-crust mix with water according to package directions. On a lightly floured surface, roll out dough from 1 pastry stick to a 9-inch circle, or roll out dough from 1/2 pastry stick to a 6-inch circle. Adjust diameter of pastry to fit size of pie you are making. Place dough on a 12-inch microwave pizza plate. Fold edge under and flute, making circle about 1 inch smaller. Sprinkle with a sugar-and-spice mixture, if desired. With a pastry wheel or sharp knife, cut in serving-size wedges, see number in chart above. Prick pastry with a fork. Microwave at 70% (MEDIUM HIGH) for time in chart above or until just beginning to brown, giving dish a half turn once. Remove any wedges that start to overbrown. Cool pastry wedges on a wire rack.

Variation
Baked Pastry Cutouts: Prepare 1/2 stick pie-crust mix with water according to package directions. Roll out dough 1/8 inch thick on a lightly floured surface. Cut into shapes with cookie cutters. Place cutouts on a 12-inch microwave pizza plate. Sprinkle with a sugar-and-spice mixture, if desired. Microwave at 70% (MEDIUM HIGH) 5-1/2 to 6-1/2 minutes or until beginning to brown. Remove any cutouts that start to overbrown. Cool cutouts on a wire rack.

How to Make Basic Lattice-Top Pie Crust

After rolling out dough, cut a circle of dough 1 inch larger than the top of the casserole for a deep-dish pie. Using a pastry wheel or sharp knife, cut a 1-inch circular strip around outside edge of pastry circle.

Remove a 2-inch piece from the circular pastry strip. Place the large strip on a pizza plate, sealing the two ends together to form a circle. Discard the 2-inch piece of pastry.

Cut remaining circle of dough into 1/2-inch wide strips. Twist half the strips and place them 1 inch apart inside circular strip on pizza plate. Twist the remaining strips and place at right angles across first strips, making a checkerboard pattern.

Fold the circular strip of dough over the ends of the checkerboard strips. Seal and flute the edge as for a regular pie crust. Sprinkle the lattice top with a sugar-and-spice mixture, if desired. After microwaving, cool. Use a spatula to loosen the lattice top and carefully place it on the pie.

How to Make Basic Crumb Pie Crust

To make crumbs for a pie crust, crush crackers, wafers or cookies in a plastic bag, then roll with a rolling pin. Or, use a food processor fitted with a steel blade to make quick work of this task.

Mix the crumbs with melted butter or margarine and sugar until evenly moistened. Then press crumb mixture firmly over bottom and sides of the pie plate. After microwaving, quickly press the crumbs against the pie plate again.

Basic Crumb Pie Crust

YIELD	9-inch pie crust	7-inch pie crust
INGREDIENTS		
butter or margarine	6 tablespoons	1/4 cup
fine graham-cracker, vanilla- or chocolate-wafer crumbs	1-1/2 cups	1 cup
sugar	3 tablespoons	2 tablespoons
PIE PLATE	9-inch pie plate	7-inch pie plate
BOWL	1-1/2-qt. mixing bowl	1-qt. mixing bowl
TIME AT HIGH (butter)	45 to 60 seconds	30 to 45 seconds
TIME AT HIGH (crust)	1-1/2 to 2 minutes	1 to 1-1/2 minutes

Lightly butter a pie plate, see size in chart above. Place butter or margarine in a bowl, see size in chart above. Microwave at full power (HIGH) for time in chart above or until melted. Stir in cracker, wafer or cookie crumbs and sugar until all crumbs are moistened. Spoon crumb mixture over bottom and sides of pie plate. Press crumbs firmly over bottom and sides of pie plate. Microwave at full power (HIGH) for time in chart above or until beginning to brown, giving dish a half turn once. Quickly press crumbs firmly against pie plate again. Cool before filling.

Variation
Gingersnap Crust: Use fine gingersnap-cookie crumbs. For a 9-inch crust, decrease butter or margarine to 3 tablespoons. For a 7-inch crust, decrease butter or margarine to 2 tablespoons. Prepare crust and microwave as above.

Tapioca Pudding Mix

SERVINGS	4 (2 cups)
INGREDIENTS vanilla or chocolate tapioca pudding mix milk	1 (3-1/4-oz.) pkg. 2 cups
BOWL	1-qt. bowl
TIME AT HIGH	3-1/2 minutes
TIME AT HIGH (after stirring)	2 to 2-1/2 minutes

Empty pudding mix into a 1-quart bowl. Gradually stir in milk, mixing well. Microwave, uncovered, at full power (HIGH) 3-1/2 minutes. Stir well. Microwave at full power (HIGH) 2 to 2-1/2 minutes or until mixture comes to a full boil, stirring once. Cover. Cool at room temperature 15 minutes, stirring twice. Serve warm or chilled.

Rice Pudding Mix

SERVINGS	4 (2-1/3 cups)
INGREDIENTS rice pudding mix milk raisins	1 (3-3/4-oz.) pkg. 2 cups 1/4 cup
BOWL	1-qt. bowl
TIME AT HIGH	4 minutes
TIME AT HIGH (after stirring)	2 to 2-1/2 minutes

Empty pudding mix into a 1-quart bowl. Gradually stir in milk, mixing well. Stir in raisins. Microwave, uncovered, at full power (HIGH) 4 minutes. Stir well. Microwave at full power (HIGH) 2 to 2-1/2 minutes or until mixture comes to a full boil, stirring once. Cover. Cool at room temperature 15 minutes; stir well. Serve warm or chilled.

Defrosting Frozen Whipped Topping

YIELD	about 4 cups	about 2 cups
INGREDIENTS frozen whipped topping	1 (8-oz.) carton	1 (4-oz.) carton
TIME AT 30%	1-1/2 minutes	1 minute

Place unopened carton of frozen whipped topping in microwave oven. Microwave at 30% (MEDIUM LOW) for time in chart above or until barely thawed. Stir gently before serving.

Basic Pudding Mix

SERVINGS	6 (3-1/4 cups)	4 (2-1/4 cups)
INGREDIENTS		
non-instant pudding mix, all flavors except lemon	1 (4-3/4- or 5-1/4-oz.) pkg.	1 (3-1/8- or 3-5/8-oz.) pkg.
milk	3 cups	2 cups
BOWL	2-qt. bowl	1-1/2-qt. bowl
TIME AT HIGH	4 minutes	3 minutes
TIME AT HIGH (after stirring)	4 to 4-1/2 minutes	3 to 3-1/2 minutes

Empty pudding mix into a bowl, see size in chart above. Gradually whisk in milk. Microwave, uncovered, at full power (HIGH) for time in chart above. Whisk well. Microwave at full power (HIGH) for time in chart above or until mixture comes to a full boil, whisking twice. Cover surface of hot pudding with plastic wrap or waxed paper. Refrigerate. Or, pour into dessert dishes and refrigerate until set.

Basic Vanilla Pudding

SERVINGS	3 or 4 (2-1/2 cups)	1 or 2 (1 cup)
INGREDIENTS		
sugar	3/4 cup	1/3 cup
cornstarch	2 tablespoons	1 tablespoon
milk	2 cups	1 cup
egg yolks, slightly beaten	2	1
butter or margarine	2 tablespoons	1 tablespoon
vanilla extract	1 teaspoon	1/2 teaspoon
BOWL	2-qt. bowl	1-1/2-qt. bowl
TIME AT HIGH (milk mixture)	6-1/2 to 7-1/2 minutes	3 to 4 minutes
TIME AT HIGH (egg yolks added)	1 minute	45 seconds

In a bowl, see size in chart above, combine sugar and cornstarch, mixing thoroughly. Whisk in milk. Microwave at full power (HIGH) for time in chart above or until mixture is thickened and bubbly, whisking three times. Stir small amount hot mixture into beaten egg yolks. Stir yolk mixture into hot mixture. Microwave at full power (HIGH) for time in chart above or until thickened, whisking twice. Stir in butter or margarine until melted. Stir in vanilla. Cover surface of hot pudding with plastic wrap or waxed paper. Refrigerate until cool enough to use in other recipes. Or, pour into dessert dishes and refrigerate until set.

Variation
Chocolate Pudding: For larger recipe, add 1 cup semisweet chocolate pieces to thickened mixture before adding egg yolks. For smaller recipe, add 1/2 cup semisweet chocolate pieces. Microwave at full power (HIGH) 30 to 60 seconds. Stir until chocolate is melted. Continue with egg yolks as above.

How to Make Basic Pudding Mix

Empty pudding mix into bowl. Gradually whisk in milk to mix well. Whisk the pudding mixture after about half the cooking time, then whisk twice during the final cooking time to prevent lumps.

To avoid making a mess, use a wide-mouth canning funnel to fill narrow parfait glasses with pudding. Butterscotch pudding layered with coconut and almonds is irresistible.

Lemon Pudding Mix

SERVINGS	6 or 7 (3-1/2 cups)	4 (2-1/3 cups)
INGREDIENTS		
non-instant lemon pudding mix	1 (4-1/2-oz.) pkg.	1 (3-oz.) pkg.
sugar	3/4 cup	1/2 cup
water	3 cups	2-1/4 cups
egg yolks, slightly beaten	3	2
BOWL	2-qt. bowl	1-1/2-qt. bowl
TIME AT HIGH	5 minutes	3-1/2 to 4 minutes
TIME AT HIGH (after stirring)	3 minutes	2 minutes
TIME AT 30%	1 to 2 minutes	1 minute

Empty pudding mix into a bowl, see size in chart above. Add sugar and mix well. Add a little of the water; mix well. Gradually stir in remaining water. Microwave, uncovered, at full power (HIGH) for time in chart above. Stir well. Microwave at full power (HIGH) for time in chart above or until mixture comes to a full boil, stirring twice. Stir 1/2 cup hot pudding into egg yolks. Return mixture to hot pudding in bowl, stirring well. Microwave at 30% (MEDIUM LOW) for time in chart above or until thickened, stirring once. Cool 5 minutes, stirring twice. Cover surface of hot pudding with plastic wrap or waxed paper. Refrigerate until cool enough to use in other recipes. Or, pour into dessert dishes and refrigerate until set.

S'More Pie

SERVINGS	6	4
INGREDIENTS		
Basic Crumb Pie Crust, page 468, made with graham crackers	9-inch crust	7-inch crust
Basic Pudding Mix, page 470, using chocolate-fudge flavor	1 (5-1/4-oz.) pkg.	1 (3-5/8-oz.) pkg.
semisweet chocolate pieces	1 (6-oz.) pkg. (1 cup)	2/3 cup
large marshmallows	20 (6 oz.)	15 (4 oz.)
graham-cracker crumbs	2 tablespoons	1 tablespoon
PIE PLATE	9-inch pie plate	7-inch pie plate
TIME AT HIGH	2-1/2 to 3-1/2 minutes	1-1/2 to 2-1/2 minutes

Prepare Basic Crumb Pie Crust with graham crackers, see size in chart above. Set aside. Prepare chocolate-fudge pudding mix. Immediately stir in chocolate pieces until melted. Cool 5 minutes, stirring twice. Pour into pie crust. Top with marshmallows. Refrigerate 8 hours or overnight. At serving time, shield bottom and sides of pie plate with foil. Microwave at full power (HIGH) for time in chart above or until marshmallows are puffed. Swirl marshmallows with a buttered spatula. Sprinkle pie with graham-cracker crumbs. Serve immediately.

Lemon Fruit Pie

SERVINGS	6	4
INGREDIENTS		
butter or margarine	5 tablespoons	3 tablespoons
lemon creme-filled cookies, crushed	16 (2 cups crushed)	10 (1-1/4 cups crushed)
Lemon Pudding Mix, page 471	1 (4-1/2-oz.) pkg.	1 (3-oz.) pkg.
lemon yogurt	1 cup	2/3 cup
fresh or drained canned fruit		
PIE PLATE	9-inch pie plate	7-inch pie plate
BOWL (butter)	1-qt. bowl	1-qt. bowl
TIME AT HIGH (butter)	1 minute	30 to 45 seconds
TIME AT HIGH (crust)	2 minutes	1 to 1-1/2 minutes

Lightly butter a pie plate, see size in chart above. Set aside. Place butter or margarine in a 1-quart bowl. Microwave at full power (HIGH) for time in chart above or until melted. Stir in cookie crumbs. Mix well. Press crumb mixture firmly into pie plate. Microwave at full power (HIGH) for time in chart above, giving pie plate a half turn once. Quickly press crumbs again firmly against bottom and sides of pie plate. Set aside to cool. Prepare Lemon Pudding Mix. Cool 5 minutes, stirring twice. Place plastic wrap or waxed paper on surface of pudding. Cool at room temperature 2 hours. Stir until smooth. Fold in yogurt. Pour into pie shell; refrigerate until set. Before serving, top with fruit.

How to Make S'More Pie

Stir chocolate pieces into hot chocolate-fudge pudding until the pieces melt. Cool the pudding mixture at room temperature for 5 minutes, stirring twice.

Pour pudding mixture into a graham-cracker pie crust. Immediately top the pie with large marshmallows, spacing the marshmallows to cover the top of the pie evenly.

Refrigerate the pie overnight. To heat before serving, shield the bottom and sides of the pie plate with a piece of foil to prevent the pudding from melting with the marshmallows.

Microwave the pie until the marshmallows are puffed and softened. Use a buttered spatula or knife to swirl the marshmallows over the pie. Serve the pie at once!

Devonshire Cheesecake Cups

SERVINGS	6
INGREDIENTS	
vanilla wafers	6
cream cheese	1 (8-oz.) pkg.
packed brown sugar	1/3 cup
egg	1
vanilla extract	1/2 teaspoon
dairy sour cream, green grapes or strawberries, brown sugar	to garnish
CUSTARD CUPS	6 (6-oz.) custard cups
BOWL	1-1/2-qt. bowl
TIME AT 10%	1-1/2 to 2 minutes
TIME AT 30%	7 to 8 minutes

Place paper bake cups in 6 (6-ounce) custard cups. Place a vanilla wafer in each paper bake cup; set aside. Unwrap cream cheese and place in a 1-1/2 quart bowl. Microwave at 10% (LOW) 1-1/2 to 2 minutes or until softened. Add 1/3 cup brown sugar, egg and vanilla. Beat with electric mixer on high speed until smooth. Pour into paper bake cups. Arrange in a circle in microwave. Microwave at 30% (MEDIUM LOW) 7 minutes, rearranging cups once. Remove any cheesecake cups that are set in center or those in which a knife inserted off-center comes out clean. Microwave remaining cheesecake cups at 30% (MEDIUM LOW) 1 minute or until done. Cool on a wire rack 1 hour. Refrigerate. Serve topped with dollops of sour cream, green grape clusters or strawberries, and a sprinkling of additional brown sugar.

Melba Cheesecake Pie

SERVINGS	6 to 8
INGREDIENTS	
Basic Crumb Pie Crust, page 468, made with graham crackers	9-inch crust
Raspberry Glaze, page 493	1 cup
cream cheese	1 (8-oz.) pkg.
all-purpose flour	1 tablespoon
sugar	1/3 cup
raspberry yogurt	1 cup
peach slices	to garnish
PIE PLATE	9-inch pie plate
BOWL	1-1/2-qt. bowl
TIME AT 10%	1-1/2 to 2 minutes
TIME AT 30%	13 to 15 minutes

Prepare Basic Crumb Pie Crust with graham crackers in a 9-inch pie plate; set aside. Prepare Raspberry Glaze; set aside. Unwrap cream cheese and place in a 1-1/2-quart bowl. Microwave at 10% (LOW) 1-1/2 to 2 minutes or until softened. Stir in flour and sugar. Add yogurt. Beat with an electric mixer on high speed until smooth. Pour into crust. Microwave, uncovered, at 30% (MEDIUM LOW) 13 to 15 minutes or until set in center, giving pie a quarter turn three times. When done, knife inserted off-center will not come out clean. Cool on a wire rack 1 hour. Refrigerate. Top with peach slices. Spoon Raspberry Glaze over pie. Refrigerate until serving time.

Peach Parfait Pie

SERVINGS	6
INGREDIENTS	
Basic Baked Pastry Shell, page 465, or Basic Crumb Pie Crust, page 468	9-inch pie shell
lemon-flavored gelatin	1 (3-oz.) pkg.
water	1-1/4 cups
peach ice cream	1 pt.
whipped topping	1 cup
additional whipped topping, peach slices, mint sprig	to garnish
PIE PLATE	9-inch pie plate
BOWL	2-qt. bowl
TIME AT HIGH	2 to 3 minutes

Prepare pastry or crumb-crust pie shell in a 9-inch pie plate; set aside. In a 2-quart bowl, combine gelatin and water. Microwave at full power (HIGH) 2 to 3 minutes or until gelatin dissolves, stirring three times. Add ice cream with a scoop or by spoonfuls, stirring until melted. Stir 1 cup whipped topping, then fold into ice-cream mixture. Whisk until smooth. Refrigerate until mixture mounds, 40 to 45 minutes. Spoon into pie shell. Refrigerate until firm, about 8 hours or overnight. Serve garnished with whipped topping, peach slices and a sprig of mint.

Variations

Raspberry Parfait Pie: Substitute raspberry-flavored gelatin for the lemon gelatin and frozen raspberry yogurt or sherbet for the peach ice cream. Garnish with fresh or frozen raspberries.

Lime Parfait Pie: Substitute lime-flavored gelatin for the lemon gelatin and lime sherbet for the peach ice cream. Garnish with fresh lime slices.

Easy Strawberry Pie

SERVINGS	6
INGREDIENTS	
Basic Baked Pastry Shell, page 465, or Basic Crumb Pie Crust, page 468	1 (9-inch) pie shell
strawberry ice cream	1 qt.
Strawberry Glaze, page 493	3/4 cup
fresh whole strawberries	2 cups
PIE PLATE	9-inch pie plate

Prepare pastry or crumb-crust pie shell in a 9-inch pie plate. Spoon ice cream evenly into pie shell. Freeze. Prepare Strawberry Glaze. Cool. Just before serving, arrange strawberries over ice cream. Spoon glaze over strawberries.

Tips

- Parfait pies may be made several weeks ahead of time and stored tightly covered in the freezer. A jumbo plastic bag makes a good freezer wrap. Remove the pie from the freezer about 30 minutes before serving time.

- To thaw frozen whipped topping for use as a garnish, see page 469.

How to Make Peach Parfait Pie

Pour lemon-flavored gelatin into 1-1/4 cups of water. Microwave until gelatin dissolves, stirring three times. When gelatin is dissolved, the liquid will be clear.

Add several scoops of peach ice cream to the hot gelatin. Stir until ice cream is melted; then add remaining ice cream. Stir in whipped topping and whisk until mixture is smooth.

Refrigerate ice-cream mixture until it mounds. Notice how the filling piles up in the pie shell after chilling. This makes a more attractive pie.

Refrigerate the pie for 8 hours or overnight. Garnish the center of the pie with fresh or canned peach slices and a sprig of mint.

Basic Old-Fashioned Custard

SERVINGS	4	2
INGREDIENTS		
milk	1-1/3 cups	2/3 cup
eggs	2	1
sugar	3 tablespoons	4 teaspoons
vanilla extract	1 teaspoon	1/2 teaspoon
ground nutmeg	to taste	to taste
hot water	to depth of 1/2 inch in baking dish	to depth of 3/4 inch in baking dish
GLASS MEASURING CUP	2-cup	1-cup
CUSTARD CUPS	4 (6-oz.) custard cups	2 (6-oz.) custard cups
BAKING DISH	8-inch square baking dish	9" x 5" loaf dish
TIME AT HIGH (milk)	2 to 3 minutes	1-1/2 to 2 minutes
TIME AT HIGH (custard)	5-1/2 to 6-1/2 minutes	3-1/2 to 4-1/2 minutes

In a glass measuring cup, see size in chart above, microwave milk at full power (HIGH) for time in chart above or until very hot but not boiling. In a medium bowl, whisk together eggs, sugar and vanilla. Gradually stir in hot milk. Divide egg mixture evenly among 6-ounce custard cups, see number in chart above. Sprinkle with nutmeg. Pour hot water into baking dish, see size in chart above, to depth given in chart above. Set custard cups in baking dish. Water should be 1 inch deep around cups. Microwave at full power (HIGH) for time in chart above or until custard is nearly set but still moves slightly in center. Give baking dish a half turn once and give individual custards a half turn once during cooking time. Check custards at minimum time and remove any that are done. Continue cooking remaining custards. Cool on a rack only until set, then serve or refrigerate. May be served warm or chilled.

Variation

Crème Brûlée: Sieve a generous coating of brown sugar over refrigerated custard. Set custards in a baking pan. Pack crushed ice around custard dishes. Broil in preheated conventional oven 5 inches from heat for 3 minutes or until brown sugar is melted.

Adapting Custard Recipes for Microwave Oven

- Individual custards work best. It is difficult to get a custard pie to set in the center before the edges are overdone.

- Generally, the same proportions of milk to egg work in the microwave oven as in conventional ovens. Use about 1 egg to 2/3 cup milk and 1 to 2 tablespoons of sugar.

- Be careful not to overcook custard or it will curdle. See the doneness test, opposite.

- Custard-type pies, such as pumpkin, are difficult to adapt to microwave cooking. To achieve a moderate degree of even cooking, these pies must be cooked at such low power levels that no time is saved over conventional baking.

How to Make Basic Old-Fashioned Custard

Whisk together eggs, sugar and vanilla until well-combined. Gradually add very hot milk to the egg mixture, continuing to whisk until all the milk is added.

Divide the egg mixture among custard cups. Sprinkle with nutmeg. Pour 1/2 inch of hot water into the baking dish. Place the custard cups in the baking dish with water.

Microwave custard in water bath until almost set, but center is not quite firm. A knife inserted between center and edge will not come out clean when custard is done. If the knife comes out clean, the custard is overdone!

To make Crème Brûlée, sieve a generous coating of brown sugar over the tops of the cooked custards. Set custard cups in the baking dish and pack with crushed ice. Broil custards in a conventional oven until the sugar is melted.

Luscious Strawberry Trifle

SERVINGS	8 to 10	4 to 5
INGREDIENTS		
golden egg-custard mix	1 (4-1/2-oz.) pkg.	1 (3-oz.) pkg.
milk	3 cups	2 cups
orange-flavored extract	1/2 teaspoon	1/4 teaspoon
dried ground orange peel	1/4 teaspoon	1/8 teaspoon
sponge-cake dessert cups	8 (1-oz.) cakes	4 (1-oz.) cakes
orange-flavored liqueur	1/4 cup	2 tablespoons
orange marmalade	1/4 cup	2 tablespoons
sliced fresh strawberries	4 cups	2 cups
whipped topping	2 cups	1 cup
additional whipped topping, fresh whole strawberries	to garnish	to garnish
BOWL (custard)	2-qt. bowl	1-1/2-qt. bowl
BOWL (trifle)	2-1/2-qt. serving bowl	1-1/2-qt. serving bowl
TIME AT HIGH	5 minutes	4 minutes
TIME AT HIGH (after stirring)	3 minutes	2 minutes

Empty custard mix into a bowl, see size in chart above. Gradually stir in milk. Microwave, uncovered, at full power (HIGH) for time in chart above. Stir well. Microwave at full power (HIGH) for time in chart above or until mixture comes to a boil, stirring once; sauce will be thin. Stir in orange extract and peel. Refrigerate only 15 minutes. Arrange half the sponge-cake dessert cups in a large glass serving bowl, see size in chart above, or in individual sherbet dishes, cutting cakes as necessary to fit dishes. Prick cakes all over with a fork. Drizzle with half the orange-flavored liqueur. Spread with half the orange marmalade. Top with half the strawberries. Pour half the custard sauce over strawberries, being sure part of the custard flows through to the cake layer. Repeat layers of cake, liqueur, marmalade, strawberries and custard sauce. Spread top with first amount of whipped topping. Refrigerate several hours. Garnish with additional whipped topping and whole strawberries just before serving.

Custard Mix

SERVINGS	6 (3 cups)	4 (2-1/3 cups)
INGREDIENTS		
golden egg-custard mix	1 (4-1/2-oz.) pkg.	1 (3-oz.) pkg.
milk	3 cups	2 cups
ground nutmeg	to taste	to taste
BOWL	2-qt. bowl	1-1/2-qt. bowl
TIME AT HIGH	5 minutes	4 minutes
TIME AT HIGH (after stirring)	3 minutes	2 minutes

Empty custard mix into a bowl, see size in chart above. Gradually stir in milk, mixing well. Microwave, uncovered, at full power (HIGH) for time in chart above. Stir well. Microwave at full power (HIGH) for time in chart above or until mixture comes to a boil, stirring once; mixture will be thin. Pour into custard cups or dessert dishes. Sprinkle with ground nutmeg. Refrigerate until set.

How to Make Luscious Strawberry Trifle

Arrange half the sponge-cake dessert cups in a glass serving bowl, cutting the cakes to fit over the entire bottom of the bowl. Prick the cakes all over with a large fork. Drizzle with half the orange liqueur.

Spread the cakes with half the orange marmalade, then top with half the fresh strawberries. Pour half the custard over all the berries, being sure part of the custard flows through to the cake layer.

Make another layer of dessert cakes and drizzle with liqueur. Spread marmalade over cakes and top with fresh strawberries. Pour remaining orange-flavored custard over the strawberries.

Spread the top of the trifle with whipped topping. Cover and refrigerate. Just before serving, garnish the trifle with whipped topping swirls and fresh whole strawberries.

Bananas Foster Chiffon Pie

SERVINGS	6	4
INGREDIENTS		
Basic Crumb Pie Crust, page 468, made with vanilla wafers	9-inch pie crust	7-inch pie crust
unflavored gelatin	1 envelope	2 teaspoons
packed brown sugar	2/3 cup	1/3 cup
egg yolks	4	2
mashed ripe bananas	1/2 cup	1/4 cup
dark rum	1/4 cup	2 tablespoons
grated lemon peel	1 teaspoon	1/2 teaspoon
egg whites	4	2
cream of tartar	1/4 teaspoon	1/8 teaspoon
packed brown sugar	2/3 cup	1/3 cup
banana yogurt	1 cup	1/2 cup
whipped cream, sliced bananas, lemon balm or mint	to garnish	to garnish
PIE PLATE	9-inch pie plate	7-inch pie plate
BOWL	1-1/2-qt. bowl	1-qt. bowl
TIME AT 30%	6 to 7 minutes	4 to 4-1/2 minutes

Prepare Basic Crumb Pie Crust, see size in chart above, using vanilla wafers. Set aside. In a bowl, see size in chart above, thoroughly mix gelatin and first amount of brown sugar; set aside. In a medium bowl, beat egg yolks, mashed bananas, rum and lemon peel with an electric mixer on medium speed until blended. Stir into gelatin mixture. Microwave at 30% (MEDIUM LOW) for time in chart above or until mixture just boils and gelatin is dissolved, stirring four times. Cool. In another medium bowl, beat egg whites and cream of tartar with electric mixer on high speed until soft peaks form. Gradually add second amount of brown sugar, beating until stiff peaks form. Fold banana mixture into egg white mixture. Fold in banana yogurt. Spoon into pie crust. Refrigerate until firm, 8 hours or overnight. Garnish with whipped cream, banana slices and lemon balm or mint.

Adapting Chiffon Pie Recipes for Microwave Oven

- Thoroughly mix the gelatin and sugar to separate gelatin granules and prevent lumping.

- Beat the egg yolks and liquid ingredients until blended, then stir into gelatin mixture.

- Microwave the yolk mixture at 30% (MEDIUM LOW) until mixture boils and gelatin dissolves, stirring often. The 30% power level is used so egg yolks cook gently. Refrigerate the yolk mixture until it mounds when spooned.

- Continue, following the conventional directions for chiffon filling, by folding the refrigerated yolk mixture into stiffly beaten egg whites.

How to Make Bananas Foster Chiffon Pie

Thoroughly combine unflavored gelatin and brown sugar. Mixing the gelatin with the sugar helps prevent lumping. Stir in egg-yolk mixture and microwave until mixture begins to boil.

Beat the egg whites until soft peaks form—look for tips on the egg whites that curl over when the whisk is lifted. Then begin beating in the brown sugar.

Beat the brown sugar into the egg whites until stiff peaks form when the whisk is lifted. At the stiff-peak stage, a rubber spatula should leave a clean trough through the egg whites.

Garnish with whipped cream, banana slices and sprigs of lemon balm or mint. To loosen the crumb crust, wrap a hot, wet towel around the pie plate for a few minutes before serving.

Café au Lait Soufflé

SERVINGS	6 to 8	3 or 4
INGREDIENTS		
unflavored gelatin	1 envelope	2 teaspoons
sugar	1/4 cup	2 tablespoons
egg yolks	4	2
cold, strong coffee	1 cup	1/2 cup
coffee-flavored liqueur	1/4 cup	2 tablespoons
egg whites	4	2
cream of tartar	1/4 teaspoon	1/8 teaspoon
sugar	1/4 cup	2 tablespoons
whipping cream, whipped	1 cup	1/2 cup
additional whipped cream, chocolate curls	to garnish	to garnish
BOWL	1-1/2-qt. bowl	1-qt. bowl
SOUFFLE DISH OR CUPS	2-qt. soufflé dish or 6 (10-oz.) cups	1-qt. soufflé dish or 3 (10-oz.) cups
TIME AT 30%	7 to 9 minutes	4 to 4-1/2 minutes

In a bowl, see size in chart above, thoroughly mix gelatin and first amount of sugar. In a medium bowl, beat egg yolks and coffee with electric mixer at low speed until blended. Stir into gelatin mixture. Microwave at 30% (MEDIUM LOW) for time in chart above or until mixture begins to boil and gelatin is dissolved, stirring four times. Stir in coffee-flavored liqueur. Refrigerate 1 to 1-1/2 hours, stirring frequently, until mixture mounds when spooned. In another medium bowl, beat egg whites and cream of tartar with electric mixer at high speed until soft peaks form. Gradually add second amount of sugar, beating until stiff peaks form. Fold coffee mixture into egg white mixture. Fold in first amount of whipped cream. Spoon into a souffle dish or individual cups, see sizes in chart above. Refrigerate until firm, 3 to 4 hours. Garnish with additional whipped cream and chocolate curls, if desired.

Cranberry Cloud Parfaits

SERVINGS	5 or 6	3 or 4
INGREDIENTS		
unflavored gelatin	1 envelope	2 teaspoons
cold water	1/2 cup	1/4 cup
fresh cranberries	2 cups	1 cup
egg whites	2	1
sugar	1 cup	1/2 cup
lemon juice	1 tablespoon	2 teaspoons
BAKING DISH	deep 2-qt. casserole	deep 1-qt. casserole
TIME AT HIGH	4 minutes	2 minutes
TIME AT 30%	6 minutes	3 minutes

In a small bowl, soften gelatin in cold water. In a casserole, see size in chart above, combine cranberries and gelatin mixture. Microwave at full power (HIGH) for time in chart above or until boiling. Stir well. Microwave at 30% (MEDIUM LOW) for time in chart above or until cranberry skins pop, stirring three times. Cool to room temperature. In a medium bowl, combine egg whites, sugar, lemon juice and cranberry mixture. Beat with electric mixer at high speed until mixture forms soft peaks, 8 to 10 minutes. Gently pile into 6-ounce parfait glasses. Refrigerate.

Apple Crisp

SERVINGS	6	3
INGREDIENTS		
granulated sugar	1/2 cup	1/4 cup
packed brown sugar	1/2 cup	1/4 cup
all-purpose flour	1/2 cup	1/4 cup
quick-cooking oats	1/2 cup	1/4 cup
ground cinnamon	1 teaspoon	1/2 teaspoon
ground nutmeg	1/2 teaspoon	1/4 teaspoon
butter or margarine	1/4 cup	2 tablespoons
pared, sliced cooking apples	6 cups (6 large apples, 2 lbs.)	3 cups (3 large apples, 1 lb.)
apple juice	1/4 cup	2 tablespoons
BAKING DISH	round, 8-inch cake dish	7-inch pie plate
TIME AT HIGH	14 to 16 minutes	7 to 8 minutes

To prepare topping mixture: In a medium bowl, combine granulated sugar, brown sugar, flour, oats, cinnamon and nutmeg. Cut in butter or margarine until mixture resembles coarse crumbs. Set aside. Butter a baking dish, see size in chart above. Place apples in baking dish. Drizzle with apple juice. Sprinkle with topping mixture. Microwave, uncovered, at full power (HIGH) for time in chart above or until apples are tender, giving dish a half turn once. Serve warm with cream or vanilla or cinnamon ice cream, if desired.

Fruit Crisp

SERVINGS	6 to 8	3 or 4
INGREDIENTS		
Apple Crisp topping mixture, above	large recipe	small recipe
fruit-pie filling	2 (21-oz.) cans	1 (21-oz.) can
lemon juice	2 tablespoons	1 tablespoon
cream or vanilla ice cream		
BAKING DISH	8-inch square baking dish	9-inch pie plate
TIME AT HIGH	10 to 11 minutes	8 to 10 minutes

Prepare topping mixture; set aside. Combine pie filling and lemon juice in a baking dish, see size in chart above. Sprinkle with topping mixture. Shield corners of square dish with small pieces of foil. Microwave, uncovered, at full power (HIGH) for time in chart above or until mixture is bubbling around edges, giving dish a half turn once. Serve warm with cream or vanilla ice cream.

Adapting Fruit Crisp Recipes for Microwave Oven

- Use a larger baking dish than called for in conventional recipes to cook fruit crisps in the microwave oven so there will be room for the fruit filling to boil up.

- Moist, buttery toppers work best. Crisps cook so quickly in the microwave oven that the topping doesn't have time to cook.

- For the freshest flavor, microwave the fruit crisps at full power (HIGH) until the fruit is barely tender.

- Microwave crisps uncovered so the topping doesn't get soggy.

How to Make Apple Crisp

Thoroughly mix granulated sugar, brown sugar, flour, oats and spices for the topping. Use a pastry blender or two knives to cut in the butter until the mixture resembles coarse crumbs.

Here's an easy way to slice apples. Cut the apple in four large pieces leaving the square core in the center. Then turn each apple piece flat side down and slice to desired thickness.

Place the sliced apples in the baking dish, then drizzle with apple juice. Sprinkle the crumb topping evenly over the apples.

Serve the warm crisp in sherbet dishes with generous scoops of vanilla ice cream or cinnamon ice cream.

Deep-Dish Rhubarb-Cherry Pie

SERVINGS	4 or 5	2
INGREDIENTS		
fresh rhubarb, sliced 1/2 inch thick	4 cups	2 cups
pitted, fresh, dark, sweet cherries	2 cups	1 cup
packed brown sugar	1 cup	1/2 cup
granulated sugar	1/2 cup	1/4 cup
all-purpose flour	1/3 cup	3 tablespoons
ground nutmeg	1/4 teaspoon	1/8 teaspoon
Basic Baked Pastry Wedges, page 466		
BAKING DISH (rhubarb mixture)	deep 2-qt. casserole	deep 1-qt. casserole
BAKING DISH (serving dish)	same deep 2-qt. casserole	2 (10-oz.) casseroles
TIME AT HIGH	10 to 11 minutes	5 to 7 minutes

Place rhubarb and cherries in a casserole, see size in chart above. In a small bowl, combine brown sugar, granulated sugar, flour and nutmeg. Mix well. Pour sugar mixture over rhubarb mixture and toss well. Cover with vented plastic wrap or lid. Microwave at full power (HIGH) for time in chart above or until fruit is just tender and mixture is thickened, stirring twice. Leave larger recipe in same casserole. For smaller recipe, divide filling evenly between two 10-ounce casseroles. Set filling aside. Prepare Basic Baked Pastry Wedges. Just before serving, carefully place pastry wedges over rhubarb-cherry filling. Serve warm.

Brandied Peach & Blueberry Pie

SERVINGS	6 to 8	3 or 4
INGREDIENTS		
peeled, sliced fresh peaches	5 cups	2-1/2 cups
fresh or frozen blueberries	1-1/2 cups	3/4 cup
peach brandy	1/3 cup	2 tablespoons
Basic Lattice-Top Pie Crust, page 466		
sugar	3/4 cup	1/3 cup
all-purpose flour	1/4 cup	2 tablespoons
ground cinnamon	1/2 teaspoon	1/4 teaspoon
ground nutmeg	dash	dash
butter or margarine	2 tablespoons	1 tablespoon
BAKING DISH	deep 2-qt. casserole	round, 8-inch cake dish
TIME AT HIGH	8 to 10 minutes	4-1/2 to 5 minutes

In a casserole, see size in chart above, gently toss together peaches, blueberries and brandy. Set aside. Prepare Basic Lattice-Top Pie Crust; set aside. In a medium bowl, combine sugar, flour, cinnamon and nutmeg. Mix well. Fold sugar mixture gently into fruit in baking dish. Dot with butter or margarine. Cover. Microwave at full power (HIGH) for time in chart above or until fruit is just tender and mixture is thickened, stirring twice. Top with Basic Lattice-Top Pie Crust just before serving.

How to Make Deep-Dish Rhubarb-Cherry Pie

Use a handy cherry pitter or a bent paper clip to remove pits from the plump Bing cherries.

Toss rhubarb and cherries with the spiced sugar-and-flour mixture. Microwave the fruit mixture until thickened and fruit is tender.

Before baking, sprinkle the pastry round with sugar and ground nutmeg, then cut into wedges with a pastry wheel.

To serve, carefully lift the baked pastry wedges with a spatula and place on top of the thickened fruit mixture.

Concord Grape Pie

SERVINGS	6
INGREDIENTS	
Basic Baked Pastry Shell, page 465,	1 (9-inch) shell
Streusel Topping, page 436	2 cups
Baked Pastry Cutouts, page 466	to garnish
Concord grapes	
(as purchased)	1-1/2 lbs.
(stems removed)	4 cups
sugar	1/2 cup
all-purpose flour	1/4 cup
ground cinnamon	1/2 teaspoon
ground nutmeg	1/4 teaspoon
lemon juice	1 tablespoon
grated lemon peel	1 teaspoon
PIE PLATE	9-inch pie plate
BOWL	1-1/2-qt. bowl
BAKING DISH	deep 2-qt. casserole
TIME AT HIGH (grape pulp)	3 to 3-1/2 minutes
TIME AT 30% (grape pulp)	4 to 5 minutes
TIME AT HIGH (thicken filling)	6 to 8 minutes
TIME AT 30% (pie)	6 to 8 minutes

Prepare Basic Baked Pastry Shell in a 9-inch pie plate; set aside. Prepare Streusel Topping and Baked Pastry Cutouts; set aside. Slip skins from grapes, setting skins aside and placing pulp in a 1-1/2-quart bowl. Cover pulp with vented plastic wrap. Microwave at full power (HIGH) 3 to 3-1/2 minutes or until boiling. Microwave at 30% (MEDIUM LOW) 4 to 5 minutes or until pulp is very soft. In a 2-quart casserole, combine sugar, flour, cinnamon and nutmeg. Mix well and set aside. Remove seeds from pulp by sieving pulp into a 1-quart glass measuring cup. You should have about 1-3/4 cups sieved pulp. Stir lemon juice, lemon peel and grape skins into pulp. Gradually stir pulp mixture into sugar mixture. Mix well. Cover. Microwave at full power (HIGH) 6 to 8 minutes or until thickened and bubbly, stirring three times. Pour into pastry shell. Sprinkle with Streusel Topping. Microwave at 30% (MEDIUM LOW) 6 to 8 minutes or until edges are bubbling and topping becomes moistened. Garnish with Baked Pastry Cutouts.

Adapting Fruit Pie Recipes for Microwave Oven

- Fruit pies are not made the same way in the microwave oven as the conventionally baked 2-crust or lattice-top pies. When prepared the conventional way and microwaved, the bottom crust is raw. Therefore, there are two choices for adapting recipes for the microwave.

- For a deep-dish pie, combine the fruit in a deep casserole. Stir together sugar, flour, cornstarch or tapioca, and liquid, in a small bowl. Then toss with the fruit. Microwave the fruit mixture at full power (HIGH) until thickened, stirring occasionally. Just before serving, top with Basic Baked Pastry Wedges or Baked Pastry Cutouts, page 466.

- To simulate a 2-crust pie, thicken the fruit mixture in a bowl or casserole in the same way as for the deep-dish pie, above. After thickening, pour the fruit mixture into a Basic Baked Pastry Shell, page 465, and top with Basic Baked Pastry Wedges or Basic Lattice-Top Pie Crust, page 466.

Apple Pie

SERVINGS	5 or 6	3 or 4
INGREDIENTS		
Basic Baked Pastry Wedges, page 466	5 or 6	3 or 4
sugar	2/3 cup	1/3 cup
all-purpose flour	2 tablespoons	1 tablespoon
ground cinnamon	1 teaspoon	1/2 teaspoon
ground allspice	1/4 teaspoon	1/8 teaspoon
pared, sliced baking apples	7 cups (7 large apples)	3-1/2 cups (3-1/2 large apples)
lemon juice	2 teaspoons	1 teaspoon
BAKING DISH	round, 8-inch baking dish	7-inch pie plate
TIME AT HIGH	10 minutes	4 to 5 minutes

Prepare Basic Baked Pastry Wedges; set aside. In a small bowl, combine sugar, flour, cinnamon and allspice. Mix well. In a large bowl, toss apple slices and lemon juice. Add sugar mixture and toss thoroughly. Spoon into a baking dish, see size in chart above. Cover with waxed paper. Microwave at full power (HIGH) for time in chart above or until apples are tender, giving dish a half turn once. Stir gently. Keep loosely covered until serving time. Just before serving, top with pastry wedges. Serve warm.

Pineapple-Apricot Streusel Pie

SERVINGS	6	4
INGREDIENTS		
Basic Baked Pastry Shell, page 465	1 (9-inch) shell	1 (7-inch) shell
Streusel Topping, page 436	2 cups	1 cup
pineapple chunks, juice-pack	1 (16-oz.) can	1 (8-oz.) can
reserved pineapple juice	1/3 cup	3 tablespoons
sugar	1/3 cup	3 tablespoons
all-purpose flour	2 tablespoons	1 tablespoon
ground allspice	1 teaspoon	1/2 teaspoon
lemon juice	2 tablespoons	1 tablespoon
canned apricot halves, drained	1 (29-oz.) can	1 (16-oz.) can
PIE PLATE	9-inch pie plate	7-inch pie plate
BOWL	2-qt. bowl	1-qt. bowl
TIME AT HIGH	2 to 2-1/2 minutes	1 to 1-1/4 minutes
TIME AT 30%	14 to 16 minutes	7 to 8 minutes

Prepare Basic Baked Pastry Shell in a pie plate, see size in chart above; set aside. Prepare Streusel Topping; set aside. Drain pineapple, reserving amount of juice listed in chart above. In a bowl, see size in chart above, thoroughly combine sugar, flour and allspice. Stir in reserved pineapple juice. Microwave at full power (HIGH) for time in chart above or until thickened and bubbly, stirring twice. Stir in lemon juice. Gently fold in apricots and pineapple chunks. Spoon into pastry shell. Sprinkle with Streusel Topping. Microwave at 30% (MEDIUM LOW) for time in chart above or until edges are bubbling and topping is moistened.

Raspberry Glaze

YIELD	1 cup
INGREDIENTS	
frozen raspberries in syrup, thawed	1 (10-oz.) pkg.
cornstarch	4 teaspoons
kirsch or crème de cassis	2 tablespoons
BOWL	1-qt. bowl
TIME AT HIGH	2-1/2 to 3 minutes

Drain raspberries, reserving syrup. Sieve raspberries; discard seeds. Combine pulp and reserved syrup. If necessary, add water to make 1 cup pulp mixture. Place cornstarch in a 1-quart bowl. Whisk in about 1/4 cup of the raspberry mixture until smooth. Whisk in remaining raspberry mixture. Microwave at full power (HIGH) 2-1/2 to 3 minutes or until mixture thickens and bubbles, stirring twice. Mixture should be thick and clear. Stir in kirsch or crème de cassis. Cool. Serve warm or chilled.

Strawberry Glaze

YIELD	1-1/3 cups	3/4 cup
INGREDIENTS		
strawberry jelly	1 (10-oz.) jar (1 cup)	1/2 (10-oz.) jar (1/2 cup)
strawberry liqueur	1/3 cup	2 tablespoons
lemon juice	1 tablespoon	2 teaspoons
cornstarch	1 tablespoon	2 teaspoons
water	2 tablespoons	1 tablespoon
GLASS MEASURING CUP	1-qt.	2-cup
TIME AT HIGH (jelly)	2 to 3 minutes	1 to 1-1/2 minutes
TIME AT HIGH (sauce)	2 to 3 minutes	1 to 1-1/2 minutes

Place jelly, liqueur and lemon juice in a glass measuring cup, see size in chart above. Microwave at full power (HIGH) for time in chart above or until jelly melts, stirring once. In a small bowl, stir together cornstarch and water until smooth. Stir into jelly mixture. Microwave at full power (HIGH) for time in chart above or until thickened and bubbly, stirring three times. Mixture should be thick and clear. Cool.

Strawberry-Glazed Pie

SERVINGS	6
INGREDIENTS	
Basic Baked Pastry Shell, page 465	1 (9-inch) shell
Strawberry Glaze, above	1-1/3 cups
fresh strawberries	5 to 6 cups
PIE PLATE	9-inch pie plate

Prepare Basic Baked Pastry Shell in a 9-inch pie plate; set aside. Prepare Strawberry Glaze; cool. No more than 3 hours before serving time, pile strawberries into pie shell, drizzling each layer with glaze. Refrigerate.

Butterscotch-Cashew Sauce

YIELD	3-1/2 cups	1-2/3 cups
INGREDIENTS		
packed brown sugar	1-1/2 cups	3/4 cup
light corn syrup	3/4 cup	1/3 cup
butter or margarine	1/4 cup	2 tablespoons
half and half	2/3 cup	1/3 cup
salted cashews	1 cup	1/2 cup
vanilla extract	1 teaspoon	1/2 teaspoon
GLASS MEASURING CUP	1-qt.	1-qt.
TIME AT HIGH	3 to 4 minutes	2 to 2-1/2 minutes

In a 1-quart glass measuring cup, combine brown sugar, corn syrup and butter or margarine. Microwave at full power (HIGH) for time in chart above or until mixture boils and sugar dissolves, stirring three times. Stir in half and half, cashews and vanilla. Serve warm or chilled. Stir before serving. Refrigerate remaining sauce.

Velvet Fudge Sauce

YIELD	4-1/2 cups	2 cups
INGREDIENTS		
semisweet chocolate pieces	1 (12-oz.) pkg. (2 cups)	1 (6-oz.) pkg. (1 cup)
evaporated milk	1 (13-oz.) can (1-2/3 cups)	1 (5-1/3-oz.) can (2/3 cup)
marshmallow creme	1 (7-oz.) jar	1/2 (7-oz.) jar
BOWL	2-qt. bowl	1-qt. bowl
TIME AT HIGH (chocolate pieces)	2 to 3 minutes	1 to 2 minutes
TIME AT HIGH (marshmallow added)	1 minute	30 seconds

In a bowl, see size in chart above, combine chocolate pieces and evaporated milk. Microwave at full power (HIGH) for time in chart above or until chocolate pieces are almost melted, stirring twice. Stir until smooth. Add marshmallow creme in spoonfuls. Microwave at full power (HIGH) for time in chart above or until marshmallow creme softens. Stir vigorously until blended. Serve warm. Refrigerate remaining sauce.

Rum Hard Sauce

YIELD	1 cup	1/2 cup
INGREDIENTS		
butter or margarine	1/2 cup	1/4 cup
powdered sugar	1 cup	1/2 cup
rum	2 tablespoons	1 tablespoon
BOWL	1-1/2-qt. bowl	1-1/2-qt. bowl
TIME AT 10%	1-1/2 minutes	1 minute

In a 1-1/2-quart bowl, microwave butter or margarine at 10% (LOW) for time in chart above or until softened. Beat in powdered sugar with electric mixer on high speed until fluffy. Beat in rum. Store in refrigerator. Serve at room temperature with plum pudding.

How to Make Champagne Fondue

Cut a block of frozen strawberries to fit in a blender or food processor fitted with the steel blade. Pour in pink champagne and process until strawberries are pureed.

Microwave champagne mixture with cornstarch until thickened. To serve, dip assorted fruits and cake cubes into warm fondue. Then roll in coconut, candies, almonds or brown sugar.

Champagne Fondue

YIELD	2-2/3 cups
INGREDIENTS	
frozen, sweetened, sliced strawberries	1 (10-oz.) pkg.
pink champagne	1-1/2 cups
cornstarch	3 tablespoons
fresh strawberries, hulled	
kiwi wedges	
melon cubes	
banana chunks	
fruitcake, plum pudding, or pound cake cubes	
flaked coconut	
chocolate candy decorettes	
finely chopped almonds	
brown sugar	
GLASS MEASURING CUP	1-qt.
TIME AT HIGH	5 to 6 minutes

Cut the block of frozen strawberries into quarters. Place strawberries and 1/2 cup champagne in a blender or food processor fitted with the steel blade. Cover and process until smooth, stirring frequently. Add cornstarch. Cover and process a few seconds. Pour into a 1-quart glass measuring cup. Stir in remaining champagne. Microwave at full power (HIGH) 5 to 6 minutes or until mixture thickens and bubbles, stirring three times. Serve warm with strawberries, kiwi wedges, melon cubes, banana chunks and cake or plum pudding cubes as dippers. Roll coated fruit or cake in coconut, chocolate candies, chopped almonds or brown sugar.

Flaming Fruit Sauce

YIELD	2-2/3 cups	1-1/4 cups
INGREDIENTS		
frozen fruit in syrup, thawed	2 (10-oz.) pkgs.	1 (10-oz.) pkg.
reserved syrup	3/4 cup	1/3 cup
cornstarch	1 tablespoon	2 teaspoons
lemon juice	1 tablespoon	2 teaspoons
fruit-flavored brandy or liqueur	1/4 cup	2 tablespoons
ice cream or sherbet		
BOWL	1-qt. bowl	1-qt. bowl
GLASS MEASURING CUP	1-cup	1-cup
TIME AT HIGH (thicken sauce)	2-1/2 to 3 minutes	1-1/2 to 2 minutes
TIME AT HIGH (heat liqueur)	20 seconds	10 seconds

Drain fruit, reserving amount of syrup listed in chart above. In a 1-quart bowl, combine cornstarch and a little reserved syrup until smooth. Stir in remaining reserved syrup and lemon juice. Microwave at full power (HIGH) for time in chart above or until thickened and bubbly. Fold in fruit. In a 1-cup glass measuring cup, heat brandy or liqueur at full power (HIGH) for time in chart above. Pour hot brandy or liqueur into a large ladle. Carefully ignite and pour over fruits. Stir when flame subsides. Serve over ice cream or sherbet.

Strawberry Banana Splits Photo on page 463.

SERVINGS	4	2
INGREDIENTS		
butter or margarine	2 tablespoons	1 tablespoon
strawberry ice-cream topping	1/2 cup	1/4 cup
banana liqueur or strawberry liqueur	2 tablespoons	1 tablespoon
chopped nuts	1/4 cup	2 tablespoons
bananas, halved lengthwise and crosswise	4	2
strawberry ice cream	1 pt.	1/2 pt.
fresh strawberries, whipped cream	to garnish	to garnish
BAKING DISH	12" x 7" baking dish	round, 8-inch baking dish
TIME AT HIGH (butter)	30 seconds	30 seconds
TIME AT HIGH (bananas)	2 to 3 minutes	1 to 2 minutes

Place butter or margarine in a baking dish, see size in chart above. Microwave at full power (HIGH) 30 seconds or until melted. Stir in strawberry topping, liqueur and nuts. Add bananas, turning gently to coat with sauce. Cover with vented plastic wrap. Microwave at full power (HIGH) for time in chart above or until bananas are warmed through, rearranging once. Spoon bananas into serving dishes. Top with scoops of ice cream. Drizzle with warm strawberry sauce from baking dish. Garnish with fresh strawberries and whipped cream.

Flaming Fruit Sauce made with frozen mixed fruit and frozen raspberries.

Basic Baked Apples

SERVINGS	4	2	1
INGREDIENTS			
baking apples	4 (6- to 7-oz.) apples	2 (6- to 7-oz.) apples	1 (6- to 7-oz.) apple
raisins	1/4 cup	2 tablespoons	1 tablespoon
packed brown sugar	1/2 cup	1/4 cup	2 tablespoons
ground cinnamon			
ground nutmeg			
bourbon or apple juice	1/4 cup	2 tablespoons	1 tablespoon
vanilla ice cream or cream			
BAKING DISH	8-inch square baking dish	9" x 5" loaf dish	1-1/2-cup casserole
TIME AT HIGH	7 to 9 minutes	5 to 6 minutes	2 to 2-1/2 minutes
STANDING TIME	10 minutes	10 minutes	5 minutes

Core apples, being careful not to cut through bottoms. Pare a small strip around top o each apple. Set apples, stem side up, in a baking dish, see size in chart above. Spoon rai sins into center of each apple. Mound brown sugar on apples. Sprinkle with cinnamo and nutmeg. Drizzle with bourbon or apple juice. Cover with vented plastic wrap. Mi crowave at full power (HIGH) for time in chart above or until almost tender, givin dish a half turn once. Let stand, covered, for time in chart above. Spoon pan juices ove apples. Serve with vanilla ice cream or cream.

Variation
Baked Pears: Select 7-ounce firm, ripe pears. Follow directions above, except for pears, use 1/4 cup brown sugar and 1/2 cup bourbon or apple juice; for 2 pears use 2 ta blespoons brown sugar and 1/4 cup bourbon or apple juice; for 1 pear, use 1 tablespoo brown sugar and 2 tablespoons bourbon or apple juice.

Applesauce

SERVINGS	6 (3-1/4 cups)	3 (1-1/2 cups)
INGREDIENTS		
pared, quartered cooking apples	6 cups (2 lbs., 10 medium apples)	3 cups (1 lb., 5 medium apples)
apple juice	1/2 cup	1/4 cup
sugar	1/3 cup	2 to 3 tablespoons
BAKING DISH	deep 2-qt. casserole	deep 1-1/2-qt. casserol
TIME AT HIGH	10 to 12 minutes	6 to 7 minutes

In a casserole, see size in chart above, combine apples, apple juice and sugar. Mix wel Cover. Microwave at full power (HIGH) for time in chart above or until apples ar tender, stirring once. Mash apples to desired consistency by hand or process in a foo processor fitted with the steel blade.

How to Make Baked Pears

Core the pears, being sure not to cut through the bottoms or the filling will fall out. Stuff the pears with raisins, brown sugar and spices, then drizzle with bourbon or apple juice.

Microwave the pears until almost tender. The standing time will finish cooking the pears. Serve the warm pears with a pitcher of cream and a shaker of ground cinnamon.

Rhubarb Sauce

SERVINGS	9 or 10 (5-1/2 cups)	4 or 5 (2-3/4 cups)
INGREDIENTS		
fresh rhubarb, cut in 1/2-inch pieces	8 cups (2-1/4 lbs.)	4 cups (1 lb. 2 oz.)
OR		
frozen unsweetened rhubarb, cut in 1/2-inch pieces	8 cups (2 lbs.)	4 cups (1 lb.)
sugar	1-1/3 to 1-2/3 cups	2/3 to 1 cup
ground cinnamon	1/2 teaspoon	1/4 teaspoon
orange juice	1/2 cup	1/4 cup
BAKING DISH	deep 3-qt. casserole	deep 2-qt. casserole
TIME AT HIGH (fresh rhubarb)	14 to 16 minutes	7 to 9 minutes
TIME AT HIGH (frozen rhubarb)	18 to 20 minutes	11 to 12 minutes

In a casserole, see size in chart above, toss together fresh or frozen rhubarb, sugar and cinnamon. Stir in orange juice. Cover. Microwave at full power (HIGH) for time in chart above or until rhubarb is tender, stirring twice.

Prunes

SERVINGS	5 or 6 (about 3 cups)	3 (1-1/2 cups)
INGREDIENTS		
dried pitted prunes	1 (12-oz.) pkg. (2 cups)	1/2 (12-oz.) pkg. (1 cup)
OR		
dried prunes, with pits	1 (16-oz.) pkg. (3 cups)	1/2 (16-oz.) pkg. (1-1/2 cups)
hot water	about 2 cups	about 1-1/4 cups
sugar	3 to 4 tablespoons	1 to 2 tablespoons
BAKING DISH	deep 1-1/2-qt. casserole	deep 1-qt. casserole
TIME AT HIGH	4 to 6 minutes	3 to 4 minutes
TIME AT 30% (prunes)	4 minutes	3 minutes
TIME AT 30% (sugar added)	2 minutes	2 minutes

See directions for Dried Mixed Fruit, opposite.

Dried Apricots

SERVINGS	4 or 5 (2 cups)	2 (1 cup)
INGREDIENTS		
dried apricots	1 (6-oz.) pkg. (1-1/2 cups)	1/2 (6-oz.) pkg. (3/4 cup)
hot water	about 1-1/2 cups	about 3/4 cup
sugar	1/2 cup	1/4 cup
BAKING DISH	deep 1-1/2-qt. casserole	deep 1-qt. casserole
TIME AT HIGH	4 to 5 minutes	2-1/2 to 3 minutes
TIME AT 30% (apricots)	5 minutes	3 to 4 minutes
TIME AT 30% (sugar added)	2 minutes	2 minutes

See directions for Dried Mixed Fruit, opposite.

Plumping Raisins

YIELD	about 1-1/4 cups	about 1/2 cup
INGREDIENTS		
dried raisins	1 cup (5-1/2 oz.)	1/2 cup (3 oz.)
hot water	1 cup	1/2 cup
BOWL	2-cup bowl	1-1/2-cup bowl
TIME AT HIGH	2 to 3 minutes	1-1/2 minutes
STANDING TIME	2 to 3 minutes	2 to 3 minutes

Place raisins in a bowl, see size in chart above. Add hot water to cover raisins. Cover Microwave at full power (HIGH) for time in chart above or until boiling. Let stand, cov ered, 2 to 3 minutes. Drain.

How to Make Dried Mixed Fruit

Pour enough hot water into the casserole to cover the fruit. Cover and microwave the fruit until almost tender.

Add sugar during the last few minutes of cooking time. Adding the sugar too soon will prevent the fruit from becoming tender.

Dried Mixed Fruit

SERVINGS	5 (2-3/4 cups)	2 or 3 (1-1/3 cups)
INGREDIENTS		
dried mixed fruit	1 (8-oz.) pkg. (2 cups)	1/2 (8-oz.) pkg. (1 cup)
hot water	about 2 cups	about 1 cup
sugar	1/4 cup	2 tablespoons
BAKING DISH	deep 1-1/2-qt. casserole	deep 1-qt. casserole
TIME AT HIGH	4 to 5 minutes	3 to 4 minutes
TIME AT 30% (fruit)	9 to 10 minutes	9 to 10 minutes
TIME AT 30% (sugar added)	2 minutes	2 minutes

Place fruit in a casserole, see size in chart. Add hot water to cover fruit. Cover. Microwave at full power (HIGH) for time in chart or until boiling. Stir and cover. Microwave at 30% (MEDIUM LOW) for time in chart or until tender. Stir in sugar. Cover. Microwave at 30% (MEDIUM LOW) 2 minutes or until sugar dissolves.

Defrosting Fruit in Cartons

SERVINGS	2 or 3
INGREDIENTS frozen, sweetened fruit: melon balls, strawberries or raspberries	1 (10- or 12-oz.) carton
BOWL	1-qt. bowl
TIME AT 30%	3 to 4 minutes
STANDING TIME	5 to 10 minutes

Place carton under running hot water a few seconds to loosen fruit. Remove frozen block of fruit from carton and place in a 1-quart bowl. Microwave at 30% (MEDIUM LOW) 3 to 4 minutes or until only a few ice crystals remain, stirring gently with a fork twice to separate fruit. Let stand 5 to 10 minutes.

Defrosting Loose-Pack Fruit

SERVINGS	6
INGREDIENTS frozen loose-pack, unsweetened fruit: blueberries, cherries, strawberries or rhubarb	1 (16-oz.) pkg.
BOWL	1-qt. bowl
TIME AT 30%	4-1/2 minutes
STANDING TIME	5 to 10 minutes

Empty frozen fruit into a 1-quart bowl. Microwave at 30% (MEDIUM LOW) 4-1/2 minutes or until only a few ice crystals remain, gently stirring twice. Frozen loose-pack rhubarb will take 7 minutes at 30% (MEDIUM LOW). Let stand 5 to 10 minutes.

Defrosting Fruit in a Pouch

SERVINGS	3 or 4
INGREDIENTS frozen, sweetened fruit in a pouch: peach slices, strawberries, mixed fruit or cranberry-orange relish	1 (10-oz.) pkg.
TIME AT 30%	2-1/2 to 3 minutes
STANDING TIME	5 to 10 minutes

With scissors or a sharp knife, cut a small "X" in center of pouch. Place, slit side up, in the microwave oven. Microwave at 30% (MEDIUM LOW) 2-1/2 to 3 minutes or until only a few ice crystals remain, flexing pouch twice to rearrange fruit. Let stand 5 to 10 minutes.

Defrosting Packaged Cake

SERVINGS	6 to 8	8	6 to 8
INGREDIENTS frozen packaged cake	1 (17-oz.) loaf cake, 8" x 3-1/2"	1 (17- or 18-oz.) frosted, 3-layer cake, 6-inch square or round	1 (12- to 14-oz.) frosted, 1-layer cake, 6-1/2-inch square or 8" x 5" oblong
TIME AT 10%	2 minutes	4 minutes	3 minutes
STANDING TIME	3 to 5 minutes	10 minutes	5 to 10 minutes

If cake is boxed, remove from carton. Remove any paper cover or protective collar. Place on a serving plate, if desired. If cake comes in a foil pan, leave in the pan for defrosting in the microwave. Microwave cake, uncovered, at 10% (LOW) for time in chart above. Let stand for time in chart above.

Defrosting Packaged Cheesecake

SERVINGS	6 to 8	4 to 6
INGREDIENTS frozen packaged cheesecake	1 (23-1/2-oz.) cheesecake	1 (17-oz.) cheesecake
TIME AT 10%	4 to 5 minutes	4 minutes
STANDING TIME	10 minutes	10 minutes

If cheesecake is boxed, remove from carton. Remove paper cover. Do not remove cheesecake from container. Microwave, uncovered, at 10% (LOW) for time in chart above. Let stand 10 minutes.

Defrosting Packaged Cream or Meringue Pie

SERVINGS	5 or 6	5 or 6
INGREDIENTS frozen packaged cream or meringue pie	1 (20-oz.) meringue pie (7 inches in diameter)	1 (14-oz.) cream pie (7 inches in diameter)
TIME AT 10%	5 minutes	3 minutes
STANDING TIME	15 minutes	10 minutes

Remove pie from carton. Remove any paper cover or protective collar. Do not remove pie from pie pan. Microwave pie, uncovered, at 10% (LOW) for time in chart above. Let stand for time in chart above.

Fruit-Nut Crispy Bars

YIELD	48 bars	30 bars
INGREDIENTS		
crisp rice cereal	4 cups	2 cups
chopped dried apricots	1/2 cup	1/4 cup
chopped candied cherries	1/2 cup	1/4 cup
chopped nuts	1/2 cup	1/4 cup
butter or margarine, cut up	1/4 cup	2 tablespoons
large marshmallows	30	15
BAKING DISH	12" x 7" baking dish	8-inch square baking dish
BOWL	4-qt. bowl	2-qt. bowl
TIME AT HIGH	1-1/2 minutes	1 minute

Measure cereal, apricots, cherries and nuts; set aside. Butter a baking dish, see size i
chart above. Place butter or margarine and marshmallows in a bowl, see size in cha
above. Microwave at full power (HIGH) for time in chart above or until melted. Stir t
blend. Quickly stir in cereal, fruits and nuts. With buttered fingers, press gently int
baking dish. Cool completely before cutting into bars.

Brownie Mix

YIELD	54 to 60 brownies
INGREDIENTS	
brownie mix	1 (20-1/2- to 23-3/4-oz.) pkg.
BAKING DISHES	2 round, 8-inch cake dishes
TIME AT HIGH (each layer)	4-1/2 minutes

Prepare brownie mix as directed on package for cake-like or fudgy brownies. Divid
batter evenly between 2 round, 8-inch cake dishes. Microwave 1 dish at a time, uncov
ered, at full power (HIGH) 4-1/2 minutes, giving dish a quarter turn after 2 minute
When done, brownies will be evenly puffed and almost dry on top. Cool on a flat, hea
proof surface. Cool completely before cutting into bars.

Tips

- Drop cookies become hard and dry in the microwave oven. There is little time saved an
  they bake unevenly. In addition, the microwave oven is so small that cookies must b
  baked in many batches.
- Refrigerated slice-and-bake cookies and packaged uncooked frozen cookies are a dis
  aster in the microwave oven. Even baking a few at a time, some cookies burn whil
  others stay raw.
- Date-Bar Mix turns an unappetizing grey when baked in the microwave oven and is ver
  dry in texture.

How to Make Peanut-Brickle Layer Bars

Spoon sweetened condensed milk evenly over the candy-and-nut mixture. This is *not* evaporated milk. Sweetened condensed milk is much thicker and sweeter than evaporated milk.

Cool completely before cutting into bars. The mixture continues to firm as it cools. Glasses of ice-cold milk make the perfect accompaniment for these rich, chewy bars.

Peanut-Brickle Layer Bars

YIELD	48 bars	30 bars
INGREDIENTS		
butter or margarine	1/4 cup	2 tablespoons
peanut-butter-cookie crumbs	1 cup	1/2 cup
peanut-butter-flavored baking pieces	1 cup	1/2 cup
almond-brickle baking pieces	1 (6-oz.) pkg. (1-1/4 cups)	1/2 cup
flaked coconut	1 (3-1/2-oz.) can (1-1/3 cups)	1/2 (3-1/2-oz.) can (2/3 cup)
salted peanuts, chopped	1/2 cup	1/4 cup
sweetened condensed milk	1 (14-oz.) can (1-1/3 cups)	1/2 (14-oz.) can (2/3 cup)
BAKING DISH	12" x 7" baking dish	round, 8-inch baking dish
TIME AT HIGH (butter)	1 minute	30 seconds
TIME AT HIGH (cookies)	7 to 8 minutes	4 to 4-1/2 minutes

Place a 2-inch diameter jar in center of a baking dish, see size in chart above. Place butter or margarine in baking dish. Microwave at full power (HIGH) for time in chart above or until melted. Stir in cookie crumbs. Press into bottom of baking dish around jar. Sprinkle with peanut-butter pieces, almond-brickle pieces, coconut and peanuts. Spoon condensed milk evenly over all. Microwave, uncovered, at full power (HIGH) for time in chart above or until set in center, giving dish a half turn once. Cool completely before cutting into bars.

Grandmother's Plum Pudding

SERVINGS	12	6
INGREDIENTS		
butter or margarine	1/2 cup	1/4 cup
packed brown sugar	3/4 cup	1/3 cup
bread, torn	3 slices	2 slices
milk	1/4 cup	2 tablespoons
eggs	2	1
dark rum	1/4 cup	2 tablespoons
vanilla extract	1 teaspoon	1/2 teaspoon
prepared mincemeat	1 cup	1/2 cup
all-purpose flour	3/4 cup	1/3 cup
baking soda	3/4 teaspoon	1/4 teaspoon
salt	1/2 teaspoon	1/4 teaspoon
ground cinnamon	1 teaspoon	1/2 teaspoon
ground cloves	1/2 teaspoon	1/4 teaspoon
ground nutmeg	1/2 teaspoon	1/4 teaspoon
chopped mixed candied fruits and peels	1 cup	1/2 cup
chopped pared apple	1 cup	1/2 cup
chopped pecans	1/2 cup	1/4 cup
Rum Hard Sauce, page 494		
BAKING DISH	6-cup microwave ring mold	6 (6-oz.) custard cups
BOWL	3-qt. bowl	1-1/2-qt. bowl
TIME AT 10%	1-1/2 minutes	30 to 45 seconds
TIME AT 30%	18 to 19 minutes	4 to 6 minutes
TIME AT HIGH	2 minutes	2 minutes

Generously grease a ring mold or custard cups, see sizes in chart above. In a bowl, se
size in chart above, microwave butter or margarine at 10% (LOW) for time in cha
above or until softened. Cream brown sugar and butter or margarine. Add bread, mill
eggs, rum and vanilla. Beat with electric mixer at high speed until blended. Batter wi
appear curdled. Stir in mincemeat. In a medium bowl, combine flour, baking soda, sa
cinnamon, cloves and nutmeg. Mix well. Toss mixed candied fruits and peels, apple
and pecans with flour mixture. Stir into butter or margarine mixture. Spoon evenly int
prepared ring mold or custard cups. Microwave at 30% (MEDIUM LOW) for time i
chart above, giving mold a quarter turn twice or rearranging custard cups once. Micro
wave at full power (HIGH) 2 minutes or until a wooden pick inserted in center come
out clean and top is only slightly moist. Cool on a rack 15 minutes. Loosen sides. Inve
on a serving plate. Serve warm with Rum Hard Sauce.

Heating Canned Plum Pudding

SERVINGS	4 to 6
INGREDIENTS	
canned plum pudding	1 (15-oz.) can
BAKING DISH	1-qt. casserole
TIME AT 70%	3 to 4 minutes

Remove pudding from can. Place in a 1-quart casserole. Cover. Microwave at 70%
(MEDIUM HIGH) 3 to 4 minutes or until warmed through.

Toasted-Almond Cake Roll

SERVINGS	6 to 8
INGREDIENTS	
slivered blanched almonds	2 cups (7-1/2 oz.)
baking powder	3/4 teaspoon
egg whites	4
egg yolks	4
powdered sugar	1/2 cup
vanilla extract	1 teaspoon
almond extract	1/4 teaspoon
Cocoa Fluff Filling, see below	2 cups
Chocolate Glaze, page 513	1/2 cup
OR	
powdered sugar	
BAKING DISH	12-inch square microwave baker
TIME AT HIGH (almonds)	4 to 5 minutes
TIME AT HIGH (cake)	6 minutes
STANDING TIME	1 minute

Spread almonds in a 12-inch square microwave baker. Microwave at full power (HIGH) 4 to 5 minutes or until toasted, stirring twice. Grind almonds or process in food processor using the steel blade. Measure 1-1/2 cups. Stir in baking powder; set aside. Line same microwave baker with waxed paper cut long enough to extend over ends of baking dish. Butter top side of waxed paper where it touches bottom of dish. In a small bowl, beat egg whites with electric mixer on high speed until stiff peaks form. In a large bowl, combine egg yolks, 1/2 cup powdered sugar, vanilla and almond extract. With electric mixer on high speed, beat mixture until thick and lemon colored, 3 to 5 minutes. Stir nut mixture into yolk mixture. Fold in egg whites. Spread batter evenly in prepared baking dish. Microwave at full power (HIGH) 6 minutes or until a wooden pick inserted in center of cake comes out clean. Let stand 1 minute. Using extended ends of waxed paper, lift cake out of dish. Place on a wire rack. Immediately cover with a damp cloth towel. Cool 50 to 60 minutes. Prepare Cocoa Fluff Filling. Prepare Chocolate Glaze, if using. To serve, remove towel. Spread Cocoa Fluff Filling on cake. Roll up jelly-roll fashion, peeling off waxed paper as cake is rolled. Be careful not to roll too tightly. Drizzle cake roll with Chocolate Glaze or sprinkle top of roll with additional powdered sugar.

Cocoa Fluff Filling

YIELD	2 cups
INGREDIENTS	
dessert-topping mix	1 envelope
cold milk	1/2 cup
vanilla extract	1/2 teaspoon
sweetened cocoa powder	1/4 cup

In a deep bowl, mix dessert topping mix, milk, vanilla and cocoa powder. Beat with electric mixer on high speed until peaks form. Continue beating until smooth and fluffy, about 2 minutes.

How to Make Toasted-Almond Cake Roll

Microwave the cake in a baking dish lined with waxed paper. Notice the waxed paper is cut long enough so the ends may be used to lift the cake from the baking dish to the cooling rack.

Remove the cake from the baking dish and place it on a cooling rack. Immediately cover the cake completely with a damp towel for 50 to 60 minutes. This keeps the cake moist enough to roll.

Spread the cooled cake with Cocoa Fluff Filling. Carefully roll up the cake, jelly-roll fashion, peeling off the waxed paper as the cake is rolled. Do not try to roll the cake too tightly or it may crack.

Drizzle the cake roll with Chocolate Glaze or sprinkle the roll lightly with powdered sugar. Use a serrated knife to slice cake roll. Lift the slices with a serving spatula.

Cake-Mix Layer Cake

YIELD	2 (8-inch) cake layers (12 to 16 servings)
INGREDIENTS cake mix with pudding in the mix	1 (2-layer-size) pkg.
BAKING DISHES	2 round, 8-inch cake dishes
TIME AT 30% (each layer)	6 minutes
TIME AT HIGH (each layer)	3-1/2 to 5 minutes*

Line bottoms of 2 round, 8-inch cake dishes with waxed paper rounds cut to fit. Prepare cake mix as directed on package. Divide batter evenly between dishes. Microwave 1 layer at a time, uncovered, at 30% (MEDIUM LOW) 6 minutes. Give dish a quarter turn. Microwave at full power (HIGH) 3-1/2 to 5 minutes, giving dish a quarter turn once. When done, top of cake is slightly moist and springs back when touched in center. A wooden pick inserted in center of cake comes out clean. Run a knife around edge of cake to loosen from dish; *immediately* invert on a heatproof surface covered with waxed paper. Carefully peel waxed paper circle from cake layer. Cool. Repeat with second cake layer.

*Devil's-food cake may take about 1 minute longer at microwave full power (HIGH).

Defrosting Tube Cakes or Cake Layers

SERVINGS	12 to 16	6 to 8
INGREDIENTS frozen unfrosted cake	1 (12-inch) fluted tube cake	1 (8-inch) cake layer
BAKING DISH	serving plate	serving plate
TIME AT HIGH	2-1/2 to 3 minutes	1 minute
STANDING TIME	5 minutes	5 minutes

Unwrap frozen cake. Place on a serving plate. Microwave, uncovered, at full power (HIGH) for time in chart above or until cake is warm to the touch. Let stand 5 minutes.

Tips

- Cakes such as angel, sponge and chiffon that rely heavily on eggs for leavening, do not work at all in the microwave oven.

- Cakes do not brown in the microwave oven. If a cake is glazed instead of frosted, choose a dark cake such as chocolate or spice. The lack of browning is easily disguised with frosting.

- Microwaved cakes have a fluffier texture and rise higher than conventionally baked cakes.

- Microwaved cakes bake and cool more quickly than conventionally baked cakes.

How to Make Cake-Mix Layer Cakes

Cut waxed paper rounds to fit the bottom of baking dishes. Divide the batter evenly between the two dishes.

The cake is done if the top springs back when touched in center and a wooden pick inserted in center comes out clean.

Cake-Mix Cupcakes

SERVINGS	6	4	2	1

INGREDIENTS
cake-mix batter
  with pudding
  in the mix
	3/4 cup	1/2 cup	1/4 cup	2 tablespoons

CUSTARD CUPS	6 (6-oz.) custard cups	4 (6-oz.) custard cups	2 (6-oz.) custard cups	1 (6-oz.) custard cup
TIME AT 30%	8 minutes	5 minutes	2-1/4 minutes	1-1/2 minutes
TIME AT HIGH	30 seconds	15 seconds	none	none

Place paper bake cups in 6-ounce custard cups, see number in chart above, or in a microwave muffin dish. Spoon 2 tablespoons batter into each paper bake cup; cups should be less than half full. Arrange custard cups in a circle in microwave oven. Microwave no more than 6 at a time, uncovered, at 30% (MEDIUM LOW) for time in chart above. Rearrange custard cups once or give muffin dish a half turn once during cooking time. If baking 1 or 2 cupcakes, a wooden pick inserted in center should come out clean after cooking time at 30%. If microwaving 4 or 6 cupcakes, microwave at full power (HIGH) for time in chart above or until a wooden pick inserted in center comes out clean. Place cupcakes on a wire rack; cool.

Note: Most 2-layer cake mixes will make 32 to 40 cupcakes.

How to Make Cake-Mix Tube Cakes

A microwave turntable makes turning the cake easy and helps maintain a level top. Insert a wooden skewer between the edge and tube to test for doneness. Skewer should come out clean.

When the cake is completely cooled, drizzle it with Versatile Powdered-Sugar Glaze, opposite or one of the frostings on page 514. This is an ideal cake to serve for a large gathering.

Cake-Mix Tube Cakes

YIELD	1 (12-inch) tube cake (12 to 16 servings)
INGREDIENTS cake mix with pudding in the mix	1 (2-layer-size) pkg.
BAKING DISH	12-cup microwave fluted tube dish
TIME AT 30%	16 minutes
TIME AT HIGH	4 to 6 minutes

Generously grease a 12-cup microwave fluted tube dish. Sugar tube dish completely. Shake out excess sugar. Prepare cake mix as directed on package. Pour into prepared tube dish. Microwave, uncovered, at 30% (MEDIUM LOW) 16 minutes, giving dish a quarter turn once. After time at 30%, give dish a quarter turn. Microwave at full power (HIGH) 4 to 6 minutes or until done, giving dish a quarter turn once. When done, a wooden skewer inserted in center of cake will come out clean; there may be a few moist spots on top of cake even when cake is done. *Immediately* invert on a heatproof surface covered with waxed paper. Leave inverted tube dish over cake 10 minutes. Remove tube dish. Cool cake completely before frosting or glazing.

Chocolate Glaze

YIELD	1 cup	1/2 cup
INGREDIENTS		
unsweetened chocolate squares	2 oz. (2 squares)	1 oz. (1 square)
butter or margarine	1/4 cup	2 tablespoons
sifted powdered sugar	2 cups	1 cup
vanilla extract	1/2 teaspoon	1/4 teaspoon
hot water	2 tablespoons plus 1 to 2 teaspoons	3 to 5 teaspoons
BOWL	1-1/2-qt. bowl	1-qt. bowl
TIME AT HIGH	1 to 1-1/2 minutes	1 to 1-1/4 minutes

Place chocolate and butter or margarine in a bowl, see size in chart above. Microwave at full power (HIGH) for time in chart above or until butter or margarine is melted. Stir until chocolate is melted and mixture is smooth. Stir in powdered sugar and vanilla. Mix well. Gradually stir in enough hot water to give mixture a drizzling consistency.

Versatile Powdered-Sugar Glaze

YIELD	3/4 cup	1/3 cup
INGREDIENTS		
butter or margarine	1/4 cup	2 tablespoons
sifted powdered sugar	2 cups	1 cup
vanilla extract	1 teaspoon	1/2 teaspoon
hot water or fruit juice	1 tablespoon plus 1 to 2 teaspoons	1 to 2 teaspoons
grated orange or lemon peel, if desired	1/2 teaspoon	1/4 teaspoon
BOWL	1-1/2-qt. bowl	1-qt. bowl
TIME AT HIGH	1 minute	30 seconds

Place butter or margarine in a bowl, see size in chart above. Microwave at full power (HIGH) for time in chart above or until melted. Stir in powdered sugar and vanilla. Mix well. Gradually stir in enough hot water or hot juice to give mixture a drizzling consistency. Stir in peel, if desired.

Melting Baking Pieces

YIELD	1 to 1-1/3 cups	2/3 cup
INGREDIENTS		
chocolate, peanut-butter or butterscotch pieces	1 (12-oz.) pkg. (about 2 cups)	1 (6-oz.) pkg. (about 1 cup)
GLASS MEASURING CUP	1-qt.	2-cup
TIME AT HIGH	2 to 2-1/2 minutes	1-1/2 to 2 minutes

Empty pieces into a glass measuring cup, see size in chart above. Microwave at full power (HIGH) for time in chart above or until just melted, stirring twice. Stir again before using.

Creamy Butterscotch Frosting

YIELD	4 cups	2-1/4 cups
INGREDIENTS		
butterscotch pieces	2 (6-oz.) pkgs.(2 cups)	1 (6-oz.) pkg. (1 cup)
butter or margarine	1/2 cup	1/4 cup
dairy sour cream	1 cup	1/2 cup
vanilla extract	2 teaspoons	1 teaspoon
powdered sugar	1 lb. (about 5 cups)	8 oz. (about 2-1/2 cups)
BOWL	1-1/2-qt. bowl	1-1/2-qt. bowl
TIME AT HIGH	2 minutes	1 to 1-1/2 minutes

In a bowl, see size in chart above, combine butterscotch pieces and butter or margarine. Microwave at full power (HIGH) for time in chart above or until melted, stirring twice. Stir until mixture is smooth. Cool. Stir in sour cream and vanilla. With an electric mixer on medium speed, gradually beat in powdered sugar until mixture reaches a spreading consistency. Store frosted cake in refrigerator.

Snowdrift Frosting

YIELD	5-1/2 cups	2-1/2 cups
INGREDIENTS		
sugar	1 cup	1/2 cup
water	1/3 cup	3 tablespoons
cream of tartar	1/4 teaspoon	1/8 teaspoon
vanilla extract	1 teaspoon	1/2 teaspoon
egg whites	2	1
GLASS MEASURING CUP	1-qt.	2-cup
TIME AT HIGH	2 to 3 minutes	1 to 1-1/4 minutes

In a glass measuring cup, see size in chart above, combine sugar, water and cream of tartar. Microwave at full power (HIGH) for time in chart above or until mixture boils and sugar dissolves, stirring three times. With an electric mixer on high speed, slowly add hot syrup and vanilla to egg whites in a 1-1/2-quart bowl. Continue beating at high speed until stiff peaks form, 3 to 5 minutes. This frosting does not keep longer than a day.

Melting Chocolate

YIELD	3 squares	2 squares	1 square
INGREDIENTS			
unsweetened or semisweet chocolate squares	3 (1-oz.) squares	2 (1-oz.) squares	1 (1-oz.) square
BOWL	1-cup bowl	custard cup	custard cup
TIME AT HIGH	1-1/4 to 1-3/4 minutes	1 to 1-1/2 minutes	1 to 1-1/2 minutes

Unwrap chocolate and place in a bowl, see size in chart above. Microwave at full power (HIGH) for time in chart above or until just melted, stirring once. Stir before using.

Cake-Mix Layer Cake, page 510, with Creamy Butterscotch Frosting

Easy Cherry Upside-Down Cake

YIELD	2 (8-inch) cake layers (12 servings)
INGREDIENTS	
cherry pie filling	1 (21-oz.) can
canned peach slices, well-drained, diced	1 (16-oz.) can
lemon juice	2 tablespoons
chopped nuts	1/2 cup
flaked coconut	1/2 cup
yellow cake mix with pudding in the mix	1 (2-layer-size) cake mix
BAKING DISH	2 round, 8-inch cake dishes
TIME AT 30% (each layer)	6 minutes
TIME AT HIGH (each layer)	8 to 9 minutes

Generously grease bottoms of 2 round, 8-inch cake dishes. Combine pie filling, peaches, lemon juice, nuts and coconut. Spread evenly in cake dishes; set aside. Prepare cake mix according to package directions. Spoon batter evenly over fruit mixture in the 2 cake dishes. Microwave 1 layer at a time, uncovered, at 30% (MEDIUM LOW) 6 minutes. Give dish a quarter turn. Microwave at full power (HIGH) 8 to 9 minutes, giving dish a quarter turn once. When cake is done, top is slightly moist and springs back when touched in center. Run a knife around edge of cake to loosen from dish. *Immediately* invert onto a serving dish. Let cake dish stand over cake 2 minutes. Remove cake dish. Any filling that slides off can be spooned back onto cake. Serve warm.

Variations
Easy Apple-Date Upside-Down Cake: Substitute apple pie filling for the cherry pie filling. Substitute 1 cup chopped dates for the peaches. Increase chopped nuts to 1 cup. Prepare as directed above, decreasing microwave time at full power (HIGH) to 6 to 7 minutes. Invert and cool as above.

Easy Raisin-Apple Upside-Down Cake: Substitute raisin pie filling for the cherry pie filling. Substitute 2 cups chopped pared apple for the peaches. Prepare as directed above. Microwave, invert and cool as above.

Reheating Upside-Down Cake

SERVINGS	2	1
INGREDIENTS		
upside-down cake	2 (2-inch) wedges	1 (2-inch) wedge
PLATE	2 small plates	1 small plate
TIME AT HIGH	45 to 60 seconds	30 seconds

Place cake wedges on small serving plates. Microwave at full power (HIGH) for time in chart above or until warmed through.

Tips

- Packaged upside-down cake mixes do not work well in the microwave oven. It's best to bake these cake mixes conventionally.
- Packaged cakes with a pudding layer on the bottom and cake on the top do not work well in the microwave oven. Bake these cakes conventionally for best results.

Mix together cherry pie filling, canned peaches, lemon juice, nuts and coconut. Spread the fruit mixture evenly in greased cake dishes.

Prepare yellow cake mix. Divide the batter equally between the two cake dishes. Spread the batter evenly over the fruit layer.

Cake will be slightly moist on top when done. Run a knife around the edge of the cake to loosen from dish.

Immediately invert the cake onto a serving dish. Let the cake dish stand over the cake 2 minutes, then remove.

Gingerbread Mix

YIELD	1 round (8-inch) cake (6 servings)
INGREDIENTS gingerbread mix	1 (14.5-oz.) pkg.
BAKING DISH	round, 8-inch cake dish
TIME AT HIGH	8 to 9 minutes

In a large bowl, prepare gingerbread mix as directed on package. Place a 2-inch diameter jar in center of a round, 8-inch cake dish. Pour batter into dish around jar. Microwave, uncovered, at full power (HIGH) 8 to 9 minutes, giving dish a quarter turn every 2 minutes. When done, top of cake should appear almost dry and spring back when touched lightly with finger. A pick inserted off-center will come out clean. Cool 10 minutes on a flat heatproof surface. Twist jar and remove. Serve warm in wedges.

Pound Cake Mix

YIELD	2 loaf cakes (12 servings)
INGREDIENTS pound cake mix	1 (16-oz.) pkg.
LOAF DISHES	2 (9" x 5" or 8" x 4") loaf dishes
TIME AT 30% (each loaf)	8 to 10 minutes
TIME AT HIGH (each loaf)	2-1/2 to 3-1/2 minutes

Line bottoms of loaf dishes, see size in chart above, with waxed paper cut to fit. Prepare pound cake mix as directed on package. Divide batter evenly between loaf dishes. Shield the top of both ends of loaf dishes with small pieces of foil. Microwave 1 dish at a time, uncovered, at 30% (MEDIUM LOW) 8 to 10 minutes. Remove foil from loaf dish. Give dish a quarter turn. Microwave at full power (HIGH) 2-1/2 to 3-1/2 minutes or until a skewer inserted in center comes out clean. Loosen edge of cake with a knife. Invert cake immediately on a heatproof surface covered with waxed paper. Peel waxed paper from bottom of cake. Cool. Repeat with second loaf.

Snack Cake Mix

YIELD	1 (8-inch) cake layer (6 to 8 servings)
INGREDIENTS snack cake mix	1 (13.5- or 14-oz.) pkg.
BAKING DISH	round, 8-inch cake dish
TIME AT 30%	6 minutes
TIME AT HIGH	3 to 4 minutes

Place a 2-inch diameter jar in center of a round, 8-inch cake dish. Prepare cake mix as directed on package except mix in a large bowl instead of in a baking pan. Pour batter into cake dish around jar. Microwave, uncovered, at 30% (MEDIUM LOW) 6 minutes. Give dish a quarter turn. Microwave at full power (HIGH) 3 to 4 minutes or until top is almost dry to the touch and a wooden pick inserted off-center comes out clean. Cool 10 minutes on a flat heatproof surface. Twist jar and remove. Cut into wedges. Serve warm.

Index

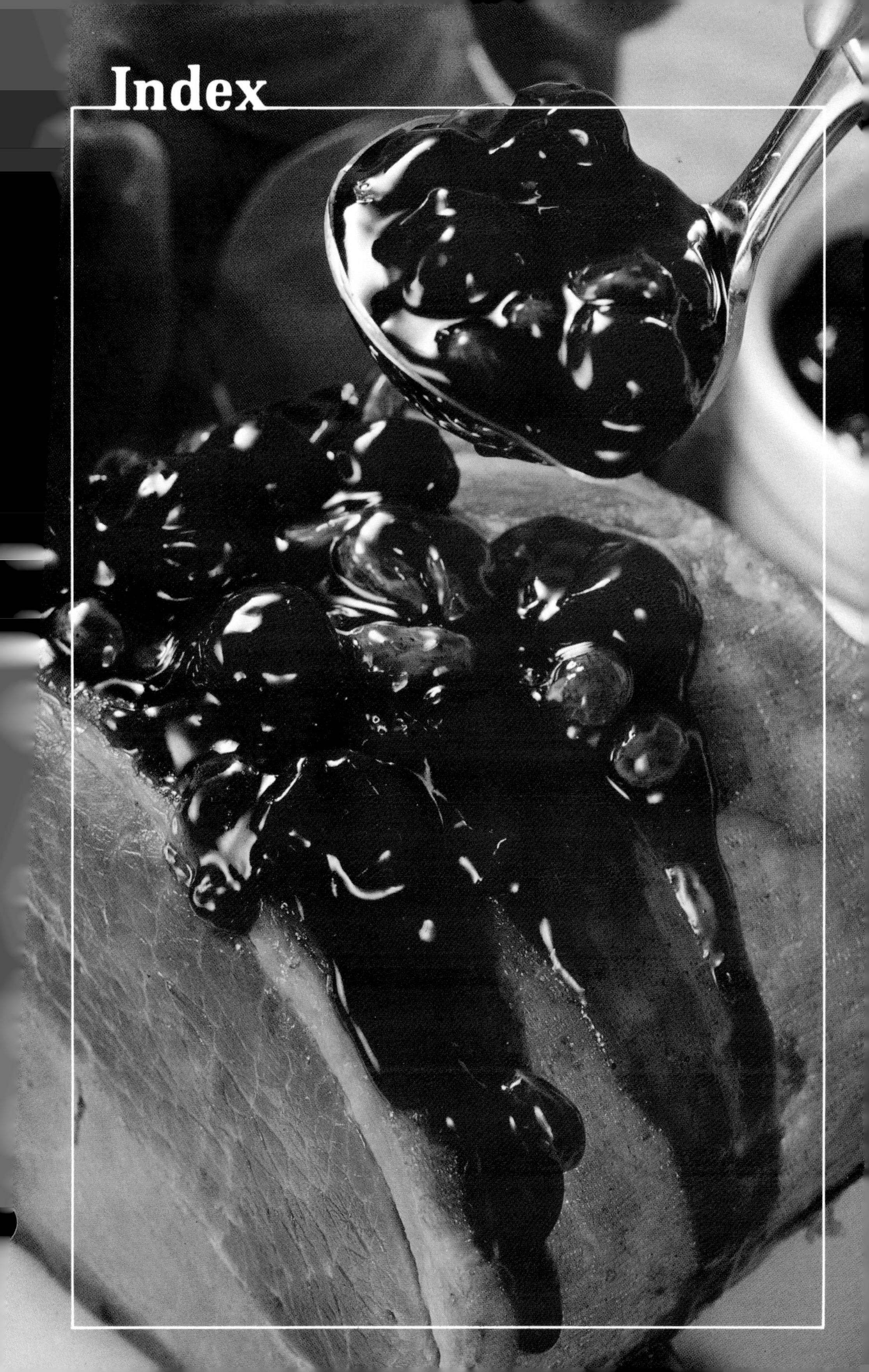

Shown on the divider: Ham with Cherry Glaze

Index

Index

Index

Index

Index

Index

Index

Index

9.8842030529117942